D1559649

THE LATIN NEW TESTAMENT

The Latin New Testament

A Guide to its Early History,
Texts, and Manuscripts

H.A.G. HOUGHTON

OXFORD
UNIVERSITY PRESS

OXFORD
UNIVERSITY PRESS

Great Clarendon Street, Oxford, OX2 6DP,
United Kingdom

Oxford University Press is a department of the University of Oxford.
It furthers the University's objective of excellence in research, scholarship,
and education by publishing worldwide. Oxford is a registered trade mark of
Oxford University Press in the UK and in certain other countries

First Edition published in 2016
Impression: 1

Published in the United States of America by Oxford University Press
198 Madison Avenue, New York, NY 10016, United States of America

British Library Cataloguing in Publication Data
Data available

Library of Congress Control Number: 2015946703

ISBN 978-0-19-874473-3

Printed in Great Britain by
Clays Ltd, St Ives plc

To David,
with thanks

The research leading to these results has received funding from the European Union Seventh Framework Programme (FP7/2007–2013) under grant agreement no. 283302 (COMPAUL: 'The Earliest Commentaries on Paul as Sources for the Biblical Text').

Preface

The Latin tradition supplies some of the earliest sources for the history of the New Testament text. Moreover the Bible was read and studied in this language for over a millennium by some of the world's most influential scholars and theologians. The manuscripts which transmit the text also provide a window on intellectual culture, book production, and religious practice across the centuries. Their evidence is supplemented by biblical quotations in Christian texts from Antiquity until the Renaissance.

The present volume seeks to offer an orientation to the early history of this tradition, a guide to the resources available for further study of the Latin New Testament, and an account of its significance for the biblical text. Recent developments in the field are such that the introductory chapters which have served for several decades are now in need of updating and expansion.[1] Berger's *Histoire de la Vulgate*, written well over a century ago, is often still cited as the only monograph to cover the whole Latin Bible even though it has both temporal and geographical limitations. Some of the information in specialist studies has yet to reach a wider audience. Almost all publications on the New Testament continue to employ an outdated set of sigla for Latin manuscripts. In a climate of renewed interest in biblical textual criticism and manuscript study, fuelled in part by the ever-increasing numbers of fully-digitized codices available on the internet, the time is ripe for a new manual which will enable further work to take proper account of previous scholarship. In fact, the approach adopted here goes beyond previous surveys, largely structured around the description of key manuscripts, by integrating the evidence of Latin Christian writers. This results in a more continuous historical approach, illustrating the spectrum of the development of the New Testament text in Latin.

Latin versions of the Bible are often treated under the two headings of Old Latin (Vetus Latina) and Vulgate. This traditional characterization, relying partly on the testimony of ancient authors, presents a picture of an early period of variety and confusion which was superseded by a single authorized version produced around the end of the fourth century. There are numerous problems with this account. For a start, the New Testament books of the Vulgate were not a fresh translation but a revision of existing versions carried

---

[1] e.g. Fischer 1972, Metzger 1977, and Elliott 1992. Several important works have appeared during the preparation of this book, chief among which are the first two volumes of the *New Cambridge History of the Bible* (Carleton Paget & Schaper 2013; Marsden & Matter 2012) and van Liere's *Introduction to the Medieval Bible* (2014). The focus of the latter on a later period of reception and exegesis, with numerous examples from the Old Testament, offers an excellent complement to the present undertaking.

out by more than one person. Jerome was only responsible for the Gospels, and even he seems to have made fewer alterations in the latter half of his work. The revised texts also took several centuries to gain acceptance, and were only identified by the name 'Vulgate' late in their history. The Latin New Testament is therefore a continuum in which a particular form of text eventually gained predominance, a situation comparable to that of the later hegemony of the Byzantine 'Majority' text in the Greek tradition. What is more, readings from ancient forms persist in later Latin manuscripts and Christian authors, resulting in the phenomenon of 'mixed texts' bearing witness to a greater or lesser extent of 'contamination' in the textual tradition. Secondly, the early multiplicity of Latin translations has become much more difficult to sustain following work on the monumental Vetus Latina edition in the latter half of the twentieth century. For each of the books which has so far appeared, both Old and New Testament, the evidence appears to point towards a single Latin version standing behind the whole of the surviving tradition.[2] This is not to say that there were not multiple independent translations in the earliest times, but if this were the case then they have left few, if any, traces. The variety between the different forms of text which have been preserved can be explained as the result of numerous later interventions, some one-off or haphazard, others more consistent, revising a Latin version in order to bring it into accordance with a Greek source or the canons of grammar and style. The overall direction in the creation of the Vulgate is the elimination of paraphrase towards the goal of formal equivalence with whichever Greek form was adopted as a standard. Attempts to identify certain earlier textual forms as 'African', 'Italian', or 'European' have largely been abandoned, along with the designation of the Old Latin texts as *Itala*. The long period during which different Latin texts circulated and influenced each other often makes it difficult to distinguish between different strands. The Vulgate tradition itself, too, is not monolithic. Nevertheless, the relative stability of the fifth-century revision and the existence of a widely-accepted critical text in the form of the Stuttgart Vulgate makes it simple in practical terms to use this as a measure against which to define differing Latin New Testament traditions. In the present volume, 'pre-Vulgate' is used as a synonym for 'Old Latin' where a form is attested prior to the fifth century; 'non-Vulgate' simply indicates a reading which differs from the editorial text of the Stuttgart Vulgate regardless of the period at which it may have arisen.

There are three parts to this book. Part I is a historical overview of evidence for the Latin New Testament focusing on the Old Latin tradition, which broadly covers the first millennium. This survey brings together details about the use of the Bible and the development of the text from a variety of sources,

---

[2] See pages 12–14.

including observations in Christian authors, their exegetical writings and the textual affiliation of their scriptural quotations, and the New Testament manuscripts surviving from this period. The account is broadly chronological, but also ordered by geographical area: manuscripts are generally mentioned at the point at which they were copied, although in some cases their text may reach back far earlier. Reference is therefore also made to the Vetus Latina text-types. Part II consists of a guide to the principal resources currently available for research into the text or history of the Latin New Testament, followed by an account of the place of Latin within the wider textual history of these writings. Each of the five sections of the New Testament (Gospels, Pauline Epistles, Acts of the Apostles, Catholic Epistles, and Revelation) is considered in turn, with details of the main witnesses and the contribution of Latin evidence in selected readings or passages. Part III focuses on manuscripts. After a summary of features found in Latin biblical manuscripts, explaining different paratextual elements and trends in book production, a catalogue is given of the major Latin New Testament manuscripts. The list comprises all witnesses featuring in the New Testament part of the register maintained by the Vetus Latina Institute in Beuron, which oversees the publication of the earliest Latin evidence, and the main manuscripts in the two principal editions of the Vulgate, the Stuttgart Vulgate of Weber, Gryson, et al. and the Oxford Vulgate of Wordsworth, White, et al. An internet address has been provided for complete or substantial sets of digitized images made available online, usually by the holding institution. There is an extensive bibliography, which permits references to secondary literature in the body of the text to be kept as short as possible.

In the absence of a single authoritative list of Latin New Testament manuscripts comparable to the Gregory-Aland *Kurzgefasste Liste* for Greek New Testament manuscripts, referencing is always an issue.[3] In Part I, I have in general used the customary Latin names for biblical codices along with a standard siglum. For Old Latin witnesses the sigla follow the Vetus Latina system, consisting of VL followed by a number. For Vulgate manuscripts, I have created a siglum based on the edition and, where necessary, the section of the New Testament in which it is cited, but using only the minimal information required to differentiate witnesses. This consists of the letters 'Vg', a superscript capital [S] or [O] for the Stuttgart or Oxford editions respectively and a superscript lower-case letter for the five sections of New Testament mentioned above ([e p a c r]), followed by the alphabetic siglum used in that edition at that point. Thus 'Vg F' will always be Codex Fuldensis, since F is used in both the Stuttgart and Oxford Vulgates for Codex Fuldensis throughout the New Testament; 'Vg[Sp] R' indicates manuscript R in the Pauline Epistles section of the Stuttgart Vulgate, which must be distinguished from

---

[3] A database is currently being compiled at Birmingham which, it is hoped, will form the basis of such a catalogue.

the different manuscript R used in this edition for the Catholic Epistles ('Vg^Sc R'). Although slightly cumbersome, this system is transparent and means that reference can immediately be made to the relevant entry in the Catalogue of Manuscripts (Chapter 10), where further information is provided including other sigla which identify that manuscript. A table of concordances between different editions is provided as Appendix 1, which also includes the alphabetic sigla used for the Old Latin manuscripts. When treating Christian authors and works, the Vetus Latina abbreviations have been supplied in brackets. This is the most economical system of referring to Latin Christian writings, and is laid out in full in the Vetus Latina *Repertorium* (Gryson 2007); unless otherwise indicated, patristic texts have been cited from the critical edition listed therein.[4]

A handbook like this relies heavily on previous scholarly work, especially critical editions and catalogues. Chief among these are the resources produced by the Vetus Latina Institute, many by its pioneering and indefatigable directors: Bonifatius Fischer (1945–73), Hermann Josef Frede (1973–98), and Roger Gryson (1998–2013). Without their remarkable contribution to biblical scholarship, this book could not have been written. Ongoing research on the Latin Bible is charted in the *Bulletin de la Bible latine*, which appears at regular intervals in the *Revue bénédictine*: since 1964 this has been edited by Pierre-Maurice Bogaert, whose encyclopaedic knowledge and sound judgement are to be seen in the accompanying comments. The Catalogue of Manuscripts in the present volume is based on the comparison of a number of different sources, most of which exhibit minor discrepancies: where possible, these have been resolved through reference to the original. The Vetus Latina *Register* (Gryson 1999) and *Repertorium* (Gryson 2007) have been taken as authoritative in questions of chronology. In addition to the links and online resources mentioned in this book, a number of associated resources may be found at <www.vetuslatina.org> and I also hope to provide corrections and updates at <https://sites.google.com/site/haghoughton/lnt>: readers are encouraged to bring any such suggestions to my attention. This is an exciting time to be working in the field of textual scholarship, with the advent of digital media offering greater access than ever before to primary documents, and the situation is changing rapidly even in so well-established a field as the Latin New Testament.

Another of the benefits of the electronic age has been the potential for improved collaboration. It has been an honour and a pleasure to work with distinguished scholars on a variety of projects, and I would like in particular to thank colleagues on the International Greek New Testament Project and at the Institute for Textual Scholarship and Electronic Editing at the University of

---

[4] An explanation of the system is given on pages 118–19. A list of the author sigla may be downloaded from <www.vetuslatina.org>.

Birmingham. The writing of this book was undertaken as part of my leadership of the COMPAUL project investigating the earliest commentaries on Paul as sources for the biblical text, funded by the European Research Council: I am glad to acknowledge their financial support, as well as that of the UK Arts and Humanities Research Council for other activities including my doctoral work and the Vetus Latina *Iohannes*. My team members Christina Kreinecker, Rosalind MacLachlan, Catherine Smith, Susan Griffith, and David Parker deserve a special tribute. Several of them were kind enough to read a draft of the whole book as did Benjamin Haupt and Josephine Houghton: their suggestions have made the text considerably more user-friendly. Alba Fedeli assisted with contacting Italian libraries and publishers, and I am grateful to the various bodies which granted permission to reproduce images of items from their collections. I should also like to express my gratitude to Edith Haynes for a collection of editions of the Latin New Testament assembled by her late husband Philip, to which I have constantly referred. Tom Perridge, Karen Raith, and the other members of Oxford University Press have been models of efficiency and encouragement; thanks too to Michael Janes and Gayathri Manoharan. Among those who offered personal support and encouragement as I worked on this book, I particularly thank Josephine and Polly Houghton for ensuring that I had both the space necessary for writing and plentiful tea and cake.

I would like to dedicate this book to David Parker, who showed me that New Testament scholarship can be a vocation and has been an advocate, example, and friend throughout my academic formation.

Birmingham, Petertide 2015.

Contents

Part II: Texts

Part III: Manuscripts

List of Images

List of Abbreviations

Abbreviations for Christian authors and their works in the *Repertorium* are not given here, although they are provided in brackets on their first occurrence in Part I. A list of authors may be downloaded from <http://www.vetuslatina.org>.

Secondary literature is indicated by the author–date system used in the Bibliography.

BAV	Biblioteca Apostolica Vaticana
BL	British Library
BM	Bibliothèque municipale
BnF	Bibliothèque nationale de France
CLA	Codices Latini Antiquiores
CLLA	Codices Liturgici Latini Antiquiores
GA	Gregory-Aland (in manuscript sigla)
MS	manuscript
NA	Nestle-Aland *Novum Testamentum Graece*
NA27	Twenty-seventh edition (1993)
NA28	Twenty-eighth edition (2012)
PL	Patrologia Latina
UBS	United Bible Societies' *Greek New Testament*
UBS4	Fourth edition (2001)
UBS5	Fifth edition (2014)
Vg	Vulgate
Vg^O	Oxford Vulgate
Vg^S	Stuttgart Vulgate
VL	Vetus Latina (in manuscript sigla)

Divisions of the New Testament:

e	Gospels (*Euangelia*)
a	Acts of the Apostles (*Acta Apostolorum*)
p	Pauline Epistles (*Epistulae Paulinae*)
c	Catholic Epistles (*Epistulae Catholicae* or *Epistulae Canonicae*)
r	Revelation (*Apocalypsis*)

Part I

History

The five chapters in this section provide an account of the historical development of the Latin New Testament from earliest times until the late Middle Ages. As an effort has been made not to duplicate information in different parts of the book, readers may wish to refer to some of the later chapters for further information. Those with little or no experience of working with manuscripts may find it helpful first of all to read Chapter 9, which provides an overview of the features and contents of Latin New Testament manuscripts. A summary of the Latin tradition for each of the New Testament writings is given in Chapter 8, while a detailed description of most of the manuscripts mentioned is found in the Catalogue in Chapter 10. The abbreviations for Latin authors and their writings are those of the Vetus Latina *Repertorium* described on pages 118–19: further background information on individuals and their works is available on numerous websites and in encyclopaedias. Technical terms are generally explained on their first occurrence, noted in the Index of Subjects at the back of the book.

1

From the Origins to the End of the Third Century

The origins of the Latin New Testament are unknown. No-one is explicitly identified as a translator or reviser of the Bible before the end of the fourth century. Jerome and Augustine's comments on the origins and previous history of the Latin translation have often been accepted without question, even though they are writing some two centuries later in justification of their own endeavours. A more reliable account has to be pieced together from surviving writings contemporary with the adoption of Latin in the early Church and the evidence of the biblical text itself. This results in a focus on Roman North Africa, where the shift from Greek to Latin appears to have preceded the same development in Italy and elsewhere in the Roman Empire. Nevertheless, the paucity of texts preserved from this time means that significant gaps remain and it can be difficult to contextualize the evidence which survives.

THE SCILLITAN MARTYRS

The earliest dated reference in Latin to the books of the New Testament is found in the proceedings of the trial of a group of Christians in Carthage, known as the Scillitan Martyrs, held on 17 July 180 (A-SS Scilitani):

> *Saturninus proconsul dixit: Quae sunt res in capsa uestra?*
> *Speratus dixit: Libri et epistulae Pauli uiri iusti.*[1]

> Saturninus the proconsul said: What are the objects in your carrying case?
> Speratus said: Books and letters of Paul, a righteous man.

While the unpunctuated text of Speratus' reply appears to attribute both 'books' and 'letters' to Paul, it has been suggested that a comma should be

---

[1] The most recent edition and study is Ruggiero 1991.

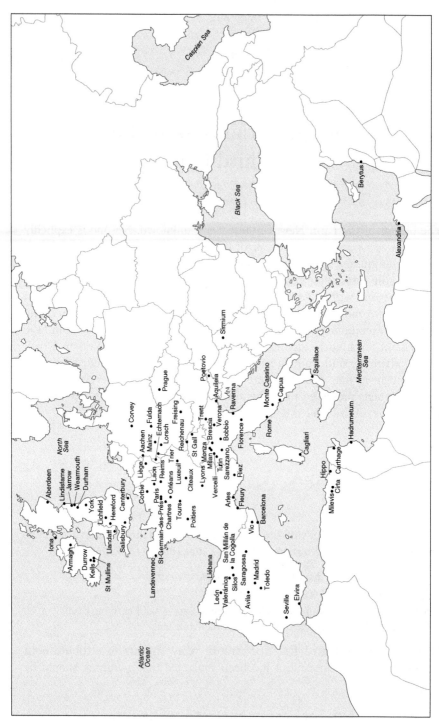

Image 1 Map of Principal Locations

placed after *libri* and that the word should be interpreted as 'gospel books'.[2] Equally, it might be that Speratus originally qualified *libri* with a word which was not familiar to the court stenographer (e.g. *libri euangeliorum*, 'books of the Gospels'), which was simply omitted from the record. Although the trial proceedings are in Latin, the administrative language of Roman North Africa, the language of the Christian texts themselves is unspecified: they may still have been Greek, although a quotation of 1 Timothy 6:16 by one of the martyrs resembles a form found in the fifth-century African writer Quodvultdeus (QU). These proceedings are the oldest Latin example of a series of court records involving Christians ('Acts of the Martyrs') which were collected and circulated; there are also similar Greek texts from elsewhere in the Mediterranean. In some churches, especially in Africa, there was a tradition of reading out the record during the annual commemoration of each martyr.

TERTULLIAN

The first Christian author to write in Latin whose works survive is Tertullian (TE), active in North Africa at the end of the second century. Tertullian's earliest writings date from around 196 or 197, and his output spans two decades. Later works show evidence of Tertullian's adoption of the doctrines of Montanism; the *Passion of Perpetua and Felicity* (A-SS Per), an extended set of martyr acts written in Latin at the beginning of the third century, is believed to have been written by one of Tertullian's circle. Tertullian wrote in Greek as well as Latin: although only his Latin works are extant, these bear witness to his knowledge of both languages (e.g. *De baptismo* 15 and *De corona* 6). The entire New Testament canon is represented in his quotations with the exception of 2 Peter, and 2 and 3 John.[3] Although scriptural passages are found throughout his works, two writings are particularly significant for the history of the biblical text. In *Adversus Praxean* (TE Pra), Tertullian uses the Gospel according to John as the basis for a carefully-constructed refutation of Monarchianism. *Adversus Marcionem* (TE Marc) is an attack on Marcion, who several decades before had produced a form of the New Testament consisting of an expurgated text of the Gospel according to Luke and ten of the Pauline Epistles: the rest, Marcion alleged, had been corrupted by a group which he called Judaizers. In books four and five of *Adversus Marcionem* Tertullian examines Marcion's treatment of Luke and Paul respectively, transmitting vital information about the nature and extent of this lost edition. Additionally, a set of prologues for the Pauline Epistles which appear to derive from

---

[2] Thus Elliott 1992:201.   [3] Thiele 1972:93 and Frisius 2011:13–15.

Marcion's edition are transmitted only in Latin tradition: they are first attested from the middle of the fourth century.[4]

Tertullian's biblical text poses numerous problems. He rarely, if ever, cites the same verse twice in exactly the same form, sometimes even within the same work. For example, the opening verse of John begins *in principio* at TE Pra 13.3 but *a primordio* at TE Pra 16.1. *De anima* and *De baptismo* have versions of John 3:5 both of which correspond to known Greek forms yet have little in common with each other:

> *nisi quis nascetur ex aqua et spiritu non inibit in regnum dei.* (TE an 39)
> *nisi quis renatus fuerit ex aqua et spiritu sancto non intrabit in regno caelorum.* (TE ba 13.3)

> Unless someone will be born of water and the spirit, they will not go in to the kingdom of God.
> Unless someone shall have been born again of water and the holy spirit, they will not enter the kingdom of heaven.

Such examples can easily be multiplied. One suggestion is that Tertullian was using more than one version, reproducing Marcion's text at one point and his own elsewhere, but the phenomenon is observable in the biblical books not included in Marcion's New Testament and works not directed against Marcion. Furthermore, there is no external evidence that Marcion's Gospel circulated in any other language than Greek.[5] A more comprehensive explanation is that Tertullian was not working with a fixed form of the Latin Bible but produced his own translation as necessary, comparing Marcion with another Greek text of the biblical passage, and perhaps using different Greek manuscripts in other works. Support for this is found in the lack of overlap between Tertullian's biblical text and the majority of surviving Old Latin forms. This distance from the rest of the Latin tradition is observed in the Vetus Latina editions, which use the siglum X to indicate text-types reconstructed from Tertullian's quotations and other early authors who probably relied on a Greek original.[6] Nonetheless, there remain occasional similarities between Tertullian's quotations and Latin biblical manuscripts which suggest that he might have used a translation of the New Testament. Furthermore, two of his comments imply the existence of a Latin version of at least the Pauline Epistles. In *De monogamia*, he contrasts a Latin text of 1 Corinthians 7:39 omitting the second occurrence of *uir eius* ('her husband') with the reading *in Graeco authentico*, 'in the authentic Greek' (TE mon 11). Similarly, he says *sicut inuenimur interpretatum* ('as we find it translated') of a particular reading in Galatians 4:24 at TE Marc 5.4.[7]

---

[4] On Marcion's edition, see the works of Schmid and Roth in the Bibliography. The prologues are considered on page 172.
[5] See Regul 1969 (against Tenney and Higgins), Birdsall 1970:345, Fischer 1972:20, 45 [1986:184, 214], and Roth 2009.
[6] For an introduction to the Vetus Latina edition and text-types, see Chapter 6.
[7] Compare also the reference to *quidam enim de Graeco interpretantes* ('For some, translating from the Greek', TE Marc 2). Studies of Tertullian are listed in the *Chronica Tertullianea et*

'CHRISTIAN LATIN'

Tertullian was a pioneer in the development of a Latin Christian vocabulary. Faced with the challenge of translating Greek terms which had a special Christian significance, Latin writers had three main options. Where a Greek word had been given an additional meaning (for example, μάρτυς coming to mean 'martyr' as well as 'witness') this further sense could be attributed to an existing Latin word through the process of 'semantic extension'. So, in some sources, the Latin for 'witness', *testis*, is also found in the sense of 'martyr'. The second possibility was to create a calque, a new Latin word in which each morphological element corresponded to the Greek: the exact match between the words for 'to enliven', ζῳο-ποι-εῖν and *uiui-fic-are*, is an example of this. Finally, the Greek term itself could be borrowed, usually becoming naturalized into Latin morphology: the word for 'overseer' or 'bishop', ἐπίσκοπος, was thus adopted as a noun, *episcopus*, for the technical Christian usage. In the earliest Christian writings, there is considerable fluidity in this technical lexicon. Numerous examples may be seen in Tertullian and other early biblical translations of initial attempts to create a Latin vocabulary through semantic extension which were later replaced with borrowings, for instance the use of *tinguere* to mean 'to baptize' as well as 'to dye' on the model of the Greek βαπτίζειν, or *minister* corresponding to διάκονος ('deacon').[8] Conversely, such texts may also have a liberal sprinkling of Greek borrowings for which a Latin term was normally preferred, such as *horoma* for *uisio* in the *Passion of Perpetua and Felicity* (A-SS Per 10.1). This bears witness to the bilingualism of early Latin Christian communities.

The origin of the use of Latin in a Christian context is usually associated with the liturgy. Just as, several centuries earlier, a scriptural reading in Hebrew was sometimes followed by an impromptu translation called a *targum* for the benefit of those attending Jewish worship not familiar with the language, the same is likely to have been the case in Christian gatherings. The only direct evidence we have of this practice is the account by the Spanish pilgrim Egeria, sometimes known as Aetheria, of her visit to the Holy Land between 381 and 384 (IT Ae). She explains how in Jerusalem the services were conducted by the bishop entirely in Greek, but there was a priest on hand who translated the sermon and biblical readings into Syriac and the same was done for those who understood only Latin. An origin in oral paraphrase is more plausible than the suggestion that Christian scriptures were translated into Latin primarily as a missionary strategy for reading by unbelievers, although examples of the

---

Cyprianea of the *Revue des études augustiniennes*: in the Bibliography of the present volume, see also Aalders, Frisius, Haendler, O'Malley, Petzer, Quispel, Rönsch, and von Soden. Many of the older works are now obsolete, and new studies by Büsch and Haupt are in progress.

[8] Coleman 1987 describes such words as 'winners' or 'losers', according to whether or not they became standard.

reading of the Bible by non-Christians mentioned by Tertullian and others are given below. Nevertheless, the early text of the Latin New Testament in surviving manuscripts stems from a written translation corresponding closely to Greek: it has even been proposed that it was originally an interlinear version written between the lines of a Greek text.[9]

The distinctiveness of the Latin language used by Christians with its Greek influence and unusual forms, some of which become standard in later Latin, led a group of twentieth-century scholars known collectively as the Nijmegen School to propose that 'Christian Latin' was a separate language (or *Sonder-sprache*).[10] Not only did it feature numerous innovations for technical terms but it also appeared to have a different vocabulary for words which had no specialist Christian connotations. Examples of these include *confortare* ('to comfort'), *proximare* ('to approach'), or *refrigerium* ('relief'). The theory also interpreted comments from early authors about 'our writings' as an indication of Christian linguistic peculiarity, as in the following line from Tertullian:

> *tanto abest ut nostris litteris annuant homines ad quas nemo uenit nisi iam Christianus.* (TE an 1.4)

> It is so remote that people agree to our writings, to which no-one comes unless they are already Christian.

In context, though, it was availability and use rather than language which posed a hindrance to potential users. From the beginning, the *Sondersprache* concept appeared to be an overstatement because the characteristics of Christian discourse were limited to the lexicon. Morphology and syntax were unaffected, apart from the influence of a Greek original on translations. Furthermore, vocabulary in Christian texts which is absent from classical Latin is sometimes attested in the early playwrights, especially Plautus, or other works written in a lower register.[11] These terms therefore appear to be indicative of popular speech and form part of a continuum of colloquial Latin which eventually led to the Romance languages. The high volume of evidence preserved from ecclesiastical writers may have given the misleading impression that the phenomenon was distinctively Christian, rather than setting it within the broader context of non-literary and post-classical forms. Latin translations of the Bible and significant early writers such as Tertullian undoubtedly had an influence on Christian vocabulary and figures of speech (for example, some of the Semitic constructions transmitted through the Greek of the Septuagint), but there is no indication that non-Christians found it hard to read texts by their Christian contemporaries for linguistic

---

[9] Against 'missionary translation', see Harris 1989:299 and Burton 2000:78–9. The suggestion of an interlinear original is found most recently at Cimosa 2008:14.

[10] Schrijnen and Mohrmann; other authors indebted to this model include Palmer, O'Malley, and García de la Fuente.

[11] See further Adams 2013.

reasons. Indeed, there are numerous exhortations for non-believers to read the Bible for themselves, as in Tertullian's *Apology*:

> *inspice dei uoces, litteras nostras, quas neque ipsi supprimimus et plerique casus ad extraneos transferunt.* (TE ap 31.1)

> Consult the words of God, our scriptures, which we do not ourselves hold back and which many situations bring to those outside the community.

Similar encouragements from Augustine are quoted below.[12] While the 'plain register' (*sermo humilis*) of the biblical translations may have been an embarrassment for more literary converts, it was also treated as a virtue by apologists and contrasted with the esotericism of other religious discourse.[13] The full *Sondersprache* hypothesis now finds few adherents, although careful linguistic analysis may still identify aspects of language use peculiar to Christian groups, as has sometimes been the case in subsequent generations.[14]

CYPRIAN AND THE FIRST LATIN BIBLES

The biblical quotations of Cyprian, bishop of Carthage from 248/9 to 258, provide evidence for a Latin translation of the New Testament in third-century Africa. His numerous works, all in Latin, have a consistency in their scriptural text which indicates that they derive from a fixed version. A further indication of Cyprian's reliance on a standard Latin form may be seen in a difference in vocabulary between his own writing and his biblical text, such as his use of *caritas* and *gloria*.[15] There are even examples in Cyprian's quotations of what seem to be copying errors within Latin biblical tradition, such as *ut suscitentur* for *ut iudicentur* at 1 Peter 4:6. If this is the case, it demonstrates that several generations of copies had preceded the text used by Cyprian. His two collections of *testimonia*, biblical extracts grouped under particular thematic headings, are of particular value: the three books of *Ad Quirinum* (CY te) date from 248 or 250 while *Ad Fortunatum* (CY Fo) is slightly later. The text-type reconstructed from Cyprian's quotations in the Vetus Latina edition is given the siglum **K**.[16] The oldest surviving Old Latin gospel

---

[12] See pages 21–2.

[13] For *sermo humilis* see Auerbach 1965. Augustine describes his own disappointing first encounter with Christian scripture in the *Confessions* (AU cf. 3.5.9; see Burton 2007:112–14).

[14] Scholarly opposition to the *Sondersprache* theory is exemplified by Braun 1985, Coleman 1987, and Fredouille 1996; Burton 2008 and 2011 offer a reappraisal.

[15] See Frede 1972:464.

[16] Von Soden 1909 remains the most recent study of Cyprian's text, although there is much useful information in Fahey 1971: see also works by Bévenot, Corssen, Pallás, and Sanday in the Bibliography and the *Chronica Tertullianea et Cyprianea* (page 142).

manuscript, VL 1 (Codex Bobiensis), has a similar form of text and is sometimes referred to as k.[17] Although it was copied in Africa in the fourth century, its text appears to antedate Cyprian. This is most clearly shown by the ending of Mark, illustrated in Image 2. VL 1 is the only gospel manuscript in Greek or Latin which has the 'shorter ending' by itself, while Cyprian seems to be familiar with the 'longer ending' of Mark 16:9 onwards.[18] Cyprian's text of John in *Ad Fortunatum* is very similar to that of VL 2 (Codex Palatinus), while his citations of Acts are close to VL 55 (the Fleury Palimpsest).

There are a number of writings attributed to Cyprian which, although not authentic, may well be of a similar date and offer important evidence for early versions of the biblical text. *De montibus Sina et Sion* (PS-CY mont) has an intriguing form of John 2:19–21, reading *fanum* (a word often used in conjunction with pagan religious sites) rather than *templum*.[19] There is some controversy over the date and location of *De aleatoribus* (PS-CY al): it has been dated as early as the end of the second century in Rome, but current preference is for a fourth-century African origin because its biblical text seems to be drawn from the *testimonia* in Cyprian's *Ad Fortunatum*.[20]

Although there is surprisingly little overlap between Cyprian's text and the biblical quotations of Tertullian, Cyprian features a number of the innovative early forms described above which were later replaced, such as *baptiziator* rather than *baptista* (e.g. Matthew 3:1, 11:12), *similitudo* for *parabola* (e.g. Matthew 13:35–6), *praessura* for *tribulatio* (e.g. Romans 5:3–4, 8:35), and even *agape* for *caritas* (e.g. Romans 8:35). There are preferences for certain renderings such as *nequam* for *malum* ('evil'), *quoadusque* for *donec* ('until'), *ploratio* for *fletus* ('lament'), and even *quoniam* rather than *quia* or *quod* ('because') and *fui* rather than *eram* ('I was'). Because many of these forms are peculiar to these African witnesses they are often described as 'African' readings or renderings, although they should not be considered as evidence for an African dialect of Latin (*Africitas*).[21] A quick glance at the alternatives will show that most are forms common to Latin authors in general. In the present study, the designation 'archaic' is preferred to 'African' to represent these early terms which, although they may have been current in the community where the translation was first made, soon fell out of favour.

There is a degree of freedom in the earliest text which contrasts markedly with the traditional description of these as slavishly literal translations, full of

---

[17] See further pages 22 and 210 below.

[18] See pages 160–1. The phrase *cum dominus dixerit . . . in baptismo praeterita peccata dimitti* in CY ep 27.3 may allude to Mark 16:16.

[19] On the avoidance of existing religious vocabulary by Latin Christians, see Burton 2000:134.

[20] See further Daniélou 1970, Heine 2004:131–2, and the *Repertorium*.

[21] The idea of *Africitas* was proposed by Sittl in 1882 but soon fell out of favour: Capelle 1913 and Löfstedt 1959 demonstrate that these terms were not confined to Africa. A full list of New Testament examples of such vocabulary is given in Valgiglio 1985:313–16. On regional diversity in Latin see Adams 2007, summarized in Galdi 2011.

vulgarisms and infelicities, committing numerous grammatical and stylistic solecisms by reproducing Greek constructions.[22] Words or phrases are sometimes omitted or paraphrased, especially if they are repetitive or explanatory in function.[23] Burton has shown how the Old Latin Gospels often bear witness to considerable linguistic sensitivity on the part of the translators.[24] Although there are frequently orthographical errors and nonsense readings in the oldest surviving manuscripts, the translation itself is not the work of an incompetent. Indeed, to have sufficient expertise both to read Greek and to write Latin is an indication of a relatively advanced degree of education. Augustine's dismissive comment in *De doctrina christiana* has long been overapplied:

> *ut enim cuique primis fidei temporibus in manus uenit codex graecus et aliquantulum facultatis sibi utriusque linguae habere uidebatur, ausus est interpretari.* (AU do 2.11.16)

> For, in the first days of the faith, whenever a Greek manuscript came into the possession of someone who believed himself to have a modicum of ability in both languages, he hazarded his own translation.

In context, this refers to translations of the Old Testament, where Semitic idioms and points of obscurity may have resulted in greater confusion. The general direction is from a periphrastic early version (consistent with the Cyprianic text) towards an ever closer correspondence with a Greek text, culminating in the form adopted as the Vulgate.[25] Jerome comments in the preface to his revision of the Gospels:

> *si enim latinis exemplaribus fides est adhibenda, respondeant quibus: tot sunt paene quot codices.*[26] (HI Ev)

> If trust is to be placed in Latin originals, let them tell us which ones: there are almost as many as there are manuscripts.

The nature of the distinction between *exemplaria* ('originals') and *codices* ('manuscripts') is not immediately obvious, and may represent Jerome's rhetorical attempt to establish the priority of his text founded on a new comparison with Greek: Latin copies were never 'original' and Jerome goes on to describe even his own version of the Gospels as a light revision of an existing text.[27]

---

[22] e.g. Palmer 1954:185.

[23] This can even extend to entire verses, e.g. Matthew 5:44, 5:47, 8:5, 9:34, 12:47. Augustine used an African version of the book of Sirach in which certain verses were missing (AU re 1.21.3).

[24] Burton 2000:77–148; see also Thiele 1972:97.

[25] For the same direction in the Syriac New Testament tradition, see Williams 2004.

[26] Numerous forms are found of the text of this well-known line, some repeating *exemplaria* in the final phrase.

[27] See page 32. Plater & White 1926:6 translate *exemplaria* as 'types of text', while Kamesar 2013:660 has 'text forms': while these remove the difficulty of the phrase, they risk being anachronistic.

So was there one initial Latin translation of the New Testament, which then underwent numerous revisions, or were there multiple independent translations from which a handful—and eventually one in particular—became dominant? If we leave to one side the potentially unreliable comments of later authors and turn to the surviving textual evidence, the balance of probability favours the former. Editors of Old and New Testament books in the Vetus Latina series have reached the conclusion that in each case a single Latin translation underlies all the surviving evidence for the Old Latin tradition.[28] This does not remove the possibility that other translations were made at an early stage, but little if anything of these remains. As noted above in the case of Tertullian, variation in Latin biblical quotations in the initial centuries is often likely to indicate direct use of a Greek source rather than an alternative Latin version in circulation. Even the Gospels, for which the surviving manuscript evidence goes back furthest, display shared features for which the simplest explanation is a single common original. These range from the sequence Matthew–John–Luke–Mark in the majority of Old Latin codices to common omissions, patterns of rendering and even particular words.[29] Individual forms may have been substituted here and there, absent text supplied and paraphrases brought into closer conformity with a Greek source, but the overall shape remains remarkably consistent. Furthermore, as early as the middle of the fourth century, there is evidence for a conservatism in Latin Christian culture pertaining specifically to the biblical text.[30]

Occasions when the Latin tradition agrees on a reading not or poorly attested in Greek provide evidence in favour of a single original translation. One of the best known examples is Mark 9:15, where all pre-Vulgate Latin manuscripts have *gaudentes*, 'rejoicing' rather than 'running', apparently due to the misreading of προστρέχοντες as προσχαίροντες (as found in Codex Bezae).[31] At Luke 1:9, early Latin tradition agrees on *introitus eius*, 'his entrance', even though Greek witnesses only have τῷ λόγῳ, 'word'. Most Old Latin manuscripts reverse the sequence of phrases in Luke 9:62, with 'looking backwards' before 'putting his hand to the plough'. A second indication of the general uniformity of the Latin tradition is agreement on a particular reading in one location when multiple alternative renderings are attested elsewhere. Although the choice of word may in some cases be prompted by sensitivity to context, this is not always the case. For example,

---

[28] For the New Testament, see Birdsall 1970:371, Fischer 1972:24–8 [1986:188–91], Thiele 1972:95, Elliott 1992:202, Petzer 1995:123; Burton 2000:61, and Houghton 2013; for the Old Testament, see Haelewyck 1996 (and Cimosa 2008:20–1 on the entire Bible).
[29] These are set out in Burton 2000:29–74, where a fuller discussion is found of the examples in the following paragraphs.
[30] See the quotation from Ambrosiaster on page 26. A few years later, the same tendencies are manifest in the hostile reception accorded to Jerome's new version (e.g. AU ep 71.5).
[31] See further Burton 2000:59.

although there are five different translations preserved of the relatively rare Greek word for 'inn', τὸ κατάλυμα, at Luke 22:11 and Mark 14:14, at Luke 2:7 all but one manuscript has *diuersorium*. Again, every instance of ὁ λίθος ('stone') in Matthew is translated by *lapis* apart from Matthew 27:60, where all Old Latin manuscripts (apart from one known to be influenced by the Vulgate) have *saxum*, despite reading *lapis* for the same stone seven verses later. The verb 'to eat', ἐσθίω, is normally translated by *manducare*, but almost all manuscripts switch to *edere* at Matthew 15:27 and *cenare* at Matthew 26:26. The treatment of words which occur only once in the Greek New Testament is also instructive. These include ἀμαράντινον at 1 Peter 5:4 and ἐπιούσιον in the Lord's Prayer at Matthew 6:11 and Luke 11:3. If the surviving manuscripts derived from independent translations, one would expect variation in these unusual words for which there was no obvious Latin equivalent, rather than universal agreement on *immarcescibilem* and *cottidianum* respectively. Even the more common word τέκτων ('builder') in Matthew 13:55 and Mark 6:3 is always rendered by *faber*, while at John 21:5 almost all witnesses have *pulmentarium* for the unique προσφάγιον. It has been suggested that the early Latin translators may have had some connection with Jewish communities because of their treatment of technical terms: the use of *cena pura* rather than *praeparatio* for παρασκευή ('the day of preparation') appears to reproduce a Jewish practice.[32]

There are also practical reasons which may explain how a single translation could become widespread. Books circulated relatively quickly and easily around the Mediterranean. If a Latin translation were known to exist already, users might have preferred to make a copy of that (with their own adjustments) rather than start from scratch. While the need for Latin copies of the New Testament probably arose at around the same time in different communities, meaning that early translators may have worked in parallel, it is not impossible that a single original could have exerted a wide influence through multiple subsequent copies. The likelihood of this would be increased if, like Jerome's Gospels later on, it had some form of prestige through association with an authoritative writer or ecclesiastical figure. It is worth observing that, despite the probable origin of Latin translations in an oral context, all the surviving evidence is literary.

Nonetheless, the theory of a single translation of all biblical books in the early third century is not without its problems, given both the ongoing debate at this time about the scriptural canon and the nature of biblical codices. Pandects, that is manuscripts containing the Old and New Testament in a single volume, are unknown until the appearance of the Greek Codex Vaticanus (GA 03) and Codex Sinaiticus (GA 01) around the end of the fourth century. Even after that

---

[32] e.g. VL 2 in John 19:14, 31 and 42; see Burton 2000:144; Adams 2007; Bogaert 2013:506.

it was still the norm for books to be circulated in smaller collections, such as the Gospels or the Pauline Epistles. The earliest Latin pandects appear to have been assembled in the fifth century from multiple manuscripts.[33] It therefore remains possible that the single versions claimed to underlie the surviving Latin tradition had various origins: while Africa provides the earliest evidence for the Gospels, the Pauline Epistles may have originated elsewhere.[34] A detailed survey of the translation technique in different books is needed to determine whether or not this is the case. At the same time, the loss of most of the early Latin New Testament manuscripts makes it difficult to quantify the amount of revision and extent of variation across Latin tradition. Almost all pre-Vulgate witnesses have a greater or lesser number of readings which are now unique to them but which may have had wider currency in manuscripts which no longer survive.

An early revision of the Latin text of the Gospels around the time of Cyprian is attested in a set of *capitula* (chapter titles), part of the prefatory material commonly found in later gospel manuscripts. By a remarkable accident of preservation, this series (KA Cy) is only present in a handful of much later manuscripts, which have a Vulgate form of the biblical text.[35] Nevertheless, the affiliation of the passages quoted in these lengthy summaries corresponds very closely to the text of Cyprian and VL 1. The inclusion of the story of the Woman taken in Adultery (John 7:53–8:11) suggests that these *capitula* post-date Cyprian, who does not quote the passage. On the other hand, some of the renderings are more ancient than Cyprian, indicating different layers in the biblical text even at this early stage. Another set of *capitula* for Matthew (KA D) also has similarities with VL 1. The provision of chapter titles and other paratextual information goes hand in hand with a revision of the biblical text as part of the creation of a new edition of the Bible.

CHRISTIAN AUTHORS IN EUROPE

Greek continued to be the first language of the early Church at the turn of the third century in Europe, as shown by Irenaeus of Lyons and Hippolytus of Rome. Even so, there is also evidence for the use of Latin at this time. In the Greek text of the *Shepherd of Hermas*, the Latin word *statio* is borrowed as a way to speak of 'fasting'.[36] Jerome identifies Victor, bishop of Rome in the

---

[33] See pages 87–8 on VL 7, a ninth-century copy of an earlier collection.
[34] See page 170.   [35] See pages 88–9.
[36] Parable 5. Mohrmann 1949 claims that στατίωνα ἔχω is a technical term pointing to the development of Latin Christianity in Rome, but in inscriptions the word is used of military service: this would also fit the context. In subsequent centuries, the word *statio* comes to mean a copyist's workshop: see Bischoff 1990:184.

190s, and his contemporary Apollonius as 'Latins' (*latinorum*; HI ill 53), implying that their theological treatises and writings against the Montanists may have been in Latin. However, there was ongoing traffic between the metropolis and the colonies. Many prominent Roman Christians were of North African origin, including Pope Victor and possibly also Minucius Felix, whose apologetic treatise *Octavius* (MIN) is set in Rome. Cyprian corresponded regularly with Roman clergy, including the presbyter Novatian (NO). Few of Novatian's writings have survived, because of his excommunication as a heretic. The most substantial is his treatise *De trinitate* (NO tri). His biblical text has sometimes been claimed to be a separate Roman tradition (*Vetus Romana*) or even a witness for the gospel harmony known as the Diatessaron, but is textually similar to later Italian tradition, especially VL 3 (Codex Vercellensis) in the Gospels.[37]

The tradition of referring to the Old Latin versions as *Itala* derives from a comment by Augustine on the Old Testament:

> *in ipsis autem interpretationibus, Itala ceteris praeferatur; nam est uerborum tenacior cum perspicuitate sententiae.* (AU do 2.15.22)

> As for the translations themselves, the *Itala* is preferable to the rest; for it keeps more closely to the words and gives the sense with clarity.

The word *Itala* has been much debated, with some scholars suggesting that it is corrupt and others that it referred to Jerome's Vulgate.[38] However, the adjective *Italus* is used elsewhere by Augustine (AU ord 2.5.15 and 2.17.45) and, given his designation of other biblical manuscripts as African (e.g. AU re 1.21.3), the best interpretation is that this is a geographical term indicating pre-Vulgate translations of Italian origin, perhaps those which he encountered during his time in Milan.[39] Another observation later in the same paragraph indicates that certain places were renowned for the quality of their biblical texts:

> *libros autem Noui Testamenti, si quid in latinis uarietatibus titubat, graecis cedere oportere non dubium est, et maxime qui apud ecclesias doctiores et diligentiores repperiuntur.* (AU do 2.15.22)

> As for the books of the New Testament, if the variety of Latin manuscripts leads to any uncertainty, there is no doubt that they should give way to Greek ones, especially those which are found in more learned and responsible churches.

---

[37] Loi 1974; Mattei 1995 (cf. Baumstark 1930).

[38] Schildenberger 1952 has a summary of proposals. As the passage relates to the Old Testament, Quentin 1927 suggested that a form of *Aquila* should be read; the Vulgate hypothesis, inadequately based on Augustine's text of the Gospels, is found in Burkitt 1896 and 1910a. Burton 2012:168 glosses it as 'the Italian [version]'.

[39] Bogaert 1998:43 and 2006:522, and Lancel 2002:176 state that Augustine took biblical codices from Milan back to Africa.

The use of *Itala* for the entire tradition, or even just Old Latin texts which do not preserve the most archaic features, is therefore unduly restrictive and has generally been abandoned.

Some third-century Latin writers continued to use Greek biblical texts. This is the case for Victorinus of Poetovio (also known as Ptuj or Pettau), who wrote a commentary on the Apocalypse (VICn Apc) before his martyrdom in the Diocletianic persecution around the year 304. Like Tertullian, Victorinus is referred to by the siglum X (or Y) in the Vetus Latina edition, to indicate his dependence on Greek: the text of Revelation in the biblical lemmata in the commentary appears to be Victorinus' own translation. The original version of this work is preserved in a single manuscript: most later users encountered it in the form of an edition made by Jerome (HI Apc), although the biblical text in this version was reworked by a series of later revisers.[40] Victorinus also wrote a commentary on Matthew, which is now lost. His gospel quotations exhibit frequent harmonization.[41]

EARLY TRANSLATIONS OF OTHER WORKS

The date of the translation of Irenaeus' *Adversus Haereses* (IR), written in Greek around 180, is unknown: it may be third-century, or from around the end of the fourth.[42] The biblical quotations in this writing are often of textual interest. It is not clear whether they were translated directly or whether reference was made to an existing Latin version. The date of translation is also unknown for the Latin versions of Clement's First Epistle to the Corinthians (CLE-R) and the 'Vulgate' version of the *Shepherd of Hermas* (HER V). It has even been suggested that these predate Tertullian.[43] Along with the translation of the Epistle of Barnabas (BAR) produced in Africa before Cyprian, which appears to rely on an existing translation of the Latin Bible, they offer interesting comparisons for the translation technique and vocabulary of the Latin Bible.[44]

The Muratorian Fragment (or Muratorian Canon; AN Mur) has been the focus of a considerable amount of scholarly attention, as one of the earliest surviving lists of canonical books. Preserved in a manuscript of the seventh or eighth century (Milan, Biblioteca Ambrosiana, Cod. J 101 sup.), it was redis-covered by Muratori in 1740. The fragment mentions four Gospels, the Acts of

---

[40] See further Dulaey 1991.

[41] Dulaey 1993 has even suggested that Victorinus used a gospel harmony, although har-monization is very common in early Latin translations and quotations from memory.

[42] Various reconstructions have been made of the biblical text: Sanday, Turner et al. 1923, Kraft 1924, and Schäfer 1951. See also Chapman 1924, Vogels 1924, and Lundström 1985.

[43] Thiele 1972:93. Tornau & Cecconi 2014 offer a new edition of HER V.

[44] See Heer 1908; Frede 1972:467.

the Apostles (attributed to Luke), thirteen letters of Paul, one of Jude and two of John, and the Apocalypses of John (i.e. Revelation) and Peter. The status of the latter is said to be dubious; there is no reference to the epistle to the Hebrews, and letters of Paul to the Laodiceans and Alexandrians are dismissed as forgeries. The order of the Pauline correspondence is unusual (Corinthians, Ephesians, Philippians, Colossians, Galatians, Thessalonians, Romans) and it is not clear whether the Catholic Epistles precede Acts or the Apocalypse. The dating of the text hinges on the reference to the *Shepherd of Hermas* at the end of the list:

> *Pastorem uero nuperrime temporibus nostris in urbe Roma Hermas conscripsit sedente cathedra urbis Romae ecclesiae Pio episcopo fratre eius et ideo legi eum quidem oportet se publicare uero in ecclesia populo neque inter prophetas completo numero neque inter apostolos in finem temporum potest.*[45]

> Most recently, in our own times in the city of Rome, Hermas wrote *The Shepherd* while his brother bishop Pius was occupying the episcopal seat of the church of the city of Rome. Therefore he should indeed be read, but he can neither be read aloud to the people in church among the prophets, whose number is complete, nor among the apostles, as he is after their times.

The death of Pius I in 157 means that the earliest possible date for the list is around the year 170, although most scholars hesitate to take this at face value.[46] Armstrong suggested that the Muratorian Canon could have come from the prologue to Victorinus of Poetovio's lost *Commentary on Matthew*, but Guignard's recent study offers compelling reasons to identify it as a fourth-century Latin translation of a Greek original.[47] The order of the Gospels, with Luke and John at the end, is another argument in favour of its origin in Greek tradition.

In conclusion, the adoption of Latin in the early Church was a gradual development, lasting at least a century. The origins of the translation of the New Testament are obscured by the continuing use of Greek texts by authors familiar with both languages who made ad hoc translations of their biblical quotations into Latin. Even so, a Latin translation of most if not all books of the Bible, probably made in the first half of the third century, was used by Cyprian in North Africa. What is more, the surviving evidence for each book points to a single original translation which was subsequently revised in different ways on numerous occasions. This accounts both for peculiarities shared across the whole of Latin tradition and the diversity of texts arising from internal revision or comparison with Greek. Examples of such revision

---

[45] The Latin orthography of the fragment is very poor; this corrected text is taken from Armstrong 2008 (Metzger 1987 has an alternative text and translation).

[46] Verheyden 2013:396–9 locates the fragment in Rome around 200; Henne 1993 also goes for an early dating, while Sundberg 1973 and Hahneman 1992 favour the fourth century.

[47] Armstrong 2008; Guignard 2015.

are already attested by the time of Cyprian, along with paratextual material to aid readers. Claims of a distinctive form of language in the early Church, often described as 'Christian Latin', are difficult to sustain. Nevertheless, the early biblical translations, including features from an initial period of experimentation, exert a strong and lasting influence on most Christian writing in Latin throughout its history.

2

The Fourth Century and the Beginning
of the Vulgate

As Christian centres became established throughout the Roman Empire, Latin gained ground as the language of theological discourse and ecclesiastical administration. The oldest surviving manuscripts of the Latin New Testament were copied in the fourth century. These bear witness to a variety of textual forms, showing that multiple revisions had already introduced considerable diversity. However, a process of convergence may also be observed, culminating in the revision of the Gospels made by Jerome towards the end of the century. The writings of the earliest Latin Christian authors, Tertullian and Cyprian in particular, were extremely influential in subsequent generations, especially among those with little or no facility in Greek. Their texts, and collections of biblical extracts known as *testimonia*, perpetuated ancient forms of the Latin New Testament alongside the ongoing revisions.[1] At the same time, the genre of biblical commentary flourished in the hands of Latin authors in the fourth century, creating a distinctive tradition of Latin exegesis closely connected to the scriptural text.

SPAIN AND AFRICA

Lactantius, a Christian poet born in Africa, composed his seven books of *Diuinae Institutiones* (LAC in) in Nicomedia, now in Turkey, before his death in Trier in Germany in 325. Many of the scriptural citations in this, as well as other minor works, were taken from Cyprian's *testimonia* although Lactantius may also bear witness to an additional biblical tradition.[2] Another

---

[1] On *testimonia* in general, see Monat 1985 and Albl 1999; for the updating of Cyprian's *testimonia* to reflect later forms of biblical text, see Bévenot 1961; Petitmengin 1968; Frede 1972:470.
[2] Wlosok 1961; Monat 1982a & 1982b; Andrist 2007.

contemporary poet, Juvencus, produced a versified form of the Gospels (JUV). Extracting the underlying biblical readings from metrical texts can be prob- lematic, but recent studies indicate that these *Libri Euangeliorum* preserve numerous early forms alongside those of revisions.[3] The work was very popular and was used by both Prudentius (PRU), a fellow Spaniard, and Paulinus of Nola (PAU-N), who was ordained in Barcelona.[4] Three Spanish bishops in the latter half of the fourth century were particularly influential. Pacian of Barcelona (PAC) produced works on penitence and baptism, counting Lactantius, Cyprian and Tertullian among his sources: his biblical text, unsur- prisingly, transmits early readings.[5] Gregory of Elvira (GR-I; the city's Latin name was Illiberis) wrote a commentary on the Song of Songs, a treatise *On Faith* (GR-I fi) using Tertullian, Novatian and others, and exegetical sermons based on a Latin *florilegium* of Origen (GR-I tr). His biblical citations are often of interest for the pre-Vulgate text. Priscillian of Avila composed a series of ninety canons for the Pauline Epistles (PRIS can). These provide details of themes shared by multiple epistles and are found in numerous later manu- scripts.[6] Priscillian is also an early witness to the Epistle to the Laodiceans, a pseudepigraphic letter of Paul inspired by Colossians 4:16. Although this pastiche based on lines from the authentic epistles was originally composed in Greek, probably in the third century, it is attested in Latin Bibles from the sixth century onwards.[7]

Throughout the fourth century, Africa was riven by the Donatist contro- versy concerning the validity of clergy who had renounced Christianity in the face of persecution. Both sides claimed to be in continuity with Cyprian and to be the true Catholic Church in North Africa. Despite descriptions of the sect by Optatus (OPT), the fourth-century bishop of Milevis, and others which focus on its destructive and violent elements, Donatists made significant contributions to biblical scholarship. Sets of chapter titles for the Acts of the Apostles and the Hebrew prophets reflect Donatist concerns such as persecu- tion and rebaptism, and were clearly composed in this milieu: they continued to be copied in biblical manuscripts several centuries after the condemnation of the sect at the Conference of Carthage in 411.[8] Whether or not they originate from Donatist circles, two sets of Old Latin *capitula* for the Gospels may be traced back to the middle of the fourth century. Type I (KA I) features readings transmitted only in African writers (such as *officium deo facere* in John 16:2), while Type A (KA A) mentions several topics which could be connected with the controversy. Another practical aspect of Donatist book

---

[3] Orban 1995, Heinsdorff 2003; see also Green 2006, 2007.

[4] For Prudentius' biblical text, see the works of Charlet and Grasso in the Bibliography.

[5] See Ferreres 2004.   [6] See page 202.

[7] Tite 2012 gives a recent analysis of the Latin letter.

[8] Tilley 1997 offers an overview of Donatism. On *capitula*, see Bogaert 1982 and Houghton 2011. On Optatus' biblical text, see Buonaiuti 1916; Marone 2005 and 2008.

production is the stichometric list discovered by Mommsen and dated by him to the year 359, sometimes called the 'Cheltenham canon'.[9] This gives the number of lines (*stichoi*) in each book of the Bible and the works of Cyprian, and was used by scribes to calculate the cost of copying. The list confirms that the standard unit for measuring the length of Latin texts was one line of hexameter verse, as found in Vergil. The letters of James and Jude are missing from this canon, as is Hebrews.

Tyconius, one of the major biblical scholars of the fourth century, was a Donatist. His commentary on Revelation (TY Apc), composed around 380 but no longer extant, has recently been reconstructed from its re-use in the later commentaries of Caesarius of Arles, Primasius of Hadrumetum, and Beatus of Liébana.[10] Tyconius also wrote the *Liber Regularum* (TY reg), which includes a set of seven rules for scriptural interpretation. These were influential for Augustine, who cites them at AU do 3.42. In fact, it has been suggested that one of the reasons that the first edition of *De doctrina Christiana* was left unfinished in the middle of the third book was Augustine's use of a Donatist source.[11]

There are several fourth-century documents which provide details about the availability of biblical books in North Africa. A set of court records, the *Gesta apud Zenophilum*, describes the confiscation of church property in Cirta. The subdeacon Catullinus handed over a single very large codex (*codicem unum pernimium maiorem*) which was stored in the church, but the other books were kept at home by the readers: a search of six of their houses results in the confiscation of a further thirty-two codices and four unbound fascicles (*quiniones*).[12] This number of copies was not unusual, as Optatus confirms:

> *bibliothecae refertae sunt libris; nihil deest ecclesiae; per loca singula diuinum sonat ubique praeconium; non silent ora lectorum; manus omnium codicibus plenae sunt; nihil deest populis doceri cupientibus.* (OPT 7.1)

> The libraries are stuffed with books; the church lacks nothing; throughout each locality the sacred message resounds everywhere; the mouths of the readers are not silent; the hands of all are full of manuscripts; nothing is lacking for the crowds who wish to be instructed.

A few decades later, Augustine urges both Christian and non-Christian readers to read the Bible for themselves:

> *cottidie codices dominici uenales sunt, legit lector; eme tibi et tu lege quando uacat, immo age ut uacet: melius enim ad hoc uacat quam ad nugas.* (AU s 114B.15)

---

[9] See Mommsen 1886, Sanday 1891, Bischoff 1990:182–4, Rouse and McNelis 2000 and Bogaert 2003. The two manuscripts in which this list is preserved are St Gall, Stiftsbibliothek 133 and Rome, Biblioteca Nazionale Centrale, Vitt. Em. 1325 (formerly Cheltenham, Phillipps 12266).

[10] Gryson 1997 and 2000–3.   [11] See AU ep 41, and TeSelle 1970 [2002:182].

[12] See Fischer 1963b [1985:38] for other references to biblical codices in the Diocletianic period.

codices nostri publice uenales feruntur: lux non erubescit. emant, legant, credant;
aut emant, legant, irrideant. nouit scriptura illa reos tenere qui legunt et non
credunt. circumfertur uenalis codex sed ille qui praedicatur in codice non est
uenalis . . . eme tu codicem et lege, nos non erubescimus. (AU s 198.20)

The Lord's manuscripts are daily on sale, and readers read them; buy one for
yourself and read it when you have time—in fact, make time for it: it is better to
have time for this than for trifles.
Our manuscripts are put on sale in public: the daylight does not blush for shame.
Let them buy them, read them, and believe them; or let them buy them, read them,
and laugh at them. Scripture knows how to call to account those who read and do
not believe. A manuscript is carried around for sale, but the one whom its pages
proclaim is not for sale . . . Buy a manuscript and read it: we are not ashamed.

Statements such as this contrast with the relatively small proportion of
members of ancient society who were able to read. Even so, while there is
undoubtedly some hyperbole in these exhortations, their force would be
entirely lost if they bore no relation to everyday life. Famous preachers such
as Augustine drew huge numbers to church, and there was clearly a ready
market for transcriptions of sermons as well as theological treatises to be read
at home or in informal gatherings.

VL 1 (Codex Bobiensis), the oldest surviving Latin gospel book, was copied
in the fourth century (see Image 2). The page is square and relatively plain in
appearance, similar to some of the earliest Greek Gospels written on papyrus:
although this is a parchment manuscript, it has been suggested that its
exemplar was papyrus.[13] It probably contained all four Gospels, in the order
John–Luke–Mark–Matthew, although only portions of the latter two survive.
The manuscript features *nomina sacra* ('sacred names'), a set of abbreviations
for words such as 'God', 'Lord', and 'Jesus' reflecting early Christian practice in
Greek, but these are unusual in form: for example, on line 11 of the image, ʜꞀˢ
can be seen in place of the more customary Ꞁʜꜱ (from the Greek *ΙΗΣΟΥΣ* for
Iesus). There are spaces of two to three characters at sense breaks in the body
of the text (lines 4 and 10 of the image) and new sections of text begin on a
fresh line with the initial letter projecting into the margin. It has been
suggested that the copyist was not a Christian: *Helion*, the name of the sun
god, is found in place of *Heliam* in Mark 15:34, while the form of Matthew
6:12 was initially written as *quanto ergo differt homo Ioue* ('how much,
therefore, does a man differ from Jove?') rather than *oue* ('from a sheep').
On the other hand, such errors (along with *ueni ad regnum tuum*, 'I have come
to your kingdom', rather than *ueniat regnum tuum* in the Lord's Prayer,
Matthew 6:10) may simply be further examples of the copyist's inaccuracy
or poor orthography.

[13] Lowe 1934–71 (CLA IV 465 ad loc.). Further details of the manuscript are given on
page 228.

Image 2 VL 1: **Codex Bobiensis** (Turin, Biblioteca Nazionale Universitaria, 1163 (G.VII.15), folio 41ʳ), showing the shorter ending of the Gospel according to Mark. © Ministero dei Beni e delle Attività Culturali e del Turismo, Biblioteca Nazionale Universitaria di Torino. Reproduction forbidden.

COMMENTATORS IN ITALY AND GAUL

Biblical exposition in Italy had numerous connections with Africa. These are embodied in Marius Victorinus (sometimes referred to as Victorinus Afer), who composed commentaries on some, perhaps all, of the Pauline Epistles in Rome after the year 363. An African grammarian (*rhetor*) who converted to Christianity around fifteen years before his death, his approach reflects his secular rhetorical training and his interest in philosophy. Victorinus' surviving writings on Galatians, Ephesians, and Philippians (MAR Gal, Eph, Phil) indicate that his commentaries on Romans and the Corinthian correspondence have been lost.[14] The biblical lemmata (the verses quoted before each section of commentary) enable the reconstruction of the earliest continuous Latin text for the three extant letters, although the manuscript tradition is late and very slim. Victorinus makes surprisingly few references in his commentaries to Greek texts or earlier Christian authors, but he does show knowledge of the Marcionite prologues to the Pauline Epistles.[15] In his other main theological work, four books addressed to the Arian Candidus (MAR Ar), the situation is quite different: Victorinus quotes extensively from the Gospel according to John in both Latin and Greek. His quotation of John 1:18 with the singular ἐν κόλπῳ ('in the breast'), apparently unattested in any Greek manuscript, seems to be an error of memory. The multiplicity of variant Latin forms in his quotations, especially those of the initial verses, has led to the conclusion that he was translating directly from a Greek text and deliberately varying the rendering of certain prepositions or leaving key terms untranslated in order to make theological points.[16]

Another contemporary African expositor who settled in Italy was Fortunatianus, bishop of Aquileia (FO-A). Jerome records that, at the request of Constantius, emperor from 337 to 361, Fortunatianus 'wrote commentaries on the Gospels, with ordered headings, in a terse and simple style'.[17] This work has recently been rediscovered, leading to the identification of numerous instances of its re-use in later writings which include those of his successor Chromatius.[18] Fortunatianus centred his work on Matthew, supplementing it with short portions from Luke and John. The commentary also includes a series of section headings. He does not mention any of his sources by name, but they include Tertullian and the lost *Commentary on Matthew* by Victorinus of Poetovio. There is strong influence from Origen throughout: references to a translator suggest that Fortunatianus relied on a Latin version of Origen.

Hilary, bishop of Poitiers from around 350, also wrote a commentary on Matthew (HIL Mt). This not only transmits an Old Latin biblical text but also provides the earliest evidence for one of the sets of *capitula* for this Gospel (KA A). The majority of forms unique to Hilary in the lemmata seem, however, to represent his own adjustments to the biblical text rather than

---

[14] See Cooper 2011:70.   [15] Schäfer 1970a, 1970b; Jongkind 2015:394.

[16] Bruce 1979.

[17] *Fortunatianus, natione Afer, Aquileiensis episcopus, imperante Constantio in euangelia titulis ordinatis breui sermone et rustico scripsit commentarios.* (HI ill 97).

[18] The principal manuscript is Cologne, Dombibliothek, MS 17, identified by Lukas J. Dorfbauer in 2012. On the other sources, see the works of Dorfbauer in the Bibliography; Houghton 2015a shows that the biblical text matches other fourth-century Italian witnesses.

readings of an otherwise unattested version.[19] For example, at Matthew 2:20, he reads *reuertere cum puero et matre eius* ('to return with the boy and his mother') in place of *accipe puerum et matrem eius* ('to receive the boy and his mother'): this appears to be motivated by a desire to avoid repeating the same phrase as found in Matthew 2:13 at the beginning of the lemma. On other occasions, he adds a verb (e.g. *iurabis* in Matthew 5:34) or changes the form (e.g. *iudicabitis* for *iudicantes* in Matthew 19:28) in order to make the sentence complete when the whole verse is not cited in the lemma. One of the tell-tale signs that Hilary is responsible for these changes is the addition of *cum* after *donec* (e.g. Matthew 12:20), a characteristic phrase in his own writings. There is also a considerable amount of harmonization with the other Synoptic Gospels, which may be attributed either to Hilary or his source. Although Hilary knew Greek, and appears to have used Origen in the original language, the variations in his gospel citations are not consistent with the use of a Greek text. His other major works include tractates on the Psalms (HIL Ps) and twelve books on the Trinity (HIL tri). There are suggestions that certain fragments may derive from lost commentaries on the Epistles.[20]

In several manuscripts as well as one of Augustine's works (AU Pel 4.4.7), an anonymous commentary on thirteen Pauline Epistles (not including Hebrews) is ascribed to Hilary. A reference to Damasus as the current pope shows that it was composed between 366 and 384, probably in Rome. The similarity of the author's style to that of Ambrose of Milan (to whom the work is also sometimes attributed) prompted Franciscus Lucas Brugensis to coin the epithet Ambrosiaster, by which the commentary is now generally identified (AMst).[21] The work was subject to extensive authorial revision, resulting in no fewer than three recensions of Romans (α, β, γ) and two of all the other Epistles (α, β).[22] Its biblical text consistently presents an Old Latin version predating all surviving manuscripts of the Epistles. There are numerous similarities with the Pauline text of Marius Victorinus: although Ambrosiaster used Victorinus' commentary, the textual tradition of his lemmata seems to be an independent witness to a similar form. The significance of this text is shown by the fact that Ambrosiaster is the most-cited Latin author in the apparatus of the Nestle-Aland Greek New Testament.[23] However, Ambrosiaster disapproved of reliance on Greek scholarship. Indeed, he maintained that the Latin tradition was superior to the Greek texts at hand:

---

[19] See Doignon 1975, from which all the examples are taken. Doignon's critical edition replaces the earlier study of Bonnassieux.

[20] Feder 1916:227–34. Hilary's text of Romans and other verses from the Pauline Epistles has been investigated by Doignon.

[21] Krans 2013; see also Souter 1905 and Lunn-Rockliffe 2007.

[22] Dating in Cooper & Hunter 2010.

[23] For figures (based on NA27), see Houghton 2012:390. Ambrosiaster's entire Pauline text is reconstructed in Vogels 1957, which is more accurate than the CSEL edition (see Frede 1972:471–2).

et tamen sic praescribere nobis uolunt de graecis codicibus, quasi non ipsi ab inuicem discrepent. . . . constat autem quosdam latinos porro olim de ueteribus graecis translatos codicibus, quos incorruptos simplicitas temporum seruauit et probat. . . . nam hodie quae in Latinis reprehenduntur codicibus, sic inueniuntur a ueteribus posita, Tertulliano et Victorino et Cypriano. (AMst Rm 5.14)

However, some people desire that we should explain in a manner based on Greek manuscripts, as if they did not differ from each other. . . . But it is agreed that certain Latin manuscripts were translated long ago from old Greek ones, which have been preserved unchanged as proven by the straightforwardness of earlier times. . . . For the things which are criticized in Latin manuscripts today are found expressed in the same way by the early authors, Tertullian, Victorinus, and Cyprian.

The same writer also produced a series of brief *Quaestiones* ('Investigations') on the Old and New Testament in Rome around 370 (AMst q). Like the commentary, this work was revised by the author: the 127-chapter version edited by Souter can be supplemented by manuscripts with a 150-chapter form.[24] A handful of short works may also be by Ambrosiaster, although this writer is no longer identified with Isaac the Jew, the author of *Fides Isatis ex Iudaeo* (AMst fi).[25] In the Vetus Latina edition, the biblical text of Ambrosiaster's works is usually described as text-type I, typical of fourth-century Italy, although there are some differences in the Gospels (see page 30).

The oldest surviving Italian gospel book is VL 3 (Codex Vercellensis). Tradition ascribes the copying of this manuscript to Bishop Eusebius of Vercelli, who died in 371: this is palaeographically possible both in terms of date and location, although the link is impossible to prove. It contains all four Gospels in the standard Old Latin order Matthew–John–Luke–Mark. The presentation is relatively plain, although red ink is used at the beginning of each Gospel. The manuscript contains an early form of text, later than that of Cyprian but featuring several parallels with Novatian. A handful of readings, including the light after Jesus' baptism at Matthew 3:15, have been described as characteristic of the Diatessaron, although these are more likely to have been incorporated as part of ongoing tradition rather than from any direct influence of the Diatessaron or Syriac sources. In John, VL 3 resembles the biblical quotations of Lucifer, bishop of Cagliari (LUC), who died in the same year as Eusebius. Lucifer's continuity with African tradition is demonstrated by his use of both Cyprian and Lactantius in *Moriundum esse pro Dei filio* (LUC mor). His New Testament text varies from book to book: in Luke and Acts, he matches VL 4 and 51 respectively, both witnesses to text-type I. Elsewhere, however, he is identified as the Vetus Latina text-type D, an early form with a particular connection to southern Italy.[26]

---

[24] See Bussières 2011.

[25] Lunn-Rockliffe 2007:34–41. A Latin equivalent for *Isaac* is, coincidentally, *Hilarius*.

[26] On Lucifer's biblical text, see further Coleman, Piras, and Vogels in the Bibliography.

In the Pauline Epistles, Lucifer's text is similar to an anonymous commentary on all fourteen Pauline Epistles composed in Rome in either 397 or 405. This is preserved in a single ninth-century manuscript, currently held in Budapest (AN Paul).[27] Although this commentary is set out in a lineated form with alternating sections of text and exegesis, fluctuations in the sequence of the latter suggest that it originated as marginal annotations in a scriptural codex: the continuous text of the Epistles in the commentary, which differs slightly from the quotations in the exposition, has been given the siglum VL 89 as if it were a biblical manuscript. The tenor of the commentary is anti-Pelagian, which has led to the suggestion that its author may have been an expositor called Constantius although Dunphy proposes that the exposition may have been translated from Greek.[28] Extracts from the work were partially incorporated into later recensions of Pelagius' commentary.

EARLY GREEK–LATIN BILINGUAL MANUSCRIPTS

The most significant feature of other biblical manuscripts which accord with the Vetus Latina text-type **D** is that they are bilingual. The oldest surviving Latin manuscript of the Pauline Epistles, VL 75 (Codex Claromontanus), was copied in Italy in the middle of the fifth century. This, along with later bilingual codices of Paul, is believed to go back to an ancient bilingual archetype created in the middle of the fourth century or possibly even earlier.[29] The Greek text is written on the *verso* (the left-hand page of each opening), the place of honour in late Antique bilingual codices.[30] It is written in short lines, enabling easy comparison between the two languages, and it seems that there has sometimes been mutual interference between their text. VL 75 also contains the so-called *Catalogus Claromontanus*, a list of biblical books and their stichometric lengths. This is added in space which may have been left for the Epistle to the Laodiceans, between the end of Philemon and the beginning of Hebrews (foll. 467v–468v). The list may have been translated from a Greek source. The books are in an unusual order, including the sequence Matthew–John–Mark–Luke. Hebrews and some of the shorter Pauline Epistles are missing, while four non-canonical writings are mentioned: the Epistle of Barnabas, the Shepherd of Hermas, the Acts of Paul, and the Revelation of Peter.[31]

---

[27] Edition in Frede 1974; see also pages 248–9 below.
[28] De Bruyn 1992; Dunphy 2013, 2014, and 2015.
[29] Parker 2008:259–61 notes that Fee reckons that the archetype (Z) could go back to the early third century. The designation of the text-type as D derives from Tischendorf's siglum for VL 75.
[30] McGurk 1994a:6; there is useful tabulation of data on bilingual manuscripts in Parker 1992:50–69.
[31] On stichometry, see page 21.

Two other documents from the end of the fourth century bear witness to a different bilingual textual tradition in the Pauline Epistles. VL 85 is a fragment found in Egypt with two verses of Ephesians. It appears to come from a Greek–Latin manuscript of all the Epistles. The study of Paul in both languages in Egypt at this time is also shown by Dublin, Chester Beatty Library, P. Chester Beatty Ac. 1499. This is a Greek–Latin glossary and grammar which, on folios 11–14, contains readings from certain letters of Paul (AN glo Paul).[32] The densely written pages consist of individual Greek words followed by their Latin equivalents. These occur in the same sequence in which they appear in the letters, offering a partial representation of the text of 2 Corinthians, Galatians, and Ephesians along with the first verse of Romans after Galatians.

The most famous bilingual New Testament manuscript is VL 5, Codex Bezae, copied around the year 400, possibly in the legal centre of Berytus (modern Beirut). It currently comprises the four Gospels in the standard Old Latin order, a Latin page from 3 John and most of the Acts of the Apostles. The manuscript is of considerable textual interest as it provides the earliest or only occurrence of certain passages in Greek. It is also the oldest surviving biblical manuscript to contain the story of the woman taken in adultery (John 7:52–8:11), and the only witness to the 'Cambridge pericope' in Luke (illustrated in Image 3; text on page 163). The text of Acts in VL 5 is notable for the amount of additional material, which amounts to a separate recension around one-third longer than the standard text and is often described as the 'Western' text. Parker has shown that this manuscript was copied from two earlier bilingual manuscripts: one containing the Gospels in the order Matthew–Mark–John–Luke, produced in the late third or fourth century with two columns per page and much shorter lines, and another of Acts with a single column on each page, in which the Latin text was adjusted to match the Greek.[33] He suggests that the manuscript was created for liturgical reading in both languages, and may already have been old-fashioned when it was produced. After some initial corrections, very little attention appears to have been paid to the Latin text, although some missing leaves were replaced when the manuscript was in Lyons in the first half of the ninth century. Despite the textual peculiarities of the manuscript, the overall character of the Latin version corresponds with the rest of Latin biblical tradition: there are a handful of early readings shared with the most ancient sources, but in the Gospels the text is relatively close to the version immediately preceding the Vulgate (text-type I). This reflects the ongoing revision of the Latin translation and its being brought into ever closer conformity with Greek texts, as the very close correspondence between the two traditions in Codex Bezae bears witness.

---

[32] This is 𝔓99 in the Gregory-Aland list; the critical edition is Wouters 1988, with details of the New Testament text in Wachtel & Witte 1994:lxvii–xc.
[33] Parker 1992.

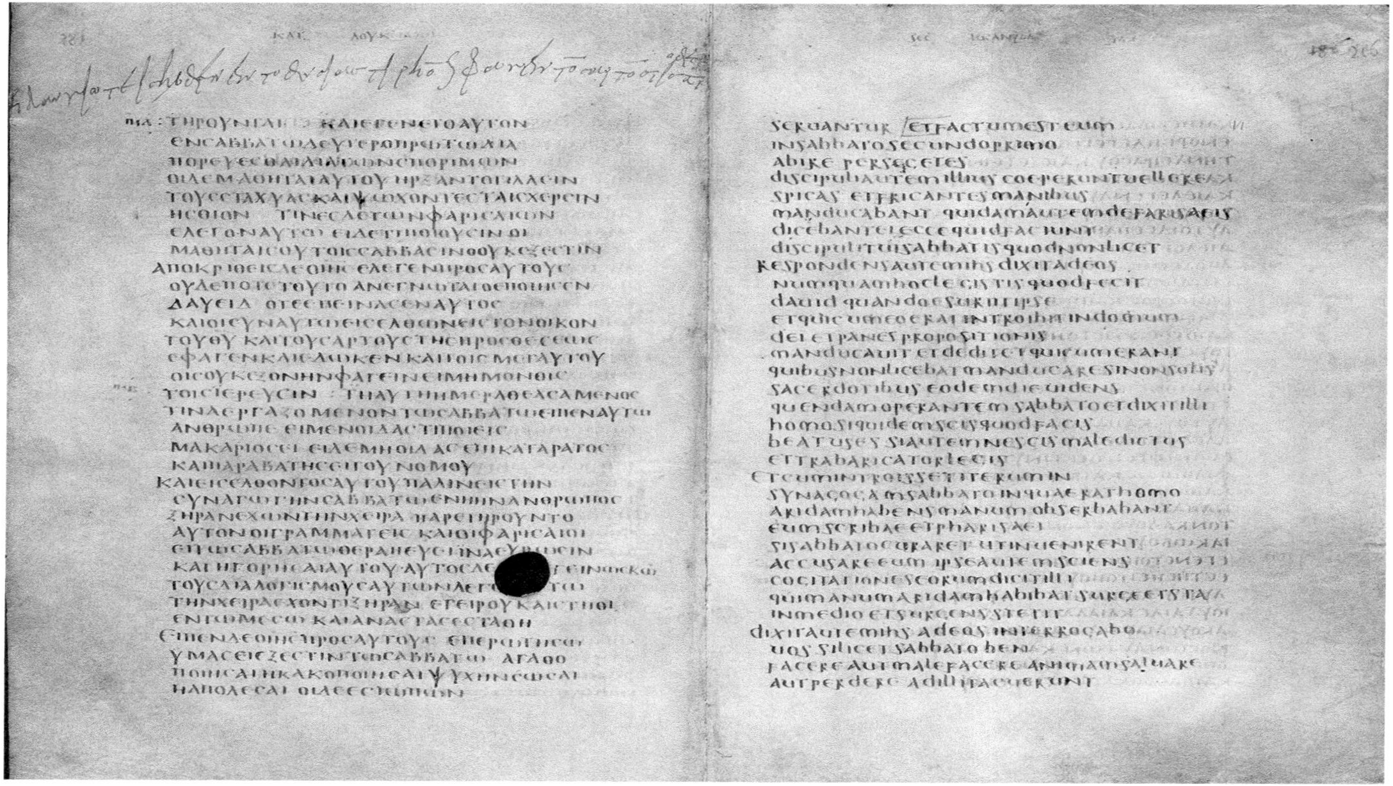

Image 3 VL 5: **Codex Bezae** (Cambridge, University Library, MS Nn. II.41, folios 205ᵛ–206ʳ), showing the 'Cambridge pericope' at Luke 6:4. Reproduced by kind permission of the Syndics of Cambridge University Library. Also available at <http://cudl.lib.cam.ac.uk/view/MS-NN-00002-00041/392>.

NORTH ITALY

The Vetus Latina text-type I is typical of northern Italy in the fourth century. It may be equivalent to the 'Italian' texts approved by Augustine (see page 15). Although it was noted above that Ambrosiaster is the principal representative of this type in the Pauline Epistles, there are some differences between his text and the characteristics of this type in the Gospels. For example, the latter consistently prefers *quia* rather than *quoniam* for the Greek ὅτι ('that, because') and *testimonium perhibere* as a rendering of μαρτυρεῖν ('bear witness'): Ambrosiaster retains a considerable proportion of instances of *quoniam* and has a variety of translations for μαρτυρεῖν. This suggests that the Gospels may have undergone a further stage of revision. Apart from the Pauline Epistles, text-type I is the best-attested form in surviving Old Latin manuscripts, from the fifth-century gospel books to the thirteenth-century VL 51 (Codex Gigas). The exact time and place of this revision are unknown. The series of chapter titles for the Gospels which usually accompany this biblical text (KA I) derive from a much earlier form of text. The correspondences between text-type I and the biblical quotations of Ambrose, bishop of Milan from 374 to 397, confirm the currency of this form of text in Italy in this period. Ambrose's most extensive work on the New Testament is his Commentary on Luke (AM Lc), composed around 390. This is partly based on the writings of Origen. Ambrose also drew on earlier Greek writers for his treatises *On faith* (AM fi) and *On the Holy Spirit* (AM sp). Readings peculiar to Ambrose or the Milanese tradition are identified in the Vetus Latina edition as text-type M.[34]

Other Italian writers in the latter half of the fourth century also provide evidence for text-type I, although they too reveal the influence of their predecessors. Zeno of Verona (ZE) left two volumes of tractates, which number Cyprian, Hilary of Poitiers, and a Latin translation of the Protevangelium of James (AP-E Jac) among their sources.[35] Faustinus, a presbyter at Rome, composed *On the Trinity against the Arians* (FAUn Ar) and other works using Ambrose and Hilary of Poitiers. Filastrius of Brescia used Hippolytus for his treatise on heresies (FIL), which was later turned into an acrostic poem (PS-GAU Fil).[36] The extensive sermon collections of Chromatius of Aquileia and Maximus of Turin are complicated by a number of different reference systems. Chromatius is of particular note for his sermon-commentary on Matthew (CHRO Mt), expounding an Old Latin text similar to that found in the *Liber de diuinis scripturis* (PS-AU spe; see page 39), although his frequent

---

[34] On Ambrose's biblical text, see the works of Caragliano, Rolando, Marzola, and Muncey.
[35] Frede 1981. It is impossible to relate the text of AP-E Jac used by Zeno to the three surviving Latin translations: on these, see Kaestli 1996.
[36] Portarena 1946.

dependence on his predecessor Fortunatianus has now been brought to light by Dorfbauer. Several portions of Chromatius' commentary were previously numbered as separate homilies (CHRO h), while others are transmitted in the Latin Chrysostom (see CHRO h Et). Most of Chromatius' sermons (CHROs) were discovered in a fuller form by Lemarié (CHRO h Lem), although the numeration of these is identical.[37] The corpus of Maximus of Turin (MAX) includes numerous pieces by his homonymous episcopal successor in the late fifth century (MAX II.). There are various overlaps between the collections of sermons and homilies (MAX s and MAX h), which have both been superseded by Mutzenbecher's edition of most of the authentic pieces (MAX s Mu), some of which use Ambrose's *Commentary on Luke*.

JEROME AND THE VULGATE GOSPELS

The Latin version of the Bible now known as the Vulgate is indissolubly linked with the name of Jerome (Hieronymus in Latin, hence the abbreviation HI). Born in Stridon in Dalmatia in 347 or 348, he initially studied in Rome, followed by periods in Trier and Aquileia, before heading to Antioch in 373–4 where he learnt Greek. After this he spent five years in Chalcis in Syria, where he was introduced to Hebrew, and then moved briefly to Constantinople where he began translating Greek texts. Having returned to Rome for six years, where he undertook the revision of the Latin Gospels, he left in 385 to spend the final three decades of his life as a scholar and ascetic near Bethlehem. Much of Jerome's literary output took the form of translations or editions of the works of others. As noted on page 16 above, he was responsible for the form in which Victorinus of Poetovio's *Commentary on Revelation* was best known (HI Apc). Some works are direct translations, such as Origen's *Homilies on Luke* (HI Lc) or Didymus the Blind's treatise *On the Holy Spirit* (HI Did). Others rely to such an extent on Origen that it is possible to reconstruct lost portions of his underlying Greek text, as is the case with Jerome's commentaries on Matthew, Galatians, Ephesians, Titus, and Philemon.[38] The same is true of some of Jerome's Old Testament commentaries, although most of these were produced in conjunction with his translations of the Scriptures based on a Hebrew text, which constitute the majority of the Old Testament in the Vulgate.[39]

One of the problems with determining Jerome's activity is that his writings are very often the only available evidence, many of which were written in a

---

[37] On Chromatius' biblical text, see Auwers 2011.
[38] Heine 2002, Cain 2011; see also Kamesar 2013:670 on the secular literary models for Jerome's commentaries.
[39] See further Fischer 1971 [1985:342–3]; Bogaert 2012:69–70 and 78–9.

polemical context. He also had a tendency towards exaggeration. Jerome's revision of the Gospels, carried out between 382 and 384, is described in the dedicatory letter to Pope Damasus which is attached as a preface (HI Ev). In it he relates that Damasus prompted him to undertake a 'new work' (*nouum opus*, the opening words of the preface), to edit 'copies of the Scriptures scattered throughout the world' (*exemplaria scripturarum toto orbe dispersa*) using Greek sources. The remainder of the preface refers only to the Gospels, however, and it seems unlikely that Jerome edited the entire New Testament despite his multiple claims to have 'restored the New Testament to the authority of the Greek'.[40] Furthermore, Jerome states that his work, far from being a new translation, was at most a light revision:

> *quae ne multum a lectionis latinae consuetudine discreparent, ita calamo imper-*
> *auimus ut, his tantum quae sensum uidebantur mutare correctis, reliqua manere*
> *pateremur ut fuerant.* (HI Ev)[41]

> In order that these [Gospels] would not differ greatly from the customary Latin reading, I directed my pen only to correct errors which seemed to change the sense, and allowed the rest to remain as it had been.

His most obvious innovation was to put the Gospels in the order Matthew–Mark–Luke–John, matching Greek tradition. This meant that he was able to add the Eusebian apparatus, a system which identifies material shared between Gospels using two types of marginal numbers and an initial set of canon tables.[42] The presence of these section numbers in certain gospel manuscripts with the earlier Latin order of the Gospels (such as VL 5 and VL 10) suggests that the system may have been adopted elsewhere independently of Jerome. However, the full apparatus, even in manuscripts with an Old Latin text, bears witness to the influence of Jerome's version: in fact, the Eusebian apparatus is far more widespread in Latin than in Greek gospel codices.

Jerome's revised text was not called the Vulgate until much later.[43] Indeed, at the end of the fourth century, *editio uulgata* ('common edition') referred to the Latin translation of the Old Testament based on the Septuagint. Despite its association with Pope Damasus and the wide circulation it enjoyed soon after its completion, Jerome's revision of the Gospels took some time to become established. This is shown by the number of Old Latin codices surviving from

---

[40] *Nouum testamentum graecae reddidi auctoritati* (HI ep 71.5); *Nouum testamentum graecae fidei reddidi* (HI ill 135); see also HI ep 112.20 to Augustine. For traces of later editing in the correspondence between Damasus and Jerome, see Bogaert 2013:517.

[41] The widespread reading *temperauimus*, in place of *imperauimus*, would give the sense that Jerome 'restrained' his pen.

[42] A full description of the Eusebian apparatus is given on page 200. Canon tables are illustrated in Image 15.

[43] The first reference appears to be the Council of Trent (1545–63): see Sutcliffe 1948, Allgeier 1948, and Bogaert 2012.

subsequent centuries, not to mention the textual affiliation of biblical quotations in Christian writers. Nonetheless, it is a convenient shorthand to use the term Vulgate, albeit anachronistically, to indicate the versions which later constituted this collection.

Jerome seems to have based his revision of the Gospels on a Latin manuscript with the text-type I. The Vulgate text of the Gospels is very close to this Old Latin form, corresponding to his statement above that very little was altered. The continuity between Jerome's text and earlier versions (as well as the mixture of texts found in many Old Latin manuscripts) means that it is sometimes difficult to identify the changes for which he was responsible.[44] Among the correction of so-called 'errors which seemed to change the sense' may be included the use of *consummaretur* in John 19:28 ('might be accomplished', corresponding to $\tau\epsilon\lambda\epsilon\iota\omega\theta\hat{\eta}$ and not $\pi\lambda\eta\rho\omega\theta\hat{\eta}$) and the well-known introduction of *supersubstantialem* for $\dot{\epsilon}\pi\iota\sigma\dot{\nu}\sigma\iota\sigma\nu$ in the Matthaean version of the Lord's Prayer.[45] Other interventions add nuance to the narrative. For instance, at Matthew 2:7, the use of *clam* ('in secret') rather than *occulte* ('in private') for $\lambda\dot{\alpha}\theta\rho\alpha$ depicts Herod's meeting in a negative light. Jerome rendered $\theta\dot{\alpha}\rho\sigma\epsilon\iota$ on the lips of Jesus with *confide* ('have faith') rather than *constans esto* ('stand firm'), emphasizing the theological aspect of the command.[46] Jerome's own preferences also shine through: the use of *comedere* in the Gospels matches its omnipresence in his translation of the Hebrew Scriptures, while $\pi\lambda\dot{\eta}\nu$ is consistently translated by *uerumtamen*. Again, *ostium* rather than *ianua* was Jerome's preferred term, and at the key passage of John 10:1–9 he seems to have reinstituted this word, perhaps also motivated by its classical sense of 'entrance' rather than a physical door. The more literal correspondence in Jerome's revision with a Greek text is witnessed by his treatment of diminutives: at Matthew 4:5 he introduced *pinnaculum* for $\pi\tau\epsilon\rho\dot{\nu}\gamma\iota\sigma\nu$ ('pinnacle'), in John 2:15 he seems to have rendered $\sigma\chi\sigma\iota\nu\dot{\iota}\omega\nu$ by *funiculis* ('strands of cord') and at John 13:27 and 13:30 *buccellam* corresponds to $\tau\dot{\sigma}\ \psi\omega\mu\dot{\iota}\sigma\nu$ ('morsel'). In fact, Jerome reintroduced Greek terms into the text, often with a technical sense, such as *anathematizare* in Mark 14:71 and *parasceue* for the 'day of preparation' in John. He also paid particular attention to the form of proper nouns. Some of the differences in Jerome's version derive from the Greek text on which he relied. It has often been observed that the Vulgate moves away from the so-called 'Western' text towards a form closer to the later standard (*koine* or Byzantine text), although attempts at more detailed classification

[44] Some differences are listed in the Oxford Vulgate (I. 662–4); the figure of 3,000 changes given in Vogels 1928a is an exaggeration (Fischer 1972:62 [1986:236]). On Jerome's translation technique, see Hulley 1944, Harrison 1986, and Burton 2000 (especially 192–9). Many of the following examples are taken from Harrison 1986:201–36.

[45] See also page 159 below.

[46] Matthew 9:2, 9:22, *cf.* 14:27; Mark 6:50; John 16:33; contrast Mark 10:49 where it is said by the crowd.

tend to founder.[47] In practice, Greek witnesses used by Jerome and other revisers would each have had their own peculiarities.

Jerome lost momentum as his revision of the Gospels progressed. He intervened most frequently in Matthew and least so in John, suggesting that he treated the Gospels according to his revised order. For example, in Matthew and Mark he often replaced a finite verb with a participle matching the Greek, but this is less common in Luke and John. He also became less consistent in his interventions. In the parable of the Wicked Tenants, he altered *colonus* to *agricola* throughout Matthew 21:33–44, made the change sporadically in Mark 12:1–11, but allowed *colonus* to stand throughout Luke 20:9–18. The translation of the word for 'chief priest' (ἀρχιερεύς) tends to be *princeps sacerdotum* in Matthew, *summus sacerdos* in Mark, and *pontifex* in John.[48] Up to the end of John 14, Jerome substituted *mandatum* for *praeceptum*, but the latter is allowed to remain in John 15:10 and 15:12. Similarly, every occurrence of δοξάζειν ('to glorify') up to and including John 12:23 is translated by *glorificare* but from John 12:26 onwards the preferred Old Latin rendering, *clarificare*, is used on sixteen of seventeen occasions: in fact, Jerome himself stated in a letter (HI ep 106.30) that his decision to preserve *clarifica* at John 17:5 was deliberate. In the final chapter of John, although the distinction between ἀγαπᾷς and φιλεῖς in Jesus' questions to Peter is kept, there is no attempt to match the pattern of differences in the commands to 'feed my sheep'. Furthermore, the inclusion of *sic* in John 21:22 and 23 is a Latin innovation which Jerome did not bother to adjust. There are also occasions when he seems to have introduced extraneous readings through inadvertence, such as changing the literal *auribus* (ὦτα) to *cordibus* at Luke 9:44, or writing *ouile* rather than *grex* in John 10:16.

There are several indications that Jerome was responsible for the revision of the Gospels only and not the rest of the New Testament. When he discusses questions of translation affecting the Gospels he quotes forms matching his revised version, but he never cites readings characteristic of the Vulgate in the other New Testament books. What is more, in his commentary on four of the Pauline Epistles, he criticizes the existing Latin translation and provides his own alternative. For example, at Galatians 5:9, he adjusts the lemma of his commentary to read *modicum fermentum totam conspersionem fermentat* ('a little yeast leavens the whole mixture') and observes:

> male in nostris codicibus habetur: *modicum fermentum totam massam corrumpit,* et sensum potius interpres suum, quam uerba apostoli transtulit. (HI Gal 3.5)

---

[47] Summaries in Fischer 1972:63–4 [1986:237–8], Metzger 1977:355–6, Petzer 1995:125, and Bogaert 2013:514. It was once thought that Jerome's Greek text was similar to Codices Sinaiticus and Vaticanus, but this is no longer the case.

[48] See further Burkitt 1908.

Our manuscripts are wrong in reading '*a little yeast spoils the whole lump*' as the translator has conveyed his own understanding rather than the words of the apostle.

It is most unlikely that Jerome would have allowed this form to persist in this letter and the identical phrase at 1 Corinthians 5:6 if he had been responsible for the Vulgate text of these Epistles. Other proofs of the separate origin of the rest of the Vulgate New Testament are considered later in this chapter.[49] Many of Jerome's quotations thus represent Old Latin readings, including references to the Gospels predating his revision. However, there are some discrepancies between his citations of the same verse in different works, including forms unique to him. In several cases, this is likely to have arisen from Jerome's reliance on a Greek source from which he translated the biblical quotation as well as the accompanying observations. He frequently refers to earlier writers, especially Origen, in order to explain his decisions about the correct reading of the text. These, and Jerome's other explicit observations about differences between biblical manuscripts, provide a special type of evidence for the history of the New Testament text, although some of these comments themselves may have been repeated from his sources.[50]

RUFINUS OF AQUILEIA

Rufinus of Aquileia, a friend of Jerome prior to their theological disagreements at the end of the fourth century, was another prolific translator. Between his return to Rome in 397 and his death in Sicily in 411, Rufinus produced Latin versions of various Greek authors, including Basil (RUF Bas), Eusebius (RUF Eus), the Pseudo-Clementine *Recognitions* (RUF Cl), and above all Origen. His complete translation of Origen's ten-volume commentary on Romans (RUF Rm) is the only source for this text apart from a few Greek fragments. Earlier in his life, Rufinus had spent time in Egypt and Jerusalem and encountered such Greek theologians as Didymus the Blind, Cyril of Jerusalem, and Epiphanius of Salamis; his translation of Eusebius was dedicated to Chromatius of Aquileia. One of the differences between Jerome and Rufinus was the extent to which they thought translators should also function as editors: Rufinus himself adopted a more interventionist approach than that advocated by Jerome. Like many translators, Rufinus appears to have translated most of the biblical quotations directly from his source. However, there is also evidence that in certain commentaries he replaced the lemmata preceding each comment with a form of text taken from an Old

---

[49] See also Sparks 1970:520, Lagrange 1916–18, and Cavallera 1920.
[50] See Souter 1941, Metzger 1979, and Donaldson 2009 and 2013.

Latin manuscript. In the case of the Romans commentary, Rufinus may even have revised the biblical text himself.[51] Although he has sometimes been proposed as the reviser of the other books in the Vulgate New Testament, there is no direct evidence to link Rufinus with this. Nevertheless, the scriptorium established by his disciples Pinian and Melania appears to have played a major role in the collection and transmission of early Latin Christian literature and created several of the surviving fifth-century manuscripts of these works.[52]

AUGUSTINE OF HIPPO

The most prolific Latin Christian author in antiquity was Augustine, bishop of Hippo from 395 to 430. His textual affiliation in the New Testament is similar to that of Jerome. Having spent several years in Milan as a follower of Ambrose, he became familiar with biblical scholarship in northern Italy before his return to Africa, and he continued this connection with a regular exchange of books and letters throughout his episcopate. Augustine's early exegetical works on the New Testament, commentaries on the Sermon on the Mount (AU s dni), Galatians (AU Gal), and a couple of attempts at Romans (AU Rm, AU Rm in), feature extensive reference to an Old Latin text. Several extracts from his substantial work on Christian teaching, *De doctrina Christiana* (AU do), are quoted above in Chapter 1, describing the variety of Latin biblical texts and his preference for the *Itala*.[53] Augustine's sermons have different forms of biblical text according to the place and time at which they were preached, indicating that Augustine used a local gospel book when preaching.

Augustine's correspondence with Jerome shows that he had a copy of the Vulgate Gospels by the year 403:

> *proinde non paruas deo gratias agimus de opere tuo, quod euangelium ex graeco interpretatus es, quia et paene in omnibus nulla offensio est, cum scripturam graecam contulerimus. unde, si quisquam ueteri falsitati contentiosus fauet, prolatis collatisque codicibus uel docetur facillime uel refellitur. et si quaedam rarissima merito mouent, quis tam durus est qui labori tam utili non facile ignoscat, cui uicem laudis referre non sufficit?* (AU ep 71.6)

---

[51]   On this, and his biblical text more generally, see Bardy 1920, Vogels 1955a, Chadwick 1959, Hammond Bammel 1985, and Lo Cicero 2002. The layout of the Latin version of the *Commentary on Romans* and Rufinus' scribal practice is considered in detail in Hammond 1978 and Hammond Bammel 1979.

[52]   See Hammond Bammel 1984.

[53]   Pages 11 and 15. Among the many works on Augustine's biblical text in the Bibliography, those of Bogaert, Houghton, La Bonnardière, Mizzi, and Schirner offer an orientation to earlier scholarship.

Accordingly, we give no small thanks to God for your work on translating the Gospel from Greek, because it is almost without fault when we compare it with a Greek Bible: when these manuscripts are brought out and compared, anyone argumentative who prefers an error of the old version will be either corrected most easily or refuted. Although very few things are truly inspirational, who is so set in their ways as not readily to justify such a useful task, to which it is insufficient to respond with praise?

In the same year as this letter, Augustine published *On the Agreement of the Evangelists* (AU Ev), a detailed study in four books dealing with parallels between the Gospels and, in particular, the resolution of discrepancies. The gospel text throughout is clearly that of Jerome's revision. The Eusebian apparatus would have greatly facilitated Augustine's identification of parallel passages, although he makes no explicit acknowledgement of this; it is also tempting to interpret the comparison with Greek in the quotation above as part of his preparation for this work. In his exegetical method, Augustine rarely questions the wording of the text but instead tries to find an interpretation which reconciles both accounts. For example, he harmonizes the different words of John the Baptist in Matthew 3:11 and John 1:27 by suggesting that they were either spoken at different times or represent two extracts from a single saying (AU Ev 2.12.29). The same approach is also found a few years later in Augustine's *Tractatus in Iohannis euangelium* (AU Jo), a commentary on John in 124 sermons. The first fifty-four were written up by stenographers as they were preached in church, and the rest dictated in private.[54] Again, the gospel text almost entirely corresponds to that of Jerome's revision. Occasional Old Latin readings, particularly in the middle of the preached sermons, represent reversion to his 'mental text', the form he produced when citing from memory. In later works, even this type of quotation accords with the Vulgate Gospels.[55]

In his polemical works, Augustine cites his opponents at length, thereby preserving their writings. These include biblical verses as originally cited by Manichees, Arians, and Donatists: unsurprisingly, many of the archaic characteristics associated with 'African' texts are present. Indeed, the Manichee Faustus has the addition of the 'flying Jesus' at Luke 4:29–30 which is believed to be a characteristic of the Diatessaron.[56] Although Augustine himself was alert to these differences, he stated on more than one occasion that he would not comment on discrepancies in the form of quotations unless it affected his argument.[57] In addition to the stenographic records of his sermons, some of Augustine's debates

[54] AU ep 23A*.3.6.
[55] Houghton 2008a.
[56] For the Manichaean use of the Diatessaron (perhaps mediated through the words of Mani rather than in a Latin translation), see Quispel 1972.
[57] AU Pet 2.61 and 2.99. Instances of Augustine revising his argument on the basis of a different version of a scriptural text may be seen in his *Retractationes* (AU re 1.7, 1.10, 1.21, and 2.12).

were taken down by shorthand secretaries. His confrontation with Felix the Manichee (AU Fel) in 404 includes long declamations from biblical manuscripts which happened to be on hand: the quotation from Luke 24 is clearly a Vulgate text but those from Acts and the Pauline Epistles are Old Latin. A parallel to this is found in the *Libellus aduersus Fulgentium Donatistam* (PS-AU Fu), attributed to Augustine but probably composed in Africa between 430 and 450. Here, the Catholic interlocutor uses a Vulgate form of text while all the biblical quotations of his Donatist opponent correspond to Old Latin versions. This detail alone suggests that the work is not entirely fictional, unless the textual affiliation is being used as a caricature.

It has sometimes been claimed that Augustine himself was responsible for a revision of the text of certain Latin biblical books.[58] The basis for this, however, is more a reflection of the amount of material preserved in Augustine than evidence of his own philological activity: although he occasionally refers to correcting Latin texts based on Greek manuscripts (e.g. AU ep 261.5), Augustine denies acting as a translator and there is no indication of this in the two catalogues of his works (AU re and POS ind). In a notice preserved among his letters, Augustine refers to a 'responsibility for the Scriptures' (*cura scripturarum*) placed on him by two episcopal councils, but this seems most likely to refer to his annotations on the Septuagint, the *Locutiones in Heptateuchum* (AU loc) composed around the same time.[59]

Many of Augustine's other writings focus on the New Testament. The scriptural references in *De Trinitate* (AU tri) reveal the different stages in its composition: Book 1, composed around 400, has an Old Latin affiliation in its gospel quotations, while the rest of the work, from 411 to 420, follows the Vulgate. Two volumes of *Quaestiones* on Matthew and Luke (AU q Ev), with a further appendix on Matthew (AU q Ev app), were composed around the same time. Augustine broke off his exposition of the Gospel according to John in Easter 407 to preach a series of ten sermons covering the First Epistle of John (AU 1 Jo) based on an Old Latin text. The first half of Book 20 of the *City of God* (AU ci) contains a sequence of lengthy quotations from Matthew, the Apocalypse, and certain Epistles, as Augustine appears to work through the New Testament books in sequence. While the gospel text corresponds to the Vulgate, the other books retain an Old Latin affiliation.

One of Augustine's last works was a collection of *testimonia*, the *Speculum quis ignorat* (AU spe). There are many unusual features to this selection of biblical passages, including some of the earliest uses of the word 'verse' (*uersus*) as a system of navigation: while this is unsurprising in the Wisdom books of the Septuagint, which were often laid out as poetry, it is less

[58] De Bruyne, followed by Thiele in his early works: refutations are listed in Frede 1972:466.
[59] AU ep 213.5, referring to the Councils of Numidia (probably Milevis in 416) and Carthage in 419.

obvious in the New Testament. The order of the New Testament books, with Acts following the Gospels, is inconsistent with Augustine's list in AU do 2.8.13. Most striking of all is the fact that this is the only work in which Augustine quotes the Vulgate version of Acts, the Epistles, and Revelation. For this reason, doubt has been cast on its authenticity. However, the composition of the *Speculum* is described in the biography of Augustine written by Possidius (POS vi), and the handful of quotations in the authorial sections do correspond to Augustine's characteristic forms in other works.[60] It therefore appears that biblical text was substituted at a relatively early point in the textual tradition, affecting all surviving copies.

Another collection of biblical *testimonia* with the title *Speculum* is attributed to Augustine, also known as the *Liber de diuinis scripturis* (PS-AU spe). This seems not to be authentic, but is an earlier compilation made in Italy around the year 400. The passages are arranged thematically under 144 headings with extensive quotation from the whole New Testament apart from Hebrews, 3 John, and Philemon. Both the order of the Gospels and the textual affiliation confirm that the scriptural sources were Old Latin. This work features in the apparatus of several editions of the New Testament, sometimes with the siglum *m* even though it is not a biblical manuscript.[61]

PELAGIUS

The earliest evidence for the text of the first thirteen Pauline Epistles as found in the Vulgate is generally held to be the commentary by Pelagius composed in Rome between 406 and 410 (PEL Rm etc.). Following his condemnation as a heretic, Pelagius' name became disassociated from the work. It continued to circulate in a revised and expanded version made around 430 by one of his followers, perhaps Caelestius, but later attributed to Jerome (PS-HI Rm etc.). Much of the additional material in this later version came from the anonymous Budapest Commentary (AN Paul) which Pelagius himself seems to have used as a source; later on, the Pseudo-Jerome commentary was again reworked with yet more interpolations. In the original Pelagian commentary the running text of each Epistle is split into small units, sometimes of only two or three words, and punctuated by similarly brief authorial comments. Pelagius' technique involves frequent paraphrase, which makes it difficult to isolate any particular biblical affiliation: some forms coincide with existing versions whereas others are clearly

---

[60] See Vaccari 1961.
[61] See Appendix 1; *m* derives from Mai, who rediscovered the original form. The siglum in NA and UBS is *Spec.*

reworkings which never existed in a biblical codex, such as the poetic *lumina*, 'lights', for *oculi*, 'eyes' at PEL Gal 5.14.

Pelagius' original version is only known from two manuscripts, both identified at the beginning of the twentieth century. The earlier is a ninth-century manuscript with biblical lemmata close to the Vulgate (A: Karlsruhe, Badische Landesbibliothek, Aug. 119); the other (B: Oxford, Balliol College, MS 157) was copied in the fifteenth century but has an Old Latin version of the Epistles very close to the Book of Armagh (VL 61). On the grounds that later editors normally adjusted biblical texts to match the Vulgate, it was initially thought that the Balliol manuscript was more likely to represent the source used by Pelagius.[62] However, evidence from biblical references in the commentary sections, Pauline quotations elsewhere in the work, the form of text in the Pseudo-Jerome version, and passages quoted by other authors has led to a reassessment. Several scholars have concluded that Pelagius used the Vulgate; others acknowledge that the authorial text is closer to the Karlsruhe manuscript but falls short of being the first unequivocal evidence for the Vulgate version of the Epistles.[63] The Old Latin text must therefore have been introduced in a context where this version was customary. The biblical text was also substituted in one of the interpolated manuscripts of Pelagius, which features a number of different Old Latin readings.[64]

Various fragments of other writings by Pelagius survive, including extracts from *On the Trinity* (PEL tri). The *Letter to Demetrias* also found in the Pseudo-Jerome corpus is now considered to be authentic Pelagius (PEL Dem, PS-HI ep 1), unlike *On the Hardening of Pharaoh's Heart* (PS-PEL ind) which was once used as a guide to his style. Pelagius' most prolific disciple was Julian, bishop of Eclanum in the first half of the fifth century, and the addressee of two polemical works by Augustine (AU Jul and AU Jul im). Julian wrote several Old Testament commentaries based on the work of Jerome, and also adopted Jerome's text of the Gospels. He was responsible for translating Theodore of Mopsuestia on the Psalms (JUL-E Ps); the Latin version of Theodore's commentary on the minor Pauline Epistles (THr), the only extant form of this work, also seems to have originated in Pelagian circles. In this commentary, the biblical text was translated directly from the Greek, although some influence from the Vulgate has been detected.[65]

The interest in translation within the Pelagian community, combined with the earliest attestation of the Vulgate text of the latter part of the New Testament, has led to the suggestion that the revision of these books was undertaken by one of its

---

[62] Souter 1922–31.

[63] In favour of the Vulgate are Frede and Thiele followed by de Bruyn, Fröhlich, and Stelzer; the latter position is adopted by the 'Bonn School' of Schäfer, Borse, Nellessen, Tinnefeld, and Zimmermann.

[64] V: Paris, BnF, latin 653; see VL 81 on page 245.

[65] Frede 1972:467.

members. The principal evidence for the identity of the translator is the prologue to the Pauline Epistles which begins *Primum quaeritur*: this includes views concerning Hebrews which run counter to Jerome and was written in Rome by someone at odds with the local community. Indeed, following the rediscovery of Pelagius' Pauline commentary, it was proposed that he himself was responsible for the Vulgate text of the Epistles, as he also quotes from the prologue.[66] More recently, the preferred candidate has been a Pelagian known as Rufinus the Syrian, who also had connections with Jerome and came to Rome around the same time as his namesake Rufinus of Aquileia.[67] The only writing attributed to Rufinus the Syrian is a *Liber de fide* (PS-RUF fi), composed in Rome before 411 when it was the object of Augustine's criticism in *De peccatorum meritis* (AU pec 1). However, both Augustine's knowledge of this work and the very existence of Rufinus the Syrian are contested.[68] The safest approach is to admit that the reviser of the books other than the Gospels in the Vulgate New Testament remains unknown, although the work appears to have been carried out in Rome after 393 (the quotation from HI ill 5 in the prologue) and before 410 (the latest date for Pelagius' commentary).

The whole of the latter part of the Vulgate New Testament has a common origin. There is a noticeable difference in translation technique between the Gospels and the other writings: while Jerome introduces various forms for which no basis can be discerned in Greek, almost all of the innovations in the Vulgate of the other books represent Greek readings. What is more, the alterations made to Acts and the Catholic Epistles appear to reflect a Greek text similar to that of the early majuscule manuscripts rather than the later Greek text used by Jerome in the Gospels.[69] There are, however, some similarities between Augustine and Jerome's quotations of the Catholic Epistles and the Vulgate, suggesting that they drew on a similar Latin source to that used by the reviser. Like Jerome's reordering of the four evangelists, the sequence of books was changed by the reviser on the basis of a Greek tradition: in the Pauline Epistles, Colossians was made to follow Ephesians and Philippians (as in the *Primum quaeritur* prologue), while James was placed first among the Catholic Epistles.

The fourth century thus laid the foundations for much of the rest of the history of the Latin New Testament. Biblical scholarship in both North Africa and Italy contributed to the development of Latin exegesis. There was an increasing use of Greek authors, often in translation. Commentaries by Hilary of Poitiers, Ambrose, Jerome, and Augustine became standard texts for later

---

[66] De Bruyne 1915; cf. Souter 1922:156–7. The text of *Primum quaeritur* is printed in the Stuttgart Vulgate, 1748–9; see also Scherbenske 2010.

[67] See Fischer 1972:21, 49 and 73 [1986:184, 220, 251] and Fröhlich 1995:220–2 with references, as well as Bogaert 2012:78 and 2013:517–18.

[68] Dunphy 2009, 2012.

[69] See further Fischer 1972:61, 64, 68, and 73 [1986:244–51] and Thiele 1972:118–19.

generations, while other commentators such as Fortunatianus and Pelagius underwent a more complicated reception. The prominence of Italian forms of the Latin Bible was sealed by Jerome's revision of the Gospels and an unknown reviser's extension of the same principles to the rest of the New Testament: in time, these would be adopted, along with Jerome's translation of the Hebrew Scriptures and Latin versions of the deuterocanonical books, as the Vulgate, the official Bible of the Roman Catholic Church.

3

Competing Texts: The Fifth to the Seventh Centuries

Christian literary activity in North Africa was considerably diminished after the death of Augustine and the establishment of the Vandal kingdom. Italy was the centre for the production of Latin biblical manuscripts and exegetical works in the fifth and sixth centuries, although the seventh century saw developments further afield, including Spain and the Insular regions of Britain and Ireland. The newly-revised text of the New Testament by Jerome and his unknown counterpart took some time to become established, despite its early adoption in influential commentaries. Most fifth-century New Testament manuscripts continue to have an Old Latin affiliation. The gradual alteration of biblical manuscripts towards what was to become the Vulgate resulted in 'mixed texts', combining features of both Vulgate and pre-Vulgate tradition. A similar mixture arose from the reintroduction of earlier readings to Vulgate texts: the sixth-century gospel books produced in North Italy are a good example of this. One of the editorial innovations of this period was the creation of manuscripts containing the whole New Testament and even pandects comprising the whole Bible, often with a new set of prologues or *capitula*.

EARLY ITALIAN MANUSCRIPTS

Although Jerome's revision of the Gospels was adopted by Augustine and other contemporaries, the majority of biblical codices surviving from the following century have an Old Latin form of text. Of these, VL 2 (Codex Palatinus, shown in Image 4) is the most distinctive. The codicology is characteristically early, with the Old Latin order Matthew–John–Luke–Mark, the absence of introductory material and divisions of the text, and the use of silver ink on purple parchment. The outsize capitals used for the first letter in each column are a feature of antique book production which is also seen in the copy of Augustine's *De doctrina*

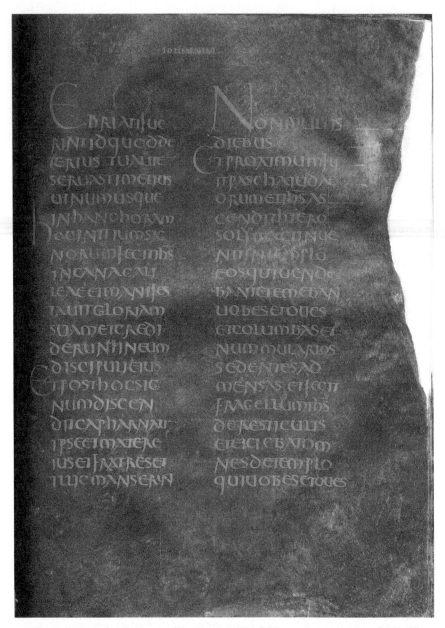

Image 4 VL 2: Codex Palatinus (Trento, Castello del Buon Consiglio, s.n., folio 49^r) at John 2. © Castello del Buonconsiglio, Trento.

christiana believed to have been produced in his lifetime in Hippo.[1] Textually, the manuscript retains numerous ancient features but is later than VL 1, although there are very few points at which both codices are extant. In the Synoptic Gospels VL 2 agrees with the citations in the *De physicis* ascribed to Marius Victorinus (PS-MAR phy) and written in Africa in or before the fourth century, while in John it corresponds almost exactly to Cyprian's *testimonia*. It therefore represents an African text of the late third century, although it was probably copied in Italy like other purple codices. The renderings are surprisingly inconsistent, suggesting that the text had already undergone various revisions; it is also possible that it is a composite form derived from several sources.[2] It has been suggested that certain mistakes in VL 2 involve the incorporation of marginal material.[3] Among its early textual characteristics are the omission of repetitive or superfluous phrases and several examples of harmonization, such as the introduction of the Matthaean form of Jesus' prediction into John 13:38.[4]

Jerome's disdain for luxury manuscripts is expressed in one of his letters:

inficitur membrana colore purpureo, aurum liquescit in litteras, gemmis codices uestiuntur et nudus ante fores earum Christus emoritur (HI ep 22.54).[5]

Parchment is dyed with purple hue, gold liquefies into writing, books are covered in jewels, and Christ is dying naked before their doors.

It is therefore appropriate that most of the early surviving purple gospel books are Old Latin witnesses, although some also reveal the influence of Jerome's revision. For example, VL 4 (Codex Veronensis, illustrated on the cover of this book) and VL 17 (Codex Vindobonensis), copied in Italy at the end of the fifth century, are written in silver and gold ink on parchment dyed purple. Both have the Gospels in the Old Latin sequence, and are the principal witnesses for the text-type I in the Synoptic Gospels. In John, VL 4 initially presents a slightly earlier form of text, but around John 10:13 it switches back to its other affiliation. However, VL 4 also has the Eusebian apparatus introduced by Jerome, added by the first hand or an early corrector. VL 22 (Codex Sarzanensis) is a poorly-preserved purple codex copied around the beginning of the sixth century. It consists of part of the end of Luke and the opening of John, following the same sequence as the Vulgate. Quire signatures show that a further portion of John is actually six sheets from a separate manuscript, VL 22A, bound with VL 22 at an early date. This difference is also observable in the renderings of λόγος ('word'):

---

[1] St Petersburg, National Library of Russia, Q.v.1.3. On the use of capitals for the first letter of each column, even when they appear in the middle of a word (as in Image 4, column 1), see Lowe 1925 and Bischoff 1990:27 and 189.

[2] For the renderings, see the tables in Burton 2000; Boismard 1993 examines overlapping passages in VL 2 and VL 3.

[3] e.g. Matthew 24:42, Luke 11:28, John 10:40. See De Bruyne 1910.

[4] See page 145 below.

[5] Jerome also refers scornfully to 'books . . . copied on purple parchment in gold and silver' (*libros . . . in membranis purpureis auro argentoque descriptos*) in his *Prologue to Job* (HI Jb pr H).

VL 22A prefers *sermo* while VL 22 has *uerbum*. Overall, the texts of both witnesses are more archaic than the other Italian manuscripts although they have affinities with VL 4 and 14. In certain places their readings are without parallel, but the damage to the parchment caused by the metallic ink means that there are substantial lacunae in which the text can no longer be read. VL 22 has evidence of a system of chapter divisions using Greek numerals but no Eusebian apparatus. This composite manuscript was rediscovered in the reliquary of a 'St Rufinus': the liturgical prominence of the gospel book and associations with individual bishops and saints explains why most of the surviving Old Latin biblical manuscripts are of the Gospels.[6]

Other fifth-century Italian gospel codices written on more conventional materials offer further evidence for the pre-Vulgate text. The most complete is VL 8 (Codex Corbeiensis). This is the third main witness for text-type I in the Synoptics (with VL 4 and 17), and the principal manuscript of this form in John. Despite the relatively thoroughgoing revision underlying this text of the Gospels, VL 8 also preserves ancient renderings such as *moechatio* rather than *adulterium* in John 8:3–4.[7] The manuscript is set out in paragraphs marked by slightly larger capital letters projecting into the margin. Before each Gospel it has *capitula* (KA I), with the corresponding numbers in the body of the text: on each occasion, the first line of the chapter is written in red with the number in the margin (see Image 5). VL 12 (Codex Claromontanus, not to be confused with VL 75) begins with an Old Latin version of Matthew, again reflecting the North Italian form preceding Jerome's revision. The other Gospels were added to this manuscript in the seventh century with the text and sequence of the Vulgate. Several fragments survive from similar codices. VL 19 consists of a double page of Mark with the same Italian pre-Vulgate text. VL 16 is divided between four manuscripts in three libraries: the remaining portions indicate that it had the Old Latin order of the Gospels and was probably copied in Rome. Its text is close to VL 3 in the Synoptic Gospels and VL 8 in John. The four pages of Luke preserved in VL 21 match the earlier Italian text in VL 3.

Some Old Latin texts are preserved as the underwriting in palimpsests, manuscripts which have been reused by the erasure of the original text and overwritten with a new one.[8] The earliest manuscript of Acts, Revelation, and the Catholic Epistles in Latin, VL 55 (the Fleury Palimpsest), was probably also copied in Italy in the fifth century. Unfortunately only eighteen pages remain of this manuscript. The order is unusual, with Revelation preceding Acts. The text in these books stems from an early revision made slightly after the time of Cyprian. In contrast, the surviving portions of the Catholic Epistles are a later version, matching text-type T which formed the basis for the Vulgate. Two

---

[6] See the figures on page 194.   [7] See Mazzini 1973.
[8] Declercq 2007 observes that 26 of the 150 manuscripts palimpsested before the ninth century feature biblical texts. For more on palimpsests, see Lowe 1964b and Bischoff 1990:11.

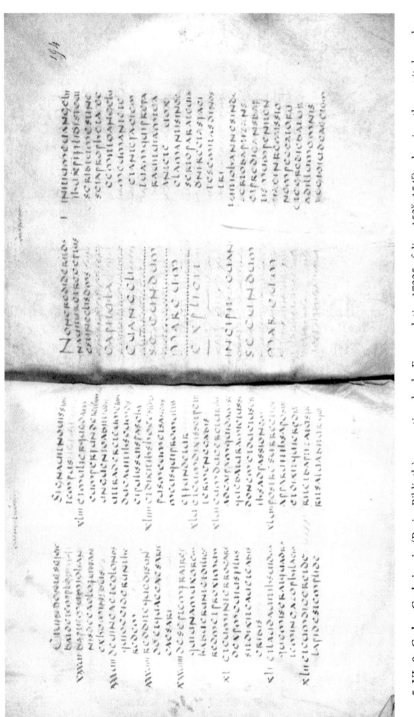

Image 5 VL 8: **Codex Corbeiensis** (Paris, Bibliothèque nationale de France, latin 17225, folios 153ᵛ–154ʳ), showing the *capitula* and beginning of the Gospel according to Mark. Also available at <http://gallica.bnf.fr/ark:/12148/btv1b9065916g/f158.item>.

palimpsests of Matthew, also of Italian origin, differ from the standard double-column layout of the contemporary gospel books mentioned above: VL 43, like VL 55, has a single column, whereas VL 45 has three. The context of VL 43 is intriguing, too: rather than being a copy of the canonical Gospels, the other surviving fragments indicate that Matthew was accompanied by Latin versions of the Gospel of Thomas (AP-E Tho) and the Gospel of Nicodemus (AP-E Nic).[9] Some ancient readings have been detected in the seventeen verses preserved in VL 45: along with VL 55, they demonstrate that a variety of textual forms were in circulation in fifth-century Italy.

The complement to these Old Latin codices are the earliest manuscripts of the Vulgate, which reach back to within a few decades of the revision. The oldest surviving copy of Jerome's text of the Gospels is the Vulgate manuscript S (Vg^{Se} S, Image 6). Around half the text is extant. Possibly copied in Verona in the early decades of the fifth century, it has been suggested that some of the marginal notes may derive from observations added to the exemplar or a more distant ancestor of the codex by Jerome himself.[10] The Gospels are in the Vulgate order, and have the Eusebian apparatus in the margin. Underneath the canon number, however, the parallel sections in the other Gospels are also listed, making the initial canon tables added by Jerome superfluous.[11] The text is written in paragraphs, indicated by initials projecting into the margin. Although the manuscript is not particularly well written, its age makes it of special interest for the Vulgate text. The diffusion of Jerome's Gospels around Italy is also attested in colophons in later manuscripts copied from fifth- or sixth-century exemplars.[12]

A tiny fragment of John, VL 23, although listed in the Vetus Latina *Register*, is more likely to be another fifth-century Vulgate witness. There is nothing distinctively Old Latin about the text of this manuscript. However, as in Vg^{Se} S, a Eusebian section in the margin is followed by a canon number in a different colour and references to parallel passages in Matthew and Luke. The layout appears to be in two columns with paragraphs indicated by projecting letters. Excavated in Egypt at the turn of the twentieth century, the fragment seems to come from a small format copy of the Gospel according to John: measuring roughly 10 by 8 cm, it is hard to imagine that it contained more than one Gospel despite the presence of the Eusebian apparatus. VL 33 is an even smaller codex of John copied in Italy in the early sixth century, consisting of 263 pages just 7.2 by 5.6 cm. It may have functioned as an amulet: the book was found in a reliquary in Chartres in 1712. There are around twenty-five words on each

---

[9] Burton 1996 suggests that this manuscript has Gothic connections: see page 230 below.
[10] Bischoff 1941; McGurk 1994a:6.   [11] See page 200.
[12] Several examples are given by Bogaert 2013:518–19, including Vg^{O} EP (exemplar from Lucullanum but claimed to be Jerome's own copy); Angers, BM, 24 (20) (a Roman exemplar); Munich, Bayerische Staatsbibliothek, Clm 6212 (copied in Ravenna).

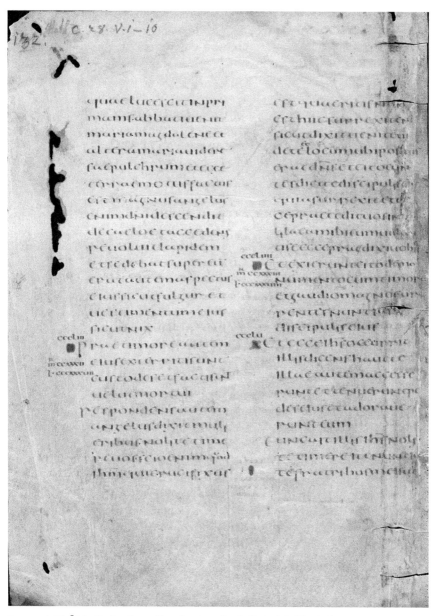

Image 6 Vg^{Se} S: **Codex Sangallensis 1395** (St Gall, Stiftsbibliothek 1395, page 132) at Matthew 28, showing the Eusebian apparatus in the margin. Also available at <http://www.e-codices.unifr.ch/de/csg/1395/132/>.

page, and no marginal material. Certain pages, including the initial four folios, are in a different, less-practised hand to the majority of the manuscript: this may have been someone of repute whose contribution would enhance the prestige of the book, perhaps even the person who commissioned its production. Overall the text corresponds to the Vulgate, but there are occasional Old Latin readings in the first six chapters, with a particular concentration at the beginning of John 5: several of these are unique to this manuscript, such as *testamentum* for *testimonium* in John 1:7, *pecuaria* for *probatica* in 5:2, *aeger* for *languidus* in 5:7, and *lectum* for *grabattum* in 5:9 and 12.

CHRISTIAN WRITERS AND CONCILIAR DOCUMENTS

The evidence for the adoption of the Vulgate text of the New Testament in authors of the fifth century is mixed. Among the large body of material pseudonymously attributed to Augustine, some use Old Latin texts (e.g. PS-AU Fu), some rework Augustinian material, and others use the Vulgate.[13] The use of Augustine as a source by other writers, whatever form of text may have been in their local codices, may also complicate the picture. Nonetheless, the Vulgate appears initially to have gained ground in North Italy. The sermons of Petrus Chrysologus (PET-C), bishop of Ravenna until his death around 450, usually follow the revised text. The same is usually true of the writings of popes such as Zosimus (ZO), Leo the Great (LEO), Simplicius (SIM), Gelasius I (GEL), and Hormisdas (HOR). Most of these are letters, which were assembled in two major sixth-century collections, the *Collectio Arelatensis* (COL-AR) and the Roman *Collectio Avellana* (COL-AV). The latter is five times larger, containing 244 letters spanning the years 367 to 553.

The proceedings of early episcopal councils provide some information about the reception and use of the New Testament.[14] The first council of Hippo in 393 (CO-Hipp 1) and the third council of Carthage in 397 (CO-Carth 3) are significant for establishing the contents of the biblical canon. The minutes of the Conference of Carthage (DO) between Catholic and Donatist bishops in 411, preserved in a single manuscript, shed light on the process of the preparation of official records by shorthand scribes. The *Decretum Gelasianum* (Decree of Gelasius) is often combined with texts claiming to represent a council held under Pope Damasus. While a Roman origin is generally accepted for these documents, neither the attribution to Damasus nor Gelasius holds up and the work may derive from the sixth century.[15] A list of biblical

[13] See pages 38–9.   [14] See further Munier 1972, 1974 and Gaudemet 1985.
[15] van Liere 2014:61; earlier work includes von Dobschütz 1894.

books in the conciliar portion gives the New Testament in the unusual order of Gospels, Acts, Paul, Revelation, and Catholic Epistles. Within this, the Pauline Epistles are listed in the sequence Romans, Corinthians, Ephesians, Thessalonians, Galatians, Philippians, and Colossians, while in the Catholic Epistles Peter precedes James. The enumeration of over sixty non-canonical books in the Gelasian section not only includes many of the apocryphal gospels, apostolic acts, and pseudepigraphal revelations but also a number of early Latin authors from Tertullian to Faustus of Riez. Strangely, Cyprian appears on both this list (as Thascius Cyprianus) and a preceding list of authoritative Greek and Latin writers (as Caecilius Cyprianus).[16]

The great Ecumenical Councils (CO), identified in the Vetus Latina *Repertorium* by their volume number in the modern *Acta Conciliorum Oecumenicum* series, are transmitted in a number of versions. Some of the translations are early, such as the portion of the *Collectio Palatina* in the Quesnel collection made in the time of Leo the Great (CO 1,5 Q), or the Tours version of certain volumes of the Council of Ephesus (CO 1,2 and 1,3). The principal Latin editions of these proceedings were produced in the early sixth century by Rusticus the Deacon (RUS:CO) and an anonymous Scythian monk (SCY:CO) perhaps to be identified with John of Tomi (JO-T). Where original Latin evidence or extracts from Greek writings are included, these are identified by their author (e.g. CYR:CO for Cyril of Alexandria). Despite their historical and theological importance, these translated texts convey little information about the Latin Bible: their significance is primarily for the sources they preserve and which are sometimes quoted in later writings.

GREEKS, GOTHS, AND ARIANS

As the knowledge of Greek decreased in the West, various translators continued the work of Jerome, Rufinus, and the Pelagians. A Latin version of Eusebius of Emesa (EUS-E) was produced in Gaul around the beginning of the fifth century. Its biblical quotations appear to have been translated directly from the Greek. The most substantial translated corpus is that of the Latin Chrysostom, which seems to have been begun around the same time in Italy: Augustine drew on an early selection of Chrysostom's homilies. The fullest collection (CHRY) was printed by Frobenius in Basle in 1558: the volume and page numbers of this edition are used to identify the individual pieces. However, many were rendered into Latin by contemporaries of the printer such as Oecolampadius. Where ancient translators or editors have been identified, the sermons are assigned to their output: the Pelagian deacon Anianus of Celeda translated the first twenty-five

---

[16] The earliest witness to the full text is the eighth-century Ragyndrudis Codex (Fulda, Hochschul- und Landesbibliothek, Bonif. 2).

of Chrysostom's homilies on Matthew (ANI h), seven sermons on Paul (ANI s), and possibly other works too around the year 420, while in the middle of the sixth century John of Naples (JO-N) collected thirty-one Latin sermons of Chrysostom which may have been translated a century or so earlier. Other pieces in the Latin Chrysostom are original Latin works from fifth-century collections including the *Collectio Escurialensis* (AN h Esc) and *Collectio Armentarii* (AN h Arm), both of which were assembled in Campania although the individual sermons have African origins. The corpus also features an incomplete Arian commentary on Matthew (AN Mt h) based on a version of Origen independent of Jerome. Certain sermons were attributed to Augustine and are found too in the collections edited by Mai (PS-AU s Mai) and Caillau (PS-AU s Cai) or the four volumes of the Monte Cassino *florilegium* (PS-AU s Cas). Other attributable works include the first four of Jerome's homilies (HI h) and seven sermons now identified as parts of Chromatius' *Commentary on Matthew* (CHRO Mt).

Bilingual manuscripts are witnesses to the relationship between Latin and Greek in the Christian world. Both VL 5 and VL 75, whose text has already been described, were copied in the fifth century, probably in Greater Syria and Italy respectively.[17] The only surviving Greek-Latin bilingual of Acts, VL 50 (the 'Laudian Acts'), was produced slightly later, in the sixth or seventh century. Sardinia has been suggested as the most likely location, although Rome is also possible. In this codex, both languages appear in parallel columns on the same page. Unlike the other bilinguals, Greek is found on the right and Latin on the left, while the lines are much shorter: many consist of only a single word. The Latin has been described as a pedantic rendering of the Greek, based on a 'European' Old Latin text.[18] The translation clearly predates the creation of this manuscript, as longer lines in the Latin column displace the Greek. Although the Greek column features *nomina sacra*, the full form is given in Latin.

The changing political situation, with the rise of the Goths, meant that bilingual manuscripts were also created with a Latin text alongside Wulfila's mid fourth-century translation from Greek into Gothic. In fact, there are a number of readings peculiar to the Latin and Gothic versions more generally, which may derive from Wulfila's occasional consultation of a Latin source: these include the addition of 'and the Holy Spirit' in Luke 1:3 (cf. Acts 15:28), and 'his entrance' rather than 'his word' in Luke 1:29.[19] The surviving Gothic–Latin codices were all produced in North Italy, although their formats vary. VL 79 (Codex Carolinus), four palimpsest leaves from a fifth-century copy of Romans, has the languages in two columns. In VL 36, a slightly later fragment of two pages of Luke, they each occupy a page. In both cases, the Gothic holds the place of honour on the left. As with the Greek bilinguals, there is some

---

[17] See pages 27–9.   [18] Parker 2008:289–90.
[19] Falluomini 2012, especially 338–42, and 2015:17, 101; see also Gryson 1990.

interaction between the two versions; the Latin texts have some pre-Vulgate readings although there are also Vulgate characteristics in VL 36.

Far more substantial than either of the Gothic-Latin fragments, however, is VL 10 (Codex Brixianus), a sixth-century gospel book possibly copied in Ravenna whose text may also derive from a bilingual manuscript.[20] Codicologically, VL 10 is strikingly similar to the contemporary Codex Argenteus (Uppsala, University Library), the principal witness to the Gothic version of the Gospels: both are written in silver and gold ink on purple parchment in single columns; the Eusebian sections are numbered in the left margin, sometimes decorated with tapering lines; these numbers are reproduced in an artistic colonnade at the bottom of each page with those of parallel passages in the other Gospels, although there are no canon numbers; the Gospels are in the sequence Matthew–John–Luke–Mark. Despite this order, the text of VL 10 is predominantly Vulgate, with a handful of Old Latin readings and a few variants which have been attributed to Gothic influence, such as *uerax* ('true') rather than *bonus* ('good') in John 7:12.[21] Before the Gospels, VL 10 has a unique preface on the problems of translating the Bible, referring to a comparison between Greek, Latin and Gothic and with an implied criticism of Jerome, written some time in the first half of the fifth century.[22] Preceding this is a set of Eusebian canon tables which appear to be of different origin to the rest of the manuscript and, unusually, provide the opening text of each section. This is Old Latin in its affiliation, often diverging from the gospel text in the main part of the manuscript.[23] Finally, there are also longer divisions in the margins of the Gospels consisting of Roman numerals preceded by the letters 'LEC', presumably for *lectio* ('reading'), also decorated like the marginalia of the Codex Argenteus.[24]

Like the Goths, a number of Latin writers of the fourth and fifth century espoused the doctrines of Arian Christianity. Some are known by name, such as Augustine's opponent Maximinus (MAXn), the bishop of a Gothic congregation in Africa. Maximinus used also to be identified as the author of much of the *Collectio Arriana Veronensis* (AN Ver), a manuscript copied around 500 containing four Arian writings and a number of sermons, as well as some Gothic marginalia.[25] The Latin works are now attributed to

[20] Burkitt 1900, Gryson 1990:22–5, Falluomini 2015:33.
[21] Further examples in Falluomini 2015:101–3.
[22] Henss 1973: the text is reproduced with a translation in Falluomini 2015:178–80. See also Falluomini 2012:339–40 and 2015:105–6.
[23] VL 46 is a later witness to these textual canon tables.
[24] On the presence of *laiktsjo* ('lection') in the margin of Gothic manuscripts, see Falluomini 2015:40.
[25] This manuscript also contains VL 49, an eighth-century marginal note with two verses of John 12 in a non-Vulgate form, and VL 183, marginal readings from Isaiah and Jeremiah.

an unknown Arian writing in Africa who used Cyprian and other sources. A similar Arian miscellany is found in a palimpsest codex in Bobbio (AN Bob), consisting of fragments of writings produced in Illyria in the late fourth century; another manuscript of Wulfila's translation was later overwritten in Bobbio with the Vulgate in an Irish semi-uncial script (Milan, Biblioteca Ambrosiana, I.61 sup).[26] Augustine wrote a response to an anonymous Arian sermon (AN Ar): both are transmitted together. The translator of parts of Origen's commentary on Matthew (ORI Mt and ORI ser) was also an Arian, and may be identical with the author of an incomplete commentary on Matthew (AN Mt h) produced by an Arian Latin speaker in the second or third quarter of the fifth century, possibly also in Illyria. These Arian sources often have a distinctive Latin biblical text, sharing renderings such as *aduocatus* for παρά-κλητος ('paraclete') and numerous other pre-Vulgate forms without any obvious theological bias.

Maximinus' quotations have been the subject of a detailed investigation which observes their close similarity with VL 13 (Codex Monacensis), a manuscript which corresponds to the biblical lemmata of the Arian commentary on Matthew.[27] This is a gospel book with the Old Latin sequence of evangelists, copied in the sixth or seventh century in Illyria or North Italy. Its biblical text cannot be easily classified: many of its renderings are more distant from the Vulgate than the North Italian text-type I yet still provide parallels for readings in Ambrose and Augustine. On some occasions (especially in John) it agrees with older readings present in VL 14; elsewhere there are parallels with VL 11. It has been observed that this text reaches back to the fourth century.[28] At the same time, there are places where VL 13 appears to have been influenced by Jerome's revised text or, at the very least, independently compared with a Greek manuscript and made to correspond more closely. This is the first manuscript in this survey to have decorations in more than two colours: the titles and some capitals feature red, pink, green, olive, and yellow. There are other adornments to initials and titles, many in the form of birds, and the use of *hederae* (ivy-leaf shapes to fill in blank space, represented by ❧ in modern typography).[29] There is no Eusebian apparatus; however, the outsize capitals and lines in colour frequently correspond to the divisions in VL 10 marked with 'LEC', providing another link with Arian tradition.

[26] See Falluomini 2015:34–5; there is a partial collation of the gospel text in McNamara 1992.
[27] Gryson 1978; see also Falluomini 2015:104.
[28] Fischer 1980 [1986:301], who suggests Sirmium as a possible place of copying.
[29] On *hederae*, which may be functional as well as decorative, see Parkes 1992:27–8.

LECTIONARIES AND HARMONIES

The development of a fixed cycle of liturgical readings brought with it a demand for lectionaries containing the portions of text appointed for particular days. In the early fifth century, the bishop was still responsible for the choice of biblical passages read in public worship, at least outside the major feasts. Augustine was thus able to deliver his commentaries as sermons preached during the liturgy.[30] Several of the gospel manuscripts already described in this section have liturgical notes added in the margin by later hands. The earliest surviving Latin lectionary, however, is VL 32 (the Wolfenbüttel Palimpsest). Copied in the first half of the sixth century, this contains readings from a wide range of Old and New Testament books. It appears to be of French origin, corresponding to the sequence of the Gallican lectionary probably developed by Claudianus Mamertus (CLAU) in 470–4. The surviving portion of the manuscript was made into a palimpsest around 700. The texts are of differing origin. As is usual, the biblical canticles follow the traditional Old Latin form. The readings from the New Testament in general correspond to the Vulgate; there are some Old Latin readings in the Pauline Epistles, and in certain Catholic Epistles the lections derive from the text-type **T** preceding the Vulgate. Some of the Gospel passages are in fact harmonizations or combinations of texts: these include the Cleansing of the Temple and the Passion narrative. Certain passages which appear more than once, most notably Jesus' commission to Peter in John 21, have completely different texts, transmitting an Old Latin form in one lection and the Vulgate in another. The oldest Roman lectionary to be preserved (Würzburg, Universitätsbibliothek, M.p.th.f.62) has lists of gospel and epistle readings reflecting the liturgy of Rome in the middle of the seventh century).[31] Early sacramentaries also provide biblical citations from a liturgical context. The Leonine Sacramentary (S-L) which includes texts from Pope Gelasius (GEL:S-L), is the first; the Gelasian Sacramentary itself is later (S-Ge). One particularly notable lectionary is VL 111 (the *Liber Commonei*; Oxford, Bodleian Library, Auct. F.4.32) which contains readings from the Old Testament for the Easter Vigil preceding the reforms of Gregory the Great. The texts are given in two forms: one column has the Latin while the other has the transliterated Greek of the same text, in order to enable a reader without Greek to read the original form aloud during the solemn ritual.[32]

---

[30] For the initial development of systems of lections based on the evidence of Ambrose, Augustine, Peter Chrysologus, Maximus of Turin, and Leo the Great, see Willis 1962a. The overall reference work for Latin liturgical manuscripts is CLLA.

[31] Morin 1910, 1911; Frere 1934, 1935; Dyer 2012:671; see also page 90.

[32] Fischer 1952 [1986:18–50]. The manuscript was copied in Wales in the early ninth century and includes a runic alphabet.

An alternative approach to the text of the Gospels was provided by Victor, bishop of Capua (VIC-C), who also created the oldest surviving Latin manuscript to contain all the books of New Testament, Codex Fuldensis (Vg F; Image 7). In his preface, written on 2 May 546, Victor tells how he discovered a harmony of the Gospels which he then brought in line with the text of Jerome's revised version and supplemented with the rest of the New Testament. Victor believed his source to be Tatian's Diatessaron, a gospel harmony created in the second century in Greek or Syriac.[33] Codex Fuldensis combines the text of the four Gospels in 182 numbered sections: in the outer margins of its tall, narrow pages the Eusebian apparatus is given with details of the parallel passages, while the sources are also indicated in red before each section of text (M^T for Matthew, M^R for Mark, Lc for Luke, and Io for John). As the text of the Gospels has been thoroughly conformed to the Vulgate, this manuscript does not offer any textual evidence for an Old Latin harmony. Nonetheless, it does give an indication of the structure of the Diatessaron and is also the earliest surviving Latin gospel harmony, which became a popular genre in the Middle Ages: harmonies deriving from Codex Fuldensis are described as *Unum ex quattuor*, based on Victor's preface. The manuscript offers a very good text of the Vulgate for all the New Testament books. It is the oldest witness to the Latin version of the pseudepigraphical Epistle to the Laodiceans, inserted between Colossians and 1 Timothy, and also to the pseudo-Hieronymian Prologue to the Catholic Epistles (PROL cath), although the Johannine Comma (1 John 5:7–8) is absent. The omission of 1 Corinthians 14:34–35 appears to have been an oversight, as these verses are added in the margin by the first hand.

Despite Victor's reference to an earlier harmony, no evidence for an Old Latin gospel harmony survives in manuscript form. It could be that this was a concordance based on *capitula*, perhaps connected with the Eusebian canon tables which include textual extracts.[34] Schmid has shown how the variations in later Latin and vernacular harmonies can be traced to the incorporation of local readings from unharmonized texts and a marginal commentary which later became part of the tradition.[35] While there may have been one or more Old Latin gospel harmonies, their existence is not required to explain the differences between surviving witnesses. Furthermore, as harmonization is a common feature both in biblical quotations and in manuscripts of the earliest Latin text of the Gospels, the identification of readings characteristic of the Diatessaron is fraught with difficulty. A more promising line of research is on the sequence of the material as an indication of the use of a gospel harmony. A recent example of this is found in an analysis of the *Carmen Paschale* composed by Sedulius around 431 (SED carm).[36] The order of the biblical

[33] See Petersen 1994:45–50, which includes a text and translation of Victor's preface.
[34] These are found in VL 10, 39, 40, and 46; see also Bogaert 2013:511.
[35] Schmid 2005, 2012.   [36] Norris 2014; see also Green 2006, 2007.

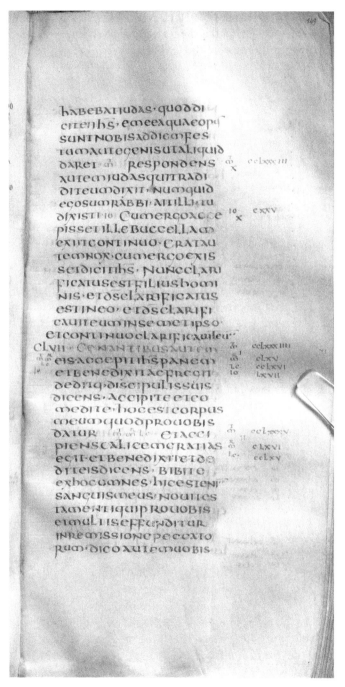

Image 7 Vg F: Codex Fuldensis (Fulda, Hochschul- und Landesbibliothek, Cod. Bonif. 1, folio 149ʳ): chapter 157 of the Diatessaron with source indications and marginal Eusebian apparatus. By kind permission of the Hochschul- und Landesbibliothek Fulda. Also available at <http://fuldig.hs-fulda.de/viewer/image/PPN325289808/301/>.

episodes in this poetic account of the Gospels appears to follow the same sequence as Codex Fuldensis, but the quotations have an Old Latin affiliation. In the companion prose version, the *Opus Paschale* (SED pa), Sedulius follows the Vulgate text.

CASSIODORUS

The innovation of the Latin biblical pandect containing the entire Old and New Testament is often attributed to the sixth-century Roman statesman Cassiodorus (CAr), although there is evidence that it emerged in the previous century.[37] Having built up a vast personal library, which later moved to the Lateran basilica in Rome, Cassiodorus sought to integrate classical literature with Christian teaching. His scheme of reading, the *Institutiones* (CAr in), was the curriculum for the monastery he founded at Vivarium (near Squillace in southern Italy). In this work Cassiodorus sets out his principles on the production of books and textual criticism, including an appeal to the importance of ancient copies and a description of biblical manuscripts in three formats. One is a single-volume pandect written in a relatively small hand (*minutiore manu*) containing all the canonical books of the Old and New Testaments in 636 leaves. Its text was arranged throughout in sense-lines, also known as *per cola et commata*, extending the format introduced by Jerome in his translation of the Hebrew Prophets. Another is a larger volume, the *codex grandior*, of 760 leaves, which also had illustrations. The third is a 'standard' edition of the Bible in nine volumes. The textual affiliation of the *codex grandior* and nine-volume Bible is unclear: based on Cassiodorus' text elsewhere, Fischer maintains that the *codex grandior* had Jerome's revision of the Gospels but an Old Latin text for the rest of the New Testament, while the nine-volume Bible was Old Latin throughout. Others hold that the nine-volume Bible had the same Vulgate text as the pandect.[38] The picture of a scribe in Codex Amiatinus (Vg A), a pandect connected with Cassiodorus' edition, could be a depiction of Cassiodorus himself. At his feet is a smaller book, which has been identified with the smaller pandect, while he is writing on larger format pages (possibly the *codex grandior*). The bookcase behind him contains nine horizontal volumes with titles matching the disposition of Scripture described in the *Institutiones*; the last three contain the New Testament with the titles on the spines: Four Books of the Gospels (*Euang. L. III[I]*),

---

[37] See page 87.
[38] See Fischer 1962, O'Donnell 1979, Gribomont 1985b, and O'Loughlin 2014.

twenty-one Letters of the Apostles (*Epist. Ap. XXI*), and two books of the Acts of the Apostles and Apocalypse (*Act. Ap. Apoc. L. I[I]*).[39]

The initial chapters of the *Institutiones* include a list of the exegetical works and commentaries in Cassiodorus' library in biblical order. This features several lost works, such as Augustine's commentary on James, Jerome's commentaries on the Letters to the Corinthians, Thessalonians, Colossians, and Timothy, and an exposition of the Pauline Epistles by Peter of Tripoli based entirely on excerpts from the works of Augustine. The significance of Augustine in this period may also be seen in the anthology of his works created at the beginning of the fifth century by Eugippius (EUGI), abbot of Lucullanum near Naples. This is an important source for the transmission of Augustine's works.[40] Cassiodorus also speaks of a number of translations of Greek works which he commissioned, including Chrysostom's sermons on Hebrews, translated by Mutianus (MUT), Didymus on the Catholic Epistles, translated by a certain Epiphanius, and Clement of Alexandria on the Catholic Epistles. These are followed by chapters listing the contents of Scripture which function as a concordance between the descriptions found in Jerome, Augustine, and the Septuagint (CAr inst 1.12–14).

Cassiodorus' main work of biblical exposition was his commentary on the Psalms (CAr Ps), composed during the decade he was resident in Constantinople. However, towards the end of his life, he began a revision of Pelagius' commentary on the Pauline Epistles. Despite its being transmitted under the name of Gelasius, Cassiodorus recognized that it was Pelagian in its theology and resolved to create a more acceptable version. He was only responsible himself for the edition of Romans (CAr Rm); the remaining books were revised by his followers (CAr 1Cor–Phlm). For a long time, this version was erroneously associated with the African bishop Primasius. After his work on Romans, Cassiodorus says in his work on orthography (CAr orth) that he produced a book of scriptural *tituli*. This appears to have been a compilation of chapter headings for each biblical book, although these have not been identified with any extant series. His next writing was the *Complexiones* (CAr cpl), a summary of the whole of the New Testament apart from the Gospels. This only survives in a single manuscript, copied around 700. Cassiodorus divided the text into numbered sections, beginning each part of his commentary with this number followed by a quotation of the first verse of the passage. These are Old Latin in their affiliation. Although much of the work is a paraphrase of the biblical text, Cassiodorus drew on numerous sources including the commentaries on Revelation by Victorinus of Poetovio, Tyconius, and Jerome, as well as his contemporary Primasius.

---

[39] This text is taken from Ricci 2000. Arguments for the identification with Cassiodorus are found in Meyvaert 1996; see also Bogaert 2012:76.

[40] Eugippius is also mentioned in the colophon to Vg[O] EP which claimed to derive from Jerome's own copy of the Gospels (see page 74).

LATER ITALIAN GOSPEL BOOKS
AND GREGORY THE GREAT

An Italian revision of the text of the Gospels was made around the beginning of the sixth century. The principal witness to this is the sixth-century Harley Gospels (Vg^S Z), which seems to derive from an Old Latin manuscript corrected towards the Vulgate.[41] Its text combines numerous pre-Vulgate readings with a good early form of Jerome's revision matching the tradition of Vg^{Se} S. There also appear to have been attempts to smooth the Latin grammar and style. It has been suggested that this sort of text was the source for the Gospels in Alcuin Bibles.[42] Vg^{Oe} P is a sixth-century copy of Luke with a Vulgate text, also of Italian origin. The ongoing currency of pre-Vulgate readings is seen in mixed-text gospel books. These may either be Old Latin manuscripts which were partially brought into agreement with the Vulgate, or manuscripts of Jerome's revision into which earlier readings were reintroduced. Several originate from north Italy in the sixth or early seventh century. One of the earliest is the Burchard Gospels (Würzburg, Universitätsbibliothek, M.p.th.f.68), a sixth-century Italian gospel book with a mixed text very close to the much later VL 15.[43] Codex Foroiuliensis (Vg^O J) has a number of indications of early origin, such as the absence of canon tables, a unique set of *capitula*, and certain pre-Vulgate readings, yet it also has Jerome's preface. The Split Gospels (Vg^S P) were copied from two exemplars and also have unusual elements in their *capitula*: they are the earliest witness to a series (KA Ben) which features a number of Old Latin readings.

The gradual shift from Old Latin to Vulgate is also seen in the writings of Pope Gregory the Great (GR-M). These include a series of forty homilies on the Gospels (GR-M Ev): like Augustine's *Tractates on John*, some of these were dictated while others were delivered during the liturgy. Two recensions survive: one has rather loose citations featuring Old Latin forms, while the other corresponds to the Vulgate. Both biblical versions were present in Rome at the time and used interchangeably.[44] In his *Moralia on Job* (GR-M Jb 35.20.48), Gregory states that Paul wrote fifteen epistles, but only fourteen were held to be canonical: this is presumably a reference to the Epistle to the Laodiceans. A Vulgate text is also found in the gospel books commissioned by Gregory for his missionary activities. Although their link with Gregory is debated, the two books known as the 'Gospels of St Augustine' (Vg^{Oe} O and

---

[41] Fischer 1971 [1985:373–7], 1972:60 [1986:234].

[42] Fischer 1963b [1985:54] and Jullien 2004.

[43] Fischer 1965 [1985:172] suggests that the Burchard Gospels originated in Rome; see also page 80 below.

[44] Manselli 1963; Étaix 1986; Gribomont 1986; Bogaert 2012:73. Bischoff 1990:190 notes that Troyes, BM 504, copied in Gregory's scriptorium, may contain corrections in the author's own hand (see also Parkes 1992:18, 171).

Vg^O X) are both manuscripts of this type. Their text is comparable to the Harley Gospels; the Cambridge manuscript (Vg^O X) contains a fine full-page evangelist picture at the beginning of Luke along with a set of twelve scenes depicting the Passion narrative and the raising of Lazarus, by far the most advanced illustrations in a Latin gospel book of this period. Produced for a wealthy patron, such as a pope, these offer an interesting comparison with other sixth-century works of Christian art in the West, such as the mosaics in the Basilica at Ravenna.[45]

Several fragments copied in the seventh century, mostly from gospel manuscripts, attest to the continued use of Old Latin texts. A replacement leaf was produced for the last page of Mark's Gospel in VL 16 from an Old Latin exemplar. VL 18 consists of parts of a gospel lectionary produced in North Italy and later palimpsested: its text corresponds to the pre-Vulgate text-type I. VL 25, a single page of John, also has affinities with this type (including the reading *perticae* ('pole' instead of 'hyssop') at John 19:29) as well as some Vulgate readings. The two extant pages of VL 26, by contrast, preserve a much older text of Luke: this has been corrected towards a later pre-Vulgate form, with some changes which appear to derive from comparison with Greek. In the eighth and ninth century, interlinear glosses were added in Latin and Old High German. VL 80 is half a leaf of Romans in a fine large uncial script: the text is similar to the Old Latin form found in Augustine and VL 64.

AFRICA AND SPAIN

African writers exhibit a variety of forms of biblical text in the decades after Augustine. Arnobius the younger (AR) was an African monk living in Rome in the first half of the fifth century, although the series of short expositions of the Gospel of John based on the Synoptics once attributed to him (AR exp) is now thought to be a much later composition.[46] Anti-Arian works are preserved from the pens of Quodvultdeus (QU), a bishop of Carthage who moved to Campania in 439, Vigilius of Thapsus (VIG-T), and Fulgentius of Ruspe (FU). Fulgentius, writing in the early sixth century, was the most prolific: his text of the Gospels normally follows Jerome's revision, but in the other books of the New Testament he corresponds to Old Latin forms. A manuscript of Hilary of Poitiers' *De Trinitate*, copied before 509, may have been corrected by Fulgentius during his period of exile in Sardinia.[47] Some intriguing works are pseudonymously attributed to Vigilius. The twelve books of *On the Trinity*

---

[45] See further Wormald 1954 and pages 204–6 below.   [46] Dorfbauer 2014a.
[47] Rome, Archivio San Pietro, Basilicanus D.182 (CLA I 1a); see Bischoff 1990:185.

(PS-VIG tri) appear to be by a variety of authors. Book nine is identical to the *Fides Damasi* (PS-DAM fi), previously thought to be by Gregory of Elvira but now attributed to fifth-century Gaul; book twelve is also transmitted in the guise of a translation of Athanasius (ATH), although the correspondence of its biblical quotations with late African sources indicates that it is more likely to be a Latin original. Other books have been dated as early as the late fourth century, although the majority of the work appears to be from the fifth century; parts of books ten and eleven are quoted by Augustine. Another work roughly contemporary with Vigilius is three books against an Arian called Varimadum (PS-VIG Var), with frequent quotations from an Old Latin version of the New Testament.[48] Finally, the *Commentary on Revelation* by Primasius (PRIM), bishop of Hadrumetum in modern Tunisia until his death around 560, is of particular interest: his sources included both Tyconius' lost commentary and Jerome's version of Victorinus of Poetovio, as well as Augustine's *City of God*. In turn, Primasius was used as a source by others including Cassiodorus.

Connections between Africa and Spain are shown in the story of Donatus, an African monk who introduced a monastic rule to Spain in the middle of the sixth century. Escaping the barbarian incursions by boat, he brought with him almost seventy monks and a large number of books (*copiosisque librorum codibus*).[49] One of the latest African biblical manuscripts, which also travelled to Spain, is the older part of VL 64 (the Freising Fragments). This consists of twenty-eight leaves from a copy of the Pauline Epistles produced in Africa in the latter half of the sixth century. Their text is a distinctive Old Latin form, very close indeed to the text of Galatians used by Augustine in his commentary. It appears to be a mixed form of various Old Latin types, corrected on the basis of a Greek manuscript.[50] The second part of the manuscript, copied in Spain in the early seventh century, comprises replacement leaves for the earlier half and portions of the Catholic Epistles.

The Vulgate text of both the Old and New Testaments appears to have travelled to Spain very soon after it was produced. One of Jerome's letters (HI ep 71.5) relates how a Lucinius from the Spanish province of Baetica sent scribes to Bethlehem to copy his writings, including the biblical translations. Around a century after Priscillian's fourth-century arrangement of the Old Latin version of Paul's letters into canons, there appears to have been a further Spanish edition of at least part of the biblical text drawing on both Priscillian and the Vulgate by a reviser whose identity is unclear. The strongest evidence for this revision is in the editions of Proverbs and the Pauline Epistles attributed to a bishop Peregrinus: in addition to incorporating a more orthodox form of Priscillian's canons, the latter include a distinctive set of *capitula*

---

[48] See further Schwank 1961.
[49] The tale is related by Ildefonsus of Toledo (ILD vir 3).   [50] De Bruyne 1921.

(KA Sp), prologues, and other prefatory material such as lists of names and Old Testament quotations. Some of the readings in Peregrinus' text confirm that he was reliant on a Vulgate manuscript from Italy.[51] Another Spanish text of uncertain origin from the same period is an exegetical work on the Gospels, *Interpretatio Euangeliorum*, by Epiphanius Latinus (EP-L), who may have been a fifth-century bishop of Seville. Further evidence for the availability of Jerome's writings in the region is seen in the use of his version of Victorinus' *Commentary on Revelation* by the Portuguese bishop Apringius (APR) in the early sixth century. In 542, the Frankish king Childebert besieged Saragossa and, according to Gregory of Tours, 'brought back twenty cases for gospel books, all decorated with pure gold and precious stones.'[52] The lack of Spanish biblical manuscripts from this time may be associated with such upheavals.

With the conversion of the Visigothic rulers from Arianism to Catholicism, the early seventh century saw a flourishing of biblical scholarship in Spain. One of the principal figures was Isidore (IS), archbishop of Seville up to his death in 636. Famous for his etymological writings, Isidore also composed a number of commentaries on the Old Testament. Extracts from his biographical work *De ortu et obitu patrum* (IS ptr) are sometimes found as prefaces in biblical codices, but Isidore wrote a set of prologues for all biblical books (IS pro) which appears to have accompanied his own edition of the Bible. However, no surviving biblical manuscript has the complete set of prologues or the order of books matching his prologues.[53] Instead, the distinctive Spanish tradition of the Latin Bible is associated with John, bishop of Saragossa (Zaragoza) from 619. This took the form of a pandect containing both the Old and the New Testament with a characteristic layout in three columns, and the order Gospels, Pauline Epistles, Catholic Epistles, Acts, and Revelation (epcar).

A seventh-century manuscript of John's edition appears to have been the exemplar for the ninth-century Codex Cavensis (Vg C) as well as underlying the great tenth-century codices.[54] Although its text was Vulgate in affiliation it preserved Old Latin readings, especially in the form of marginal alternatives and glosses. In some of the later manuscripts, these non-Vulgate forms were reintroduced into the body of the text. A different combination of Old Latin and Vulgate is seen in VL 67 (the León Palimpsest). This is the oldest surviving Latin biblical pandect, a large format manuscript copied in Toledo in the seventh century but re-used three centuries later. The surviving pages show that, while its text of the Pauline Epistles is Vulgate, the Catholic Epistles and part of Acts have an Old Latin affiliation with similarities to Cyprian and

---

[51] Fischer 1963b [1985:47–53]; Frede 1976b.

[52] *Uiginti euangeliorum capsas detulit, omnia ex auro puro ac gemmis praetiosis ornatas* (GR-T hist 3.10).

[53] Fischer 1963b [1985:80]. On Isidore's contribution to punctuation, see Parkes 1992:20–2.

[54] See pages 96–7 and 255. These witnesses are identified by the siglum Σ in Vetus Latina editions.

Tyconius, as well as the fifth-century Portuguese writer Orosius. In addition to a substantial body of contemporary work pseudonymously ascribed to Isidore (PS-IS), there are various writings by the seventh-century bishops of Saragossa, Braulio (BRAU), brother of John, and his successor Taius (TA), consisting mostly of extracts from Gregory the Great. The works of their counterparts in Toledo, Ildefonsus (ILD) and Julian, rely on Jerome and Isidore. Julian of Toledo's *Antikeimenon* (JUL-T ant) offers explanations of apparent contradictions in no fewer than 221 passages of the Bible.[55]

FRANCE

Jerome's revised text of the Gospels was known in France in the early fifth century. The most extensive New Testament citations in the writings of Eucherius, bishop of Lyons until his death around 450, appear in his two volumes of *Instructiones* (EUCH inst). His gospel text corresponds largely to the Vulgate, albeit with a handful of earlier readings. The second book of the *Instructiones* includes a guide to Hebrew and Greek words, weights and measures, and other specialist terminology in the Bible, and was later included among the scholarly apparatus at the end of Theodulf Bibles.[56] Salvian, author of four books *To the Church* (SALV eccl) and eight *On divine guidance* (SALV gu), also broadly corresponds to Jerome's version. In contrast, Avitus of Vienne (AV), famous for his poetry and correspondence, appears to use the Vulgate of the Old Testament but an Old Latin text for the New Testament. Faustus, a fifth-century bishop of Riez in Provence, used Augustine for his treatise *On grace* (FAU-R gr) and Jerome's translation of Didymus (HI Did) in his own work *On the Holy Spirit* (FAU-R sp). Few, if any, of the sermons attributed to him are authentic in their present form: most are the work of his younger contemporary Caesarius of Arles, although there is one sermon of Caesarius which may preserve a lost sermon of Faustus (CAE s 211).

The *Commentary on the Apocalypse* by Caesarius of Arles (CAE Apc), written shortly after 510, takes the form of eighteen sermons and draws on Victorinus of Poetovio and Tyconius. There are no fewer than 238 sermons by Caesarius, which have been divided into three classes: around half are original compositions; others are portions of existing works assembled by Caesarius; the remainder are largely unaltered pieces from earlier preachers. His chief dependence is on Augustine, but others include Rufinus, Maximus of Turin,

---

[55]　O'Loughlin 1993.　　　[56]　See page 85.

Gregory of Elvira, and Quodvultdeus. Non-Vulgate readings in the biblical text may well derive from these sources. In addition, over 130 of Caesarius' sermons are found among those later ascribed to Augustine (PS-AU s). The seventh-century collection of seventy-six homilies, known as Eusebius Gallicanus (EUS-G h), includes much material found in Caesarius or attributed to him; it has been suggested that this is, in fact, a corpus of Faustus of Riez.[57] An anonymous commentary on all four Gospels, known as Pseudo-Theophilus of Antioch (PS-THl), was written in Gaul between 470 and 529, drawing on Eucherius and other authors.[58]

Towards the end of the sixth century, Gregory of Tours, famous for his *History of the Franks* (GR-T hist), composed several works on martyrs including the *Miracles* in eight books (GR-T mir), three of which are devoted to his predecessor Martin. Like Avitus, Gregory's New Testament text continues to preserve a higher proportion of Old Latin rather than Vulgate readings. A contemporary of Gregory, traditionally known as Abdias, produced an *Apostolic History* in ten books (ABD), also known as the *Virtutes apostolorum*. Although based on Greek sources such as the Apocryphal Acts of the Apostles, possibly in translation, this is an original Latin work which occasionally features non-Vulgate forms in its biblical quotations.[59]

IRELAND AND BRITAIN

The missionary activity of Gregory the Great had been preceded by the voyage of Patrick to Ireland in the fifth century. A few of Patrick's works have been preserved (PAT), mostly with Old Latin biblical quotations although he cites the Vulgate form of Acts.[60] Indeed, by the time of Gregory, Irish monks were returning to preach in mainland Europe. Perhaps the most famous is Columbanus (COL), founder of several monasteries including Luxeuil in France and Bobbio in Italy, where he died in 615. The Old Latin scriptural books brought by Patrick were to characterize the Irish biblical text for centuries to come.[61]

The oldest surviving Irish Latin gospel book is VL 14 (Codex Usserianus primus), written around the year 600 in Ireland (Image 8). Its layout is characteristic of pre-Vulgate tradition: the order of the Gospels is Matthew–John–Luke–Mark; the margins have not been preserved but it seems unlikely that there was any Eusebian apparatus; the title of Luke has the archaic *cata* rather than *secundum*. Most of the biblical text is distinctively Old Latin, often

---

[57] Étaix in Gryson 2007:470.   [58] Gorman 2003b; Hen 2003.
[59] See Steinová 2011.   [60] Bieler 1947; Fischer 1972:35 [202]; see also Cordolliani 1950.
[61] On Columbanus' biblical text, see Lomiento 1966.

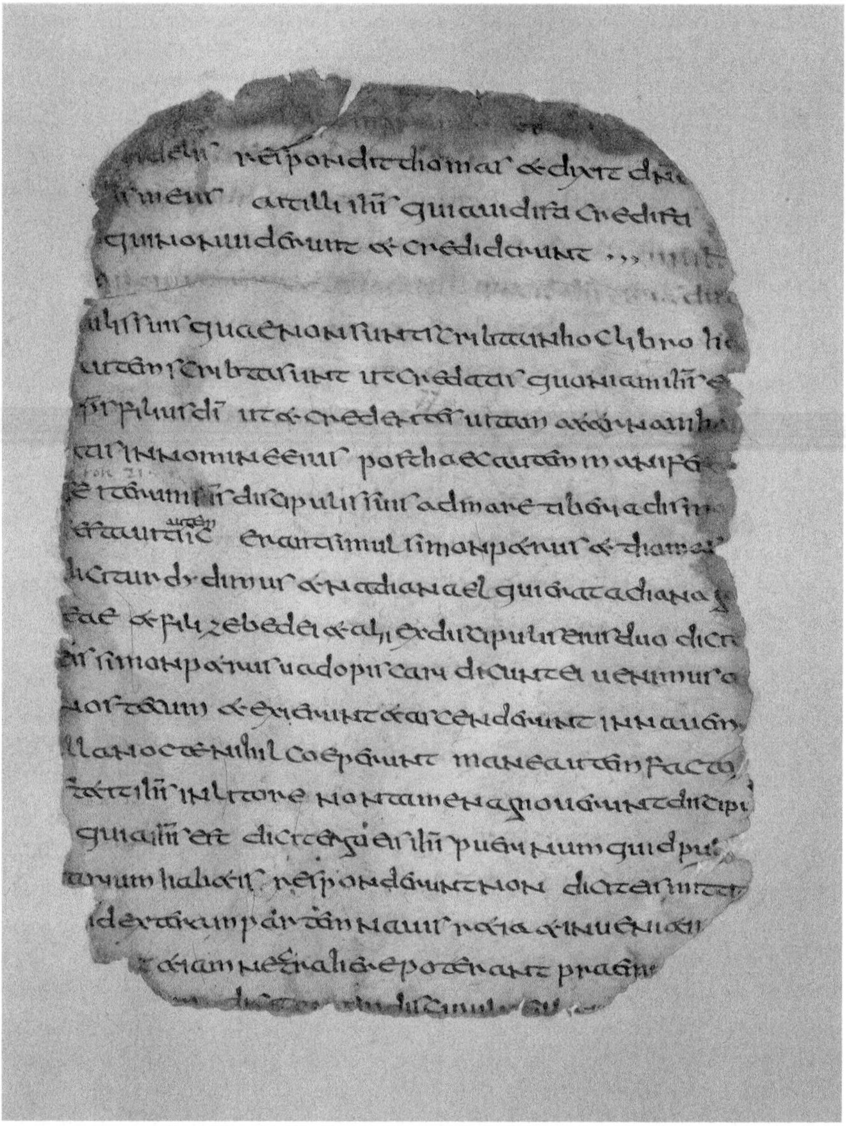

Image 8 VL 14: Codex Usserianus primus (Dublin, Trinity College, MS 55, folio 77ʳ), showing the beginning of John 21 and a rubricated chapter title. By kind permission of the Board of Trinity College Dublin.

matching that of Hilary of Poitiers and preserving some very early readings. VL 14 has parallels with other surviving Old Latin manuscripts, especially VL 4 in the first half of John and VL 12 in Matthew, with which it has been described as forming a 'Gallo-Irish' group. There are also certain readings shared with VL 13, and others typical of Irish texts.[62] However, a few features have points of contact with Jerome's revision. Between John and Luke there is a list of Hebrew names and their Latin equivalents.[63] All four Gospels are divided into numbered chapters, the first line of which is written in coloured ink; these correspond to the Type I divisions (see the fourth/fifth line on Image 8). The form of the *Pericope Adulterae* is almost identical to the Vulgate, although the unique placing of the chapter number after this passage, at John 8:12, indicates that this may have been a secondary insertion.[64]

Significant Christian literary activity in the Insular regions of Ireland and Britain and the Celtic lands of Wales, Cornwall, and Brittany is first attested in the sixth and seventh centuries.[65] Gildas, the Welsh abbot of Rhuys in Brittany, composed his *De excidio et conquestu Britanniae* (GI exc) between 515 and 530. In contrast with others' dependence on earlier authors or *testimonia* collections, Gildas seems to have made a fresh compilation of biblical illustrations on kings and rulers by working through the Bible from start to finish. O'Loughlin's recent study has shown that, broadly speaking, Gildas used Jerome's translation for much of the Old Testament but read certain books, including the Minor Prophets and the whole of the New Testament in an Old Latin form.[66] The changes in affiliation are likely to reflect the grouping of biblical books in separate codices. A commentary on Mark, long known as Pseudo-Jerome (PS-HI Mc), is now attributed to Cummianus, a seventh-century Abbot of Durrow (CU-D Mc). Theodore, archbishop of Canterbury in the second half of the seventh century (THr-C), a native Greek speaker from Tarsus, used the Vulgate for his commentary on the Gospels.[67] The travelling of texts across Europe is seen in the epitome of Gregory the Great's *Moralia*: this summary was composed in Ireland by Lathcen (LATH) only a few decades after the work was written. Around the same time, the Irish monk Aileran the Wise produced a mystical interpretation of the genealogy of Jesus in Matthew (AIL prog) using a variety of earlier sources. He also composed a poem on the Eusebian canons, putting into rhyming Latin verse the number of agreements between the four Gospels (AIL Eus), which is incorporated in some biblical manuscripts.[68]

The earliest complete Insular gospel book is the Book of Durrow (Vg^S D), copied in the second half of the seventh century. This displays a number of the artistic features which reached their culmination in the following centuries: outsize decorative initials and text on the first page of each Gospel, evangelist symbols, and 'carpet pages'. The last-mentioned are abstract or geometric

---

[62] For Irish interpolations, see pages 159–67.   [63] See page 198.
[64] Chapter 16 in KA I normally comes at John 8:1; see Houghton 2011:321.
[65] See further Bieler 1964 and 1974; Grosjean 1955; Kelly 1988 and 1989.
[66] O'Loughlin 2012, replacing a short earlier survey by Burkitt.
[67] Bischoff & Lapidge 1994; McGurk 1995.
[68] See De Bruyne 1912 and Howlett 1996, as well as page 202.

designs using a variety of colours, which usually precede the portrait of each gospel writer. The evangelist symbols in the Book of Durrow differ from the customary identification, and may go back to an Old Latin source.[69] Matthew 1:18 begins with a decorated *chi-rho* monogram, typical of Insular tradition.[70] Textually, the Book of Durrow is a good early witness to the Vulgate, unlike later Insular codices. It also includes the full Eusebian apparatus and chapter titles. Various locations have been suggested as its place of production, including the monasteries of Iona in Scotland or Durrow in Ireland, although the most likely are Lindisfarne or Durham in Northumbria.

A partially preserved copy of the Gospels, VL 19A, originates from around the same time and place. This was a large codex, almost twice the size of the Book of Durrow, but was later taken apart and used as endpapers in the bindings of other manuscripts. The larger initials and other decorations show typical interlace design and have infill in red, orange, yellow, blue, and green. Although the primary affiliation of the surviving fragments of Matthew and Mark is with the Vulgate, four chapters of Mark have an Old Latin text similar to that of VL 14. This example of 'block mixture' is likely to have arisen from the use of a second manuscript to supply text missing from the principal exemplar. This manuscript also features a phonetic Latin representation of Greek text of the Lord's Prayer in three decorative frames at the end of Matthew.

To sum up, the three centuries following the revision of the Latin Bible which later became known as the Vulgate saw continuing interaction between this text and earlier traditions. As biblical books tended still to circulate individually or in small groups, Christian writers could use an Old Latin form in one book but the Vulgate in another. This inconsistency is replicated in the earliest pandects or complete New Testaments, where the textual affiliation of the constituent sections may vary. Even within a book some manuscripts exhibit a mixture of Old Latin and Vulgate, either through the use of multiple exemplars or the activity of correctors. Liturgical use introduced a new type of biblical manuscript, the lectionary, and the oldest Latin gospel harmony was also created in this period. The influence of Greek writings on Latin Christianity diminished, although there was productive contact for a time between the Latin and Gothic versions, including a distinctive biblical text common to Arian sources. The assembly of large sermon collections, as well as pseudonymous writings and the extensive re-use of earlier authors, complicates the identification of the biblical text for certain writers. Nevertheless, individual scholars such as Cassiodorus, Isidore, and John of Saragossa play an important part in the editing and transmission of biblical texts, as the geographical reach of Latin Christianity became ever greater.

---

[69] See page 206.   [70] See pages 159 and 207.

4

The Eighth and Ninth Centuries

Old Latin manuscripts continued to be used and copied in the eighth and ninth centuries, although surviving examples are more scarce than in the previous period and come from a wider variety of locations. The production of complete Bibles or New Testaments in one or two volumes became common, as seen first in the pandects created in the Northumbrian scriptorium of Wearmouth–Jarrow and then in the early ninth-century editions overseen by Alcuin and Theodulf. At the same time, the gospel book becomes a vehicle for the flourishing of indigenous artistic traditions, extending from astonishingly intricate Insular creations such as the Lindisfarne Gospels and the Book of Kells to the golden splendour of the books produced for the court of Charlemagne. The Carolingian period also sees a resurgence of biblical commentary, much of it stimulated by Irish scholars associated with monasteries on the European continent.

BEDE AND NORTHUMBRIA

The Venerable Bede, a scholar and monk at the twin Northumbrian monasteries of Wearmouth and Jarrow, was the most prolific author on the Latin Bible since Augustine. His works drew on the diverse collection of copies of earlier writers and scriptural codices assembled by the monasteries' founder, Benedict Biscop, on multiple visits to Rome in the late seventh century. Bede's best-known work is his *History of the English Church and People* (BED hist), completed four years before his death in 735. He produced commentaries on Mark, Luke, Acts, and the Catholic Epistles (BED Mc, Lc, Act, cath), which were structured according to the divisions of the biblical text: the commentaries on Mark and Luke are preceded by a series of chapter titles (KA C). Bede also gave indications of the principal sources in the margins, such as AU for Augustine or HI for Jerome: it has been estimated that only one-tenth of the writing is original to Bede.[1] Unfortunately, these marks have only been

---

[1] Gorman 2002; see also Ray 1982, Contreni 2012:520–2.

haphazardly copied in the manuscript tradition and rarely feature in modern editions. In addition, Bede composed two books of homilies on the Gospels (BED h) and tractates on Revelation (BED Apc), relying heavily on Augustine's sermons and the commentaries of Tyconius, Primasius, and Jerome's edition of Victorinus of Poetovio. Bede also wrote exegetical works on books of the Old Testament, technical treatises about the calendar, metre and orthography, and ancillary texts such as a list of place names in Acts (BED nom). One of Cuthbert's letters refers to a translation of John into English by Bede, although this does not survive: it may have been one of the earliest English–Latin interlinear glosses.[2] Bede was responsible for a series of chapter titles for all the books of the Bible apart from the Gospels, and prologues for the Pauline Epistles, which were even adopted in the mediaeval *Glossa ordinaria* commentary.[3]

The Wearmouth–Jarrow scriptorium is renowned for the production of one of the most famous Vulgate manuscripts, the Codex Amiatinus (Vg A, Image 9). This is a large format pandect of the entire Latin Bible. Every book is set out *per cola et commata*, the layout of most modern editions of the Vulgate. In his *Lives of the Abbots* (BED abb 1.15), Bede recounts how Ceolfrid, abbot of both monasteries from 690 until just before his death in 716, brought back a pandect of the old translation (*uetusta translatio*) from Rome and made three copies of the new translation, one for each monastery and one as a gift for the Pope. The last was Codex Amiatinus, which Ceolfrid was carrying with him on his way to Italy when he died; the dedication in the manuscript was later altered, changing the donor's name from Ceolfrid, abbot of the English, to Peter, abbot of the Lombards. Scholarship on this manuscript has been beset by a number of persistent misunderstandings.[4] Until the end of the nineteenth century, it was thought that Codex Amiatinus was written by an Italian hand, or in Italy itself. Long considered to be a copy of Cassiodorus' *codex grandior*, it has even been suggested that the first quire of this new manuscript was originally part of the *codex grandior* itself. The fact that the pandect imported by Ceolfrid was Old Latin indicates that this was not the exemplar for the Vulgate text in Codex Amiatinus: the assembly of books was the work of the scholarly community at Wearmouth–Jarrow.[5] Although there is still some hesitation about the presence of the *codex grandior* in Northumbria, this is the simplest explanation for the format and certain features of Codex Amiatinus. In his treatises on the Temple and the Tabernacle (BED aed, BED tab), Bede claims to have seen illustrations of both buildings, as found in the *codex grandior*, even though only

[2] Marsden 2012:218.
[3] For the *glossa ordinaria*, see Chapter 5 (pages 104–5); Meyvaert 1995 identifies Bede's prologues (PROL Eln) and *capitula* (KA Eln in Paul, KA Tur elsewhere).
[4] See Gorman 2003.
[5] Fischer 1962: the Psalms have the greatest number of Insular features, while the Gospels are a copy of a Neapolitan gospel book, liturgical notes included.

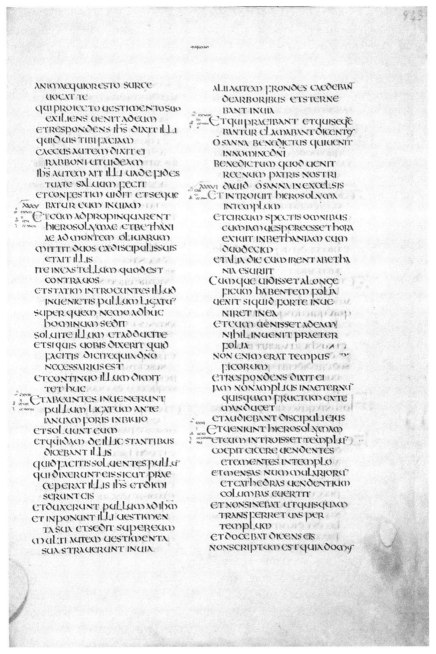

Image 9 Vg A: Codex Amiatinus (Florence, Biblioteca Medicea Laurenziana, MS Amiatino 1, folio 843ʳ) at the beginning of Mark 11, showing the layout *per cola et commata*. By permission of Ministero dei Beni e delle Attività Culturali e del Turismo. All further reproduction in any medium is forbidden.

the latter is found in the first quire of Codex Amiatinus. As explained on page 58, although the image of the copyist in this quire is identified in the caption as Ezra, there are good reasons for thinking that it may be a depiction of Cassiodorus himself.

Of the two sister manuscripts produced with Codex Amiatinus, only fragments of one remain. This is the Ceolfrid Bible (London, BL, Add. MSS 37777 and 45025), extant in parts of 3 and 4 Kings. The creation of these three Bibles may be linked with a grant of land to the monastery in 692 in order to raise the animals to supply the parchment required, although this could simply reflect the extent of the literary activity at Wearmouth–Jarrow at this time.[6] Another contemporary product of this Northumbrian scriptorium, in addition to several Durham gospel books (see pages 67–8 and the next section), is the Cuthbert Gospel (Vg^{Oe} S). This seventh-century copy of the Gospel according to John is still in its original binding. It was buried with St Cuthbert in his coffin at either his death in 687 or, more likely, his reinterment in 698 and discovered when his remains were translated to Durham in the early twelfth century. The Vulgate text is written in a clear uncial hand with little decoration apart from some rubricated initials, which correspond to the *capitula lectionum* found in Codex Amiatinus (KA C). There are four marginal annotations indicating passages to be read at the funeral liturgy. There can be little doubt that Bede was involved with the production of biblical manuscripts. In his *Commentary on Acts* and the later *Retractation* attached to the commentary he quotes multiple forms of text including Codex Amiatinus, the unique Latin text in the Laudian Acts (VL 50), and additional Old Latin forms.[7] Nevertheless, as the Vulgate text becomes ever more well established in this period, Bede is one of the latest authors used as a source for reconstructing the Vetus Latina.

INSULAR GOSPEL MANUSCRIPTS

Insular gospel books of the eighth century include a number of manuscripts of exceptional quality. One of the earliest and most remarkable is the Lindisfarne Gospels (Vg^{O} Y), copied by a single hand believed to be that of Eadfrith, bishop of Lindisfarne between 698 and 721. The 'carpet pages' preceding each Gospel and the decorated initials feature extraordinarily intricate details and geometric patterns. The biblical text is that of Jerome's revision, laid out in short sense-lines in two columns, with full Eusebian apparatus and magnificent initial canon tables (see Image 15). Ancillary material includes a set of chapter titles

---

[6] Bischoff 1990:9–10 notes that sheep parchment was specially used for these three pandects.
[7] Laistner 1937; see also Marsden 1998.

for each Gospel (KA C) and a table of liturgical readings including a reference to St Januarius, patron saint of Naples. Both these suggest that the exemplar for the manuscript came from Italy, and may even have been the same gospel book used for Codex Amiatinus.[8] An interlinear translation was added around 970, the earliest surviving version of the Gospels in Anglo-Saxon.

The Durham Gospels (Durham, Cathedral Library, A.II.17) are closely connected to the Lindisfarne Gospels. They may have been produced in the same place, and the same corrector made alterations to both manuscripts. The first page of John, one of the few illustrated pages to survive in the Durham Gospels, has a very similar layout and decoration to that in the Lindisfarne Gospels. However, the text of the Durham Gospels, although Vulgate, comes from a different tradition, and they are copied in the Insular style with a single column of long lines on each page. Punctuation was later added to the manuscript, dividing the text into sense-lines.[9] These Durham Gospels are not to be confused with their neighbour on the shelf of the cathedral library, an eighth-century gospel book made up of three parts (Vg^O Δ, sometimes called Codex Dunelmensis).[10] The affiliation of this second manuscript is also Vulgate, but there are textual variations between the various sections as well as codicological differences: the first part is written in uncial script, while the supplements are in Insular majuscules with a different presentation of the Eusebian apparatus. The text of John is similar to that in Codex Amiatinus. If a multiple-part manuscript such as this were used as an exemplar, the copy would demonstrate block mixture, with different textual affiliations in different sections. This is the case of the fragmentary Durham gospel book described earlier (VL 19A, page 68).

The Echternach Gospels (Vg^O EP) have connections with several of the preceding manuscripts. Copied in the last decade of the seventh century, probably in Northumbria, they feature a number of different Vulgate forms across the gospel text with resemblances to Vg^O Δ in the Synoptic Gospels. For a long time, it was thought that the same copyist wrote the Durham and Echternach Gospels.[11] Marginal Latin glosses throughout the text report alternative readings found in Insular witnesses. The Echternach Gospels also have a glossary of Hebrew names before each gospel: the antiquity of these is

---

[8] Fischer's collations show that these two manuscripts agree in 5870 of his 5960 units of variation (98.5%; see pages 124–5).

[9] The Durham Gospels are not included in any of the principal editions of the Vulgate and are therefore absent from the Catalogue below, although they are number 13 in McGurk 1961a. For studies, including a facsimile, see Verey and Gameson in the Bibliography. The agreement of their text with the Stuttgart Vulgate is 93.4% in Fischer's collation (see previous note).

[10] The classmark A.II.17 also includes nine pages at the end from an uncial gospel book copied in Wearmouth–Jarrow around 700, with portions of Luke 21–23. Gameson 2010:28 suggests this may have been the exemplar for the Lindisfarne Gospels.

[11] Bruce-Mitford 1989; Brown 2003:262.

shown in the use of the archaic *cata* rather than *secundum* before Matthew and Mark. Finally a colophon, reproduced from one of the source manuscripts, connects this manuscript with the earliest tradition of the Vulgate Gospels and provides another link between Northumbria and Naples:

> *Proemendaui ut potui secundum codicem de bibliotheca Eugipi praespiteri quem*
> *ferunt fuisse s(an)c(t)i Hieronimi indictione VI p(ost) con(sulatum) Bassilii u(iri)*
> *c(larissimi) anno septimo decimo.* (fol. 222ᵛ; original orthography)

> I have made corrections as I was able according to a manuscript from the library of Eugippius the priest, which they say belonged to Saint Jerome, in the sixth indiction after the consulate of the most noble Basilius, in the seventeenth year.

Eugippius has already been mentioned above; the consular dating assigns the activity of the corrector to the year 558.

The replacement of the Old Latin text with the Vulgate in Northumbria is exemplified in VL 9A (Codex Fossatensis), a fine late eighth-century gospel book. Although the text of the Gospels is predominantly Vulgate, there are numerous readings which go back to an early Old Latin text, such as *abiit* rather than *perrexit* in John 8:1. It appears that the text stems from an Old Latin manuscript which had been corrected towards the Vulgate, perhaps over the course of several generations of copies. The same process can be seen in corrections to VL 9A itself: *nati sunt* in John 1:13 is written over an erasure which may have originally read *natus est*, and *saluifica me* in John 12:27 replaces *saluum me fac*. There are also doublets in the manuscript, where corrections in the exemplar have been included alongside the text they were intended to replace: examples of this include *ubi est diuersorium meum et refectio mea* ('where is my accommodation and my lodging') at Mark 14:14 and *si dilectionem habueritis ad inuicem ad alterutrum* ('if you have love to each other to one another') at John 13:35. A significant proportion of readings are not preserved in any other gospel book. Some have parallels in pre-Vulgate writers or early forms of the Greek text, which testify to the antiquity of the fossilized remnants of the earlier text.

Five prominent Insular manuscripts are often treated as a textual group in the Gospels, identified according to their sigla in the Oxford Vulgate (DELQR): the Book of Armagh (VL 61; D in the Oxford Vulgate); the Egerton Gospels (Vg^{Oe} E); the Lichfield Gospels (Vg^{Oe} L); the Book of Kells (Vg^{O} Q); and the MacRegol, or Rushworth, Gospels (Vg^{Oe} R). These were all copied in the late eighth or early ninth century in differing locations, but share a number of interpolations which characterize an Insular Vulgate text.[12] Nonetheless, they vary considerably in presentation, contents and layout, and in some cases even their text finds closer parallels in other manuscripts rather than members of this group.

---

[12] These appear in Matthew 8:24, 10:29, 14:35, 24:31, and 27:49, Mark 13:18, Luke 23:2 and 24:1, and John 19:30 and 21:6. Further details are given in Chapter 8.

The earliest appear to be the Lichfield Gospels (Vg^{Oe} L), whose origin is unknown: Northumbria, Scotland, Wales, and Lichfield itself are among the suggested locations. Only the first volume of this manuscript remains, containing Matthew, Mark, and the beginning of Luke. There are several full-page illuminations, including evangelist portraits, a carpet page, and decorative initial pages for each book, including the *chi-rho* monogram in Matthew. It was housed for a time in Llandeilo Fawr or Llandaff, and some of the earliest written Welsh is found in the margins of the manuscript. There are textual similarities with the Hereford Gospels (Hereford, Cathedral Library, MS P. I.2), another eighth-century gospel book which may have been produced in Wales. The MacRegol Gospels (Vg^{Oe} R) take their name from the copyist and illustrator named in the colophon, who was possibly a ninth-century abbot of Birr in Ireland. They are also known as the Rushworth Gospels after one of their subsequent owners. The layout is similar to the Lichfield and Hereford Gospels, lacking initial canon tables and Eusebian apparatus; like the Lindisfarne Gospels, they have an early Anglo-Saxon interlinear translation, added by the scribes Farman and Owun in the late tenth century. In the latter half of Luke, the MacRegol Gospels have a significant proportion of non-Vulgate readings; they also have an unusual form of Matthew 21:29–31 matching that of Spanish manuscripts and the Greek Codex Vaticanus.[13]

The Book of Kells (Vg^O Q) is the most richly decorated of all Insular gospel books, with ornate zoomorphic initials throughout the manuscript as well as full-page pictures. It begins with a fine set of canon tables, although the Eusebian apparatus is not present alongside the text. As in Codex Fossatensis, a number of doublets combine readings from different Latin traditions. For example, at Matthew 6:16, the most widely-attested reading is *exterminant* ('wipe out'), whereas a handful of manuscripts have *demoliuntur* ('disfigure'): the Book of Kells combines these, reading *demuliuntur exterminant*. The incorporation of a marginal gloss with an alternative reading can be seen at Luke 23:15, where *in alio sic remisi eum ad uos* ('in another: thus I have sent him back to you') is found in the text preceding the standard form *nam remisi uos ad illum* ('for I sent you back to him'). Apart from such links with the other members of this group, the text is close to the form of the Vulgate in the Book of Durrow (Vg^S D), another manuscript linked with the island of Iona.[14]

The Book of Armagh (VL 61) contains the entire Latin New Testament preceded by texts relating to St Patrick, some written in Old Irish, and followed by Sulpicius Severus' *Life of St Martin* (SUL Mart). Written in Irish minuscule script, rather than the majuscule of the Insular gospel books, the colophon records that it was commissioned by Torbach, bishop of Armagh in 807–8, and copied there by the scribe Ferdomnach. The unusual collection of biblical and non-biblical texts reflects the significance of Patrick as founder of the bishopric.

---

[13] See Metzger 1994:44–6 and the Oxford Vulgate. [14] See page 68 above.

The Gospels are followed by the Pauline Epistles, the Catholic Epistles, and Revelation, with Acts in final place. The decoration is relatively sparse, although there are evangelist symbols and a few decorated initials as well as some use of colour. The textual affiliation of the biblical books varies: the Gospels display Insular Vulgate characteristics, but there are Old Latin readings in Acts and the Apocalypse, both of which have been characterized as unique recensions. The Pauline Epistles are Old Latin throughout, with the same form of text found in the lemmata of the Balliol manuscript of Pelagius' commentary; similarly, two copies of Bede's *Commentary on the Apocalypse* in Durham have a lemma text close to that of VL 61.[15] One striking feature of the manuscript is the use of the Greek alphabet: this is found in the running titles (where the Gospels have the Greek preposition κατά rather than the Latin *secundum*) and words such as *amen*, usually written as AMHN. However, Greek letters are also substituted apparently at random for their phonetic Latin equivalents, giving forms such as NHMO (for *nemo*) or AMBYΛΛNC (for *ambulans*). This bizarre practice finds its apogee in the Lord's Prayer (Matthew 6:9–13, fol. 36) which is entirely transliterated into Greek. Along with the extensive paratextual material, which includes prologues to the Pauline Epistles named as those of Hilarius (actually Ambrosiaster) and Pelagius, this suggests that the book was intended for scholarly use; it is typical of the arcane learning sometimes displayed in Irish biblical codices.

VL 35 (the Book of Mulling) is a gospel book which shares a number of features with VL 61, written in three similar minuscule hands with the occasional use of Greek letters. It postdates the seventh-century founder of the Tech-Moling monastery (now St Mullins), although four leaves of a contemporary manuscript from the same scriptorium containing portions of Matthew and Mark were found in the shrine of St Moling. VL 35 has illuminated initials and evangelist portraits. Despite the Vulgate order of the Gospels, it features a relatively high number of Old Latin readings and, like VL 9A above, probably derives from an Old Latin ancestor corrected towards the Vulgate. Certain passages, the most substantial being Luke 4–9, have a much higher concentration of Old Latin forms, suggesting that they were not as thoroughly corrected: this is the only Latin manuscript with *paucis uero opus est uel etiam uno* ('truly, there is need of few things or even one') at Luke 10:42, a conflate reading found in some early Greek manuscripts. In the rest of VL 35 isolated earlier forms remain in a predominantly Vulgate text, either because they were overlooked by correctors or because a copyist ignored a correction. At the end of the manuscript is a liturgical text and a line drawing which has been interpreted as a diagram of the monastery.[16]

Another mixed-text gospel book copied in Ireland is VL 28 (Codex Usserianus secundus or the Garland of Howth). Produced around the year

---

[15] See Sparks 1951.   [16] See Nees 1983.

800, this has a particularly strong Old Latin element in the latter half of Matthew. It also has peculiar orthographic features, notably *–iarunt* rather than *–erunt* in the third-person plural. VL 44 is a contemporary fragment of Luke, also of Irish origin, which is both palaeographically and textually very close to VL 28.

Only the Egerton Gospels (Vg^{Oe} E) of the DELQR group were not copied in the British Isles. Instead, they demonstrate the spread of Insular traditions to the European mainland, being copied in western France in the ninth century. The script is the Caroline (or Carolingian) minuscule developed on the European continent and the decoration is much plainer, but the interlacing and zoomorphic initials together with the use of colour in the enclosed parts of capital letters betray Insular influence. This is also seen in the orthography (e.g. *aeuangelium* for *euangelium*) and the use of the phrase *item nunc orditur* ('likewise now begins') in an incipit, as well as the overall complexion of the biblical text.[17] The same features are present in VL 30 (Codex Gatianus), a copy of the four Gospels in half-uncial script made in Brittany around the year 800. Its text combines characteristics of the Insular Vulgate group with additional Old Latin elements, similar to VL 35. It is the sole biblical manuscript to transmit a handful of readings only otherwise found in pre-Vulgate authors, such as *panibus meis* in John 6:26. A third ninth-century gospel book of probable Breton origin is VL 11A, written in uncials. Its text exhibits block mixture: certain passages have a consistently Old Latin affiliation similar to VL 8 and VL 11. In one of these, beginning at Matthew 3:1, a corrector has brought the text in line with the Vulgate for four pages. The manuscript has little in the way of paratext or decoration, with no Eusebian apparatus or prefaces. In the incipit to each Gospel, the use of *sequentia* ('continuation') is a further Insular feature; this also occurs before the enlarged title at Matthew 1:18. The copyist of the manuscript was particularly prone to omitting passages through the error known as eyeskip or homoeoteleuton (jumping between identical sequences of letters): many words or part-verses are missing, giving rise to nonsense readings.

MONASTERIES IN CONTINENTAL EUROPE

The Irish monastic centres instituted by Columbanus on the continent flourished during the ninth century. The monastery of St Gall in Switzerland, named after one of Columbanus' companions, was well known for the quality of its scriptorium. At the end of the eighth century its principal scribe was

---

[17] McGurk 1996:122 connects *item nunc orditur* with Brittany.

Winithar, whose characteristic handwriting can be seen in a number of codices. Three contain the latter part of the New Testament (Vg^{Sar} S, Vg^{Sp} S, Vg^{Sc} S), based on an exemplar with a similar text to Codex Fuldensis. He was succeeded by Wolfcoz (780–825), who undertook a systematic correction of the manuscripts.[18] A second wave of Irish monks followed: they often took Latinized forms of their names, such as Moengal (Marcellus) who directed the school around 850. Irish monks were often identified by the appellation *Scottus*, and a ninth-century catalogue of books in the St Gall library includes a number of 'books written in the Irish way' (*libri scottice scripti*), a reference to the use of Insular minuscule script.[19] Moengal appears to be one of a number of scholars who developed a renewed interest in the Greek text of the Bible several hundred years after it had largely passed out of use in the West.[20] The library of St Gall still contains a number of grammars and glossaries with Greek written in the characteristic Western majuscule script, featuring some confusion between letters and erratic punctuation and word division.

A set of three bilingual biblical codices from the second half of the ninth century are associated with St Gall, although they may have been produced in Columbanus' monastery of Bobbio and transferred to St Gall by Irish pilgrims. They consist of a Psalter (Basle, Universitätsbibliothek A.VII.7; VL 334), a gospel book (VL 27; Codex Sangallensis), and a copy of the Pauline Epistles (VL 77; Codex Boernerianus). Unlike the earlier bilingual tradition with Latin and Greek on facing pages or columns, these are interlinear: Latin glosses are written above each word. In fact, two or three alternative renderings are supplied for certain Greek terms, separated by *l* (the abbreviation for *uel*, 'or'). There are also grammatical observations or glosses indicated by ·*i*· (the abbreviation for *id est*) along with a series of letters in the margin which may be linked to particular linguistic features.[21] In the case of VL 27, the interlinear Latin version was based on a Vulgate text similar to the Egerton Gospels (Vg^{Oe} E). Although some of the alternative renderings correspond to Old Latin forms, there is no reason to consider this manuscript an Old Latin witness. The situation is less clear with regard to VL 77. As its Greek text matches the distinctive bilingual tradition in the Pauline Epistles, it is possible that the Latin translation was also influenced by the corresponding Old Latin form. As with the other two manuscripts, however, a number of alternative renderings are included with no claim to derive from a Latin biblical manuscript.

The St Gall collection includes two other gospel books in Insular script. Both may have been produced in Ireland around the year 800, although VL 47 is already listed in the ninth-century monastery catalogue. This is a copy of

---

[18] Fischer 1971 [1985:399–400]; Schaab 1999.

[19] The catalogue, probably produced under Abbot Hartmut in 882, lists forty-one biblical manuscripts, of which thirty-one may be identified with surviving volumes.

[20] See Kaczynski 1988 and Esposito 1990.   [21] See also pages 203–4 below.

John by itself with full Eusebian apparatus in the margin. An Old Latin text is present in the first three chapters, which a later corrector has partly brought into line with the Vulgate; elsewhere there are a few earlier forms typical of the Insular Vulgate text. The four Gospels in VL 48 are a more ornate production with richly-coloured initials, evangelist portraits, a carpet page (before the *chi-rho* monogram), and full-page illustrations of the crucifixion and of Christ and the apostles at the end of the manuscript. The opening chapters of Matthew have one of the most non-Vulgate Old Latin texts to be found in surviving manuscripts. The rest of the manuscript conforms to the customary Insular form, with parallels in VL 61 and the MacRegol Gospels (Vg^{Oe} R). VL 20, also in St Gall, is a double page from a liturgical book in Irish minuscule containing a lection from John 11; it has an Old Latin affiliation similar to VL 14.

The nearby monastery of Reichenau is situated on an island in Lake Constance (the Bodensee). In the ninth century, a period in which its abbot was shared with St Gall, it too had an extensive library. VL 78 (Codex Augiensis), another Greek–Latin bilingual copy of the Pauline Epistles, was produced here around the same time as VL 77. In fact, the identical lacunae prove that both manuscripts used the same exemplar for their Greek text. The Latin portions are treated differently: whereas VL 77 offers an interlinear translation, in VL 78 a Vulgate text with a few local readings has been copied in the outside column of each page, its short lines roughly corresponding to the Greek in the other column. Einsiedeln, another monastery connected with St Gall, was also known for the production of books.

French monastic centres were equally famous as places of learning. Particularly important in the development of Latin minuscule script were Luxeuil and its daughter foundation Corbie.[22] Following several decades of experimentation with different types of cursive writing, Corbie is considered the birthplace of Caroline minuscule with the production of the multiple-volume Maurdramnus Bible between 772 and 780.[23] Some of the biblical manuscripts owned or created by the monastery, most of which are now divided between Paris and St Petersburg, have Old Latin affiliations. Confusingly, several are known as Codex Corbeiensis: the principal biblical representatives are VL 8 (see pages 46–7), VL 9, and VL 66. The latter two were both copied in Corbie. VL 9 is an eighth-century copy of Matthew. It has numerous ancient readings, particularly in the latter half of the Gospel, and was later bound with a Vulgate copy of the first four chapters of Mark. VL 66 bears testimony to the antiquarian interests of the monastery in the ninth century: it contains a treatise by Novatian (NO cib), the pre-Cyprianic Latin translation of the Epistle of Barnabas (BAR), and a unique recension of the Epistle of James. Assigned the

---

[22] See Ganz 1990; examples of script are given in Bischoff 1990:104–7; 194–5.

[23] Five volumes of the Old Testament survive in Amiens, BM, 6, 7, 9, 11, 12, with two further leaves in Paris, BnF, latin 13174; the New Testament is lost.

Vetus Latina text-type F, its text has similarities with quotations in Pope Innocent I, Chromatius of Aquileia, and Jerome's commentary on Zechariah (HI Za), and is therefore likely to derive from Italy shortly before the year 400. VL 76 (sometime called Codex Sangermanensis, although also connected with Corbie) is the third of the ninth-century Pauline bilinguals. This is a copy of VL 75 and its paratextual features, including the place of origin of each Epistle and the catalogue of biblical books. Each opening of VL 75 has been combined in a single two-column page, with Greek on the left and Latin on the right. Nonsense readings in the Greek confirm that the copyist's principal language was Latin, such as a misreading of the correction to the *nomen sacrum* at Galatians 6:16. Fragments of a fourth Pauline bilingual, VL 83 (Codex Waldeccensis), copied in the tenth century from VL 75 or VL 76, have been linked with Corbie or its daughter monastery Corvey in Westphalia, founded by Adalard in 822.

The scriptorium at Echternach, an abbey in Germany founded by the English monk Willibrord in 698, may not have been responsible for the Echternach Gospels (Vg^O EP) but it did produce several members of a group of gospel books.[24] The best known of this group is VL 15 (Codex Aureus Holmiensis), copied in southern England around the year 775. With lavishly coloured polychrome canon tables and evangelist portraits, the manuscript is named after the gold ink used on the purple leaves which alternate with pages of white parchment. On many pages, letters or rows are picked out in silver or red ink to form patterns. One of the finest golden pages is the *chi-rho* monogram page, attesting to the Insular origin of this manuscript. Despite numerous Vulgate features including Jerome's preface, the order of the books and the Eusebian apparatus with parallel passages, the gospel text has a number of Old Latin readings. The highest concentration of these occurs in the second half of Mark and the beginning of Luke; some have very little other attestation, such as *prostitutione* rather than *fornicatione* in John 8:41. The oldest surviving representative of this textual group appears to be the sixth-century Burchard Gospels (see page 60), which was in Northumbria by the end of the seventh century: this was corrected at an early stage, with many of the non-standard readings erased. One feature shared by many of these witnesses is the lengthy interpolation at Matthew 20:28 of a text resembling Luke 14:8–10, present in many Old Latin codices as well as some Vulgate gospel books (see page 159). The Echternach-related manuscripts are the Augsburg Gospels (Augsburg, Universitätsbibliothek, Cod. I.2.4°.2), the Trier Gospels (Trier, Dombibliothek, 134 [Schatz 61]), and the Maaseyck Gospels (Maaseick, Sint-Catharinakerk, s.n.), all from the first half of the eighth century.[25] To these may be added the Barberini Gospels (Vatican,

---

[24] See also Schroeder 1983.
[25] On this group, see further Netzer 1994 and Fischer 2010.

BAV, Barberini lat. 570) and possibly also the Fleury Gospels (Paris, BnF, latin 256), the Ghent Livinus Gospels (Ghent, Sint Baafs Katedraal, s.n.), and Douai, BM 12. Several gospel books copied at Fulda in the ninth century belong to this group as well. Founded in 744 by one of the companions of the English missionary St Boniface, this monastery in central Germany became a place of pilgrimage as well as a centre of learning and book production in the Carolingian empire.[26]

CHARLEMAGNE, ALCUIN, AND THEODULF

The scholarly activities associated with the court of Charlemagne had a significant impact on the text and production of the Bible. Concerned by the poor quality of books in circulation, Charlemagne gave strict instructions in his *Admonitio Generalis* of 789 about the creation of copies to be used in schools:

> *et si opus est euangelium, psalterium et missalem scribere, perfectae aetates hominum scribant, cum omni diligentia.* (1.60).

> If it is necessary to copy a gospel book, psalter or missal, let mature experienced persons copy them with all care.

In the biography of his son, Louis the Pious, the claim is even made that Charlemagne spent his final days correcting the Gospels from Greek and Syriac, but this seems to be hagiographical imagination. The earliest version of the Bible to emerge from the Carolingian court was the Bible of Angilram, produced by Charlemagne's chaplain some time before 791.[27] Ten gospel books copied in Aachen between 781 and 814 are known as the 'Ada Group', centred on the two-part Ada Gospels possibly produced for Charlemagne's sister (Trier, Stadtbibliothek, 22, also known as the Trier Golden Gospels). Each has a fine set of evangelist portraits, and some are written in gold ink, such as the Ingolstadt Gospels (Vg^{Oe} I) and the purple Abbeville Gospels (Abbeville, BM, 4 [1]). The two finest members of the group are the Lorsch Gospels (Alba Iulia, Batthyaneum, s.n., and Vatican, BAV, Pal. lat. 50), with carved ivory covers reviving a practice from late antiquity, and the Harley Golden Gospels (London, BL, Harley 2788), written entirely in gold on white parchment with several illustrations.[28] Tradition has it that the Coronation Gospels (also

---

[26] Bischoff 1990:93 includes the suggestion that some of the cursive script in Codex Fuldensis may be in the hand of Boniface himself.

[27] Metz, BM 7 (VL 145, as Tobit and Judith are Old Latin); the manuscript was destroyed in 1944 but photographs survive. For a summary of the Bibles of Charlemagne, see Bogaert 2012:79–84; on Charlemagne's own activity, see Berger 1893:118–19 and 186–8; Fischer 1971 [1985:214]; Ganshof 1974.

[28] On the Ada Gospels, and this group in general, see Berger 1893:259–77.

known as the Vienna Golden Gospels; Vienna, Hofburg, Schatzkammer Inv. XIII 18), used by the emperor to take his oath of office in December 800, were found in his tomb when it was opened 200 years later.

Alcuin of York, the tutor of Charlemagne and his family, wrote in a letter following his appointment as abbot of Tours in 796 that he had 'a command of the lord king to emend the Old and New Testament' (*Domini regis praeceptum in emendatione ueteris nouique testamenti. [Epistula* 165]). In conjunction with his treatises on grammar and orthography, Alcuin's principal goal was the correct punctuation and Latin usage rather than the use of text-critical principles to determine the earliest readings.[29] His letters show that the revision was finished in 800 and the pandect was presented to Charlemagne the following Christmas. Alcuin's version was not designated an official text for the whole empire, even though it appeared in a copy which had been commissioned by the emperor. Instead, it was the remarkably efficient working practices of the Tours scriptorium which made its manuscripts so influential. Up to twenty copyists would work on unbound quaternions simultaneously, sometimes even using different exemplars for the same book, and each text was scrupulously compared with its original after copying. There are extant forty-six complete Bibles and eighteen gospel books which were copied at Tours in the first half of the ninth century.[30]

The five most important early Tours Bibles are grouped together in the Stuttgart Vulgate under the siglum Φ, which derives from Alcuin's nickname *Flaccus*. Four were copied in Tours around 800: the 'Moutier-Grandval Bible' (Codex Grandivallensis, Vg^S Φ^G, illustrated in Image 10) and three others now in Paris (Φ^E), St Gall (Φ^T), and Bamberg (Φ^B). The fifth, Codex Vallicellianus (Vg^S Φ^V), was produced slightly later and in Reims.[31] All of these are pandects of the Old and New Testaments, characterized by a distinctive layout, script, and set of contents. The manuscripts are written on large sheets of parchment, around 50 by 38 centimetres; they consist of 350–450 pages, written in two columns (although Φ^V has three) of 50–52 lines. There is a clear hierarchy of letter size and type of writing (see Image 10): the main titles are in display capitals; rustic capitals are used for subordinate indications, such as the subscriptions at the end of each book; the gospel prologues are in half-uncial script; the biblical text, after a few initial lines in uncial, is in a regular Caroline minuscule.[32] There are relatively few abbreviations, most of which are

---

[29] On Alcuin's contribution to punctuation, see Parkes 1992:30–2 and 35.

[30] Ganz 1994:53. The textual studies of Fischer are unsurpassed; see also works by Bullough, Ganz, Glunz, Jones, Jullien, Kessler, Lobrichon, McKitterick, and Rand in the Bibliography.

[31] Lists of Tours Bibles are found in Fischer 1965 [1985:124–7] and Ganz 1994:61–2. Another early witness to Alcuin's recension not included in either the Oxford or Stuttgart Vulgates is the St Adelbert Gospels (Gniezno, Chapter Library, MS 1): see Gryglewicz 1964 and Bolz 1971. In later times, Rome, St Paolo fuori le mura, s.n. (Φ^P) was an influential copy of Alcuin's text: Nardin et al 1993 is a study and facsimile.

[32] See Petitmengin 1990b, Bischoff 1990:206, and Ganz 2012:331.

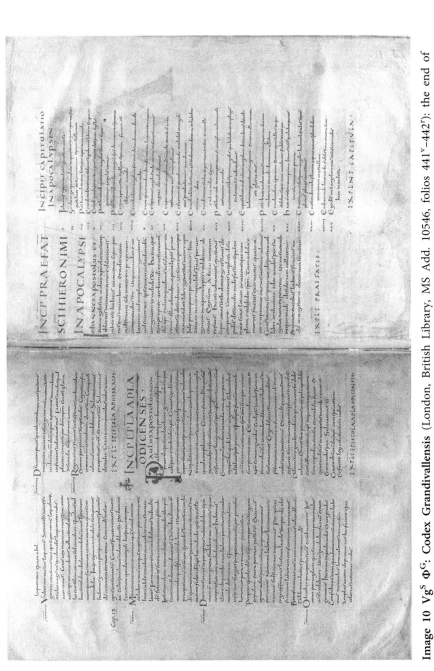

Image 10 Vg^S Φ^G: Codex Grandivallensis (London, British Library, MS Add. 10546, folios 441^v–442^r): the end of Hebrews, followed by Laodiceans and the preface and *capitula* to Revelation. © The British Library Board. Also available at <http://www.bl.uk/manuscripts/Viewer.aspx?ref=add_ms_10546_f441v>

indicated by a superscript line. New sections begin with a rubricated capital projecting slightly into the margin. The order of the New Testament in most Tours Bibles consists of the Gospels, Acts, Catholic Epistles, Pauline Epistles, and Revelation (eacpr), although some manuscripts have the Pauline Epistles after Revelation. Each book is preceded by a prologue and set of *capitula*, with corresponding chapter numbers in the margin of the text. In addition to the Eusebian apparatus and canon tables for the Gospels, some Tours Bibles also have the *Concordia Epistularum* associated with Pelagius in a decorated arcade before the Pauline Epistles. The attribution of all the prefaces to Jerome, as well as the full adoption of his version of the Old Testament from the Hebrew, played a large part in the acceptance of his translation as the Vulgate.

Alcuin's source texts have long been the subject of debate. It is known that he requested books from York, and his *Commentary on John*, which is structured according to the distinctive Type C *capitula* found in Northumbrian manuscripts, also features a form of John 5:4 matching Codex Amiatinus (Vg A). This work is predominantly based on Augustine, but Alcuin also used Bede and Gregory the Great and provided a considerable amount of original material.[33] Although early Tours manuscripts have the same series of *capitula* before the Gospels, their text is much closer to the Harley Gospels (Vg^S Z) than Codex Amiatinus.[34] In Acts, their source was similar to Codex Fuldensis (Vg F): they also have readings from an Italian text of the Pauline Epistles. Alcuin appears to have used manuscripts circulating locally rather than seeking out exemplars of particular note.[35] He made relatively few changes to his source copies, despite the gradual accumulation of some four thousand readings across the whole Bible attributed to his revision.

In many cases, Tours Bibles feature longer forms, either harmonizations or interpolations, which became standard in mediaeval tradition and persist into the Clementine Vulgate. Two examples of forms which appear to be peculiar to Tours Bibles are *praescientiam* rather than *praesentiam* in 2 Peter 1:16, and *conseruata* in Jude 13. The use of multiple source manuscripts means that each Tours Bible has a different textual complexion: for instance, the Bamberg Bible (Φ^B) has a substantial proportion of Old Latin readings in Acts and the Pauline Epistles. Much of the paratextual material was taken over from the exemplars.[36] However, Alcuin composed dedicatory poems for specially commissioned manuscripts, some of which were adopted more widely. Written in classical metres, these epitomize his literary learning; the recurrence of certain phrases and structures can be used to show Alcuinian authorship of otherwise

---

[33] Gorman 2009.   [34] Fischer 1965 [1985:131–2].   [35] Fischer 1963b [1985:93].

[36] For the different prologues and *capitula* in Tours Bibles, see Fischer 1971 [1985:274, 287–310]. De Bruyne's series KA Tur (now identified as the work of Bede) is not found in Bibles produced in Tours. Even Type P^i in the Gospels, which Fischer suggests may have originated in Tours, is now thought to have been composed at least three centuries earlier (Houghton 2011:344–6).

unattributed verses. One peculiarity of poems 68 and 69, which list the sections of the New Testament, is that they both place Paul between Acts and the Catholic Epistles, a sequence which is not attested in any Tours Bibles.[37]

Variation among Tours Bibles and gospel books enables the reconstruction of different stages in the history of the scriptorium. The sequence of some Old Testament books differs, as does the placement of Colossians. Laodiceans is only present in later manuscripts, normally before 1 Thessalonians. Jerome's letter to Paulinus of Nola on the study of the scriptures (beginning *Frater Ambrosius*, HI ep 53) was introduced as the opening text in Tours Bibles under Fridugisus, Alcuin's immediate successor and abbot from 803–34. Adalhard, abbot from 834–43, presided over a revision of the gospel text. Nevertheless, because of the working practices of the scriptorium, the relative age of Tours manuscripts cannot be determined from their text: there is little continuity in the distribution of 'old' and 'new' readings in copies of the Gospels made in the ninth century.[38] Instead, the key is provided by their decoration and illustrations.[39]

At the same time as Alcuin was preparing his edition for Charlemagne, a revision of the Latin Bible was also being undertaken by Theodulf, abbot of Fleury and bishop of Orléans from 798 to 818. A refugee from southern France, Theodulf drew on the Spanish tradition of biblical pandects established by John of Saragossa. His edition follows the order of books set out by Isidore and includes the Priscillian apparatus to the Pauline Epistles from the fifth-century edition associated with Peregrinus. Theodulf's approach was more scholarly than that of his contemporaries in Tours. He referred to the Bible as a *bibliotheca* ('library'), which he divided into five sections: the New Testament consists of the *Ordo Euangelicus* (Gospels) and the *Ordo Apostolicus* (Acts, Epistles, and Revelation). He also added a number of non-biblical texts: Isidore's *Chronicle* (IS chr), the second book of Eucherius' *Instructiones* (EUCH inst) which was at that time attributed to Jerome, a biblical glossary known as the *Clavis Melitonis* (PS-MEL V), and the *Liber de diuinis scripturis* (PS-AU spe) which Theodulf later adjusted to the biblical text of the Vulgate and abbreviated.[40] He also paid attention to textual variation, marking variants in the margin: $\bar{a}$ indicates readings from Alcuin's edition, $\bar{s}$ those in Spanish witnesses, $\bar{\imath\jmath}$ those in both, and $\bar{al}$ those in others.[41] These marginal

---

[37] On Alcuin's poetry, see the texts in Fischer 1971 [1985:222–47 and 276–8] and Ganz 1994:55–6. Alcuin's own handwriting has been identified in one of the Tours manuscripts: see Bischoff 1990:45.

[38] Figures in Fischer 1972:17–9 [180–2].

[39] See page 207 and the works of Kessler and Rand.

[40] On the lists of Hebrew names in Theodulf Bibles, see Szerwiniack 1994.

[41] The Mesmes Bible (Θ^{M}) also has $\bar{r}$, the significance of which is unclear; another Theodulf Bible (Paris, BnF, latin 11937) has marginal variants in the Old Testament which relate to Hebrew marked with $\bar{h}$.

readings, however, were sometimes re-incorporated into the text by copyists. Theodulf kept an unbound exemplar in the scriptorium to which he added corrections and adjustments. Individual books were revised in between the production of Bibles, as is shown by the interrelationships of the principal witnesses.[42] Unlike the later Tours Bibles, Theodulf did not include the Epistle to the Laodiceans, although the Johannine Comma is present in his text of the Catholic Epistles.[43]

The oldest surviving example of Theodulf's text appears to be a manuscript now in Stuttgart (Württembergische Landesbibliothek, HB.II.16; Θ^S in the Vetus Latina edition): in the New Testament, only the Pauline Epistles and two of the Catholic Epistles are extant. Codex Hubertianus (Vg^O H; VL Θ^H), a heavily-corrected manuscript originally produced in Tours, is the earliest witness to Theodulf's Gospels. In this copy, a text similar to Codex Amiatinus (Vg A) has been brought into agreement with the version typified by Harley 1775 (Vg^S Z); corrections in the Pauline Epistles may represent further reworking by Theodulf. Like the Spanish pandects, it has three columns to a page. Codex Aniciensis (Le Puy, Cathedral; VL Θ^A) was written under Theodulf's direction around 800.[44] This still has the Old Latin version of the *Liber de diuinis scripturis* and no references to Alcuin's Bible. The Psalms and Gospels are copied in silver and gold ink on parchment dyed dark purple. The script is small, with over sixty lines per column. Book titles are characteristically placed in circles, with a thick decorated border. The Theodulf Bible par excellence is the magnificent Mesmes Bible, also known as Codex Theodulfianus (Vg^O Θ, VL Θ^M). This is the first witness with variants from Alcuin, and the Vulgate form of the *Liber de diuinis scripturis*. Apart from these four manuscripts and two later copies (Paris, BnF, latin 11937: Θ^G, and Copenhagen, Royal Library, NKS 1: Θ^K), little remains of Theodulf's editions, which were largely eclipsed by the productions of Tours.[45]

OLD LATIN MANUSCRIPTS

Pre-Vulgate texts continued to be copied in the eighth and ninth centuries. VL 11 (Codex Rehdigeranus) is a gospel book produced in Aquileia in the first half of the eighth century. The Gospels are in the Vulgate order, with Eusebian sections in the margins but no canon numbers: like VL 10, parallel sections in

---

[42] Fischer 1963b, 1965 [1985:135–47]; Dahlhaus-Berg 1975.   [43] See pages 178–9.

[44] Paris, BnF latin 4, also known as Codex Aniciensis, is unrelated: it is a complete Bible, also originally in Le Puy.

[45] Ninth-century fragments of Theodulf's Old Testament have also been found at Solothurn: see <http://www.e-codices.unifr.ch/en/list/one/sl/0003>. On the use of Theodulf's Bibles, see Chevalier-Royet 2006.

the other Gospels are presented in a decorative arcade at the foot of the page. Its textual affiliation is mixed: Matthew and Mark are close to the Vulgate, whereas Luke and John correspond to the Vetus Latina text-type I. The *Pericope Adulterae* was originally absent but has been supplied in the margin by a corrector. VL 86 was originally a two-volume Bible from which only some apocryphal Old Testament books and the Pauline Epistles are preserved. The latter present an Old Latin form very close to that of Ambrose: as the manuscript was copied in Monza or perhaps Milan itself, this may represent a local tradition. The insertion of the final doxology of Romans at the end of chapter 14, a point which Origen claims was the end of this letter in Marcion's recension, is a further ancient feature of the text. VL 86 also has summaries of the Epistles which are only otherwise found in the fourth-century anonymous commentary (VL 89). The table of contents reveals that VL 86 included the pseudonymous Third Epistle to the Corinthians (extracted from the Apocryphal Acts of Paul), although the relevant pages are now missing.[46]

VL 7 (Codex Sangermanensis; also Vg G: see Image 16) is the latter half of a two-volume Bible produced at St-Germain-des-Prés around 810. Several of the Old Testament books are Old Latin, as is Matthew: VL 7 closely matches the lemmata of the commentary by Hilary of Poitiers (HIL Mt) even though it also has Eusebian apparatus in the margin. There are a few Old Latin readings in the other Synoptic Gospels, but in the rest of the New Testament the manuscript is the best witness to the Vulgate.[47] The copyist included in John a set of *hermeneiai*, a system of divination attached to particular biblical verses.[48] In addition, there are exegetical glosses in Acts, Revelation, and the Catholic Epistles from Bede and other Insular sources, some written in shorthand, and alternative marginal readings in some of the Pauline Epistles (including Greek words). The manuscript is incomplete: the opening of the *Shepherd of Hermas* follows Hebrews, while the codex begins in the middle of a set of biblical canticles from the Gallican tradition.[49] Despite its textual interest, this manuscript is not a high-quality production but is written in an untidy minuscule with some non-standard orthography, such as *locor* for *loquor*. It appears that its model was a fifth-century pandect, the earliest known example of this type of Bible in Latin, assembled by an anonymous editor.[50] The evidence for this is two subscriptions, which provide the earliest attestations of the use of pandect and *bibliotheca* ('library') for the Bible.[51] At the end of Esther, the editor states that they collected all of Jerome's translations into a single volume (*fecique*

---

[46] See Bogaert 2012:90.

[47] For a comparison of the texts of Vg A, F, and G, see Fischer 1972:66–80 [1986:241–59].

[48] *Hermeneiai* are also found in Codex Bezae: see Outtier in Parker & Amphoux 1996.

[49] These are the Odes: see further page 90.   [50] See Bogaert 2013:510, 521–2.

[51] The first use of *bibliotheca* is often attributed to Isidore (IS ety 6.6.1): see Contreni 2012:518.

pandectem, fol. 69ʳ), and added non-canonical works including the *Shepherd of Hermas*.[52] The second, found after Hebrews and before Hermas, reads:

> *bibliotheca Hieronimi presbyter Bethleem secundum grecum ex emendatis exemplaribus conlatus.* (fol. 187r)

> The library of Jerome, the priest of Bethlehem, compared according to the Greek, from corrected copies.

This shows how, in subsequent centuries, Jerome's revision became associated with the whole of the New Testament, despite the peculiar features of this particular manuscript with its combination of Old Latin and Vulgate texts.

VL 65 (Codex Harleianus) is an attractive minuscule manuscript, featuring large coloured initials with an interlace design. Written in northern France, probably Reims, in the ninth century, it contains the Pauline and Catholic Epistles and the first part of Revelation. One of its copyists, Iuseus, provided a dedication in runes. Although the overall textual complexion of the manuscript is Vulgate, certain portions of the Catholic Epistles are Old Latin, as is a supplement providing the final four chapters of Hebrews. Another example of the use of an earlier text to replace lacunae is VL 88, a manuscript of the latter part of the New Testament and the major and minor Prophets. Copied in the ninth or tenth century on the Franco-German border, it is entirely Vulgate apart from one page of 2 Corinthians with an Old Latin text practically identical to VL 64. VL 82, the remains of a bifolium with an Old Latin text of Hebrews, comes from a contemporary minuscule manuscript also possibly of German origin.

Following the Viking invasion of Tours and Marmoutier in 852, the locus of production shifted to Reims. Codex Vallicellianus (Vgˢ Φⱽ; see page 82), an Alcuin Bible produced in Reims, was used as the exemplar for the Bible of Hincmar, archbishop from 845–82 (Reims, BM, 1–2). Hincmar also commissioned a luxury purple gospel book with a fine binding:

> *euangelium aureis argentisque describi fecit litteris, aureisque muniuit tabulis et gemmis distinxit pretiosis.*[53]

> He caused the Gospel to be written in gold and silver letters, and endowed it with gold covers and adorned it with precious stones.

Other golden Gospels were also produced in northern France in the later ninth century until the focus of production shifted to the Rhine under the Ottonian dynasty.

Ancillary texts in biblical manuscripts may also transmit Old Latin readings. The earliest series of gospel *capitula*, KA Cy, composed in the first half of

---

[52] The same text is found after Esther in VL 62; transcriptions in Berger 1893:24 and 67.

[53] *Historia Remensis* 1.3.5, quoted in Berger 1893:282. This manuscript is identified with Reims, BM, 38. Other Franco-German gospel books and sacramentaries are listed at Berger 1893:283–4.

the third century, are only attested in manuscripts of the ninth century and later (Vatican, BAV, Barberini lat. 637; Munich, Bayerische Staatsbibliothek, Clm 6212; Florence, Biblioteca Medicea Laurenziana, Edili 125; Paris, BnF, lat. 277; Berlin, Staatsbibliothek, Hamilton 82).[54] Similarly, VL 46, a ninth-century French gospel book, is a further witness to the biblical verses quoted in canon tables in VL 10 (see page 53). VL 39 and VL 40, produced around the same time, have a slightly different series of extracts in their initial canon tables, again with some non-Vulgate elements. In all cases, the affiliation of this paratextual material differs from that in the rest of the manuscript.

LITURGICAL BOOKS

Lectionaries in this period often have a Vulgate text of the Old Testament and a mixed text in the New Testament.[55] Some liturgical manuscripts from the beginning of the eighth century with an Old Latin affiliation are written in uncial script: VL 24 is an Old Latin lection from John 13 in a Gallican sacramentary, while VL 41 consists of the first third of Matthew divided into readings as used in Verona; its text is similar to the much older VL 4 (Codex Veronensis) which served as a local text over many years. VL 49 is also found in the chapter library in Verona: it is an eighth-century note in the margin of an Arian collection of sermons with an Old Latin text of two verses from John. VL 57 and 87 are two separate North Italian lectionaries which were at one time bound together: the former contains readings from Acts which correspond to VL 51; the latter is part of a collection of Pauline readings with some Old Latin forms.

One of the earliest surviving Vulgate lectionaries is the Luxeuil Lectionary (VL 251, Vg^{Sc} L), written around 700 in the characteristic minuscule of its birthplace. The late eighth-century *Comes* of Murbach (Besançon, BM, 84) is the oldest lectionary featuring the full text of both Epistles and Gospels in liturgical order. It is contemporary with a magnificent purple lectionary from North Italy (Paris, BnF, latin 9451). The origin of the word *comes* (also in the form *Liber comitis* or *Liber comicus*) is contested: the lectionary could be seen as a 'companion' volume (Latin *comes*), but it has also been suggested that the term derives from the use of *comma* to denote a biblical pericope.[56] VL 71 is an early example of a Spanish *Liber comicus* type of lectionary,

[54] The Munich manuscript features a colophon saying that it is from an exemplar corrected for Ecclesius, bishop of Ravenna in the 520s.

[55] See further the works of Gochee.

[56] For *comma*, see Dyer 2012:671–2. On the *Comes* of Murbach, see Wilmart 1913. The *liber comicus* and *liber misticus* are described on pages 97–8.

most of which dates from the tenth century onwards. Copied in Southern France around 800, it was later palimpsested. Most of the readings, from throughout the Latin Bible, are Vulgate, but there are Old Latin elements in the Catholic Epistles. A number of Carolingian lectionaries survive, which followed earlier Roman practice: the Catholic Epistles, Acts, and Revelation were read from Easter to Pentecost and the Pauline Epistles from after Christmas until just before Lent (Septuagesima).[57] Several complete Bibles from the ninth century onwards have their books in the order in which they were read during the liturgical year.[58] The *Capitulare euangeliorum de circulo anni* ('Chapter list of the Gospels from the yearly cycle'), a list of readings identified by Eusebian section numbers, is found in numerous Vulgate gospel books from the ninth century onwards; the equivalent list of readings from the Epistles is a *Capitulare lectionum* ('Chapter list of readings').[59] All Saints' Day was not observed in the Frankish empire before 835, and is missing from these lists in early Franco-Saxon gospel books.

Liturgical readings are also contained in missals alongside ritual texts. Most of the biblical passages correspond to the Vulgate, but there are occasional differences which preserve textual forms current at this time. The Bobbio Missal (M-Bo) and the Missale Gothicum (M-Go) are both Gallican mass books copied around 700.[60] The Mozarabic Missal (M-M), from the Christian community in Spain under Moorish rule, has particularly extensive scriptural coverage. The Stowe Missal (M-St; Dublin, Royal Irish Academy, MS D.II.3) was produced in Ireland around the beginning of the ninth century, and is bound with a collection of gospel extracts (the Stowe St John). Other liturgical sources sometimes cited in editions of the Bible include the Ambrosian Missal (M-A), the Gallican and Mozarabic Antiphonaries (ANT-G, ANT-M), and the Roman Missal and Responsory (M-R, RES-R).

A series of canticles taken from scriptural sources, also known as the Odes, is found in a number of manuscripts of this period, sometimes following the psalter (as in VL 7 and VL 250). The seventh-century Verona Psalter is a bilingual manuscript of the Psalms and Odes with the Greek text written in Latin letters. The Odes stem from early Greek tradition, and are present in the fifth-century Codex Alexandrinus (GA 02).[61] The New Testament Odes are all from Luke, consisting of the *Magnificat* (Luke 1:46–55), the *Benedictus* (Luke 1:68–79), and the *Nunc Dimittis* (Luke 2:29–32). The Latin versions of these hallowed liturgical texts differ from the Vulgate text of Luke, either because they were taken from an Old Latin witness or because they were translated

---

[57] See Martimort 1992, Dyer 2012, and Ganz 2012:326–8.
[58] These include VL 135; see Bogaert 2014a.
[59] See page 203. The *capitulare euangeliorum* are classified in Ranke 1847; see also Klauser 1972.
[60] See further Legg 1917; Lowe 1920; Wlimart, Lowe & Wilson 1924; Hen & Meens 2004.
[61] Knust & Wasserman 2014 offer an introduction to the Odes and a study of their text.

separately. One or more of the Odes is found in VL 254 (the Bangor Antiphonary, from the end of the seventh century), VL 256 and 257 (Irish collections of hymns), VL 258 (the Book of Lindisfarne, copied in Mercia in the second half of the eighth century), and VL 263 (a late bilingual Psalter).

COMMENTARIES AND HARMONIES

Manuscripts of scriptural commentaries overlap with the direct tradition of the New Testament. VL 37 and 38 are eighth- and ninth-century copies of Jerome's *Commentary on Matthew* (HI Mt) in which the lemmata preceding each portion of commentary have been expanded from an Old Latin source. Two copies of Bede's *Commentary on the Apocalypse* have a lemma text similar to VL 61. VL 81 consists of the first three chapters of Hebrews copied after a version of Pelagius' *Commentary on Paul* in a manuscript written about 800. In fact, the lemmata in the preceding commentary are a substitution of Pelagius' text by a different version with a partial Old Latin affiliation.[62] The same situation is found in Ambrosiaster's *Commentary on Paul*: two eighth-century manuscripts (Amiens, BM, 87 and Vienna, Österreichische Nationalbibliothek, 743) have an Old Latin text of the lemmata at variance with the form used by the author. One of the most remarkable examples of Old Latin lemmata in a later commentary manuscript is VL 89, the only witness to the anonymous commentary on Paul composed in Rome at the end of the fourth century (AN Paul; see page 27). This was copied around the year 800 in St Amand, preserving the pre-Vulgate text of the Epistles.

Several biblical commentaries composed in this period have Insular connections.[63] An eighth-century copy of the Pauline Epistles with a text similar to VL 61 features interlinear glosses written in Ireland (Würzburg, Universitätsbibliothek M.p.th.f. 12).[64] Smaragdus of Saint Mihiel, a monk believed to be of Irish origin who founded the monastery in Northern France by which he is known, was a secretary of Charlemagne who composed a large number of homilies. His *Expositio libri comitis* is an assembly of writings from earlier authors which relate to the portions of the Gospels and Epistles in the lectionary for Sundays and feast days. Another compilation with Insular roots is the *Catechesis Celtica* (AN Wil), a series of exegetical pieces surviving in a single manuscript (Vatican, BAV, Reg. lat. 49). Its sources include Bede's *Commentary on Luke*.[65] Although the biblical text usually corresponds to

---

[62] VL 81 is manuscript V in Souter 1922–31; its non-Vulgate readings only occasionally overlap with the Old Latin text in the Balliol manuscript (see page 40).

[63] Bischoff 1954; Gorman 2000; Ó Cróinín 2000; Contreni 2012:522–3.

[64] Stern 1910; Breen 1996; Picard 2003. In the Vetus Latina edition it is given the siglum W.

[65] McNamara 1994; a new edition is being prepared by Rittmueller.

the Vulgate, the treatment of the Wedding at Cana in John 2 provides several unique readings which may represent a paraphrase or fresh translation. The most substantial compilation is known as the 'Reference Bible' (German *Das Bibelwerk*); the title in the manuscripts is *Pauca problesmata de enigmatibus in tomis canonicis*. This is a collection of patristic material deployed in question-and-answer format to address problems based on the Old and New Testaments. It includes extracts from Ambrose, Jerome, Augustine, John Cassian, Eucherius, Isidore, and Gregory the Great introduced by name.[66] Other works on the New Testament with probable Irish connections are transmitted pseudonymously, usually under the names of Jerome or Bede. These include an exposition of the four Gospels from the second half of the seventh century (PS-HI Ev) and an eighth-century commentary on John (PS-HI Jo), both of which were written on the Continent. The latter relies heavily on Fortunatianus of Aquileia and Augustine, while both share sources with another anonymous commentary on John, produced around 780 in Salzburg (PS-BED Jo) along with a similar work on Luke (PS-BED Lc).[67]

Ambrosius Autpertus, the abbot of San Vicenzo al Volturno in the second half of the eighth century, wrote a ten-book exposition of Revelation (AM-A Apc) using the fourth-century commentary of Tyconius, a revision made around 700 of Jerome's version of Victorinus' commentary, and Primasius; Ambrosius is also often dependent on Gregory the Great. A few years later, his contemporary Beatus, abbot of Liébana in Asturia, produced a commentary on Revelation (BEA Apc). A second edition, revised by the author, appeared in 784. Beatus used Tyconius, a sixth-century revision of Jerome's version of Victorinus, and Apringius. Claudius of Turin (CLAU-T), also of Spanish origin, was commissioned by Charlemagne's son Louis the Pious to write a commentary on Genesis. After completing it in 811, he expounded other books of the Bible. Most of these commentaries remain unpublished; several have been transmitted under the names of other authors, such as Eucherius and Atto of Vercelli. Claudius issued a commentary on 1 and 2 Corinthians in 820, and later completed all the Pauline Epistles. These, along with his commentary on Matthew, circulated widely in the ninth century. Claudius followed Bede's example of including indications of his sources in the margin, even identifying his own contributions with CL.[68] Sources are also specified by name in the commentary on Romans attributed to Helisachar, chaplain of Louis the Pious (Paris, BnF, latin 11574), where extracts from Augustine, Ambrosiaster, Origen, Pelagius, and other writers have been assembled along

---

[66] See Bischoff 1954 and Contreni 2012:524; there is no edition of the New Testament, but the earliest manuscript, the ninth-century Paris, BnF, latin 11561, is fully available online: <http://gallica.bnf.fr/ark:/12148/btv1b90668240>.

[67] Brearley 1987; O'Loughlin 1999b; Dorfbauer 2014b.

[68] Gorman 1997:312–16.

with the differing forms of the biblical text found in their commentary.[69] A commentary on Matthew by Paschasius Radbertus, abbot of Corbie in the first half of the ninth century, combines patristic scholarship with a renewed focus on the biblical text.[70]

Another approach to earlier Latin authors is seen in the commentary on Paul produced by Florus of Lyons in the middle of the ninth century. This line-by-line exposition of the Epistles is made up of over two thousand excerpts from the writings of Augustine. Although Florus relied in part on Augustinian *sententiae* ('extracts') compiled by Paul of Aquitaine, the majority of the commentary is his own work. It provides a very valuable witness to the textual tradition of Augustine, including fragments of some works not otherwise extant. Nevertheless, by the twelfth century this commentary was widely attributed to Bede, with some manuscripts even identifying the work as the compilation of Peter of Tripoli mentioned by Cassiodorus.[71] Florus was famed for his knowledge of literature, including some ability in Greek. Numerous ninth-century manuscripts from his library in Lyons are written or annotated in blue ink in his characteristic hand, including some of the codices of Augustine from which he assembled his extracts. VL 5 (Codex Bezae) is also known to have been in Lyons, and Florus may have been involved in the provision of the ninth-century supplementary pages replacing those which had been lost; it has also been suggested that Florus had access to VL 75 and the Theodulf Bible from Le Puy.[72]

Sedulius Scottus, an Irish monk and grammarian teaching at Liège around 845, composed several expository works based largely on extracts from earlier writers. The most significant are commentaries on Matthew (SED-S Mt) and on the fourteen Pauline Epistles, also known as the *Collectaneum in Apostolum* (SED-S Rm, etc.). Pelagius, for which Sedulius is an important witness, is among the early sources quoted in the Pauline commentary. Sedulius appears to have used a mixed-text manuscript similar to VL 61.[73] He has also been identified as the copyist of VL 250, a Greek–Latin bilingual manuscript of the Psalter and the Odes, which he adjusted to bring it into closer correspondence with the Greek text. Johannes Scotus Eriugena, a Neoplatonist philosopher and theologian who taught at the French court, was a fellow countryman and contemporary of Sedulius. In addition to a commentary on the Greek text of the Gospel according to John, Eriugena also produced a series of glosses based on the Bible of Theodulf.[74] He is famous for his translation and commentary on Pseudo-Dionysius, and his opposition to the doctrines of predestination espoused by the monk Gottschalk (Godescalc). The St Gall bilingual gospel book (VL 27) includes the name Gottschalk in

---

[69] This is currently being edited by Boodts.   [70] Contreni 2012:532.
[71] See page 59.   [72] Charlier 1945:84.
[73] Frede 1961 and 1972:469; Löfstedt 1989–91; Frede & Stanjek 1996–7; Sloan 2012.
[74] Contreni & Ó Néill 1997.

the margin as well as a possible abbreviation for Sedulius, although these appear to be later additions.

The most prolific of the Carolingian exegetes was Hrabanus Maurus. A pupil of Alcuin, he became head of the school at Fulda where he taught Walafrid Strabo before ending his days as archbishop of Mainz, the city of his birth, in 856. Hrabanus composed biblical commentaries drawing heavily on earlier Latin authors, especially Jerome, whom he often reproduced verbatim. Like Bede and Claudius of Turin, he included abbreviations in the margins identifying his sources. His commentaries on Matthew and Paul embody the single-volume biblical anthology which dominated Carolingian scholarship. Indeed, it has been claimed that, in this period, the writings of the Church Fathers began to be accorded greater precedence than the biblical text itself in setting the parameters for scriptural interpretation.[75]

Alongside the standard texts of the Latin Bible, the gospel harmony began to increase in popularity, paving the way for vernacular harmonies. There are four surviving ninth-century copies of Codex Fuldensis (Vg F), one of which is St Gall, Stiftsbibliothek, 56, made in Fulda itself. This manuscript unites both traditions: the Latin harmony text is written on the left column of each page, with an Old High German translation on the right.[76] Another product of Fulda is the *Heliand*, a German poem on the life of Christ, commissioned by Louis the Pious and based on a gospel harmony. Louis was the dedicatee of a harmonized gospel in German rhyming couplets composed by Otfrid of Weissenburg. A pupil of Hrabanus Maurus, Otfrid also made a collection of biblical commentaries, and was responsible for some of the earliest glossed biblical manuscripts.[77]

The eighth and ninth centuries thus constitute a pivotal point in the history of the Latin New Testament. Editions of the whole Bible in one or two volumes with a fixed set of prefatory material establish the revised biblical text from the turn of the fifth century, ascribed in its entirety to Jerome, as the standard form. The pandects of Wearmouth–Jarrow draw on earlier Italian models, while Spanish tradition lies behind the edition of Theodulf, itself overshadowed by single-volume Bibles from the scriptorium of Tours. Illustration and decoration become an ever more important element in manuscript production, from the famous Insular gospel books to the cycles of illustration in Carolingian codices. Old Latin texts continue to be transmitted through

---

[75] Contreni 2012:525–31; he observes that only seventy surviving Latin biblical commentaries were composed between 500 and 750, while no fewer than two hundred and twenty were produced by fifty-one identifiable authors between 750 and 1000. For more on Carolingian exegesis, see the other works of Contreni.

[76] Rathofer 1973; Schmid 2012. The other witnesses, which have 184 capitula rather than the 181 in Codex Fuldensis, are described in Schmid 2012:129.

[77] Bischoff 1990:118; Ganz 2012:335.

earlier commentaries and paratextual material, as well as biblical manuscripts themselves. The combination of creativity and antiquarianism in Irish Latin tradition spreads across the European continent, resulting in a burgeoning of exegetical scholarship. Extracts from existing Latin tradition, with each source carefully identified, are assembled to forge a new encyclopaedic approach in a single-volume commentary. These innovations are central to further developments in the Latin New Testament as it enters the High Middle Ages.

5

The Tenth Century Onwards: Scholarship and Heresy

The early history of the Latin New Testament is essentially complete by the end of the ninth century and the developments outlined in the previous chapter. No Christian author is cited in the Vetus Latina edition after this period, and the affiliation of the vast majority of Bibles is Vulgate. Nevertheless, several of the codices copied between the tenth and fourteenth century provide evidence for the pre-Vulgate text. The context for these manuscripts includes the flourishing of Spanish Bible production, the creation of the *Glossa ordinaria*, Italian Giant Bibles linked to ecclesiastical reform, and Paris Bibles. In the fourteenth century, the rise of commercial booksellers in place of monastic scriptoria and the dissociation of the study of the biblical text from the copying of Bibles mark a new state of affairs which continues to the end of the manuscript period and the invention of printing.

SPANISH PANDECTS AND LECTIONARIES

From the tenth century, large-format codices containing the whole Bible, sometimes in multiple volumes, became common in many parts of Europe. The Spanish tradition includes a number of manuscripts which represent the seventh-century revision by John of Saragossa (see page 63). These normally take the form of pandects with three columns on each page, such as Codex Toletanus (Vg^O T), copied in southern Spain in the middle of the tenth century. A similar text is found in the contemporary Codex Complutensis 2 (Madrid, Biblioteca de la Universidad, MS 32), Madrid, Biblioteca Nacional, lat. 2, Montpellier, BM, 6, and the Bible of Huesca (VL 134; Madrid, Museo Arqueológico 485) copied over a century later. Certain books of the Old Testament are Old Latin in affiliation; elsewhere, these Bibles preserve occasional non-Vulgate readings current in Spain and southern France. The same is true of manuscripts representing an edition of the Bible created by the famous copyist Florentius in the monastery of Valeránica around 940.[1] The principal representatives are VL 91 and VL 95. These, along with the rest of the series VL 91–6, feature Old Latin forms in marginal glosses, although in the New Testament these are only found alongside the Catholic Epistles. VL 93 and 94 are printed texts with indications of variant readings, while only the first, Old Testament, volume of VL 96 is extant. Several of these appear to be related to a lost tenth-century manuscript known as the Valvanera Bible, which may also have been produced at Valeránica.[2]

VL 109 (Codex Complutensis 1, also known as the first Bible of Alcalá; Image 11) was copied in the tenth century from a manuscript produced at least three hundred years earlier.[3] Portions of the Old Testament are Old Latin: in Ruth, its text is related to that used by Claudius of Turin for his commentary, while elsewhere there are liturgical influences and relationships with other Spanish manuscripts. In the New Testament, it displays some similarities with VL 61, perhaps deriving from a Gallican tradition, although the order of books and the three-column format correspond to Spanish practice. The text of Hebrews in VL 109 is closely related to that of VL 89, transmitting a Roman text of the fourth century. In the sixteenth century, the manuscript was given to the Complutense University by Cardinal Ximenez, who was instrumental in the creation of the first printed multilingual edition of the Bible, the Complutensian Polyglot. During the Spanish Civil War in the 1930s, VL 109 was severely damaged. Its original state can still be seen in photographs taken in 1914.

VL 62 (the *Biblia de Rosas*) is an eleventh-century Bible in four volumes with three columns to a page, made in the diocese of Vic. As with the earlier Spanish codices, a completely non-Vulgate text is only found in the deutero-canonical books. However, the Acts of the Apostles contain earlier readings in the text and margin as well as an Old Latin portion in chapters 11 and 12. This is the older of the two manuscripts with the set of *capitula* for the Gospels known as KA Cat, an expansion of an earlier type which incorporates some additional Old Latin material.[4] Another set of *capitula* (KA Vich) is peculiar to this locality: found in two manuscripts also of this period held by the Town Museum in Vic, it seems to be a reworking of a different series based on the Vulgate. This renewal of earlier forms suggests a particular focus on editorial activity in eleventh-century Catalan Bible production.

The Spanish lectionary tradition also transmits a distinctive form of biblical text. There are two principal types of lectionary: the *Liber comicus* (or *comitis*) contains the readings for Sundays and Feast Days, while the *Liber misticus* (or

---

[1] In the Vetus Latina editions, manuscripts of Florentius' edition are given the siglum Λ, while the earlier text is identified as Σ.

[2] See Williams 1999:186–7. The Valvanera Bible was probably destroyed in the fire of 1671 at the Escorial: VL 94 is a copy of some of its marginal glosses.

[3] Fischer 1963b [1985:75].   [4] See Houghton 2011:335–7. The other is San Millán, 3.

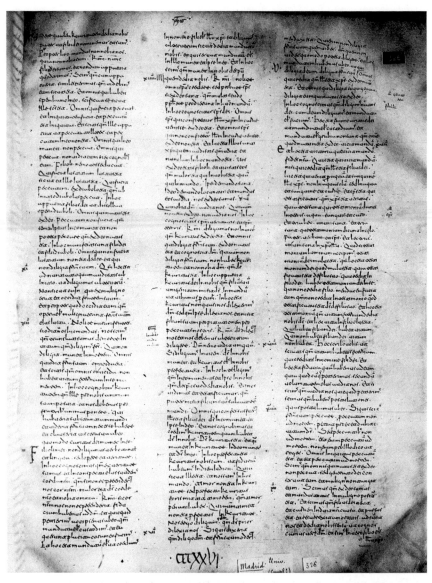

Image 11 VL 109/Vg X: Codex **Complutensis primus** (Madrid, Biblioteca Histórica, Universidad Complutense, BH MSS 31, folio 326ʳ), showing the Johannine Comma at 1 John 5:7. By kind permission of the Universidad Complutense. Image Courtesy of the Hill Museum & Manuscript Library.

mixtus) provides lections for offices and masses. This textual type is sometimes denoted by the siglum τ with a superscript letter, although most manuscripts have been allocated VL numbers. The dating of these witnesses is precise when the year of production is given in a colophon, but can be very uncertain on palaeographical grounds alone. VL 68 (Comes Toletanus) and VL 72, a *liber misticus* also held in Toledo, have been dated to both the ninth and twelfth centuries, while VL 70 (Comes Aemilianus) was copied in 1073 by the abbot of San Millán, slightly after VL 69 (Comes Legionensis). Two eleventh-century lectionaries originate from Silos, VL 56 (Comes Silensis) and VL 73, another *liber misticus*. These witnesses may be divided into two principal strands of tradition: an older text, represented by VL 68 and 71 (*Comes Carcasonensis*; pages 89–90 above), and a more recent text in the five other manuscripts, for which VL 56 is the chief witness. There are numerous points of similarity both with the Spanish continuous-text tradition and the Mozarabic liturgy (M-M, ANT-M; see page 90). VL 259–62 and 271 are also Spanish liturgical manuscripts. VL 260 is the tenth-century León Antiphonary, an important codex with musical notation in neumes, although its biblical text is heavily abbreviated and appears identical to ANT-M. The others are four *libri mistici*: the most significant for the New Testament are VL 262 and 271, which seem to have a higher proportion of Old Latin readings than the standard Spanish texts. VL 60 was completely destroyed in the Spanish Civil War. This thirteenth-century lectionary had a Vulgate text of Paul but two short passages from the first chapter of Acts with an Old Latin affiliation. The increasing influence of Roman liturgy led to a prohibition at the Council of León in 1090 on using the traditional Visigothic script for copying liturgical books in Spain.[5]

Outside Spain, lectionaries are less common, although liturgical evidence may continue to preserve unusual forms of text. VL 31 is an eleventh-century manuscript from North Italy containing a number of rituals. One is the *ordo scrutiniorum* (AN scru), a liturgy with fifteen brief readings which seems to go back to the end of the sixth century. The lections include portions of the Synoptic Gospels, Romans and 2 Corinthians: some match the Vulgate but others are Old Latin. Latin continued to be the language of North African liturgy: VL 74 is two leaves from a tenth-century lectionary found in Sinai containing readings from Acts and Revelation with an Old Latin affiliation. The antiphonary with which VL 74 is bound indicates the opening lines of readings from Acts and the Epistles in a non-Vulgate form.[6] Christian grave inscriptions near Tripoli from around the same time also have Old Latin biblical verses (INS En Ngila). Liutprand of Cremona uses an Old Latin text which corresponds to VL 75 in his sermons delivered in 960. He may have had recourse to such a bilingual manuscript on his diplomatic missions to Constantinople.[7]

---

[5] Bischoff 1990:100.   [6] Fischer 1964 [1986:145].   [7] Frede 1986.

ATLANTIC BIBLES

On the other side of the Mediterranean, large Bibles produced in northern Italy in the eleventh and twelfth centuries are known as Atlantic Bibles, after the giant Atlas.[8] These are associated with the reforms of Pope Gregory VII: some were used as control texts for the revised liturgy, while others were commissioned by lay people and presented to monasteries. They are very similar in format and decoration. Three textual stages have been identified, for which the revisers used Tours Bibles.[9] Rome was the principal centre of production, although several have been associated with Tuscany.[10]

The Atlantic Bibles inspired numerous similar productions across Europe, linking monasteries with the Gregorian reform. The Stavelot Bible (London, BL, Add. MS 28106–7) was copied between 1093 and 1097 in Holland, while three large Norman Bibles were produced which soon made their way to England: the Saint-Calais Bible, now in Durham, the Gundulf Bible once in Rochester, and the two-volume Lincoln Bible. These are adorned with numerous coloured initials featuring figures and foliage, while red, blue, and green inks are used for titles and capital letters. Large-scale twelfth-century English Romanesque Bibles form part of the same tradition, including the Bury St Edmunds, Winchester, Dover, and Lambeth Bibles. Contemporary accounts of their manufacture show that these were outsourced to professional craftsmen rather than being produced entirely within monastery scriptoria.[11] The Bible of William of Hales (Vg^O W), copied in Salisbury in 1254, represents the subsequent generation of this type of production.

Non-standard versions of the text could still be included in some of the outsize thirteenth-century Bibles. The largest Latin Bible in existence is VL 51, aptly known as the Codex Gigas ('Giant Codex'), originally measuring almost one metre in height and half a metre in width. Written in Bohemia between 1204 and 1227, it has an unusual set of contents: the Old Testament is followed by Josephus' *Antiquities* and *Jewish War*, Isidore's *Etymologies*, and some medical texts; next come the New Testament and the *Chronicle of Bohemia* by the twelfth-century Cosmas of Prague. The *Rule of St Benedict* was originally included too. Although the majority of the biblical text corresponds to the Vulgate, two of the New Testament books are Old Latin: VL 51 is one of the principal witnesses to the Vetus Latina text-type I in Acts and Revelation, matching quotations in Lucifer of Cagliari, Ambrosiaster, and the *Liber de diuinis scripturis* (PS-AU spe). A handful of Old Latin readings are found in the other books, typical of Vulgate witnesses from southern France and

---

[8] On the terminology (*Riesenbibel* in German) see Ayres 1994:125.
[9] See van Liere 2012:98–9 and the works of Lobrichon.
[10] Ayres 1994, especially 144–51; see also Yawn 2004.   [11] See Thomson 2001.

Bohemia. VL 59 (Codex Demidovianus) was also a very large-format manuscript of the Bible, with the whole New Testament on sixty pages. Copied in Burgundy in the second half of the thirteenth century, it belonged to Paul Demidov in Moscow when C.F. Matthaei cited it in his bilingual edition of the New Testament published in Riga between 1782 and 1788. The manuscript was subsequently lost, with the result that Matthaei's edition (in which the orthography had been standardized) is the only evidence for its readings. Although included in the Vetus Latina *Register*, it appears to furnish little in the way of Old Latin evidence.

SECTARIAN TEXTS

Two Old Latin witnesses may be associated with the Cathar movement. Both VL 6 (Codex Colbertinus) and VL 54 (Codex Perpinianensis) contain the whole of the New Testament and were copied in southern France in the twelfth century. The former has a stronger Old Latin affiliation. In the Gospels, there are multiple textual layers: an archaic text for much of Mark and Luke, a marked similarity to the fifth-century VL 8 elsewhere, some Vulgate influence, and numerous unique readings. For example, VL 6 and VL 1 are the only manuscripts which consistently have the ancient rendering *secreto* for κατ' ἰδίαν ('in private') in Mark as well as a distinctive text of Mark 12:21–3.[12] In Luke, only VL 2 and VL 6 have *consecuti estis* rather than *habetis* at Luke 6:24 and *manducantes* rather than *edentes* at Luke 10:7 (cf. 12:45), while VL 6 is the sole manuscript with *claritate* rather than *gloria* or *maiestate* at Luke 9:31. VL 6 also contains some Old Latin readings in the Acts of the Apostles, while the rest of the New Testament is predominantly Vulgate. The Pauline Epistles are placed last, and include the Epistle to the Laodiceans. In VL 54, the principal Old Latin element is in the first half of the Acts of the Apostles. This is a mixed text featuring a number of longer forms which may go back to the fifth century. Its unusual renderings include *benenuntiare* rather than *euangelizare*, *conuentio* for *synagoga*, and *magnum falsum uatem* for *pseudopropheta*; Dorcas is also translated as *Damula*.[13] There are also a few non-Vulgate readings in Paul characteristic of texts from southern France.

---

[12] See further the extensive lists of readings at Haelewyck 2013:90–102.
[13] Berger 1893:77–9; other readings characteristic of Languedoc are found on 81–2.

LATER GOSPEL BOOKS

Insular and Celtic manuscripts continue to transmit a characteristic text of the Gospels in this period. VL 29 (Codex Sangermanensis secundus) is a gospel book copied in Brittany in the tenth century which has a number of similarities with the DELQR group (see page 74). Unusually for an Insular text it is written in Caroline minuscule, although it also features initials decorated with interlace designs and enlarged letters at Matthew 1:18 and Luke 1:5. Liturgical indications have been incorporated into the text of John: numerous paragraphs begin *in illo tempore* ('at that time'), the standard opening for a lection, and sometimes even include the day on which the passage is appointed to be read and end with *finis*. This has occasionally led to the rearrangement of the biblical text: attempts to restore the original have often resulted in further confusion.

Irish Gospels copied from the tenth century onwards are often in a small format, known as 'pocket gospel books'.[14] These were made for private use, written in a dense and often highly-abbreviated Insular minuscule. Some copies are named after their scribe, such as the Cadmug Gospels (Fulda, Hochschul-und Landesbibliothek, Bonifatianus 3) and the Gospels of Mael Brigte (London, BL, Harley 1802). The latter, produced in Armagh in 1138, includes material written in Irish and numerous Latin interlinear and marginal notes in the Synoptic Gospels. The Cadmug Gospels are abbreviated through the omission of a short portion in the middle of each book. This is also the case in the Book of Deer (Cambridge, University Library, Ii.VI.32; Image 12), in which only John is complete; an Office for the Visitation of the Sick is inserted between the opening sections of Mark and Luke. Although the hand is similar to Irish scribes of the early tenth century, this pocket gospel book is believed to be the earliest extant manuscript produced in Scotland. As well as some written Gaelic, there are Latin marginalia indicating that the book was at the monastery of Deer, near Aberdeen, in the early twelfth century. The text of all these pocket gospels includes Insular features present in the DELQR group and other Irish manuscripts such as VL 48 and VL 61. They also share characteristic traits of Irish orthography, such as –bt– for –pt– (e.g. *babtizo* for *baptizo*), –ss– for –s– (e.g. *circumcissio* for *circumcisio*), and a set of abbreviations.[15]

On the European continent, pride of place is held by the magnificent gospel books of the Ottonian dynasty. A disproportionate number of golden gospel books with richly bejewelled covers were produced in Germany in the tenth and early eleventh centuries. Perhaps the finest is the Pierpont Morgan Golden Gospels (New York, Pierpont Morgan Library, M. 23), written in gold uncial letters on fine purple parchment in Trier by no fewer than sixteen scribes.[16] Another is the

---

[14] McGurk 1956; Farr 2011.   [15] See page 192.

[16] Lowe 1972:389ff. The book was subsequently owned by King Henry VIII of England.

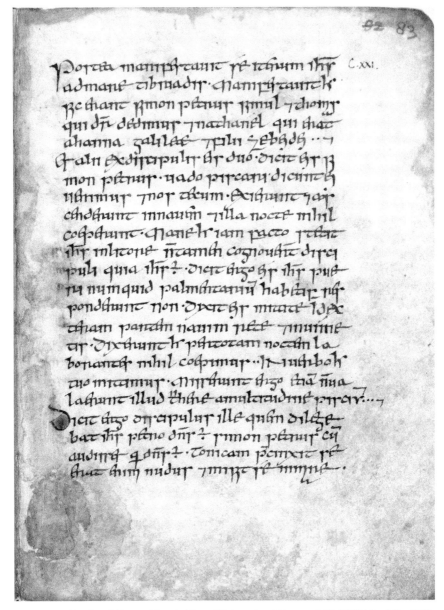

Image 12 Book of Deer (Cambridge, University Library, MS Ii.VI.32, folio 83ʳ), showing Insular abbreviations and the interpolation at John 21:6. Reproduced by kind permission of the Syndics of Cambridge University Library. Also available at <http://cudl.lib.cam.ac.uk/view/MS-II-00006-00032/166>

eleventh-century Echternach Golden Gospels (Nuremberg, Germanisches Natio-
nalmuseum): Echternach and Corvey were centres of production for both gospel
books and lectionaries in the Ottonian period. Several Ottonian codices also
contain illustrations of scenes from the Gospels and decorative pages painted to
resemble the luxury cloth used for wrapping books.[17]

BIBLICAL REVISIONS AND
THE *GLOSSA ORDINARIA*

Further efforts to revise the Bible demonstrate the continuing diversity of textual
forms. Olbert, abbot of Gembloux in the middle of the eleventh century, is
reported in the abbey chronicle to have collected one hundred biblical manuscripts in order to produce a pandect.[18] The biography of Lanfranc, archbishop
of Canterbury from 1069–89, tells how he worked on the text of both the Bible
and the Church Fathers, although there are no manuscripts of his revision
known to survive. He may also have produced a commentary on the Pauline
Epistles.[19] The revision of the Bible by Stephen Harding, abbot of Cîteaux, is
preserved in four volumes copied in 1109 (Codex Divionensis: Dijon, BM,
12–15). Harding collated Latin and Greek manuscripts and excised numerous
interpolations.

The assembly by scholars of patristic extracts to illuminate the New Testament text culminates in the development of all-in-one editions of text and
commentary, chief among which is the *Glossa ordinaria*. The initial format of
manuscripts of the *Glossa* consists of three columns to a page, with the biblical
text in the middle: the inside column is much narrower than the others. There
are interlinear glosses above the words of the Bible in addition to the patristic
extracts on either side. This layout is similar to earlier glossed books of the ninth
and tenth centuries and is also used in VL 63, a twelfth-century copy of Acts.
The biblical text of VL 63 is flanked by an exposition on either side drawing on
Bede and Hrabanus Maurus: although its textual affiliation is primarily Vulgate,
there are over one thousand Old Latin readings.[20] In later copies of the *Glossa
ordinaria* the separation between the columns becomes less strict and the
biblical text is only distinguished by being in larger script.

For a long time, the *Glossa ordinaria* was attributed to the ninth-century
scholar Walafrid Strabo, but it has recently been shown to originate in the

---

[17] Lowden 2012:49; see also Metz 1957 and Mayr-Harting 1991.
[18] van Liere 2014:95.
[19] Collins 2007, although Lobrichon 2012:550 observes that the manuscripts claimed to
represent Lanfranc's commentary predate him by a century.
[20] Gryson 1999:97 gives a figure of 1384 differences from the Oxford Vulgate.

early twelfth century in Laon.[21] Anselm of Laon (d. 1117) is believed to be responsible for the *Glossa ordinaria* on the Psalms, Pauline Epistles, and John: the latter quotes Eriugena's *Commentary on John* which is only extant in a single manuscript, in Laon. Anselm may also have produced the *Glossa* on Luke. The majority of the other books of the Bible appear to have been glossed by Anselm's brother Ralph and Gilbert of Auxerre (sometimes called Gilbert the Universal).[22] The *Glossa ordinaria* is reliant on earlier compilations: in the Pauline Epistles, there are notable similarities with the commentary attributed to Lanfranc. The *Glossa* itself was soon revised and expanded. Anselm's gloss on Paul became known as the *parua glosatura* as it was considerably enlarged first by Gilbert of Poitiers (d. 1154, also known as Gilbert de la Porrée or Gilbertus Porretanus) into the *media glosatura*, and later by Peter Lombard, who created the *magna glosatura*. Gilbert's version includes marginal indications of sources such as Augustine, Jerome, Ambrose (although the actual source is Ambrosiaster) and Haymo of Auxerre. It may have been Gilbert who took the *Glossa ordinaria* to Paris, where it achieved its popularity through its use in the schools, forming the subject of lectures by Peter Lombard and his student Petrus Comestor in the middle of the twelfth century. Subsequent New Testament exegesis was usually indebted to such glosses: the commentary of Hugh of St Cher on the whole Bible, written in the 1230s, both used and superseded the *Glossa ordinaria* within a century of its creation. Three decades later, Thomas Aquinas created the *Catena aurea*, the first compilation of patristic extracts to go by the name *catena* ('chain'). The continued appearance of non-Vulgate readings in these and later writers, such as the fourteenth-century *postillae* of Nicholas of Lyra (commentaries for insertion after the biblical text, *post illa uerba*) or Laurence of Brindisi in the sixteenth century, stems from their quotation of patristic sources with the biblical text unchanged.[23]

PARIS BIBLES

The rise to prominence of Paris as a centre of scholarship in the twelfth and thirteenth centuries was reflected in the activities of monastic establishments such as the Augustinian abbey of St Victor and the Dominican convent of St James (Saint-Jacques) and the university which developed from the cathedral school.[24] So-called 'Paris Bibles' were produced in great numbers from the

[21] Smith 2009; Andrée 2008, 2011.

[22] Thus Smith 2012:366; a slightly different division of labour is reported in van Liere 2014:155.

[23] For *postillae*, see Courtenay 2012:566.

[24] For the background, see Spicq 1944 and Courtenay 2012, as well as the works of Dahan, Light, Smalley, Smith, and Ruzzier.

thirteenth century onwards. The term refers to a particular type of text and set of contents: their textual affiliation is identical to that of many glossed Bibles, while the distinctive sequence of books included the order Gospels, Pauline Epistles, Acts, Catholic Epistles, and Revelation (epacr). These were followed by a list of Hebrew names (*Interpretatio hebraicorum nominum*), beginning *Aaz apprehendens*, an expansion of Jerome's glossary attributed to Stephen Langton, who taught theology in Paris before his appointment as Archbishop of Canterbury in 1207.[25] Each book was preceded by a prologue, although the selection varies between codices.[26] Early copies also have lists of *capitula*, although in later manuscripts the chapter numbers stand by themselves in the margin. From around 1230, the Paris Bibles have the same set of chapter divisions as modern Bibles, traditionally attributed to Stephen Langton too, although it slightly predates him.[27] Some Paris Bibles also have extensive sets of cross-references in the margin, made possible by the standardization of the chapters, which meant that the Eusebian apparatus for the Gospels was no longer copied.

The Paris Bibles did not represent an official recension, but instead derived from the city's importance as a centre for students and the associated book trade.[28] In practice, their text largely derived from the Tours Bibles, and consistent forms of layout were developed in small format pandects or two-volume Bibles. The presentation normally comprised two columns of text in gothic script, running titles at the top of each page, and larger initials at the beginnings of paragraphs (an early example is shown in Image 13). Decoration was often restricted to the use of red and blue for the titles, running titles and initials, although the initial letter of a book could be illuminated with a miniature.

The production of Bibles in Paris by professional workshops meant that the study of its text became separated from the copying of biblical codices. Several groups of scholars compiled *correctoria* or *correctoriones*, lists of variant readings based on Greek and Latin manuscripts as well as biblical quotations in early authors.[29] Sometimes these were written in the margins of a scriptural codex, but they appeared more often as separate volumes, arranged in an apparatus following the sequence of biblical books. Three of the four principal collections are associated with Paris: the *Correctorium Parisinense*, the *Correctorium Sorbonicum*, and the *Correctio Biblie*. The last

---

[25] The attribution is called into question in Dahan 2010; see also Szerwiniack 1994.

[26] Light 1994:164–6 notes that two New Testament prologues are introduced in the Paris Bibles apparently from the *Glossa ordinaria*: *Matheus cum primo* [S 589] before Matthew, and *Omnes qui pie uolunt uiuere* [S 839] before Revelation. The latter was erroneously attributed to Gilbert de la Porrée.

[27] Saenger 2008; see also d'Esneval 1978 and Light 1994:172. Numbered verses were not introduced until the invention of printing; the present system may be traced back to the Greek and Latin New Testament published in Geneva in 1551 by Robert Estienne (Stephanus).

[28] van Liere 2012:103; on the text see the works of Light and McKitterick 1994b:65.

[29] Dahan 1997, 2004; Linde 2012.

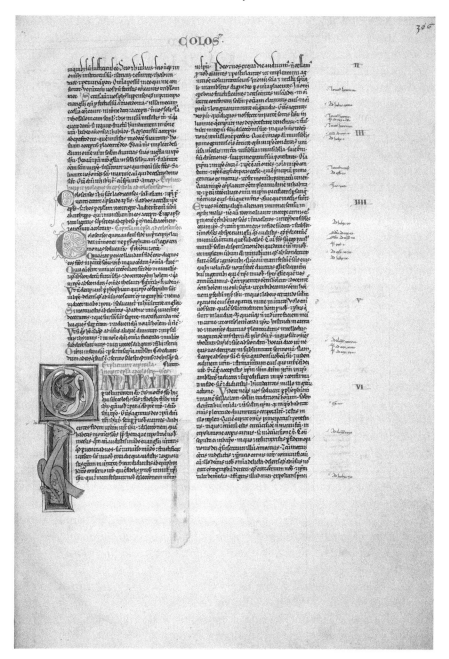

Image 13 An early Paris Bible (Paris, Bibliothèque nationale de France, latin 14233, folio 306ʳ), showing the prologue, *capitula* and beginning of Colossians. Also available at <http://gallica.bnf.fr/ark:/12148/btv1b9072553q/f314.item>

of these was the work of Hugh of Saint Cher, who, with his fellow Dominicans at the abbey of St James, was engaged on the first concordance of the Bible (*Concordantia sacrorum bibliorum*). In order to narrow the field of reference, the Dominicans divided each biblical chapter into seven sections indicated by the letters a–g. Shorter chapters were only divided into four, a–d. This achieved wide diffusion, and was soon followed by a second concordance revised by three English friars (*Magnae concordantiae anglicanae* or Saint-Jacques II) which provided more context.[30] The same Dominican scholarship also resulted in a revision of the biblical text, known as the Bible of Saint-Jacques, with emendations based on Latin, Greek, and Hebrew manuscripts. This was criticized by Roger Bacon (*c.*1215–92), who, as a Franciscan, favoured the more conservative *Correctorium Vaticanum* produced by his fellow friars such as William of Mara (de la Mare) and Gerard of Huy.[31] In general, the *correctoria* did not influence the text of the Bible until the advent of printing but they were used to provide a range of alternative readings for discussion in biblical commentaries.

HARMONIES, GLOSSES, AND THE REDISCOVERY OF GREEK

Eighteen Latin gospel harmony manuscripts survive from the twelfth and thirteenth centuries. Seven of these feature a series of marginal annotations and extracts from the *Glossa ordinaria*. It appears that these alternatives were sometimes incorporated into the text when a Latin manuscript was used as the basis for a vernacular harmony, as in the case of the Liège Diatessaron.[32] In addition to the *Unum ex quattuor* type, favoured by mediaeval scholars, other harmonies were created from the twelfth century onwards. The Latin gospel harmony of Clement of Llanthony was the source for the *Pepysian Harmony*, a Middle English gospel harmony in a manuscript once owned by Samuel Pepys, through an intermediate Anglo-Norman translation. Some commentaries were based on harmonies, including Petrus Comestor's *Historia Scholastica*. One twelfth-century Bible (Cambridge, Corpus Christi College 48) has a unique method of presentation for comparing the Gospels. They are copied in four parallel columns of different widths in order to make each cover the same number of pages: marginal Eusebian apparatus is also provided, as matching pericopes rarely coincide despite the novel layout.

The rise of the vernacular tradition is apparent in glossed manuscripts. One of the latest to have a partial Old Latin affiliation is VL 58 (Codex Wernigerodensis),

---

[30] Rouse & Rouse 1974; Courtenay 2012:562–3.
[31] This is cited in the Oxford Vulgate as *cor. vat.* [32] Schmid 2012:127–32.

copied in Bohemia in the second half of the fourteenth century. This pocket copy of the entire New Testament has glosses in Czech added between the lines and in the bottom margin. It is essentially a Paris Bible, with the characteristic order of books and marginal cross-references using the Dominican system, but has a mixed-text form of Acts featuring several of the longer, 'Western' readings. A similar text was the basis of the Provençal translation, indicating that it may also be connected with southern France. Although the Pauline Epistles are closer to the Vulgate, they feature a number of explanatory glosses and doublets incorporated into the biblical text, typical of later tradition.

Bilingual codices also offered a means of engaging with the Greek tradition. After the ninth-century examples of Irish scholarship on the continent, there is a gap of some three or four centuries before the next surviving bilingual Greek–Latin New Testament manuscript (Florence, Biblioteca Medicea Laurenziana, Conv. Soppr. 150 [GA 620]), copied in the twelfth century and containing the Epistles and Revelation. Between the late thirteenth and fifteenth centuries, twelve Greek–Latin bilinguals demonstrate humanist interest in the original language.[33] There is even a thirteenth-century Greek–Latin–Arabic trilingual of the Epistles and Acts (Venice, Bib. Marciana, Gr. Z. 11 [GA 420]). Most of these have each language in a separate column: the Greek is normally on the left, the traditional place for the original language, although three of the later manu-scripts have the Latin in this position. Two fourteenth-century manuscripts at the Vatican have different formats, an interlinear gospel book (Vatican, BAV, Urb. gr. 4 [GA 1269]) and a copy of the rest of the New Testament with the Latin as the outer column on each page (Vatican, BAV, Ottob. gr. 258 [GA 628]). Many of these later manuscripts are incomplete, usually with gaps in the Latin translation. Paris, BnF, grec 54 (GA 16) is a typical example.[34] Its Latin column, in an elegant humanist hand with very few abbreviations and only occasional use of *nomina sacra*, is about two-thirds of the width of the Greek. Neither language is written in sense lines and synchronization is often lost. The entire Greek text is present but the Latin is missing in the latter part of Mark and John and all of Luke apart from four verses in the middle of the Gospel. The translation is clearly modelled on the Vulgate, yet there are departures from this text: the use of *testificare* rather than *testimonium perhibere* may reflect a desire to correspond to the single word in Greek, but other differences, such as *uidit* rather than *inuenit* in John 1:43 and 45, cannot be explained with reference to the other column.

The growing awareness of discrepancies between the Latin and Greek texts revealed by bilingual manuscripts and early printed Bibles, such as the Com-plutensian Polyglot and the editions of Erasmus, led to the restoration of the Greek as the definitive New Testament and ended the millennium of Latin

---

[33] For a summary, see Parker 1992:62–6. [34] See Maxwell 2014.

predominance in the West. Even Erasmus himself, after preparing a critical edition based on manuscripts of the Vulgate, adjusted the Latin text to meet later stylistic criteria.[35] His acceptance of the priority of the Greek is well known from the story of the Johannine Comma (1 John 5:7–8) which he omitted from his edition on the grounds that it was not found in Greek despite being widely attested in Latin. Only when he was presented with a Greek codex containing these lines did he include it in his third edition of 1522, although it was suggested that these verses had been translated from the Vulgate especially to confound him.[36] Erasmus himself translated the final verses of Revelation from Latin as they were missing from his Greek source.[37] His edition formed the basis of the *Textus Receptus*, the 'Received Text' of the Greek New Testament printed by Robert Étienne (Stephanus) in Paris in 1550.

As scholarly proficiency in Greek was restored, Latin versions became less necessary for textual study although the Vulgate continued to be the standard text for the Roman Catholic Church. New translations appeared occasionally, such as the Latin version of the New Testament by the French Protestant Theodore Beza which highlighted differences between the Greek and the Vulgate: the three were printed in parallel columns in his edition of 1565.[38] Less than two centuries later, however, attention had shifted to differences within the Latin versions themselves and the edition by Pierre Sabatier of the most ancient Latin biblical translations, which marked the beginning of modern scholarship on the Vetus Latina.

---

[35] See Erasmus, *Epistle* 695.   [36] See de Jonge 1980, and pages 178 and 181 below.

[37] See page 182 below, Metzger 1994:8*, and Parker 2008:227–8.

[38] Beza's version should not be confused with the text of Codex Bezae, VL 5, which he presented to the University of Cambridge.

Part II

Texts

This section is concerned with the text of the Latin New Testament in scholarly editions and in biblical tradition more broadly. Chapter 6 provides a user's guide to the principal critical editions of the Latin New Testament, including the Vetus Latina series, the Stuttgart Vulgate, and the Oxford Vulgate. There is also information on the presentation of Latin evidence in the Greek *Editio Critica Maior* and the two most popular hand editions, UBS5 and NA28. A concordance between the different witness sigla used to identify Latin manuscripts in critical editions is provided in Appendix 1. Some considerations when using the Latin tradition in support of a Greek reading are outlined in Chapter 7. Chapter 8 offers an overview of the Latin evidence for each of the New Testament writings: it may be useful to refer to the Catalogue in Chapter 10 for further details of individual manuscripts.

6

Editions and Resources

The first part of this chapter provides details of the four principal scholarly editions devoted to the Old Latin Bible: Sabatier's eighteenth-century edition, which still remains the only Old Latin edition of certain books; the Vetus Latina series and its associated publications; the *Itala* edition of gospel manuscripts by Jülicher; and the Vetus Latina Hispana project, which only covers the Old Testament. This is followed by an introduction to the Stuttgart Vulgate edited by Weber and Gryson, the standard scholarly edition of the fifth-century text, and the Oxford Vulgate, whose main editors were Wordsworth and White. The Clementine Vulgate and the *Nova Vulgata* are described separately. Information on the presentation of Latin evidence in Greek editions focuses on the *Editio Critica Maior* and the hand editions of NA28 and UBS5.

There are numerous other resources for scholarly research on the text of the Latin New Testament. Editions and transcriptions of certain manuscripts are available in both printed and electronic form; photographic facsimiles can now be supplemented with complete sets of digital images, many of which are noted in Chapter 10. Specialist publications exist for the identification and study of biblical paratexts, including prefaces, series of *capitula*, and textual divisions. A number of studies have gathered the biblical quotations of a Christian author for one or more books, sometimes with a reconstruction of their text. Online databases, including the *Vetus Latina Database*, also offer collections of quotations arranged by verse. Finally, some bibliographical resources are mentioned which list publications relating to the Latin New Testament.

A) SABATIER

The first printed edition of an Old Latin version of the complete Old and New Testaments was undertaken by a Benedictine monk of the Maurist congregation, Dom Pierre Sabatier (often Latinized as Petrus Sabatier). Sabatier died in 1742 while his edition was still in press. Although the title page of *Bibliorum Sacrorum Latinae Versiones Antiquae seu Vetus Italica* ('The Ancient Latin

Versions of the Holy Bible, or the Old Italian') gives the date of publication of each volume as 1743, it was not completed until 1749.[1] The edition consists of three large format volumes with a total of over 3,000 pages. The first two cover the Old Testament and the third contains the New Testament. Sabatier's practice was to print the text of the Vulgate (entitled *Vulgata Nova*) on the inside column of each page and that of an Old Latin witness in the outer column. For the Gospels, he used VL 6 (Codex Colbertinus, under its old shelfmark of Colbertinus 4051). For Acts, he used VL 50 (the Laudian Acts, from an edition by Thomas Hearn in 1715), supplying the last two chapters from the text of Bede's commentary and other sources. The text of the Pauline Epistles comes from VL 75 (Codex Claromontanus, with the old shelfmark 2245) and VL 76 (at that point still in Paris, known as Sangermanensis 31). For the Catholic Epistles, he used VL 66 for James (with the shelfmark Corbeiensis 625, from Martianay's edition), while the other letters are pieced together from patristic quotations (largely Augustine, including his commentary on 1 John). The lemma text of Primasius' commentary, which had been printed as early as 1544, is taken as the Old Latin form of Revelation.

In the lower half of each page, Sabatier gives an apparatus of information pertaining to readings in the Old Latin version, including Greek texts. The principal Latin manuscripts cited in the Gospels are as follows:

Cantabr. (VL 5);
Clarom. (VL 12);
Corb. (VL 9 in Matthew 1–12, VL 8 in the other Gospels; in Matthew 13–28, VL 9 has the siglum *Corb. 1* and VL 8 *Corb. 2*);
Fossat. (VL 9A);
Maj. Mon. (Vg^{Oe} E);
S. Gat. (VL 30);
S. Germ. 1 or Sang. 1 (VL 7);
S. Germ. 2 or Sang. 2 (VL 29);
S. Mart. Turon. (Vg^{O} MT).

VL 5 is also cited in Acts as *Cantabr.* or *Cantabrig.*, along with readings from the Fleury palimpsest (VL 55, cited as *Reg. 5367*) and the Luxeuil Lectionary (VL 251, with the siglum *Luxoviense*). As with the principal witnesses, some of these are taken from earlier editions rather than direct consultation of the manuscript. The readings are given in full, as are biblical quotations from a variety of Christian authors ranging from Irenaeus to Gregory the Great and Bede. References are given to the page or column number of the edition consulted for each work, normally the Benedictine editions of the seventeenth

---

[1] The 'new edition' published by Didot in Paris in 1751 is identical to the earlier editions apart from the title page; the volumes were also reprinted by Brepols in 1976, with the addition of an appendix listing manuscripts used by Sabatier. Digitized versions of the originals are available, e.g. <https://archive.org/details/Sabatier3>.

and eighteenth centuries. In section 3 of the preface to Volume 1 (pp. xxxix–lxii), Sabatier lists and discusses each of his patristic sources, including anonymous writings. The preface to Volume 3 includes a ten-page discussion of the term *Itala*, engaging with previous scholarship, especially that of Bentley. For the Gospels and Acts, *capitula* are presented from a manuscript treated as Old Latin; in the other books, they are supplied from the Vulgate.

Sabatier chose his manuscripts for the Old Latin column based on their state of preservation. In the preface, he presents a number of indications of the antiquity of his chosen text for the Gospels despite its late date and notes that, for the first six chapters of John, where VL 6 is very close to the Vulgate, he had initially decided to present the text of VL 8 as the Old Latin version but was subsequently dissuaded. He treats VL 5 as a special case in the Gospels as it is a bilingual. For Acts, he suspends judgement over the relative antiquity of the text of VL 5 and VL 50, but selects the latter as more of the book is extant. In the Pauline Epistles, he recognizes that VL 76 is a copy of VL 75 but takes the corrected text as definitive, noting first-hand readings in VL 75 as marginal variants (with the siglum *Ms. Reg.*). Sabatier's dating of manuscripts reflects their age at the time of writing: for example, the indication '*annor(um) circiter* 1200' for VL 75 puts its date of copying in the early sixth century (1200 years before 1740).

Despite the mass of material, Sabatier's edition is now only of antiquarian interest in the New Testament as it has largely been replaced by the more comprehensive Vetus Latina edition and Jülicher's *Itala*. Most of the oldest manuscripts are missing from his apparatus for the Gospels: in the rest of the New Testament, other early witnesses are now available which were unknown to Sabatier, such as VL 64 or VL 89. The patristic information is impressive but the early editions from which the text is taken have now been superseded.

B) VETUS LATINA

The Vetus Latina edition is a full, modern presentation of the surviving evidence for the early Latin versions of the Bible. Its title characterizes it as the successor to Sabatier: *Vetus Latina: Die Reste der altlateinischen Bibel nach Petrus Sabatier neu gesammelt und herausgegeben von der Erzabtei Beuron* ('Vetus Latina: The Remains of the Old Latin Bible newly collected after Pierre Sabatier and edited by the Archabbey of Beuron'). The original plan was for the publication of the entire Bible and ancillary material in 27 volumes, although several have been subdivided. At the time of writing, the following instalments had been published for the New Testament:

Vol. 17. Mark (Haelewyck 2013–; in progress)
Vol. 19. John (Burton, Houghton, MacLachlan, and Parker 2011–; in progress)

Vol. 21. Romans (Eymann 1996; introduction only)
Vol. 22. 1 Corinthians (Fröhlich 1995–8; introduction only)
Vol. 24/1. Ephesians (Frede 1962–4)
Vol. 24/2. Philippians and Colossians (Frede 1966–71)
Vol. 25/1. Thessalonians, Timothy (Frede 1975–82)
Vol. 25/2. Titus, Philemon, and Hebrews (Frede 1983–91)
Vol. 26/1. Catholic Epistles (Thiele 1956–69)
Vol. 26/2. Revelation (Gryson 2000–3)

The publication is overseen by the Vetus Latina-Institut, based at the Archabbey of Beuron in South Germany. The plan to create a 'new Sabatier' in the early twentieth century was initiated by Joseph Denk, a parish priest in Freising. Following the methods of the newly-founded *Thesaurus Linguae Latinae*, he compiled a set of around 400,000 index cards, each with Old Latin evidence for a single verse from manuscripts or quotations in Christian authors.[2] On his death in 1927, these were housed in the Archabbey of Beuron where, in 1945, the Vetus Latina-Institut was founded by Bonifatius Fischer. The index cards were augmented and revised as new editions of manuscripts and patristic writings were published, and formed the basis for each of the early editions of biblical books in the Vetus Latina series: the editor would take all the cards for a particular verse, ensure that they were up to date, discard any which were irrelevant and, having prepared the other parts of the edition, transcribe each card into an apparatus. Once the volume was published, the cards were no longer required and were normally destroyed, although the files were kept open for updates from subsequent publications. In 1999, the remaining collection was photographed and, from 2002, made available online by subscription as the *Vetus Latina Database*.[3] Although much of the initial work was centred on Beuron, in recent years editors and teams based elsewhere have taken responsibility for individual volumes. The most significant contributions have been made by the first three directors of the Institute: Bonifatius Fischer (1945–73), Hermann Josef Frede (1973–1998), and Roger Gryson (1998–2013), as well as Walter Thiele who served as acting director in the 1970s. The Institut publishes annual progress reports (Vetus Latina *Arbeitsbericht*) featuring contributions from all current editors, which may include items of broader interest.

Before describing the format of the Vetus Latina editions, the two key works of reference which make up the first volume of the edition should be introduced. These are the official lists of Old Latin manuscripts (known as the *Register*) and patristic writings with sigla and editions (known as the *Repertorium*). The first

---

[2] For bibliography on Denk, including his own articles, see Gryson 2007:16 and Frede 1972:477.

[3] <www.brepolis.net>. In 2006, Brepols Publishers announced their intention to capture the text of citations from published editions in order to replace the missing cards (Vetus Latina *Arbeitsbericht* 2006:37), but this project appears to have been abandoned.

edition was published by Fischer in 1949 (*Verzeichnis der Sigel für Handschriften und Kirchenschriftsteller*), but this has subsequently been expanded and updated by both Frede and Gryson. The current editions are:

Vol. 1/1. *Repertorium.* (fifth edition: Gryson 2007)[4]
Vol. 1/2. *Register.* (Gryson 1999; Gryson 2004)

The *Register* lists all manuscripts identified as containing evidence for the Old Latin biblical text, assigning each a Vetus Latina number (as used in the present volume). Each part of the Bible is allocated a series of numbers: 1–49 for the Gospels; 50–74 for Acts, the Catholic Epistles and Revelation; 75–89 for the Pauline Epistles; 100–218 for Old Testament books and Apocrypha. The entire second volume (Gryson 2004) is taken up with manuscripts of the Psalter (300–485): because the Roman and Gallican Psalters co-existed for centuries alongside Jerome's Vulgate version, the tradition is particularly extensive. There are two further groups: 91–96 comprise Spanish Bibles with Old Latin glosses in the margin; 250–275 list manuscripts with the biblical canticles (also known as the Book of Odes). The only New Testament canticles are the *Magnificat* (Luke 1:46–55), *Benedictus* (Luke 1:68–79) and *Nunc Dimittis* (Luke 2:29–32), but several of these liturgical manuscripts include lections from other biblical books with Old Latin features. Some Psalters also have liturgical sentences or passages from New Testament books, most notably VL 411, 414, and 415.

Much of the information from the *Register* is reproduced in the Catalogue of Latin New Testament Manuscripts in the present volume. In the *Register*, each entry has up to six sections: H (*Handschrift*) gives information about the codicology and history; I (*Inhalt*) summarizes the contents; E (*Edition*) lists editions of the witness; Z (*zitiert in*) details biblical editions in which the witness is cited; T (*Text*) offers a brief summary of the textual characteristics of the manuscript; L (*Literatur*) is a selected bibliography. The entries are written in German or French. At the end of the second volume (Gryson 2004), there is a list of updates to the first volume and an index of manuscripts arranged by library.

Although the *Register* is the official list of manuscripts and provides the system of reference which should be universally adopted, it has a number of peculiarities. First, manuscripts are usually listed in respect of the first biblical section with Old Latin material (in the order given above). Thus VL 7, the second volume of a complete Bible with an Old Latin text of Matthew and four Old Testament books, is listed in the Gospels section, while VL 61, a complete New Testament, is thoroughly Old Latin in the Pauline Epistles but also has some Old Latin readings in Acts and Revelation and so is numbered among

---

[4] Although the title page of Gryson 2007 is in French (*Répertoire*), in the preface he introduces the Latin form *Repertorium*, which is employed in the *Vetus Latina Database*.

the Acts manuscripts. An exception is VL 109, listed among the manuscripts of the Octateuch because of its Old Latin version of Ruth even though it also has an Old Latin text in Hebrews (compare also VL 135). Some of the lectionaries with Old Latin material appear in the Acts series (VL 56, 68–73), while other closely related manuscripts are in the Canticles section (e.g. VL 262, 271). The same manuscript which has a marginal addition assigned the number VL 49 is also identified as VL 183. A second convention which can be confusing is that manuscripts included in the *Register* may be cited under another *siglum* in books where they are not deemed to be Old Latin. So, in the shorter Pauline Epistles, VL 7 is cited as G, VL 91 is cited as Λ^L, VL 109 is cited as X and most lectionaries are presented in the form τ^{56}, τ^{68}, τ^{69}, etc., even though the Luxeuil lectionary (only described as Old Latin in Canticles) is always given as VL 251.[5] Third, as a finite series of numbers is allocated to each biblical section, newly-identified Old Latin witnesses have to be given an alphabetical suffix (e.g. VL 9A, 11A, 19A). Fourth, not all manuscripts are Old Latin: none of the extant text in VL 23 differs from the Vulgate, and the marginal Eusebian apparatus points to its being a Vulgate source. The status of mixed-text manuscripts is unclear: VL 15 is included in the *Register* but its close relations, some of which are more distant from the Vulgate in particular passages, are not.[6] Finally, despite the *Register*'s title, not all the witnesses are biblical manuscripts. VL 37 and 38 are lemmata in manuscripts of Jerome's *Commentary on Matthew*, while VL 89 consists of the lemmata in the anonymous Budapest commentary on Paul; VL 42 refers to marginal glosses in a manuscript of Juvencus; VL 49 is a marginalium in a collection of Arian writings. For VL 39 and 40, the Old Latin reference is not to the main part of the gospel book but the titles in the initial canon tables. These would be better treated as patristic or ancillary sources rather than in the main series of gospel witnesses.

The *Repertorium* complements the *Register* by providing sigla for the other sources in which Old Latin material is preserved. These are not just early writers but also paratextual material in biblical manuscripts such as prologues (PROL) and *capitula* (KA), lections in missals and sacramentaries (M- and S-), episcopal councils (CO) and their canons (CAN), and similar collective works.[7] The system of abbreviations normally consists of two parts: the first, beginning with one or more capital letters, indicates the author or source; the second, usually lower case (apart from proper nouns, which begin with a single capital), gives the work or subdivision where needed. Thus TE ba is Tertullian's *De baptismo*, HIL Mt is Hilary of Poitiers' *Commentary on Matthew* and VICn-P Chr refers to the work *De Iesu Christo Deo et homine* by the fifth-century French poet Victorinus (not to be confused with Victorinus of

---

[5] These are noted in the Catalogue below; see also Appendices 1 and 2.

[6] See page 80 and Fischer 2010.

[7] On paratextual material, see further pages 196–204 below.

Poetovio, whose siglum is VICn, or Victor of Capua, indicated by VIC-C). The author's abbreviation is put in square brackets for works by a different author transmitted within that corpus (e.g. [AU] ep 72, which is actually Jerome's response to Augustine's *Epistula* 71 but included in the collection of Augustine's letters; among Jerome's writings the same document is listed as HI ep 102). There are numerous anonymous works (AN), some of which refer to individual manuscripts. Pseudonymously-attributed works are preceded by PS-. Translated works are listed by their Greek author where the translator is unknown (e.g. ORI for Origen, BAS for Basil), or under the works of the identified translator (e.g. RUF for Rufinus). At the end of the second volume there is an eight-page list of writers without their own siglum: many of these are correspondents preserved in the corpus of a more famous writer, authors of hymns (HYM), prayers (ORA), and saints' lives (A-SS), or those included in collections (COL-).

The entries in the *Repertorium* are given in alphabetical order of siglum, apart from pseudonymous works which are appended after an author's authentic corpus. If a work siglum begins with a number, the first letter is used for the sequence: AU 1 Jo therefore follows AU Jo. On the right of each entry, the number identifying the work in the *Clavis Patrum Latinorum* (Dekkers & Gaar 1995) is given in square brackets.[8] If the number is in italics, it refers to the *Clavis Patrum Graecorum*; preceded by *CA* or *CAV* this indicates the *Clavis Apocryphorum* of the Old or New Testaments. Dates and locations are given for each author, where known. The title of the work is followed by a short description, sometimes specifying the time and place of its composition. This is followed by bibliographic details of the best current edition; if an earlier edition was used for a Vetus Latina volume, its reference is also given. At the end of each entry appears the abbreviation for that work in the *Thesaurus Linguae Latinae* (*TLL*) and the *Clavis Patristica Pseudepigraphorum Medii Aevi* of Machielsen (Mach). Entries in parentheses indicate that, despite its appearance in one corpus, the work should be cited from another. Thus the first sermon of Faustus of Riez (FAU-R s 1) is better described as number 187 among those of Caesarius of Arles (CAE s 187).[9] An entire entry in square brackets means that although this author or work was cited in earlier Vetus Latina volumes, such as Pseudo-Gaius (PS-GAI) or Virgilius of Salzburg (VIR-S), it should no longer be included.

The *Repertorium* is extremely useful in providing the most economical yet transparent system of sigla for patristic writings. Furthermore, it not only

---

[8] The *Clavis* aims to provide a list of all patristic works, each assigned a number, with details of the most recent edition (as well as their location in Migne's *Patrologia Latina*) and bibliography on their Latinity, textual tradition, etc. This is a useful complement to the *Repertorium*, but it does not have a series of abbreviations or give details about the relationships of different writings. There are concordances to the numbers in the *Clavis Patrum Latinorum* and the *Clavis Patrum Graecorum* at the back of the second volume of the *Repertorium*.

[9] See page 64 above.

offers cross-references for works identified in more than one way but also gives information about texts re-used or cited in other works. So, for example, in the entry for the *Sermo de supremo iudicio* by Eligius of Noyon (ELI s), it is observed that this text was later incorporated in full in his *Life* (A-SS Eli) and uses seven sermons of Caesarius of Arles, Pelagius' commentary on 1 Timothy, and other sources including a piece once believed to be a translation of a work by Basil the Great (PS-BAS adm). As further research can alter attributions or change the date assigned to individual writings, each edition of the *Repertorium* may differ. The current version is available electronically as part of the *Vetus Latina Database*. Like the *Register*, the entries in the *Repertorium* are written in German and French; it also includes an introduction to the Vetus Latina edition in both languages.[10]

The first volume of the Vetus Latina edition to be published was Genesis, edited by Bonifatius Fischer in 1951–4. This set the template for subsequent biblical books. No manuscript survives of Genesis with an Old Latin affiliation throughout. The text therefore had to be reconstructed from quotations in early Christian authors, following the model of Sabatier. Unlike Sabatier, however, Fischer identified different stages in the pre-Vulgate history of the book. When the Latin text appeared to have been revised based on comparison with a Greek witness, this was described as a separate text-type. Each text-type was identified and localized based on the author in whose work it was first attested, although some achieved much wider diffusion. The sigla for text-types and sub-types used so far in the New Testament are as follows:[11]

X A very early form, probably an ad hoc translation made by the author directly from Greek (e.g. Tertullian and the Latin Irenaeus). In 2 Peter, it is used to indicate doubt that citations in Jerome and Paulinus derive from a Latin Bible.
Y The text of Victorinus of Poetovio for Revelation, also dependent on Greek.
K The earliest complete Latin translation, originating in Africa in the early third century (Cyprian, Pseudo-Cyprian).
C A revision of the early translation found in later African writers (e.g. Optatus, Quodvultdeus).
D A 'European' revision of the early translation, connected in the Pauline Epistles with the Greek–Latin bilingual tradition (e.g. Lucifer of Cagliari). In Revelation, this siglum instead designates Old Latin readings from VL 61.
R A form only found in Lucifer of Cagliari.
I A text circulating in Italy in the middle of the fourth century; often the form which was revised to produce the Vulgate (Ambrose, Rufinus, Jerome).
J A sub-type of I in contemporary Italian sources.
M A form only found in Ambrose of Milan; a sub-type of I.
F In James, the text of VL 66 (also Chromatius).

---

[10] Gryson 2007:15–43.

[11] In the Old Testament books, additional text-types are found such as E (a European text where D and I are in agreement); Petzer 1993a assigned VL 5 the provisional text-type B in Acts.

A A text only found in Augustine, sometimes with African readings, sometimes a sub-type of I.

S A form found in Spanish sources, sometimes with African connections (e.g. Tyconius). It also includes earlier readings present in Peregrinus' edition of the Vulgate.

T A text circulating in Africa, Spain, Gaul, and elsewhere in Europe around the same time as the Vulgate.

G Old Latin readings surviving in pre-Carolingian Gaul.

V The editorial text of the Stuttgart Vulgate.

Not all of these are found in each book, and some only appear occasionally. Their identification depends on the judgement of each editor, and is fraught with difficulties. Only fresh translations and the Vulgate revision are known to derive from thoroughgoing comparison with a Greek text; other variants described as text-types may be punctual alterations not extending through the whole of a biblical book. The definition of a text-type as based on a Greek source excludes intra-Latin variation such as stylistic improvement or linguistic updating, although in practice it can be difficult to distinguish the two.[12] In addition, given the description of most text-types as revisions, it is impossible to tell whether passages where no intervention was made were also compared with the Greek but not altered, or were simply passed over. Where more extensive Old Latin material is preserved in biblical manuscripts (such as the Gospels), the use of quotations to reconstruct texts is less necessary: although surviving scriptural codices may have been subject to contamination or partial adjustment, the same is true of the biblical quotations in Christian authors. Furthermore, unusual forms in individual authors may derive from the use of Greek writers, either in an existing Latin version or an ad hoc translation, and may not reflect a Latin biblical text in circulation.[13] The advantage of text-types, however, is that they align the Latin material based on points of contact with the Greek, enabling developments to be easily identified and avoiding the repetition in the apparatus of a Greek edition of multiple Latin sources which stem from a single text-form.

A typical page of the Vetus Latina edition, illustrated in Image 14, is divided into three sections. At the top comes the *schema* of the Old Latin text-types arranged in chronological order underneath a Greek text, which is usually that of Nestle-Aland.[14] Variants to each text-type are noted underneath. It is a principle of the edition that each variant only appears once in the *schema*, under the line of the text-type from which it is believed to derive, and also that, despite the smaller typeface, variants are to be accorded the same significance

---

[12] See further pages 143–50 below.   [13] See page 151.

[14] Variants in the Greek tradition are noted under the principal line of text. Mark is exceptional in giving a parallel text of three different Greek manuscripts, each representing a different form of text.

561   Ad Timotheum I   5,10-11

ἀγαθῷ ἐπηκολούθησεν. 11 νεωτέρας δὲ χήρας παραιτοῦ· ὅταν γὰρ καταστρηνιάσωσιν

```
                                ×                    ×
X         iuvenculas      viduas          quae postquam × in deliciis habuerunt
K         iuniores autem  ‖ praeteri ×    cum enim indeliciatae fuerint
                            evita                      deliciatae
D bonum subsecuta est  adulescentiores ‖  ‖ devita ×   ‖   ‖ in deliciis egerint
I    ‖    ‖    ‖        iuniores  ‖  ‖     ‖  ×      ‖  ‖  ‖   ‖   ‖
                        iuveniores                quae
V    ‖    ‖    ‖        adulescentiores ‖  ‖    ‖  ×    ‖    ‖ luxuriatae fuerint
     ×                                 ×                 cumque      autem
  ×     ×    ×
  num opus
```

11   *desunt* 76* 64 1Rμᴮᴬ 32 251 Pᴛ⁵⁶·⁶⁹·⁷⁰ 410 412 414 415 417, Wien ser. nov. 3750

× PS-AU spe 141 (Var): — αγαθω 2401
persecuta est ? HI Za   fuerit subsecuta ? AM: *vide supra*

11   11 **X TE, K CY**
iuvenculas ? TE   iuniores 77† Γᴮ; CY; AMstᵗˣᵗ; cf AU mon; vg; THrᵗˣᵗ (Var)· ᶜᵒᵐ ¹/₂; PS-HI ep 12; SED-S; {RUF Cl ep; THrᶜᵒᵐ ¹/₂ (Var)}   iuveniores CY (Var); THrᵗˣᵗ· {ᶜᵒᵐ ¹/₂}   adulescentiores 75 77 78 89 61 (adolisc.) 86 V(adhul. Φᵀ; adol. HENᶜᴹZᶠQΔᴴθᵂ²ᵩᴱ²σᴴ Ωᵂ; adolisc. Zᴹ²ᴴ²Φᴮᴳⱽ; adulisc. A*K*S(-ciores) LVY (-ciores) Zᴹ*ᴴ*ᴸᶜ*θⱽ²Φᴱ*σᵂᴿ); CY (Var); AMstᶜᵒᵐ; cf KA A; AM; HI; PEL > CAr; THrᵗˣᵗ (Var); PS-AU spe; FU; [CAE]; cf FEol; PS-HIL-A   adulescentes ? cf KA A (Var); {cf HI ep 123,14ᶜᵒᵐ}   {adulescentulas ? cf HI ep 79; 123,5; cf 123,14ᶜᵒᵐ (Var); RUF Gr; AU Ps > CAE}: cf 1 Tm 5,14; Tt 2,4
× K*Zᴸ*; *in initio*: AM Abr (Var); HI ep 123,14; AU vg (Var); THrᶜᵒᵐ; [CAE]; PS-HIL-A: — δε 241 522 642 𝔐ᶜᵒᵈ
praeteri CY   evita CY (Var); AU vg; cf FUᶜᵒᵐ; CAr cpl   devita 75 77 78 89 61(div.) 86 V(devi•ta S; d *in ras.* ? H); CY (Var); AMst; cf AM vid; Abr; HI; PEL > CAr 1 Tm; AU vg (Var); THr; PS-AU spe; FUᵗˣᵗ; [CAE]; PS-HI ep 12; PS-HIL-A   (in viduis iunioribus . . .)

cave ? cf AU mon   quae (. . .) postquam ? TE   quae cum ? AM Jb; AST; HI ep 123; AN Mt h
cumque Zᴹ*ᴴ*
× 61 Zᴹ*ᴴ*; TE; AM Jb; AST; HI ep 22; 54; 79; 123; Is; Ez; AN Mt h   autem KΦᶻ; CY (Var): < *supra*
in deliciis habuerunt christum ? TE   indeliciatae fuerint in christo CY   deliciatae fuerint in christo CY (Var); cf HIL?   ∼ in christo deliciatae fuerint ? cf PAU-N   delicatae fuerint in christo CY (Var); cf HIL (Var)?   in deliciis egerint in christo 75 89(diliciis); CY (Var); AMstᶜᵒᵐ; AU; PS-AU spe   in christo deliciis vitam egerint ? cf AMstᶜᵒᵐ   in deliciis fuerint in christo CY (Var)   luxuriatae fuerint in christo 77(luxoriate) 78 61(luxuriatae) 86 V(luxuriati Δᴸ; eri *in ras. et* nt *supra lin.* L); cf AM; HI *exc* ep 123; PEL > CAr; THr; FU; [CAE]; IS; PS-HI ep 12   ∼ in christo luxuriatae fuerint ? AST   luxuriatae fuerint adversus christum ? cf MUT   luxuriatae fuerint × × ? cf AM Jb; AN stat (Var)   lascivierint in christo ? HI ep 123ᵗˣᵗ   lasciviatae fuerint in christo ? HI ep 123ᵗˣᵗ (Var)   fornicatae sint in iniuriam christi ? cf HI ep 123ᶜᵒᵐ   deluserint christum ? AN Mt h   per luxuriam abiecerint christum ? cf PS-IGN

educavit (-bit D; edocavit LΣ) si hospitalis fuit si sanctorum pedes lavit si adflictis abundanter praebuit si. . .(= I) . . . est. didicisti catalogum virtutum tuarum   123,3,2 (74,17): /quae liberos (-ris Ψ) educavit (edoc. KDΨ; × × × A*), quae in bonis operibus habuit testimonium, quae tribulantibus (-atis A²B) de sua substantiola ministravit (subm. AΠ)/5   Is h 6,3 (273,9): /si sanctorum inquit pedes lavit (-vant B). si autem vis apertius audire quomodo vidua lavat pedes sanctorum/Tt 2,3. 4/lavantes sordes pedum iuvencularum (cf Tt 2,4). et istae viduae dignae sunt ecclesiastico honore, quaecumque sanctorum pedes lavant sermone spiritalis doctrinae, sanctorum vero non masculorum/2,12   Za 2 (809,109): /in bonis operibus habens testimonium, si educavit liberos, si recepit hospitio, si sanctorum pedes lavit, si in tribulationibus positis ministravit, si omne opus bonum persecuta est (< Didymus: επι εργοις καλοις μαρτυρουμενη, ει ετεκνοφρονησεν, ει εξενοδοχησεν, ει αγιων ποδας ενιψεν, ει θλιβομενοις επηρκεσεν, ει παντι εργω καλω επηκολουθησεν) PS-HIL ap 11 (84,22): /discat filios educare pie/2,9 (cf 1 Tm 5,4; 2,15)   IS off 2,19,3 (808B): /si fuerit in operibus . . . (= V). . .habens. utique sicut Tabitha (cf Act 9,36). si filios educavit. subauditur deo. si hospitio suscepit si . . . (= V). . .subministravit. hoc est aegrotis vel in carcere positis (cf Mt 25,36). si omne. . .(= V). . .est. breviter uni-

versa concludens ut in omnibus sint exempla vivendi (cf 1 Tm 4,12) (< PEL 1 Tm)   MAX s Mu 67,2 (281,36): Rm 10,15/hos pedes lavari praecepit dominus (cf Jo 13, 14), sicut apostolus ait de vidua: si sanctorum pedes lavit PEL Phlm 7 (537,13): Phlm 7/quos hospitio recipiens refecisti/Phlm 8   1 Tm 5,10 (494,18): /in operibus bonis. si ex tempore viduitatis suae ista omnia custodivit. testimonium habens. sicut Tabitha (cf Act 9,36). si filios educavit (edoc. VE*RG; edocuit SMN) subauditur deo. si hospitio recepit (-cipit ERMG) si sanctorum pedes lavit (lavavit G). . .cui non sufficiat hospitio recipere (susc. H₁) sed etiam hospitum pedes manu propria lavare. si tribulationem patientibus subministravit. hoc est in carcere positis vel aegrotis (cf Mt 25,36). si omne. . .(= V). . .est. breviter universa conclusit/   PEL:PS-AU vit 15 (1046): /in operibus. . .(= V). . .educavit, quod subintellegitur deo, si hospitio. . .(= V). . .est/5 . . .ut aut filios deo et non saeculo educent, aut hospitio recipiant advenam, aut sanctorum pedes. . .lavent   RUF Gr 5,6,1 (173,11): quis nudum operuit et peregrinum introduxit in domum suam? quis sanctorum pedes lavit? quis tribulantibus subministravit (ει επτωχοτροφησατε, ει εξενοδοχησατε, ει αγιων ποδας ενιψατε)   Rm 10,20 (1280A): laborant cum docent adolescentulas sobrias esse, diligere viros (cf Tt 2,4), filios enutrire/Tt 2,5; 1 Tm 5,4/hospitio recipere, sanctorum

Image 14 The *Vetus Latina* Edition (VL 25/1, ed. H.J. Frede, page 561), showing the beginning of 1 Timothy 5:11. © Verlag Herder, 1980.

as readings in the principal line.[15] The continuity between different Latin forms is apparent in the use of quotation marks (" or »), indicating the persistence of the main word in the text-type above. Text-types may begin or end in the middle of a verse, according to whether or not the evidence is extant. The symbol × indicates that a word present at that point elsewhere in the tradition is absent. Letters in italics indicates that the form has been reconstructed (for example, from a quotation in which it appears in a different grammatical form). A line of sigla in small type under the schema at the beginning of each verse gives details of witnesses not present in that verse (*desunt*).

The middle section is the *critical apparatus*, with information about the attestation of each reading. When new text-types are introduced, details of the source are provided: in Image 14 we thus learn that Tertullian lies behind text-type X and Cyprian behind type K. Again, the readings appear in chronological order and are followed by the sigla of the manuscripts and Christian authors in which they are found. Comparative material is supplied from other languages, such as Greek (sometimes designated by the siglum 𝕲), Syriac (𝕾), Gothic (𝔚) and Coptic (𝔅 and 𝕮). Dependencies between different sources are noted by the symbols < (derives from) and > (source for). If a question mark follows the reading (as in the first word of 1 Timothy 5:11, *iuvenculas?*), it indicates doubt as to whether the form was ever found in a Latin biblical manuscript; a question mark following a siglum expresses uncertainty whether the witness genuinely attests that reading. If a witness supports more than one reading, the number of occasions is expressed as a fraction, e.g. $^2/_4$ for two of four instances.

The bottom third of the page is the *witness apparatus* in which the full text is given of each of the Latin sources, beginning with the manuscripts (in numerical order) and followed by the patristic material (in alphabetical order of siglum). In order to save space, if a witness is identical with a text-type for the whole verse, the biblical text is replaced by the letter of the text-type (as in the case of the readings from Isidore in Image 14). Omitted material not relevant to the biblical text is indicated by . . . or { . . . }. Other symbols used in the witness apparatus include / at the beginning or end of a text to indicate that it is immediately preceded or followed by the neighbouring verse. If the verse is not neighbouring, this is indicated by a number or biblical reference. Thus '15/' indicates that the text of this verse is preceded by that of verse 15 of the same chapter. In biblical manuscripts, however, / indicates a line break. Variants in the textual tradition of a patristic work are also included when they may be of relevance to the biblical text; these are generally marked as (Var),

---

[15] In Image 14, the first word of 1 Timothy 5:11 is repeated for text-type **I** (*iuniores*) because of the intervention of a different reading in text-type **D** (*adulescentiores*); the same is true for text-type **V**.

although in some cases where variants derive from a different textual form the manuscript siglum is provided, e.g. CY (A) or PEL (B).

The three parts of the page are therefore interrelated, with the editorial reconstruction in the *schema*, the exact attestation of each unit in the *critical apparatus*, and the whole verse in context in the *witness apparatus*. This means that users can see a reading in the *schema* as part of, or a variant to, a text-type, identify all the manuscripts or authors in which it is found through the *critical apparatus*, and check its original context and exact form in the *witness apparatus*. Although most of the New Testament books follow the same pattern, each has its own peculiarities, explained in the introduction. The most divergent presentation is that adopted in the edition of John, where the *schema* presents the exact text of each manuscript rather than text-types, and the *critical apparatus* and *witness apparatus* are restricted to patristic quotations and other secondary material.[16]

The introduction to each of the Vetus Latina volumes includes a full description of each of the manuscripts used, an account of the constitution of the text-types for each book, and details of the relation of the Latin version to other traditions. The text of some shorter manuscripts is occasionally transcribed in full, and the introduction may include an edition of the paratextual material.[17] In the case of Mark, lengthy lists of significant readings are provided for the main manuscripts. At the end of most volumes are lists of corrections or additions, as well as an index of manuscripts and patristic sources.

The Vetus Latina edition is complemented by the series *Aus der Geschichte der lateinischen Bibel* (AGLB; 'From the History of the Latin Bible'). This features monographs on related topics as well as editions of key witnesses, including VL 86 (Frede 1964) and VL 89 (Frede 1974), Sedulius Scottus' commentaries on Matthew (Löfstedt 1989, 1991) and Paul (Frede & Stanjek 1996, 1997), and Rufinus' translation of Origen's commentary on Romans (Hammond Bammel 1990, 1997, 1998). Other material pertinent to the New Testament includes studies of the Latin vocabulary of the Johannine epistles (Thiele 1958), the Latin text of 1 Peter (Thiele 1965), the Prologues to the Gospels (Regul 1969), Hebrews and the Pauline corpus (Schlossnikel 1991), and the Latin gospel harmony tradition (Schmid 2005). There are also two volumes of Bonifatius Fischer's collected papers with new pagination and updated bibliography (Fischer 1985 and 1986), studies of Origen and Rufinus (Hammond Bammel 1996), and a *Festschrift* (Gryson 1993).

The four-volume collation of Latin gospel manuscripts in this series by Bonifatius Fischer (1988–1991) represents one of the earliest sustained uses of computers in New Testament textual research. Fischer first produced a list of all surviving Latin gospel manuscripts copied in the first millennium, totalling almost 500 witnesses. These were each given a two-letter siglum: a capital

---

[16] For an explanation of the layout of John, see Houghton 2013.
[17] See pages 137–8 below.

letter representing a general grouping often based on script (such as N for Northumbria, H for Insular manuscripts, W for Spanish lectionaries, and X for Old Latin) and a lower-case letter to identify individual manuscripts. Thus Na is Codex Amiatinus, Hq is the Book of Kells, and Xk is Codex Bobiensis; the editorial text of the Stuttgart Vulgate is given the siglum Xz.[18] Four lengthy passages (*Abschnitte*) were selected from each gospel as follows:

11: Mt 2:19–4:17	12: Mt 8:2–9:8	13: Mt 16:9–17:17	14: Mt 26:39–58; 27:29–46
21: Mc 2:12–3:21	22: Mc 7:32–8:35	23: Mc 10:17–52	24: Mc 14:22–62
31: Lc 6:17–49	32: Lc 8:12–43	33: Lc 10:40–11:32	34: Lc 23:35–44; 24:8–13, 24–49
41: Io 2:18–3:31	42: Io 7:28–8:16	43: Io 12:17–13:6	44: Io 20:1–21:4

The manuscripts were then transcribed and collated. Each variant reading was identified by a five-digit number with a letter offering a provisional description of the source. For example, 21265x refers to passage 21, variant 265, reading x, the form *quanta* attested in five Old Latin manuscripts at Mark 3:8 rather than the Vulgate *quae*. Differences in word order are treated separately in addition to other types of variation; nonsense orthographical variants and lacunae tend to be grouped under a normalized form. The published totals cover 5,953 variant units, although not all manuscripts are present in each: sources extant in fewer than 50 units were discarded, giving a total of 462 witnesses. Fischer's aim was to produce a 'three-dimensional' analysis of each manuscript, showing how closely each was related to all the others. This would assist in identifying textual groups in addition to exemplars and copies. Unfortunately, he died before this could be completed: a posthumous publication provides an analysis of manuscripts related to Codex Aureus (VL 15) as well as the overall figures of agreement for the entire sample.[19] The percentages of agreement in each test-passage can also be reconstructed from unpublished files, which help to identify block mixture. The collations demonstrate that there is a remarkable stability in the Vulgate text of the Gospels up to the year 1000, with 294 of the 462 witnesses agreeing 95 per cent or more with the Stuttgart Vulgate, and a further 99 in the bracket of 90–95 per cent.

C) JÜLICHER, *ITALA*

The four volumes of *Itala: Das Neue Testament in altlateinischer Überlieferung* ('Itala: The New Testament in Old Latin Tradition') begun by Adolf Jülicher

---

[18] The full list is given in Fischer 1987 and Fischer 2010 and reproduced in each volume of collation. These sigla are included in the Catalogue of Manuscripts below, as is an indication of the percentage agreement with the Stuttgart Vulgate over all test passages.

[19] Fischer 2010.

are an edition of the principal Old Latin gospel manuscripts. Despite draw-backs in their conception, they provide useful information in the absence of Vetus Latina editions of the Gospels. The first instalment, Matthew, appeared in 1938, the year of Jülicher's death; this and Mark (1940) were seen through the press by Walter Matzkow, who died in the Second World War. Luke (1954) and John (1963) were published by Kurt Aland, who also oversaw second, improved editions of the Synoptic Gospels (Mark in 1970, Matthew in 1972, Luke in 1976). This multiple editorship has sometimes led to the description of the volumes as Jülicher-Matzkow-Aland.

Each volume contains information from between sixteen and eighteen Old Latin witnesses, all listed in the Vetus Latina *Register*, although Jülicher employs the earlier, alphabetical sigla developed by Lachmann. Adopting Augustine's terminology (see page 15), Jülicher divides the tradition into two lines, *Itala* and *Afra*, which are displayed in parallel for each verse. The witnesses present in each line are listed in the top margin of the page. The *Afra*, on the lower line, consists of a transcription of VL 1 and VL 2, which only overlap for six verses of Mark and portions of Matthew 13–15; where neither of these is extant, the line is absent. The *Itala* consists of a text reconstructed from all the other witnesses, deemed to be of European origin, sometimes with several lines of variant readings below in smaller type. This bifurcation of the tradition is problematic, not allowing for smaller subgroups or changes in affiliation within manuscripts (e.g. the African element in VL 6). The identification of VL 2 as an African witness is contested, while the indiscriminate use of some mixed texts, especially VL 11 and 15, means that certain readings only found in the Vulgate are presented as if they were Old Latin. Most perplexing of all is Jülicher's failure to provide his criteria for reconstructing the principal line of the *Itala*.[20] Generally speaking, he follows VL 4, sometimes against all other witnesses, but on other occasions different manuscripts and combinations are preferred.

In the initial volumes, the text of the manuscripts was taken from existing printed editions. For the second edition, some corrections were introduced from photographs and other collations. The siglum *vg* denotes the editorial text of the Oxford Vulgate, while (*vg*) indicates a reading present in at least one of Jülicher's *Itala* manuscripts which is also found in a minimum of three Vulgate manuscripts.[21] The other editorial signs are relatively straightforward. Square brackets ([...]) are used to indicate text which has been reconstructed or was only visible to earlier editors; in the case of VL 3, double square brackets (⟦ ... ⟧) enclose portions of text which were legible to the seventeenth-century

---

[20] This even mystified his successors, as Aland explains in the introduction to the first edition of Luke (see Fischer 1972:35 [1986:202]).

[21] As the Oxford Vulgate includes a number of mixed texts, these readings cannot straight-forwardly be identified as Vulgate or Old Latin.

editors but not those of the early twentieth century. As in the Vetus Latina edition, inverted commas (") in the *Afra* line indicate that the same word is present as in the principal *Itala* line, regardless of any intervening variants. In the lines of variant readings, however, the same symbol indicates a repetition of the variant immediately above, not the reading of the main text.

D) VETUS LATINA HISPANA

Around the same time as the Vetus Latina-Institut was founded, the Spanish scholar Teófilo Ayuso Marazuela inaugurated the Vetus Latina Hispana. Given the presence of Old Latin readings in several Spanish biblical manuscripts and the importance of the marginal glosses in the certain codices, especially in the books of the Old Testament, this project aimed to gather the Spanish evidence for the early Latin Bible.[22] The first volume (Ayuso Marazuela 1953) offers a full survey of the state of the question in Latin biblical scholarship. It provides a list of Old Latin manuscripts of both Old and New Testament books, almost one thousand Christian authors, and an extensive bibliography not restricted to Spanish sources. The only editions to be published were the Psalter and the Octateuch: the latter appeared in 1967, five years after Marazuela's death. Furthermore, Marazuela invented his own numbering system for the 204 codices he used (166 of which were held in Spanish libraries), also used in his articles. Although a Spanish text-type is reconstructed in some of the Vetus Latina editions of New Testament writings, the late date of most manuscripts and the piecemeal nature of the data means that it is difficult to develop a coherent picture of a Spanish tradition in the absence of the wider Old Latin context. More recent Spanish scholarship has continued to focus on glosses in the Old Testament in a series entitled *Las glosas marginales de Vetus Latina*.

E) STUTTGART VULGATE

The principal hand edition and reference text of the Vulgate is the Stuttgart Vulgate, first prepared by Robert Weber and a committee of four other scholars for the German Bible Society in 1969. The fourth edition was revised by Roger Gryson, hence the alternative description as Weber-Gryson. The current edition is the fifth (2007). The text was used as the basis for a five-volume concordance

---

[22] See pages 96–9.

prepared by computer (Fischer 1977), and its text has remained unchanged since the third edition (1983). For the Old Testament, Weber based his text on the Roman Vulgate (completed by the time of the fourth edition in 1994), while the New Testament took as its source the Oxford Vulgate (see below). The Introduction, detailing the history of the edition, is given in four languages including English. The order of the books follows that of the Clementine Vulgate, matching most modern editions. This is also the case for the verse numbering, although there are some differences between the Stuttgart Vulgate and the standard Greek texts. Most only affect the division of pairs of verses, although the splitting of John 6:51 into two means that all subsequent verses in the chapter differ and there are seventy-two rather than seventy-one in total. The edition also provides a text of the *Nouum opus* and *Primum quaeritur* prefaces and the Eusebian canon tables.

The text is set out in sense-lines, *per cola et commata*, as in the Oxford Vulgate, with no other punctuation. Capitals are used for *nomina sacra*, proper names and the beginning of sections in the Gospels. Parallel passages are noted in the margin: the numbers in bold refer to groups of verses which are similar to material appearing elsewhere. The Eusebian apparatus is included at the relevant point in the text in Roman numerals. The editorial text is relatively similar to the Oxford Vulgate: in the whole of John's Gospel there are only ninety-five differences, of which eight are differences in word division (such as *priusquam* rather than *prius quam*) and twenty-one are orthographic alternatives, the Stuttgart Vulgate preferring -*np*- for -*mp*- and -*f*- rather than -*ph*-.[23] The figures are similar for other books: over the entire New Testament, there are 772 differences between the first edition of the Stuttgart Vulgate and the Oxford Vulgate.[24] Even though the editors' goal was to produce a hand edition of the Latin Vulgate in general, the editorial text is a reconstruction of the earliest form, i.e. Jerome's revised text of the Gospels and the rest of the New Testament from the early fifth century. It is not a guide to the mediaeval Vulgate, although later manuscripts and early printed editions are occasionally included in the apparatus.

The witnesses in the edition are listed on pages xlvi–xlvii of the introduction and on a separate green card; they are also described in the Catalogue of Manuscripts in the present volume. Certain sigla refer to different manuscripts in different writings, such as R (a Vatican manuscript in the Pauline Epistles but a Verona manuscript in the Catholic Epistles) and no fewer than four manuscripts designated as S. All the witnesses present for that page are listed in the margin of the critical apparatus: those in parentheses are only partially extant. They are divided into three categories. The top line indicates the 'primary witnesses' which are reported in every variation unit in order of

---

[23] These minor differences are not listed in the critical apparatus of the Stuttgart Vulgate.
[24] Fischer 1972:50–1 [1986:221–2], where the data is also divided by book.

priority. These are SNAMZ in the Gospels, GFA in Acts, GAR in Paul, FGA in the Catholic Epistles, and FGAΛ in Revelation. Other manuscripts, listed in the middle line, are only cited in the apparatus when they support readings attested by members of the other two categories. Their text cannot, therefore, be reconstructed from the information in this edition. Among the 'secondary witnesses', the siglum Φ represents the agreement of up to five manuscripts of Alcuin's recension. The third line of witnesses consists of four editions, which are always cited when present even if they do not agree with any primary witness. The Clementine Vulgate of 1592 and the Oxford Vulgate are given the sigla ꞓ and ꝺ respectively. Variations in the Vulgate text-type as reconstructed in the Beuron Old Latin edition are given as ꞗ, while White's *editio minor* of the Oxford Vulgate is cited as ꞷ in the four epistles where it differs from ꝺ (1 Corinthians to Ephesians).[25] In the apparatus, a full stop (.) is used after a siglum to indicate that no other Vulgate manuscript is listed with that reading in the major editions: forms unique to the Clementine Vulgate are thus all indicated by 'ꞓ'. The siglum 𝕲 is used to refer to the Greek text.

Five apocryphal or pseudepigraphical books are included in the appendix at the end of the edition, the last of which is the Epistle to the Laodiceans (p. 1976). This is edited from seven manuscripts, whose sigla do not necessarily correspond to those in the canonical New Testament, and Harnack's edition (ꜧ).

F) OXFORD VULGATE

The Oxford Vulgate, *Nouum Testamentum Domini nostri Iesu Christi latine secundum editionem sancti Hieronymi* ('The New Testament of our Lord Jesus Christ in Latin according to the edition of St Jerome'), is also known as Wordsworth-White after its two principal editors, John Wordsworth, bishop of Salisbury from 1885–1911, and Henry Julian White, dean of Christ Church, Oxford, from 1920–34. It is the fullest edition of the Vulgate New Testament, with a substantial critical apparatus recording the readings of over fifty Vulgate manuscripts (indicated by Roman and Greek capital letters), numerous Old Latin witnesses (in lower-case italics), Christian authors—especially outside the Gospels—and several editions. In addition, frequent reference is made to Greek manuscripts: these are also listed using the traditional capital letters, so need to be carefully distinguished from the Latin witnesses. As in the Stuttgart Vulgate, the same sigla can designate different witnesses in the different sections of the

---

[25] See page 130.

New Testament, most notably O which refers to five separate manuscripts, one in each section![26] Some witnesses have the same sigla as in the Stuttgart Vulgate, but others do not; see further Appendix 1 of the present volume. Across the whole New Testament, the siglum *vg* is used for the agreement of four earlier editions: Stephanus 1538 (ℭ), Hentenius 1547 (ℌ), the Sixtine Vulgate of 1590 (ℭ), and the Clementine Vulgate of 1592 (ℭ). Other Latin editors cited include Erasmus' sixth edition of 1705 (*Erasm.*), Tischendorf 1864 (*Tisch.*), and Bentley (*Bentl.*, from the manuscript of his proposed edition, Cambridge, Trinity College, B.17.5).

The edition was published in fascicles, which are normally bound into three volumes as follows:

> *Pars prior: Quattuor euangelia.* ed. J. Wordsworth and H.J. White, Oxford 1889–98.
>
> *Pars secunda: Epistulae Paulinae.* ed. J. Wordsworth and H.J. White, with A. Ramsbotham, H.F.D. Sparks and C. Jenkins, Oxford 1913–41.
>
> *Pars tertia: Actus Apostolorum, Epistulae Canonicae, Apocalypsis Iohannis.* ed. J. Wordsworth and H.J. White, with H.F.D. Sparks and A.W. Adams, Oxford 1905–54.

Of the books published after White's death, Adams edited the Johannine Epistles and Sparks edited the other Catholic Epistles, Hebrews, and Revelation. In 1911, White produced a hand edition of the whole New Testament (*Novum Testamentum Latine Secundum Editionem S. Hieronymi*), consisting of the books which had thus far been edited (the Gospels, Acts, and Romans) and a provisional text of the others. In the rest of the main edition the editorial text of the Epistles to the Corinthians, Galatians, and Ephesians differs slightly, but the other books are identical with the *editio minor*. This preservation of White's provisional text rather than the establishment of a new text based on the full spread of evidence has been criticized as one of the weaker points of the edition: there is a higher proportion of differences between the Oxford and Stuttgart Vulgates in these books.[27]

The selection of manuscripts includes all the major traditions, with Codex Amiatinus (A) being the principal witness. Most of the oldest and most important Vulgate manuscripts are featured, with the exception of St Gall 1395 (Vg^Se S) and the Book of Durrow (Vg^S D) in the Gospels. There are witnesses to the recensions of Alcuin (B outside the Gospels, K, V) and Theodulf (Θ, H), as well as the thirteenth-century Bible of William of Hales (W) which is included as a representative of the mediaeval tradition (with a nod to Wordsworth's bishopric). The editors divide the gospel manuscripts

---

[26] In the system of the present volume, these are identified as Vg^O O^e, Vg^O O^a, Vg^O O^p, Vg^O O^c, and Vg^O O^r.

[27] Fischer 1955, 1972:51–2 [1986:223]; Lo Bue 1955.

into a class of earlier, less interpolated witnesses (A Δ S Y and the first hand of H; O X; J M P; F EP; Z) and a number of regional texts (the Insular group D E L Q R; a Gallic group B BF G; the Spanish witnesses C T) along with I and U, which are unclassified. However, the manuscripts with Northumbrian connections (A Δ S Y U D E L Q R) go back to the same sixth-century Neapolitan gospel book used as a model at Wearmouth–Jarrow, while several of the other witnesses may also be connected with the same Italian tradition (F G M). In opposition to these stand the manuscripts related to Z, including O J X and B, as well as the texts of Alcuin, Theodulf, and the Carolingian witness I.[28] In the Gospels, a full transcription of Codex Brixianus (VL 10) is given underneath the editorially-reconstructed text, reproducing that of Bianchini's edition of 1740. The rationale for this was to provide an example of the form of Old Latin text ('*Itala*') which was used by Jerome as the basis of his revision, although recent scholarship suggests that other manuscripts, such as VL 4 or 8, would have been more appropriate.[29]

The manuscripts used for each New Testament writing are listed before its text, with full descriptions in the introduction to each volume. The text is printed *per cola et commata*, based on the sense-lines of Codex Amiatinus; the verse and chapter divisions are taken from Stephanus' edition and the canon numbers are based on Tischendorf. A few words are enclosed in square brackets ([. . .]), indicating that they are later glosses which have become embedded in the tradition; words between daggers († . . . †) are judged to be genuine but poorly-attested readings. The edition provides a considerable amount of paratextual material, including prefaces, the Eusebian canon tables, the text of Priscillian's canons to the Pauline Epistles, and several *capitula* lists. There are broader studies in the preface and appendix to the first volume, including surveys of Greek words translated in different ways in Latin tradition, the orthography of Codex Cavensis (Vg C), the Greek manuscripts used by Jerome, and lists of orthographic errors; the appendix also includes additional Gospel *capitula* lists and a list of errata. Much of the research underlying this edition was published in the Oxford *Old-Latin Biblical Texts* series (see page 136). Although the volumes of the Vetus Latina edition offer an even more thorough survey of the textual history of the Latin Bible, the Oxford Vulgate remains a magnificent achievement. Notwithstanding the superior editorial text of the Stuttgart Vulgate and its own dependence on some unreliable editions of manuscripts and Christian authors, the Oxford Vulgate continues to provide a rich treasury of readings and material not otherwise easily accessible.[30]

---

[28] See Fischer 1972:54–5 [1986:226–7].
[29] According to Fischer 1955 [1986:56] the use of VL 10 was prompted by F.J.A. Hort.
[30] For criticism of certain sources used for the Oxford Vulgate, see Fischer 1955 [1986:60–2].

G) THE CLEMENTINE VULGATE,
THE *NOVA VULGATA*, AND
ELECTRONIC VULGATES

The standard Bible of the Roman Catholic Church until 1979 was the Clementine Vulgate, prepared for Pope Clement VIII in 1592. Its roots go back to the Council of Trent in 1546, which had called for an accurate edition of the Vulgate to be authorized by the Pope. The first result of this was the Sixtine (or Sistine) Vulgate, produced in 1590 by Pope Sixtus V. Following the Pope's death later that year this was withdrawn on the grounds of the number of misprints, although it has been suggested that political motives lay behind this.[31] The Clementine Vulgate retained the name of Sixtus on its title page (*Biblia Sacra Vulgatæ Editionis Sixti Quinti Pontificis Maximi iussu recognita atque edita*; 'The Holy Bible of the Common/Vulgate Edition identified and published by the order of Pope Sixtus V'), and is therefore sometimes known as the Sixto-Clementine Vulgate. Although the Sixtine Vulgate had introduced a new division of verses, the Clementine Vulgate restored the verse-division of Stephanus' 1551 edition. Both of these editions and the two forerunners on which they were based (Stephanus and Hentenius) are cited in the Oxford Vulgate; the Stuttgart Vulgate only gives the readings of the Clementine Vulgate.

At the beginning of the twentieth century, awareness of the inadequacies of the Clementine text increased. In 1906, Michael Hetzenauer produced a new edition of the Clementine Vulgate based on its three printings in 1592, 1593, and 1598 and incorporating officially-authorized corrections; that same year, Eberhard Nestle printed the Clementine version with an apparatus showing variants from the Sixtine Vulgate, the Oxford Vulgate, and some other Latin editions and manuscripts, with the title *Novum Testamentum Latine*. The next year, 1907, saw the inauguration of the Roman Vulgate project, undertaken by Benedictine monks in Rome. This resulted in a major critical edition of Jerome's Latin Old Testament, along with the apocryphal books, finally completed in 1995. The Clementine Vulgate is often a better guide to the text of the mediaeval Vulgate than critical editions of the earliest attainable text. The current standard reference edition is that of Colunga & Turrado 1946, a form of which is available online.[32] A bilingual edition of the New Testament in Greek and Latin by Augustinus Merk was first published in 1933 and subsequently revised in eight editions up to 1957. This reproduces the text of the Clementine Vulgate of 1592.

The Second Vatican Council, which had called for a revision of the Latin Psalter, also inspired a new version of the whole Bible. The intention behind

---

[31] See Metzger 1977:348; Reynolds & Wilson 1991:169. On the history of the Clementine Vulgate, see Höpfl 1913.

[32] See van Liere 2012:109. The electronic text is at <http://vulsearch.sourceforge.net/>.

this *Nova Vulgata*, also known as the *Neovulgata*, was to create a Latin version based on current critical texts of the Hebrew Bible and Greek New Testament, in order to provide a firmer ground for scholarly study.[33] The New Testament, published in 1971, was based on the first edition of the Stuttgart Vulgate; the whole Bible was issued in 1979 and promulgated as the official Latin text of the Roman Catholic Church in the papal encyclical *Scripturarum Thesaurus*.[34] A second edition followed in 1986, with an apparatus detailing changes from earlier editions of the Vulgate. The text may be found online at the official Vatican website: <http://www.vatican.va/archive/bible/nova_vulgata/documents/nova-vulgata_index_lt.html>. There are approximately 2,000 differences between the *Nova Vulgata* and the critical text of Jerome's revision of the Gospels in the Stuttgart Vulgate, most of which are very minor.[35] Following the appearance of the *Nova Vulgata*, Nestle's *Novum Testamentum Latine* was revised by Kurt and Barbara Aland: the Clementine text was replaced with the *Nova Vulgata* and an apparatus added showing differences from eleven other editions, including the Stuttgart, Oxford, Sixtine, and Clementine Vulgates; the first edition of 1984 was followed by a second edition in 1992. The *Nova Vulgata* is also the Latin text in the Alands' bilingual edition, *Novum Testamentum Graece et Latine*.

As electronic texts of the Vulgate are often unclear about their source, it has been observed that the orthography of Genesis 3:20 offers a helpful means of distinguishing the three principal versions.[36] The *Nova Vulgata* gives the proper noun as *Eva*, the Clementine Vulgate has *Heva*, and the Stuttgart Vulgate reads *Hava*. Unfortunately, the dependence of the *Nova Vulgata* on the Stuttgart Vulgate means that there is no single way of identifying all the different versions of the New Testament. The following characteristic readings, however, are found in the genealogy in the first chapter of Matthew (unique readings are highlighted):

Matt.	Clementine	Stuttgart	Oxford	*Nova Vulgata*	Other
1:3	Zaram	Zara	Zara	Zara	
1:3	Esron	Esrom	Esrom	Esrom	
1:5	Rahab	Rachab	Rachab	Rahab	Raab (Stephanus)
1:6	rex	rex	rex	om.	
1:7	Abiam	Abiam	Abia	Abiam	
1:7	Abias	Abia	Abia	Abia	
1:12	Salathiel	Salathihel	Salathiel	Salathiel	
1:14	Sadoc	Saddoc	Sadoc	Sadoc	

[33] See further Stramare 1987:149–75; Cimosa 2008, especially 12–13 and 62–8.
[34] The text of this, and of the introduction to the *Nova Vulgata*, is printed in Cimosa 2008:171–91; see also 89–93 on the history of the edition.
[35] Figure from Cimosa 2008:79.
[36] Sources Chrétiennes briefing, 'Les études bibliques sur Internet', 16 April 2010.

H) LATIN EVIDENCE IN GREEK EDITIONS

The early date and textual significance of the Latin translation mean that it is cited in most of the major editions of the Greek New Testament. The first instalment of the *Novum Testamentum Graecum Editio Critica Maior*, covering the Catholic Epistles (ECM 2013), reports the text-types reconstructed in Thiele's Vetus Latina edition. Versional evidence is cited towards the end of each variation unit: the bold L: denotes Latin, which is followed by the letters indicating each text-type. A double-headed arrow, ↔, indicates that the Latin could represent multiple Greek forms. Although the Latin witnesses are listed under Greek readings in the main volume of text, the original Latin text (with English and German translation) is sometimes provided in the versional apparatus in the volume of supplementary material (pp. 102–44): this also has a full listing of the meaning of each siglum (pp. 63–70). No Latin sources are listed in the patristic section (pp. 33–62). Subsequent volumes on Acts and John are proceeding hand in hand with work on the Old Latin evidence.

In the most recent edition of the Nestle-Aland *Novum Testamentum Graece* (NA28, 2012), the Latin evidence is described on pages 68*–69*, with a full listing of the manuscripts and their contents in the first appendix. Manuscript readings are based on Jülicher's *Itala* for the Gospels and the published Vetus Latina editions for the rest of the New Testament; in the absence of editions of Acts and Romans to Galatians, evidence has been taken straight from the manuscripts. The critical apparatus relies on a dichotomy between the Old Latin and Vulgate: 'latt' indicates the entire Latin tradition, 'lat' the Vulgate and part of the Old Latin tradition, 'it' most or all of the Old Latin manuscripts, and 'vg' the Vulgate editions. Individual manuscripts are referred to using the traditional alphabetical sigla (see NA28: 815–9 and Appendix 1 in the present volume). Of the seventy-six patristic sources listed on pages 80*–81*, thirty-four are Latin. Among these, 'Spec' is the testimonia collection *Speculum (Liber de diuinis scripturis)*.[37] It appears that the original source for many of the Christian writers listed in Nestle-Aland was Tischendorf's edition (see below), although all references have subsequently been updated and verified. A number of citations of Latin witnesses (especially editions of the Vulgate) in the apparatus of NA27 have been removed from NA28.

The United Bible Societies' *Greek New Testament* (UBS5, 2014) has a fuller presentation of the Latin, following a slightly different approach. Across the New Testament a total of sixty-three manuscripts are cited as Old Latin witnesses (although some are mixed texts), listed on pages 31*–33*. They are identified by the standard alphabetical sigla, superscript to 'it' (for *Itala*), and are always enumerated separately even when they correspond to the same

[37] See page 39.

text-type.[38] As with Nestle-Aland, references to the Vulgate ('vg') are confined to the principal editions. No fewer than sixty-one Latin Church Fathers are included, listed on pages 41*–43*. The nomenclature may seem inconsistent, but it follows a pattern: where geographical modifiers are part of the siglum used in the critical apparatus, they are hyphenated (e.g. Faustus-Milevis); where they are simply supplied in this list for identification they are subordinated (e.g. Faustus, of Riez).[39] Two of the sources are listed by title rather than author: Rebaptism (Pseudo-Cyprian *De Rebaptismate*) and Speculum (Pseudo-Augustine *Liber de diuinis scripturis*). In addition, two biblical manuscripts are actually the lemmata from Pauline commentaries: it[b] (VL 89) and it[o] (manuscript B of Pelagius).[40] In the critical apparatus, if the same verse is cited more than once in a different form, the number of quotations corresponding to each version is given as a fraction, e.g. Augustine[5/7]. This figure, however, offers no indication of the relative value of each reading based on the context of the citation.

Among the earlier editions of the Greek New Testament, Tischendorf's *Editio Octava Maior* (Tischendorf 1869–72) is of particular use for its citation of Latin evidence. When Latin manuscripts do not obviously correspond to a reading preserved in the Greek tradition, Tischendorf includes the Latin word in his apparatus. Quotations from Latin authors are also given in the original language. One downside, however, is that Tischendorf, like Sabatier, often abbreviates the reference for patristic writings to the volume and page of the edition he used, which can make it very difficult to track down the original quotation. In the second book of *Prolegomena* supplied by Ezra Abbott and Caspar René Gregory (volume 3.2 of the edition, published in 1894), pages 948–1108 contain an account of the Latin evidence in Latin. This includes a description of the Old Latin manuscripts, a description of Vulgate manuscripts to which Tischendorf also gave alphabetical sigla (e.g. 'am' for Codex Amiatinus), and a list of 2,228 Vulgate New Testament manuscripts. Although some of the holding institutions and classmarks have changed over the last 120 years, this list remains unrivalled in its scope.[41]

On the inclusion of Old Latin evidence in other printed editions of the Greek New Testament, see Elliott 1984. It is worth noting that Latin manuscripts and authors are extensively cited in the International Greek New Testament project's volumes of Luke (1984, 1987).

---

[38] See also Appendix 1.

[39] The lists of Latin evidence are identical between UBS4 and UBS5, except for a typographical error in the entry for 'Caesarius, of Arles'. In the case of Julian-Eclanum and Paulinus-Nola the geographical identifier is not necessary to differentiate the siglum.

[40] See pages 27 and 40.

[41] An electronic version is currently in preparation at the University of Birmingham.

I) INDIVIDUAL MANUSCRIPTS

In the past, much of the preparatory work for editions of the biblical text involved editions of individual manuscripts, and this is once more the case in the digital age. The increasing online availability of books from the nineteenth century and earlier means that access to this material is often very easy, although it must be remembered that earlier scholarship is often now dated (following the discovery of new manuscripts or other advances in knowledge) and, like its successors, is rarely flawless. More and more holding institutions are publishing full digitizations of their manuscripts, which enable the verification of queries against the original: the internet address for each manuscript known to be available in this way is included in the Catalogue of Manuscripts below. Editions and transcriptions of individual manuscripts are also listed in the Catalogue: the present section describes the major series of scholarly publications.

Giuseppe Bianchini, a contemporary of Sabatier, published one of the principal early editions of Old Latin manuscripts in 1749. This consists of a full transcription of VL 3 and 4 in two columns on facing pages: the lines, but not the columns, are those of the original manuscripts. In Matthew, Bianchini gives a transcription of VL 8 and VL 10 without lineation at the foot of the page: in the other gospels, which follow the Old Latin order, VL 8 is condensed to an apparatus of variant readings, along with non-Vulgate forms from VL 30 and Vg^{Oe} E, while VL 10 continues throughout. An appendix in a further volume provides the lineated text (in five columns) of two early Vulgate manuscripts, Codex Foroiuliensis (Vg^O J) and Codex Perusinus (Vg^{Oe} P). The main volumes, featuring VL 3, 4, 8, and 10, were reprinted in a similar format by Migne in PL 12.

Many of Tischendorf's transcriptions appear in the *Monumenta sacra inedita* series of his discoveries. Among the Latin witnesses are full editions of VL 2 (1847), VL 75 (1852), and VL 50 (1870). The creation of the Oxford Vulgate was preceded by the publication of transcriptions in the Oxford *Old-Latin Biblical Texts* series (OLBT), several edited by Wordsworth and White themselves. Seven volumes appeared between 1883 and 1923, comprising editions of VL 7 (Matthew only; Wordsworth 1883), VL 1, 16, 19, 20, and 21 (Wordsworth, Sanday, and White 1886), VL 13 and 25 (White 1888), VL 53 (White 1897), VL 8 and 55 (Buchanan 1907), VL 4 (Buchanan 1911a), and Irenaeus' New Testament text (Sanday, Turner et al. 1923). Although Hoskier's edition of VL 28 (Hoskier 1919) also claims to be part of a series *Old Latin Biblical Texts*, this is a one-off from a different publisher. Buchanan went on to publish four volumes of *Sacred Latin Texts* between 1912 and 1916, including editions of VL 65, Vg^{Op} O, and Vg^{Or} O in Paul and Revelation. This later work was unfortunately marred by Buchanan's over-active imagination, including the reconstruction of non-existent first-hand readings underneath what he perceived to be corrections.[42]

---

[42] See Sanders 1922 and Metzger 1977:311–12.

Collectanea Biblica Latina, inaugurated in Rome in 1912 in conjunction with the edition of the Roman Vulgate, comprises seventeen volumes with editions of Latin biblical manuscripts and, later, analytical studies. Those pertaining to the New Testament cover VL 11 (Vogels 1913), VL 3 (Gasquet 1914), VL 64 (De Bruyne 1921), and VL 251 (Salmon 1944, 1953). Volumes 10–15 are dedicated to the Psalter; the last volume, also on the Psalter, appeared in 1988. Between 1917 and 1957, the archabbey of Beuron published a series called *Texte und Arbeiten*. Its forty-eight instalments include Dold's editions of VL 18 (1923), VL 24 (1952), VL 32 (1936), VL 79 (1950), and VL 84 (1944). Following the establishment of the Vetus Latina-Institut in Beuron, this was succeeded by the series *Aus der Geschichte der lateinischen Bibel*, described above. Other German-language scholarship on the Latin Bible is found in the early volumes of the *Bonner Biblische Beiträge*. These include editions of VL 6 (Vogels 1953) and Ambrosiaster's text of the Pauline Epistles (Vogels 1957), as well as studies of the Latin text of the Pauline Epistles (Vogels 1955a, Zimmermann 1960, Nellessen 1965).

The use of digital tools to edit the New Testament, pioneered by the International Greek New Testament project (IGNTP) and the *Institut für neutestamentliche Textforschung* (INTF), means that complete transcriptions of biblical books, and sometimes whole manuscripts, are also being published online. Encoded in extensible markup language (XML) according to the standards of the Text Encoding Initiative, these electronic files are easy to search, manipulate, and update, and are made available under a Creative Commons licence for scholarly re-use.[43] A digital edition of the Vetus Latina codices of John, featuring full transcriptions of each manuscript was published online in 2007 at <www.iohannes.com/vetuslatina>. The same is planned for the principal Pauline Epistles at <www.epistulae.org>. A complete electronic edition of Codex Bezae, with a transcription based on new high-resolution images, was released by Cambridge University Library in 2012: details of this are given in the entry for VL 5 in the Catalogue below (page 212). Other bilingual manuscripts, as well as many other Greek witnesses, can be found online in the *New Testament Virtual Manuscript Room*, <http://ntvmr.uni-muenster.de/>.

J) ANCILLARY MATERIAL

Latin manuscripts transmit possibly the largest amount of paratextual material of all traditions of the New Testament. Texts of the different series of prefaces, prologues, and *capitula* are found in a variety of publications and may be referred

---

[43] See further Parker 2012 and Houghton 2014a.

to in different ways. The *Repertorium* uses the abbreviation PROL for anonymous prologues, but identifies them within an author's corpus when the source is known (e.g. IS pro for Isidore's prologues, AMst Rm pr for Ambrosiaster's prologue to Romans); *capitula* are identified by the siglum KA followed by the abbreviation for the biblical book and then the series identifier (e.g. KA Mt B for series B in Matthew). The most comprehensive list of Latin prologues is provided in Stegmüller 1981 and ten further volumes. Each item is assigned a number, traditionally prefixed by S: thus S 595 is Stegmüller's reference for Jerome's preface to the Gospels (HI Ev), while S 809 is the anonymous preface to the Catholic Epistles (PROL cath). Stegmüller's inventory only quotes the opening and last lines of each item; the inclusion of *capitula* is haphazard, in entries for individual manuscripts rather than critical editions (e.g. S 9127 for KA Hbr Sp, S 3235.14 for KA Iac A). All eleven volumes of Stegmüller have been made available online at <http://www.repbib.uni-trier.de/> and can be searched by a number of fields including number, author, and textual content.[44]

Critical texts of Jerome's preface to the Gospels (*Nouum opus*, HI Ev [S 595]) and the translator's preface to the Pauline Epistles (*Primum quaeritur*, PROL Paul 1 [S 670]) are provided in the Stuttgart Vulgate. The editors of the Oxford Vulgate tended to reproduce ancillary items as found in individual manuscripts rather than create an edition. The fullest assembly of the complete texts of prefaces and *capitula* was made anonymously for the use of the editors of the Roman Vulgate (De Bruyne 1914 [also 2014] and 1920a). These volumes are only provisional, with no complete introduction or lists of witnesses, and contain a number of typographical errors. For the Old Testament, they have been superseded by the critical editions: in the New Testament, updated texts are found in some of the Vetus Latina volumes (*capitula* in John, prologues and *capitula* in Revelation, and an account of all the Pauline material in the preface to 1 Thessalonians), but full critical editions are otherwise still lacking. It is import-ant to note that De Bruyne splits the fourteen sets of gospel *capitula* into two sections (De Bruyne 1914:240–69 and 270–311); this volume also contains a presentation of the location of textual divisions, some of which correspond to series of *capitula*, although the inaccurate typography renders this only a general guide and all details require verification. De Bruyne's sigla for *capitula* remain in general use, whereas those for the prologues have been replaced by Stegmüller and the *Repertorium*. A list of prefaces, prologues and *capitula* drawn principally from De Bruyne and Stegmüller, with updates from later literature, is available at <www.vetuslatina.org/paratext>.[45]

---

[44] The *Repertorium* does not include cross-references to Stegmüller, but these are available in the online list at <www.vetuslatina.org/paratext>.

[45] Individual works on the paratext of the Latin Bible in the Bibliography include the other writings of De Bruyne, Regul 1969, Dahl 1978, Meyvaert 1995, Bogaert 1982, Houghton 2011, and Jongkind 2015; Berger 1893 and 1902 continue to supply useful information.

K) BIBLICAL QUOTATIONS

The evidence of biblical quotations in Christian writers is invaluable for the early history of the Latin Bible. In addition to the witness apparatus of the Vetus Latina editions and the *Vetus Latina Database* (described above), there are a number of other resources and studies concerned with patristic citations. The most comprehensive is the *Biblia Patristica*, begun by the *Centre d'Analyse et de Documentation Patristique* (CADP) in Strasbourg in 1965. This is an index of scriptural references created in conjunction with other research centres, including the Vetus Latina-Institut. Seven chronologically-ordered volumes were produced, of which three contain Latin material: the first (1975) and second (1977), covering the second and third centuries, and the sixth (1995), devoted to Hilary of Poitiers, Ambrose of Milan, and Ambrosiaster. These printed books do not provide the text of each quotation but only a reference to a critical edition which is listed at the beginning. A broad sweep of references is included, ranging from verbatim quotations and loose allusions. When the project ended in 2000, the archives were taken over by Sources Chrétiennes. The published data, along with 100,000 further entries for authors including Jerome, has now been made freely available online as Biblindex, an index of biblical quotations and allusions in early Christian literature at <www.biblindex.org>. At present, this still only provides references to editions. The authors included in the database are listed in a drop-down menu on the homepage. The search facilities return all the entries for a biblical verse or passage, which can be further restricted by date, geographical region and author or work, although not currently by language. The results offer a maximal selection, which can be reduced by reference to the original writing: bibliographical details for the edition as well as the page and line number of the reference are provided for each online entry. Unverified references are noted in red, while citations with parallels in more than one gospel are identified by the letter E and usually assigned to Matthew. As the database grows and references are checked, this is likely to become the first port of call for finding biblical quotations after the major critical editions of the Bible.

   The online edition of the *Patrologia Latina* (PL), a 217-volume edition of Latin Christian writings produced by Jacques-Paul Migne between 1844 and 1855, can also be used for finding the text of quotations.[46] Biblical references observed by the editor are recorded in parentheses, so a search of the full database (or a subset of volumes) will return all references listed. The correct format must first be identified, such as 'Joan. XIX, 13' for John 19:13 or 'Galat. V, 24' for Galatians 5:24. However, this is not exhaustive as it will not identify each verse in quotations of multiple verses where a format such as 'Joan. XIX, 12, 13' or 'Joan. XIX, 13–16' is used. Furthermore, Migne's edition has long been obsolete for most writings

---

[46] The address is: <http://pld.chadwyck.co.uk/>. A subscription is required.

and the text should be verified in more recent critical editions. Volumes 218–21 of the edition contain a set of indexes published in 1862–5. There is no biblical index as such but a range of topics including lists of scriptural commentaries (index 43, vol. 219 col. 101) and homilies (index 186, vol. 221 col. 19), key exegetical passages (by book and chapter only, index 44, vol. 219 col. 116), and New Testament themes (index 42.13, vol. 219 col. 98).

Three principal modern series of critical editions of Latin patristic writings are in progress. The *Corpus Christianorum*, started in 1947 by Eligius Dekkers with the intention of replacing Migne, is organized into subgroups including the *series latina* (CCSL) for the earliest authors, and the *continuatio medievalis* (CCCM) for later texts. Since 1953 almost 200 volumes of CCSL and over 250 of CCCM have appeared.[47] The scope of the *series latina* is summarized in the *Clavis Patrum Latinorum* (CPL; Dekkers & Gaar 1995), which assigns a number to each Latin Christian work written before 735, as well as offering a brief bibliography comparable to the Vetus Latina *Repertorium*. The *Corpus Scriptorum Ecclesiasticorum Latinorum* (CSEL) is sometimes known as the 'Vienna Corpus' or *Corpus Vindobonense* (CV), although it is now based in Salzburg. Publication began in 1866, and there are now around a hundred volumes, often complementing those of the *Corpus Christianorum*.[48] *Sources chrétiennes* (SC or SChr), founded in 1943, produces editions of Christian writings with a French translation on the facing page.[49] In addition, certain texts have been edited in smaller series (such as AGLB, see page 124) or separately, including articles in journals such as the *Revue bénédictine*. Information on an author's biblical text is often provided in the editorial introduction to a critical edition; lists of scriptural references may be given in an index, and sometimes there is a separate *apparatus fontium* ('list of sources') on each page. Even so, the identification of biblical quotations or allusions can vary both in accuracy and comprehensiveness from editor to editor.[50] Scholars of the biblical text are also advised to check variant readings in the critical apparatus to verify that the editor has selected the form of the quotation most likely to be authorial.[51]

Biblical quotations may also be found through keyword searches in electronic textual corpora. The most comprehensive collection of Christian writings in Latin is the *Library of Latin Texts* (LLT) published by Brepols.[52] This is an expansion of the original *Cetedoc Library of Christian Latin Texts* (CLCLT): it includes all of the *Corpus Christianorum* editions as well as an increasing number from other series.

---

[47] Published volumes and work in progress can be seen at <www.corpuschristianorum.org>.
[48] See further <www.csel.eu>. [49] See <www.sources-chretiennes.mom.fr>.
[50] For examples, see Frede 1972:470–2.
[51] See further Willis 1966a and Houghton 2014d.
[52] There are two databases: LLT-A, comprising critically-edited texts, and LLT-B, with more uniform corpora. Like the *Vetus Latina Database*, these and a 'Cross-Database Search tool' are accessed through <http://www.brepolis.net/>. A subscription is required.

As biblical references may have been adapted to their context, or contain non-standard readings (particularly in the early Latin tradition), a certain amount of ingenuity and wildcard searching is required. Concordances of the Vulgate (Fischer 1977 and Bergren 1991) are useful tools in tracing potential quotations of particular passages. A bilingual concordance of the Bible in Greek and Latin is planned to follow the completion of the Vetus Latina edition.[53] Attention must also be paid to the coverage of each corpus: Harmon 2003 offers helpful cautionary advice in this respect, both in terms of writings not included and one author's re-use of another. One major drawback of electronic corpora is that they currently only offer an editorial text and do not include information about different forms of biblical quotations in the manuscript tradition.

Reconstructions of the biblical text used by a particular author can offer a considered appreciation of the surviving evidence. The most extensive in the Latin tradition was the *Biblia Augustiniana*, a project to collect all Augustine's biblical quotations: only the third volume contains New Testament material, consisting of 1 and 2 Thessalonians, Titus and Philemon. In addition to the references to literature on individual authors given in Part I, the following list provides details of reconstructions or surveys of one or more New Testament books in roughly chronological order:

> Tertullian: Rönsch 1871 (NT); von Soden 1927 (Paul); Aalders 1932 and 1937 (Gospels); Tenney 1947 (Luke); Higgins 1951 (Luke); Pagani 1976 (Matthew); Petzer 1991a (Acts).
> Irenaeus: Sanday & Turner 1923 (NT); Kraft 1924 (Gospels); Schäfer 1951 (NT).
> Cyprian: von Soden 1909 (NT); Pagani 1976 (Matthew).
> Marius Victorinus: Bruce 1969 (John).
> Hilary of Poitiers: Doignon 1975 (Matthew), Doignon 1978 (Romans).
> Ambrose: Rolando 1945–6 (Luke); Caragliano 1946 (John); Muncey 1959 (NT); Marzola 1953, 1965, 1971 (NT).
> Ambrosiaster: Vogels 1957 (Paul).[54]
> Lucifer of Cagliari: Vogels 1922a and 1922b (Luke, John); Coleman 1927, 1946, and 1947 (Acts, Paul).
> Zeno of Verona: Frede 1981 (NT).
> Filastrius of Brescia: Portarena 1946 (Bible).
> Chromatius of Aquileia: Auwers 2011 (Bible).
> Maximinus: Gryson 1978 (NT).
> Rufinus: Hammond Bammel 1985 (Romans).
> Pelagius: Frede 1961 (Ephesians), Borse 1966 (Colossians); De Bruyn 1993 (Romans); Stelzer 2013 (2 Corinthians).

[53] According to Cimosa 2008:22, work on this is ongoing at the Benedictine Abbey of Mariendonk and a draft copy may be found at the *Centre de recherches sur la Bible latine* at Louvain-la-Neuve.
[54] The sigla used for manuscripts in Vogels' reconstruction of the biblical text differ from the sigla in his posthumous edition of the commentary.

Augustine: Milne 1926 (Gospels); Mizzi 1954 and 1962 (Matthew); Thiele 1955 (James); *Biblia Augustiniana*; La Bonnardière 1957 (Hebrews); Willis 1962b (Hebrews); Petzer 1991b (Acts); Houghton 2008b (John).

Gildas: O'Loughlin 2012 (Bible).

Some of these surveys have been criticized for inaccuracies or mistaken precon-ceptions about an author's biblical text (e.g. Milne 1926, Muncey 1959) and most of those published before 1950 rely on editions which are now obsolete. None-theless, the study of an individual author's biblical text and citation practice are essential to the correct deployment of their evidence in editions of the New Testament as well as shedding light on the forms of text they knew and used.[55]

L) BIBLIOGRAPHICAL RESOURCES

The Bibliography of the present volume aims to include all major publications on the early Latin New Testament from the last century. These are referenced for each manuscript in the Catalogue of Manuscripts, supplementing the informa-tion in the Vetus Latina *Register* (Gryson 1999). Bibliography on individual Christian writers, including works on their biblical text, is provided in the Vetus Latina *Repertorium* (Gryson 2007) as well as the *Clavis Patrum Latinorum* (Dekkers & Gaar 1995). The *Corpus Christanorum Lingua Patrum* series in-cludes a list of works on Christian Latin (Sanders and Van Uytfanghe 1989).

A number of scholarly journals print lists of recent publications in addition to book reviews. The most important for the study of the Latin Bible is the *Bulletin de la Bible latine* (BBL), an annotated bibliography edited since 1964 by Pierre-Maurice Bogaert, which appears every two years in the *Revue bénédictine*. Prior to 1995, it was published with its own pagination in order to be bound separately: this was also the case with its predecessor, the *Bulletin d'ancienne littérature chrétienne latine* published with the *Revue bénédictine* from 1921 to 1959, which had a special section on the Bible. Since 1955, the *Revue des études augustiniennes et patristiques* has included bibliographies of recent work on Augustine, Tertullian, and Cyprian.[56] The annual Vetus Latina *Arbeitsbericht*, published by the Vetus Latina-Institut, provides a report of work in progress and a full list of the state of the edition: the most recent may be downloaded from the Institute's website <www.vetus-latina.de>. The an-nual *Bulletin d'information et de liaison* of the Association Internationale d'Études Patristiques/International Association of Patristic Studies lists recent publications and work in progress in various thematic areas, including the Bible: this, too, is available online <http://www.aiep-iaps.org/bulletin>.

---

[55] For the SBL *New Testament in the Greek Fathers* series and other work on the Greek tradition, see <www.igntp.org/patristic.html>.

[56] Works from 1975–94 are also published in Braun et al. 1999.

7

Latin as a Witness for the Greek New Testament

The text of the Latin New Testament bears witness to its transmission history, its connection with theological developments, and changes in language and literary style. It can also supply evidence for the forms of the Greek text underlying the translation or used for revision and emendation. Using the Latin and other early versions as a source for the Greek New Testament, however, requires careful analysis taking a number of factors into consideration.[1] Latin and Greek are relatively similar in their linguistic structure, both being inflected languages with nouns which are declined in a case-system and verbal conjugations. Even in these, though, they do not correspond exactly: Greek has no ablative case, for example, while Latin has no verbal aorist, middle voice, or perfect active participle. The prolonged period of contact between the two languages means that there was considerable mutual influence, revealed in the exchange of vocabulary and also the borrowing of certain grammatical structures.[2] Nonetheless, unlike the Harklean version of the Syriac, the Latin translation of the New Testament is not a word-for-word equivalent which can easily be retroverted to reconstruct its Greek source. Instead, a single Latin form may be used to render a number of different Greek words or constructions, while multiple Latin versions may derive from an identical Greek text. Furthermore, much of the variation between Latin texts does not represent different forms in Greek but internal Latin developments reflecting stylistic, phonetic, orthographic, or other considerations. It is therefore helpful to distinguish 'renderings', different Latin translations of the same underlying Greek text (the *Vorlage*), from 'readings', competing forms of text within the same tradition, be it Latin or Greek.

As seems to be the case for most translations with a history of several centuries, the earliest Latin version was the loosest, often paraphrasing and

---

[1] Fischer 1972 [1986:259–74] offers the classic account of 'Limitations of Latin in representing Greek' (translated into English in Metzger 1977); see also Plater & White 1926:28–40, Williams 2004 and 2012, Jimenez Zamudio 2009.

[2] See, for example, Burton 2000:172–91 and Galdi 2011:574–5.

sometimes even omitting material which appeared to be superfluous.[3] For example, Luke 12:21 and the final clause of John 4:9, both of which serve an explanatory function, are absent from the earliest Latin texts. Repetitive phrases are often simplified, such as the double verb in John 10:38 (*ut cognoscatis et credatis*, 'that you may know and believe'), the omission of *anni illius* from John 11:51 ('for that year', repeated from 11:49) and *in diebus illis* from Acts 2:18 ('in those days'; cf. 2:17). Even specific details may be omitted, such as the women's names in Mark 16:2 in VL 1. Complicated Greek constructions are another place where the early translation is sometimes omissive. For example, the omission of the difficult clause between *Martha* in Luke 10:41 and *Maria* in the next verse has been described as 'a deliberate excision of an incomprehensible passage'; a similar explanation has been given for the absence of the latter half of 1 Corinthians 7:35.[4]

The fact that some Greek words are transliterated, or structures replicated contrary to Latin usage, should not automatically lead to the characterization of the translation as incompetent: early Latin translations often display considerable ingenuity and some artistry in rendering Greek.[5] The borrowing of Greek words (usually incorporated into Latin morphology), preference for Latin forms whose structure exactly matches those of Greek (such as *re-surrec-tio* corresponding to ἀνά-στα-σις), the creation of calques following the same model, and the semantic extension of existing Latin words also reflect the development of a Christian vocabulary, with technical or specialized aspects.[6] The incorporation of specific Greek terms or constructions may offer fairly solid evidence for the *Vorlage*, yet this does not necessarily represent the most ancient text. At Matthew 19:12, for example, the earliest Latin translation appears to have been *castrauerunt* but the Greek term was borrowed in VL 3 as *eunuchizauerunt*, a reading which persists in a handful of Vulgate manuscripts. Burton observes that the earliest translators were keener than later revisers to avoid Greek loanwords.[7] Old Latin texts also reveal sensitivity to contextual constraints in the choice of Latin renderings, such as *mulier* or *uxor* depending on whether the Greek ἡ γυνή means 'woman' or 'wife', and *nuntius* rather than *angelus* when ἄγγελος does not denote a divinely-sent messenger.[8] In general, when the transmitted Greek is invariant and the Latin version offers a close match, the two may reasonably be connected.

Even in the earliest Latin tradition there is a degree of harmonizing interference. This may take the form of the creation of 'scriptural formulae' on

[3] On the origin of the Latin translation, see pages 12–14 above.
[4] Metzger 1994:129 and Sparks 1970:529 respectively. More examples are given by Thiele, who also notes a number of examples of interpolations in the Catholic Epistles (1972:98–113).
[5] See further Burton 2000.
[6] Other examples are given in Burton 2011:489–93; Plater & White 1926:54–64 has a list of semantic extensions in the Vulgate. See also pages 7–9 above on 'Christian Latin'.
[7] Burton 2000:97. Compare the examples of Jerome's Greek borrowing on page 34 above.
[8] Burton 2000:87–94.

occasions where they are not employed in the *Vorlage*. For example, VL 11, 11A, and 15 have *dico enim uobis* ('for I say to you') in place of *et* before Jesus' pronouncement at John 3:13, despite there being no parallel for this in surviving Greek witnesses. A slightly less obvious case may be seen in the construction at the beginning of John 4:17, where VL 2 and 13 read *respondit mulier dicens* ('the woman replied, saying') even though it seems that all surviving Greek manuscripts have two finite verbs: the introduction of a present participle resembles the Hebrew speech formula which became part of Greek and Latin biblical register through the Septuagint.[9] There are numerous instances of harmonization within and between the Gospels, reflecting familiarity with the different accounts at the expense of word-for-word correspondence. For example, at John 13:38, VL 2 substitutes the reference to the cock at Matthew 26:75 (*priusquam gallus cantet ter me negabis*, 'before the cock crows you will deny me three times') for the Johannine wording (*non cantabit gallus donec me ter neges*, 'the cock will not crow until you deny me three times'). The simplest explanation is that the translator is responsible for the harmonization, rather than positing an otherwise unattested Greek form. In Matthew 21:39, however, where the Old Latin tradition inverts the order of the verbs with *occiderunt* preceding *eiecerunt*, there is a Greek parallel in two surviving manuscripts (GA 05 and 038). As the Latin sequence matches that of the standard text of the parallel passage at Mark 12:8 it is therefore possible that this harmonization took place independently. A similar example involves Matthew 17:2, where most Old Latin manuscripts read *alba sicut nix* ('white as snow'). This is found in other versions and the Greek text of Codex Bezae, but it is impossible to say whether it is based on the Greek reading or is an independent harmonization to Matthew 28:3. For this reason, harmonizing readings constitute weak evidence at best for the influence of a Greek source or even a gospel harmony.[10]

Subsequent Latin forms of text appear to be revisions of an earlier translation rather than completely new versions.[11] The overall tendency is to bring the biblical text into closer correspondence with a Greek model: where the manuscript used for comparison differed from the translation's *Vorlage*, this could result in the introduction of new readings. Differences in rendering, however, are as likely to have arisen through internal Latin revision as through comparison with Greek, if not more so: an obsolescent or regional form may have been replaced, or a word may have been introduced which was felt to be more theologically or contextually suitable, without reference to the original language. Such pairs of renderings, as in *uerbum* and *sermo* for ὁ λόγος, *lux* and *lumen* for τὸ φῶς, and *populus* and *plebs* for ὁ λαός, have often been used to describe

---

[9] Surprising instances of looseness in the text of Mark in VL 6 and 9A are reported in Haelewyck 2013:97–102 and Houghton 2016 respectively.

[10] Thus also Fischer 1972:48 [1986:219].   [11] See pages 12–14.

manuscripts in terms of their 'translation colouring' (*Übersetzungsfarbe*).[12] The downside of this approach, however, is that it leads to binary results because it is rare for a single Greek word to have more than two common Latin renderings. Multiple options such as *magnificare, glorificare, honorificare, honorare,* and *clarificare* for δοξάζειν, or *is, ille,* and *iste* for αὐτός are the exception rather than the norm. This polarity may explain why the 'African' and 'European' dichotomy has long characterized approaches to Old Latin tradition. A particularly good example of changing Latin usage is seen in the verb 'to eat': the most ancient biblical form is *edere,* but the revisions have *manducare,* which took on the sense 'to eat' around the middle of the third century; Jerome has a marked preference for *comedere.*[13] The choice of synonyms is therefore unlikely to contribute much to the reconstruction of the *Vorlage.*

Other variations can also be explained as stylistic or internal adjustments to the Latin. While corresponding Greek alternatives are attested in many cases, these may have arisen independently as editors in either language sought to smooth the narrative flow or copyists made conscious or subconscious harmonizations or adjustments. For example, the changes from the first to the third person in 1 John 2:4 and 4:20 are not secure evidence for revision based on Greek.[14] In each case, the burden of proof lies in showing that the Latin is causally connected to the Greek and not coincidental. Knowledge of the looseness of early translators should caution against using versional evidence to reconstruct Greek forms which are not preserved, but the same criteria should also be applied even when the Greek tradition does appear to provide a parallel. The breadth of attestation of the reading in each tradition, despite the haphazard nature of the evidence which survives, is also to be taken into account. The fact that similar alterations may have been employed by translators in different languages means that the agreement of two or more versions without a Greek parallel may be coincidental rather than representing a lost form. For example, the entire Latin tradition reads *secuti sunt eum* at Mark 1:20 ('they followed him'), a literal translation of the harmonizing reading ἠκολούθησαν αὐτῷ attested in a handful of Greek manuscripts, but it is debatable whether this would have been adjusted by editors comparing the existing Latin text with Greek copies which read ἀπῆλθον ὀπίσω αὐτοῦ ('they went away behind him').

In general terms, Latin texts offer relatively secure evidence for the omission and addition of phrases, although the possibility that these may represent paraphrase or gloss in the earliest translations must also be considered. One example, which may even be an error in the original Latin translation, is the omission of the middle of Luke 12:19 from *posita* to *bibe* (κείμενα to πίε in

---

[12] The practice is adopted in Vogels 1928b and Burton 2000, although hesitations are expressed in Burton 2012:186.
[13] Burton 2000:162–4.   [14] Thus Thiele 1972:98.

Greek). This is not found in the earliest strand of Old Latin tradition and could be a line missing from the Greek source or overlooked by the translator: the only Greek parallel is in Codex Bezae. In the case of single words, particularly auxiliary verbs, the likelihood of a causal relationship between Latin and Greek is far lower. Where there is a semantic difference involving a verb or noun, it is usually possible to align Latin evidence with existing Greek readings. The reconstruction of a Greek form otherwise unattested should only be undertaken in the face of compelling evidence: the possibility of semantic extension in the Latin, or even the deliberate use of an alternative word either as a translator's interpretative intervention or through a misunderstanding or misreading of an attested Greek form must be borne in mind. For example, at Matthew 13:29–30 variation in the Latin and Syriac tradition suggests that ἅμα ('together') was misread as ἀλλά ('but').[15] Error within the Latin tradition is sometimes the most plausible explanation of a difference, as in the forms *descendentium* (Luke 19:37) and *discumbentium* (John 21:12) in place of *discentium*. It is also the case that similar errors can happen in both languages: for example, the *nomina sacra* abbreviations DS and DNS (for *deus* and *dominus*) may lead to confusion independent of the Greek forms κc and ΘC, while at Colossians 2:7, the apparently visual alternation between *abundantes* and *ambulantes* could be matched by περισσεύοντες and περιπατοῦντες in Greek.

Certain elements of Greek cannot be rendered directly into Latin, including missing parts of the verbal paradigm and the definite article. The latter may be represented by a relative clause or appear to be omitted. For example, at 1 Peter 1:11, the same underlying Greek (τὸ ἐν αὐτοῖς πνεῦμα) is rendered by *qui in eis erat spiritus* in text-type T but *in eis spiritus* in the Vulgate. Conversely, the demonstrative pronoun can be used in Latin on certain occasions, most notably *hic mundus* (ὁ κόσμος), when the Greek has nothing more than an article.[16] The lack of a distinction between aorist and perfect in Latin means that both ἐλάλησα and λελάληκα correspond to *locutus sum*. Again, the absence of a perfect active participle and a present passive participle from Latin means that some Greek constructions have to be rewritten.[17] This could take the form of relative, temporal, or causal clauses (with *cum, dum, quando, quia, qua, ut*), correlation rather than subordination, or even recasting in Latin-only constructions such as the ablative absolute. A translator's choice on one occasion may not be the same for the next instance. The participle ὤν ('being'), which does not exist in Latin, offers a good example: one option is to use some form of *esse* ('to be'), as at James 3:4, where τηλικαῦτα ὄντα is

---

[15] Burton 2000:58–9; the similarity between AMA and AΛΛA is more obvious in majuscule script.
[16] See further Abel 1971 and Hofmann & Szantyr 1963–5.
[17] Eklund 1970 deals with issues regarding the Latin present participle.

rendered by *quae tam inmensae sunt* (text-type S), *tam magnae sunt . . . autem* (text-type T), and *cum magnae sint* (Vulgate); alternatively, a verb may be repeated or supplied, as in the extreme example of Acts 27:2 where ὄντος in the genitive absolute corresponds to *erat, ascendit, nauigabat,* and *perseuerante* in different witnesses. The Greek use of the infinitive is normally changed to a periphrastic form in Latin, usually with *ut,* although at 1 Peter 2:5, no fewer than six forms are found for ἀνενέγκαι ('to offer'): *offerre, afferre, offerentes, offerte, ad offerendas,* and *ut afferatis.* The tense of verbs often fluctuates in the Latin tradition regardless of the Greek *Vorlage.* This is exacerbated by sound changes leading to the interchange of *i* and *e* (e.g. *dicit* and *dicet*) and *b* and *u* (e.g. *saluauit* and *saluabit*). Another common change involving nasal consonants can result in confusion between participles and finite forms, such as *ignorans* and *ignoras.*[18] The use of μέλλειν ('to be about to') to indicate the future in Greek often poses problems to Latin translators: for example, at John 11:51, *incipiebat Iesus mori pro gente* ('Jesus was beginning to die on behalf of the people') is a hyper-literal rendering of ἔμελλεν Ἰησοῦς ἀποθνῄσκειν ὑπὲρ τοῦ ἔθνους.

As with demonstratives, the rendering of other *uerba minora,* such as conjunctions and prepositions, is another area in which there is considerable looseness and Latin forms can at best only tentatively be matched to Greek. For example, the choice between *a, de,* and *ex* often seems to be a mark of differentiation between text-types (as in the Pauline phrase *ex mortuis,* 'from the dead'), regardless of the Greek form (ἐκ, ἀπό, etc.). Existing overlaps in biblical Greek between the use of εἰς ('into') and ἐν ('in'), rendered in Latin by *in* with the accusative and ablative respectively, are further complicated by the weakness of final *–m* in Latin, meaning that *in honorem* and *in honore* can both correspond to either εἰς τιμήν or ἐν τιμῇ (e.g. Romans 15:7, Colossians 2:23, 2 Timothy 2:20–1). The repetition of prepositions with compound verbs in Greek is rarely found in Latin, while the nuances of such compounds may be rendered by a completely different word. Overlap is often attested in the rendering of different connectives: there are examples of δέ matching the Latin *autem, uero, sed, et, -que, igitur, itaque, ergo,* and *enim,* while οὖν can be translated in a variety of ways.[19] Independently, *autem* and *enim* are frequently exchanged in Latin.[20] There is no Latin equivalent to μεν which signals the first half of an antithesis; *utique* is sometimes used for ἄν when it indicates the subjunctive, but this particle is often omitted.

Latin should rarely, if ever, be used to support variations in word order, because this is fluid in inflected languages. Although there are potential

---

[18] A similar phenomenon results in *uoluptas* ('voluptuousness') in place of *uoluntas* ('will'), leading to unexpected alternatives in verses such as John 1:13!

[19] Parker 1985.

[20] Although this may sometimes be explained as the misinterpretation of the Insular symbols for these words (see page 192), the phenomenon is too common solely to be scribal confusion.

correspondences between the two traditions, as shown in Jerome's re-ordering of *me misit* to *misit me* in the Vulgate Gospels on the model of the Greek ὁ πέμψας με, it is impossible confidently to decide on occasions when both forms are preserved in Greek. Scribal confusion over the form of foreign words means that Latin is rarely secure evidence for the form of proper nouns, although certain traditions may be aligned with alternatives such as *Hierusalem* and *Hierosolyma*, or *Nazarenus* and *Nazoraeus*.[21] Some words borrowed from Greek keep their original morphology, such as *liber Geneseos* ('the book of Genesis', with the Greek genitive γενεσέως); the Greek accusative, ending in *-n*, is found in a number of proper nouns (e.g. *Barabban*).[22] Latin idiom can also result in discrepancies. For instance, the plural form of certain nouns may be customary in Latin where Greek prefers a singular, such as *tenebrae* ('shadows') for ἡ σκοτία ('darkness'); others are interchangeable, notably *caelum* and *caeli* for 'heaven'.[23] The Latin superlative is often found where Greek witnesses only attest a positive, as in *nequissimus* for πονηρός and *carissimus* for ἀγαπητός (Ephesians 6:16 and 21). The creativity of translators is another factor for consideration. A basic rule of thumb is that, if an attested form of Greek text could even loosely underlie a Latin form, it is superfluous to posit a different *Vorlage*. If the transmitted Greek is invariant, most Latin forms may normally be considered to derive from it. Where there are multiple Greek readings, it is often impossible to distinguish between alternative Greek readings on the basis of Latin forms, since the latter could be derived from either. Certain developments, such as harmonizations or the interchange of nouns and pronouns, may happen independently: although it may be attractive to connect such readings, in such cases it is usually better to be agnostic about a causal connection unless the similarity is particularly striking.[24]

The Vetus Latina text-types are predicated on the revision of a Latin translation based on comparison with a Greek witness. However, as observed above (page 121), it is difficult to be sure about the thoroughness with which these revisions were carried out and the extent to which changes were made. Some users may have extensively revised a single passage on the basis of a Greek text available to them, while others may have made thoroughgoing stylistic Latin changes but only altered a few readings, perhaps on the basis of a second Latin witness which reflected a Greek variant.[25] The only two Latin versions which we know to have been dependent on a Greek text from start to finish are the earliest Latin translation, no longer preserved, and Jerome's

---

[21] The spellings *Caiaphas* and *Iscariotes*, in place of *Caiphas* and *Scarioth*, derive from comparison with Greek.

[22] According to Plater & White 1926:33, this is a particular feature of Vg A.

[23] Other examples include *lignum, caro, aqua, uentis, sanitas, manus* (Fischer 1972:88 [1986:268–9]).

[24] See further Frede 1972:460.

[25] For biblical textual criticism in antiquity, see Hulley 1944 and Schirner 2014.

revision of the Gospels, yet even the latter says that he restricted his interventions, the extent of which decrease as his work proceeds.[26] The citation of Latin evidence in an apparatus of the Greek text using textual groupings, rather than as individual witnesses, avoids the incorrect impression that each manuscript is an independent source for that Greek reading. In this respect, the text-types, while artificial and perhaps also a patchwork of different editorial interventions, are useful. For instance, the correction of Mark 5:23 from the overly literal *nouissime habet* ('she has on the edge') in VL 1 to *in extremis est* ('she is at the point of death') only needs to have happened once to appear in the rest of Latin tradition.[27] Conversely, VL 13 is the only Old Latin manuscript to read *alba sicut lumen* ('white as light'), the standard Greek text of Matthew 17:2. As this removes the harmonization in the rest of Latin tradition, including the Vulgate, it is likely to have been prompted by comparison with Greek, even though this manuscript is not normally assigned a separate text-type. The fact that a punctual intervention in just one biblical manuscript may reflect comparison with the Greek means that there is also a case for citing individual witnesses when these differ from the rest of the tradition. The practice of the Vetus Latina edition is to treat this as a variant to the text-type of equal significance to the main line, meaning that on such occasions the text-type is split between different Greek forms.[28] It is worth remembering that the age of the Latin witnesses rarely if ever corresponds to the point at which their biblical text was in contact with Greek tradition: the initial translation predates all witnesses, while most subsequent revisions were made some time before the surviving manuscripts were copied. Furthermore, the concept of a text-type in Latin differs from the geographical text-types ('Alexandrian', 'Western', etc.) which used to be used to describe Greek tradition but have now fallen out of favour. Even though Latin texts may share features typical of Greek recensions, particularly in the Acts of the Apostles, the connection between the two languages always took place through the comparison of individual manuscripts, each with its own peculiarities and unique readings.[29]

Biblical quotations in Latin authors are at an additional remove from the Greek tradition: not only are these translations but they are subject to further alterations through adjustment to their context or quotation from memory, as well as being dependent on the transmission history of the work in which they are found.[30] This is not to say that they are completely without value. Some writers, such as Tertullian, relied on a Greek text of the New Testament. Scriptural commentaries usually preserve a complete text of the book which is being expounded, potentially equivalent to an extra Latin manuscript of that book especially if it can be shown that the form of text transmitted is likely to

---

[26] See page 34 and the quotation from the *Praefatio in Euangelia* on page 32.
[27] See Burton 2000:133.   [28] See pages 121–4.
[29] See further Petzer 1995:124–5.   [30] Frede 1972 and Houghton 2012.

have been that used by the commentator. A distinction between 'primary citations' and 'secondary citations' has been proposed to identify those which are likely to have been drawn directly from a biblical codex and those which may instead have been quoted from memory; the latter may be subject to 'flattening', the loss of details due to their being taken out of their original context, or another form of adaptation.[31] An example of this is seen in John 6:44, where all biblical manuscripts have *nemo potest uenire ad me* ('no-one can come to me'). The most common form of this verse in Latin authors, going back all the way to Tertullian, is *nemo uenit ad me* ('no-one comes to me'). Six verses earlier, in place of the biblical form *descendi de caelo non ut faciam uoluntatem meam* ('I descended from heaven not that I might do my will'), several writers begin John 6:38 with *non ueni facere uoluntatem meam* ('I did not come to do my will'), a form popularized by Hilary of Poitiers and Augustine which even makes it into the Rule of Benedict.

A related problem with citational evidence is the possibility that authors are dependent on another secondary source for their biblical text, quoting it from a collection of *testimonia* or another treatise which could have been in a different language or a Latin translation which is no longer extant. Even when Christian writers make an assertion about the reading of one or more New Testament manuscripts this may not be based on first-hand testimony.[32] In terms of their transmission, the phenomenon of 'Vulgatization' is some- times observed in the adjustment of an author's biblical text to a form current at a later period. However, this is by no means universal, and in many cases the persistence of non-standard forms suggests that the original text has been transmitted faithfully. The use of patristic quotations to establish different Vetus Latina text-types means that their textual evidence is evaluated and taken into account in these reconstructed forms: if Christian writers are used directly, their evidence must be carefully assessed before it can be cited in support of readings present in biblical tradition, let alone used as the basis of a hypothetical form which does not otherwise survive.[33]

Translations of Greek writings generally produce ad hoc renderings of the biblical quotations in the text. Although such forms are undoubtedly influ- enced by the text of Latin versions known to the translator, they stand apart from the transmission of the Latin Bible. Often they exhibit minor differences from surviving Latin biblical manuscripts, but their claim to represent a Latin version no longer preserved is weak, even though they may derive from the same Greek text. Where a Greek author paraphrased or adjusted the biblical

---

[31] On primary and secondary citations, see Houghton 2008a; for 'flattening', Houghton 2010b.

[32] Metzger 1979; Donaldson 2009, 2013.

[33] For examples of the variety in quotations which bear no relation to a biblical manuscript, see Frede 1972:460–1.

text, this too will be reflected in the translation: it is possible that the flattened form of John 6:38 quoted above goes all the way back to Origen. Another problem with translated sources is that it is often difficult to date the Latin versions of individual Greek works: some, such as Clement of Rome (CLE-R), the *Didache* (DIDe), and Irenaeus (IR) appear to be very early. The majority, however, date from around the end of the fourth century, in conjunction with the translation projects of Jerome and Rufinus and the theological controversies which inspired them.

There are a number of overlaps between the Latin New Testament and other early versions, especially translations into Coptic, Syriac, and Gothic. Although Wulfila, translator of the Gothic version, worked from Greek, it seems that he also had recourse to Latin manuscripts. In addition, as Latin and Gothic texts circulated in the same geographical area, common readings are not surprising.[34] Readings shared with Coptic and Syriac manuscripts but not otherwise attested in Greek are more intriguing. In certain cases these may go back to a Greek *Vorlage* which is now lost. However, the potential for similar translation phenomena to occur independently of language (such as the alteration of connectives and verbal forms, the interchange of nouns and pronouns, the omission of material considered to be superfluous) means that similarities must be carefully analysed before a shared origin can be confirmed.[35] For example, Birdsall claimed that the omissions common to VL 1 and Syriac versions in Matthew 4:17 are original, but these are currently considered to be independent abbreviations of the text.[36] There is one family of Arabic gospel manuscripts which appears to have been translated from a Latin exemplar in the year 946.[37]

In conclusion, while the antiquity of the early Latin tradition makes it an important witness for the textual transmission of the New Testament, matters of linguistic relationships and translation technique must be carefully considered before using Latin evidence to support readings in Greek tradition. There are several overlaps between the application of versional evidence and that of biblical quotations in Christian writers. Such secondary, or indirect, evidence should rarely be taken in support of omissions, as words or phrases present in a *Vorlage* may simply have been passed over; harmonization is a common phenomenon, which can happen independently in similar or slightly different ways. Even additions, such as explanatory glosses, may be secondary. The reconstruction of forms no longer attested in direct Greek tradition should only be undertaken with the greatest caution. A guiding principle is

[34] See page 52, as well as Burton 1996 and 2002; Falluomini 2012:341–2 and 2015:17, 105–14.
[35] See Chase 1895, Williams 2004 and 2012. Klijn 1969 suggests that agreements between the Old Latin and Old Syriac versions go back before 170 but do not derive from the Diatessaron.
[36] Birdsall 1970:330; contrast Metzger 1994:10.   [37] Kashouh 2011:275–6.

that, if a reading can be explained as a development internal to the Latin tradition, this should be preferred to any other explanation. It is also important to remember that the attestation by more than one Latin witness of a particular reading does not mean that the Latin sources provide independent evidence for the corresponding Greek form: the variation only needs to have been introduced on one occasion for it to spread more widely within Latin tradition. The identification of text-types based on points of contact between Latin and Greek texts offers a means of avoiding the misleading citation of multiple Latin sources as witnesses for a single instance of variation relating to a Greek text.

8

The Text of the Early Latin
New Testament

A full textual commentary on the Latin New Testament is beyond the scope of
the present volume. In this chapter, the early Latin tradition of each New
Testament book is described in turn. Information is given about the availability
of the books in critical editions, with details of the textual history and text-
types, the extant manuscripts, and early commentaries. The different series of
capitula are also enumerated and put in context. Each section concludes with a
discussion of textual features or passages of special significance for the textual
history of the New Testament. For the sake of simplicity, witnesses continue to
be described as Old Latin or Vulgate despite the continuity in Latin tradition.

A discussion of selected variant readings in the New Testament, in which
Latin evidence is often mentioned, is found in the textual commentary on the
United Bible Societies' edition of the Greek New Testament.[1] Latin sources are
also quoted and discussed in the companion volumes to the Greek *Editio
Critica Maior*. The only commentary devoted to the Old Latin New Testament
is structured according to whether a Latin form is deemed to be a literal or
non-literal rendering of its Greek *Vorlage*. This not only makes it difficult to
use but begs a number of questions about translation technique which have
already been raised in Chapter 7.[2]

A) GOSPELS

The oldest surviving part of the Latin New Testament is the Gospels, where
several manuscripts preserve evidence for the forms of text which preceded
Jerome's fifth-century revision. For the most part, these codices preserve an

---

[1] Metzger 1994.
[2] Valgiglio 1985; extracts are reproduced in Cimosa 2008:25–37. For the Latin language of the
biblical translations, see Vineis 1974 and Ceresa-Gastaldo 1975, as well as Burton 2000.

earlier and wider selection of readings than the biblical quotations in Christian authors. Their texts are available in the *Itala* of Jülicher, Matzkow, and Aland, from which they are often cited in the apparatus to NA28 and UBS5.[3] The Vetus Latina editions of Mark and John currently in progress provide fuller information, as well as patristic evidence. The Latin gospel harmony tradition is a later development, although harmonized readings and features sometimes claimed to be characteristic of the Diatessaron are also found in early Latin gospel manuscripts; the oldest extant Latin harmony, Codex Fuldensis (Vg F), is dependent on the Vulgate.[4] The revision of the Gospels undertaken by Jerome and now known as the Vulgate was based on a Greek text. In the sixth century, this appears to have split into two branches because of internal Latin adjustments: a Neapolitan text, underlying Codex Amiatinus (Vg A), other Northumbrian manuscripts, and Vg F, and the preservation of a text closer to Jerome, represented by the fifth-century St Gall Gospels (Vg^{Se} S). The latter underwent further internal revision in Italy at the beginning of the sixth century, as seen in the Harley Gospels (Vg^S Z). Almost all gospel manuscripts of the period have an admixture of earlier readings, some so prevalent as to constitute a 'mixed text' of Vulgate and Old Latin forms. The gospel text of the Tours Bibles appears to have been based broadly on the Italian revision with a number of readings from the Neapolitan tradition.[5]

The variety of the Old Latin texts, stemming from a period when Latin and Greek speakers within the Church were in close communication, means that a number of the different readings in these early manuscripts may have arisen from comparison with Greek witnesses. Comparison of the two traditions reveals a number of parallels between early Latin texts and Greek manuscripts which are slightly removed from the mainstream. In many cases, the Greek column of the bilingual Codex Bezae (GA 05; VL 5) offers the only parallel for a well-attested Latin form. Other manuscripts with similarities to the Latin tradition include Codex Sinaiticus (GA 01) and the Freer Gospels (GA 032), as well as two groups of minuscule manuscripts, Family 1 and Family 13. A change in the Greek text underlying Latin witnesses in the fourth century has been connected with the arrival of Greek scholars and writings in the West during the Arian controversy, although it could also reflect the growing text-critical awareness of Jerome, Augustine, and their contemporaries.[6]

Equally, a process of internal Latin development was also under way during the third and fourth centuries, including the creation of a Latin Christian vocabulary and the adjustment of biblical translations towards more standard linguistic forms despite their pervasive influence on the language of Christian

---

[3] These editions are described in Chapter 6.   [4] See page 56.

[5] See further Fischer 1985:373–7 [1971].

[6] On the Arian explanation, see Frede 1972:465. For debate about the Greek text underlying the Vulgate, see pages 33–4 and 41 above.

writers. The translation technique in the Old Latin Gospels has been analysed by Burton, who provides numerous indicators of a single common source underlying the Gospels as well as identifying subsequent revisions prior to the Vulgate (which he terms 'European') based on changes in the Latin renderings of certain Greek words: the Synoptic Gospels all stem directly from the original translation, although the different Gospels have been revised in different ways; in John, there appear to be two different branches of intermediate Latin texts, one of which was taken by Jerome as the base for the Vulgate.[7]

Fischer also upholds the hypothesis of one original Latin translation for the whole of the New Testament.[8] According to his reconstruction of the history of the Gospels, the closest surviving witness to the earliest form is VL 1 and other witnesses to text-type K, although the text in Cyprian appears already to have undergone revision. Elements of this archaic (or 'African') text remain in several other Old Latin manuscripts, including VL 2, 3, 5, 6, 9, 21, and 26. Of these, VL 3 stands at the centre of an older group with VL 16 and 21 and writers such as Lucifer of Cagliari and Jerome. This is equivalent to text-type D, a form of text which may also be seen in VL 2. The higher proportion of archaic forms in VL 2, however, normally leads to its classification as a separate form, text-type C. The mid fourth-century Italian text, text-type I, is best represented by VL 4 (in the Synoptic Gospels), VL 8, and 17, and quotations in writers such as Ambrose, Hilary, and Chromatius; several other Old Latin manuscripts, including VL 13, 14, and 22, are more distantly related to this form. Certain witnesses, most notably VL 6, preserve multiple Old Latin types, while there are numerous 'mixed text' manuscripts which either alternate between Old Latin and Vulgate portions or combine readings from both traditions. Notwithstanding these overall text-types, it is possible that individual codices may bear witness to occasional or more extensive revision based on comparison with Greek, especially when a single Old Latin manuscript stands alone.[9]

Some of the ancillary texts for the Gospels are of considerable antiquity.[10] The earliest *capitula*, KA Cy, date from the middle of the third century. Several others which preserve Old Latin texts are likely to have been composed for fourth-century editions, principally KA I, which may also originate in Africa, and KA A (and their abbreviated form, KA B). There is also pre-Vulgate material in KA Cat, KA D, KA Ben, and KA I[for] (the latter only found in Vg[O] J). KA P[i] date from early in the history of the Vulgate, prior to their abbreviation in KA W (attested in a sixth-century manuscript). KA In are similar in age.

---

[7] Burton 2000:29–74, especially 58 and 74. [8] Fischer 1972:30–9 [1986:196–207].

[9] e.g. page 150 above.

[10] The texts of these are available at <www.vetuslatina.org/paratext>; see also Chapter 6 section j (pages 137–8). The dates given in this paragraph are extrapolated from Houghton 2011.

KA C, with the heading *capitula lectionum*, stem from the Neapolitan exemplar used in Northumbria for Vg A and Vg^O Y: in John, KA Win are a later version of this. KA Vic are peculiar to two Spanish manuscripts of the eleventh and twelfth century, while KA Z are found in a single twelfth-century witness. The 'anti-Marcionite' prologues, PROL Pa, were written in the middle of the fourth century, while the 'Monarchian' prologues, PROL Mo, come from the end of the century.[11] Jerome introduced his preface explaining the Eusebian apparatus before his text of the Gospels (*Nouum opus*, HI Ev [S 595]); the preface to his commentary to Matthew (*Plures fuisse*, HI Mt [S 596]) and extracts from his *De uiris illustribus* (HI ill) and lists of Hebrew words (HI nom) were added later. *Sciendum etiam* [S 601], although also attributed to Jerome, was not composed until the eighth century.[12] Other prefaces include those written by Isidore, poems by Aileran and Alcuin, and anonymous prologues to each Gospel associated with Ireland (PROL Ir) and Spain (PROL Sp).

Matthew

Matthew is preserved in seventeen continuous-text manuscripts with a consistent Old Latin affiliation (VL 1, 2, 3, 4, 5, 6, 7, 8, 9, 10, 12, 13, 14, 16, 28, 41, 48). VL 43 and 45 are fragments of two pages or fewer; there are also nine mixed-text or predominantly Vulgate witnesses listed in the Vetus Latina *Register* (VL 9A, 11, 11A, 15, 19A, 27, 29, 30, 35), three lectionaries (VL 18, 31, 32), four sets of canon tables with text (VL 10, 39, 40, 46), and two copies of Jerome's commentary (VL 37, 38). VL 1, the earliest surviving Latin gospel book, is extant for the first half of Matthew, while VL 2 only survives in the latter half. VL 9 consists of Matthew alone, while in VL 7 and 12 only Matthew has an Old Latin affiliation and the other New Testament writings correspond to the Vulgate. Burton shows that all the surviving Old Latin manuscripts of Matthew derive from a single common source: within this, the Passion narrative represents an earlier stratum which could represent an earlier separate form, perhaps of liturgical origin.[13]

In addition to having the largest number of surviving manuscripts, Matthew is well served by early Latin commentators. The newly-rediscovered fourth-century commentary on the Gospels by Fortunatianus of Aquileia (FO-A) focuses on Matthew, and is itself dependent on a lost commentary on Matthew by Victorinus of Poetovio (VICn).[14] Roughly contemporary with Fortunatianus is Hilary of Poitiers' commentary (HIL Mt), written around 353.[15] Augustine composed a two-book exposition of the Sermon on the Mount in 394 (AU s dni)

---

[11] Texts for these are given on page 197.   [12] Shepard 2012a:345.
[13] Burton 2000:36–44.   [14] Dorfbauer 2013a and 2013b.
[15] On its biblical text, see Doignon 1975 and pages 24–5 above.

and *Quaestiones* on Matthew and Luke (AU q Ev, AU q Ev app) a decade later.[16] Chromatius of Aquileia produced a commentary on Matthew in a series of sermons in the same period (CHRO Mt), relying heavily on Fortunatianus. Jerome's four-volume commentary on Matthew (HI Mt, written in 398) was based on Origen and other Greek sources: Latin translations of Origen's commentary were made in the middle of the fifth century (ORI Mt, ORI ser).[17] Several anonymous commentaries are probably also fifth-century, including Pseudo-Theophilus (PS-THl), AN Mt and, from an Arian setting, AN Mt h.[18] After this, there is a gap before the flourishing of Insular scholarship in the eighth and ninth centuries with the commentaries of Frigulus (FRI, which has recently been shown to be dependent on Fortunatianus),[19] Sedulius Scottus (SED-S Mt), Pseudo-Alcuin (PS-ALC Mt), Pseudo-Jerome (PS-HI Ev), a series of *Quaestiones* (AN q Mt), and some anonymous Irish fragments (AN Löf). There is also a ninth-century commentary written in Germany and ascribed to Salonius (PS-SALO Mt).

The Old Latin version of the Beatitudes (Matthew 5:1–12) attested in Cyprian's *testimonia* (CY te) has *felices* ('happy'), although all surviving gospel codices, including VL 1, have *beati* ('blessed'). In the Lord's Prayer, the earliest Latin tradition and most Vulgate manuscripts have the present tense for 'forgive', *dimittimus*, at Matthew 6:12 but a handful of Vulgate witnesses have the perfect (*dimisimus*, 'have forgiven'), an early Greek reading found in GA 01* and 03. After *in temptatione* in the next verse, a number of Latin authors including Hilary of Poitiers, Jerome, Ambrose, and Chromatius add *quam sufferre non possumus* ('which we cannot bear'): this may be of liturgical origin.[20] VL 1 has a short doxology at the end of the Lord's Prayer, but this is absent from the other Old Latin witnesses and the discussions in Tertullian and Cyprian. There are a few readings in VL 3 which appear to be shared with the Diatessaron. The light in the water following Jesus' baptism at Matthew 3:15 is also found with a slightly different wording in VL 7, which reads:

> *et cum baptizaretur Iesus lumen magnum fulgebat de aqua, ita ut timerent omnes qui congregati erant.*

> And when Jesus was baptized, a great light began to shine from the water, so that all who had gathered were afraid.

Most Old Latin manuscripts have two interpolations in Matthew 20:28. The first usually reads:

> *uos autem quaeritis de pusillo crescere et de maiore minores esse.*

> But you seek to grow from what is small and to be smaller from what is greater.

---

[16] Discussion of the biblical text in Mizzi 1954; Mees 1966 also considers the text of Matthew 5.
[17] See Souter 1937 and 1941.   [18] See pages 54 and 65 above.
[19] Dorfbauer 2015.
[20] See Doignon 1977. It is also found at 1 Corinthians 10:13 in VL 77 and 78.

This is followed by a longer passage similar, but not identical, to Luke 14:8–10:

> *intrantes autem et rogati ad cenam nolite recumbere in locis eminentioribus ne*
> *forte clarior te superueniat et accedens qui ad cenam uocauit te dicat tibi: adhuc*
> *deorsum accede et confundaris. si autem in loco inferiori recubueris et superuenerit*
> *humilior te, dicet tibi qui te ad cenam uocauit: accede adhuc superius et erit hoc*
> *tibi utilius.*

> But when you are invited to a dinner and go in, do not sit in the more prominent
> places in case someone more important than you should then arrive, and the one
> who asked you to dinner should come and say to you 'Go lower down' and you
> should be shamed. But if you have sat in a lower place and one less worthy than
> you should then come, the one who asked you to dinner will say to you 'Go
> further up' and this will be to your advantage.

These are both present in Fortunatianus' commentary, as is the addition at
Matthew 24:41 from the parallel passage at Luke 17:34, *duo in lecto unus*
adsumetur et unus reliquetur ('Two people are on a bed: one will be taken and
one will be left') although VL 3 reads *tecto* ('roof') for *lecto* ('bed'). The whole
of Matthew 23:14 is missing from the earliest Latin witnesses and the Vulgate,
although it is included by an intermediate strand of pre-Vulgate tradition (VL
4, 6, 8, 10, 11, 12).

Matthew was the first gospel to be revised by Jerome, and he makes a
number of comments about readings known to him. For example, he was
familiar with some manuscripts which read *operibus suis* ('by her works')
rather than *filiis suis* ('by her children') at Matthew 11:19, and others which
omitted Matthew 16:2–3, even though none of these have been preserved. At
Matthew 6:11 all Old Latin manuscripts have *cotidianum* for ἐπιούσιον (as in
the English 'daily bread'), but Jerome introduced a calque, *supersubstantialem*.
By the time he reached Luke, however, Jerome was less interventionist and
allowed *cotidianum* to remain in Luke 11:3. Jerome also knew the Old Latin
tradition in Matthew 21:29–31 that it was the second son (*nouissimus*; VL 2, 3,
4, 5, 8, 11, 12) who did the will of the father, even though he failed to keep his
promise. He explained this by suggesting that Jesus' interlocutors deliberately
gave the incorrect answer![21]

In Insular tradition, the first seventeen verses of Matthew are re-interpreted
as a separate genealogical text, the 'Book of the Birth of Jesus Christ' (from the
opening words of Matthew 1:1, *Liber generationis Iesu Christi*). Matthew 1:18
is treated as the beginning of the gospel itself, with decoration of the initial
letters ₰ (the *chi–rho* of the *nomen sacrum* for Christ).[22] There are no fewer
than five interpolations in Matthew which are considered characteristic of
Insular tradition: the addition of *erat autem illis uentus contrarius* in 8:24 ('but
the wind was against them', cf. Mark 6:48); *sine patris uestri uoluntate qui est*

---

[21] HI Mt 3.   [22] See further McGurk 1956:257–8.

in caelis at 10:29 ('without the will of your father who is in heaven'); *uenerunt
et adorauerunt eum* at 14:35 ('they came and worshipped him'); *cum coeper-
unt autem fieri* at 24:31 ('but when they began to be'); *alius autem accepta
lancea pupungit latus eius et exiit aqua et sanguis* after 27:49 ('but another,
having taken a spear, pierced his side and water and blood came out', cf. John
19:30). Some of these are attested in Old Latin witnesses and thus represent
early harmonizations which survived in part of Vulgate tradition.

Mark

There are twelve consistently Old Latin manuscripts of Mark (VL 1, 2, 3, 4, 5,
6, 8, 10, 13, 14, 16, 17) along with one two-page fragment (VL 19). Thirteen
manuscripts are mixed-text or predominantly Vulgate (VL 7, 9A, 11, 11A, 12,
15, 19A, 27, 28, 29, 30, 35, 48): of these, VL 9A, 11A, and 19A have significant
Old Latin portions. There are also two lectionaries (VL 31, 32), and four sets of
canon tables with text (VL 10, 39, 40, 46). Burton also discerns a single
common source for the extant manuscripts of Mark, albeit different in places
from the other Synoptic Gospels.[23] Haelewyck's Vetus Latina edition includes
rich lists of information about Latin readings and their Greek parallels in the
introduction.[24] His identification of text-types corresponds to those outlined
by Fischer, described above. As in Matthew, the distribution of VL 1 and VL 2
is largely complementary, with the former only extant in the second half of
the Gospel. Not only does VL 6 feature a complicated mix of text-types K, C, I
and the Vulgate but it also contains a surprisingly large number of readings
peculiar to this manuscript, many of them expansions. In addition to the
Vetus Latina edition, Haelewyck is also responsible for the Latin part of the
Marc multilingue project, which includes transcriptions and a French translation of VL 1, 2, 5, and 8.[25]

Considered in antiquity as an abbreviation of the other Synoptic Gospels,
Mark is not well served by Latin commentators. The authenticity of the ten-
sermon commentary attributed to Jerome has recently been brought into
question again and may be a translation of a Greek work.[26] The only surviving
Latin commentaries dedicated to this book are by Cummianus of Durrow in
the first half of the seventh century (CU-D Mc, previously PS-HI Mc) and
Bede a century later (BED Mc), although it is also covered in the fifth-century
Pseudo-Theophilus commentary (PS-THl).

The most famous textual problem in Mark concerns the end of the Gospel.[27]
VL 1 is the only witness in any language for the 'Shorter Ending' by itself, not

---

[23] Burton 2000:48.   [24] Haelewyck 2013–; see also 1999 and 2003.
[25] See <http://www.safran.be/marcmultilingue/>. The Vulgate text is given from Vg^Se s.
[26] Haelewyck 2013–:21–3.   [27] See, for example, Aland 1969.

followed by the 'Longer Ending' of Mark 16:9–20. Its text (illustrated in Image 2) reads:

> *omnia autem quaecumque praecepta erant et qui cum puero erant breuiter exposuerunt. post haec et ipse Iesus adparuit et ab orientem usque usque in orientem misit per illos sanctam et incorruptam praedicationis[28] salutis aeternae. amen.*

> But those who were also with the boy [for *Petro*, Peter?] told in brief everything which they had been instructed. After this, Jesus himself appeared too and sent the holy and unchanging <message> of the preaching of eternal salvation through them from the east all the way right to the east [west?]. Amen.

The 'Shorter Ending' is not found in any other Latin manuscript: the 'Longer Ending' is attested by VL 6, 8, 13, and 16 as well as Vulgate witnesses (including VL 11 and 15). Several Old Latin codices lack the conclusion of this Gospel, because Mark is last in the Old Latin sequence and the pages at the end of a manuscript are most vulnerable to damage.

As a key early witness to the text of Mark, VL 1 contains a number of significant readings, including expansions. For instance, in the first half of Mark 14:41, it reads:

> *et uenit tertio et ubi adorauit dicit illis: dormite iam nunc, ecce adpropinquauit qui me tradit. et post pusillum excitauit illos et dixit: iam hora est, ecce traditur . . .*

> And he came a third time and when he worshipped he says to them 'Sleep on now; behold the one who betrays me has arrived.' And after a little, he woke them up and said 'Now it is time, see he is handed over . . .'.

Similarly, there is a gloss after Mark 16:4 which describes the resurrection:

> *subito autem ad horam tertiam tenebrae diei factae sunt per totam orbem terrae et descenderunt de caelis angeli et surgent in claritate uiui dei; simul ascenderunt cum eo et continuo lux facta est. tunc illae accesserunt ad monimentum . . .*

> But suddenly at the third hour the shadows of the day came across the whole globe and the angels descended from the heavens and they will arise in the glory of the living God; at the same time they ascended with him and straightaway it was light. Then the women went to the tomb . . . .

Other markers of the secondary nature of its text include the relocation of Mark 10:25 before 10:24, in order to provide a more logical sequence, and a misreading of the Greek in Mark 9:49: *omnia autem substantia consumitur* ('but all substance is consumed') represents οὐσία rather than θυσία. On the other hand, it also contains some shorter readings, such as *nemini dixeris in castello* at Mark 8:26. VL 2 attests to some interesting forms, including a

---

[28] The word *praedicationis* was initially omitted and added in the bottom margin (indicated by the symbol *hd*); however, only *prae* appears to be original and the rest of the word has been rewritten.

strangely garbled version of the Aramaic phrase in Mark 5:41, reading *tabea acultha cumhi*. It has been observed that the final *–i*, also found in VL 2 and the Vulgate, reflects the Aramaic feminine ending.[29]

At Mark 1:41, four Latin codices state that Jesus was 'angry' (*iratus*; VL 3, 5, 8, 14) rather than 'full of compassion'. The only Greek evidence for this is the reading ὀργισθείς in Codex Bezae, which may have been influenced by the Latin side. In fact, *iratus* could have arisen as an internal Latin development, stemming from the misreading of *miseratus*; the earliest Latin reading is *misericordia actus*, while Jerome appears to have introduced *misertus eius* in the Vulgate. A similar situation is found at Mark 15:34 where, in place of 'forsaken', the earliest Latin tradition appears to support 'scorned' (*maledixisti* VL 1, *exprobrasti* VL 6, *in opprobrium dedisti* VL 17), corresponding to ὠνείδας on the Greek side of Codex Bezae. Although the phrase 'the Son of God' in Mark 1:1 is missing in parts of the Greek tradition (reflected in Victorinus of Poetovio, Rufinus' translation of Origen and several of Jerome's quotations), there is no clear Latin support for its absence.

Several Old Latin witnesses have an interpolation at the end of Mark 13:2 based on Mark 14:58, although the wording differs. The earliest witness is Cyprian, who reads *et post triduum aliud excitabitur sine manibus* ('after three days another will be raised up without hands'; CY te 1.15). There is only one interpolation in Mark characteristic of Insular witnesses, the addition of *fuga uestra* ('your flight') in Mark 13:18, which actually corresponds to the majority of Greek manuscripts; some witnesses have *uel sabbato* ('or on the sabbath'), again with Greek support: both derive from the parallel passage at Matthew 24:20.

Luke

There are eleven consistently Old Latin manuscripts of Luke (VL 2, 3, 4, 5, 6, 8, 10, 11, 13, 14, 17) and six fragments of four pages or fewer (VL 16, 21, 22, 26, 36, 44). Ten manuscripts are mixed-text or predominantly Vulgate (VL 7, 9A, 11A, 12, 15, 27, 28, 29, 30, 35, 48), among which VL 35 features a consistently Old Latin portion in Luke 4–9. There are three lectionaries (VL 18, 31, 32), and four sets of canon tables with text (VL 10, 39, 40, 46). The oldest texts are VL 2 and 3, while significant early material is preserved in VL 6. The other manuscripts generally represent the Italian text, led by VL 4, 8, and 17. VL 10, given in full in the Oxford Vulgate, reflects a different Greek text on a number of occasions in this Gospel. Burton observes that although the surviving Old Latin versions of Luke share a common origin, a higher proportion of archaic

---

[29] Metzger 1994:74–5.

readings (such as *similitudo* rather than *parabola*) are preserved in European traditions and can be used to differentiate between subgroups.[30]

Among the handful of commentaries on Luke, Ambrose of Milan holds pride of place (AM Lc, written in 390).[31] Contemporary with this are Augustine's *Quaestiones* (AU q) and an Arian commentary (AN Lc). Fortunatianus of Aquileia (FO-A) only considers Luke 2–5. After the fifth-century Pseudo-Theophilus (PS-THl), there is then a gap before Bede's commentary from the beginning of the eighth century (BED Lc) and another a few years later also attributed to Bede (PS-BED Lc).[32]

Luke provides the three New Testament items always numbered among the biblical Odes.[33] It is interesting to note that some Old Latin sources name Elizabeth rather than Mary as the speaker of the *Magnificat* (VL 3, 4, 11 and Nicetas of Remesiana; see also the Latin Irenaeus, Jerome's translation of Origen, and the widespread series of *capitula* KA A).[34] The re-use of other verses in a liturgical context may also preserve an Old Latin form. For example, the angelic greeting to the shepherds at Luke 2:14 is found as both *gloria in excelsis* and *gloria in altissimis*: despite the adoption of the latter in the Vulgate, the former continues to be widespread in liturgical and pictorial representations for many centuries. It is also common for Lukan references to the Old Testament to be extended. Almost all Latin witnesses, including the Vulgate, continue the quotation of Isaiah 61:2 at Luke 4:19 with the phrase *et diem retributionis* ('and the day of retribution') despite minimal attestation in Greek. Similarly, at Luke 3:22 Old Latin witnesses, including Hilary of Poitiers and manuscripts known to Augustine, incorporate a line from Psalm 2:7, 'you are my son, today I have begotten you' (*filius meus es tu, ego hodie genui te*).

VL 5 has a unique addition at the end of Luke 6:4, known as the 'Cambridge pericope', incorporating an *agraphon* (a tradition about Jesus circulating separately from the New Testament). It reads:

> *eodem die uidens quendam operantem sabbato et dixit illi homo si quidem scis quod facis beatus es si autem nescis maledictus et trabaricator legis.*

> On the same day, seeing a man working on the Sabbath, he said to him: Man, if you know what you are doing, you are blessed; but if you do not know, you are cursed and a transgressor of the Law.

There are comparable insertions of unusual material in other manuscripts. VL 2 has a text in Luke 23:5 which Epiphanius attributes to Marcion (a shorter form is found in VL 6):

> *et filios nostros et uxores auertit a nobis non enim baptizantur sicut et nos nec se mundant.*

---

[30] Burton 2000:48–57.   [31] See Rolando 1945–6.
[32] See Laistner 1937, Hen 2003, and Gorman 2003b.   [33] See page 90.
[34] See Bogaert 1984; Metzger 1994:109; Kloha 2013.

And he alienates our sons and wives from us, for they are not baptized as also we are, nor do they purify themselves.

At the end of Luke 23:48, VL 7 adds a line which has parallels in both the Diatessaron and the *Gospel of Peter*:

dicentes uae uobis quae facta sunt hodie propter peccata nostra; adpropinquauit enim desolatio Hierusalem.

Saying, 'Woe to you on account of our sins that have been committed this day! For the desolation of Jerusalem has drawn near.'

Early Latin tradition more generally provides support for several other additions, including Jesus' rebuke to the disciples at Luke 9:54–6, the angel and the bloody sweat at Luke 22:43–44 and a reference to abolishing the law at Luke 23:2. The last of these continues to be found in Insular Vulgate manuscripts, as does the addition of the names *Maria Magdalena et altera Maria* in Luke 24:1. There are also a number of instances of verses missing from Old Latin gospel books, such as the whole of Luke 5:39 and 23:17 and Jesus' prayer for forgiveness in Luke 23:34.

Other pre-Vulgate features in Luke include the re-ordering of the Temptations in VL 4, 6, 10, 11, 13, and 14, transposing Luke 4:5–8 and 9–12 in order to match Matthew 4:5–11. VL 5 likewise adjusts the genealogy at the end of Luke 3 to bring it into conformity with that of Matthew. A reading unique to the Latin tradition (apart from the Greek of Codex Bezae) is the colourful reference to 'a basket of dung' (*cophinum stercoris*) at Luke 13:8. There are two forms of the text of the Last Supper in Old Latin manuscripts, both of which involve the omission of one of the cups (Luke 22:20): VL 3, 5, 8, 11, and 17 have the order cup first, then bread, while VL 2 and 4 appear to have changed the sequence back to bread, then cup. VL 11 supplies the name of the robbers at Luke 23:32, reading *Ioathas et Maggatras*. In contrast, VL 14 names the latter as *Capnatas* and VL 6 reads *Zoatham et Camma* at both Matthew 27:38 and Mark 15:27. A misinterpretation of the place name leads to the naming of the two disciples at Luke 24:13 as *Ammaus et Cleophas* in VL 2, 4, 8 and 14. A further misreading is found in VL 3, 4, 8, 11, 13, 14, and 17 at Luke 16:26, where *qui ueniunt...transire* derives from ἐλθόντες rather than θέλοντες. Within the Vulgate tradition, Luke 6:35 was altered at some point from *nihil desperantes* ('despairing of nothing') to *nihil inde sperantes* ('hoping for nothing from it'), which is arguably closer to the Greek.

The Vetus Latina *Arbeitsbericht* of 2014 includes the announcement of a new edition of Luke to be undertaken by Thomas Johann Bauer, the current director of the Institute. A study of the early Latin text of Luke 5 is included in a *Festschrift* for two of his predecessors.[35]

[35] Amphoux 1993.

John

There are eleven consistently Old Latin manuscripts of John (VL 2, 3, 4, 5, 6, 8, 10, 11, 13, 14, 22) along with three fragments (VL 16, 22A, 25). Fifteen manuscripts are mixed-text or predominantly Vulgate (VL 7, 9A, 11A, 12, 15, 23, 27, 28, 29, 30, 33, 34, 35, 47, 48): of these, VL 11A, 33, and 47 have significant Old Latin portions. There are also four lectionaries (VL 18, 20, 24, 32; cf. VL 49), and four sets of canon tables with text (VL 10, 39, 40, 46). VL 33 and 47 consist of John alone, which is also the case for several Vulgate witnesses (e.g. Vg^{Oe} S). The oldest surviving text is VL 2, which often matches Cyprian's quotations. VL 3 offers an early European form; the other more archaic texts are VL 4 (in the first half of the gospel), 5 (which often uniquely matches its Greek text), 13 (although it also betrays Vulgate influence or independent comparison with Greek), 14, and 22. A second group of manuscripts reflect the fourth-century Italian text which preceded the Vulgate: VL 8 is the best example, joined by VL 4 (in the second half of the Gospel), 6, 11, 11A, and 16. Full transcriptions of the Old Latin manuscripts of John are available at <http://www.iohannes.com/vetuslatina>.

The principal ancient commentary was by Augustine in the form of 124 sermons (AU Jo) on Jerome's revised text.[36] The eighth and ninth centuries saw commentaries ascribed to Bede (PS-BED Jo), Jerome (PS-HI Jo), and Salonius (PS-SALO Jo), as well as the slightly earlier Pseudo-Jerome commentary on all four gospels (PS-HI Ev) and the commentary of Alcuin. A series of expositions of John, Matthew, and Luke attributed to Arnobius the Younger (AR exp) has recently been shown to be a much later composition.[37] Fortunatianus of Aquileia (FO-A) only treats the first two chapters.[38]

The Latin tradition provides the earliest evidence for the *Pericope Adulterae* of John 7:53–8:11. It is missing from VL 3, 10, 13, and the first hand of VL 11 but present in all other gospel books, albeit with minor variations in certain phrases corresponding to those found in Greek (e.g. 'beginning from the eldest' and 'up to the youngest').[39] Most Old Latin manuscripts also include the angel stirring the waters in John 5:3b–4, although it is absent from VL 5, 10, 11, 11A, and 13, and Jerome did not include it in the Vulgate. Three manuscripts have an extra phrase in John 6:56: VL 3 and 8 read *si acceperit homo corpus filii hominis quemadmodum panem uitae habebit uitam in illo* ('if a man receives the body of the Son of Man as the Bread of Life he will have life in him'); VL 5 has a slightly different form matching its unique Greek text of this interpolation.

As with the Beatitudes in Matthew, the opening of John is very stable: all surviving Latin manuscripts have *uerbum* for λόγος in John 1:1, even though

---

[36] On its biblical text, see Houghton 2008b.   [37] Dorfbauer 2014a.
[38] See Houghton 2015a.
[39] A full apparatus is given in Fischer 1991; among the many surveys, Becker 1963 is the most comprehensive. The extent of the missing pages of VL 4 indicates that these verses were present.

some Christian writers (principally Tertullian) show that *sermo* could have existed as an alternative rendering.[40] At John 1:13, Tertullian, some other writers and VL 4 and 9A have the singular *natus est*, reinterpreting the verse as a description of Jesus. Latin witnesses also support the reading *electus*, or a doublet *electus filius*, in John 1:34. The earliest Latin form of John 7:1 appears to be *non enim habebat potestatem* ('for he did not have the ability') rather than *non enim uolebat* ('for he did not wish'): this corresponds to a poorly-attested reading in Greek and other versions. VL 3 and Augustine add *et totum corpus* ('and the whole body') at the end of John 13:9, which has been taken to reflect full immersion baptism; the presence of *semel* ('once') and *iterum* ('again') in quotations of 13:10 may also relate to baptismal controversies.[41] At John 19:39, one group of pre-Vulgate manuscripts read *perticae*, 'on a pole', rather than *hyssopo*, 'on hyssop'. This may stem from haplography in Greek (ὑσσῷ for ὑσσώπῳ).

John appears to have been the last gospel to be revised by Jerome, and there are some occasions on which he appears to have introduced erroneous readings. At John 10:16, *unum ouile*, 'one fold', is peculiar to the Vulgate and, unless Jerome's text read αὐλή in place of ποίμνη, is less accurate than the Old Latin *unus grex* ('one flock').[42] Similarly, Jerome seems to have introduced *docebit* ('he will teach') for ὁδηγήσει ('he will guide') in John 16:13, although this may be an early misreading of the late Latin form *ducebit* (for *ducet*) early in the transmission of the Vulgate. Jerome also conflated the two earlier forms of John 21:22–23, reading *si sic eum uolo manere*, 'if I wish him to remain thus', despite the absence of *sic* from Greek tradition (apart from Codex Bezae). This variant formed the subject of discussions of the primacy of the Greek and Latin text, as well as discussions about celibacy.[43] Again, in the early history of the Vulgate, *discentium* ('the disciples') in John 21:12 was replaced by *discumbentium* ('those reclining'), under the influence of the context.

There are two interpolations which are found in Irish Vulgate manuscripts of John. A line from the Synoptic parallels at Matthew 27:41 and Mark 15:38 is added at the end of John 19:30, reading:

cum autem expirasset uelum templi scissum est medium a summo usque deorsum.

When he had breathed his last, the veil of the Temple was cut in half from the top to the bottom.

Similarly, the disciples' response from the miraculous catch of fish in Luke 5:5 is inserted into John 21:6 as follows:

dixerunt autem per totam noctem laborantes nihil cepimus; in uerbo autem tuo mittemus.

---

[40] Burton 2000:92 attributes this stability to the theological significance of the passage.
[41] See Houghton 2008b:303–4 and Petersen 1994:380–4.   [42] See Metzger 1977:354–5.
[43] See Metzger 1994:220–1 and Reynolds and Wilson 1991:152.

But they said: 'After working all night we have caught nothing: yet at your command we will cast.'

This text can be seen in the Book of Deer on line 16 of Image 12. VL 29 has the Lukan *laxabo* ('I will loosen') in place of *mittemus*.

B) ACTS OF THE APOSTLES

The development of the Latin version of Acts, and, indeed, the so-called 'Western' text more generally, has given rise to various complicated theories found in studies such as the classic survey of Jülicher 1914 and Boismard & Lamouille 1984. From his preliminary work towards the Vetus Latina edition, Petzer concluded that the surviving Latin witnesses of Acts all derive from a single version, often revised: even the Vulgate preserves traces of the most ancient Latin forms.[44] Fischer concurs but notes that there is some uncertainty as to when longer readings characteristic of the 'Western' text entered the Latin tradition. It is likely that some were in the Greek text used as the initial *Vorlage*, but others may have been introduced into the Latin tradition at a later point.[45]

The earliest surviving witnesses are quotations in Cyprian (text-type **K**), followed by a later revision (text-type **C**) found in VL 55, 74, and Augustine. The text immediately preceding the Vulgate (text-type **I**) attested by Lucifer of Cagliari and Ambrosiaster is most consistently found in VL 51 (Codex Gigas, 'gig'), accompanied by several lectionaries (VL 52, 57, 60, and 67). Two of the most significant manuscripts are Greek–Latin bilinguals: VL 5 (Codex Bezae, 'd'), the principal witness to the 'Western' text, and, from a different tradition, VL 50 (the 'Laudian Acts', 'e'), whose Latin text sometimes matches the 'Western' witnesses in contrast to its Greek side. There are also mixed texts: VL 54 ('p') combines elements from all surviving versions, ending up with an extended text which may go back as far as the fifth century; conversely VL 53 appears to be a revision postdating the Vulgate, based on a Greek text and eliminating the 'Western' interpolations. VL 61, 62, and 63 transmit a handful of Old Latin readings in Acts, while the Spanish lectionary tradition occasionally has marginal glosses (VL 56, 68, 69, 70, 71, 72, 73, 259, 262, 271). VL 53, 58, and 59 are primarily Vulgate.

The prefatory material to Acts is not as early as that for the Gospels, apart from a set of chapter titles from a fourth-century Donatist edition (KA Act

---

[44] Petzer 1993a, 1995:123.

[45] Fischer 1972:82 [1986:262]. Other early recensions of Acts are also found in the Greek tradition, e.g. 𝔓127. It is sometimes claimed that the 'Western' text is earlier than the standard form, but its characteristics mostly take the form of secondary expansions.

Don).[46] The principal prologue, PROL Act Mo, was composed at some point
in the fifth century. Lists of places, names, Old Testament citations and at least
one prologue and set of *capitula* are all of Spanish origin (PROL Act Lo, PROL
Act No, PROL Act Te, PROL Act Sp, KA Act Sp) and probably to be
connected with the seventh-century edition.[47] The other *capitula* are only
datable from their first surviving manuscript. Early Vulgate tradition is represented by KA A (found in Vg F and, later, Tours Bibles), KA C (in Vg A) and
KA Tur, composed by Bede. Manuscripts of the eighth and ninth century have
KA Sp^r (VL 7) and KA In (Vg^S I); KA Eln is not attested until the twelfth
century.

The earliest Latin commentary on Acts is that of Cassiodorus, which also
treats the Catholic Epistles and Revelation (CAr cpl); a single commentary on
Acts alone is not found until Bede (BED Act), who also published a revised
form two decades later.[48] Arator's *Historia Apostolica* (ARA) is a sustained
exegesis of Acts, including prose summaries relating to an Old Latin version.[49]
The text of Acts adopted in the Vulgate is believed to be the work of the same
reviser as the rest of the New Testament apart from the Gospels, although
different strands are preserved within the Vulgate tradition: the best manuscript for the Vulgate text of Acts is Vg G (VL 7), followed by Vg A and Vg F,
each of which appears to represent a different branch.[50] Alcuin's text is closest
to the last of these.

The attestation of longer readings varies across the Latin tradition. In some
cases there is plenty of Greek support, as in the addition of Acts 8:37 or the
extra clause *qui cum aduenerit loquetur tibi* ('who will speak to you when he
arrives') in most Old Latin witnesses at the end of Acts 10:32. In Acts 5:15, the
various Latin additions correspond to the alternatives preserved in the Greek
of Codex Bezae and the Laudian Acts. In contrast, the inclusion of Acts 18:4
is primarily attested in Latin tradition (VL 5, 51, 55 and the Clementine
Vulgate), as is the additional material before and at the opening of Acts
16:1: for these, Codex Bezae is the only Greek witness. At Acts 5:29, the re-
writing of the end of the verse to supply the answer to Peter's question and
identify him as the sole speaker of Acts 5:30 appears to be restricted to Latin
tradition and one Coptic manuscript. There are also examples of harmonization in Latin tradition, such as the detail in Acts 1:18 that Judas hanged
himself, based on Matthew 27:5. VL 51 and 54 re-order parts of Acts 7:3–4
in order to match the sequence in Genesis. Omissions are more rare, although
the absence of *et . . . salus* in Acts 4:12 from Latin witnesses may be a deliberate
abbreviation.

Some of the extra phrases present in Latin tradition were incorporated by
Erasmus and feature in the Greek *Textus Receptus*. These include an insertion

---

[46] Bogaert 1982.   [47] See page 63.   [48] Laistner 1937.
[49] See Deproost & Haelewyck 1993.   [50] See the tables in Fischer 1972:66 [1986:241].

in Acts 9:5–7 based on Acts 26:14 and 22:10, and the addition *hic dicet tibi quid te oporteat facere* ('he will tell you what you should do') in Acts 10:6.[51] Acts 15:34, 23:25, and 28:29 are all found in pre-Vulgate tradition as well as the Clementine Vulgate and the *Textus Receptus*, bearing witness to the longevity of these additions.

Certain manuscripts feature unusual readings, especially VL 55, the earliest surviving continuous-text witness. At Acts 4:13–16 it seems to have a fuller form of the 'Western' text than VL 5, while it is the only witness to two details which characterize the paralysed man in Acts 14:8–9 as a Jewish proselyte: *habens timorem dei* ('having the fear of God') in the first verse and *libenter* ('gladly') in the latter.[52] VL 51 is the sole Latin manuscript to add *lingua hebraica* in Acts 22:7, although it is also found in the Harklean Syriac.[53] It also has 'two' rather than 'seven' sons of Sceva at Acts 19:14 matching 'both', the standard text of 19:16. A longer form of Acts 27:34 occurs in VL 51, reading:

> *ideo hortor uos accipere escam. hoc enim pro uestra salute est. spero enim in deo meo quia nullius uestrum capillus de capite cadet.*
>
> For this reason, I urge you to take the food. For this is for your safety. For I hope in my God that no hair will fall from the head of any of you.

Some forms represent errors in Greek or Latin witnesses, such as *potestate* in Acts 3:12 (for *pietate*), or *gloria* for *dextera* in Acts 5:31 (deriving from δόξῃ in place of δεξιᾳ).[54]

The Vetus Latina edition of Acts is currently in preparation at Mainz, where it has been accompanied by unpublished studies of its text in Cyprian, Lucifer of Cagliari, and Bede. Preliminary collations of the manuscripts by verse are available for download from the project website (<http://nttf.klassphil.uni-mainz.de/> with a link to *Kollationsdateien*). Earlier work towards this edition may be seen in the articles of Petzer on Acts 6, Tertullian, and Augustine.[55]

C) PAULINE EPISTLES

Ten of the fourteen Pauline Epistles have been edited in the Vetus Latina series by Hermann Josef Frede (Ephesians to Hebrews: Frede 1962–4; 1966–71; 1975–82). In anticipation of a Vetus Latina edition of the four principal letters (Romans, 1 and 2 Corinthians and Galatians), a collation of early witnesses is currently in preparation by the present author; full transcriptions are available at <http://www.epistulae.org/>. For these remaining books, the critical apparatus of the Oxford Vulgate is valuable, and Latin evidence, especially early

---

[51] See further Metzger 1994:8*, 318, 325.   [52] Metzger 1994:373.
[53] Metzger 1994:430.   [54] Metzger 1994:290.   [55] Petzer 1988, 1991a, and 1991b.

authors, is cited in NA28 and UBS5. Frede's edition includes almost 200 manuscripts, enabling the identification of various subgroups representing different stages in Vulgate tradition.[56]

In Latin, the Pauline Epistles always seem to have circulated as a collection comprising at least the thirteen core letters, initially as a self-contained corpus and later as part of a New Testament. Hebrews is normally also present, although sometimes shows evidence of different treatment, while some Vulgate manuscripts include the pseudonymous Epistle to the Laodiceans and, very rarely, 3 Corinthians.[57] The surviving textual evidence for the Pauline Epistles in Latin is not as ancient as that of the Gospels, although they are also believed to derive from a single original translation. According to Fischer, this gave rise to two branches. On one side an early African form, text-type K (only preserved in quotations) was revised in the third century to become text-type I. Text-type D, in his opinion, was a separate development from the initial version, using the same vocabulary as text-type I but with different readings. Frede, however, believes that text-type D is the most ancient and did not originate in Africa, not least because Hebrews was absent from the early African biblical canon. In his account, text-type K was a branch of D attested only in Africa, without Hebrews. Fischer thinks that the Vulgate derived from an Old Latin text which was a mixture of types D and I (perhaps similar to VL 61 and the lemmata of manuscript B of Pelagius).[58] The different text-types are also characterized by their order of the epistles: the principal witnesses to text-type I have Phil–Eph–Col–12Thess, while a later subgroup (including Priscillian, Pelagius, and many Vulgate witnesses) has Eph–Phil–12Thess–Col; text-type D has Eph–Col–Phil–12Thess; the Vulgate (V) follows the Greek model with Eph–Phil–Col–12Thess.[59] The text adopted as the Vulgate appears to have been revised at the end of the fourth century in Rome, probably in Pelagian circles: Pelagius' own commentary seems to be the earliest witness to this form.

Only fifteen manuscripts are listed in the Pauline Epistles section of the Vetus Latina *Register* (VL 75–89), although other witnesses are described elsewhere. The oldest complete manuscript is VL 75 (Codex Claromontanus), copied in the middle of the fifth century, with the bilingual text-type D also found in Lucifer of Cagliari. In the earlier epistles (Romans to Colossians), the Latin text of VL 75 appears to have been revised and is often quite close to the Vulgate; from 1 Thessalonians to Hebrews, it is older and more distinctive. VL 89, the lemmata of the Anonymous Commentary, is another witness to text-type D; this form is also found in Hebrews in VL 109. Text-type I is first

---

[56] Many of these manuscripts are listed in Appendix 2.

[57] On these two epistles, see Bogaert 2012:90: 3 Corinthians is only present in the Bible of Biasca (Vg[S] B; page 266) and the contents list of VL 86.

[58] Fischer 1972:24 [1986:244].   [59] See further page 196 and Frede 1964:160–8.

attested in Novatian and Marius Victorinus, followed by Ambrosiaster, Ambrose, and Rufinus. Frede and Fischer classify VL 64 and the quotations of Augustine as early witnesses to text-type I, although these are sufficiently distinct from Ambrosiaster and other witnesses that they could be considered as a separate text-type, possibly with an African connection. VL 86, from North Italy, is a more clear-cut instance of type I. Four small fragments contain portions of Romans (VL 79—a Gothic–Latin bilingual—and VL 80), Ephesians (VL 85), and Hebrews (VL 82). VL 135 is Old Latin in the last two chapters of Romans. Of the Greek–Latin bilingual codices, only VL 75 and 85 are genuinely independent Old Latin witnesses: VL 76 and 83 are descended from VL 75; VL 77 is an ad hoc interlinear translation; VL 78 is Vulgate. Despite the practice in some editions of the Greek New Testament, it is rarely worth citing the Latin text of these later bilinguals as witnesses independent from their Greek side. The other manuscripts in the *Register* are mostly Vulgate (VL 51, 54, 58, 65, 67, 81, and 88), apart from one page of 2 Corinthians in VL 88 which is Old Latin. Pauline lectionaries are also Vulgate (VL 87, 251), including the Spanish lectionary tradition (VL 56, 68, 69, 70, 71, 72, 73, 259, 262, 271); VL 84, a list of lections, is a mixed text. The three principal manuscripts of the Pauline Epistles used in the Stuttgart Vulgate are G (VL 7), A (Vg A), and R (Vg^{Sp} R). G has a better text in all letters apart from Titus and Philemon, in which the text of A, which may derive from Rome, is best.[60] The original text of F (Vg F) features a number of Old Latin readings, which Victor corrected according to R, a consistent text of North Italian origin. Alcuin's text stands somewhere between A and R.

The early Latin commentary tradition on Paul is unusually rich. Marius Victorinus wrote on several letters, of which three survive (MAR Gal, Eph, Phil). Ambrosiaster's extensive commentary (AMst) covers thirteen epistles but not Hebrews, with a later authorial revision.[61] Jerome's commentaries on four shorter epistles are often dependent on Origen (HI Gal, Eph, Tt, Phlm); Rufinus translated Origen's *Commentary on Romans*, substituting an Old Latin form for the biblical lemmata (RUF Rm).[62] Augustine's early work includes a commentary on Galatians (AU Gal) and two expositions of parts of Romans (AU Rm, AU Rm in) as well as numerous exegetical sermons. The anonymous Budapest commentary on Paul includes Hebrews (AN Paul): its biblical text is referred to as VL 89, and it appears to have originated as a series of marginal comments in a codex of the Epistles in Rome in 397 or 405. Pelagius' commentary on the thirteen Epistles (PEL) was written in Rome

---

[60] Tables of comparison in Fischer 1972:70–1 [1986:248]; see also 1971 [1985:382–4].

[61] See page 25. In most manuscripts of Ambrosiaster, the end of 1 Corinthians and the beginning of 2 Corinthians have been replaced with Pelagius' commentary on the missing portion, presumably due to damage in an exemplar which lies behind the entire tradition. See Souter 1922:51–60.

[62] See Bardy 1920 and the works of Hammond-Bammel.

between 406 and 411, incorporating material from AN Paul. The original form only survives in two manuscripts, one with a Vulgate text (A) and one with an Old Latin text (B).[63] An early revision of Pelagius' commentary goes under the name of Cassiodorus, although Cassiodorus only reworked Romans himself (CAr Rm, etc.). The Pseudo-Jerome commentary on Paul is also a version of Pelagius with substantial interpolations (PS-HI Rm, etc.), while there are even traces of Pelagius in Sedulius Scottus' ninth-century commentary, the *Collectaneum in Apostolum* (SED-S Rm, etc.). The Greek commentary on Paul of Theodore of Mopsuestia (THr) was soon translated into Latin, probably in the circles of Julian of Eclanum in fifth-century Italy. Only Galatians to Philemon is extant; the Greek lemmata appear to have been rendered ad hoc by the commentator.

The earliest Latin prefatory material to Paul comprises the Marcionite prologues (PROL Ma) known to Marius Victorinus and a set of *capitula* which may be of Donatist origin (KA C for the thirteen epistles and KA H in Hebrews).[64] At the end of the fourth century, Priscillian of Avila created an edition including his canons to the Epistles (PRIS can [S 656, 672]).[65] The reviser of the Vulgate, around the year 400, was responsible for the preface *Primum quaeritur* (PROL Paul 1 [S 670]) and the *Argumentum* to Romans (PROL Rm Arg [S 674]). Both of these were sometimes attributed to Pelagius, as was the *Concordia Epistularum* (AN conc [S 646]): Pelagius does bear partial witness to a set of prologues to the individual epistles which drew on the 'Marcionite' prologues (PROL Pel). *Primum quaeritur* was re-used in prologues to the Epistles from the fifth and sixth centuries (PROL Paul 3 and 4 [S 669 and 651]). Later manuscripts include prefatory material taken from Ambrosiaster, Jerome, and Isidore. As with Acts, lists of names and quotations appear to be of seventh-century Spanish origin (PROL No, PROL Te; cf. KA Sp). The most widespread series of *capitula*, which may go back to at least the fourth century, is KA A (KA M in Romans, with an abbreviated form A^{br} or M^{br}), present in both Vg F and Vg A. Vg F also has a set of anti-Pelagian chapter titles in Romans, KA Ant (or KA Antipel), which extends to the rest of the Epistles in other manuscripts. One set of prologues and *capitula* has been identified as the work of Bede (PROL Eln, KA Eln). KA R is found in the eighth-century VL 84 (Vg^{SP} R), while the full form of KA S is only found in VL 89: KA R, S, and T are often mixed with each other, and are found in some Tours Bibles. However, KA B also has a Tours connection, appearing before some letters in Vg^S Q and Vg^S Φ^V. KA Ost, only found in a manuscript from Lyons, begins each list with the word *ostendit*. Different sets of *capitula* are

---

[63] See page 40.
[64] For more on the Marcionite prologues, see Jongkind 2015 and page 198; the *capitula* are discussed in Bogaert 1982:11.
[65] See further pages 20 and 62–3.

found before Hebrews: KA Hbr Z are a translation and completion of the Greek Euthalian material for this letter. [66]

In addition to work on the early commentators, including a complete reconstruction of Ambrosiaster's Pauline text (Vogels 1957) and a summary of the major early commentaries (Souter 1927), there are a number of monographs on the Latin Pauline tradition. Many of the earlier studies require updating in the light of the Vetus Latina edition, including Frede's overview of the manuscripts (Frede 1964).[67] Individual epistles have been treated as follows: 1 Corinthians (Fröhlich 1995–8; Kloha 2006); 2 Corinthians (Zimmermann 1960); Galatians (Zimmer 1887; Schäfer 1935, 1939); Ephesians (Frede 1958); Colossians (Borse 1966); 1 Thessalonians (Nellessen 1965); 1 Timothy (Tinnefeld 1963); Titus (Wolgarten 1968); Hebrews (Schäfer 1929; von Harnack 1931; Frede 1987; Schlossnikel 1991). Doignon considers the text of Romans in Hilary of Poitiers and a number of individual verses in other Epistles.

The final chapters of Romans and the placing of the concluding doxology (16:25–27) are a well-known textual crux.[68] Three Latin manuscripts have the doxology after Romans 14:23 (where it is repeated in most Greek witnesses): VL 86, which omits it from Romans 16, and two Vulgate manuscripts in Munich.[69] The space left after 14:23 in the Greek text in VL 77 suggests that the doxology was present in the Latin manuscript used for the translation (compare John 7:53ff. in VL 27). The abbreviated form of the letter attributed to Marcion is believed to have ended at this point. Tertullian refers to Romans 14:10 as 'at the end of the epistle' (TE Marc 5.14) and Cyprian does not quote from Romans 15 or 16. The *Concordia Epistularum* does not have any reference after Romans 14, and neither do the earliest series of *capitula* (KA Rm A (and A[br]) and KA Rm Ant) apart from a reference to the doxology—presumably at the end of Romans 14. Jerome mentions that the doxology is absent from the end of Romans 16 in several manuscripts. While the rest of VL 75 is written in sense lines, these verses are written continuously, suggesting that they were added from a separate source. Romans 16:24 is absent from a number of early Latin witnesses as well as the Vulgate, but present in Ambrosiaster and VL 61. (It can be seen added by a second hand in the first column of VL 7 in Image 16.) There is no independent Latin evidence for the absence of the references to Rome in 1:7 and 1:15, nor, indeed, the omission of *qui sunt Ephesi* from Ephesians 1:1, although Tertullian, the Marcionite Prologue to Colossians, and the earliest Prologue to Ephesians note that Marcion knew this letter as Laodiceans.

---

[66] Blomkvist 2012.
[67] Compare also Ziegler 1876a, Diehl 1921, Plooij 1936, and Thiele 1969.
[68] See Gamble 1977, Metzger 1994:470–3, and Parker 2008:270–4.
[69] Munich, Bayerische Staatsbibliothek, Clm 17040 and 17043; see Schumacher 1929.

The Latin tradition of the Pauline Epistles is characterized by a number of doublets and glosses. For example, *clarificate et portate deum* ('glorify and bear God') in 1 Corinthians 6:20 is attested from earliest times (Cyprian, Tertullian, Ambrosiaster): *portate* apparently arises from the Greek variant ἄρα τε (or ἄραγε) in place of δή, reinterpreted as ἄρατε. At 1 Thessalonians 2:7 the Stuttgart Vulgate reads *lenes* ('gentle'), as found in the majority of Greek manuscripts (ἤπιοι), but the earlier Latin versions have *paruuli* ('children'), from νήπιοι: VL 7 has a doublet, *lenes paruuli*, which may in fact have been in the archetype of the Vulgate tradition. A similar situation occurs with *confidenter palam* at Colossians 2:15.[70] The double form in Hebrews 11:37, *secti sunt temptati sunt* ('they were cut down, they were attacked'), corresponds to the majority of Greek manuscripts (ἐπρίσθησαν ἐπειράσθησαν). Instances of glosses or harmonizations in Old Latin manuscripts include the additions of *aut iam iustificatus sum* ('or I have already been justified') in Philippians 3:12 and *fideli* and *fidelem* at 1 Corinthians 7:14. Numerous others occur in Vulgate tradition, such as *(quod uolo) bonum* and *(quod odi) malum* ('the good I wish' and 'the bad I hate') in order to clarify the Apostle's desires at Romans 7:15.

The significance of translation in theological development is nowhere clearer than at Romans 5:12, where the Latin version used by Augustine allowed him to develop the doctrine of Original Sin. The Greek ἐφ' ᾧ may simply mean 'in that' or 'because', but the literal rendering *in quo* connects the final clause with the 'one man' from earlier in the verse, suggesting that it is he 'in whom all have sinned'.[71] Paul's teaching about the rôle of women also provides instances of textual development. At 1 Corinthians 11:10, most Latin witnesses read *potestatem*, corresponding to ἐξουσίαν ('authority'). However, the use of 'veil' to gloss this word is found in several versions and Christian authors, and *uelamen* has replaced *potestatem* in VL 7 and 58. Latin manuscripts are among the witnesses which delay 1 Corinthians 14:34–35 until after 14:40; it has been suggested that in Codex Fuldensis, a scribal note and addition in the bottom margin was intended to result in the omission of these verses from liturgical reading.[72] The Latin translation of Hebrews 11:11 takes Sarah as the subject of the verb (*et ipsa Sarra sterilis uirtutem in conceptionem seminis accepit*, 'and barren Sarah herself received power to conceive'), despite the problems associated with the Greek phrase.[73] The only variant forms occur in Augustine and Jerome, who both omit *sterilis*; Augustine reads *uirtutem accepit ad emissionem seminis* ('received power to send forth seed'), while Jerome's paraphrase runs *accepit uirtutem ad recipiendum semen* ('received power to accept seed').

Liturgical influence may be seen in the account of the Last Supper at 1 Corinthians 11:24. VL 51 and later Vulgate manuscripts (including Alcuin and

---

[70] See Doignon 1994.   [71] See Harbert 1989.
[72] Metzger 1994:499–500; on this variant, see also Parker 2008:275–7.
[73] See Metzger 1994:602.

the Clementine Vulgate) add *accipite et manducate* ('take and eat') as Jesus'
opening words. Although the Stuttgart Vulgate matches the Greek of NA28
with *pro uobis* alone, in other Vulgate editions and manuscripts *quod pro uobis
tradetur* ('which will be handed over for you') is found instead. In place of
tradetur, which has no Greek support here, earlier Latin witnesses correspond
to κλώμενον ('broken'), with *frangitur* in VL 75 and Ambrosiaster, *frangetur* in
VL 77 and 78, and *confringetur* in VL 89. Most Latin witnesses have the
expansion *domini nostri Iesu Christi* at Ephesians 3:14, but it is absent from
Jerome's commentary and VL 59.

Some variations depend on similarities in forms, either in Greek or Latin.
The variation between καυθήσωμαι ('burn') and καυχήσωμαι ('boast') at 1
Corinthians 13:3 is well known, although the Latin tradition unanimously
supports the former, reading *ardeam* from Tertullian and Cyprian onwards. In
2 Corinthians 1:12, both ἐν ἁπλότητι ('in simplicity') and ἐν ἁγιότητι ('in
holiness') are supported by Latin witnesses. Conversely, where the same words
appear as a doublet in Greek and Old Latin manuscripts at 2 Corinthians 11:3,
the Vulgate only reads *simplicitate* while quotations in Latin authors just have
sanctitate.[74] Jerome observes that some Greek manuscripts read καιρῷ rather
than κυρίῳ in Romans 12:11: while he prefers the latter, the former is supported by Cyprian and Ambrosiaster as well as the bilinguals. Likewise, Latin
tradition is split between μαρτύριον (*testimonium*) and μυστήριον (*mysterium*)
in 1 Corinthians 2:1. At Ephesians 4:19, *desperantes* in all Latin sources derives
from the Greek ἀπηλπικότες ('hopeless'); Jerome's suggestion of *indolentes*
may reflect the alternative ἀπηλγηκότες ('lost all feeling'). The pre-Vulgate
tradition of Ephesians 5:14 attests to ἐπιψαύσει(s) ('will touch'), apart from
Ambrose with *inlucescet*: this comes from ἐπιφαύσει ('will enlighten'), as does
inluminabit in the Vulgate. At 2 Thessalonians 2:13, the Vulgate's *primitias*
('first-fruits') restores the earliest Greek form (ἀπαρχήν); *ab initio* and *a
principio* in earlier Latin witnesses come from ἀπ' ἀρχῆς ('from the beginning'). The reading *placuerunt* rather than *latuerunt* in some Vulgate manuscripts at Hebrews 13:2, including Codex Fuldensis and Alcuin's recension,
('they gave pleasure' rather than 'they were unaware') is an erroneous substitution of a more common Latin word.

There is very early Latin evidence for *resurgemus* ('we will arise') rather than
dormiemus ('we will sleep') in 1 Corinthians 15:51, along with the assertion
that **non** omnes immutabimur ('we will *not* all be changed'). The initial Latin
form of Galatians 3:14 appears to be *benedictionem*, matching εὐλογίαν rather
than ἐπαγγελίαν. Pre-Vulgate tradition has *Petrus* throughout Galatians,
which has been replaced by *Cephas* in the Vulgate when this is also present
in Greek. The omission of *in domino* from Ephesians 6:1 is, according to

---

[74] Metzger 1994:515.

Tertullian, a form characteristic of Marcion's text, but it is also absent from Cyprian, Ambrosiaster, and VL 89. At Colossians 2:2, all pre-Vulgate witnesses apart from Ambrose do not include *patris*, although VL 61, 75, and other Old Latin sources read *quod est Ch,ristus*. The addition of *Iesu* seems to be peculiar to the Vulgate. In some Latin traditions, 1 Thessalonians 5:21 is connected with an *agraphon* about becoming trustworthy bankers (γίνεσθε τραπεζίται δόκιμοι).[75] Although Latin manuscripts have *homo peccati* (ὁ ἄνθρωπος τῆς ἁμαρτίας, 'the man of sin') in 2 Thessalonians 2:3, the forms *delinquentiae homo* and *homo delicti* in Tertullian appear to reflect the earlier Greek reading ἀνομίας ('the man of lawlessness'). At 1 Timothy 5:19, the phrase *nisi sub duobus et tribus testibus* ('except with two or three witnesses') was missing from some manuscripts known to Jerome, and is not attested in VL 89, Cyprian, Ambrosiaster, or Pelagius. Conversely, even though *discede ab huiusmodi* ('depart from such a man') is found in 1 Timothy 6:5 as early as Cyprian, it appears to be secondary.[76] Almost all Latin texts have *gratia dei* (χάριτι θεοῦ, 'by the grace of God') at Hebrews 2:9. However, the reading χωρὶς θεοῦ ('apart from God') was known to Ambrosiaster (*sine deo*) and Jerome (*absque deo*) and appears in the margin of VL 7.[77]

Two verses are of particular significance for the history of the Latin version. The omission of the last two words of 2 Corinthians 10:12 and the first two words of the following verse seems to be due to eyeskip, and was never rectified in the Old Latin tradition: the Vulgate restores *nos autem* at the beginning of 10:13. However, this shared error in all Latin versions (corresponding to the Greek of the bilinguals) may point towards a single original translation. At 2 Timothy 2:17, the reading *ut cancer serpit* ('creeps like a crab/cancer') is found throughout the Latin tradition. It seems to be a mistranslation of ὡς γάγγραινα νομὴν ἕξει ('will spread like gangrene'), although Frede suggests that it may derive from an unattested Greek form νεμεθῇ rather than νομὴν ἕξει.[78] If Tertullian's reference *et sermones serpentes uelut cancer* ('and words creeping like a crab', TE hae 7.7) is a reference to this verse, it could demonstrate that he knew a Latin version of this Epistle.

D) CATHOLIC EPISTLES

In Latin manuscripts, the title *Epistulae Canonicae* (used in the Oxford Vulgate) is preferred to *Epistulae Catholicae*: Augustine, Cassiodorus, the earliest set of prologues and the translation of Clement of Alexandria, amongst others, only attest to the former; Jerome, however, has the latter, as does the

---

[75] See Doignon 1993.   [76] Metzger 1994:575–6.
[77] Parker 2008:275–7.   [78] Frede 1975–82:721; Bogaert 1988:143.

prologue of Theodulf, and it is adopted in the Vetus Latina edition and Stuttgart Vulgate. Cyprian refers to 1 Peter as *Epistula Petri ad Ponticos* ('The Letter of Peter to the inhabitants of Pontus'; CY te 3.36–39), based on the opening verse. Augustine's peculiar designation of 1 John as *Epistula Iohannis ad Parthos* ('The Letter of John to the Parthians') has been explained as a corruption of the Greek *parthenos* ('virgin'), a reference to the tradition of John's virginity.

Thiele's edition of the Catholic Epistles (1956–69) was the first part of the New Testament to be completed in the Vetus Latina series. In addition, he produced separate studies of several letters (1 John 1958; James 1959; 1 Peter 1965). According to Thiele's analysis, the original translation was very close to text-type K (reconstructed from VL 55, Cyprian, and occasionally Lactantius), which subsequently underwent various parallel developments, seen in the text-types C, A, M, R, S, and T, largely based on quotations in Christian authors. The last of these has a similar range of vocabulary to text-type I in the Pauline Epistles, although it is closer to the Greek tradition: it formed the basis of the Vulgate and, indeed, is almost identical to the Vulgate in James. The principal witnesses to type T are VL 55, 64, and Cassiodorus, followed by VL 32, 65, and 67 in certain epistles. Text-type F is only present in James, attested by Chromatius and Innocent as well as VL 66: like the Vulgate, it appears to be a development from type T involving thoroughgoing comparison with a Greek text, in this case similar to Codex Vaticanus, and the introduction of particular renderings. The Greek form underlying the Vulgate is closer to Codex Alexandrinus (GA 02) and GA 33.[79] Thiele's edition includes information from an increasing number of Vulgate manuscripts, although the final range of witnesses is not as wide as that cited by Frede for the Pauline Epistles.[80]

Old Latin texts of the individual Epistles are split between multiple manuscripts: James is found in VL 66 and 67; 1 Peter and 1 John appear in VL 55, 64, 65, and 67; 2 Peter is in VL 55; 2 John is in VL 67; 3 John is partially in VL 5 and 67. There is no complete Old Latin manuscript of Jude, although VL 51 and 54 are cited by Thiele throughout his edition. The Spanish lectionary tradition is of particular note for its marginal glosses in the Catholic Epistles (VL 56, 68, 69, 70, 71, 72, 73, 259, 262, 271). VL 53, 58, and 59 are primarily Vulgate. Augustine's ten sermons on 1 John (AU 1 Jo) are the earliest Latin commentary to survive on this letter. According to AU re 2.58, Possidius, and Cassiodorus, Augustine also wrote a commentary on James, but this has not been preserved. Latin translations of both Clement of Alexandria (CLE-A) and Didymus the Blind (EP-SC en) on the Catholic Epistles were made in the sixth century. Cassiodorus's commentary known as the *Complexiones* includes the

---

[79] For the vocabulary of text-type F and the Greek correspondences, see Thiele 1972:115, 118–19.
[80] See further Appendix 2.

Catholic Epistles (CAr cpl). Bede's commentary on these letters (BED cath) was composed a few decades after an anonymous Irish commentary (AN cath), which was used as a source for a series of tractates ascribed to Hilary of Arles (PS-HIL-A). The Vulgate text of the Catholic Epistles is believed to have been produced at the same time as the rest of the latter half of the New Testament, despite differences in relation to earlier Latin tradition which are especially noticeable in James and 1 Peter. The principal witnesses in the Stuttgart Vulgate are G (VL 7), Vg F, and Vg A. Again, their quality varies: F offers the purest text in James and 1 Peter, while G is best from 2 Peter onwards. Alcuin's text is somewhere between A and F. The Clementine Vulgate bears witness to various later accretions.

The most widely-attested series of *capitula* for the Catholic Epistles, present in Vg A and Vg F amongst others, is KA A, which De Bruyne suggested may be of Donatist origin.[81] The standard preface to the collection, *Non ita ordo est* (PROL cath [S 809]), also first preserved in Vg F, is not the work of the translator but probably dates from the second half of the fifth century. Of the other series of *capitula*, KA Sp is from the seventh-century Spanish edition and KA Tur is by Bede; KA C is not attested before the twelfth century. All that can be said about the main set of prologues to the individual epistles is that they were composed before 700: extracts from Jerome and Isidore are also used as prefaces.

The most debated verses of the Catholic Epistles are 1 John 5:7–8, also known as the Johannine Comma.[82] The additional mention of 'the Father, the Word and the Spirit' (*pater uerbum et spiritus*) appears to have originated in Latin tradition, possibly as a gloss at the end of the fourth century. The reference to these verses in the prologue to the Catholic Epistles (PROL cath) indicates their presence in the fifth century. The earliest form has the sequence *in terra . . . in caelo*, attested by Priscillian, the Pseudo-Augustine *Speculum*, the *De trinitate* ascribed to Vigilius of Thapsus and numerous later writers, as well as VL 64, the Spanish witnesses in the Vetus Latina *Register* (VL 59, 67, 91, 94, 95, 109), the first hand of VL 54, and a large number of Vulgate manuscripts. The text in VL 109 can be seen in Image 11, in line 22 of the third column (with the alternative *sps* in the margin). The Greek version found in the *Textus Receptus* and some later minuscule manuscripts is a translation of a secondary Latin form present in a handful of later Vulgate manuscripts and a correction to VL 54. This inverts the two clauses, reading *in caelo pater uerbum et spiritus sanctus et hi tres unum sunt et tres sunt qui testimonium dant in terra* ('in heaven, the Father, Word and Holy Spirit, and these three are one, and there are three who bear witness on the earth'). Some witnesses replace *uerbum* with *filius*, giving the standard sequence 'the Father

---

[81] Bogaert 1982:11.   [82] See further Thiele 1959, de Jonge 1980, Metzger 1994.

and the Son and the Holy Spirit': although Cyprian twice has this phrase alongside the words *tres unum sunt,* the absence of other references to the immediate context discount this as a reference to the Johannine Comma. The addition is completely lacking from the earliest surviving Latin quotation of these verses, the African treatise *De rebaptismate* composed around 256, as well as Ambrose, Rufinus, Augustine, Quodvultdeus, and other authors.[83] There is one Carolingian manuscript which includes on the back page four patristic testimonies concerning the form of this passage.[84]

The Latin tradition of the Catholic Epistles is characterized by interpolations to an even greater extent than the Pauline Epistles.[85] Many of these are noted in the margins of the later Spanish codices (VL 91–5), including the additional phrase *quod quidem secundum illos blasphematur, secundum nos autem honoratur* ('which indeed is blasphemy to them, but is honourable to us') at 1 Peter 4:14, which is attested as early as Cyprian; in Vg A, it takes the form *ab aliis blasphematus a uobis autem honorificatus* ('blasphemed by others, but honoured by you'). This matches the majority of Greek manuscripts, but is not included in the editorial text of the Stuttgart Vulgate.[86] Likewise, 1 Peter 1:20 features an additional sentence in Spanish Vulgate tradition, also reflected in the Spanish *capitula*:[87]

> *ipse ergo qui et praecognitus est ante constitutionem mundi et nouissimo tempore natus et passus est ipse accepit gloriam quam deus uerbum semper possedit sine initio manens in patre.*
>
> He, therefore, who was also known before the foundation of the world and was born and suffered in the last time himself received the glory which God the Word always possesses without beginning, remaining in the Father.

Most Latin witnesses have an addition in the middle of 1 Peter 3:22: the earliest form is *qui degluttit a morte ut uitae heres esset* ('who swallowed from death that he might be an inheritor of life'), although other witnesses including Vg A and the Spanish tradition read *degluttiens mortem ut uitae aeternae heredes efficeremur* ('swallowing death that we might be made inheritors of eternal life'). Metzger, following Harnack, suggests that this is a translation of a Greek gloss.[88] The extra phrase is missing from the earliest Vulgate tradition and Rufinus. Spanish witnesses feature interpolations in both 1 John 5:9 and 5:20, neither of which has any parallel in Greek. The earliest source for the addition after *uenit* in 5:20 is Hilary of Poitiers, reading *et concarnatus est propter nos et passus est et resurgens de mortuis adsumpsit*

---

[83] For more on this controversial passage, see Thiele 1959, de Jonge 1980, Metzger 1994:647–9.
[84] Paris, BnF, latin 13174: see Berger 1893:103.   [85] See Thiele 1972.
[86] On this variant, see further Thiele 1972:100.
[87] The addition is not found in Bede; Metzger 1994:617 misreads the Oxford Vulgate apparatus.
[88] Metzger 1994:624.

nos ('and he was enfleshed for us and suffered and, rising from the dead, received us'). Later tradition, including the fourth-century *Contra Varimadum* and the Pseudo-Augustine *Speculum* have a different phrasing, beginning *et carnem induit* ('and he put on flesh').[89]

As the earliest surviving Latin manuscript of James, VL 66 is often of special interest. At James 1:12, its omission of *deus* has been linked with the Jewish practice of avoiding direct reference to God. This could also be reflected in *dominum* in James 3:9 where other Latin witnesses prefer *deum*, but *dominum* corresponds to the earliest Greek text. The use of *exploratores* ('spies') rather than *nuntios* ('messengers') in VL 66 at James 2:25 is apparently in order to avoid interpreting the Greek ἀγγέλους as angels. In James 5:7, VL 66 is among the Latin witnesses which inappropriately add 'fruit' to qualify 'the early and the late'; some Vulgate manuscripts add 'rain' (*imbrem*).[90] The Pseudo-Augustine *Speculum* sometimes offers evidence for early forms. At the end of James 4:1, it adds *et sunt uobis suauissima* ('and these are the sweetest things for you'): the superlative suggests that this is an ancient Latin reading.[91] It also contains an addition in 2 John 11, reading: *ecce praedixi uobis ne in diem domini condemnemini* ('See, I have forewarned you, so that in the day of the Lord you may not be condemned'). A slightly different form is found in a handful of Vulgate manuscripts (including a corrector in VL 54) and was adopted in the Sixtine Vulgate. The Pseudo-Augustine *Speculum* and Lucifer of Cagliari both include *sanctorum angelorum* ('of the holy angels') in Jude 6, a reading only otherwise attested in a quotation of Clement of Alexandria. The same two witnesses have *cinis* ('ash') in Jude 7, absent from Greek tradition but parallelled in the Harklean Syriac. Cyprian is the earliest Latin witness for a gloss at the end of 1 John 2:17, *quomodo et ipse manet in aeternum* ('just as he abides for ever'), parallelled in Sahidic but without Greek support. At 1 John 4:3, the Latin tradition is split between *negat* (Cyprian) or *non confitetur* (Ambrose and Spanish witnesses), deriving from μὴ ὁμολογεῖ ('does not confess'), and *soluit* (Irenaeus, Tyconius and the Vulgate) corresponding to λύει ('releases').[92]

A couple of errors appear to go back to the archetype of the Vulgate. At James 5:13, it appears that the translator mistakenly read *aequo animo et psallat*, 'in happiness, let him also sing', changing the sense of the Greek ('if anyone is happy, let him sing'). The Vulgate form of 1 John 5:6, *Christus est ueritas* ('Christ is truth'), seems most likely to have arisen from an early misreading of the *nomen sacrum* for 'spirit' (SPS) as that for 'Christ' (XPS). Only two Greek manuscripts contain this reading: GA 629, a fourteenth-

---

[89] For an analysis of the Vulgate tradition of this verse, see Thiele 1972:118.
[90] Metzger 1994:614.   [91] Thiele 1972:106.
[92] Commentators who have argued for the originality of the latter are listed in Metzger 1994:644–5.

century bilingual, in which the Greek is secondary to the Latin, and GA 61 (Codex Montfortianus). The latter is a sixteenth-century codex into which the Johannine Comma seems to have been incorporated in order to confound Erasmus: the presence of this variant as well, stemming from an internal Latin error, confirms that a Latin source lies behind these verses in this manuscript.

E) REVELATION (APOCALYPSE)

In Latin manuscripts the title of this book is transliterated from the Greek as *Apocalypsis Iohannis*, although there is evidence for the use of *Reuelatio* in Christian authors. The recent Vetus Latina edition by Gryson (2000–3) provides a state-of-the-art account of the Latin text and has been accompanied by new editions of several of the more significant Latin commentaries.[93] Gryson includes information from a wide range of Vulgate manuscripts, which gives an indication of textual developments in later tradition (see Appendix 2).

Of the Old Latin manuscripts, the earliest form of text is the portions of the palimpsest VL 55 (text-type K). Only VL 51 comes close to having an Old Latin text of the whole book: it is the principal witness for text-type I from Revelation 2:19 onwards, supported by quotations in Ambrose, Ambrosiaster, and Jerome. The two lections in VL 74 correspond to the text found in Augustine, and there are also Old Latin readings in VL 61 (which are marked as text-type D in the edition). Gryson cites VL 54 and 58 along with several lectionaries (VL 251, 259, 262, 271) and collections of canticles (VL 330, 414, 415). The Vulgate text seems to have been the work of the same reviser as for Acts and the Epistles, based on a manuscript with text-type I; the principal witness is G (VL 7), closely followed by Vg A. There is a strong connection between the Vulgate and the form of Greek text in Codex Sinaiticus (GA 01). A few manuscripts are found which only contain this book: some are illustrated Apocalypses, which appear to go back to an early stage (e.g. Vg^O Σ, the Trier Apocalypse); others combine it with a commentary (e.g. Vg^S I with Bede, Codex Hafnianus with Apringius).[94]

The standard prologue to Revelation (PROL Apc Mo [S 834/835]) draws on the 'Monarchian' prologue to John and was probably composed in the latter half of the fifth century: it is first attested in Vg F. There is no preface in Vg A or VL 7. Although De Bruyne prints eleven sets of *capitula*, there are only three principal series. KA Apc A, which he suggests are of Donatist origin, feature vocabulary consistent with a fourth-century African origin: they are present in Vg^S I and Vg^{Oa} M.[95] KA Apc B are found in Vg F and Vg^{Sar} S as well

---

[93] cf. Gryson 1997, which supersedes earlier studies such as Vogels 1920 and Vogt 1965.
[94] On illustrations, see page 206.   [95] See Bogaert 1982:11.

as some Tours Bibles. KA Sp are restricted to Spanish manuscripts which have an identical prologue (PROL Apc Spa [S 831]) and probably derive from the seventh-century edition. Of the other *capitula* which are not variants of those already listed, KA Apc Compl are unique to VL 109, KA Apc Tur are the work of Bede, and KA Apc M are present in VL 61; KA Apc Carth, KA Apc Scor, and KA Apc Val are only found in individual late manuscripts.[96]

The key textual evidence for Revelation is to be found in the Latin commentary tradition. The earliest is that of Victorinus of Poetovio (VICn Apc), produced in the third century using a Greek text. This is designated text-type **Y**. Jerome made a revision of this commentary in 398 (HI Apc), which exists in three recensions: **Y**, from 470; **Φ**, around 500, which expands many of the biblical lemmata using a later Italian form of pre-Vulgate text (text-type **J**); **S**, around 700. The commentary of the African Donatist Tyconius (TY Apc), written in the late fourth century, was re-used by numerous later commentators. Gryson's reconstruction of this lost work draws on Caesarius of Arles (CAE Apc), Primasius (PRIM), and Beatus of Liébana (BEA Apc). Old Latin forms in Tyconius are identified as text-type **S**, while the lemmata in Primasius are text-type **C**. Caesarius also used the original form of Victorinus' commentary; the anonymous seventh-century gloss (AN Apc) relied on both Tyconius and Victorinus as did Bede for his commentary (BED Apc). Finally, Cassiodorus' *Complexiones* (CAr cpl) include comments on Revelation. Bogaert 2014b offers a summary of the text of Revelation in Latin authors.

There is a special relationship between the Latin text of Revelation and the Greek *Textus Receptus*, stemming from Erasmus' use of a Latin manuscript to supplement his Greek source.[97] The most notorious instance involves his retroversion of the last six verses from Latin as his Greek codex was lacunose: at Revelation 22:19, he therefore includes the reading 'from the book of life'. This stems from a Latin copying error of *de libro uitae* in place of *de ligno uitae* ('from the tree of life'), perhaps under the influence of the other occurrences of *liber* in this verse. It is first attested in Ambrose and later appears in the Clementine Vulgate. At Revelation 15:3, Old Latin witnesses with *gentium* derive from ἐθνῶν ('peoples'), while the Vulgate's *saeculorum* represents αἰώνων ('generations'). The reading ἁγίων ('saints') in the *Textus Receptus* appears once again to have Latin roots, stemming from a misreading of the abbreviation *s(ae)c(u)lorum* as *s(an)ctorum* (compare *scorum* in VL 95).[98] The addition of *et ego Iohannes* at the beginning of Revelation 21:2, found in numerous later Latin manuscripts, including Tours Bibles and the Clementine Vulgate, is also present in the *Textus Receptus*. Copying errors in the Latin

---

[96] See Gryson 2000–3:54–77 for texts and analysis.

[97] Metzger 1994:8*; Parker 2008:227–8.

[98] Metzger 1994:680. Note, however, that there is no evidence in the Vetus Latina edition which supports his observation that '"saint" is also read by several Latin writers'.

tradition include *tuba* ('trumpet') rather than *turba* ('crowd') in Vulgate manuscripts at both Revelation 19:1 and 19:6. At Revelation 15:6, the Vulgate *lapide* appears to derive from a misreading of λίνον ('linen') as λίθον ('stone') in a Greek exemplar; the same word appears in 18:12, although here an alternative reading λίθον ('stone') is attested alongside ξύλου ('wood').

The majority of Latin witnesses have 666 (*sescenti sexaginta sex*) as the number of the beast in Revelation 13:18. One Vulgate manuscript (Düsseldorf, Universitätsbibliothek, Ms. B 3, copied in Corbie in the ninth century) reads *sescenti sedecim*, 616, corresponding to the earliest surviving Greek sources. 616 is also found in a handful of Christian writers including Tyconius, Caesarius of Arles, and the Donatist *Liber genealogus* (AN gen), which cites Victorinus of Poetovio and identifies the intended reference as Nero. A variant in Cassiodorus has 690, while alternative forms in the anonymous seventh-century commentary on the Apocalypse (AN Apc) include 667 and 646. Numbers are often confused in transmission: at Revelation 14:20, VL 55 gives the distance as ∞*ac*, probably a misreading of *MDC* (1600). VL 51 is the only witness with *mille quingentis* (1500); AN Apc has 1060.

Part III

Manuscripts

Chapter 9 is an introduction to characteristic features of manuscripts of the Latin New Testament, in order to provide an orientation to the technical aspects of the entries in the Catalogue in Chapter 10. It deals with matters such as the layout of text, different scripts, the order of books, and illustrations. A description is given of the fourth-century Eusebian apparatus for locating passages found in more than one gospel, and the differing layouts of canon tables and marginal references in gospel codices. Other paratextual material includes biblical prologues and chapter lists (*capitula*), the development of which has already been treated in Chapter 8. The Catalogue of Latin New Testament manuscripts in Chapter 10 comprises all manuscripts in the three principal editions of the early Latin New Testament: information on these editions is given in Chapter 6, while differences in sigla are described in Appendix 1. Other manuscripts mentioned in the Vetus Latina edition or of interest for their gospel text are listed in Appendix 2 and Appendix 3. The Index of Manuscripts is ordered by library, offering an alternative means of identifying witnesses.

9

Features of Latin New Testament Manuscripts

Manuscripts of the New Testament constitute a significant proportion of the surviving Latin codices from Antiquity and the Middle Ages. The last century of studies in palaeography and codicology has resulted in a much better appreciation of these documents as artefacts. Among the chief contributors have been E.A. Lowe, editor of *Codices Latini Antiquiores* (CLA), which features images of all manuscripts copied before the ninth century, Bernhard Bischoff, whose publications include a standard introduction to Latin palaeography, Leonard Boyle, and Patrick McGurk.[1]

A) MATERIAL AND FORMAT

There are no surviving papyrus manuscripts of the Latin New Testament. Even though VL 23 and 85 have a papyrus shelfmark at their holding institution because of their Egyptian provenance, both are fragments of parchment.[2] All the early witnesses, beginning with VL 1, are written on parchment. Paper was not used in the first thousand years of Latin biblical manuscripts: the only item in the Catalogue in Chapter 10 which is written on paper is VL 58, produced in Bohemia in the late fourteenth century. A relatively high proportion of early Latin gospel books are written on purple parchment (VL 2, 4, 10, 17, 22, 22A; see Image 4). Although this practice was scorned by Jerome (see page 45 above), it leaves its traces in Vulgate manuscripts: VL 15, a particularly lavish production, has alternating leaves of plain and purple parchment, while some Theodulf Bibles (e.g. Vg^{Se} Θ) have the Gospels on purple parchment and plain

---

[1] Bischoff 1990; Boyle 1984; McGurk 1961a and 1994a. Reynolds & Wilson 2013 describes the transmission of Classical literature. For the Greek New Testament, see Parker 2008.

[2] For Latin Christian texts on papyrus, including an eighth-century codex of Augustine, see Bischoff 1990:8.

for the rest of the New Testament. Others have significant pages painted purple or deep blue to mimic the effect of the ancient sheets which were dyed purple with the pigment of the *murex* shell. These include Codex Amiatinus (Vg A, fol. 3–4 of the first quire) and Codex Cavensis (Vg C), while Codex Ingolstadiensis (Vg^{Oe} I) has painted purple panels.

A single leaf of parchment is also known as a folio. The front, which is on the right-hand side of an 'opening' of two sides, is called the *recto*, and the back the *verso*. One face is the outer side of the animal skin, the hair side, on which follicles can still sometimes be seen; the flesh side is smoother and tends to hold the ink better over time. Openings are normally arranged so that both visible pages are the same side of the skin. Vellum is a type of parchment which has been prepared in such a way as to make hair and flesh sides indistinguishable.[3] Folios are normally only numbered on the *recto*, with the suffixes –r and –v used to indicate the front or back. If each side is given its own number, locations are referred to as 'pages' rather than 'folios'. A sheet of parchment folded in half to make two folios (four sides) is called a bifolium. Manuscripts are made up of gatherings of several folded sheets sewn together along the spine. These are also called quires. The standard quire consists of four folded sheets (a quaternion), making up eight folia (sixteen pages), although the number can vary. The 'ruling pattern' consists of holes pricked into the quire to mark the space for the text to be copied, with lines scored between them using a dry point and straight edge (such holes are visible on Image 11 between the second and third columns). The size of the written area of the page (the 'text block'), which may be in multiple columns, is often given in manuscript descriptions because margins may have perished or been trimmed each time the manuscript was rebound. Insular manuscripts follow a different practice for the arrangement of hair and flesh sides in a quire, allowing the two to face each other with a hair side on the first page. They also have a distinctive ruling pattern, and tend to be written not on sheepskin but on calfskin, which is more suitable for colour painting.[4]

Black or brownish ink is the norm, with red ink (rubrics) used in moderation from the fourth century onwards.[5] In VL 3 and 5 the first three lines of each gospel are written in red, which is also used for book titles in VL 5. The fifth-century VL 8 is the earliest Latin gospel book with the first line of each chapter written in red. In his preface to the Vulgate, Jerome specifies that the Eusebian apparatus should be written in two colours, implying that *minium* (red) for the canon numbers was universally available alongside black.[6] On purple parchment, silver replaces black as the standard ink, while gold corresponds to red. VL 2 has the opening lines of each gospel in gold, while

---

[3] Bischoff 1990:9.   [4] Bischoff 1990:9–10, 20–2; Gameson 1994:31; Parker 2008:60–1.
[5] For more on ink and writing materials, see Bischoff 1990:16–19.
[6] See page 200 below.

VL 4 uses gold for the first page of each book: both manuscripts have gold *nomina sacra* (described below). The use of gold ink on plain parchment is comparatively rare and restricted to luxury productions of the Carolingian and Ottonian scriptoria.[7] Other colours are used for the decoration of initials and pictures (see 'Decoration' below): the late sixth-century Gospels of St Augustine (Vg^O X) offer an exceptionally early instance of full-page colour illustrations; VL 13, from around the same time, is the oldest manuscript with a pre-Vulgate text to feature multiple colours used to decorate capital letters. The use of red letters for the words of Christ is not attested in the first millennium: the earliest example in Chapter 10 is the Passion narratives in VL 62 from the eleventh century.[8] The use of green or blue ink for the opening lines of biblical books is not widespread until Atlantic Bibles.

The earliest type of Latin gospel book had roughly square pages, with the text in a single column (e.g. VL 1; Image 2).[9] This is seen in fifth-century manuscripts with other parts of the New Testament (e.g. VL 5, 55, and 75; Image 3). Two-column manuscripts could also be square, such as VL 4, 8, 16, and 22 (see Image 5), although the 'portrait' format which became standard was already present in the fourth century (VL 2 and 3; see Image 4). The use of enlarged letters (*litterae notabiliores*) for the first letter of each column, regardless of where it occurs in the word, is a very ancient practice.[10] Double columns are the norm for pandects such as Vg A and G, Tours Bibles, Atlantic Bibles, and Paris Bibles. Nevertheless, single-column biblical manuscripts remain common, especially in the Insular world and places which experienced Irish influence: VL 14, 20, 24, 28, 29, 30, 44, 47, and 48 are all written in long lines (see Image 8), as are the Book of Durrow (Vg^S D) and Vg^{Oe} E, L, Q, and R; the biblical books produced by Winithar at St Gall in the eighth century are also single columns (Vg^{Saprc} S). Miniature codices are usually too small to have multiple columns. The oldest examples for the Latin New Testament are VL 33 (from sixth-century Italy) and Vg^{Oe} S (seventh-century Northumbria). This is also true of the Irish pocket gospel books from the ninth to eleventh centuries (Image 12).[11] The long, narrow format of Vg F is unusual, if not unique (Image 7). Three columns tend to be characteristic of Spanish tradition, probably starting with the seventh-century pandects. They are found in early Theodulf Bibles, as well as the large Spanish codices of the ninth century onwards. The fifth-century VL 45, from North Italy, is a remarkable and early exception. In the later period, manuscripts of the *Glossa ordinaria* tend to have

---

[7] See pages 80–1 and 103–4 above.

[8] Nevertheless, Charlemagne's Coronation Gospels (see pages 81–2) have the words of Christ in uncial script and the rest of the text in minuscule (Berger 1893:275).

[9] McGurk 1994a:8–11 provides information on page size and shape, and the number of columns.

[10] See Lowe 1925.   [11] See further McGurk 1956; Farr 2011.

three columns, with the biblical text in the central column. This is also true of certain commentaries, such as the twelfth-century VL 63. The expansiveness of the margins is an indicator of the luxury of the production, although in the case of larger Bibles the size of the sheet was dependent on the parchment available.

B) SCRIPT, ABBREVIATIONS, AND PUNCTUATION

The script of Latin New Testament manuscripts conforms to broader trends in book production. The only examples of biblical manuscripts in rustic capitals (also known as *capitalis*) are both from Egypt (VL 23 and 85), although this style continues to be used for headings in later manuscripts as part of a hierarchy of scripts (e.g. the explicits in Image 10).[12] The majority of early New Testament manuscripts are written in capital letters known as 'uncial', based on Jerome's reference in his Preface to Job (HI Jb H):

ueteres libros . . . uncialibus ut uulgo aiunt litteris

Old books . . . in inch-high/uncial letters, as they commonly say.[13]

Italian uncial is the standard (Image 7), and served as the model for the script developed in Wearmouth–Jarrow for the great Northumbrian manuscripts (Image 9). A less common form is *b-d* uncial with a distinctive form of these two letters (as in VL 5, Image 3). Hammond Bammel has suggested that half-uncial script was developed in the early fifth century in the circles of Rufinus of Aquileia for scholarly productions.[14] Examples in biblical manuscripts are rare, although they include VL 53 and Vg[Se] S (Image 6). Many later codices, however, are written in Irish or Anglo-Saxon half-uncial (e.g. VL 14, Image 8). 'Majuscule' is a general term for capital letters. Minuscule (lower-case) script was developed in northern France in the late eighth century. The most common variety is named after Charlemagne ('Caroline minuscule' or 'Carolingian minuscule'), and adopted in the Tours Bibles (Image 10). Again, local forms developed, such as Insular minuscule in Britain and Ireland (Image 12), Visigothic minuscule in Spain (Image 11), and Alemannic minuscule in Germany and Switzerland, as well as versions peculiar to specific monasteries such as Luxeuil.[15] The adoption of Gothic script, also known as *textura* or *textualis*, which is found in most Romanesque and Paris Bibles (Image 13),

---

[12] See Bischoff 1990:57–61.
[13] Text in the Stuttgart Vulgate (Weber, Gryson, et al. 2007:732); examples in Bischoff 1990:66–72.
[14] Hammond Bammel 1984.   [15] See Bischoff 1990:83–127.

seems to have been popularized by the *Glossa ordinaria*.[16] This provided the model for the typeface of the first printed Bibles of Gutenberg.

Even before the development of minuscule, capital letters were still sometimes joined together as 'ligatures', especially at line ends in order to save space: the most common are *–nt* and *–unt*, found in the earliest manuscripts (e.g. VL 1 and 2: see the end of line 9 on Image 2 and the last characters of column 1 on Image 4). Later copyists often displayed their virtuosity by using a number of scripts. In a few manuscripts, normally of Insular origin, some Latin characters are transliterated into Greek as a mark of learning (e.g. VL 35 and 61, but also VL 13).

Abbreviations are rare in the earliest Latin manuscripts, with the exception of *nomina sacra*. These 'sacred names' correspond to Christian practice in Greek, where divine titles (such as God, Father, Lord, Jesus, Christ, and Spirit) are abbreviated as two- or three-letter forms with a line above. Latin Bibles follow suit for the words *deus* (DS), *iesus* (IHS), *christus* (XPS), *spiritus* (SPS), and *dominus* (DNS), although not *pater*; the final letters vary according to grammatical case. For *Iesus* and *Christus*, the first two letters of the Greek word were borrowed with the Latin termination, giving forms such as IHU or XPM. A second layer of Greek *nomina sacra* (including Jerusalem, Israel, heaven, and mother) is less well attested in Latin: forms such as *isrl* (for *Israhel*) tend to occur in manuscripts with many other abbreviations. Conversely, Latin writers appear to have given *sanctus* ('holy') the status of a *nomen sacrum* from a relatively early stage (SCS), possibly because it was frequently found in collocation with the other terms: *noster* too is often abbreviated in the context of other *nomina sacra* (NR). Some fluidity is seen in the oldest Latin *nomina sacra*. VL 1 features a range of peculiar forms with varying combinations such as HI[S] for *Iesus* (Image 2, line 11), DOM for *dominus*, and a monogram based on the *chi-rho* symbol (℟) for *Christus*. Other early manuscripts have DMS for *dominus* (e.g. VL 75); VL 5 has DMS in the Gospels, but DNS in Acts. Rufinus of Aquileia appears to have introduced IS rather than IHS in his works: he also preferred DOM for *dominus*.[17] Around the eighth century, Irish scribes restored the Greek lunate *sigma* in the nominative of the Greek-based forms, reading IHC and XPC: this practice was also adopted in Carolingian scriptoria.[18] VL 11 is unusual in using XRS (also present in Vg[Sp] s). The origin of the practice of *nomina sacra* is still a matter of debate, and it is intriguing that there is not more explicit discussion of it by Latin authors. Differences in the forms of Latin *nomina sacra* have also been taken as indications of geographical origin, since they occur in inscriptions carved into burial stones or buildings.[19]

---

[16] See Bischoff 1990:127–36.   [17] Hammond Bammel 1979.
[18] Bischoff 1990:87 and 154; see also Horsley & Waterhouse 1984.
[19] Hälvä Nyberg 1988; Felle 2006.

The commonest abbreviations in uncial script are the use of a superline for *n* or *m*, often at the end of lines (e.g. Image 2, lines 5 and 11). These are sometimes distinguished by the placing of one or two dots below the line when *m* is intended (VL 4, cover; Vg F, Image 7, lines 18 and 30). Traube suggests that this practice, like the *nomina sacra*, was borrowed from Greek biblical tradition.[20] The ending *–bus* is abbreviated as *–b·* and *–que* as *–q·* in early manuscripts (e.g. Image 7, line 22). A system soon develops for reasons of economy, with words such as *dix(it)*, *dic(it)*, *q(uo)d*, *n(on)*, and *–er(unt)* all having the letters in parentheses replaced by an overline. Later innovations include the creation of symbols for words and syllables such as *per, pro, quia, quod, quam*, the ampersand (&) for *et*, and so on.[21] Many Latin abbreviations appear to have originated in Ireland. The symbols ʜ for *autem* and ǂ for *enim* are peculiar to Insular manuscripts (ʜ features in Image 12, lines 2, 10, and 16). Others were adopted in continental minuscule scripts, including *con–* represented as ɔ–, *eius* as ꝫ, *et* as ⁊, and *est* may be abbreviated as $\bar{e}$ or ÷ (Image 12 has ⁊ in line 3 onwards, and a form of ÷ in line 12, 21, and 22).[22] The use of ·$\bar{e}$· for *est* originated in Tours.[23] Some of these standard abbreviations are comparable to Latin shorthand, or 'Tironian notes', which is occasionally seen in marginal comments (e.g. VL 7).[24]

Sound changes are also reflected in spelling conventions, with the use of the digraphs æ and œ and the *e-caudata* ('e with a tail', ę). The latter is found in place of *ae* in the eighth century, becoming very common in the tenth and eleventh centuries before being replaced by *e* alone in the twelfth century.[25] Later manuscripts tend to assimilate consonants, as in *app–* and *suff–* instead of *adp–* and *subf–* respectively. The development of consonantal *u* and *i* to *v* and *j* respectively takes place at different times: the former is relatively early, as seen in betacism (*b* for *u*) in VL 5, whereas the latter is largely a late mediaeval innovation.

The earliest New Testament manuscripts are written with no breaks between words (*scriptio continua*) and straight left and right margins (see Image 2).[26] The beginning of sense units on a new line, together with ekthesis (letters projecting into the margin), and the use of outsize or capital letters (known as *litterae notabiliores*, 'more prominent letters') constitute the most basic form of

---

[20] Traube 1907:241; Bischoff 1990:151.

[21] Handbooks such as Capelli 2011 give a full account, as do an increasing number of websites.

[22] For more on these abbreviations see Bischoff 1990:80–1, 86, and 119, as well as Lindsay 1910 and 1915 and Bains 1936.

[23] Bischoff 1990:178.

[24] These include ⁊, known as the 'Tironian *et*'; this should not be confused with the *positura*, also shaped like a '7', for marking the end of paragraphs (Parkes 1992:22, 24, 43).

[25] Bischoff 1990:122.

[26] On the challenges of reading *scriptio continua* see Parkes 1992:67.

punctuation. Bilingual codices favour short sense lines, in order to keep the two languages in correspondence (e.g. VL 5, 50, and 75; see Image 3). In his preface to Isaiah (HI pr Is), Jerome stated that he had introduced this format, which he describes as *per cola et commata*, into his translations of the prophetic books.[27] In Codex Amiatinus (Vg A; Image 9), it has been extended to the entire Bible, with each short sense unit marked by ekthesis and little in the way of other punctuation. This type of line division, however, is relatively inefficient as it leaves a lot of unused parchment. The most common layout in biblical manuscripts is to have longer sections with a higher proportion of words split between lines, and straight margins on each side. This can be seen in the earliest surviving manuscript of Jerome's text of the Gospels (Vg^{Se} S; Image 6). In Insular manuscripts, text is often copied in blank space left at the end of the previous section or on the following line after the opening part of a new section. These are called 'runovers', and are separated from the rest of the text by diagonal lines or other markings.[28]

The full system of punctuation developed by grammarians in the fourth century consists of dots (*distinctiones*) at three different heights relative to the line: a high point (*distinctio*), middle point (*media distinctio*), and low point (*subdistinctio*).[29] This is largely absent from contemporary biblical manuscripts, in which blank spaces of differing lengths are sometimes used to indicate breaks (e.g. Images 2 and 5). Regular gaps between words appeared to have been introduced by Irish scribes in the seventh century (Image 8). The separation of words by dots (interpunction) is occasionally found as an intermediate stage, as in VL 11A. Insular copyists employed a number of other devices to assist readers of Latin texts, including a 'diminuendo', capital letters in decreasing size, at the beginning of a new section. They often used combinations of dots to signify pauses, in which the number of marks was equivalent to the significance of the break, although such patterns merge into decorative devices. Carolingian scriptoria developed a simplified form of the earlier system of punctuation, comprising a binary distinction between high points at the end of sentences and medial points for intermediate pauses. However, the late eighth century also saw the adoption of different symbols, later known as *positurae*, for liturgical readings. These are made up of dots and lines, with the *punctus uersus* (;) at the end of a sentence, the *punctus eleuatus* (⸵) in the middle of a sentence, and a new symbol, the *punctus interrogatiuus* (.⸮) corresponding to the modern question mark. From the tenth to the twelfth centuries, the *punctus flexus* (.ꞌ) was inserted for minor pauses in the middle of sense-units. In many cases, the punctuation in surviving New

[27] See further Parkes 1992:15–16.

[28] See McGurk 1994a:12; Irish scribes call this practice 'turn in the path' or 'head under wing' (Brown 1980:77).

[29] Details in this paragraph are taken from Parkes 1992:13–40.

Testament manuscripts has been added or revised by later hands, frequently involving the introduction of a more recent system into an older manuscript (e.g. VL 8).

Quotations, normally from the Old Testament, may be indicated in a number of ways. Some New Testament codices use indentation (e.g. VL 8, Image 5, column 4) or rubrication (e.g. VL 75). A marginal symbol known as a *diple*, initially shaped like a horizontal arrow-head (>), is often placed at the first line or beside each line of a quotation. In later manuscripts this becomes simply a short wavy line. *Diplai* are often used in copies of biblical commentaries to indicate the scriptural lemma.[30]

C) CONTENTS AND PARATEXT

Manuscripts of the entire Bible, or even just the New Testament, are unusual before the ninth century. Constraints of space, as well as custom, meant that books generally circulated in subgroups. The illustration of the bookcase in Codex Amiatinus has the New Testament divided into three volumes: the Gospels, the Epistles, and Acts and Revelation.[31] The two principal collections in surviving manuscripts are the Gospels and the Pauline Epistles. Figures from CLA show that forty-one surviving manuscripts of the Gospels and eleven of the Pauline Epistles were copied before 600, while 119 gospel manuscripts and twenty-five of the Pauline Epistles are preserved from 600 to 800. The figure for the rest of the New Testament (Acts, Catholic Epistles, and Revelation) is just five and seven respectively.[32]

Exceptions to the standard groupings are rare: Vg^{Spc} K consists of both the Pauline and the Catholic Epistles, as does Vg^{Sl} Q; VL 66 combines the Letter of James with patristic texts (cf. Vg^{Sc} R, with all the Catholic Epistles); VL 7 includes the *Shepherd of Hermas* after the New Testament, while VL 51, VL 61, and the Theodulf Bibles also have non-biblical material. Some manuscripts consist of single books, John and Revelation being the most common (e.g. VL 33, 47, Vg^{Oe} S, and Vg^{O} Σ). Lectionaries provide only the passages read in the liturgy: these may be confined to the Gospels (sometimes called an 'evangelistary') or the Epistles (e.g. VL 87), but the majority contain extracts from throughout the New Testament.[33] Irish

---

[30] See McGurk 1961b and Parkes 1992:22.   [31] See pages 58–9.

[32] This information, deriving from data in CLA, comes from McGurk 1994a:4. Fischer 1963b [1985:98–9] includes a list of biblical manuscripts in CLA: there are 108 from Italy, 67 from Germany, 47 from England, 47 from France, and 35 from Ireland. See also Parker 2008:63 and 75.

[33] See further page 203 below.

Pocket Gospels often have an abbreviated text.[34] It is, of course, impossible to be sure of the contents of manuscripts which are now fragmentary, although details such as page numbers or quire signatures may offer a guide: for example, Codex Bezae cannot have contained the entire New Testament although a substantial portion is missing between the end of Mark and 3 John, which may have been sufficient to contain Revelation and the other Johannine Epistles.

The order of the constituent subgroups in complete New Testaments and lists of canonical books varies.[35] The modern sequence, with Paul following Acts (eapcr), is found in Codex Amiatinus (Vg A; also VL 54, 95, Vg Φ^V). A number of manuscripts place the Pauline Epistles after Revelation (eacrp; e.g. VL 6, 7, 51; Vg^S Φ^T, s). Tours Bibles tend to have Paul between the Catholic Epistles and Revelation (eacpr; Vg^S Φ^E, Φ^G), an order which persists into the thirteenth century (Vg^O W). In Theodulf Bibles and the Spanish tradition, Paul follows the Gospels and Acts is located between the Catholic Epistles and Revelation (epcar; VL 67, 91, 92, 109; Vg^O C, T, Θ). VL 61 places Paul second and Acts at the end (epcra). The pseudonymous Letter to the Laodiceans is found in several New Testament manuscripts (e.g. Vg F, VL 6, 51, 58, 61, 62, 91, 109); 3 Corinthians, by contrast, is very poorly attested (Vg^S B and the table of contents in VL 86). A few biblical codices are ordered according to the sequence of liturgical lections for the year, such as VL 135 and Vg^S B.[36] Very occasionally, the Gospels are omitted from later New Testament manuscripts because of the use of a separate gospel book for the liturgy.

Most Old Latin gospel books have the evangelists in the sequence Matthew–John–Luke–Mark, sometimes described as the 'Western' order. There is evidence for a variety of early sequences: VL 1 has Mark followed by Matthew, while Matthew–Mark–John–Luke was found in the ancestor of VL 5 and Mommsen's stichometry.[37] Jerome explicitly mentions in his preface to the Gospels that he put the books into the same order as Greek (Matthew–Mark–Luke–John) in order to include the Eusebian apparatus. Several sequences are found for the Pauline Epistles, with or without Hebrews or Laodiceans.[38] The principal variation involves the placing of Colossians:

---

[34] See page 102.

[35] For lists of different sequences of biblical books, see Berger 1893:331–9 and the works of Bogaert and Frede mentioned below.

[36] See further Bogaert 2012:80 or Bogaert 2014a, which includes a list of thirty-seven such manuscripts from the ninth century onwards.

[37] Bogaert 1999 and 2013:513–14 gives details of other sequences of gospel books. Several different sequences of the evangelists are found in the opening sections of Fortunatianus of Aquileia's commentary, but the chapter titles suggest the sequence Matthew–Luke–John–Mark.

[38] These are summarized in Frede 1964:161–2; see further Frede 1966–71:290–303.

Eph–Col–Phil–12Thess	VL 75
Phil–Eph–Col–12Thess	VL 86 (also Marius Victorinus and Ambrosiaster).
Eph–Phil–12Thess–Col	Pelagius and some Vulgate manuscripts
Eph–Phil–Col–12Thess	VL 7, 54, 78, Vg A, many Vulgate manuscripts
Eph–Phil–12Thess–Col–Laod	VL 61, Vg F, Vg^{Op} M
Eph–Phil–12Thess–Col . . . Hbr–Laod	VL 51, 109
Eph–Phil–Col–Laod–12Thess	Spanish Vulgate manuscripts (Vg C, Peregrinus).
Eph–Phil–Col–12Thess . . . (Laod Hbr)	VL 77
Eph–Phil–Col–12Thess . . . Hbr–Laod	Vg^{Oa} U
Eph–Phil–Col–12Thess–Hbr–12Tim–Tt–Phm	Vg^{Sp} S

The pre-Vulgate tradition of the Catholic Epistles put the two Epistles of Peter first, although no Old Latin manuscripts with all seven letters survive. Augustine's *Speculum* and the stichometric list of VL 75 have the order Peter–James–John–Jude, while Peter–John–James–Jude is supported by the list in the Breviarium Hipponense adopted by the Council of Carthage in 397 and seems to underlie VL 55 and the Pseudo-Augustine *Speculum*.[39]

The first line of paratextual material in biblical codices is the title of each book, given as an *incipit* before the text and an *explicit* after the final verse. Early Latin gospel manuscripts and authors borrow the Greek word for 'according to', *cata* (e.g. VL 1, 2, Cyprian). Although *secundum* is soon established as the standard form, *cata* continues to be found in later manuscripts such as the ninth-century VL 61 and certain sequences of chapter titles (see below). The names of the evangelists are fairly consistent, although *Lucanus* is found instead of *Lucas* in some Old Latin witnesses (e.g. VL 3, 8, 16, 21, Cyprian and Fortunatianus of Aquileia). The Pauline Epistles, along with the latter Epistles of Peter and John, often have *eiusdem* ('from the same person') rather than repeating the author's name. As noted in Chapter 8, the Catholic Epistles tend to be designated as the *Epistulae Canonicae* in Latin manuscripts, while Revelation is universally referred to as *Apocalypsis*.[40] An abbreviated form of the title normally appears at the top of each page, known as the 'running title'. A few Insular manuscripts have *O Emmanuel* as the running title in place of the name of the evangelist (Cadmug Gospels and the Liber Commonei). Additional material is frequently added to the explicit. In VL 1 and VL 13, it is recorded that Mark ends 'happily' (*explicit feliciter*; in VL 13 this is written in Greek letters; see also Philippians in VL 89), while VL 14 adds the word for 'peace' (*pax*) three times.[41] In the Pauline Epistles, there is a tradition in both Greek and Latin of adding details of the location at which the

[39] See Thiele 1956–69:4.   [40] See pages 176 and 181.
[41] For other Insular practices, see Bischoff 1990:44.

letter was believed to have been written. This is also found in the Marcionite prologues.[42] A colophon is often found at the end of a volume, in which the name of the copyist may be mentioned: a number of manuscripts are known by the name of their copyist, especially in Irish and Spanish tradition.[43]

Biblical prologues are generally identified by the numbers assigned by Stegmüller.[44] Jerome's *Preface to the Gospels*, a dedicatory letter to Pope Damasus also known as the *Epistula ad Damasum*, is found in most copies of the Vulgate Gospels.[45] It is often identified by its opening words, *Nouum opus* (HI Ev [S 595]), and accompanied by *Plures fuisse*, the preface to Jerome's commentary on Matthew (HI Mt [S 596]) or, later, *Sciendum etiam* [S 601]. Some codices with Northumbrian connections have a Latin translation of Eusebius of Caesarea's *Letter to Carpianus*, beginning *Ammonius quidam* ([S 581], e.g. VL 9A and Vg^{Oe} Y). VL 10 has a unique preface to the Gospels from a Gothic milieu discussing the problems of biblical translation (*Sanctus Petrus apostolus*).[46]

Prologues to the individual gospels are rarely present in Old Latin tradition, but the two series commonly found in Vulgate manuscripts date back to the fourth century.[47] The most widespread are known as the 'Monarchian' prologues (PROL Mo), because they were originally believed to derive from Monarchian circles in Rome in the second or third century. Subsequent scholarship has suggested that they are Spanish in origin, possibly from the circles of Priscillian. Their original sequence matches that of Old Latin gospel codices. Each gives brief details about each evangelist, beginning as follows:

> *Matthaeus ex Iudaea sicut in ordine primus ponitur*... [S 590, 591]
> *Marcus euangelista dei et Petri in baptismate filius*... [S 607]
> *Lucas Syrus natione Antiochensis arte medicus*... [S 620]
> *Hic est Iohannes euangelista unus ex discipulis dei*... [S 624]

They appear to have been composed in response to a set of 'anti-Marcionite' prologues (PROL Pa), written in the middle of the fourth century, which only survive for the latter three gospels:

> *Marcus adseruit qui colobodactylus est*... [S 604]
> *Est quidem Lucas Antiochensis Syrus*... [S 612]
> *Euangelium Iohannis manifestatum est*... [S 623]

---

[42] e.g. VL 75; see Amphoux 2013.

[43] Some colophons are copied unaltered from exemplars: see pages 48 and 74 above.

[44] See Chapter 6 section j (page 138).

[45] A critical edition appears in the Stuttgart Vulgate (Weber, Gryson, et al. 2007:1515–16).

[46] See page 53.

[47] On both groups, see Regul 1969; Norelli 1990 reaffirms a Marcionite origin for the Monarchian prologues, although this is surprising given Marcion's advocacy of a single Gospel.

The 'anti-Marcionite' prologue to Luke is the only one to be included in VL 8. Alternatives to these two sets of prologues are only found in a handful of Irish and Spanish manuscripts, and are late derivatives. Other prefatory material sometimes found before each gospel includes a list of Old Testament citations made by the evangelist (PROL Te [S 10236]), and Jerome's glossary of Hebrew words in that book (HI nom [S 10235]). An abbreviated form of the latter is first attested in VL 14, but clearly predates the seventh century and is found in a number of Insular manuscripts, including Vg^{Oe} Q. The list was considerably expanded for the Paris Bibles in the thirteenth century.[48] Brief biographies from Jerome's *De uiris illustribus* (HI ill) or Isidore's *De ortu et obitu patrum* (IS ptr) are sometimes used to introduce each author. In Insular manuscripts, the first seventeen verses of Matthew are reinterpreted as a prologue, with a decorated *chi-rho* page beginning Matthew 1:18; this is also the case to a lesser extent at Luke 1:5 (e.g. VL 11A and 29).

Primum quaeritur (PROL Paul 1 [S 670]), an introduction to the entire Pauline corpus, is found before the Epistle to the Romans in the Vulgate. This was the work of the translator responsible for the revision of these letters, and probably the rest of the New Testament. The *argumentum* for Romans (PROL Rm Arg [S 674]) appears to be from the same pen. The most common set of prologues for the individual Pauline Epistles by far are the Marcionite prologues (PROL Ma [S 677, etc.]), preserved only in Latin tradition. There has been considerable debate as to whether these derive from Marcion's collection of selected letters of Paul, suggested by the identification of Ephesians as Laodiceans as well as the correspondence between the original set of seven prologues and the unusual order of Marcion's collection reported by Tertullian (Galatians, Corinthians, Romans, Thessalonians, Ephesians/Laodiceans, Colossians, and Philippians). The most recent evaluation puts forward a strong case in favour of their Marcionite origin.[49] They are attested in Marius Victorinus and Latin manuscripts from the fourth century onwards in a revised form which includes additional prologues in order to provide one for each canonical Epistle. These were also adopted as the standard prologues to Paul in Paris Bibles.[50] Alternative sets of Pauline prologues include one attributed to Pelagius (PROL Pel), one of French and two of Italian origin (PROL Fr, PROL It 1 and 2), and a series composed by Bede (BED pr/PROL Eln). In addition, lists are sometimes provided of the quotations from the Old Testament in each Epistle.

The most common prologues to Acts and Revelation, composed before the sixth century, draw on the 'Monarchian' prologues to Luke and John: *Lucas*

---

[48] See McGurk 1994b, 1996; Szerwiniack 1994 and page 106 above.

[49] Jongkind 2015; I am grateful to the author for a pre-publication copy of this study, which includes a text and translation. The classic survey (which argues for a non-Marcionite origin) is Dahl 1978.

[50] See Light 1994:167.

natione syrus cuius laus in euangelio canitur (PROL Act Mo; S 640) and *Iohannes apostolus et euangelista* (PROL Apc Mo; S 834/5). Other prologues are found before Acts, as well as lists of names, places, and biblical citations. The principal prologue to the Catholic Epistles is a later addition, not by the translator, which includes a polemic about the omission of the Johannine Comma: *Non ita* (or *idem*) *ordo est apud graecos* (PROL cath; S 809). Like the 'Monarchian' prologues to Acts and Revelation, this is first attested in Vg F. Individual letters are often prefaced by the biographical material from Jerome or Isidore mentioned above. Alternatives to the 'Monarchian' prologue of Revelation are a preface of Spanish origin, Isidore's prologue, Jerome's biography of the evangelist, or even an extract from Jerome's *Epistula* 53 to Paulinus of Nola stating that Revelation has as many signs as words (*tot habet sacramenta quot uerba*): this letter is used as a preface for the Bible in Vg A and Tours Bibles.

The creation of sets of chapter titles (*capitula*) is already attested in the third century: one series for the Gospels predates Cyprian (KA Cy), while Donatists created their own sets for the other books of the New Testament.[51] In manuscripts, they are introduced by a variety of terms including *breues, breuiarium, tituli, elenchus, breues causae, capitulatio, capitula lectionum*. No fewer than thirteen types are attested for each Gospel, of which around half appear to derive from Old Latin texts. Their chronology has already been discussed in Chapter 8. The titles were linked to numbered divisions in the text, although the two sometimes become separated: marginal chapter numbers in some manuscripts do not correspond to the initial titles (e.g. VL 9A). The length of the divisions varies considerably: Matthew, for example, ranges from twenty-eight to one hundred chapters. VL 8 has one of the earliest full sets (Image 5), but unexpected numbers in the margin or text of other Old Latin manuscripts may indicate the presence of chapters in their exemplar (e.g. Matthew 28:1 in VL 3). In Vulgate tradition, the *capitula* normally come between the prologue and the biblical text (e.g. Image 10), although in certain manuscripts the *capitula* for a group of books are placed at the beginning of the collection (e.g. VL 7). The use of Greek numerals for chapters is an indication of North Italian origin.[52] One series of *capitula* has been identified as the work of Bede.[53] In the early Tours Bibles and Paris Bibles, the series of *capitula* varies from manuscript to manuscript although a degree of standardization emerges later on. Latin *capitula* do not correspond to the divisions or titles of the Greek *kephalaia*, although one set of *capitula* for Hebrews is a translation of Euthalian material (KA Heb Z).

---

[51] Technically, *capitula* refers to the divisions of the text and *tituli* to the initial set of titles, but it is customary to refer to the titles as *capitula* as well (cf. the siglum KA in the Vetus Latina *Repertorium*). For more on the divisions and history, see Bogaert 1982 and Houghton 2011.

[52] Fischer 1965 [1985:178]. The claim that *capitula* beginning with *Ubi* are of Spanish origin (Enciso 1954 and Vives 1957) is not borne out by further investigation.

[53] Meyvaert 1995; see page 70.

The Eusebian apparatus included by Jerome is a system for identifying shared material between the four Gospels. It consists of two parts: an initial set of ten canon tables showing the different types of agreement, and a series of numbers in the margin of the biblical text. Each Gospel is divided into sequentially numbered 'Eusebian sections' (or sometimes 'Ammonian sections'), the usual figures being 355 in Matthew, 233 in Mark, 342 in Luke, and 232 in John. The ten 'Eusebian canons' cover the various permutations of overlap: Canon I lists the sections which contain material paralleled in all four Gospels (see Image 15), Canons II–IV similarities between three Gospels, Canons V–IX agreements in two Gospels only, and Canon X, split into four, material unique to each Gospel.[54] Jerome states that the section numbers and canon numbers in the margin should be written in different colours:

> *hic nigro colore praescriptus sub se habet alium ex minio numerum discolorem, qui ad decem usque procedens indicat, prior numerus in quo sit canone requirendus.*
>
> The first number, written in a dark colour, has another number underneath it in a different colour from red pigment, which goes up to ten and indicates in which canon table the first number should be sought.

Despite the reference only to a single section number, from a very early stage the numbers of the parallel sections from the other gospels were also added in the margins (e.g. VL 23, Vg[Se] S; see Image 6). This is clearly secondary to Jerome as it obviates the need for the initial canon tables. Nevertheless, they were generally retained and become ever more decorated. In fact, the Eusebian apparatus is far better attested in Latin manuscripts than in Greek tradition.[55] In Greek canon tables, the numbers are usually given in groups of four, whereas in their Latin counterparts they tend to be in groups of five, or with no divisions at all: VL 7, with groups of four, is an exception.[56] Nordenfalk identifies three different types of Latin canon tables: the first, 'shorter Latin series', occupies twelve pages, while the second and third both have sixteen pages.[57]

Alternatives to Jerome's implementation of the Eusebian apparatus suggest that he was not the only scholar to transfer it to Latin. In VL 10 (which preserves the Old Latin order of the Gospels) and VL 11, the section numbers are written alongside the text and the corresponding passages in the other gospels are identified by number in four decorative arches at the bottom of each page. In VL 5, the section numbers but not the canon numbers are written alongside the Greek text. Further evidence of pre-Vulgate use of the

---

[54] The system does not provide for agreements between (a) Mark, Luke, and John or (b) John and Mark.

[55] See Thiele 1981; O'Loughlin 2010.

[56] See further McGurk 1993. Other examples of groups of four in canon tables are Erlangen, Universitätsbibliothek, 10 (page 295) and Munich, BSB, Clm 6212; Vg A switches from five to four.

[57] Nordenfalk 1938.

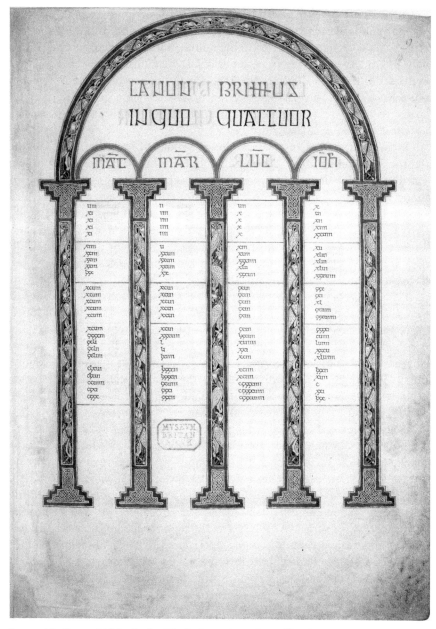

Image 15 Canon Tables in the Lindisfarne Gospels: Vg^O Y (London, British Library, MS Cotton Nero D.IV, folio 10^r), a page from the initial canon tables. © The British Library Board. Also available at <http://www.bl.uk/manuscripts/Viewer.aspx?ref=cotton_ms_nero_d_iv_f010r>

Eusebian divisions is provided by the four manuscripts which include the opening words of each section in the initial canon tables with an Old Latin text (VL 10, 39, 40, and 46).[58] Errors in the numeration of the Eusebian apparatus may often serve as markers of genealogical relationship: for example, the exemplar of Jerome's Vulgate appears to have placed several section numbers one verse early.[59] The Eusebian section numbers were also used to identify gospel passages in lists of liturgical lections, such as the *Capitulare euangeliorum de circulo anni* (described below).

On the model of the Eusebian canons, Priscillian of Avila developed canons for the Pauline Epistles. These group together similar material from the fourteen epistles under ninety headings, preceded by a preface (*Prologum subter adiectum . . . multis occupatus necessitatibus . . . corrigere mentes* [PRIS can pr; S 672, 656]). Each canon is identified by a number preceded by the letter K, which may also appear in the margin of the biblical text.[60] These are a staple of Spanish biblical manuscripts, but are by no means confined to them: they are also adopted in Theodulf Bibles and other codices. Priscillian may have been inspired by Jerome's treatment of the Eusebian apparatus, as both refer to the use of contrasting colours of ink.[61] An alternative concordance to the Pauline Epistles is the *Concordia epistularum* attributed to Pelagius, which groups the thirteen epistles under fifty-six headings (AN conc; S 646). This is found in Vg A, F, and a number of Tours Bibles and Atlantic Bibles. The headings of the two series are easily differentiated: Priscillian's canons usually begin with *Quia*, and the titles of the Pelagian concordance titles all begin with *De*. Some Tours Bibles have the Pelagian concordance in a set of arcades similar to the Eusebian canon tables.

Several poems are included among the ancillary material of New Testament manuscripts. The four evangelists and their symbols are the subject of a number of short verses found at the beginning of the Gospels or alongside illustrations. Some extracts are taken from Sedulius' *Paschale Carmen* (e.g. VL 62) or Juvencus (e.g. Cadmug Gospels). Three of the most common poems concern the content and division of the Eusebian canons; Aileran's *Quam in primo speciosa quadriga* (AIL Eus; S 843), Alcuin's *Textum si cupies canonis* (S 851), and the anonymous *In primo certe canone* (S 848). Although the other books of the New Testament have inspired less poetry, a particularly ingenious poet managed to conclude a poem on the Pauline Epistles (*Uersus quot et*

---

[58] For examples of this in other witnesses, see McGurk 1955:194.

[59] See the Stuttgart Vulgate for Matthew 123, 226, 231, and 343; Mark 4 and 185; Luke 2, 3, and 106 (and also the canon number for John 180).

[60] On the use of the marginal K to denote chapters in classical texts, see Parkes 1992:12 and 27; Parkes also notes the possible use of K to indicate corrections in manuscripts copied *per cola et commata* (1992:125 note 73).

[61] The text of PRIS can is given in the Oxford Vulgate (II.20–32).

quibus missae sunt epistolae, S 681) with a mnemonic for all fourteen in a single quasi-hexameter line:

> *Ro cor bis gal ephe phi co te bis timo bis ti phil hebre.*
> Romans, Corinthians twice, Galatians;
> Ephesians, Philippians, and Colossians;
> Thessalonians twice, and Timothy's two;
> Titus, Philemon, and one to Hebrews.

Lectionary manuscripts are each affiliated to a particular liturgical tradition.[62] Each extract is usually preceded by an indication of the appointed day for the reading and its source. The beginning of a lection is often adjusted to enable it to be read out of context: *fratres* ('brethren') is usually added as the first word in extracts from the Epistles, while *in illis diebus* ('in those days') or *dixit Iesus discipulis suis* ('Jesus said to his disciples') may preface readings from the Gospels. The influence of lectionaries can sometimes be seen in continuous-text manuscripts, with liturgical indications added in the margins by later hands (e.g. VL 13) or the incorporation of the initial formulae (e.g. VL 29). The reverential addition of *dominus* before *Iesus* (e.g. VL 11A) may also reflect lectionary influence. The Passion narratives are occasionally marked up for dramatic reading, for example by the insertion of a cross above the words of Jesus (e.g. Vg^{Oe} R). Many gospel books have a table of liturgical readings, the *Capitulare euangeliorum de circulo anni* [S 852]. Beginning with the Christmas reading *In natale domini* and normally ending with the second week after Pentecost (*Ebd. II post Pentecosten*), these 192 entries enable the gospel book to be used as a lectionary.[63] The individual readings are identified by the Eusebian section number in each gospel, with the opening and closing words provided in the table for precision. This table is widely attested in manuscripts from the ninth century onwards.

Various other miscellaneous material may be found in the margins or at the beginning or end of New Testament manuscripts. Proper nouns often identify the book's owners, written in normal characters, runes (e.g. VL 9A, 65), or even Ogham (Stowe St John). Random letters or words are sometimes described in catalogues as 'testing of the pen' (*probatio pennae*), and could have been added at any point in the history of the manuscript. Missing text is sometimes noted by the letters *hd* (*haec desunt*), with the corresponding text added in the margin with the letters *hp* (*haec pone*) or *sr* (*sequitur*).[64] In addition to the use of the margin by correctors, it is occasionally employed by copyists for noting alternative readings (e.g. VL 88, 91, 95, 109, etc., Vg^{Oe} EP)

---

[62] See above, pages 55, 89–90, and 97–9.

[63] For the *Ordo lectionum per circulum anni,* a list of lections for the entire year in early Roman office books, see Klauser 1972 and Bogaert 2012:72.

[64] Compare *hd* at the end of the penultimate line of Image 2. Other ways of indicating corrections are explained in Bischoff 1990:172.

or, in later manuscripts, cross-references (VL 58 and the Paris Bibles; see Image 13). There is sometimes an indication that a manuscript has been compared with its exemplar in the scriptorium, with the word *contuli* or *req(uisitum)*.[65] Books may be followed by stichometric numbers indicating the total lines. These are found in Old Latin witnesses (e.g. VL 64) as well as several ninth-century productions (e.g. VL 7, VL 61, Vg^{Sp} R, Vg^{Sp} S, Vg^O L): the total lines for Romans in VL 7 can be seen in the last line of the first column in Image 16. Numerals were often garbled during transmission and do not necessarily relate to the preceding text: sometimes the *stichoi* appear to correspond to Greek rather than Latin texts.[66]

D) DECORATION

The earliest Latin New Testament manuscripts have little in the way of decoration to the text, apart from lines or dashes surrounding the book titles (e.g. VL 1 and 5). From the sixth century, capital letters start to attract decoration either through the use of several colours of ink or the introduction of zoomorphic elements such as animal and bird heads or leaves (e.g. VL 13).[67] Outsize initials afford the opportunity for more complex ornamentation, whether in the form of interlace and geometric patterns (seventh century onwards) or, eventually, human figures (e.g. VL 6). The latter develop from around the ninth century, as in the Moutier-Grandval Bible (Vg^S Φ^G), with a head of Paul in the first initial of Romans, or the depiction of John on Patmos in Revelation in Vg^S I. They reach their apogee in Romanesque Bibles of the thirteenth and fourteenth centuries; the Paris Bibles produced for academic purposes are less lavish. The Eusebian apparatus also affords an opportunity for artistic creativity, either in the architectural structures enclosing the initial canon tables (see Image 15) or the arcades at the bottom of the page in VL 10 and 11.[68]

The style of the illustrations in a few manuscripts could derive from classical models. The Gospels of St Augustine (Vg^O X), produced in Italy in the sixth century, provide the earliest surviving full-page colour illustrations in a Latin New Testament manuscript. The two surviving pages feature twelve scenes from the Passion and twelve episodes from the Gospel according to Luke with a picture of the evangelist. Their depiction of events in the life of Christ is

---

[65] See page 27 and Bischoff 1990:43.

[66] Bogaert 2003:167–70; see also pages 21 and 27 above.

[67] Bischoff 1990:197, who notes that the decoration in VL 13 also includes imitations of jewellery.

[68] See pages 53 and 86–7.

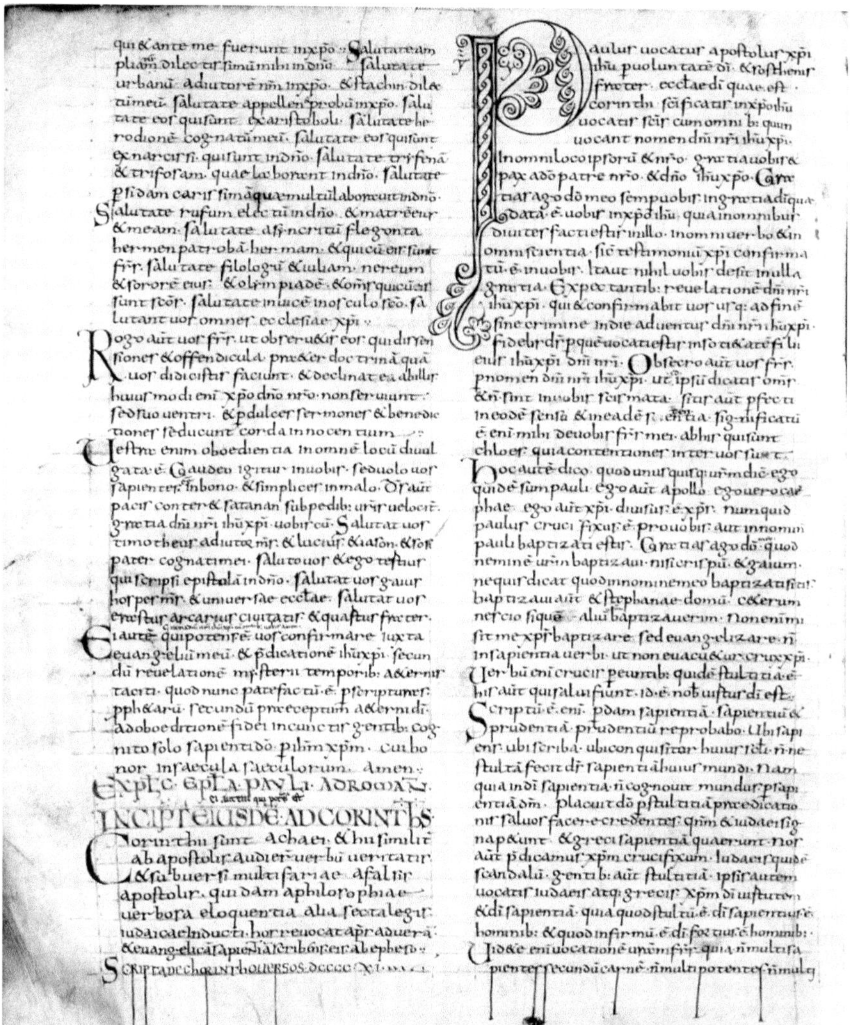

Image 16 VL 7, Vg G: Codex Sangermanensis primus (Paris, Bibliothèque nationale de France, latin 11553, folio 164ᵛ), showing the end of Romans and beginning of 1 Corinthians. Also available at <http://gallica.bnf.fr/ark:/12148/btv1b9065916g/f158. item>

unique in surviving Latin tradition, although there are contemporary parallels in Greek and Syriac manuscripts.[69] The Trier Apocalypse (Vg^O Σ) has a series of seventy-four full-page colour images whose exemplar may go back to fifth-century Italy. A large number of single-volume illustrated Apocalypses were produced from the ninth century onwards, of which the Trier Apocalypse and Valenciennes, BM, 99, are the earliest.[70] Bede records that Benedict Biscop brought back a series of paintings from Italy to Wearmouth–Jarrow in 675, including a cycle based on the Apocalypse, to hang in the monastery church.

The first quire of Vg A (Codex Amiatinus) has two illustrations which have been connected with those of Cassiodorus' sixth-century *codex grandior*. These comprise an illustration of the Tabernacle, across a single opening, and a copyist seated in front of a bookcase containing a nine-volume Bible. Cassiodorus' *Institutiones* indicate that his pandect also featured an illustration of the Temple in Jerusalem, which is not present in Vg A. Instead, its other pages contain three diagrams of different systems of grouping the books of the Bible and a page with a painted series of roundels describing the contents of each book of the Pentateuch. The only other picture in Vg A is a magnificent full-colour image preceding the New Testament. A central roundel depicts Christ in majesty, flanked by two angels, against a background of dark blue concentric circles studded with white points, while in the corners of the rectangular frame are the four evangelists, each with their symbol.

The association of each Gospel writer with the four creatures listed in Revelation 4:7, a man, lion, ox and eagle, is found in numerous early Christian writers although the correspondences vary. The earliest surviving reference, in Irenaeus of Lyons, identifies Matthew with the man, John with the lion, Luke with the ox, and Mark with the eagle.[71] This is the same sequence as the most common order of the Gospels in Old Latin codices, and also features in the seventh-century Book of Durrow (Vg^S D). Nevertheless, the standard sequence in Latin and Greek tradition identifies Mark with the lion and John with the eagle. Evangelist symbols are particularly favoured in Insular tradition. The Echternach Gospels (Vg^O EP) has only a full-page symbol before each Gospel rather than a human figure, while other gospel books with evangelist portraits also include a symbol page depicting all four creatures (e.g. Vg^S D, Vg^{Oe} L, Vg^O Q). Full-page portraits of evangelists occur across all traditions of the New Testament, although allusion to the evangelist symbols

---

[69] e.g. the Rossano Gospels (GA 042), also from the sixth century, written in Greek on purple parchment with scenes from the life of Christ or the Syriac Rabbula Gospels from 586: see Lowden 2012.

[70] Morgan 2012:409; 418–20.

[71] IR hae 3.11.8, also found in FO-A; see also AU Ev 1.6.9 where the Irenaean sequence is rejected in favour of Matthew–Mark–Luke–John; discussion in Bogaert 2001.

in these illustrations tends to be peculiar to Latin tradition.[72] In Irish manuscripts, the evangelists are always presented facing the reader directly rather than in profile.[73]

Insular gospel books from the seventh century onwards have a particular set of illustrations, in addition to evangelist portraits and a four-symbols page. 'Carpet pages', entire pages with a colourful geometric design (Vg^Se D; Vg^Oe L, Q, Y), are found either at the beginning of the manuscript or before each Gospel. The opening page for each book is highly stylized, with the initial letters woven into a full-page design and decorated with interlacing patterns. This is also the case for the *chi-rho* at Matthew 1:18, based on the *nomen sacrum* which begins the verse (*xpi autem generatio*).[74] The illustration of Matthew sometimes appears opposite this page rather than at the beginning of the Gospel. At the end of VL 48, copied in Ireland at the end of the eighth century, are full-page colour pictures of the Crucifixion and Christ in Majesty (or possibly the Last Judgement). The Book of Mulling (VL 35) contains a line drawing at the back of the manuscript which may be a plan of the monastery.

A sequence of five images became standard for gospel books copied in Tours around 830. This consisted of the four evangelist portraits and an initial Christ in Majesty surrounded by the evangelists and their symbols, comparable to that described above in Codex Amiatinus. Later in the ninth century, two more illustrations were added at the beginning of Tours Gospels depicting the emperor on his throne and the twenty-four elders adoring the lamb (from Revelation 5:8). Two styles of decoration can be discerned in these manuscripts.[75] The Moutier-Grandval Bible (Vg^S Φ^G) is a lavish production, although it has no evangelist portraits. It features full-page colour pictures of Christ in Majesty before the Gospels and the book with seven seals flanked by evangelist symbols after the conclusion of Revelation, and decorated arcades for the canon tables and the concordance to the Epistles. Miniature illustrations are added in outsize capitals: in Acts, these include human heads and the Lukan evangelist symbol, while capitals in Romans contain Paul and a man with a sword. Initial illustrations of Christ in Majesty are also found in the eighth-century VL 39 and, more surprisingly, at the beginning of the Pauline commentary in VL 89. Certain Latin scholars in the time of Charlemagne, however, among them Theodulf and Claudius of Turin, were iconoclasts, disapproving of sculpture and human representation.

Spanish pandects are illustrated in a distinctive style.[76] Chief among them is the tenth-century Codex Legionensis (VL 91 and also 133). In the Old Testament, one or more columns of the page are interrupted or displaced in

---

[72] Portraits are, very occasionally, found at the end of the Gospel, as in the Stowe St John, Autun, BM, 3, and possibly also VL 35: see further McGurk 1956:258–9 and 1961a:16.
[73] McGurk 1956:261. [74] See also page 159 above, and McGurk 1956:257–8.
[75] See Bischoff 1990:209. [76] See further Williams 1999.

order to accommodate colourful representations of the biblical passage. These are less common in the New Testament, apart from Revelation, which seems to be a special case (e.g. VL 62). Illustrations were an integral part of the *Commentary on the Apocalypse* by the eighth-century Beatus of Liébana.[77] The ever-increasing use of images in mediaeval picture Bibles, such as the *Bible moralisée* or the *Biblia pauperum*, some of which had Latin rather than or as well as vernacular text, is beyond the scope of the present volume.[78] Even so, the full-page image of the devil in Codex Gigas (VL 51) led to its being known as the 'Devil's Bible'.

Bindings are also part of the decoration of manuscripts, although in most cases the original binding has perished or been replaced. One of the earliest to survive is the late seventh-century tooled leather cover of the Cuthbert Gospel (Vg^{Oe} S). Jerome's comment about 'jewelled gospel books' (see page 45) shows that the practice of creating luxurious bindings was already prevalent at the end of the fourth century. The magnificent casings of gospel books at the court of Charlemagne, and later the Ottonian dynasty, stand in the same tradition. The incorporation of carved ivory panels, a feature of luxury late antique bindings, was reintroduced in Carolingian times; decorative metalwork and precious stones are also found in particularly lavish productions. In Ireland, biblical manuscripts were often treated as relics and kept in a case, or shrine (e.g. VL 35).[79]

[77] Bischoff 1990:211.   [78] See van Liere 2014:248–53.
[79] McGurk 1994a:20.

10

Catalogue of Latin New Testament Manuscripts

This chapter offers brief descriptions of the manuscripts cited in the principal editions of the Latin New Testament. All of the manuscripts listed in the New Testament section of the Vetus Latina *Register* (Gryson 1999) are included in the first section. Details from the *Register* have been supplemented from other lists (e.g. McGurk 1961a, Metzger 1977, Elliott 1992) as well as fresh research. Manuscripts 9A, 11A, and 19A have been identified since the publication of the *Register*. The next two sections describe Vulgate manuscripts. The Stuttgart Vulgate uses relatively few manuscripts, and not all are consistently cited in the apparatus.[1] The Oxford Vulgate has a much fuller selection, including many famous witnesses. This catalogue can therefore be used alongside all of these editions, as well as others such as NA28 and UBS5 (see the conversion tables in Appendix 1). Other manuscripts occasionally cited in the the Vetus Latina edition are listed in Appendix 2, while Appendix 3 contains additional manuscript of interest for their text of the Gospels. The index of manuscripts in Fischer 1985 and 1986, Berger 1893, McGurk 1961a, and the prefaces to the Vetus Latina editions may be consulted for further details of these.

Holding institutions are listed in their original language apart from the location; some manuscripts are split across more than one library. If the manuscript does not have a shelf number, this is indicated by 's. n.' (*sine numero*). The approximate page size is given in brackets after the number of pages; the measurement following the number of columns is the approximate size of the text block. In order to take account of variation within manuscripts, these have been rounded to the nearest half-centimetre. For gospel manuscripts, the siglum from Fischer's collation is given, followed by the percentage agreement with the Stuttgart Vulgate over all test-passages. If the figure for any single test-passage differs from the average by more than 10 per cent, details are provided.[2] Abbreviated references to

---

[1] See page 129 above.
[2] Fischer 1988–91, 2010; see page 125, where a list of test-passages is also provided. For example, Mark[23] indicates test-passage 23 in Mark.

the Bibliography are provided for each manuscript. Most of the editions are described in Chapter 6. TM indicates the number in the online Trismegistos catalogue, incorporating the Leuven Database of Ancient Books <www.tri smegistos.org>. The original references for the writings of Fischer are followed by details of his two volumes of collected works (Fischer 1985 and 1986) in which the bibliography has been updated. The information given under further literature is not intended to be exhaustive: only the most substantial and/or recent publications are given, and the editions should also always be consulted.

A) THE VETUS LATINA *REGISTER*

VL 1

Turin, Biblioteca Nazionale Universitaria, 1163 (G.VII.15)
   Codex Bobiensis. Portions of Mark and Matthew.
   Copied in Africa in the fourth century. Uncial script.
   96 folios (19x16 cm). One column of 14 lines (13½x12 cm). Parchment; black ink.
   The beginning of the manuscript is lost, which is likely to have contained John, Luke and the first half of Mark. The extant text is Mark 8:8–11, 8:14–16, 8:19–16:8 (with the short ending) and Matthew 1:1–3:10, 4:1–14:17; 15:20–36. There is no marginal apparatus or other paratext. The text represents the earliest African strand of the Latin Gospels. Paragraphs are indicated by ekthesis and blank space on the previous line, with spaces in the text to mark sense breaks. The *nomina sacra* are unusual in form (see page 191). Parts of the manuscript are now illegible due to the decay of the parchment caused by the ink.
   Facsimile: Cipolla 1913 <https://books.google.co.uk/books?id=iM_sMgEACA AJ>. (CLA IV 465). Image 2 in the present volume.
   Edition: Wordsworth, Sanday, and White 1886; Turner 1904a. Cited in Vetus Latina, *Itala* (k) and Oxford Vulgate (k). Fischer Xk: 46.6 per cent (ranging from 35.2 per cent in Mark[24] to 58.9 per cent in Matthew[11]).
   Further literature: Turner & Burkitt 1904; von Soden 1909; De Bruyne 1910; Hoogterp 1930; Bakker 1933; McGurk 1961a no. 106; Mizzi 1965; Fischer 1972:31–2 [1986:196–8]; Palmer 1976; Parker 1991; Helderman 1992; Hilhorst 1994; Haelewyck 1999:44–9; Burton 2000:16–17. TM 66572.

VL 2

   i) Trent, Museo Nazionale (Castello del Buon Consiglio), s. n.
   ii) Dublin, Trinity College, 1709
   iii) London, British Library, MS Add. 40107

   Codex Palatinus. Four Gospels (Matthew–John–Luke–Mark).

Copied in North Italy (Trent?) in the fifth century. Uncial script.

230 folios (35½x26 cm). Two columns of 19–20 lines (22x17½ cm). Purple parchment; silver and gold ink.

i) contains Matthew 12:50–13:11, 13:33–24:49, 28:3–20; Mark 1:21–4:7, 4:20–6:9, 12:38–9, 13:25–6, 13:34–5; Luke 1:1–8:29, 8:49–11:3, 11:25–24:53; John 1:1–18:11, 18:26–21:25; ii) contains Matthew 13:12–23; iii) contains Matthew 14:11–22. An eighteenth-century copy (Rome, Bib. Vallicelliana U. 66) includes the text of Matthew 13:23–33, now lost. There is no prefatory material or marginal apparatus. The text is a later strand of early tradition than VL 1, often close to Cyprian. Parts of John (especially John 10) have a similar text to VL 3.

Images: iii only) <http://www.bl.uk/manuscripts/Viewer.aspx?ref=add_ms_40107_f001r>. (CLA IV 437; II p. 17; Suppl. p. ix). Image 4 in the present volume.

Editions: Tischendorf 1847; Souter 1922b; <http://iohannes.com/vetuslatina> (John). Cited in Vetus Latina, *Itala* (e) and Oxford Vulgate (e). Fischer Xe: 52.8 per cent.

Further literature: von Soden 1909; De Bruyne 1910:441; Burkitt 1920; Vogels 1925, 1926a; McGurk 1961a no. 104; Mizzi 1965; Fischer 1972:32–3 [1986:198–201]; Boismard 1993; Haelewyck 1999:43, 49; Burton 2000:17–18. TM 66281.

VL 3

Vercelli, Archivio Capitolare Eusebiano, s. n.

Codex Vercellensis. Four Gospels (Matthew–John–Luke–Mark).

Copied in Italy, probably Vercelli, in the second half of the fourth century. Uncial script.

634 pages (25½x16 cm). Two columns of 24 lines (17x10½ cm). Parchment; black ink with rubrication for the first three lines of each Gospel.

This manuscript is now severely deteriorated, in part because of its use when taking oaths. Pages are missing containing Matthew 25:2–12; Luke 11:12–26, 12:37–59; Mark 1:22–34, 15:15–16:20; Mark 16:7–20 have been added at the end in a Vulgate form. The text is early. There is no prefatory material or marginal apparatus, although a chapter number is preserved at Matthew 28:1. Paragraphs are marked by ekthesis.

Images: <http://purl.org/itsee/parker2008/VL3>. (CLA IV 467).

Editions: Bianchini 1749; Gasquet 1914 (with several misprints and reconstructions based on VL 4, but an improvement on Belsheim 1894); <http://iohannes.com/vetuslatina> (John). A new edition by Heyworth is in progress using multispectral imaging. Cited in Vetus Latina, *Itala* (a) and Oxford Vulgate (a). Fischer Xa: 60.7 per cent (ranging from 44.1 per cent in Mark[24] to 77.6 per cent in Matthew[11]).

Further literature: Souter 1911; Vogels 1919; Turner 1927; McGurk 1961a no. 108; Fischer 1972:36 [1986:204]; Haelewyck 1999:38; Burton 2000:21. TM 66574.

VL 4

Verona, Biblioteca Capitolare, VI

Codex Veronensis. Four Gospels (Matthew–John–Luke–Mark).

Copied in Italy, probably Verona, at the end of the fifth century. Uncial script. 395 folios (28x22 cm). Two columns of 18 lines (17½x15 cm). Purple parchment; silver and gold ink.

A few pages are missing, containing Matthew 1:1–11, 15:12–22, 23:18–27; John 7:44–8:12; Luke 19:26–21:29; Mark 13:11–16, 13:27–14:24; 14:56–16:20. A representative of the Italian text of the late fourth century, although John 1:1–10:12 is slightly earlier. The first page of each Gospel is in gold. The Eusebian apparatus is written in the margins in gold and silver, although this may have been added later.

Images: <http://iohannes.com/vetuslatina>. (CLA IV 481).

Editions: Bianchini 1749; Belsheim 1904; Buchanan 1911a; <http://iohannes.com/vetuslatina> (John). Cited in Vetus Latina, *Itala* (b) and Oxford Vulgate (b). Fischer Xb: 71.6 per cent (ranging from 57.6 per cent in Mark[21] to 82.6 per cent in John[44]).

Further literature: Sanders 1922; Mercati 1925; McGurk 1961a no. 109; Fischer 1972:36 [1986:203–4]; Spagnolo & Marchi 1996; Haelewyck 1999:38–42; Burton 2000:19–20, 72–3. TM 66588.

VL 5

Cambridge, University Library, Nn. II. 41

Codex Bezae Cantabrigiensis. Four Gospels (Matthew–John–Luke–Mark); 3 John; Acts.

Copied around 400, possibly in Berytus. Uncial script (b-d uncial).

406 folios (26x22 cm). A Greek–Latin bilingual manuscript, with the Greek on the left page and the Latin on the right. One column of 33 lines (18½x14½ cm). Parchment; black ink with the first three lines of each book in red.

The opening of the manuscript is missing, as are several quires after the Gospels which may have contained Revelation and the Johannine Epistles; 3 John 11–15 is found on the reverse of the first pages of Acts in Greek. The following portions are lacunose, although those marked with † have been provided on ninth-century replacement leaves: Matthew 1:1–11, 2:21–3:7†; 6:8–8:27; 26:25–27:2; John 1:1–3:16; 18:2–20:1†; Mark 16:6–20†; Acts 8:21–10:3; 20:32–21:1, 21:8–9, 22:3–9, 22:21–28:31. The text of Acts is the longer, so-called 'Western' text. In the Gospels, there are early Latin readings although the overall shape is close to the Vulgate. Throughout the manuscript there are harmonizations between the Latin and the Greek. The text is written in sense lines. Eusebian section numbers are found in the margin of the Greek pages. In Mark there are hermeneiai (fortune-telling phrases) in Greek written across the bottom margin.

Images: <http://cudl.lib.cam.ac.uk/view/MS-NN-00002-00041/>. (CLA II 140). Image 3 in the present volume.

Editions: Full transcription alongside digital images above, replacing Scrivener 1864 (also downloadable from <http://epapers.bham.ac.uk/1664>). Cited in Vetus Latina, Sabatier (*Cantabr.*, using a copy made for Bentley), *Itala* (d) and Oxford Vulgate (d). Fischer Xd: 59.6 per cent (ranging from 42 per cent in Luke[34] to 75 per cent in John[41]).

Further literature: Jülicher 1914; Ropes 1926; Stone 1946; Thiele 1956:90*-1*; Mizzi 1963; Mizzi 1968; Fischer 1972:39–42 [1986:208–11]; Birdsall 1986; Parker 1992; Parker & Amphoux 1996, esp. Auwers 1996; Burton 2000:22–3. TM 61777.

VL 6
Paris, Bibliothèque nationale de France, latin 254
Codex Colbertinus. New Testament (eacrp) including Laodiceans.
Copied in southern France in the twelfth century. Late Caroline minuscule script.
146 folios (26x16½ cm). Two columns of 40 lines (17½x9½ cm in the first half and 18x10½ cm in the second). Parchment; black ink with decoration in red, green, and blue and illustrations at the beginning of each gospel.
The Old Latin element is principally in the Gospels and Acts, with a substantial archaic portion in Mark and Luke and a later Italian Old Latin text in Matthew and John; Revelation and the Epistles are Vulgate. The manuscript begins with *Plures fuisse, Nouum opus* and canon tables (no divisions). Each Gospel has a prologue and *capitula* (KA I), with Eusebian apparatus (including parallel passages) in margins. Acts also has *capitula* and a prologue and is followed by a note on the *Passion of Peter and Paul* also found in VL 109; the other writings only have prologues, including *Primum intellegere* (S 669), *Epistolae Pauli* (S 651), and *Primum quaeritur* (S 670) before the Pauline Epistles.
Images: <http://gallica.bnf.fr/ark:/12148/btv1b8426051s>.
Editions: Vogels 1953; <http://iohannes.com/vetuslatina> (John). Cited in Sabatier (*Colb.*, his text of the Gospels), Vetus Latina (with the siglum Ω^C when not Old Latin), *Itala* (c), and Oxford Vulgate (c). Fischer Xc: 68.3 per cent (ranging from 50.8 per cent in Luke[34] to 95.8 per cent in John[41]).
Further literature: Berger 1893:74–6, 402; Fischer 1972:34 [1986:200–1]; Frede 1975:74–5; Fröhlich 1995:111–12; Haelewyck 1999:42; Burton 2000:27.

VL 7
Paris, Bibliothèque nationale de France, latin 11553
Codex Sangermanensis (primus). The second volume of a Latin Bible, containing the Odes, Wisdom Literature, Old Testament Apocrypha, New Testament (eacrp), and the beginning of the Shepherd of Hermas.
Copied in St-Germain-des-Prés around 810. Caroline minuscule script.
189 folios (40x33 cm). Two columns of 46–52 lines (34–35x25–27 cm). Parchment; black ink with minimal decoration.
This manuscript goes back to a pandect assembled in the fifth century, probably in Rome. The New Testament came from three separate volumes (Gospels,

Acts–Revelation, Pauline Epistles), as shown by the titles copied in the manuscript. Matthew is Old Latin, and there is a decreasing Old Latin element in the other Gospels; the rest of the New Testament is Vulgate. In 2 Thessalonians, this manuscript alone preserves readings which appear to be that of the Vulgate archetype; in Acts it is the best Vulgate witness by far, and it is also the leading Vulgate witness in the Epistles and Revelation. Preceding Matthew are canon tables (divisions of 4) and *capitula* for all four Gospels (KA I). The first line of each chapter is written in capitals; Eusebian apparatus is present in the margins (but not with parallel passages). John also features Latin hermeneiai (fortune-telling phrases) corresponding to those in VL 5. Acts is preceded by a unique series of *capitula* (KA Act Sp^r), but there are none for the latter books; Acts, the Catholic Epistles, and Revelation all have marginal glosses in shorthand (Tironian notes), including some words in Greek. Many of these are taken from the commentaries of Bede. There are some ninth-century corrections which bring the manuscript into line with Alcuin's text. Stichometry is present. Readings from the first volume as well as text now missing from this second volume are reported by Stephanus in his Vulgate editions of 1532 and 1538–40; these portions had been lost by the late seventeenth century.

Images: <http://gallica.bnf.fr/ark:/12148/btv1b9065958t>. Image 16 in the present volume.

Editions: Sabatier (*Sang. 1*, Gospels); Wordsworth 1883 (Matthew); <http://iohannes.com/vetuslatina> (John). Cited in Vetus Latina, *Itala* (g^1), Stuttgart Vulgate (G), and Oxford Vulgate (G or g^1). Fischer Pg: 88.3 per cent (ranging from 72.9 per cent in Matthew[12] to 97 per cent in John[44]).

Further literature: Harris 1888; Berger 1893:65–72, 408; Fischer 1963b: 576–86 [1985:81–89]; Fischer 1965 [1985:147–8]; Frede 1966: 35–41; Fischer 1971 [1985:390]; Fischer 1972:62–80 [1986:240–50]; Frede 1973; Frede 1975:37–40; Fröhlich 1995:52–3; Burton 2000:26; Bogaert 2013:510.

VL 8

Paris, Bibliothèque nationale de France, latin 17225

Codex Corbeiensis (secundus). Four Gospels (Matthew–John–Luke–Mark).

Copied in Italy in the fifth century. Uncial script.

190 folios (28x25 cm). Two columns of 24 lines (17x17 cm). Parchment; black ink with rubrication.

There are numerous small lacunae as well as the following more substantial missing portions: Matthew 1:1–11:26; John 17:16–18:9, 20:23–21:8; Luke 9:48–10:20, 11:45–12:6. The latter three Gospels are preceded by *capitula* (KA I). The anti-Marcionite preface to Luke (PROL Lc Pa) follows the *capitula*. The first line of each chapter is in red with a marginal number; there is no Eusebian apparatus. The text is an Italian form from the late fourth century, very close to the type used by Jerome for his revision of the Gospels.

Images: <http://gallica.bnf.fr/ark:/12148/btv1b9065916g>. (CLA V 666). Image 5 in the present volume.

Editions: Bianchini 1749; Belsheim 1887; Buchanan 1907; <http://iohannes.com/vetuslatina> (John). Cited in Sabatier (*Corb.*, *Corb. 2*), Vetus Latina, *Itala* (ff²), and Oxford Vulgate (ff²). Fischer Xf: 70.5 per cent (ranging from 53.6 per cent in Mark[24] to 83.5 per cent in John[41]).

Further literature: Sanders 1922; McGurk 1961a no. 61; Fischer 1972:34–6 [1986:200–3]; Vezin 1987; Haelewyck 1999:43; Burton 2000:20. TM 66834.

VL 9

St Petersburg, Russian National Library, O.v.I.3
Codex Corbeiensis (primus). Matthew.
Copied in Corbie (France) in the first half of the eighth century. Cursive and pre-Caroline minuscule script.
78 folios (21x15 cm). Two columns of 19 lines (18½x11 cm). Parchment; black ink.
The text of Matthew has a Vulgate overlay, particularly in the first nine chapters, but there are a number of archaic readings, and an Old Latin portion around Matthew 16–17. There are initial *capitula* (KA B). The manuscript was bound with a Vulgate copy of Mark 1:1–5:2 written in half uncial in the eighth century (O.v.I.2).
Images: (CLA XI 1623).
Editions: Belsheim 1881. Cited in Sabatier (*Corb.*, *Corb. 1*), *Itala* (ff¹), and Oxford Vulgate (ff¹). Fischer Xo: 83.8 per cent (ranging from 52.4 per cent in Matthew[13] to 94.1 per cent in Matthew[12]).
Further literature: McGurk 1961a no. 129; Fischer 1972:38 [1986:206]; Burton 2000:28. TM 67789.

VL 9A

St Petersburg, Russian National Library, F.v.I.8
Codex Fossatensis. Four Gospels (Matthew–Mark–Luke–John).
Copied in England, probably Northumbria, in the late eighth century. Anglo-Saxon majuscule/Insular half-uncial script.
215 folios (34x24 cm). Two columns of around 25 lines (27½x20 cm). Parchment; black ink with decoration in red, yellow, and blue.
The manuscript begins with *Nouum opus, Plures fuisse, Eusebius Carpiano* and the prologue and *capitula* to Matthew (KA C) before the richly-decorated canon tables. The other gospels also have the same *capitula* but a different set of chapter divisions. Eusebian apparatus is found in all gospels, but missing from the latter half of Matthew. The text is Vulgate with several early readings, especially in the second half of Mark.
Images: *Insular Gospels* 2001. Certain pages at <http://iohannes.com/vetuslatina> and <http://www.helsinki.fi/varieng/series/volumes/09/bleskina/>. (CLA XI 1605).
Editions: <http://iohannes.com/vetuslatina> (John). Cited in Sabatier (*Fossat.*), Vetus Latina. Fischer Ec: 88.8 per cent (ranging from 65.4 per cent in Mark[24] to 97.8 per cent in Matthew[13]).

Further literature: McGurk 1961a no. 126; McGurk 1993:248–51; Gameson 1994:35; Kockelkorn 2000; Houghton 2010a; Bleskina 2012; Houghton 2016. TM 67770.

VL 10

Brescia, Biblioteca civica Queriniana, s. n. ('Evangelario purpureo')
   Codex Brixianus. Four Gospels (Matthew–John–Luke–Mark).
   Copied in North Italy, possibly Ravenna, in the sixth century. Uncial script.
   419 folios (28x21½ cm). One column of 20 lines (18½x12 cm). Purple parchment; silver ink with gold for the first three lines of each gospel.
   The following portions are missing: Matthew 8:16–26; Mark 12:5–13:32, 14:53–62, 14:70–16:20. The first quire of canon tables with quotations is from a different source. The Gospels are preceded by a unique preface, *Sanctus Petrus apostolus.* Eusebian sections are in an arcade in the bottom margin, with lection numbers in the left margin. The text is close to the Vulgate but has some similarities with the Gothic version.
   Images: (CLA III 281).
   Editions: Bianchini 1749; Oxford Vulgate (printed under the editorial text); <http://iohannes.com/vetuslatina> (John). Cited in Vetus Latina (John), *Itala* (f), and Oxford Vulgate. Fischer Jg: 81.7 per cent.
   Further literature: Burkitt 1900; McGurk 1961a no. 93; Henss 1973; Fischer 1972:37 [1986:205]; Gryson 1990; Haelewyck 1999:43; Burton 2000:27; Falluomini 2012:339–40, 2015:101–3, 178–80. TM 66390.

VL 11

Berlin, Staatsbibliothek Preußischer Kulturbesitz, Depot Breslau 5
   Codex Rehdigeranus. Four Gospels (Matthew–Mark–Luke–John).
   Copied in North Italy (Aquileia) in the first half of the eighth century. Uncial script.
   296 folios (cut to 30½x25 cm). Two columns of 20 lines (21–22½x19–19½ cm). Parchment; black ink with rubrication at the beginning of chapters.
   The following text is lacking: Matthew 1:1–2:15; Luke 11:28–37; John 1:1–16, 6:32–61; 11:56–12:10; 13:34–14:22; 15:3–15; 16:13–21:25. Eusebian sections are provided in an arcade at the bottom of the page; there are chapter numbers in the left margin. Prologues and *capitula* are present before Mark (KA I) and Luke (KA B). The text is an Italian Old Latin form of the late fourth century, although Matthew and Mark are close to the Vulgate. Reports that the manuscript was destroyed in 1945 are incorrect.
   Images: (CLA VIII 1073; also CLA IX p. 57).
   Editions: Vogels 1913; <http://iohannes.com/vetuslatina> (John). Cited in Vetus Latina (John), *Itala* (l), and Oxford Vulgate (l, based on Tischendorf). Fischer Xl: 84.2 per cent (ranging from 68.5 per cent in Luke[34] to 94.2 per cent in Matthew[11]).
   Further literature: McGurk 1961a no. 110; Fischer 1972:36–8 [1986:203–5]; Haelewyck 1999:44; Burton 2000:27; Haelewyck 2013:12. TM 67212.

VL 11A

Würzburg, Universitätsbibliothek, M.p.th.f. 67

Four Gospels (Matthew–Mark–Luke–John).

Copied in the eighth or ninth century, probably in Brittany. Uncial script with Insular features.

192 folios (32x21 cm). Two columns of 20 lines (26x16 cm). Parchment; black ink.

John 18:36–21:25 is missing. There is no prefatory material or Eusebian apparatus; only Mark has a prologue. There are some chapter numbers in the margin (KA I). The text displays block mixture: only certain passages in each Gospel are Old Latin.

Images: <http://vb.uni-wuerzburg.de/ub/mpthf67/index.html>. (CLA IX 1422).

Editions: <http://iohannes.com/vetuslatina> (John). Cited in Vetus Latina (John). Fischer Bw: 84.1 per cent (ranging from 65.7 per cent in Mark[24] to 92 per cent in Luke[32]).

Further literature: Thurn 1984; McGurk 1987:176; Houghton 2009; Houghton 2016. TM 67561.

VL 12

Vatican City, Biblioteca Apostolica Vaticana, Vatic. lat. 7223

Codex Claromontanus. Four Gospels (Matthew–Mark–Luke–John).

Matthew was copied in Italy at the end of the fifth century; the other gospels were produced in northern Italy or France in the seventh century. Uncial script.

Matthew consists of 66 pages (25x20 cm); the other gospels are on 217 pages of the same size. Two columns of 23 lines (19x15 cm). Parchment; black ink.

The manuscript originally consisted only of Matthew (the sole Old Latin text, typical of an early Gallo-Irish group) with no prefatory material, but was made into a gospel book in the seventh century with the addition of the other gospels in a Vulgate form (preceded by KA I). The following portions are missing: Matthew 1:1–3:14, 14:34–18:11.

Images: <http://digi.vatlib.it/view/MSS_Vat.lat.7223>. (CLA I 53, 54).

Editions: Belsheim 1892. Cited in Sabatier (*Clarom.*), *Itala* (h; Matthew only), and Oxford Vulgate (h). Fischer Xh in Matthew: 71.5 per cent; Jh in the other gospels: 96.4 per cent.

Further literature: McGurk 1961a no. 135 & 136; Fischer 1972:36 [1986:203]; Burton 2000:23. TM 66149.

VL 13

Munich, Bayerische Staatsbibliothek, Clm 6224

Codex Monacensis or *Codex Valerianus.* Four Gospels (Matthew–John–Luke–Mark).

Copied in Illyria (possibly Sirmium) or Italy in the sixth or seventh century. Uncial script.

235 folios (25x21 cm). Two columns of 19–22 lines (16½–18x15½–16½ cm). Parchment; black ink with other colours used in decoration.

There are several lacunae (Matthew 3:15–4:23, 5:25–6:4, 6:28–7:8, 23:13–28; John 10:11–12:38, 21:9–20; Luke 23:23–35, 24:11–39; Mark 1:7–21, 15:5–36). An attempt to change the sequence of the gospels has resulted in several sections being bound in the wrong order. No prefatory material or Eusebian apparatus is present. Lectionary indications have been added in seventh-century North Italian cursive script. The text is Old Latin but with some Vulgate influence: it appears to have been revised on the basis of a Greek text.

Images: <http://daten.digitale-sammlungen.de/~db/bsb00006573/images/>. (CLA IX 1249).

Editions: White 1888; <http://iohannes.com/vetuslatina> (John). Cited in Vetus Latina, *Itala* (q), and Oxford Vulgate (q). Fischer Xq: 70.9 per cent (ranging from 56.5 per cent in Mark[22] to 80.4 per cent in Matthew[11]).

Further literature: De Bruyne 1911; Souter 1934; McGurk 1961a no. 74; Gryson 1978; Fischer 1972:36–7 [1986:203–4]; Fischer 1980 [1986:301]; Haelewyck 1999:13; Burton 2000:24; Glauche 2000; Falluomini 2015:104. TM 67390.

VL 14
Dublin, Trinity College, MS 55
Codex Usserianus primus. Four Gospels (Matthew–John–Luke–Mark).
Copied in Ireland around 600. Irish half uncial script.

180 folios, with no margins preserved. One column of 22 lines (17½x13 cm). Parchment; black ink. In Matthew and John, the first line of each chapter is in colour.

The manuscript is heavily damaged and the following portions are entirely missing: Matthew 1:1–15:16, 15:31–16:13, 21:4–21, 28:16–20; John 1:1–15; Mark 14:58–15:8, 15:32–16:20. No prefatory material or Eusebian apparatus is preserved apart from a list of Hebrew names before Luke. Some chapter numbers are visible. The text is Old Latin, typical of a Gallo-Irish group including some distinctive readings.

Images: <http://digitalcollections.tcd.ie/home/#folder_id=36&pidtopage=MS55_001&entry_point=1>, <http://digitalcollections.tcd.ie/content/36/pdf/36.pdf>. (CLA II 271). Image 8 in the present volume.

Editions: Abbott 1884; <http://iohannes.com/vetuslatina> (John). Cited in Vetus Latina, *Itala* (r¹), and Oxford Vulgate (r¹). Fischer Xr: 68.1 per cent.

Further literature: McGurk 1961a no. 84; Fischer 1963b [1985:82], 1965 [1985:196], 1972:36 [1986:203]; Parkes 1992:24; McGurk 1994b; Haelewyck 1999:44–5; Burton 2000:23. TM 66357.

VL 15
Stockholm, Kungliga Biblioteket, A.135
Codex Aureus Holmiensis. Four Gospels (Matthew–Mark–Luke–John).
Copied in Southern England (Minster in Thanet?) around 775. Uncial script.

193 folios (39½x31½ cm). Two columns of 24–26 lines (28x24½ cm). Alternating leaves of purple and white parchment; gold, silver, black, and red ink with the text often laid out in a decorative pattern.

Prefatory material comprises *Nouum opus*, *Plures fuisse* and canon tables. Each gospel is preceded by *capitula* (KA B in Matthew, KA I in the other gospels) although these do not match the numbered divisions in Matthew and Luke. Eusebian apparatus in margins. The text is essentially Vulgate (especially in Matthew and the second half of Luke) although portions are a mixed text with occasional Old Latin readings. Luke 21:8–30 is absent.

Facsimile: Gameson 2001–2. (CLA XI 1642).

Editions: Belsheim 1878; <http://iohannes.com/vetuslatina> (John). Cited in Vetus Latina, *Itala* (aur), and Oxford Vulgate (aur). Fischer Ea: 88.4 per cent (ranging from 78.5 per cent in Mark[24] to 94.5 per cent in Luke[34]).

Further literature: McGurk 1961a no. 111; Fischer 1965 [1985:159, 170], 1972:39 [1986:207]; Gameson 1994:46; Burton 2000:26; Gameson 2001; Fischer 2010. TM 67808.

VL 16

  i) St Gall, Stiftsbibliothek, 1394, pp. 51–88
 ii) St Gall, Stiftsbibliothek, 172
iii) St Gall, Kantonsbibliothek, Vadianische Sammlung, Ms. 70a
 iv) Chur, Bischöfliches Archiv, 041.0.1
  v) St Gall, Stiftsbibliothek, 1394 pp. 91–2
 vi) St Gall, Stiftsarchiv, Fragmentensammlung

iv) *Fragmenta Curiensia*; v) *Fragmentum Sangallense*. Four Gospels (Matthew–John–Luke–Mark).

Copied in Italy in the fifth century; v) is a seventh-century replacement leaf. Uncial script.

Remains of 25 folios (32x22½ cm). Two columns of 24 lines (22x18½ cm). Parchment; black ink with rubrication.

These are a few pages from a gospel book with an Old Latin text close to VL 3. The contents are as follows: i) portions of Matthew 17–21 and 26–28, Mark 7–9, 13, 15–16; ii) Mark 15 (part of a page also preserved in i); iii) verses from John 19:13–42; iv) Luke 11:11–29 and 13:16–34; v) Mark 16:14–20; vi) portions of John 14:23–18:7. The chapter numbers are written in red in Greek numerals at the top of the page in Matthew and John. There is no Eusebian apparatus. The fragment of John has some Old High German glosses written between the lines. White suggests that i) and iv) are from different manuscripts.

Images: Gamper et al. 2012; i) and v): <http://www.e-codices.unifr.ch/en/csg/1394/>; ii) <http://www.e-codices.unifr.ch/en/csg/0172/258/>. (CLA VII 978a, 978b).

Editions: Gamper et al. 2012; i), iii), iv), v) Wordsworth, Sanday, and White 1886; Bischoff 1946: 420–4; iii and vi) <http://iohannes.com/vetuslatina>. Cited in Vetus Latina, *Itala* (i and iii have the siglum n; iv has the siglum a^2; v has the siglum o) and Oxford Vulgate (same sigla as *Itala*). Fischer Xn: 64.6 per cent.

Further literature: McGurk 1961a no. 119 and 120; Fischer 1972:37 [1986:204]; Burton 2000:21–2; Haelewyck 2013:13. TM 67122 and 67123.

VL 17

Naples, Biblioteca Nazionale, lat. 3

> *Codex Vindobonensis.* Portions of Luke and Mark.
>
> Copied in Italy at the end of the fifth century. Uncial script.
>
> 143 folios (26x19½ cm). One column of 14 lines (14x14 cm). Purple parchment; silver ink with gold for the *nomina sacra*.
>
> The first 42 quires are missing, implying that this was a gospel book with the order Matthew–John–Luke–Mark. The extant text is Luke 10:6–14:22, 14:29–16:4, 16:11–23:10 and Mark 2:17–3:29, 4:4–10:1, 10:33–14:36, 15:33–40. The text is an Old Latin form current in Italy in the middle of the fourth century.
>
> Images: (CLA III 399).
>
> Editions: Belsheim 1885; Cited in *Itala* (i) and Oxford Vulgate (i). Fischer Xi: 70.9 per cent.
>
> Further literature: McGurk 1961a no. 99; Fischer 1972:36 [1986:203]; Haelewyck 1999:43–44; Burton 2000:20. TM 66503.

VL 18

i) Darmstadt, Hessische Landes- und Hochschulbibliothek, 895
ii) Donaueschingen, Fürstlich Fürstenbergische Hofbibliothek, 925
iii) Stuttgart, Württembergische Landesbibliothek, HB. VI. 114; VII, 29; VII. 64; XIV. 15

> *Fragmenta Weingartensia* or *Fragmenta Constantiensia.* Parts of a gospel lectionary.
>
> Copied in North Italy in the seventh century, but palimpsested around 800. Uncial script.
>
> 19 folios (23x17½ cm). One column of 17 lines (20x14 cm). Parchment; black ink.
>
> This is one of the earliest surviving Latin lectionaries, containing pericopes of 3 to 15 verses from Matthew, Luke and John. The text is from the later Italian Old Latin tradition but is very close to the Vulgate.
>
> Images: (CLA VIII 1175 and 1176).
>
> Editions: Lehmann 1908; Dold 1923; <http://iohannes.com/vetuslatina> (John). Cited in Vetus Latina and *Itala* (π). Fischer Xw: 89.9 per cent.
>
> Further literature: Gamber 1962; Salmon 1963; Burton 2000:25. CLLA 261. TM 67314.

VL 19

Bern, Burgerbibliothek, 611, foll. 143–4
> *Fragmentum Bernense.* Fragments of Mark.

Copied in the second half of the fifth century, probably in Italy. Palimpsested in the first half of the eighth century. Uncial script.

2 folios (cut to 18½x21½ cm). Two columns of 22 lines (15½x15½ cm). Parchment; black ink.

A witness to the fourth-century Italian text for Mark 1:2–23, 2:22–27, and 3:11–18.

Images: (CLA VII 867).

Editions: Hagen 1884; Wordsworth, Sanday, and White 1886; Cited in Vetus Latina, *Itala* (t), and Oxford Vulgate (t). Fischer Xt: 76 per cent.

Further literature: McGurk 1961a no. 113; Fischer 1972:36 [1986:203]; Haelewyck 1999:45; Haelewyck 2013:14. TM 67010.

VL 19A

i) Durham, Cathedral Library, A.II.10, foll. 2–5, 338–9
ii) Durham, Cathedral Library, C.III.13, foll. 192–5
iii) Durham, Cathedral Library, C.III.20, foll. 1–2

Fragments of Matthew and Mark.

Copied in Ireland or Northumbria in the middle of the seventh century. Insular half uncial script (with Insular minuscule at the end of certain columns).

12 folios (38½x26 cm; originally 47x33 cm). Two columns of 45–51 lines (36x25 cm). Parchment; black ink with coloured decoration.

These leaves from a gospel book were re-used as endpapers in later manuscripts. The contents are as follows: i) Matthew 27:35–28:19; Mark 1:1–4:24, Mark 10:17–14:55; ii) Matthew 14:32–18:29; 22:15–25:26; iii) Mark 4:24–6:6; Mark 8:39–10:17.[3] Most of the fragments are Vulgate, but Mark 2:12–6:5 is Old Latin, corresponding to the text of the Gallo-Irish subgroup seen in VL 14. Mark has Eusebian sections (but not canon numbers) in the margin; there is no marginal material in Matthew, but at the end of the Gospel a phonetic Latin representation of the Lord's Prayer in Greek is written in rubrics.

Images: (CLA II 147).

Editions: Cited in Vetus Latina. Fischer Ee: 82.1 per cent (ranging from 72.4 per cent in Mark[21] to 88.7 per cent in Mark[23]).

Further literature: McGurk 1961a no. 9; Verey 1969–70, 1973; Gameson 2010:24–7; Haelewyck 2013a. TM 66247.

VL 20

St Gall, Stiftsbibliothek, 1395, pp. 430–3

Fragmentum Sangallense. Lection from John.

Copied in Ireland in the eighth century. Irish minuscule script.

One bifolium, in two parts (22½x17 cm). One column of 21 lines (21x14 cm). Parchment; black ink.

---

[3] I am grateful to Dr Michael Stansfield for confirming the extent of these pages.

John 11:14–44, a reading from the Mass for the Dead, now preserved as a single fragment. The text is Old Latin, similar to VL 14.

Images: <http://www.e-codices.unifr.ch/en/csg/1395/430/>. (CLA VII 989).

Editions: Wordsworth, Sanday & White 1886; Bischoff 1946:425–7; <http://iohannes.com/vetuslatina>. Cited in Vetus Latina, *Itala* (p), and Oxford Vulgate (p).

Further literature: Berger 1893:31; Fischer 1972:36 [1986:203]. TM 67134.

VL 21

Milan, Biblioteca Ambrosiana, O.210 sup., Appendix

Fragments from Luke.

Copied in Italy in the fifth century. Uncial script.

4 folios (23x19½ cm). Two columns of 26 lines (18x17 cm). Parchment; black ink.

Luke 17:3–29, 18:39–19:47, 20:46–21:22 with an Old Latin text similar to VL 3, including a number of archaic readings. The leaves had been used in the binding of another manuscript (O.210 sup.).

Images: (CLA III 360).

Edition: Wordsworth, Sanday, and White 1886. Cited in *Itala* (s) and Oxford Vulgate (s).

Further literature: McGurk 1961a no. 98; Fischer 1972:37 [1986:204]; Burton 2000:25. TM 66462.

VL 22

Sarezzano in Tortona, Biblioteca Parrocchiale, s. n. (pars prima)

Codex Sarzanensis. Fragments of Luke and John.

Copied in North Italy at the beginning of the sixth century. Uncial script.

64 folios (30x25 cm). Two columns of 16 lines (17½x16 cm). Purple parchment; silver ink.

This manuscript was found by Amelli in 1872 in a reliquary in the Church of Sarezzano. It is bound with VL 22A. Although badly damaged, with erosion caused by the metal ink, it contains portions of Luke 24 and John 1–11. There are chapter numbers and lectionary indications in the margin. The text is an early Old Latin form, forming a subgroup in John with VL 4 and 14.

Images: 31 plates, 7 in colour, in Ghiglione 1984. (CLA IV 436a).

Editions: Godu 1936; Ghiglione 1984 (only 19 pages); <http://iohannes.com/vetuslatina> (John). Cited in Vetus Latina, *Itala* (j), and Oxford Vulgate (j). Fischer Xj: 75.1 per cent in John[41].

Further literature: McGurk 1961a no. 103; Pagano 1987; Ghiglione 1990; Burton 2000:73. TM 66542.

VL 22A

Sarezzano in Tortona, Biblioteca Parrocchiale, s. n. (pars altera)

Codex Sarzanensis. Fragments of John.

Copied in North Italy at the beginning of the sixth century. Uncial script.

6 folios (29x24 cm). One column of 16 lines (15½x15½ cm). Purple parchment; silver ink.

These pages are bound with VL 22 but come from a different manuscript. They contain an Old Latin text of portions of John 18:36–20:14.

Images: 2 plates, 1 in colour, in Ghiglione 1984. (CLA IV 436b).

Editions: Godu 1936; <http://iohannes.com/vetuslatina>. Cited in Vetus Latina, *Itala* (j), and Oxford Vulgate (j). Fischer Xj: 82.2 per cent in John[41].

Further literature: McGurk 1961a no. 102; Pagano 1987; Ghiglione 1990; Burton 2000:23. TM 66542.

VL 23

Aberdeen, University Library, Papyrus 2a

Fragmentum Aberdonense. A fragment of John.

Written in the fifth century and found in Egypt, possibly the Fayyum. Rustic capitals.

1 page (reconstructed as 10½x8 cm); the fragment itself measures about 2x4 cm. Two columns of 20–21 lines. Parchment; black ink with a red numeral.

Only parts of John 7:27–28 and 30–31 are preserved, along with Eusebian apparatus (including parallel passages) in the left margin. Despite the reconstruction of an Old Latin word order in the *editio princeps*, the text preserved corresponds to the Vulgate and the Eusebian apparatus supports its identification as Vulgate. Mercati 1953b suggested that it might be part of a Latin Diatessaron but the small format indicates that it is more likely to have been a copy of John alone.

Images: <http://iohannes.com/vetuslatina>. (CLA II 118).

Editions: Winstedt 1907; Turner 1939; <http://iohannes.com/vetuslatina>. Cited in *Itala* (23).

Further literature: Mercati 1953b; Fischer 1972:44 [1986:213]. TM 61647.

VL 24

Milan, Biblioteca Ambrosiana, M. 12 sup., pp. 119–22

Fragmentum Mediolanense. Johannine lection from a Gallican Sacramentary.

Copied around 700 in southern France; palimpsested in the ninth century. Uncial script.

4 pages (17x14 cm). One column, usually of 14 lines (15x11 cm). Parchment; black ink.

The lection is John 13:3–17. Its text corresponds to the Gallo-Irish group of Old Latin witnesses.

Images: (CLA III 354).

Editions: Wilmart 1922; Dold 1952; <http://iohannes.com/vetuslatina> (John). Cited in Vetus Latina and *Itala* (ρ). Fischer Xs: 71.1 per cent.

Further literature: Salmon 1963; Fischer 1972:36 [1986:203]; CLLA 205. TM 66456.

VL 25

Vienna, Österreichische Nationalbibliothek, lat. 502, fol. II
  Fragmentum Vindobonense. A fragment of John.
  Copied in North Italy or France in the sixth or seventh century. Uncial script.
  1 page (cut to 23½x16½ cm). Two columns of 30 lines (estimated 20x20 cm). Parchment; black ink.
  A single page with John 19:27–20:11. The text has similarities with the Italian Old Latin text preceding the Vulgate. There is no marginal material.
  Images: <http://data.onb.ac.at/dtl/3550818>, images 7 & 8. (CLA X 1481).
  Editions: White 1888; <http://iohannes.com/vetuslatina>. Cited in Vetus Latina, *Itala* (v) and Oxford Vulgate (v). Fischer Xv: 79.8 per cent.
  Further literature: McGurk 1961a no. 41. TM 67667.

VL 26

St Paul in Kärnten, Stiftsbibliothek St Paul im Lavanttal, 1/1, fol. 1–2
  Fragmentum Carinthianum. A fragment of Luke.
  Copied in the sixth or seventh century, probably in Italy. Uncial script.
  2 folios (cut to 26x20½ cm). Two columns of 32 lines (22½x19½ cm). Parchment; black ink.
  This bifolium containing Luke 1:64–2:51 is bound into another codex as a guard leaf. There are interlinear Latin and Old High German glosses. The early Old Latin text has been partially corrected towards a later Old Latin version.
  Images: (CLA X 1449).
  Edition: De Bruyne 1923. Cited in *Itala* (β).
  Further literature: McGurk 1961a no. 39; Fischer 1972:36 [1986:203]; Burton 2000:23–4. TM 67636.

VL 27

St Gall, Stiftsbibliothek, 48
  Codex Sangallensis (interlinearis). Four Gospels (Matthew–Mark–Luke–John).
  Copied in St Gall in 860/70. Irish minuscule script.
  199 folios, numbered 1–398 (22½x18 cm). A Greek-Latin bilingual manuscript. One column of 19–27 lines (16½x13 cm). Parchment; black ink with rubrication in red and yellow.
  This is a Greek gospel manuscript (GA 037), with an interlinear Latin version. The translation is based on a form of the Vulgate similar to Vg^{Oe} E but has been conformed to the grammar of the Greek in many places; alternative renderings are also supplied. It is a sister manuscript of VL 77 but preserves little Old Latin evidence. There is some Latin prefatory material in the opening pages consisting of Hilary of Poitiers' poem on the Gospels, *Nouum opus*, canon tables (no divisions), and a preface and *capitula* to Matthew (KA B). The Greek *kephalaia* are found at the beginning and inserted into the text of each gospel. John 19:17–35 is missing.
  Images: <http://www.e-codices.unifr.ch/en/csg/0048/>; Rettig 1836.

Edition: <http://iohannes.com/vetuslatina> (John). Cited in Oxford Vulgate (δ).

Further literature: Harris 1891; Frede 1964:50–79; Bischoff 1981:45–7; Kaczynski 1988; Duft 1990; Radiciotti 1998. GA 037.

VL 28
Dublin, Trinity College, MS 56

Codex Usserianus secundus; The Garland of Howth. Four Gospels (Matthew–Mark–Luke–John).

Copied in Ireland around 800. Irish majuscule script.

86 folios (24x17½ cm). One column of 26 lines (19–20½x14½–15½ cm). Parchment; black ink.

There are lacunae spanning Matthew 27:59–28:20, Mark 5:31–6:13, and Luke 1:1–13, 23:15–24:53, while in John only 5:12–10:3 is extant. There is no marginal material. The text is an Irish mixed text, with a concentration of Old Latin readings in the latter half of Matthew, where it is one of the most non-Vulgate texts.

Images: (CLA II 272).

Editions: Lawlor 1897:186–201 (Matthew); Hoskier 1919; <http://iohannes. com/vetuslatina> (John). Cited in Vetus Latina (John), *Itala* (r^2), Oxford Vulgate (r^2) and Abbott 1884. Fischer Hg: 78.9 per cent (ranging from 56.5 per cent in Matthew[14] to 85.8 per cent in Luke[31]).

Further literature: Berger 1893:42; McGurk 1961a no. 85. TM 66358.

VL 29
Paris, Bibliothèque nationale de France, latin 13169

Codex Sangermanensis secundus. Four Gospels (Matthew–Mark–Luke–John).

Copied in Brittany in the tenth century. Caroline minuscule script.

166 folios (21½x14 cm). One column of 24–30 lines (16½x10½ cm). Parchment; black ink with rubrication and coloured decoration.

The prefatory material consists of *Nouum opus, Sciendum etiam, Plures fuisse,* the *argumentum* and *capitula* to Matthew (KA A, incomplete), and then the canon tables. Eusebian apparatus varies: it is absent from Mark; Matthew and Luke have section and canon numbers in the margin; John includes details of parallel passages. There is a blank space for *capitula* before Mark and Luke; John has KA P[i]. The text is mixed, with readings shared with the Insular Vulgate manuscripts. In John, lectionary headings have been integrated into the gospel, affecting the neighbouring text.

Images: <http://gallica.bnf.fr/ark:/12148/btv1b10500013s>.

Edition: <http://iohannes.com/vetuslatina> (John). Cited in Sabatier (*Sang. 2*), Vetus Latina (John), and Oxford Vulgate (g^2). Fischer Bg: 88.8 per cent.

Further literature: Berger 1893:48, 408–9; Fischer 1972:38 [1986:206].

VL 30
Paris, Bibliothèque nationale de France, nouv. acq. latin 1587

Codex Gatianus. Four Gospels (Matthew–Mark–Luke–John).

Copied in Brittany around 800. Celtic half-uncial script.

109 folios (30½x24 cm). One column of 27–29 lines (25x19½ cm). Parchment; black ink with yellow and red decoration.

There is no prefatory material, apart from a carpet page before Matthew; *chi-rho* in Matthew is also decorated. Eusebian apparatus is in the margins in black and red. The text is mixed, with readings shared with the Insular Vulgate manuscripts. The archaic *cata* is used in some of the titles.

Images: <http://gallica.bnf.fr/ark:/12148/btv1b8423842n>. (CLA V 684).

Editions: Heer 1910; <http://iohannes.com/vetuslatina> (John). Cited in Bianchini 1749 (John to Mark); Vetus Latina (John), Sabatier (*S. Gat.*), and Oxford Vulgate (gat). Fischer Bt: 86.5 per cent.

Further literature: Berger 1893:46–7, 410; McGurk 1961a no. 63; Fischer 1965 [1985:134, 251], 1972:38 [1986:206]; McGurk 1987:176; Lemoine 2004. TM 66851.

VL 31

Milan, Biblioteca Ambrosiana, T. 27 sup.

A collection of liturgical rites, including biblical lections.

Copied in North Italy in the eleventh century. Late Caroline minuscule script.

61 folios (19x13½ cm). One column of 30 lines (14x9 cm). Parchment; black ink.

The lections occur in an *ordo scrutiniorum* (foll. 6–26) compiled at the end of the sixth century. The New Testament readings are from Matthew, Mark, Luke, Romans, and 2 Corinthians. Some are Old Latin, others Vulgate in affiliation.

Edition: Lambot 1931.

Further literature: Morin 1934.

VL 32

Wolfenbüttel, Herzog-August-Bibliothek, Weißenburg 76

Lectionarium Guelferbytanus. Gallican lectionary.

Copied in France (Clermont-Ferrand?) in the first half of the sixth century. Palimpsested around 700 in Burgundy. Uncial script.

100 folios (cut to 25½x18½ cm). One column of 26 or 28 lines (21½x16½ cm). Parchment; black ink.

Both Old and New Testament lections; the latter come from all books apart from Revelation and the shorter epistles. Some passages occur more than once, with a different text; certain lections are conflations from multiple books. The affiliation ranges from Old Latin to Vulgate.

Images: <http://diglib.hab.de/mss/76-weiss/start.htm>. (CLA IX 1391, 1392).

Editions: Dold 1936; <http://iohannes.com/vetuslatina> (John). Cited in Vetus Latina (John) and Oxford Vulgate (Romans only). Fischer Gw: 88.9 per cent (ranging from 77.7 per cent in John[44] to 92 per cent in Luke[31]).

Further literature: Morin 1937; Berti 1954; Gamber 1959; Fröhlich 1995:17–18; Carmassi 2008. TM 67531.

VL 33

Paris, Bibliothèque nationale de France, latin 10439

Codex Carnotensis. John.

Copied in Italy around 500. Uncial script.

263 folios (7x5½ cm). One column of 11 lines (5x3½ cm). Parchment; black ink.

This small-format gospel was found in an eleventh-century reliquary in Chartres in 1712. Certain pages have faded, including the initial dedicatory page. There is no other prefatory material or paratext. The affiliation is Old Latin in parts of John 1–5 and Vulgate for the rest of the gospel.

Images: <http://gallica.bnf.fr/ark:/12148/btv1b52503882m>. (CLA V 600).

Edition: <http://iohannes.com/vetuslatina>. Cited in Vetus Latina. Fischer Jc: 95.5 per cent.

Further literature: Berger 1893:89–90, 407; McGurk 1961a no. 60. TM 66731.

VL 34

Grottaferrata, Biblioteca della Badia, Γ.β.VI

Codex Cryptoferratensis. A lection from John.

The manuscript is made up of palimpsested leaves from a Greek *euchologium*. The text of John 1:1–17, which was read in both languages on Easter Day, is found in Latin. The first 14 verses correspond to the Vulgate; the last 3 are an ad hoc translation with no Old Latin ancestry.

Editions: Cozza 1867:336; <http://iohannes.com/vetuslatina>.

VL 35

Dublin, Trinity College, MS 60

Book of Mulling; Liber Moliensis. Four Gospels (Matthew–Mark–Luke–John).

Copied in Ireland (probably St Mullins) at the end of the eighth century. Irish minuscule script.

84 folios (16½x12 cm). Normally two columns of 28 lines (13x9 cm); this increases up to 47 lines (and one page of three columns) towards the end of the manuscript. Parchment; black ink.

Prefatory material includes prologues and canon tables. Eusebian apparatus in margins. The text is an Irish mixed text with a strong Old Latin element in Luke 4–9. There is a diagram on the final page which is believed to be a plan of the monastery at Tech-Moling. Four further pages from another eighth-century manuscript were found in the shrine of St Moling containing portions of Matthew 26–27 and Mark 1–6 and are kept with this manuscript; these also have a mixed text.

Images: (CLA II 276).

Editions: Lawlor 1897 (selections); <http://iohannes.com/vetuslatina> (John). Cited in Vetus Latina (John). Fischer Hm: 83.2 per cent (ranging from 58.4 per cent in Luke[32] to 92 per cent in Mark[22]). The additional manuscript is Fischer Hn: 88.3 per cent.

Further literature: Berger 1893:33–4; McGurk 1956; Willis 1959; McGurk 1961a no. 89; Willis 1966b; Doyle 1967; Doyle 1972; Fischer 1972:38 [1986:206]; Nees 1983. TM 66362.

VL 36

Formerly Giessen, Universitätsbibliothek, 651/20

Fragment of Luke.

Copied in Italy in the early sixth century, but excavated in Egypt. Uncial script.

One fragment from a bifolium, comprising a part of each page plus the central margin. (Original single page size *c.* 26x18 cm). A Gothic-Latin bilingual manuscript with the Gothic on the *verso* and the Latin on the *recto*.[4] One column of 24 or 25 lines (estimated as 19x15 cm). Parchment; black ink.

The Latin text comprises parts of Luke 23:3–6 and 24:5–9. The text has Old Latin and Vulgate readings. Eusebian sections are indicated in the margin. The manuscript was destroyed through water damage in 1945.

Images: <http://papyri-giessen.dl.uni-leipzig.de/receive/GiePapyri_schrift_ 00007340>. (CLA VIII 1200).

Edition: Glaue & Helm 1910.

Further literature: Burkitt 1910b; Henss 1973; Gryson 1990; Falluomini 2010, 2015:35–6. TM 61726.

VL 37

Boulogne-sur-Mer, Bibliothèque municipale, 42 (47)

Jerome's *Commentary on Matthew* (HI Mt).

Copied in north-eastern France at the end of the eighth century. Early Caroline minuscule script.

189 folios (29x20 cm). One column of 20 lines (22½x15½ cm). Parchment; black ink.

The biblical lemmata in this commentary have been extended by means of an Old Latin source, identical to VL 38.

Images: <http://bvmm.irht.cnrs.fr/consult/consult.php?reproductionId= 87>. (CLA VI 736).

Edition: Souter 1937.

Further literature: TM 66905.

VL 38

Vatican City, Biblioteca Apostolica Vaticana, Palat. lat. 177

Jerome's *Commentary on Matthew* (HI Mt).

Copied in Lorsch around 880. Anglo-Saxon minuscule script.

123 folios (31½x17½ cm). One column of 30 lines (24x13 cm). Parchment; black ink.

The biblical lemmata in this commentary have been extended by means of an Old Latin source, identical to VL 37.

---

[4] Gryson 1999:60 reverses the position of the languages.

Images: <http://digi.vatlib.it/view/bav_pal_lat_177>. (CLA I 79).
Edition: Souter 1937.
Further literature: TM 66175.

VL 39

Poitiers, Médiathèque François-Mitterrand, MS 17 (65)
  Gospels of Sainte-Croix of Poitiers. Four Gospels (Matthew–Mark–Luke–John).
  Copied in Amiens at the end of the eighth century. Uncial script.
  214 folios (31x23 cm). Two columns of 26–28 lines (24½x18 cm). Parchment;
black ink.
  The text of the Gospels is Vulgate. The first series of canon tables quote
an Old Latin text (also in VL 40). The prefatory material is unusual, consist-
ing of a rare translation of the *Letter to Carpianus*, the canon tables with
incipits, *Nouum opus*, a regular set of canon tables, and Aileran's poem on
the canons (AIL Eus), followed by a picture of Christ in Majesty. The list of
lections at the back of the manuscript reproduces a Roman exemplar of 740.
All gospels have *capitula* (KA I). The same set of Hebrew names is found in
Vg^{Oe} Q.
  Images: (CLA VI 821).
  Editions: Minard 1945; <http://iohannes.com/vetuslatina> (John canons).
Canon tables cited in Vetus Latina (John) as a patristic witness. The main
manuscript is Fischer Pa: 96.4 per cent.
  Further literature: Minard 1947; Fischer 1965 [1985:155–6]; McGurk 1961a
no. 64; McGurk 1994b; Palazzo 2006; Herbert 2012. TM 67601.

VL 40

Vendôme, Bibliothèque municipale, 2
  Four Gospels (Matthew–Mark–Luke–John).
  Copied in France, probably in the tenth century. Caroline minuscule script.
  158 folios (33x24 cm). Parchment; black ink.
  The text of the Gospels is Vulgate. The canon tables quote an Old Latin text
(as in VL 39).
  Images: <http://bvmm.irht.cnrs.fr/consult/consult.php?reproductionId=8644>
(four pages).
  Editions: Minard 1945; <http://iohannes.com/vetuslatina> (John canons).
Canon tables cited in Vetus Latina (John) as a patristic witness.
  Further literature: Fischer 1965 [1985:155].

VL 41

Verona, Biblioteca Capitolare, VII
  Lections from Matthew.
  Copied in Verona in the first half of the eighth century. Uncial script.
  24 folios (21½x14½ cm). One column of 19 lines (17½x11½ cm). Parchment; black ink.

The manuscript consists of Matthew 1:18–9:9 divided into lections. The text is mostly Vulgate with some influence from VL 4, which served as a local text in Verona for several centuries.

Images: (CLA IV 482).

Edition: Vogels 1952. Fischer Xu: 79.9 per cent.

Further literature: Fischer 1965 [1985:197], 1972:36 [1986:203]. TM 66589.

VL 42

Cambridge, University Library, Ff. IV.42

The Cambridge Juvencus. Juvencus, *Euangeliorum libri IV* (JUV).

Copied in Wales in the second half of the ninth century. Insular minuscule script.

55 folios (25x18½ cm). One column of 27–33 lines (21x15 cm). Parchment; black ink.

The Latin text of Juvencus was glossed by at least thirteen scribes in Latin, Old Welsh, and Old Irish. Gryson 1999 notes that some of the Latin glosses on the Gospels correspond to non-Vulgate forms paralleled in Gildas.

Images: <http://cudl.lib.cam.ac.uk/view/MS-FF-00004-00042/1>; McKee 2000a.

Edition: McKee 2000b.

Further literature: Haddan & Stubbs 1869:198; Zangemeister 1877:548–550; McKee 2000c.

VL 43[5]

Vienna, Österreichische Nationalbibliothek, lat. 563, foll. 122–77

Fragments from Matthew.

Copied in Italy in the fifth century; palimpsested in the first half of the eighth century in North Italy. Uncial script.

51 folios (20½x15 cm). One column of 10 lines (11½x8–9 cm). Parchment; black ink.

The underwriting contains portions of Matthew 26:56–28:2 (and the Gospels of Thomas and Nicodemus). Burton 1996 suggests that it was part of a Latin–Gothic bilingual.

Images: (CLA X 1485).

Edition: Philippart 1972. Fischer Xp: 72.2 per cent.

Further literature: Despineux 1988; Burton 1996, 2000:25; Falluomini 2015:103–4. TM 67671. <http://data.onb.ac.at/rec/AL00173440>.

VL 44

Cambridge MA, Harvard University, Houghton Library, Ms Typ 620

Rosenthal fragment. A fragment of Luke.

---

[5] In Metzger 1977 and earlier versions of the *Register*, the Book of Dimma (Dublin, Trinity College, MS 59) is given the number VL 43.

Copied in Ireland in the second half of the eighth century. Irish majuscule script with minuscule elements.

One page, missing three margins (23x17 cm). One column of 27 lines (23x16 cm). Parchment; black ink.

Portions of Luke 16:27–17:26 are preserved on this leaf which was used in a binding. There is a chapter number but no evidence of any Eusebian apparatus. The text is similar to VL 28.

Images: <http://nrs.harvard.edu/urn-3:FHCL.HOUGH:3429165>; Bischoff & Brown 1985 (no. 1819; plate IIIb).

Editions: Cited in *Itala* (λ).

Further literature: Burton 2000:25. TM 68689.

VL 45

Munich, Bayerische Staatsbibliothek, Clm 29270/1

A fragment of Matthew.

Copied in the fifth century in Italy; palimpsested in the late eighth century in Salzburg. Uncial script.

One fragment from a bifolium (cut to 10x22 cm) used in a binding, preserving portions of two folios and the central margin. Three columns of probably 17 lines (originally around 13x15½ cm). Parchment; black ink.

Portions of Matthew 9:17–10:10, with an Old Latin text representing an early revision with a high proportion of ancient readings. The fragment formerly had the classmark Clm 29155g.

Images: <http://daten.digitale-sammlungen.de/bsb00001703/image_11>.

Edition: Fischer 1980 [1986:279–81]. Cited in *Itala* from an earlier transcription (μ).

Further literature: Fischer 1980 [1986:275–307]; Bischoff & Brown 1985 (no. 1843); Burton 2000:25. TM 68708.

VL 46

Laon, Bibliothèque municipale, 473 bis

Four Gospels (Matthew–Mark–Luke–John).

Copied in France in the first half of the ninth century.

The text of the Gospels is Vulgate. The initial series of canon tables (foll. 1–19) quote a similar Old Latin text to those in VL 10. The manuscript has been damaged by water.

Edition: <http://iohannes.com/vetuslatina> (John canons). Canon tables cited in Vetus Latina (John) as a patristic witness. The main manuscript is Fischer Pl: 95.9 per cent.

Further literature: Fischer 1965 [1985:155–6].

VL 47

St Gall, Stiftsbibliothek, 60

John.

Copied in Ireland around 800. Irish majuscule and minuscule script.

34 folios, numbered 1–68 (26½x18 cm). One column of 26 lines (21x14–15 cm). Parchment; black ink with yellow and red decoration.

There is no prefatory material. Eusebian apparatus (with parallel passages) and chapter numbers in margins. Parts of John 1–3 are Old Latin (although there are numerous contemporary corrections in John 1); the rest is Vulgate.

Images: <http://www.e-codices.unifr.ch/en/csg/0060/>. (CLA VII 902).

Edition: <http://iohannes.com/vetuslatina>. Cited in Vetus Latina. Fischer Hu: 82.5 per cent (ranging from 68.8 per cent in John[41] to 90.9 per cent in John[42]).

Further literature: Berger 1893:56; McGurk 1961a no. 118; Mizzi 1978. TM 67046.

VL 48
St Gall, Stiftsbibliothek, 51

Four Gospels (Matthew–Mark–Luke–John).

Copied in Ireland at the end of the eighth century. Irish majuscule script.

134 folios, numbered 1–268 (29½x22 cm). One column of 24 or 25 lines (22–25x15½–16½ cm). Parchment; black ink with rubrication; coloured evangelist portraits and full-page illustrations of the crucifixion and last judgement.

There is no prefatory material or Eusebian apparatus. A carpet page precedes the decorated *chi-rho* page. This is one of the most archaic Old Latin texts of the early chapters of Matthew; the other books have an Insular Vulgate text. Luke 22:25–55 is missing.

Images: <http://www.e-codices.unifr.ch/en/csg/0051/>. (CLA VII 901).

Editions: <http://iohannes.com/vetuslatina> (John). Cited in Vetus Latina (John). Fischer Hs: 83.3 per cent (ranging from 69.1 per cent in Matthew[11] to 91.5 per cent in Luke[34]).

Further literature: Berger 1893:56, 416; McGurk 1961a no. 117; McNamara 1990, 2001, 2002. TM 67045.

VL 49
Verona, Biblioteca Capitolare LI (49), fol. 19v

Lection from John.

A marginal annotation written in Verona in the eighth century in cursive minuscule script on folio 19v. The manuscript itself was copied around 500, possibly in Verona, in uncial script, and is also designated as VL 183. It is a collection of Arian homilies.

The lection consists of John 12:12–13 (titled *Lectio de oliua*), with a distinctive early Old Latin text almost identical to VL 2.

Images: (CLA IV 504).

Editions: Gryson 1982; <http://iohannes.com/vetuslatina>. Cited in Vetus Latina as a patristic witness.

Further literature: Capelle 1910; Bischoff & Brown 1985:354; Spagnolo & Marchi 1996. TM 66611.

VL 50

Oxford, Bodleian Library, MS Laud gr. 35

Codex Laudianus, Laudian Acts. Acts of the Apostles.

Copied in Sardinia or Rome in the sixth or seventh century. Uncial script (type b).

227 folios (27x22 cm). This is a Latin–Greek bilingual manuscript. Two columns of 24 to 26 lines (20x16 cm); the Latin is in the left column and the Greek on the right. Parchment; black ink.

Acts 1:1–2 and 26:30–28:25 are missing. The text is written in short sense lines. The Latin was based on a European Old Latin text which has been accommodated to the Greek. There is no marginal material.

Images: <http://viewer.bodleian.ox.ac.uk/icv/page.php?book=ms._laud_gr._35>; see also <http://bodley30.bodley.ox.ac.uk:8180/luna/servlet> (certain pages). (CLA II 251).

Editions: Tischendorf 1870; Belsheim 1893. Cited in Sabatier and Oxford Vulgate.

Further literature: Jülicher 1914; Laistner 1937; Fischer 1972:29 [1986:194]; Walther 1980; Boismard & Lamouille 1984; Petzer 1988; Gibson 1993:22; Petzer 1993a; Parker 2008:289–90; Lai 2011. TM 61729.

VL 51

Stockholm, Kungliga Biblioteket, A. 148

Codex Gigas or *Gigas librorum.* Bible and other texts (New Testament eacrp, including Laodiceans).

Copied in Bohemia (probably Podlažice) between 1204 and 1227. Minuscule script.

309 folios (cut to 89½x49 cm). Two columns of 106 lines. Parchment; black and red ink with coloured decoration.

Only Acts and Revelation are Old Latin, in which this manuscript is the principal witness to the fourth-century Italian text. The other books are Vulgate. Laodiceans is placed after Hebrews.

Images: <http://www.kb.se/codex-gigas/>.

Editions: Belsheim 1879; Vogels 1920. Cited in Vetus Latina and Oxford Vulgate.

Further literature: Ropes 1926; Friedl 1929; Frede 1966:288–90; Fischer 1972:29 [1986:194–5]; Fischer 1975 [1985:417]; Frede 1975:15–16; Gryson 1988:419–20; Fröhlich 1995:19–20; Gryson 2000–3:10.

VL 52

Milan, Biblioteca Ambrosiana, B. 168 sup.

Fragmenta Mediolanensia. Two martyr narratives.

Copied in North Italy in the second half of the eighth century. Uncial and early Caroline minuscule script.

Three folios (26½x18½ cm). One column of 30 lines (20½x14½ cm). Parchment; black ink.

The leaves contain the Martyrdom of St Stephen extracted from Acts (6:8–7:2, 7:51–8:4), preceded by the Martyrdom of St Vincent. The text is an Old Latin form close to VL 51.

Images: (CLA III 310).

Editions: Ceriani 1866:127–8. Cited in Oxford Vulgate (g^2).

Further literature: Fischer 1955 [1986:56], 1965 [1985:193], 1972:29 [1986:195]. TM 66407.

VL 53

Naples, Biblioteca Nazionale, lat. 2

Codex Bobiensis, Codex Vindobonensis. Fragments of Acts and the Catholic Epistles.

Copied in Italy in the sixth century; palimpsested in Bobbio in the eighth century. Half-uncial script.

20 folios (cut to 23x17 cm). One column of 24 to 25 lines (17½x12½ cm). Parchment; black ink.

The text consists of Acts 23:15–23, 24:4–28:31; James 1:1–2:11, 2:16–3:9, 3:13–5:20; 1 Peter 1:1–18, 2:4–10. Acts was described by Jülicher as a recension based on the Vulgate and a Greek text, removing interpolations (see Fischer 1972:30); the two letters have a predominantly Vulgate text with some earlier readings.

Images: White 1897. (CLA III 395).

Editions: White 1897; Bick 1908. Cited in Vetus Latina and Oxford Vulgate.

Further literature: Fischer 1955 [1986:56, 61], 1972:30, 85, 88 [1986:195, 266, 269]. TM 66498.

VL 54

Paris, Bibliothèque nationale de France, latin 321

Codex Perpinianensis. New Testament (eapcr).

Copied in Roussillon in the second half of the twelfth century. Minuscule script.

240 folios (19x13½ cm). Two columns of 30 lines (13x9 cm). Parchment; black ink.

Acts 1:1–13:6 and 28:16–31 are Old Latin; the rest of the manuscript is Vulgate although there are a few earlier readings in Paul.

Images: <http://gallica.bnf.fr/ark:/12148/btv1b8442902q/>.

Editions: Berger 1895; Blass 1896; Buchanan 1911b. Cited in Vetus Latina and Oxford Vulgate.

Further literature: Berger 1893:77–9, 404; Fischer 1955 [1986:56]; Andorf 1964; Frede 1966:264, 288–90; Fischer 1972:30, 67 [1986:195, 242], 1975 [1985:417]; Frede 1975:16–17.

VL 55
Paris, Bibliothèque nationale de France, latin 6400 G, foll. 113–30
   The Fleury Palimpsest. Portions of Acts, Catholic Epistles, and Revelation.
   Copied in the fifth century, probably in Italy. Palimpsested in the seventh or
eighth century in France. Uncial script.
   18 folios (cut to 25x18 cm). One column of 23 lines (19½x17 cm). Parchment;
black ink.
   The original sequence appears to have been Revelation, Acts, Catholic Epistles.
The following portions are extant: Revelation 1:1–2:1, 8:7–9:12, 11:16–12:14,
14:15–16:5; Acts 3:2–4:18, 5:23–7:2, 7:42–8:2, 9:4–24, 14:5–23; 17:34–18:19;
23:8–24; 26:20–27:13; 1 Peter 4:17–5:14; 2 Peter 1:1–2:7; 1 John 1:8–3:20. The
text of Revelation and Acts is an early African form slightly postdating Cyprian;
the Catholic Epistles have a text immediately preceding the Vulgate.
   Images: <http://gallica.bnf.fr/ark:/12148/btv1b90671363>. (CLA V 565).
   Editions: Berger 1889; Buchanan 1907 (corrections in Buchanan 1911a:198);
Vogels 1920:209–12; Ropes 1926. Cited in Sabatier (*Reg. 5367*), Vetus Latina and
Oxford Vulgate.
   Further literature: von Soden 1909; Vogels 1920; Fischer 1955 [1986:56],
1972:27, 29 [1986:192, 194]; Gryson 2000–3:10–11. TM 66695.

VL 56
Paris, Bibliothèque nationale de France, nouv. acq. latin 2171
   Comes Silensis. Lectionary (*Liber comicus*).
   Copied in Silos in the middle of the eleventh century. Visigothic minuscule
script.
   222 folios (36x26½ cm). Two columns of 25 lines (24½x16½ cm). Parch-
ment; black and red ink with other colours in the decoration.
   There are readings from most biblical books: in the New Testament, Acts,
Epistles, and Revelation feature Old Latin readings in an otherwise Vulgate text.
This is the principal representative of the younger tradition of the *Liber comicus*.
   Images: <http://gallica.bnf.fr/ark:/12148/btv1b8457362r>.
   Editions: Morin 1893; Pérez & González 1950. Cited in Vetus Latina
(usually as τ^{56}) and Oxford Vulgate (t). Fischer Ws: 85.5 per cent (ranging
from 73.5 per cent in Matthew[14] to 95 per cent in Matthew[12]).
   Further literature: Férotin 1912:885–8; Thiele 1956:39*–40*; Frede 1975:
86–7, 1006–16; Fröhlich 1995–8:143–5; Gryson 2000–3:48.

VL 57
Sélestat, Bibliothèque Humaniste, 1A
   Lectionary containing readings from the Old Testament and Acts of the
Apostles.
   Copied in the eighth century, probably in North Italy. Uncial script.
   78 folios (18½x12 cm). One column of 17 lines (14½x9 cm). Parchment;
black ink.

Seven lections are included from Acts: 2:1–3:13, 4:31–5:11, 7:2–10, 8:9–9:22, 9:36–42, 12:1–17, 19:4–17. The text is an Old Latin form close to VL 51.

Images: <http://bhnumerique.ville-selestat.fr/bhnum/player/index.html?id=MS01A&v=161&p=1>. (CLA VI 829).

Editions: Morin 1913:440–56.

Further literature: Morin 1908; Fischer 1965 [1985:193], 1972:29 [1986:195]. TM 67609.

VL 58

Orlando (Florida), The Scriptorium, VK 799

Codex Wernigerodensis. New Testament (epacr) including Laodiceans.

Copied in Bohemia (possibly Tepl) in the second half of the fourteenth century. Minuscule script.

251 folios (14x10½ cm). One column of 33 lines (11x7 cm). Paper; black ink with rubrication.

There are a large number of interpolations in Acts which may derive from Old Latin sources; the rest of the manuscript is Vulgate, marked by the incorporation of much additional material, and features numerous Czech glosses. Laodiceans occurs between Colossians and 1 Thessalonians.

Editions: Cited in Oxford Vulgate (Acts only).

Further literature: Berger 1893:80; Blass 1896; Frede 1966:288–90; Fischer 1975 [1985:416–7]; Houghton 2015b.

VL 59

Codex Demidovianus. Bible.

Copied in Burgundy in the second half of the thirteenth century.

272 large format folios (the last 60 of which contained the New Testament). The manuscript has been lost since the late eighteenth century, but readings for the New Testament are reported in Matthaei's edition. The text is Vulgate, but related to the Florus Bible (Paris, Bibliothèque de l'Assemblée nationale, 1) and also Spanish manuscripts.

Editions: Matthaei 1782–8. Cited in Oxford Vulgate (dem); occasionally cited in Vetus Latina with the siglum λ^D.

Further literature: Berger 1893:80; Thiele 1956:14*–15*; Frede 1966:35–40; Frede 1973; Fischer 1972:69 [1986:245], 1975 [1985:419]; Frede 1975:79–81; Fröhlich 1995:124–5; Gryson 2000–3:40.

VL 60

Formerly Sarriá (Barcelona), Colegio Máximo S.J., s. n.

Lectionary with Acts and Epistles.

Copied in Catalonia in the thirteenth century, but destroyed in the Spanish Civil War. The affiliation is Vulgate apart from two pericopes on folios 112–13, which have an Old Latin text of Acts 1:15–26 similar to VL 67.

Edition: Bover 1927.

VL 61
Dublin, Trinity College, MS 52
Liber Ardmachanus; Book of Armagh. New Testament (epcra including Laodiceans) and hagiographical material.

Copied in Ireland, probably Armagh, in 807/8. Irish minuscule script.

217 folios (19½x14½ cm). Two columns of 34–40 lines (14–16x10½–12 cm). The columns are sometimes subdivided further for lists. Parchment; black ink.

The manuscript consists of texts relating to St Patrick (foll. 2–24), some written in Old Irish, the New Testament (foll. 25–190), and Sulpicius Severus' *Vita Martini* (foll. 191–220). Matthew 14:33–21:4 is missing. The affiliation is Vulgate apart from the Pauline Epistles and Old Latin readings in Acts and Revelation. Matthew is preceded by *Nouum opus*, canon tables (no divisions), and *capitula* for all four Gospels (KA I). There is a decorated *chi-rho* monogram. There are prologues and lists of Hebrew names before each Gospel and the Pelagian prologues to the Pauline Epistles, but no marginal numbers or Eusebian apparatus; the Catholic Epistles have chapter numbers; Revelation has a unique numbered summary (KA M); Acts has numerous marginal annotations and glosses. There are also stichometric numbers. Laodiceans appears between Colossians and 1 Timothy.

Images: <http://digitalcollections.tcd.ie/home/#folder_id=26&pidtopage=MS52_01&entry_point=1>,   <http://digitalcollections.tcd.ie/content/26/pdf/26.pdf> (foll. 2–48). (CLA II 270).

Editions: Gwynn 1913. Cited in Vetus Latina (not Gospels) and Oxford Vulgate (D). Fischer Hd: 88.5 per cent.

Further literature: Berger 1893:31–3, 380; Sparks 1954a; Frede 1961:59–86; Fischer 1962 [1985:32, 55]; Thiele 1965:132–6; Frede 1966:277–284; Fischer 1972:38–9, 52–5 [1986: 206–7, 224–5]; McNamara 1987; McNamara 1990: 140–160; Colker 1991:93–97; McGurk 1994b; Fröhlich 1995:21–24. TM 66356.

VL 62
Paris, Bibliothèque nationale de France, latin 6, 1–4
Biblia de Rosas, Bible de Roda. Latin Bible (eacpr including Laodiceans).

Copied in Santa Maria de Ripoll in the middle of the eleventh century. Catalan minuscule script.

566 folios in four volumes (48x33 cm). Three columns of 50–1 lines. Parchment; black ink with rubrication and decoration in blue and yellow.

The fourth volume (113 folios) begins with a list of lections, *Nouum opus*, incomplete canon tables (divisions of 5), *Ammonius quidam*, and *Plures fuisse*. All books are preceded by prologues (sometimes more than one) and *capitula*. In the Passion narratives, the words of Jesus are written in red. The Gospels have full Eusebian apparatus in the margin with parallel passages. The text of Revelation is divided to make space for illustrations on each page. 2 Timothy 4:5–Hebrews 13:25 and Revelation 12:12–16:11 and 22:14–21 are missing. The New Testament is Vulgate, apart from Old Latin readings in Acts (especially

Acts 11–12), including interlinear alternatives. Laodiceans appears between Colossians and 1 Thessalonians.

Images: <http://gallica.bnf.fr/ark:/12148/btv1b90669191>.

Editions: Cited in Vetus Latina (sometimes with the siglum κ^P) and Oxford Vulgate (R: Acts only).

Further literature: Berger 1893:24–6, 400; Fischer 1962 [1985:13, 51], 1963b [1985:86]; Thiele 1965:94–5; Frede 1966:23–4; Fischer 1972:69 [1986:246]; Klein 1972; Delcor 1974; Frede 1975:78–9; Fröhlich 1995:116–22; Gryson 2000–3:39; Contessa 2003, 2008.

VL 63

Ann Arbor MI, University of Michigan, Ms. 146

Acts of the Apostles.

Copied in England in the first half of the twelfth century.

78 folios. Acts is written in a central column, with commentary on either side taken from Bede and Hrabanus Maurus. In the fifteenth century the manuscript was bound with a thirteenth-century manuscript of Revelation and the Catholic Epistles.

The text is Vulgate with Old Latin readings.

Edition: Sanders & Ogden 1937.

Further literature: Petzer 1988.

VL 64

i) Munich, Bayerische Staatsbibliothek, Clm 6436
ii) Munich, Universitätsbibliothek, 4° 928 frg. 1-2 (=Munich, Bayerische Staatsbibliothek, Clm 6436/20)
iii) Munich, Bayerische Staatsbibliothek, Clm 6436 (from Clm 28135)
iv) Göttweig, Stiftsbibliothek, s. n.
v) Göttweig, Stiftsbibliothek, s. n. (a)
vi) Munich, Bayerische Staatsbibliothek, Clm 6436/11
vii) Munich, Bayerische Staatsbibliothek, Clm 6230
viii) Munich, Bayerische Staatsbibliothek, Clm 6436/21 (from Clm 6220 and Clm 6277)
ix) Munich, Bayerische Staatsbibliothek, Clm 6436/16

Fragmenta Frisingensia; Freising Fragments. Fragments of the Pauline and Catholic Epistles.

These fragments have two origins.

i–iv) are 28 folios (26x17½ cm) from a manuscript of the Pauline Epistles copied in the second half of the sixth century, probably in Africa. Uncial script. One column of 32 lines (21x13½ cm). Parchment; black ink.

v–ix) are 5 folios (22½x17½ cm) comprising replacement leaves for Paul and parts of the Catholic Epistles, copied in the first half of the seventh century, probably in Spain. Uncial script. One column of 32 lines (20½x13½ cm). Parchment; black ink.

The contents are as follows: i) Romans 14:10–15:13; 1 Corinthians 1:1–3:5, 6:1–7:12, 7:19–26, 13:13–14:5, 14:11–18, 15:14–43, 16:12–24; 2 Corinthians 1:1–2:10, 3:17–5:1, 7:10–8:12, 9:10–11:21, 12:14–13:10; Galatians 2:5–3:5; Ephesians 1:16–2:3, 2:6–3:16, 6:24; Philippians 1:1–20; 1 Timothy 1:12–2:15, 5:18–6:13; Hebrews 6:6–7:5, 7:8–18, 7:20–8:1, 9:27–10:9, 10:11–11:7; ii) Galatians 3:5–4:3, 6:5–18; Ephesians 1:1–1:13; iii) 2 Corinthians 5:2–12, 5:14–6:3; iv) Galatians 4:6–5:2; v) Romans 5:16–6:19; vi) Philippians 4:11–23; 1 Thessalonians 1:1–10; vii) 1 Peter 1:8–19, 2:20–3:7; viii) 1 Peter 4:10–2 Peter 1:4; ix) 1 John 3:8–2 John tit.

The text is an Old Latin form almost identical to that used by Augustine. There is no marginal material. The first page of 1 Thessalonians is divided into paragraphs of 5–6 lines. There is a stichometric indication at the end of 1 John.

Images: (CLA IX 1286a, IX 1286b, X p. 2, XI p. ix, Supp. p. ix).

Editions: De Bruyne 1921. Cited in Vetus Latina and Oxford Vulgate (r).

Further literature: Souter 1927:149–54; Schäfer 1929:69–97; De Bruyne 1931a; Schäfer 1939:11–14; Thiele 1956:43*–4*, 70*–1*; Frede 1964:102–17; Thiele 1965:91–2; Frede 1975:18–21; Fröhlich 1995:24–5. TM 67428.

VL 65
London, British Library, Harley 1772
Codex Harleianus. Pauline Epistles, Catholic Epistles, and Revelation.

Copied in northern France, probably Reims or Cambrai, in the second half of the ninth century. Caroline minuscule script.

146 folios (29x18½ cm). One column of 27–31 lines (apart from two columns on foll. 104–5); written area 22½x13½ cm. Parchment; black and red ink with coloured decorations. There is also a runic dedication written by the scribe Iuseus.

The manuscript is badly damaged; 3 John, Jude, and Revelation 14:17–22:21 are missing. The text is mostly Vulgate, with Old Latin portions at 1 Peter 2:9–4:15, 1 John 1:1–3:15, and Hebrews 10–13; the last of these was missing from the main exemplar, which was also used for Metz 7.

Images: <http://www.bl.uk/catalogues/illuminatedmanuscripts/record.asp? MSID=8617> (nine folios).

Editions: Buchanan 1912 (omitting 1 John 3:16–2 John). Cited in Vetus Latina (sometimes with the siglum Z^H) and Oxford Vulgate (Z).

Further literature: Berger 1893:50–1, 387; Schäfer 1929:102–113, 143–151; Thiele 1956; Frede 1964:142–3; Thiele 1965:92–3; Fischer 1965 [1985:158–9]; Frede 1974:129–148; Fröhlich 1995:79–80; Gryson 2000–3:25. TM 66302.

VL 66
St Petersburg, National Library of Russia, Q.v.I.39
Corbey St James. Epistle of James and other texts.

Copied in Corbie around 830. Caroline minuscule script.

24 folios (23x19 cm). One column of 21 lines (16–18x13½–15 cm). Parchment; black ink.

The manuscript contains Novatian *De cibis iudaicis*, a Latin translation of the *Epistle of Barnabas* and, on foll. 20–4, an Old Latin text of James produced around 400 in Rome.

Editions: Belsheim 1883. Cited in Sabatier, Vetus Latina, and Oxford Vulgate.

Further literature: Wordsworth 1885; Sanday 1885; Jones 1947 (esp. 388); Thiele 1956; Fischer 1965 [1985:155]; Frede 1974:255–6; Kraft 1977.

VL 67

León, Archivo Catedralicio, 15

Palimpsestus Legionensis. Remains of a Latin Bible (epcar).

Copied in the seventh century, possibly in Toledo. Palimpsested in the tenth century with Rufinus' translation of Eusebius' *Historia ecclesiastica* in Visigothic minuscule. Spanish half-uncial script.

The original manuscript consisted of around 322 folios, of which 48 remain (original size at least 48x35 cm). Two columns of 71–6 lines (36½x28½ cm). Parchment; black ink.

The New Testament portions remaining are Romans 11:2–16:6; 2 Corinthians 1:1–7:4; 12:18–end; Galatians 1:1–3:29; 1 Thessalonians 2:16–2 Thessalonians 3:2; James 4:4–1 Peter 3:14; 1 John 1:5–3 John 10; Acts 8:27–11:13, 14:21–17:25. The Catholic Epistles and parts of Acts are Old Latin, with different text-types in different portions (Acts 15:6–12 and 26–38 are very early, with similarities to Cyprian); Paul is a good Vulgate text.

Images: (CLA XI 1636 and 1637).

Editions: Fischer 1963a (Acts), Berger 1893:9–10 (1 John). Cited in Vetus Latina, and Stuttgart Vulgate (l; Acts and Paul).

Further literature: Berger 1893:8–10, 384; Thiele 1956:16*–17*, 84*ff.; Fischer 1963a [1986:74–105], 1963b [1985:73–8]; Bogaert 2012:74–5. TM 67802.

VL 68

Toledo, Catedral, Biblioteca del Cabildo, 35–8

Comes Toletanus. Lectionary (*Liber comicus*).

Copied in Toledo in the ninth century or later. Visigothic minuscule script.

112 folios (32½x26½ cm). Two columns of 30–1 lines (26x21 cm). Parchment; black ink.

The beginning and end of the manuscript is missing. This manuscript is a witness to the older *Liber comicus* tradition: there are readings from most biblical books, with occasional Old Latin forms.

Edition: Pérez & González 1950. Cited in Vetus Latina (usually as τ^{68}). Fischer Wt: 89.6 per cent.

Further literature: Férotin 1912; Rivera Recio 1948; Thiele 1956:39*–40*; Mundó 1965.

VL 69

León, Archivo Catedralicio, 2

Comes Legionensis. Lectionary (*Liber comicus*).
Copied between 1065 and 1071, possibly in León. Visigothic minuscule script.
82 of around 300 folios are extant (40x28 cm). Two columns of 26 lines.
Parchment; black ink.
There are readings from most biblical books in the younger *Liber comicus*
tradition, preserving occasional Old Latin forms (cf. VL 56).
Edition: Pérez & González 1950. Cited in Vetus Latina (usually as τ^{69}).
Fischer Wl: 92.9 per cent.
Further literature: Férotin 1912; Gryson 2000–3:49.

VL 70
Madrid, Real Academia de la Historia, Aemil. 22
Comes Aemilianus. Lectionary (*Liber comicus*).
Copied in San Millán de la Cogolla in 1073. Visigothic minuscule script.
195 folios (38½x27 cm). Two columns of 26 lines (28½x19 cm). Parchment;
black and red ink with coloured decorations.
There are readings from most biblical books in the younger *Liber comicus*
tradition, preserving occasional Old Latin forms (cf. VL 56).
Images: <http://bibliotecadigital.rah.es/dgbrah/i18n/consulta/registro.cmd?
id=67>.
Edition: Pérez & González 1950. Cited in Vetus Latina (usually as τ^{70}).
Fischer We: 86.3 per cent (ranging from 73.8 per cent in Matthew[14] to 93.7 per
cent in Matthew[12]).
Further literature: Férotin 1912; Frede 1975:86–7; Fröhlich 1995:146–7;
Gryson 2000–3:49.

VL 71
Paris, Bibliothèque nationale de France, latin 2269, foll. 17–48
Comes Carcassonensis. Lectionary (*Liber comicus*).
Copied in Septimania around 800. Palimpsested in Carcassonne in the
twelfth century. Visigothic minuscule script.
16 folios are extant (originally 38x32 cm). Two columns of 30–1 lines
(28½x21½ cm). Parchment; black ink.
This is a witness to the younger *Liber comicus* tradition. In the New
Testament, readings are extant from Matthew, Luke, John, 2 Corinthians,
Galatians, Philippians, Hebrews, James, 1 and 2 Peter.
Edition: Mundó 1956:243–74. Cited in Vetus Latina (usually as τ^{71}).
Further literature: Mundó 1954; Thiele 1956:39*–41*. TM 68773.

VL 72
Toledo, Catedral, Biblioteca del Cabildo, 35-4
Lectionary (*Liber misticus*).
Copied in Toledo around 1200 (although some sources give a ninth century
date). Visigothic minuscule script.

175+2 folios (34½x28 cm). Two columns of 27 lines (28½x22 cm). Parchment; black ink.

In the main part of the manuscript the New Testament readings are from the Gospels, Acts, Romans, 1 and 2 Corinthians, Galatians, Ephesians, Philippians, 1 Thessalonians, and Revelation. The last two leaves are from a *Liber comicus* copied in the late eleventh century with New Testament readings from Matthew, John, Romans, 1 Corinthians, 1 Thessalonians, and James. All text corresponds to the younger *Liber comicus* tradition.

Edition: Pérez & González 1950 (last two leaves). Cited in Vetus Latina (usually as τ^{72}). Fischer Wc: 90 per cent.

Further literature: Férotin 1912; Mundó 1965; Fröhlich 1995:147–8; Gryson 2000–3:50.

VL 73
London, British Library, MS Add. 30846

Lectionary (*Liber misticus*).

Copied in the tenth or eleventh century, possibly in Silos. Visigothic minuscule script.

175 folios (28½x22 cm). Sometimes one, sometimes two columns of 22–4 lines. Parchment; black, red, and green ink, with additional colours in some decorated capitals.

The New Testament readings are from the Gospels, Acts, 1 and 2 Corinthians, Ephesians, Philippians, Hebrews, and Revelation. The text corresponds to the younger *Liber comicus* tradition.

Edition: Janini 1977 (partial). Cited in Vetus Latina (usually as τ^{73}). Fischer Wo: 76.8 per cent (based on three passages in Luke and John).

Further literature: Férotin 1912; Fröhlich 1995:148–9; Haelewyck 2013:15; Gryson 2000–3:50.

VL 74
Sinai, St. Catherine's Monastery, Arab. 455, foll. 1 and 4

Readings from Acts and Revelation.

Copied in the tenth century, either in the Near East or North Africa.

2 folios (19x13½ cm). One column of 19–20 lines (16x12 cm). Parchment; black ink.

The two leaves were bound into a twelfth-century Arabic homily manuscript. The lections are Acts 10:36–40, 13:14–16, 26–30, and Revelation 20:11–21:7, both corresponding to African Old Latin sources. The text of Revelation is very close to that in Augustine. The *nomina sacra* are similar to those in VL 1. A later hand has added the beginning and end of John 20:19–23 and two short canticles.

Edition: Lowe 1964a [Fischer 1986:111–35]. Cited in Vetus Latina.

Further literature: Fischer 1964 [1986:151–5]; Lowe 1965; Vezin 1993; Gryson 2000–3:11; Gros 2002.

VL 75

  i) Paris, Bibliothèque nationale de France, grec 107
 ii) Paris, Bibliothèque nationale de France, grec 107A
iii) Paris, Bibliothèque nationale de France, grec 107B

Codex Claromontanus. Pauline Epistles.
Copied around the middle of the fifth century, probably in southern Italy.
Uncial (b-d) script.
533 folios (25x19 cm). A Greek–Latin bilingual manuscript, with the Greek
on the *verso* and the Latin on the *recto*. One column of 21 lines (15x14 cm).
Parchment; black and red ink.
    i) contains the majority of the manuscript; ii) consists of 35 leaves stolen in the
sixteenth century and catalogued as a separate manuscript on their return,
covering (in Latin) 1 Corinthians 11:23–12:5, 15:22–30, 15:44–54; 2 Corinthians
4:15–5:4; Colossians 1:16–2:12; Philippians 1:28–2:7; 1 Thessalonians 3:6–13; 2
Timothy 4:17–Titus 3:15; iii) is two replacement leaves written on a palimpsested
text of Euripides in the sixth century containing the Greek text of 1 Corinthians
14:9–17. The Latin of 1 Corinthians 14:9–17 and Hebrews 13:22–25 is missing.
The first three lines of each book are in red, as are indented quotations from the
Old Testament. Between Philemon and Hebrews, the manuscript also contains
the *Catalogus Claromontanus* in a later hand on four leaves which may have been
left blank for the entry of Laodiceans. The text is characteristic of the bilingual
tradition (text-type D), with some influence from the Greek. VL 76 and VL 83
both derive from VL 75.
    Images: <http://gallica.bnf.fr/ark:/12148/btv1b84683111> and <http://gal
lica.bnf.fr/ark:/12148/btv1b10515443k>; also <http://ntvmr.uni-muenster.de/
en_GB/manuscript-workspace/?docID=20006> (GA 06). (CLA V 521).
    Editions: Tischendorf 1852. Cited in Sabatier (*Reg. sen. Clarom.* or just
Reg.), Vetus Latina. and Oxford Vulgate (d).
    Further literature: Corssen 1887–9; Schäfer 1929; Vogels 1933; Schäfer
1935; Zimmermann 1960; Tinnefeld 1963; Frede 1964; Nellessen 1965; Frede
1974; Schlossnikel 1991; Fröhlich 1995:25–7. TM 65887; GA 06.

VL 76
St. Petersburg, National Library of Russia, F.v. XX
    Codex Sangermanensis. Pauline Epistles.
    Copied in the ninth century, possibly in France. Uncial script.
    174 folios (35½x27½ cm). A Greek–Latin bilingual manuscript. Two col-
umns of 31 lines (27½x22½ cm). The Greek is in the left column and the Latin
on the right. Parchment; black ink.
    Fourteen folios are missing, containing the Latin text of Romans 8:21–33
and 11:15–25, and Hebrews 12:8–13:25. 1 Timothy 1:1–6:15 is supplied
from the Vulgate on two replacement leaves from the late twelfth century.

The exemplar for the manuscript was VL 75, which was already missing 1 Corinthians 14:8–18: this was supplied from another Old Latin source. The *Catalogus Claromontanus* was also copied. Various corrections from VL 75 are incorporated (some erroneously), and there are occasional adjustments towards the Vulgate. VL 76 may have been the exemplar for VL 83.

 Images: <http://ntvmr.uni-muenster.de/manuscript-workspace/?docID= 20319> (GA 0319).

 Editions: Belsheim 1885. Cited in Sabatier (*Sangerm.*), Vetus Latina and Oxford Vulgate (e).

 Further literature: Frede 1964:34–49; Fröhlich 1995:28–9. GA 0319.

VL 77
Dresden, Sächsische Landesbibliothek, A. 145b

 Codex Boernerianus. Pauline Epistles (without Hebrews).

 Copied in St Gall in 860/70. Insular minuscule script.

 111 folios (25x19 cm). One column of 20–6 lines (17½x13 cm). A Greek–Latin bilingual manuscript. Parchment; black ink with red and yellow rubrication.

 This is a companion manuscript to VL 27. The Greek text of the Epistles is close to that of VL 75, but the interlinear Latin version reproduces the grammar of the Greek and appears to have been influenced by the Vulgate. Multiple alternative renderings are supplied for certain Greek words, and there are numerous marginal notes relating to biblical parallels, grammatical notes, and theological controversies. The following portions are missing: Romans 1:1–5, 2:16–25, 16:25–27; 1 Corinthians 3:8–16, 6:7–14; Colossians 1:1–8; Philemon 21–25. After a blank space for the conclusion of Philemon, the title for Laodiceans is present in Greek and Latin, but the last eleven pages of the manuscript were later filled with a Latin commentary on Matthew (Otfrid of Weissenburg). The manuscript suffered water damage in 1945.

 Images: <http://digital.slub-dresden.de/id274591448>; also <http://ntvmr. uni-muenster.de/en_GB/manuscript-workspace/?docID=20012> (GA 012). Reichardt 1909 is a monochrome facsimile which predates the water damage.

 Editions: Cited in Vetus Latina and Oxford Vulgate (g).

 Further literature: Rönsch 1882–3; Frede 1964; Frede 1974; Bischoff 1981: 45–47; Duft 1990; Fröhlich 1995:29–31; Radiciotti 1998. GA 012.

VL 78
Cambridge, Trinity College, B.17.1

 Codex Augiensis. Pauline Epistles.

 Copied in Reichenau in the last third of the ninth century. Caroline minuscule script.

 136 folios (23x18½ cm). A Greek–Latin bilingual manuscript. Two columns of 28 lines (18x14 cm). The Greek is in the inner column and the Latin on the outer column of each page. Parchment; black ink with red initials.

The Greek column occupies approximately two-thirds of the width of each page and derives from the same source as VL 77. The Latin corresponds largely to the Vulgate. Romans 1:1–3:19 is missing. There is no Greek text for Hebrews, for which the Latin occupies both columns.

Images: <http://www.stgallplan.org/stgallmss/viewItem.do?ark=p21198-zz 0027scpz>. Also <http://ntvmr.uni-muenster.de/en_GB/manuscript-work-space/?docID=20010> (GA 010).

Editions: Scrivener 1859. Cited in Vetus Latina and Oxford Vulgate (f).

Further literature: Frede 1964; Frede 1974; Fröhlich 1995:31–3; Berschin 2007.

VL 79

Wolfenbüttel, Herzog-August-Bibliothek, Weißenburg 64, foll. 255–6, 277, 280
Codex Carolinus. Portions of Romans.

Copied in North Italy at the beginning of the sixth century; palimpsested in North Italy in the eighth century. Uncial script.

Four pages (2 bifolia; cut to 26½x21½ cm). A Gothic–Latin bilingual manuscript. Two columns of 27 lines (23x18½ cm). The Gothic is in the left column and the Latin in the right. Parchment; black ink.

The extant text is Romans 11:33–12:5, 12:17–13:5, 14:9–20, 15:3–13. It corresponds to an Italian Old Latin type, with some influence from the Gothic. There are Euthalian section numbers in the margin of the Gothic.

Images: <http://diglib.hab.de/edoc/ed000006/>; <http://diglib.hab.de/mss/ 64-weiss/start.htm>. Henning 1913. (CLA IX 1388, cf. 1386).

Editions: Tischendorf 1861:155–8; Dold 1950; <http://diglib.hab.de/edoc/ ed000006/index.php?transcript=palimpsest_Ulfilas_Falluomini> (Falluomini 2007). Cited in Vetus Latina and Oxford Vulgate (gue).

Further literature: Streitberg 1910; van den Hout 1951; Butzmann 1964:204–10; Henss 1973; Dahl 1979; Gryson 1990; Falluomini 1999, 2015:27, 36–8. TM 67527.

VL 80

Heidelberg, Universitätsbibliothek, Heid. HS 1334
A fragment of Romans.

Copied in the seventh century, probably in Italy. Uncial script.

Part of one page (14½x19½ cm; original page size 30x22 cm). Two columns of 25 lines (around 24x17 cm). Parchment; black ink.

The fragment contains Romans 5:14–17, 5:19–20, 6:1–2, with a text similar to that of VL 64. It was re-used in a binding.

Images: (CLA VIII 1223).

Editions: Sillib 1906. Cited in Oxford Vulgate (p).

Further literature: Frede 1964:117–20. TM 67357.

VL 81

Paris, Bibliothèque nationale de France, latin 653, foll. 289v–292v
A fragment of Hebrews in a copy of Pelagius.

Copied around 800, possibly in Monza. Early minuscule script.

4 folios from a total of 292 (27x18 cm). One column of 23 lines (22x13½ cm). Parchment; black ink with one rubricated initial.

The text of Hebrews 1:1–4:3 follows the end of Pelagius' *Commentary on Philemon* at the end of the manuscript. The text is Vulgate with some Old Latin readings.

Images: <http://gallica.bnf.fr/ark:/12148/btv1b8492141f>. (CLA V 527).

Editions: Souter 1924. Cited in Vetus Latina and Oxford Vulgate (v).

Further literature: Schäfer 1929; Frede 1974; Frede 1983–91. TM 66656.

VL 82

Munich, Bayerische Staatsbibliothek, Clm 29270/6 (formerly Clm 29055a)
   A fragment of Hebrews.

Copied at the beginning of the ninth century, probably in Germany. South-east German minuscule script.

2 folios (1 bifolium; originally 23x15 cm). One column of 21 lines (18½x11½ cm). Parchment; black ink with rubrication.

The fragment contains Hebrews 7:8–26 and 10:23–39. The text is an Old Latin form probably of North Italian origin, with some influence from Greek.

Images: <http://daten.digitale-sammlungen.de/~db/bsb00001708/images/>.

Editions: Bischoff 1946:434–6. Cited in Vetus Latina.

Further literature: Fischer 1965 [1985:186]; Frede 1983–91:1037–47.

VL 83

 i) formerly Mengeringhausen (Waldeck), Stiftsarchiv, s.n.
ii) Marburg, Hessisches Staatsarchiv, Best. 147

Codex Waldeccensis. Fragments of the Pauline Epistles.

Copied in the second half of the tenth century possibly in Corvey or Fulda. Minuscule script.

8 folios (37x22 cm). A Greek–Latin bilingual manuscript. One column of 42 lines (27x13½ cm). The Greek is on the *verso* and the Latin on the *recto*. Parchment; black ink.

i) contains Ephesians 1:5–13 and 2:3–11 in Latin and is currently lost; ii) contains 2 Corinthians 11:33–12:14 and Titus 1:1–3:3 in Latin. The manuscript incorporates the corrections of VL 75 and may have been copied directly from this or VL 76.

Images: <http://ntvmr.uni-muenster.de/manuscript-workspace/?docID=20320> (GA 0320); Bredehorn 1999 (for ii).

Edition: Schultze 1904 (for i); Bredehorn 1999 (for i and ii).

Further literature: Frede 1964:47–8; Frede 1974:76–7; Frede 1986. GA 0320.

VL 84

Vatican City, Biblioteca Apostolica Vaticana, Regin. lat. 9, foll. 2–3

A list of lections quoting Pauline verses.

Copied in North Italy around 750. Uncial script.

2 folios (28x22 cm). Two columns of 30 lines (24½x18 cm). Parchment; black and red ink.

This list stands at the front of a Vulgate manuscript of the Pauline Epistles, giving the opening words of readings for particular feasts. The text quoted is Vulgate, but with occasional Italian Old Latin readings. The sequence of readings may be related to Codex Fuldensis (Vg F).

Images: (CLA I 100).

Editions: Dold 1944. Cited in Vetus Latina. The text of the Epistles is given under the siglum R in the Stuttgart and Oxford Vulgates; see Vg^{Sp} R below.

Further literature: Fischer 1963b [1985:63–4]; Fröhlich 1995:33–4. TM 66195.

VL 85

Florence, Biblioteca Medicea Laurenziana, P.S.I. 13.1306

A fragment of Ephesians.

Copied in the fourth or fifth century, probably in Egypt. Rustic capital script.

One strip (3x13 cm). A Greek–Latin bilingual, with Greek on the *verso* and Latin on the *recto*. Only four lines are extant on each side. The page has been reconstructed by Dahl as one column of 19–24 lines (*c.* 16x13 cm). Parchment; black ink.

The Latin text is Ephesians 6:5–6.

Images: <http://www.psi-online.it/documents/psi;13;1306>; Mercati 1953a (CLA S 1694).

Editions: Mercati 1953a; Dahl 1979. Cited in Vetus Latina.

Further literature: Mercati 1953a; Dahl 1979. TM 61867; GA 0230.

VL 86

Monza, Biblioteca Capitolare, i-2/9

Fragments of the Pauline Epistles.

Copied in North Italy (Monza or around Milan) in the middle of the ninth century. Italian minuscule script.

55 folios (26x19 cm). One column of 26 lines (21½x15½ cm). Parchment; black ink.

This damaged manuscript is the remains of the second volume of a two-volume Bible. The extant leaves contain portions of Tobit, Esther and Judith, and the Pauline Epistles: Romans 1:1–10:2, 10:6, 12:13–16, 13:8–10, 14:8–10, 14:23 (followed by 16:24–25), 15:11–16:24; 1 Corinthians 1:1–5; Ephesians 4:1–2; Timothy 4:1. The list before Romans indicates that the manuscript originally contained 3 Corinthians. The text is an Old Latin form similar to that used by Ambrose. The *capitula* are KA S.

Editions: Frede 1964:181–286. Cited in Vetus Latina.

Further literature: Berger 1893:139–40, 395; Frede 1976a; Fischer 1965 [1985:195]; Fröhlich 1995:34–5.

VL 87

Sélestat, Bibliothèque Humaniste, 1B

Fragments from a Pauline lectionary.

Copied in the second half of the eighth century, probably in Italy. Late uncial script.

8 folios (18½x12 cm). One column of 24 lines (15x9–10 cm). Parchment; black and red ink.

The following passages are preserved: Romans 11:30–36, 12:1–16; 1 Corinthians 10:17–31; 2 Corinthians 6:2–10, 6:12–18, 10:7–14; Galatians 3:24–4:7; Ephesians 5:20–33; Philippians 3:17–21, 4:4–9; Colossians 1:23–29; 1 Thessalonians 2:19–3:13; 2 Thessalonians 3:6–8. The text is predominantly Vulgate with a few Old Latin readings. The lectionary was previously bound with VL 57. The manuscript also contains a fragment of a medical text.

Images: <http://bhnumerique.ville-selestat.fr/bhnum/player/index.html?id=MS01B&v=21&p=1>.[6] (CLA VI 831).

Editions: Morin 1908; Morin 1913. Cited in Vetus Latina.

Further literature: Fröhlich 1995:35–6. TM 67611.

VL 88

Basle, Universitätsbibliothek, B.I.6

Part of a Latin Bible with Prophets and New Testament (parc).

Copied in western Germany in the ninth or tenth century. Caroline minuscule.

153 folios (48x34 cm). One column of 38–40 lines (39x25 cm); some replacement leaves have two columns. Parchment; black ink with rubrication.

Paul begins on fol. 1^r, Acts on fol. 37^r, Revelation on fol. 49^r, Catholic Epistles on fol. 54^v. From fol. 60^r (62) onwards are the Major and Minor Prophets. The text throughout is Vulgate apart from folio 21 (2 Corinthians 7:3–10:18) which has an Old Latin affiliation matching VL 64 and Augustine.

Edition: Meyer 1965.

Further literature: Berger 1893:76, 130, 376; Meyer & Burckhardt 1960:10–29; Frede 1964:119–20.

VL 89

Budapest, National Széchényi Library, Cod. Lat. 1

Anonymous commentary on Paul (AN Paul).

Copied in Saint-Amand around 800. Caroline minuscule.

106 folios (32½x17 cm). One column of 29 lines (26x12 cm). Parchment; black and red ink. One multicolour full-page illustration.

The entire text of the Pauline Epistles alternates with paragraphs of commentary. The commentary appears to have been composed in Rome at the end of the fourth century. The biblical text is an Old Latin form similar in most

---

[6] The final six images are not included in the standard navigation, but may be accessed directly by adjusting the 'p=' value in the address.

letters to VL 75 but without the secondary Greek influence of the bilingual tradition. In Hebrews the text is a Roman pre-Vulgate form comparable to VL 109. This manuscript is the principal witness to the *capitula* KA S (from 1 Corinthians to 2 Thessalonians), which are given Greek numerals.

Editions: Frede 1974 (which expands the commentary based on other sources). Cited in Vetus Latina.

Further literature: Lehmann 1939; Frede 1974; De Bruyn 1992; Dunphy 2013; Dunphy 2014; MacLachlan 2014; Dunphy 2015. TM 68774.

VL 90

This siglum has not been assigned.

VL 91, VL 133

León, Biblioteca de la Real Colegiata de San Isidoro, 2

Codex Gothicus Legionensis or *Codex Biblicus Legionensis.* Bible with Old and New Testament (epcar, including Laodiceans). The number VL 91 refers to the marginal glosses, while VL 133 is assigned to the Old Latin forms of certain Old Testament books.

Copied by the priest Sancho in 960, probably in León or Valeránica. Visigothic minuscule script.

517 folios (47x34½ cm). Two columns of 51 lines (33x26 cm). Parchment; black and red ink with multicolour illustrations.

This is the earliest surviving representative of the Spanish edition of the Bible with marginal glosses giving alternative readings in the Old Testament and Catholic Epistles. The text of all books is Vulgate, broken up by numerous images. Outside the Gospels, the New Testament text is unusually pure for a Spanish pandect, and may have links with southern Gaul. The Priscillian apparatus is found for the Pauline Epistles. VL 92 is a copy and VL 93 a collation of this manuscript.

Images: González 1997 (facsimile); <http://arachne.uni-koeln.de/item/buch/764> (selection with 160 images).

Edition: Vetus Latina (sometimes with the siglum Λ^L) and Stuttgart Vulgate (Λ; not Gospels). Fischer Sl: 96.2 per cent.

Further literature: Berger 1893:18–19, 384–5; Fischer 1961; Fischer 1963b [1985:72, 75]; Ayuso Marazuela 1960–1, 1965; González 1999 (=Dodd 1999); Gryson 2000–3:28; Schenker 2013.

VL 92

León, Biblioteca de la Real Colegiata de San Isidoro, 1.3

Three-volume Bible with Old and New Testament (epcar).

Copied in León in 1162. Visigothic minuscule script.

The volumes are of differing sizes: the New Testament is in the third volume (242 folios, 51½x35 cm). Two columns of 40–41 lines. Parchment.

This is a copy of VL 91 with some corrections towards the Vulgate.

Further literature: Berger 1893:21, 385; Fischer 1963b [1985:73]; Schenker 2013.

VL 93

Vatican City, Biblioteca Apostolica Vaticana, Vat. lat. 4859

Collation of some Old Testament books in a printed Vulgate of 1522.

A collation of certain books and marginal glosses in VL 91 made by Bishop Francisco Trujillo in preparation for the Sixtine Vulgate. It appears not to contain any New Testament material and is not cited in the Vetus Latina edition.

VL 94

El Escorial, Biblioteca de San Lorenzo, 54.V.35

Collation of biblical glosses in a printed Vulgate of 1478.

This collation appears to have been made in 1561 from two manuscripts now lost: an eighth-century Gospel book from Oviedo Cathedral and the tenth-century Valvanera Bible. The latter contained a different selection of glosses to VL 91 from the exemplar for this type of Bible. In the New Testament, glosses are found in the margins of 1 and 2 Peter, 1 John and Jude.

Edition: Vetus Latina (Catholic Epistles). Fischer allocated it the siglum Se but did not collate it.

Further literature: Fischer 1963b [1985:73]; Schenker 2013.

VL 95

Madrid, Real Academia de la Historia, 2–3

Two volume Bible, with the Old and New Testaments (eapcr).

Copied in San Millán de la Cogolla in the twelfth century. Gothic book script.

362 and 351 folios (49x35 cm). Two columns of 40 lines. Parchment; black ink with blue and red initials.

A Spanish Bible with marginal glosses: in the New Testament (Cod. 3), these are found in 1 and 2 Peter, 1 and 3 John, and Jude. They may derive from the lost Valvanera Bible rather than the VL 91 strand. Revelation is preceded by *capitula* (KA A).

Images: <http://bibliotecadigital.rah.es/dgbrah/es/catalogo_imagenes/grupo. cmd?path=1000088>.

Edition: Cited in Vetus Latina (sometimes with the siglum Λ^H). Fischer Sh: 94.6 per cent.

Further literature: Fischer 1963b [1985:73]; Gryson 2000–3:28; Schenker 2013.

VL 96

Calahorra, Archivo Catedralicio, 2

Part of a two-volume Bible.

Copied in Calahorra in 1183. 173 folios (55x37 cm). Two columns of 50 lines.

This is a copy of a manuscript similar to VL 95, preserving some of the marginal glosses. Only the first volume, containing part of the Old Testament, is preserved.

VL 109

Madrid, Biblioteca de la Universidad Complutense, 31

Codex Complutensis primus, First Bible of Alcala. Old and New Testaments, including Laodiceans (epcar).

Copied in Spain in 927. Visigothic script.

339 folios (49½x36 cm). Three columns of 64–7 lines. Parchment; black and red ink. The canon tables have zoomorphic arches and coloured decoration.

This manuscript was partially destroyed in the Spanish Civil War, but is completely preserved in a set of photographs made in 1914. Its sources go back at least to the seventh century. Parts of the Old Testament are Old Latin. In the New Testament the overall affiliation is Vulgate but there are also Old Latin elements: traces of an Italian mixed text are found in the Pauline Epistles (the text of Hebrews has similarities with VL 89) and there are alternative readings in the margins of the Catholic Epistles with Old Latin forms. There are prefaces and *capitula* for the Gospels (KA B) and, preceding Romans, for the fourteen Pauline Epistles. Revelation has a unique series of *capitula* (KA Compl). The New Testament starts on fol. 276^r with *Nouum opus, Plures fuisse,* and canon tables (no divisions). Laodiceans appears after Hebrews.

Images: <http://alfama.sim.ucm.es/dioscorides/consulta_libro.asp?ref= B20833532> (current state of manuscript). Image 11 in the present volume.

Editions: Fischer Sx: 89 per cent. Often cited in Vetus Latina as X.

Further literature: Berger 1893:22–3, 392; Revilla Rico 1917; Miquélez & Martínez 1935; Fischer 1963b [1985:72, 77].

VL 135

Milan, Biblioteca Ambrosiana, E. 26 inf.

The Bobbio Bible. Part of a two-volume Bible including the Pauline Epistles.

Copied in North Italy in the second quarter of the ninth century. Caroline minuscule script.

307 folios (44½x30 cm). Two columns of 42–4 lines (36½x25 cm). Parchment.

The biblical books are ordered according to the Roman Liturgy; Tobit, the beginning of Esther, and 2 Maccabees are Old Latin, as are the last two chapters of Romans. There are Old Latin readings throughout the Epistles, with similarities to VL 61 and 86. The original manuscript breaks off at Hebrews 8:11; there are supplementary leaves with six New Testament lections from the ninth or tenth century.

Editions: Cited occasionally in Vetus Latina as Γ^B.

Further literature: Berger 1893:138–9, 394; Fischer 1963b [1985:53–4]; Frede 1964:144–9; Fischer 1965 [1985:196–7]; Fröhlich 1995:71–2; Eymann 1996:36–7.

VL 189

See C in the Stuttgart Vulgate.

VL 251

Paris, Bibliothèque nationale de France, latin 9427

Lectionarium Luxoviense. Gallican Lectionary.

Copied in Luxeuil around 700. Luxeuil minuscule script.

246 folios (29x18 cm). One column of 22 lines (21½x12½ cm). Parchment; black and red ink. There are occasional coloured and zoomorphic initials.

There are 56 Old Testament readings and 131 New Testament readings. The text of all is Vulgate; three of the Easter Vigil canticles are Old Latin.

Images: <http://gallica.bnf.fr/ark:/12148/btv1b84516388>. (CLA V 579).

Editions: Salmon 1944. Cited in the Stuttgart Vulgate only in the Catholic Epistles (L). Also cited in Sabatier (*Luxoviense*). Fischer Gl: 87.8 per cent (ranging from 78 per cent in Matthew[14] to 90.6 per cent in Luke[34]).

Further literature: Salmon 1941; Salmon 1944, 1953; Thiele 1965:140–2; Fröhlich 1995:37–9; Gryson 2000–3:12–14; Tewes 2011:158–68. TM 66710. CLLA 255.

VL 259

London, British Library, MS Add. 30844

Missale Silense. Lectionary (*Liber Misticus*).

Copied in northern Spain (Silos?) in the eleventh century. Visigothic minuscule script.

172 folios (40x32 cm). Two columns of 22–4 lines. Parchment; black, red, and blue ink. Numerous colourful decorated initials.

In addition, folios 173–7 are from a tenth-century *Liber canticorum*, with two columns of 27 lines, containing canticles from Isaiah and Luke.

The text of the missal is Vulgate with variants typical of the Mozarabic lectionary.

Images: <http://arachne.uni-koeln.de/item/buch/971> (29 images).

Editions: Janini 1976; Fischer Wm: 88.3 per cent.

Further literature: Férotin 1912; Gryson 2000–3:14; CLLA 305.

VL 262

Toledo, Catedral, Biblioteca del Cabildo, 35-5

Liber misticus. Lectionary.

Copied in Toledo in the thirteenth century. Visigothic minuscule script.

204 folios (30½x25 cm). Two columns of 22–6 lines. Parchment; black ink.

This is a representative of the liturgical tradition found in the Mozarabic Missal. Some pages are missing.

Editions: Janini 1980 (partial); Fischer Wd: 76.9 per cent (ranging from 58.1 per cent in Matthew[14] to 89.7 per cent in John[42]).

Further literature: Férotin 1912; Mundó 1965; Janini et al 1977; Fröhlich 1995:39–41; Gryson 2000–3:14; CLLA 312.

VL 271

Toledo, Catedral, Biblioteca del Cabildo, 35-6

Liber misticus. Lectionary.

Copied in Toledo around 1000. Visigothic minuscule script.

199 folios (31x20 cm). One column of 23 lines (23x13½ cm). Parchment; black and red ink. Coloured initials.

The text is similar to the other Mozarabic lectionaries (VL 56, 69, and 70) but with additional Old Latin readings especially in 1 Peter and Revelation.

Edition: Fischer Wb: 79.6 per cent.

Further literature: Férotin 1912; Millares Carlo 1963; Janini et al. 1977; Fröhlich 1995:41; Gryson 2000–3:14–15; Haelewyck 2013:15; CLLA 313.

VL 330

Vatican, Biblioteca Apostolica Vaticana, Reg. lat. 11

The Queen's Psalter. Double Psalter with Canticles.

Copied in northern France in the second half of the eighth century. Uncial script.

The canticles include Revelation 15:3–4 in an Old Latin form.

Images: <http://digi.vatlib.it/view/MSS_Reg.lat.11>. (CLA I 101).

Edition: Cited in Vetus Latina (Apocalypse).

Further literature: Morin 1909; Gryson 2000–3:15. TM 66196.

VL 411

London, British Library, MS Add. 30851

Liturgical manuscript, including Psalter and Canticles.

Copied in Spain (probably Silos) in the tenth or eleventh century. Visigothic minuscule script.

202 folios (39x30 cm). Two columns of 25 lines (28x8 cm per column). Parchment; black ink with rubrication and coloured initials.

The manuscript consists of a Mozarabic Psalter, Mozarabic Canticles, a Book of Hymns, and an Office with hymns and antiphons. Among the last of these there is a brief lection from 1 Corinthians 16:13–14 and 2 Corinthians 13:11 on fol. 172v also found in VL 414 and 415.

Images: <http://www.bl.uk/manuscripts/Viewer.aspx?ref=add_ms_30851_fs001r>.

Edition: Gilson 1905; see also Fröhlich 1995:42.

Further literature: Porter 1935; Schneider 1938:126–158; Millares Carlo 1963; Díaz y Díaz 1988. CLLA 352.

VL 414

Santiago de Compostela, Biblioteca de la Universidad, 5

Book of Hours of Ferdinand I, including Psalter and Canticles.

Copied in northern Spain in 1055 by the copyist Petrus. Visigothic minuscule script.

226 folios (31x20 cm). One column of 22–3 lines (22x11 cm). Parchment; black ink with much decoration.

The 102 canticles include 24 only found in this manuscript and VL 415; two are from Revelation. The Office features the Corinthian liturgical sentence also in VL 411.

Edition: Cited occasionally in Vetus Latina; see also Fröhlich 1995:42.

Further literature: Férotin 1901; Fröhlich 1995:43–4; Gryson 2000–3:16. CLLA 356.

VL 415

Salamanca, Biblioteca de la Universidad, 2268

Book of Hours, including Canticles.

Copied in northern Spain in 1059 by the copyist Christoforus. Visigothic minuscule script.

187 folios (21½x13 cm). One column of 14–15 lines. Parchment; black ink.

This includes the same collection of Canticles as VL 414 with two additions. The order is slightly different, but the text is almost identical to VL 414. The Corinthian liturgical sentence of VL 411 is also present.

Edition: Cited occasionally in Vetus Latina; see also Fröhlich 1995:42.

Further literature: Férotin 1901; Fröhlich 1995:44; Gryson 2000–3:16. CLLA 358.

Addendum

Graz, Universitätsbibliothek, 1703–53

Fragments of a lectionary with an Old Latin lection in Acts.

Copied in the twelfth century.

Two parts of one folio (originally 35x30 cm, with one column of 34 lines). Parchment; black and red ink.

The lectionary comprises three passages from Acts: the first (4:9–22) is Old Latin, similar to VL 51 and Lucifer of Cagliari; the others (14:8–28 and 15:1–14) are Vulgate but with Old Latin readings.

Images: <http://sosa2.uni-graz.at/sosa/katalog/katalogisate/1703/1703-0053. html>.

Edition: Simonet 2010.

B) MANUSCRIPTS IN THE STUTTGART VULGATE

These are given in the order in which they are listed in the Stuttgart Vulgate, consisting of Roman capital letters (A–Z), Greek capital letters (Λ–Φ^V), and Roman lower case letters (k–s). The siglum in square brackets is explained above in the Preface. All Gospels are in the order Matthew, Mark, Luke, John.

A [Vg A]

Florence, Biblioteca Medicea Laurenziana, Amiatino 1

Codex Amiatinus. Bible containing Old and New Testaments (eapcr).

Copied in Northumbria at the beginning of the eighth century. Uncial script.

1030 folios (50½x34 cm). Two columns of 44–5 lines (36–7½x26 cm). Parchment; black and red ink with coloured illuminations in the prefatory material.

The format may have been modelled on Cassiodorus' *codex grandior*, while the text comes from a variety of sources. The gospels (and their *capitula*, KA C) were copied from a Neapolitan gospel book; the Pauline text is also a good Italian Vulgate. The *capitula* to Acts (KA Act C) and the Catholic Epistles (apart from James and 1 Peter) are otherwise unattested, and the text of these books displays similarities with Spanish and Insular manuscripts respectively.

Images: Ricci 2000 (CD facsimile), *Bibbia Amiatina* 2003 (reduced facsimile). (CLA III 299). Image 9 in the present volume.

Editions: Tischendorf 1850. Also cited in Oxford Vulgate (A) and occasionally in Vetus Latina (A). Fischer Na: 97.3 per cent.

Further literature: Wright 1961; Fischer 1962 [1985:9–34]; Fischer 1963b [1985:67–9]; Bruce Mitford 1969; Fischer 1972:57–60 [1986:230–3]; Alexander 1978; Corsano 1987; Petitmengin 1990a; Meyvaert 1996; Gorman 2003a (useful on earlier studies); Bogaert 2012:75–6; O'Loughlin 2014. TM 66398.

C [Vg C]
Cava de' Tirreni (Salerno), Archivio della Badia MS 1 (14)

Codex Cavensis or *Biblia de Danila*. Bible containing Old and New Testaments (epcar, including Laodiceans).

Copied in Spain in the ninth century by the scribe Danila. Visigothic minuscule script.

303 folios (32x27 cm). Three columns of 54–56 lines (27x21½ cm). Parchment; black and red ink. Decorations in blue, yellow, and green, but no illustrations apart from crosses. Five folios are stained blue or purple, with text in coloured ink and sometimes a cross shape, including Jerome's *Preface to the Gospels*.

The text is typical of the Spanish Vulgate apart from the Old Latin version of Baruch. The manuscript appears to be a copy of a pandect from the beginning of the seventh century: it may be as early as 810 although it is normally dated after 850. There are occasional Old Latin readings throughout the New Testament. For the Pauline Epistles, the manuscript reproduces the edition of Peregrinus. *Capitula*, Eusebian apparatus and other reference systems are all present. Vatican, Vat. lat. 8484 is a copy of this manuscript made for Mai in 1831.

Editions: Also cited in Oxford Vulgate (C) and occasionally in Vetus Latina (C or VL 189). Fischer Sc: 96.4 per cent.

Further literature: Ziegler 1876b; Berger 1893:14–15, 379; Lowe 1937; Ayuso Marazuela 1955–6; Millares Carlo 1963; Fischer 1963b [1985:78–79]; Fröhlich 1995:47–49; Bogaert 2012:81; Cherubini 2012; Perriccioli Saggese 2014.

D [Vg^S D][7]
Dublin, Trinity College, MS 57

Book of Durrow or *Codex Durmachensis*. Four Gospels.

---

[7] Note that VL 61 is given the siglum D in the Stuttgart Vulgate for Laodiceans.

Copied in the second half of the seventh century, probably in Northumbria. Insular minuscule script.

248 folios (24½x14½ cm). One column of 25 lines (21x12 cm), apart from *capitula* in two columns. Parchment; black ink. There are decorated initials, carpet pages and full-page evangelist symbols before each gospel; there is also a single four-symbols page.

The prefatory material consists of *Nouum opus* and canon tables. Each gospel has its own *capitula* (KA I); there are lists of Hebrew names for Matthew and John. The text is a good representative of the Vulgate. The evangelist symbols have the earlier arrangement of a lion for John and an eagle for Mark.

Images: Luce et al. 1960 (facsimile). (CLA II 273).

Collation: Fischer Ed: 93.9 per cent.

Further literature: Nordenfalk 1947; Powell 1956; McGurk 1961a no. 86; Fischer 1972:57 [1986:230]; McGurk 1994b; O'Sullivan 1994; Meehan 1996. TM 66359.

F [Vg F]

Fulda, Hochschul- und Landesbibliothek, Bonifatianus 1

Codex Fuldensis or *Victor Codex*. Harmony of the Gospels followed by the rest of the New Testament, including Laodiceans (epacr).

Copied in Capua in 546. Uncial script.

503 folios (29x14 cm). One column of 35 lines (19x6–7 cm). Parchment; black and red ink.

This is the earliest surviving Latin pandect of the New Testament. The gospel harmony is preceded by canon tables; indications of the source gospel appear in the text and margin. There are also source marks in the epistles. The entire manuscript was corrected by Victor himself in 546–7: in Paul, his corrections have a very similar text to that of Vg^{Sp} R. Later corrections and glosses in Insular uncial and Insular minuscule scripts derive from the period when the manuscript belonged to St Boniface. All books have prologues and *capitula*, although those of Acts are on a separate quire inserted in the scriptorium after the initial completion of the manuscript in April 546. The affiliation of the *capitula* is as follows: KA Act A; AN conc; KA Rm Ant, followed by KA Rm A; KA 1Cor A, etc.; KA Iac A, KA 1Pt A, etc., KA Apc B.

Images: <http://fuldig.hs-fulda.de/viewer/image/PPN325289808/1/>. (CLA VIII 1196). Image 7 in the present volume.

Editions: Ranke 1868 (with *corrigenda*). Also cited in Oxford Vulgate (F) and occasionally in Vetus Latina (F). Fischer Jf: 83.5 per cent (ranging from 52.5 per cent in Mark[24] to 98.6 per cent in John[41]; the harmony poses challenges of classification). A new edition and English translation is being prepared by Nicholas Zola.

Further literature: Chapman 1908: 78–161 (but see Fischer 1972:39 [1986:207]); McGurk 1955; Bolgiani 1962; Fischer 1963b:545–57 [1985:57–66];

Bischoff 1990:93; Petersen 1994; Schmid 2003b, 2005; Scherbenske 2010; Schmid 2012:119–20. TM 67337.

G [Vg G]
See VL 7 above.

I [Vg^S I]
Rome, Biblioteca Vallicelliana B.25^{II}
  Codex Iuvenianus, Codex Vallicellianus. Acts, Catholic Epistles and Revelation.
  Copied in the eighth or ninth century, possibly in Rome, by the subdeacon Juvenianus. Uncial script.
  101 folios (31x23 cm). One column of 30 lines (24x17½ cm). Parchment; black and red ink. Decorated and zoomorphic initials in multiple colours. Three full-page illustrations.
  The overall affiliation is with the Vulgate, but there are a handful of earlier and unusual readings. The biblical text is followed by the first book of Bede's *Commentary on Revelation*. The *capitula* for Acts are KA In, for Revelation KA A.
  Images: (CLA IV 430).
  Editions: Also cited in Oxford Vulgate (I) and occasionally in Vetus Latina (I).
  Further literature: Messerer 1961; Fischer 1965 [1985:200]; Mütherich 1976; Schmid 1992. TM 66536.

K [Vg^S K]
Karlsruhe, Badische Landesbibliothek, Aug. perg. 185
  Pauline and Catholic Epistles.
  Copied in Reichenau in the ninth century.
  88 folios (26½x17 cm). One column of 27 lines. Parchment; black ink.
  The text is a good Italian Vulgate, close to Vg A. There are prologues to each Epistle.
  Images: <http://nbn-resolving.de/urn:nbn:de:bsz:31-45394>, <http://digi tal.blb-karlsruhe.de/blbhs/content/pageview/2290274>
  Editions: Also cited occasionally in Vetus Latina (K).
  Further literature: Frede 1976b.

L [Vg^S L]
See VL 251 above.

M [Vg^S M][8]
Milan, Biblioteca Ambrosiana, C. 39 inf.
  Codex Mediolanensis. Four Gospels.
  Copied in North Italy in the second half of the sixth century. Uncial script.

---

[8] Vg^{Op} M is given the siglum M in the Stuttgart Vulgate for Laodiceans.

281 folios (27x17 cm). One column of 25 lines (18x11 cm). Parchment; black ink with rubrication.

The text is Vulgate. The first quire is missing, including Matthew 1:1–15. Other portions are replacements, including a copy of John 13–18 from the manuscript itself. Greek numerals are used for the Eusebian apparatus, which does not share the erroneous placing of Jerome's archetype.[9] There are liturgical notes in the margin from the seventh century.

Images: (CLA III 313).

Editions: Also cited in Oxford Vulgate (M). Fischer Jm: 96.9 per cent.

Further literature: McGurk 1961a no. 95; Parker 1990. TM 66410.

N [Vg^S N]

i) Autun, Bibliothèque municipale, 21 (foll. 64–136, 138–42, 105b)
ii) Paris, Bibliothèque nationale de France, nouv. acq. latin 1628 (foll. 5–14)

Fragments of the four Gospels.

Copied in Italy in the fifth century. Palimpsested in Lyons in the late eighth century. Uncial script.

83 folios (originally 31x24 cm). Two columns of 22–4 lines (21½x18 cm). Parchment; black and red ink.

One of the oldest Vulgate witnesses, with a mixture of Vulgate and Old Latin readings. *Capitula* are present on folio 10 of the Paris portion.

Images: Maître 2004 (CD-ROM; one image). (CLA VI 722).

Collation: Fischer Jn: 96.2 per cent.

Further literature: McGurk 1961a no. 48; Fischer 1972:57 [1986:230]; Maître 2004:94–7. TM 66890.

P [Vg^S P]

Split, Cathedral Library, s. n.

Codex Spalatensis. Four Gospels.

Copied in Italy or possibly in Salona in the sixth or seventh century. Half-uncial script.

309 folios (23½x17½ cm).[10] Two columns of 21 lines (18x13½ cm). Parchment; black and red ink.

The following portions are missing: Matthew 1:1–14, 4:21–8:3; Mark 15:46–16:20; John 18:12–21:25. Various Greek texts are written in transliteration, including the opening of John (fol. 246). Two exemplars seem to have been used, one for the Synoptics and one for John. *Capitula* are present before Mark and Luke (KA I) and John (KA Ben). There are liturgical notes in the margin.

Images: (CLA XI 1669).

Collation: Fischer Jy: 91.6 per cent.

---

[9] See page 202 above.   [10] McGurk 1961a gives the page size as 32x24 cm.

Further literature: Devich 1893; McGurk 1961a no. 138; Popovic 1989, 1992; McGurk 1994a:6–7. TM 67822.

R (Pauline Epistles) [Vg^{Sp} R]
Vatican City, Biblioteca Apostolica Vaticana, Regin. lat. 9
  Pauline Epistles.
  Copied in Ravenna in the middle of the eighth century. Uncial script.
  113 folios (30½x22 cm). Two columns of 29–32 lines (24½x18 cm). Parchment; black and red ink. Decorated capitals, some foliated, in red, green, and yellow.
  The first two folios are a list of Pauline lections with Old Latin affiliation (VL 84; see above). The text of the Epistles is a good Vulgate, with some earlier readings at the beginning of the collection; there are some doublets. The summaries are rare and do not match the divisions of the text. There are also stichometric numbers.
  Images: (CLA I 100).
  Editions: Also cited in Oxford Vulgate (R) and occasionally in Vetus Latina (R; VL 84).
  Further literature: Berger 1893:85; Wilmart 1937:19–23; Dold 1944; Fischer 1963b [1985:63–4], 1965 [1985:199]. TM 66195.

R (Catholic Epistles) [Vg^{Sc} R]
Verona, Biblioteca Capitolare X (8)
  Catholic Epistles and patristic works.
  Copied in Verona around the end of the seventh century. Uncial and half-uncial script.
  158 folios (19x12 cm). One column of 22–4 lines (15x10 cm). Parchment; black and red ink. Some decorative crosses.
  The patristic writings are by Augustine, Ambrose, and Leo.
  Images: (CLA IV 483).
  Editions: Also cited occasionally in Vetus Latina (R).
  Further literature: Spagnolo & Marchi 1996:58–9. TM 66590.

S (Gospels) [Vg^{Se} S]

  i) St Gall, Stiftsbibliothek, 1395 (pp. 7–327)
  ii) St Gall, Kantonsbibliothek, Vadianische Sammlung Ms. 292a
  iii) St Paul in Kärnten, Stiftsbibliothek St Paul im Lavanttal, 25.4.21a
  iv) Zürich, Staatsarchiv A.G. 19, No. II (foll. 2–5)
  v) Zürich, Zentralbibliothek, C.43
  vi) Zürich, Zentralbibliothek, C.79b (foll. 4–7)
  vii) Zürich, Zentralbibliothek, Z.XIV.5

  Four Gospels (fragmentary).
  Copied in Italy in the first half of the fifth century. Half-uncial script.

110 folios (23x18½ cm). Two columns of 23–5 lines (14½x13 cm). Parchment; black ink.

This is the oldest surviving Vulgate gospel book, which may even have been copied during Jerome's lifetime. It was subsequently dismembered and used for bindings. The Eusebian apparatus is present in the margin; the canon number is in a different colour, but parallel passages are also given. i) has 90 leaves containing portions of Matthew 6:21–John 17:18; ii) consists of seven pages with parts of Mark 1:27–9:7. Marginal comments refer to Latin variants and Greek readings, e.g. i) pp. 95, 136, 168b, and 312. The beginnings of Mark and John indicate that there were no *capitula* or prefaces. A copy of this manuscript, Vg^{Se} s (see below), can be used to supply text now lacking.

Images: i) <http://www.e-codices.unifr.ch/en/csg/1395/7/>; ii) <http://www.e-codices.unifr.ch/en/vad/0292a>; v) <http://www.e-codices.unifr.ch/en/binding/zbz/C0043/bindingF/>. (CLA VII 984; also X 984). Image 6 in the present volume.

Editions: Also cited in Tischendorf (san). Fischer Js: 98.3 per cent.

Further literature: Berger 1893:418; Turner 1931; Lehmann 1933; Dold 1933; Dold 1941; Bischoff 1941, 1946; McGurk 1961a no. 122; Bischoff 1966:101–11; Fischer 1972:57–60 [1986:230–3]; Parkes 1992:15, 161; McGurk 1994a:6. TM 67129.

S (Acts and Revelation) [Vg^{Sar} S]
St Gall, Stiftsbibliothek, 2 (p. 301–568)
Acts, Revelation, and other works.

Copied in St Gall in 760–80 by the scribe Winithar. Alemannic minuscule script.

134 folios, numbered 301–568 (24½x15½ cm). One column of 25–8 lines (21x14 cm). Parchment; black ink with rubrication; some coloured initials in green, yellow, and purple.

This was originally a separate codex in its own right, but is now bound with a copy of Numbers and Deuteronomy. Acts, whose text is close to that of Vg F, begins with *capitula* on p. 301; it is followed by Revelation with a prologue and *capitula* (KA B; p. 431 ff.). Vg^{Sc} S may be a partial copy of Revelation. The non-biblical portion starts with the *Passion of St Clement* on p. 489.

Images: <http://www.e-codices.unifr.ch/en/csg/0002/301>. (CLA VII 894).

Editions: Also cited for Acts in the Oxford Vulgate (S) and in Vetus Latina (Apocalypse: S).

Further literature: Berger 1893:120–1, 413; Fischer 1965 [1985:181]; Gryson 2000–3:21. TM 67038.

S (Paul) [Vg^{Sp} S]
St Gall, Stiftsbibliothek, 70
Pauline Epistles.

Copied in St Gall in 760–80 by the scribe Winithar. Alemannic minuscule script.

128 folios, numbered 1–258 (29x20½ cm). One column of 27 lines (21½x16½ cm). Parchment; black ink with rubrication. Coloured initials with some human and animal decoration.

All epistles are preceded by prologues and *capitula*. Hebrews comes between 2 Thessalonians and 1 Timothy. The text derives from a similar Italian source to Vg F, but was corrected towards the text of Theodulf's edition in the early ninth century. There are stichometric numbers.

Images: <http://www.e-codices.unifr.ch/en/csg/0070/>. (CLA VII 903).

Editions: Also cited occasionally in Vetus Latina (S).

Further literature: Berger 1893:117–20, 417; Fischer 1965 [1985:181–2], 1971 [1985:338]. TM 67047.

S (Catholic Epistles) [Vg^{Sc} S]
St Gall, Stiftsbibliothek, 907

Miscellany including Catholic Epistles and part of Revelation.

Copied in St Gall in 760–80 by the scribe Winithar. Alemannic minuscule script.

158 folios, numbered 1–316 (25x17½ cm). One column of 24 lines (20½x15½ cm). Parchment; black ink with rubrication.

The manuscript begins with an extensive glossary. The Catholic Epistles are found on pp. 237–97; Revelation 1:1–7:2 appears on pp. 303–18, apparently copied from Vg^{Sar} S. There are prefaces and chapter divisions (e.g. S 812 for 1 Peter).

Images: <http://www.e-codices.unifr.ch/en/csg/0907/>. (CLA VII 952).

Editions: Also cited occasionally in Vetus Latina (S in Catholic Epistles, s in Revelation).

Further literature: Berger 1893:121, 418; Fischer 1965 [1985:181–2]; Gryson 2000–3:22. TM 67096.

Z (Gospels) [Vg^S Z]
London, British Library, Harley 1775

Codex Harleianus, Harley Gospels. Four Gospels.

Copied in Italy in the sixth century. Uncial script.

469 folios (18x12 cm). One column of 25 lines (13x7½ cm). Parchment; black and red ink.

The text is arranged in sense lines. The gospels are preceded by *Plures fuisse*, the prologue to Matthew and canon tables (no divisions) in elegant coloured columns. Pages have been left blank between the preface and the beginning of each gospel for *capitula*. Eusebian apparatus is in the margins with parallel passages. The first two lines of the Passion narrative in Matthew are in red. The text is from an Italian edition of the Vulgate Gospels.[11] This is one of the

---

[11] See page 155.

principal witnesses in both the Oxford and the Stuttgart Vulgates: its text is closer to Vg^{Se} S than Vg A. The two correctors date from the sixth and ninth centuries; the latter adds liturgical indications in Tironian notes.

Images: <http://www.bl.uk/manuscripts/Viewer.aspx?ref=harley_ms_1775_f002r>. (CLA II 197).

Editions: Also cited in Oxford Vulgate (Z). Fischer Jz: 96.3 per cent.

Further literature: McGurk 1961a no. 26; Fischer 1963b [1985:54], 1971 [1985:374–7], 1972:57–60 [1986:231–3]; Popovic 1990; McGurk 1993, 1994a:19–20; Jullien 2004. TM 68772.

Λ [Vg Λ]

See VL 91; also cited occasionally in Vetus Latina (Λ^{L}).

Φ [Vg^{S} Φ]

This indicates Alcuin's recension and represents the agreement of the following five manuscripts (Φ^{B}, Φ^{E}, Φ^{G}, Φ^{T}, Φ^{V}).

Φ^{B} [Vg^{S} Φ^{B}]

Bamberg, Staatliche Bibliothek, Msc. Bibl. 1. (formerly A.I.5)

Bible: Old and New Testament (eacp).

Copied in Tours at the beginning of the ninth century. Minuscule script.

423 folios (47x35½ cm). Two columns of 49–52 lines (36½x26½ cm). Parchment; black ink with rubrication. Decorative initials and two full-page illuminations (Genesis fol. 7^{v}; Lamb of God fol. 339^{v}).

The New Testament begins on fol. 334^{v}; Revelation is missing. There are initial canon tables, and prefaces and *capitula* for each book (KA P^{i} for the Gospels, KA A for Acts, Catholic Epistles, and Revelation and a mixture of KA T, B, A, and H in Paul).

Images: <http://bsbsbb.bsb.lrz-muenchen.de/~db/0000/sbb00000032/images/index.html>.

Editions: Cited in the Stuttgart Vulgate for Acts, Pauline Epistles, and Catholic Epistles. Also cited in Oxford Vulgate (B) and occasionally in Vetus Latina (Φ^{B}). Fischer Tb: 95.6 per cent.

Further literature: Berger 1893:206–7 and 376–7 (with bibliography); Rand 1929; Fischer 1957, 1971 [1985:291–312]; Kessler 1977.

Φ^{E} [Vg^{S} Φ^{E}]

Paris, Bibliothèque nationale de France, latin 8847

Part of a pandect, including the whole New Testament (eacpr).

Copied in Tours around 800. Minuscule script.

177 folios (45x34 cm). Two columns of 40 lines (37x25–7 cm). Parchment; black and red ink.

This is one of the oldest surviving pandects from the Tours scriptorium. The New Testament begins on fol. 88^{r}; all books have prefaces, with *capitula* for the latter books (KA A for Acts and Revelation, a mixture of KA A and Tur for the Catholic Epistles, and KA A and B in Paul), but not the Gospels. Fragments of the Old Testament are preserved in other manuscripts.

Images: <http://gallica.bnf.fr/ark:/12148/btv1b8438679t>.

Editions: Collation in Jones 1935:150–66 (but see Fischer 1971 [1985:329]). Cited in Stuttgart Vulgate for Philippians to 2 Timothy. Also cited occasionally in Vetus Latina (Φ^E). Fischer Te: 95.8 per cent.

Further literature: Jones 1935; Fischer 1971 [1985:291–312, 326–30, 336]; Schroeder 1983; Ferrari 1999; Gryson 2000–3:34; Ganz 2012:332–3. TM 67824.

Φ^G [Vg^S Φ^G]

London, British Library, MS Add. 10546

Codex Grandivallensis, Moutier-Grandval Bible, Codex Carolinus (Bible of Charlemagne). Bible: Old and New Testaments (eacpr).

Copied in Tours in the first half of the ninth century. Caroline minuscule script.

449 folios (51x37½ cm). Two columns of 50–1 lines. Parchment; black ink with rubrication. Decorated capitals. Several richly coloured full-page illustrations.

The New Testament begins on fol. 349^r. There are initial canon tables, and prefaces and *capitula* for each book (KA Pi for the Gospels, KA A for Acts, Catholic Epistles, Revelation, and most of Paul, with KA M for Romans and KA H for Hebrews). Twenty-four copyists worked on this volume.

Images: <http://www.bl.uk/manuscripts/FullDisplay.aspx?ref=Add_MS_10546>; Duft et al 1971 (facsimile). Image 10 in the present volume.

Editions: Also cited in Oxford Vulgate (K) and occasionally in Vetus Latina (Φ^G). Fischer Tg: 95.7 per cent.

Further literature: Berger 1893:209–12, 389; Duft et al 1971; Fischer 1971 [1985:291–312]; Bruckner 1972; Kessler 1977; Ganz 1994; Gryson 2000–3:34; Ganz 2012:332–3.

Φ^T [Vg^S Φ^T]

St Gall, Stiftsbibliothek, 75

Bible: Old and New Testament (eacrp).

Copied in Tours around 800. Minuscule script.

836 pages (54x39½ cm). Two columns of 50–5 lines (38–9½x27 cm). Parchment; black ink with rubrication.

This is the oldest complete pandect from Tours. The New Testament begins on p. 689. There are initial canon tables and prefaces: the latter books have *capitula* (KA A for Acts and Revelation, a mixture of KA A and Tur for the Catholic Epistles, and KA A and B in Paul), but there are none before the Gospels. It was in St Gall by 883.

Images: <http://www.e-codices.unifr.ch/en/csg/0075/>. (CLA VII 904).

Editions: Also cited occasionally in Vetus Latina (Φ^T). Fischer Tt: 94.3 per cent.

Further literature: Berger 1893:127–9; Fischer 1965 [1985:126], 1971 [1985:291–312]; Fröhlich 1995:109–10; Gryson 2000–3:35; Ganz 2012:331–3. TM 67048.

Φ^V [Vg^S Φ^V]

Rome, Biblioteca Vallicelliana, B.6

Codex Vallicellianus. Bible: Old and New Testaments (eapcr).

Copied in the region of Reims around 850. Minuscule script.

346 folios (35x30½ cm). Three columns of around 54 lines. Parchment; black ink with rubrication.

There are initial canon tables, and prefaces and *capitula* for each book (KA C for the Gospels, KA Tur for Acts, Catholic Epistles, and Revelation and probably a mixture of KA M, A, and B for Paul). The text of the gospels is similar to Vg^O MT, with a number of Insular features.

Editions: Also cited in Oxford Vulgate (V) and occasionally in Vetus Latina (Φ^V). Fischer Cv: 95.9 per cent.

Further literature: Berger 1893:197–203, 413; Fischer 1963b [1985:40], 1971 [1985:291–312]; Gryson 2000–3:35; Lobrichon 2004.

k (Pauline Epistles) [Vg^{Sp} k]

Fragments of a Bible, including Pauline Epistles

  i) Orléans, Bibliothèque municipale, 19 (16), foll. 26–30
 ii) Paris, Bibliothèque nationale de France, latin 2389, foll. 41^r–8^v
iii) Orléans, Bibliothèque municipale, 19 (16), foll. 31–2

These fragments derive from two manuscripts: i+ii and iii. Copied in Italy in the second half of the sixth century. Uncial script.

i+ii consist of 13 folios (24x15 cm). One column of 25 lines (20x11 cm). Parchment; black and red ink.

  i) contains 1 Thessalonians 1:1–2:14, 4:6–5:1; 1 Corinthians 9:13–23, 10:29–11:12; preceded by some Old Testament fragments.
 ii) contains Philippians 4:6–23; Colossians 1:1–4:7 as part of a composite codex. The two epistles are separated by hederae and the titles and preface to Colossians are written in half-uncial script.
iii) consists of 1 bifolium (31½x24 cm). Two columns of 33 lines (25x20½ cm) written in sense lines. Parchment; black and red ink. The biblical coverage is Ephesians 6:6–24 and Philippians 1:1–27. The chapter divisions are similar to VL 84.

Both manuscripts originally came from Fleury.

Images: ii) <http://gallica.bnf.fr/ark:/12148/btv1b84323098>. (CLA VI 800, 801).

Editions: Also cited occasionally in Vetus Latina (J).

Further literature: Berger 1893:85, 397; Fischer 1972:68 [1986:244]. TM 66973, 66974.

k (James) [Vg^{Sc} k]

Karlsruhe, Bayerische Landesbibliothek, Fragm. Aug. 15

Fragment of James.

Copied in the first half of the seventh century, possibly in Italy. Uncial script.

2 folios; most of one bifolium (26x18½ cm). Two columns of 31 lines. Parchment; black ink.

The fragment contains James 2:6–4:4 with a Vulgate text.

Images: <http://digital.blb-karlsruhe.de/id/21575>. (CLA VIII 1114).

Edition: Holder 1914 <http://www.manuscripta-mediaevalia.de/hs/katalogseiten/HSK0721_c367_jpg.htm>.

Further literature: Fischer 1965 [1985:179]. TM 67254.

l [Vg^S l]

See VL 67 above.

r [Vg^S r]

Ravenna, Archivio arcivescovile, s. n.

Fragments from a New Testament (Acts, 1 John, and Revelation).

Copied in Ravenna in the second half of the sixth century. Uncial script.

6 folios (31x22½ cm). Two columns of 29 lines (24x20 cm). Parchment; black and red ink.

The contents are Acts 16:11–25, 17:32–18:17, 19:6–10, 19:18–22, 21:11–26; 1 John 3:17–4:11; Revelation 6:2–15.

Images: (CLA IV 411).

Editions: Also cited occasionally in Vetus Latina (J).

Further literature: TM 66516.

s (Gospels) [Vg^Se s]

Fulda, Hochschul- und Landesbibliothek, Aa 11

Second volume of a two-volume Bible, containing the New Testament (eacrp).

Copied in Reichenau in the first half of the ninth century. Caroline minuscule script.

302 folios (43x30 cm). Two columns of 36–43 lines (35½x22 cm). Parchment; black ink with rubrication.

The New Testament begins on fol. 201. The gospels are a copy of Vg^Se S, and are used in the Stuttgart Vulgate to supply text now lacking in that witness. There are some readings from Peregrinus' edition in the Pauline Epistles. Most books have prologues and *capitula* (KA B in Revelation).

Editions: Cited occasionally in Vetus Latina (σ^R). Fischer Jr: 97.2 per cent.

Images: <http://nbn-resolving.de/urn:nbn:de:hebis:66:fuldig-2418167>.

Further literature: Frede 1964:56ff.; Fischer 1965 [1985:179], 1971 [1985:291–302], 1972:57–8 [1986:231–2]; Gryson 2000–3:46–7.

s (Paul) [Vg^Sp s]

St Gall, Stiftsbibliothek, 908

Fragments of the Pauline Epistles.

Copied in northern Italy in the first half of the sixth century. Uncial script. Palimpsested twice, first around 700 with a Milan liturgy and again around 800 with glossaries in North Italy or Switzerland.

21 pages (originally 25x20 cm). Two columns of 24 lines (17½x16½ cm). Parchment; black ink.

The Pauline passages, with a good Italian Vulgate text, occur between pages 77 and 122 of the manuscript; a list is given on page 76 b–c. The following text is extant: Ephesians 6:20–24; Philippians 1:1–3:1, 3:15–19, 4:2–23; Colossians 1:1–3:10; 1 Thessalonians 4:16–5:18; 1 Timothy 1:9–2:5. There are also prologues to the epistles. The *nomen sacrum* for Christ is written xʀs.

Images: <http://www.e-codices.unifr.ch/en/csg/0908/77>. (CLA VII 957).

Editions: Also cited occasionally in Vetus Latina (I).

Further literature: Fischer 1972:68 [1986:244]. TM 67101.

In addition, there are four manuscripts used for the Epistle to the Laodiceans (given in an Appendix on page 1976 of the Stuttgart Vulgate) which are not otherwise cited in the New Testament:

B [Vg^S B]
Milan, Biblioteca Ambrosiana, E. 53 inf.

Codex Abiascensis, Bible of Biasca. Partial Bible: most of the Old and New Testaments, including Laodiceans and 3 Corinthians.

Copied in Milan in the tenth century. Minuscule script.

328 folios (52x41 cm). Two columns of 49–51 lines. Parchment; black and red ink.

The manuscript is badly damaged, with the top half of each page often lacunose. Arranged according to the Roman Lectionary, the manuscript never contained the Psalter or the Gospels. All books have *capitula* and prefaces, apart from Acts which starts at 1:21 on fol. 97^r; it is followed by the Catholic Epistles (108^r–113^v) and the Apocalypse (113^v–18^v). The Pauline Epistles are found on foll. 298–328, with much prefatory material; the apocryphal letter of the Corinthians and Paul's response (3 Corinthians) appears at the end of the corpus after Hebrews.

Images: <http://dai.ambrosiana.eu/nav?f1stId=&resId=&s2ndId=E+53+inf. &agency=MI0133&agencyType=2> (subscription required).

Editions: Cited occasionally in Vetus Latina (Γ^A).

Further literature: Berger 1893:143, 394; Fischer 1965 [1985:194].

D
See VL 61 above.

M [Vg^{Op} M]
See M (Pauline Epistles) in the Oxford Vulgate below.

Q [Vg^S Q]
Milan, Biblioteca Ambrosiana, B. 48 sup.

Pauline and Catholic Epistles, including Laodiceans.

Copied in Italy in the ninth century. 140 folios (20x14 cm). One column of 26 lines. Parchment; black and red ink.

The manuscript may be connected with the Irish teacher Dungal. Its text shows influence from Alcuin Bibles. The text is preceded by the prefaces of Pelagius and Isidore, the verses of Damasus, and the Priscillian Canons.

Editions: Cited occasionally in Vetus Latina (Γ^C).

Images: <http://dai.ambrosiana.eu/nav?f1stId=&resId=&s2ndId=B+48+sup.&agency=MI0133&agencyType=2> (subscription required).

Further literature: Fischer 1971 [1985:402].

C) MANUSCRIPTS IN THE OXFORD VULGATE

Cross-references are given to manuscripts already described for the Stuttgart Vulgate. Witnesses are listed in the following order of siglum: Roman capital letters (including double letters for BF, EP, and MT), Greek capital letters, and additional witnesses with lower-case letters. All Gospels follow the Vulgate sequence. For a full table of correspondences, see Appendix 1.

A [Vg A]

See A in the Stuttgart Vulgate.

B (Gospels) [Vg^{Oe} B]

 i) Paris, Bibliothèque nationale de France, latin 281
ii) Paris, Bibliothèque nationale de France, latin 298

Codex Bigotianus, Codex Fiscannensis. Four Gospels.

Copied in southern England in the last quarter of the eighth century. Uncial script, with prefatory material in rustic capitals.

216 and 49 folios (35x27 cm). One column of 21 lines (27x22 cm). Parchment; black and red ink. Large coloured initials with zoomorphic figures.

i) consists of 216 folios, containing the Synoptic Gospels; ii) consists of 49 folios, containing John. The text is written in sense lines. After *Nouum opus* and *Plures fuisse* the canon tables and certain other pages have been removed. There are prefaces and *capitula* (KA B).

Images: i) <http://gallica.bnf.fr/ark:/12148/btv1b8492142v>; ii) <http://gallica.bnf.fr/ark:/12148/btv1b9065974x>. (CLA V 526).

Collation: Fischer Eb: 95.7 per cent.

Further literature: Berger 1893:50, 403; McGurk 1961a no. 58. TM 66655.

B (Acts, Pauline Epistles, Catholic Epistles)

See Φ^B in the Stuttgart Vulgate.

ᚠ [Vg^O BF]

London, British Library, MS Add. 5463

Codex Beneventanus. Four Gospels.

Copied in St Vincent on the Volturno in Benevento by the monk Lupus between 736 and 760. Uncial script.

239 folios (35½x27½ cm). Two columns of 23 lines (26½x21½ cm). Parchment; black and red ink. Coloured initials and decorative patterns in the colophons.

The text is written in sense lines. There are illuminated canon tables; one set of arches is blank. These are followed by *Nouum opus* and *Plures fuisse.* Prologues and *capitula* (KA B) are present before each gospel.

Images: (CLA II 162).

Collation: Fischer Jb: 96.2 per cent.

Further literature: Berger 1893:91–2, 389; McGurk 1961a no. 18; Fischer 1965 [1985:201]. TM 66266.

C [Vg C]

See C in the Stuttgart Vulgate.

D

See VL 61 above.

E (Gospels) [Vg^{Oe} E]

London, British Library, MS Egerton 609

Gospels of Marmoutier. Four Gospels.

Copied in western France, probably Brittany, in the second quarter of the ninth century. Caroline minuscule script.

102 folios (31x21 cm). One column of 28–30 lines. Parchment; black ink, with red and yellow highlights. There are evangelist portraits, coloured zoomorphic initials and decorated canon tables.

The manuscript is missing Mark 6:56 to Luke 7:24. The text is part of the Irish-Northumbrian Vulgate group. Each gospel has a preface, but no *capitula.*

Images: <http://www.bl.uk/catalogues/illuminatedmanuscripts/record.asp?MSID=8618> (11 images).

Edition: Cited in Sabatier (*Maj. Mon.*); Bianchini 1749 (Mm; John–Mark); Fischer Be: 86.2 per cent.

Further literature: Berger 1893:47, 388; Chapman 1908; Rand 1929; Morey 1931; Fischer 1972:52–6 [1986:224–8]; Alexander 1978; McGurk 1987:189; Lemoine 2004.

E (Paul) [Vg^{Op} E]

London, British Library, MS Cotton Vitellius C. VIII, foll. 86–90

Portions of some Pauline Epistles.

Copied in Northumbria in the first half of the eighth century. Insular minuscule script.

5 folios (29½x23 cm). One column of 27 lines (25x16½ cm). Parchment; black ink with red and yellow decoration.

This manuscript consists of five folios extracted from Cambridge, Trinity College, B.10.5 (Vg^Op S). It was damaged by fire in 1731.

Images: (CLA II 133).

Further literature: TM 66237.

𝔓 [Vg^O EP]

Paris, Bibliothèque nationale de France, latin 9389

Codex Epternacensis, Echternach Gospels. Four Gospels.

Copied in Northumbria, or possibly Echternach, around 690. Insular minuscule script with some prefatory material in Insular majuscule.

223 folios (33½x26½ cm). Two columns of 24–5 lines (27x21½ cm). Parchment; black ink with rubrication. Full-page pictures with evangelist symbols before each gospel.

Nouum opus is followed by plain canon tables (no divisions). Each gospel is preceded by *capitula* (KA I), a glossary of Hebrew words and a prologue. The text is written in sense-units; Eusebian apparatus with parallel passages is in the margins. Alternative readings are reported in marginal glosses. A colophon (page 74 above) notes that an exemplar was corrected in 558 from a manuscript belonging to Eugippius.

Images: <http://gallica.bnf.fr/ark:/12148/btv1b530193948>. (CLA V 578).

Editions: Fischer Ge: 93.3 per cent.

Further literature: Berger 1893:52–3, 406; McGurk 1961a no. 59; Fischer 1965 [1985:169], 1972:56–7 [1986:229–30]; McNamara 1987; Bruce-Mitford 1989; McGurk 1994b; O'Sullivan 1994; Glaser & Moulin Fankhänel 1999:104–8; Rohr 2000. TM 66709.

F [Vg F]

See F in the Stuttgart Vulgate.

G, g¹

See VL 7.

H [Vg^O H]

London, British Library, MS Add. 24142

Codex Hubertianus. Bible with Old and New Testaments.

Copied in Tours in the ninth or tenth century. Minuscule script.

248 folios (33x24 cm). Three columns of 62 lines (25½x20 cm).

The manuscript breaks off at 1 Peter 4:3.

The text of the first hand has similarities with the Northumbrian Vulgate tradition, but this has been extensively corrected towards the Vulgate recension of Theodulf.

Editions: Cited in the Oxford Vulgate for the Gospels and Pauline Epistles. Also occasionally cited in Vetus Latina (Θ^H). Fischer Oh: 94.9 per cent.

Further literature: Berger 1893:179–81, 390; Fischer 1963b [1985:94–5]; Gibson 1993:32–3.

I (Gospels) [Vg^{Oe} I]
Munich, Universitätsbibliothek, 2° 29
  Codex Ingolstadiensis. Four Gospels.
  Copied in Aachen around 800. Uncial script.
  137 folios (32½x22½ cm). Two columns of 31 lines (25½x16 cm). Parchment; black and red ink, with incipits in gold on a purple background. Decorated initials.
  Matthew and Luke are only partially preserved.
  Images: (CLA IX 1343).
  Collation: Fischer Ai: 97.2 per cent.
  Further literature: Bischoff 2004:299. TM 67485.

I (Acts, Catholic Epistles, Revelation)
  See I in the Stuttgart Vulgate.

J [Vg^O J]

  i) Cividale del Friuli, Museo Archeologico Nazionale, 138
  ii) Venice, Biblioteca Nazionale Marciana, s. n.
  iii) Prague, National Library, Cim. 1

  Codex Forojuliensis, Codex Aquileiensis. Four Gospels.
  Copied in North Italy (Aquileia) in the sixth or seventh century. Uncial script.
  326 folios (30½x26½ cm). Two columns of 19 lines (22½x22 cm). Parchment; black and red ink.

  i) consists of 270 folios with Matthew, Luke, and part of John (John 19:24–40 and 20:19–21 and 25 are missing); ii) consists of 40 folios with Mark 1:1–12:20; iii) is 16 folios covering Mark 12:21–16:20. The manuscript has been badly damaged by damp; iii) is the best-preserved portion. *Nouum opus* is present, but there are no canon tables. The text is written in sense lines. There are two sets of *capitula* for each gospel, the first headed *breues* (KA B) and the second *capitulationes* (KA I^{for}). The latter are unique to this manuscript and preserve some Old Latin readings.
  Images: (CLA III 285; also CLA X 285).
  Editions: Bianchini 1749; Dobrovský 1778; Fischer Jj: 94.3 per cent.
  Further literature: McGurk 1961a, no. 94, 1994a:19; Scalon & Pani 1998; Bartoli Langeli et al. 2001; Houghton 2011; CLLA 246. TM 66394.

K
  See Φ^G in the Stuttgart Vulgate.

L (Gospels) [Vg^{Oe} L]
Lichfield, Cathedral Library, s. n.

Lichfield Gospels, St Chad Gospels, Llandaff Gospels. Three Gospels (Matthew, Mark, Luke).

Copied in the first half of the eighth century, possibly in Wales. Insular majuscule script.

236 pages (31x22½ cm). One column of 20 lines (25x19 cm). Parchment; black ink with rubrication. There are decorated initial pages, evangelist portraits for Mark and Luke and a four symbols page and carpet page before Luke.

The manuscript breaks off at Luke 3:9. There is no prefatory material or Eusebian apparatus. The Lord's Prayer is written at the end of Mark. Some of the additions to the manuscript include very early examples of Welsh as well as a Latin note that the manuscript was purchased in exchange for a horse.

Images: <https://lichfield.as.uky.edu/st-chad-gospels/gallery>. (CLA II 159).

Editions: <http://folio.furman.edu/lichfield/>; Scrivener 1887; Hopkins-James 1934. Fischer Hl: 86.3 per cent.

Further literature: McGurk 1961a no. 16. TM 66263.

L (Paul) [Vg^Op L]
Paris, Bibliothèque nationale de France, latin 335
Codex Langobardus. Pauline Epistles.
Copied in the eighth century. Beneventan minuscule script.
156 folios (24½x16½ cm). One column of 18 lines. Parchment; black ink with rubrication. Decorative initials at the beginning of each epistle.

The conclusion of Titus, along with Philemon and Hebrews, was copied in the tenth century. There is no marginal material, although stichometry is present.

Images: <http://gallica.bnf.fr/ark:/12148/btv1b9072418x>.

Further literature: Fischer 1971 [1985:337].

L (Catholic Epistles) [Vg^Oc L]
Paris, Bibliothèque nationale de France, latin 2328
Codex Lemovicensis. Catholic Epistles.
Copied around 800; provenance Limoges. Minuscule script.
125 folios (29x17½ cm). Two columns of 33–5 lines. Parchment; black ink with rubrication and decorative initials.

After works by Isidore and Alcuin, the Catholic Epistles occur on foll. 97–107 with no prologues or summaries. They are followed by sermons of Augustine and Caesarius of Arles. The text is a fairly pure Vulgate with some Old Latin readings typical of French witnesses, including one at James 2:13 shared with Ruricius of Limoges.

Images: <http://gallica.bnf.fr/ark:/12148/btv1b52503985b>.

Further literature: Berger 1893:405; Fischer 1965 [1985:120].

M (Gospels) [Vg^S M]
See M in the Stuttgart Vulgate.

M (Acts) [Vg^{Oa} M]
Munich, Bayerische Staatsbibliothek, Clm 6230
  Codex Monacensis. Acts of the Apostles, Catholic Epistles, and Revelation.
  Copied in Freising in the tenth century.
  127 folios (24½x18½ cm). One column of 20–2 lines (20x13½ cm). Parchment;
black ink with rubrication.
  VL 64 part vii, with text from 1 Peter, is an offset in the binding of this
manuscript. The final page of Revelation is missing. All books have *capitula*
(KA A in Revelation) and a prologue.
  Editions: Only cited in the Oxford Vulgate for Acts; Cited in Vetus Latina
(Apocalypse: M). De Bruyne 1914:370–96 (siglum F).
  Further literature: Glauche 2000; Gryson 2000–3:19–20.

M (Pauline Epistles) [Vg^{Op} M]
Munich, Bayerische Staatsbibliothek, Clm 6229
  Codex Frisingensis. Pauline Epistles, including Laodiceans.
  Copied in Freising in the second half of the eighth century. Early Caroline
minuscule script.
  135 folios (25½x17½ cm). Two columns of 23–7 lines (20½x13 cm).
Parchment; black ink.
  Laodiceans occurs after Colossians. The manuscript begins with prologues and
a concordance to all the Pauline Epistles. There is a prologue and *capitula* before
each Epistle. The text is initially close to Vg A, but there is an increasing proportion
of earlier readings in later letters. There are lectionary marks in the margins. Parts
of Jerome, *Epistula* 22 are found on the final five folios of the manuscript.
  Images: <http://daten.digitale-sammlungen.de/~db/0004/bsb00047192/im
ages/>. (CLA IX 1251).
  Further literature: Fischer 1965 [1985:187]; Glauche 2000. TM 67392.

M [Vg^{O} MT]
Tours, Bibliothèque municipale, 22
  Codex Martini (Turonensis). Four Gospels.
  Copied in the ninth century, either around the beginning or the second
quarter, possibly in Fleury. Uncial script.
  289 folios (31x23 cm). Two columns of 25 or 26 lines. Parchment; written in
gold ink. Elegant coloured canon tables.
  The text is taken from an early Tours edition of the Gospels. The manu-
script was used by French royalty for taking oaths as canons of St Martin's
Abbey. There is no Eusebian apparatus in the margins.
  Images: <http://bvmm.irht.cnrs.fr/consult/consult.php?reproductionId=
8263>, <http://www.enluminures.culture.fr/documentation/enlumine/fr/BM/
tours_021-01.htm> (canon tables).
  Editions: Cited in Sabatier (*S. Mart. Turon.*); Fischer Ot: 94.7 per cent.
  Further literature: Berger 1893:47–8, 420; Fischer 1965 [1985:147].

N [Vg^O N]

Colmar, Bibliothèque municipale 15 (38), foll. 173–238

Pauline Epistles.

Copied in the ninth century, probably on the European continent. Anglo-Saxon minuscule script.

66 folios (cut to 28½x18 cm). Two columns of 38–40 lines (26½x16 cm). Parchment; black ink. Initials decorated in red and yellow.

The manuscript currently consists of an eighth-century manuscript of the Gospels (foll. 1–172; CLA VI 749) bound with the Pauline Epistles. Hebrews 4:16–end is missing. All epistles begin with *capitula* and a preface, and have a good Vulgate text. The text is written in sense lines. Greek numerals are used for the chapters.

Images: <http://bvmm.irht.cnrs.fr/consult/consult.php?reproductionId=1930>. (CLA VI 750).

Further literature: McGurk 1961a no. 32 (Gospels); Fischer 1965 [1985:169, 178]. TM 66920.

O (Gospels) [Vg^{Oe} O]

Oxford, Bodleian Library, MS Auct. D.2.14 (Bodley 857)

Gospels of St Augustine. Four Gospels.

Copied in the seventh century, perhaps in Rome. Uncial script.

173 folios (25x19½ cm). Two columns of 29 lines (21x16 cm). Parchment; black ink with rubrication.

Matthew 1:1–4:13 is missing. The other gospels have prefaces and *capitula* (KA B). Eusebian apparatus with parallel passages is in the margins. The presentation is similar to Vg^O X. A number of readings are shared with Irish gospel books.

Images: (CLA II 230).

Editions: Fischer Jo: 94.2 per cent.

Further literature: Berger 1893:35–6; McGurk 1961a no. 32; Verey 1998; Marsden 1999; Ganz 2001. TM 66321

O (Acts) [Vg^{Oa} O]

Oxford, Bodleian Library, MS Selden Supra 30 (Bodley 3418)

Codex Oxoniensis. Acts of the Apostles.

Copied in Kent in the eighth century. Uncial script.

54 folios (23x17½ cm). One column of 24–6 lines (17–19x13–15 cm). Parchment; black ink with coloured decoration of the first letter. Acts 14:27–15:32 is missing.

Images: (CLA II 257).

Further literature: Brown 2006:54–5. TM 66343

O (Pauline Epistles) [Vg^{Op} O]

Oxford, Bodleian Library, MS Laud. lat. 108

Codex Laudianus. Pauline Epistles
Copied in the first half of the ninth century, possibly in Würzburg. Minuscule script.

117 folios (25½x19 cm). One column of 21 lines. Parchment; black ink with red and yellow decoration.

The manuscript is a copy of Würzburg, Universitätsbibliothek, M.p.th.f. 69, an eighth-century codex of the Pauline Epistles with Insular features. The epistles have prefaces and *capitula*.

Images: Oxford Digital Library (two images).

Editions: Buchanan 1914a; Tischendorf x_2.

Further literature: Berger 1893:398; Frede 1962–4:17*–18*; Fischer 1965 [1985:174]; Frede 1966–71:18.

O (Catholic Epistles) [Vg^{Oc} O]
Oxford, Bodleian Library, MS Laud. lat. 103

Codex Oxoniensis. Catholic Epistles.
Copied in Germany in the first half of the twelfth century.
Parchment; black ink with decorated initials.

O (Revelation) [Vg^{Or} O]
Oxford, Bodleian Library, MS Laud. lat. 43

Codex Oxoniensis. Catholic Epistles and Revelation.
Copied in England in the twelfth or thirteenth century.
One column (apart from the prologues). Parchment; black ink with rubrication.
The text is accompanied by a gloss. There are three prologues for the Catholic Epistles, but no prologue or *capitula* for Revelation.

Editions: Buchanan 1916. Only cited for Revelation in the Oxford Vulgate; cited in Vetus Latina (Ω^O).

P (Gospels) [Vg^{Oe} P]
Perugia, Biblioteca Capitolare 1.

Codex Perusinus. Part of Luke.
Copied in Umbria in the second half of the sixth century. Uncial script.
46 folios (32x26 cm). Two columns of 27 lines (22x19 cm). Parchment; black ink.

The manuscript contains Luke 1:26–12:8. Fragments of John found in the binding of manuscript 29 (renumbered as Biblioteca Capitolare 3) may no longer be available.

Images: (CLA IV 407).

Editions: Bianchini 1749; Fischer Jp: 93.9 per cent.

Further literature: McGurk 1961a no. 100; Fischer 1965 [1985:199]. TM 66511.

P (Pauline Epistles) [Vg^{Op} P]
Paris, Bibliothèque nationale de France, nouv. acq. latin 1063

Gospels and Epistles, including Laodiceans.

Copied in Corbie in the last third of the seventh century.[12] Merovingian cursive minuscule script.

120 folios (22x14½ cm). Two columns of 28–34 lines (19x11½ cm). Parchment; black ink. Each book begins with a zoomorphic initial and the opening lines written in red uncial script.

Matthew 1:1–26:4 is missing. The other gospels have prefaces but no *capitula*. Eusebian apparatus with parallel passages in the margin. The Pauline Epistles have prologues but only Romans has *capitula*. Laodiceans comes between Philemon and Hebrews. The manuscript breaks off at Hebrews 7:14. There are contemporary liturgical notes.

Images: <http://gallica.bnf.fr/ark:/12148/btv1b10510172h>. (CLA V 679).

Editions: Fischer Gi: 92.9 per cent.

Further literature: McGurk 1994a:20; Tewes 2011:204; Ganz 2012:326. TM 66847.

Q [Vg^O Q]

Dublin, Trinity College, MS 58

Codex Kenanensis, Book of Kells. Four Gospels.

Copied in the early ninth century, in Ireland, Scotland, or possibly Northumbria. Insular majuscule script.

340 folios (33x25 cm). One column of 17 lines (25x17 cm). Parchment; black ink with much coloured decoration, including numerous zoomorphic initials and pictures. Several full page illustrations, including four symbol pages before each Gospel, and a single four symbols page.

There are initial canon tables; each Gospel is preceded by prefaces and *capitula* (KA I); lists of Hebrew names are given for Matthew and Luke. The manuscript breaks off at John 17:13.

Images: <http://digitalcollections.tcd.ie/home/#folder_id=14&pidtopage=MS58_001r&entry_point=1>; Alton, Meyer & Simms 1950 (complete facsimile, mostly monochrome); Alexander & Fox 1990 (colour facsimile). (CLA II 274).

Editions: Fischer Hq: 89.2 per cent (ranging from 77.1 per cent in Matthew[14] to 94.3 per cent in Luke[34]).

Further literature: Berger 1893:41–2; McGurk 1961a no. 87; Brown & Verey 1972; Brown 1980; McGurk 1994b; O'Mahony 1994; Meehan 1995; Farr 1997; O'Reilly in Sharpe & Van Kampen 1998; Pulliam 2006; Meehan 2012. TM 66360.

R (Gospels) [Vg^Oe R]

Oxford, Bodleian Library, MS Auct. D.2.19 (Bodley 3964)

Rushworth Gospels, MacRegol Gospels. Four Gospels.

---

[12] The date and location follow a private communication from David Ganz (article forthcoming in *Revue bénédictine*, 2016).

Copied in Ireland around 800. Insular majuscule script.

169 folios (35x27 cm). One column of 22 lines (27x21 cm). Parchment; black ink with rubrication. There are evangelist portraits (some now missing) and large initial pages.

Luke 4:29–8:38, 10:20–38, and 15:14–16:25 are missing. There is no prefatory material or Eusebian apparatus. The highest concentration of Old Latin readings is found in the second half of Matthew and the middle of Luke. An Old English gloss was added throughout the manuscript by two scribes probably in Yorkshire in the late tenth century.

Images: <http://bodley30.bodley.ox.ac.uk:8180/luna/servlet/view/search/what/ MS. per cent20Auct. per cent20D. per cent202. per cent2019>. (CLA II 231).

Editions: Tamoto 2013. Fischer Hr: 87.1 per cent (ranging from 74.9 per cent in Luke[33] to 93 per cent in Mark[11]).

Further literature: Hemphill 1911; McGurk 1961a no. 33. TM 66322.

R (Acts)
See VL 62 above.

R (Pauline Epistles)
See R in the Stuttgart Vulgate.

S (Gospels) [Vg^{Oe} S]
London, British Library, MS Add. 89000
Cuthbert Gospel (formerly Stonyhurst St John).[13] John.
Copied in Northumbria at the end of the seventh century. Uncial script.
90 folios (13½x9½ cm). One column of 19 lines (9½x6½ cm). Parchment; black ink with red initials.

Found in the tomb of St Cuthbert in 1104. The text is arranged in sense-units, sometimes over two lines. The coloured initials correspond to the KA C divisions. There are four lection markings.

Images: <http://www.bl.uk/manuscripts/Viewer.aspx?ref=add_ms_89000>. Brown 1969 (facsimile). (CLA II 260).

Editions: Fischer Ns: 97.5 per cent.

Further literature: Mynors and Powell 1956; McGurk 1961a no. 37; Gibson 1993:26–7; Breay & Meehan 2015. TM 66346.

S (Acts)
See S (Acts and Revelation) in the Stuttgart Vulgate.

S (Pauline Epistles) [Vg^{Op} S]
Cambridge, Trinity College B.10.5
Pauline Epistles (partial).

---

[13] There is also an eighth-century set of 'Cuthbert Gospels' which take their name from their Anglo-Saxon copyist: Vienna, Österreichische Nationalbibliothek, lat. 1224 (McGurk 1961a no. 42).

Copied in Northumbria in the first half of the eighth century. Insular minuscule script.

67 folios (29½x23 cm). One column of 27 lines (25x16½ cm). Parchment; black ink with red and yellow decoration.

The manuscript begins at 1 Corinthians 7:32 and contains the rest of the Pauline Epistles up to and including Hebrews. Five folios are currently in London, cited as Vg^{Op} E. There are numerous Latin marginal and interlinear glosses. The *capitula* and preface at the beginning of each Epistle are written in two columns.

Images: <http://sites.trin.cam.ac.uk/manuscripts/B_10_5/manuscript.php>. (CLA II 133).

Edition: De Paor (in preparation).

Further literature: McGurk 1994a:18. TM 66237.

T [Vg^O T]

Madrid, Biblioteca Nacional, Vitr. 13-1 (Tol. 2-1).

Codex Toletanus. Bible with Old and New Testament, including Laodiceans (epcar).

Copied in southern Spain around 950 for Bishop Servandus. Visigothic minuscule script.

375 folios (44x32 cm). Three columns of 63–5 lines. Parchment; black and red ink.

Decorated canon tables. Eusebian apparatus with parallel passages in the margin of the Gospels; Priscillian's canon numbers in the Pauline Epistles. Laodiceans appears after Colossians. There are *capitula* before Revelation (KA Sp).

Images: <http://bibliotecadigitalhispanica.bne.es:80/webclient/Delivery Manager?pid=1723042>.

Editions: Bianchini 1740 (reprinted in PL 29: 915–1152). Occasionally cited in Vetus Latina (Σ^T). Fischer St: 93.1 per cent. (CLA XI 1654, although Lowe's dating is no longer accepted.)

Further literature: Berger 1893:12–14, 391; Lowe 1923; Smith 1924; Millares Carlo 1925; Fischer 1963b [1985:70]; Frede 1976b; Gryson 2000–3:31–2.

U (Gospels) [Vg^{Oe} U]

Utrecht, Bibliotheek der Rijksuniversiteit, 32, foll. 94–104

Fragmenta Ultratraiectina. Fragments of Matthew and John.

Copied in Jarrow around 720. Anglo-Saxon uncial script.

11 folios (31x24 cm). Two columns of 30 lines (25x19½ cm). Parchment; black and red ink, gold for the initial lines. Decorations in green, blue, and yellow.

The manuscript is bound with the Utrecht Psalter (VL 423). The first eight folios consist of prefatory material (*Nouum opus, Plures fuisse*, a prologue and KA C for Matthew), including a title page to the four gospels with a Greek invocation. These are followed by Matthew 1:1–3:4 and John 1:1–21.

Images: Birch 1873 (facsimile); van der Horst et al 1982 (facsimile). (CLA X 1587).

Editions: Fischer Nu: 97.6 per cent.

Further literature: Lowe 1952; McGurk 1961a no. 81. TM 67752.

U (Acts, Epistles, Revelation) [Vg^{Oa} U]

London, British Library, MS Add. 11852

Codex Ulmensis. Latter part of New Testament (pacr).

Copied in the ninth century, possibly in St Gall. Minuscule script.

215 folios (23½x17cm). One column of 23–5 lines. Parchment; black and red ink.

There are prefaces, marginal chapter numbers and stichometry. The text has been described as the local text of the Bodensee area and is related to Vg^{Sar} S. It was once thought to have been copied by Abbot Hartmut.

Images: <http://www.stgallplan.org/stgallmss/viewItem.do?ark=p21198-zz002971c4>.

Editions: Cited occasionally in Vetus Latina (σ^{U}).

Further literature: Berger 1893:126–7, 390; Fischer 1965 [1985:181].

V

See Φ^{V} in the Stuttgart Vulgate.

W [Vg^{O} W]

London, British Library, Royal I.B.12

Codex Sarisburiensis, *Bible of William of Hales*. Bible with Old and New Testaments (eacpr).

Copied in Salisbury by William of Hales in 1254. Gothic script.

431 folios (35x20 cm). Two columns of 51 lines (20x12 cm). Parchment; black, red, and blue ink with gold and other colours in decorated initials.

According to Glunz, the text is copied from Salisbury Cathedral MS 148. Some of the illustrations are by the 'Sarum Master'.

Images: <http://www.bl.uk/catalogues/illuminatedmanuscripts/record.asp? MSID=7160> (7 images).

Editions: Also cited occasionally in Vetus Latina (Ω^{W}; W in Mark).

Further literature: Glunz 1933.

X [Vg^{O} X]

Cambridge, Corpus Christi College, 286

Gospels of St Augustine. Four Gospels.

Copied at the end of the sixth century, possibly in Rome. Uncial script.

265 folios (24½x18 cm). Two columns of 25 lines (18½x13½ cm). Parchment; black ink with rubrication for the first line of each chapter. Full page illustrations with multiple scenes and evangelist portraits (only preserved for Luke).

The gospels begin with prefaces and *capitula* (KA B). There is Eusebian apparatus with parallel passages. The canon tables are likely to have been in a missing initial quire. Corrections have been added in a Northumbrian hand.

Images: <http://parkerweb.stanford.edu/parker/actions/page_turner.do?ms_no=286>. (CLA II 126).

Collation: Fischer Jx: 96.3 per cent.

Further literature: Berger 1893:35; Wormald 1954; McGurk 1961a no. 3; McGurk 1994a:16; Marsden 1999. TM 66230.

Y [Vg^O Y]

London, British Library, Cotton Nero D.IV

Lindisfarne Gospels, Codex Lindisfarnensis. Four Gospels.

Copied in Lindisfarne around 700. Anglo-Saxon majuscule script.

259 folios (36½x27½ cm). Two columns of 24 lines (23½x19 cm). Parchment; black and red ink with multiple colours used in decoration. Evangelist portraits, carpet pages, and large ornate initials.

Prefatory material: *Nouum opus, Plures fuisse,* and *Eusebius Carpiano* followed by decorated canon tables. Each Gospel is preceded by a preface and *capitula* (KA C); there is a list of Neapolitan feasts (also found in British Library, Royal 1.B.VII). Eusebian apparatus with parallel passages. The text is closely related to Vg A. An Old English gloss was added throughout by Aldred in Chester-le-Street in the late tenth century. In the *capitula* for John, some lectionary indications have been copied as titles within the text.

Images: <http://www.bl.uk/manuscripts/FullDisplay.aspx?ref=Cotton_MS_nero_d_iv>. Kendrick et al. 1956–60; Brown 2002. (CLA II 187). Image 15 in the present volume.

Editions: Fischer Ny: 96.6 per cent.

Further literature: Berger 1893:39–41, 385; McGurk 1955; Kendrick et al. 1956–60; McGurk 1961a no. 22; Gibson 1993:26–7; McGurk 1993; Backhouse 1994; Gameson 1994:42; O'Sullivan 1994; Brown 2003, 2011; Gameson 2013. TM 66291.

Z (Gospels)

See Z in the Stuttgart Vulgate.

Z (Epistles and Revelation)

See VL 65 above.

Δ [Vg^O Δ]

i) Durham, Cathedral Library, A.II.16, foll. 1–23, 34–86, 102
ii) Durham, Cathedral Library, A.II.16, foll. 24–33, 87–101
iii) Durham, Cathedral Library, A.II.16, foll. 103–34.

Codex Dunelmensis. Four Gospels.[14]

---

[14] Note that these are not the Durham Gospels, which bear the shelfmark A.II.17 (see page 73).

Copied in Northumbria in the eighth century. i) is in uncial script, ii) and iii) in Insular majuscule script.

134 folios (35x24½ cm). Two columns; i) and iii) have 30 lines per page, ii) has 27–8 (27x20 cm). Parchment; black ink with rubrication.

i) contains Matthew 2:13–22:15, Mark, Luke 1:57–16:15; ii) contains replacement leaves for Matthew 23:3–28:14 and Luke 16:15–end; iii) contains John 1:27–15:16 and 16:33–21:8. There is a prologue and *capitula* for Mark (KA C).

Both i) and ii) have a text similar to the Echternach Gospels (Vg^O EP), while iii) resembles Codex Amiatinus (Vg A). There are liturgical indications of different speakers in the Passion narratives. Eusebian apparatus with parallel passages is found in the margins of ii and iii.

Images: (CLA II 148 a,b,c).

Editions: Fischer i) Nd: 90.2 per cent; ii) Ne: 90 per cent; iii) Nf: 97.6 per cent.

Further literature: Berger 1893:381–2; McGurk 1961a nos 10–12; Verey 1969–70; Bruce-Mitford 1989. TM 66248, 66249, 66250.

Θ [Vg^O Θ]

Paris, Bibliothèque nationale de France, latin 9380

Codex Theodulfianus, Codex Mesmianus, Mesmes Bible. Bible: Old and New Testaments (epcar).

Copied in Orléans or Fleury around 800. Caroline minuscule script.

349 folios (32x23 cm). Two columns of 62 lines (23½x16 cm). Purple parchment with silver and gold ink in the Gospels (*ordo euangelicus*); normal parchment with black and red ink in the rest of the New Testament (*ordo apostolicus*).

This is an early copy of a Theodulf Bible. The gospels have Eusebian apparatus with parallel passages; the Pauline Epistles have Priscillian canons. In the Old Testament there is a large number of interlinear corrections and alternatives contemporary with the production of the manuscript. After the biblical text, there is a list of lections, then *De nominibus hebraeis* and the *Liber de diuinis scripturis* (PS-AU spe).

Images: <http://gallica.bnf.fr/ark:/12148/btv1b8452776m>. (CLA V 576).

Editions: Cited occasionally in the Vetus Latina edition (Θ^M). Fischer Om: 95.5 per cent.

Further literature: Berger 1893:149–76, 405–6; Fischer 1963b [1985:95]. Loewe 1969; Gryson 2000–3:27. TM 66707.

Π [Vg^O Π]

Paris, Bibliothèque nationale de France, nouv. acq. latin 1132

Codex Parisinus. Revelation.

Copied in northern France at the turn of the tenth century. Caroline minuscule script.

40 folios (29x21 cm). One column of 20 lines (23x14 cm). Parchment; black and red ink. The text alternates with numerous coloured drawings, the principal colours being blue, red, and yellow.

Revelation occupies the first 36 folios; the remaining four contain the *Fables of Avianus*. The extensive interlinear and marginal glosses were added in the fourteenth century.

Images: <http://gallica.bnf.fr/ark:/12148/btv1b8426793j>.

Σ [Vg^O Σ]
Trier, Stadtbibliothek, MS 31
   Codex Triverensis, Trier Apocalypse. Revelation.
   Copied in northern France around 800. Half-uncial and Caroline minuscule scripts.
   75 folios (26x21½ cm). One column of 19 lines (20 in the first quire). Parchment; black ink with rubrication. The biblical text alternates with full-page colour images.
   The classical parallels in the illustrations have led to suggestions that their source may date to the fifth century or earlier. The text corresponds to an Italian Vulgate, although there are extensive erasures and eleventh-century corrections. The first-hand text was, in fact, Vulgate: the corrections are adjustments to match the texts with the pictures. There is no prefatory material.
   Images: Klein & Laufner 1975 (facsimile), Klein 2001 (facsimile), <http://www.johannesoffenbarung.ch/bilderzyklen/trierer1.php> (illustrations only).
   Edition: Also cited in Vetus Latina (ϒ^T for main text, ϒ^{Tr} for readings above erasures).
   Further literature: Fischer 1965 [1985:151]; Klein & Laufner 1975; Renna 1990; Gryson 2000–3:33; Morgan 2012.

   The following are occasionally cited as additional witnesses in the Oxford Vulgate but do not appear as principal manuscripts in either of the other editions:
   arg. *Codex Argenteus.* Paris, Bibliothèque nationale de France, latin 9451. A lectionary written in silver ink on purple parchment, copied around the beginning of the ninth century. (CLA V 580). Cited for some readings in Acts. <http://gallica.bnf.fr/ark:/12148/btv1b6001307x>.
   div. *Codex Divionensis.* Dijon, Bibliothèque municipale, 15. ('Bible of Stephen Harding'); Fourth volume of a complete Bible, containing the New Testament in the order eacpr. Copied in Cîteaux in 1109. Occasionally cited as Ω^D in Vetus Latina.
   haf. *Codex Hafnianus.* Copenhagen, Univ. Bibliotek, Arnamagnaeaske Legat AM. 795 4to. Revelation, followed by Apringius' Commentary (APR). Copied in Catalonia in the twelfth century. Cited as κ^K in Vetus Latina. See description in Gryson 2000–3:38.
   m. *Speculum.* The patristic *testimonia* collection, *Liber de diuinis scripturis* (PS-AU spe in Vetus Latina).
   s (Acts, Catholic Epistles). Vienna, Österreichische Nationalbibliothek, lat. 16.

APPENDIX 1

Concordances of Manuscript Sigla

A) Old Latin

The traditional system of sigla for Old Latin witnesses was developed in Tischendorf's editions of the New Testament, culminating in his eighth edition (*Editio octava maior*) of 1869–72. This uses lower-case letters, sometimes with superscript or subscript numerals. The alphabetical series was adopted for Latin evidence in subsequent editions of the Greek New Testament, including NA28 and UBS5. It is also found in the Jülicher-Matzkow-Aland *Itala* editions of the Old Latin Gospels (see Chapter 6, pages 125–7). The major drawback is that the series begins afresh for each portion of the New Testament: witness 'e' in the Gospels is not the same as witness 'e' in Acts or witness 'e' in the Pauline Epistles. To avoid confusion, the Vetus Latina register assigns each manuscript a unique number.

Because of the overlap between alphabetical sigla, it is necessary to provide an indication of the scope of each (the books of the New Testament for which they are generally cited). The abbreviations are as follows: e=Gospels; a=Acts; p=Paul; c=Catholic Epistles; r=Revelation. The † suffix indicates that the witness is missing (or only cited in) one or more books within that scope.

For the sake of completeness, sigla are also given from Fischer's collation of gospel manuscripts (Fischer 1988–91; see pages 124–5 above), and the Oxford Vulgate (pages 129–31).

As the manuscripts are presented in the Vetus Latina order in Chapter 10, the table below is ordered by the alphabetical sigla. Greek letters appear in the sequence of their transliterated equivalent. A few rows have been duplicated in order to ensure that alphabetical order is broadly maintained in all columns.

NA28	UBS5	Tischendorf	Itala	Fischer	Oxford Vulgate	Vetus Latina	Other	Scope
a	it^a	a	a	Xa	a	3	*Verc.*	e
a^2	it^{a2}	a$_2$	a^2	Xn	a^2	16	*cur.*	e†
–		amb^{rescr}	–	–	–	AM Lc		e†
ar	it^{ar}	–	–	Hd	D	61	*arm.*	pr (NA); acpr (UBS); eapcr (Vg^O)
aur	it^{aur}	–	aur	Ea	aur	15	*holm.*	e
b	it^b	b	b	Xb	b	4	*Veron.*	e
b	it^b	–	–	–	–	89		p
β	it^β	–	β	–	–	26		e†

(continued)

Continued

NA28	UBS5	Tischendorf	Itala	Fischer	Oxford Vulgate	Vetus Latina	Other	Scope
c	it^c	c	c	Xc	c	6	*Colb.*	e (NA); ea (UBS)
–	it^{comp}	–	–	–	–	109	*compl^l*	p
d	it^d	d	d	Xd	d	5	*Bez.*	eac†
d	it^d	d	–	–	d	75	*Claro.*	p
–	–	δ	–	–	δ	27	δ	e
–	it^{dem}	demid	–	–	dem	59	*dem.*	ap
–	it^{div}	–	–	–	div	–	*div.*	pcr
–	–	–	–	Ed	durmach	–	*durm.*	e
e	it^e	e	e	Xe	e	2	*Palat.*	e
e	it^e	e	–	–	e	50	*laud.*	a
–	–	e	–	–	e	76	*germ.*	p
f	it^f	f	f	Jg	f	10	*Brix.*	e
f	it^f	f	–	–	f	78	*Aug.*	p
ff	it^{ff}	ff	–	–	ff	66	*Corb.*	c†
ff^1	it^{ff1}	ff^1	ff^1	Xo	ff^1	9	*Corb.*	e†
ff^2	it^{ff2}	ff^2	ff^2	Xf	ff^2	8	*Corb.*	e
g	it^g	g	–	–	g	77	*Boern.*	p
g^1	it^{g1}	g^1	g^1	Pg	g^1, G	7	*germ./sang.*	e†
–	–	g^2	–	Bg	g^2	29	*germ./sang.*	e
–	–	g$_2$	–	–	g^2	52		a
–	–	gat	–	Bt	gat	30	*gat.*	e
gig	it^{gig}	g	–	–	gig	51	*gig.*	ar (NA, UBS); ear (Vg^O)
gue	it^{gue}	gue	–	–	gue	79	*guelf.*	p†
h	it^h	h	h	Xh	h	12	*Claro.*	e†
h	it^h	reg	–	–	h	55		ac†r
–	–	–	–	–	haf	–		r
z	it^z	harl	–	–	Z	65	*harl.*	p†c† (NA); p †c†r (UBS, Vg^O)
aur	it^{aur}	–	aur	Ea	aur	15	*holm.*	e
i	it^i	i	i	Xi	i	17	*Vind.*	e†
j	it^j	z	j	Xj	j	22, 22A	*Sarz.*	e†
k	it^k	k	k	Xk	k	1	*Bob.*	e†
l	it^l	l	l	Xl	l	11	*Rehd.*	e
l	it^l	–	–	–	–	67	*leg.*	ac†
–	–	–	–	Sl	–	91, 133	*leg^2*	eapcr
–	–	–	–	–	–	92	*leg^3*	eapcr
λ	it^λ	–	λ	–	–	44		e†
m	it^{mon}	–	–	–	–	86		p†
–	–	m	–	–	m	PS-AU spe	*spec.*	eapcr
μ	it^μ	–	μ	–	–	45		e†
μ	it^μ	–	–	–	–	82		p†
n	it^n	n	n	Xn	n	16		e†
o	it^o	o	o	–	o	16		e†

–	it^{o}	–	–	–	–	PEL	*see note*[1]	p
p	it^{p}	p	p	Xp	p	20		e†
p	it^{p}	–	–	–	p	54		a (NA, UBS); ac (Vg^{O})
p	–	–	–	–	p	80		p†
–	it^{Ph}	–	–	–	–	63		a†
π	it^{π}	–	π	Xw	–	18		e†
–	it^{φ}	–	–	Xp	–	43		e†
q	it^{q}	q	q	Xq	q	13	*mon.*	e
r	it^{r}	–	–	–	–	57		a
r	it^{r}	r, r^2, r^3	–	–	r	64	*frising.*	p†
r	it^{q}	q	–	–	r	64	*frising.*	c†
r^1	it^{r1}	r	r^1	Xr	r^1	14	*Uss.*	e
–	–	–	–	Hg	r^2	28	*Uss.*[2]	e
–	it^{ro}	–	–	–	R	62		a
ρ	it^{p}	–	ρ		–	24		e†
ρ	it^{p}	–	–	–	–	88		p†
s	it^{s}	s	s	Xs	s	21		e†
s	it^{s}	s	–	–	s	53		ac†
–	it^{s}	–	–	–	–	87		p†
–	it^{sa}	–	–	–	–	60		a
sin	it^{sin}	–	–	–	–	74		ar
t	it^{t}	t	t	Xt	t	19	*Bern.*	e†
t	it^{t}	–	–	–	t	56	*see note*[2]	apcr
v	it^{v}	–	–	–	v	81		p†
–	it^{v}	v	v	Xv	v	25	*Vind.*	e†
w	it^{w}	–	–	–	–	58		a
w	it^{w}	gue lect	–	Gw	–	32		c†
–	–	x_1	–	–	O	–		a
–	–	x_2, laud	–	–	O	–		p
z	it^{z}	harl	–	–	Z	65	*harl.*	p†c† (NA); p †c†r (UBS, Vg^{O})
–	–	–	23	–	–	23		e†
–	–	–	–	Hm, Hn	–	35	*mull.*	e†
–	–	–	–	Jc	–	33		e†
–	–	–	–	Xu	–	41		e†

B) Vulgate

As noted in the Preface, overlaps between sigla in the two principal editions of the Vulgate have led to the creation of a single reference scheme. This is given in the first column below (LNT). The Stuttgart and Oxford Vulgate are both listed, as are sigla from Fischer's collation and Tischendorf's eighth edition (see above). Vetus Latina sigla are included when applicable. Common appellations of the manuscripts are also

---

[1] In UBS5, it^{o} in the Pauline Epistles indicates the lemma text of Oxford, Balliol College, MS 157 (see page 40 above).

[2] In NA28, the siglum t denotes the printed edition of the *Liber Comicus* rather than any single manuscript.

LNT	Oxford (Vg^O)	Stuttgart (Vg^S)	Fischer	Tischendorf	Vetus Latina	Other	Name	Scope
Vg A	A	A	Na	am	A	*am.*	Amiatinus	eapcr
Vg^{Oe} B	B	–	Eb	–	–	–	Bigotianus	e†
Vg^S Φ^B	B	Φ^B	–	–	–	–	–	apc
Vg^S B	–	B	–	–	Γ^A	–	Abiascensis	l
Vg^O BF	ᛒF	–	–	–	–	–	–	e
Vg C	C	C	Sc	cav	189	*cav.*	Cavensis	eapcr (Vg^O), eaprl (Vg^S)
VL 61	D	D	Hd	–	61	*arm.*	Armagh, Ardmachanus	eapcr (Vg^O), 1 (Vg^S)
Vg^S D	durmach	D	Ed	–	–	*durm.*	Durrow, Durmachensis	e
Vg^{Oe} E	E	–	Be	mm	–	*mm.*	Egerton	e
Vg^{Op} E	E	–	–	–	–	–	–	p
Vg^O EP	ℰP	–	Ge	–	–	–	Epternachensis	eapcr
Vg F	F	F	Jf	fu, fuld	F	*fuld.*	Fuldensis	eapcrl
VL 7	G, g^1	G	Pg	g^1	7, G	g^1	Sangallensis	eapcr
Vg^O H	H	–	–	–	Θ^H	*hub.*	Hubertianus	eapcr
Vg^{Oe} I	I	–	Ai	ing	–	–	Ingolstadiensis	e
Vg^S I	I	I	–	–	I	–	Vallicellianus	acr
Vg^O J	J	–	Jj	for	J	–	Forojuliensis	e
Vg^S Φ^G	K	Φ^G	–	–	Φ^G	*Grandv.*	Karolinus, Grandivallensis	eapcr
Vg^S K	–	K	–	–	–	–	–	p
Vg^{Sp} k	–	k	–	–	–	–	–	p
Vg^{Sc} k	–	k	–	–	–	–	–	c†
Vg^{Oe} L	L	–	Hl	–	L	*lich.*	Lichfield, Llandaff, Chad	e†
Vg^{Op} L	L	–	–	–	L	–	Langobardus	p
Vg^{Oc} L	L	–	–	–	–	*lem.*	Lemovicensis	c
VL 251	–	L	Gl	lux	251	–	Luxoviense	c

VL 67	–	1	–	67	–	–	ap
Vgˢ M	M	M	–	–	–	Mediolanensis	e
Vg^Oa M	M	–	–	–	–	Monacensis	a
Vg^Op M	M	M	–	M	–	Frisingensis	p (Vg^O), l (Vgˢ)
Vg^O MT	**M**	Ot	mt, mart	–	*mt.*	Martini Turonensis	e
Vg^O N	N	Jn	–	–	–	–	p
Vgˢ N	N	–	–	–	–	–	e
Vg^Oe O	O	Jo	bodl	–	–	St Augustine	e
Vg^Oa O	O	–	x_1	–	–	Oxoniensis	a
Vg^Op O	O	–	laud	–	–	Laudianus	p
Vg^Oc O	O	–	–	–	–	Oxoniensis	c
Vg^Or O	O	–	–	–	–	Oxoniensis	r
Vg^Oe P	P	Jp	pe, per	–	–	Perusinus	e
Vg^Op P	P	–	–	–	*long.*	Langobardus	p
Vgˢ P	–	Jy	–	–	–	–	e
Vg^O Q	Q	Hq	–	–	–	–	e
Vgˢ Q	–	–	–	Γ^C	*ken.*	Kells, Kenanensis	l
Vg^Oe R	R	Hr	–	–	–	–	e
VL 62	R	–	–	62	*rush.*	Rushworth, MacRegol	a
Vg^Sp R	R	–	–	R	–	Rosas	p
Vg^Sc R	R	–	–	R	–	Reginensis	p
Vgˢ r	r	–	–	J	–	–	ac†r
Vg^Oe S	S	–	–	–	–	–	e
Vg^Se S	S	Ns	–	–	*ston.*	Stonyhurst, Cuthbert	e
Vg^Se s	s	Js	san	–	*sang.*	Sangallensis	e
Vg^Sar S	S	Jr	–	–	–	–	a (Vg^O), ar (Vgˢ)
Vg^Op S	S	–	–	E	–	–	p
Vg^Sp S	–	S	–	S	–	–	p

(continued)

Continued

LNT	Oxford (Vg^O)	Stuttgart (Vg^S)	Fischer	Tischendorf	Vetus Latina	Other	Name	Scope
Vg^Sp s	–	s	–	–	I	–	–	p
Vg^Sc S	–	S	–	–	s	–	–	c
Vg^O T	T	–	St	tol	Σ^T	tol.	Toletanus	eapcr
Vg^Oe U	U	–	Nu	–	–	–	Ultratraiectina	e
Vg^Oa U	U	–	–	ulm	σ^U	–	Ulmensis	apcr
Vg^S Φ^V	V	Φ^V	Cv	vallic	Φ^V	vall.	Vallicellianus	eapcr
Vg^O W	W	–	–	–	Ω^W	–	Sarisburiensis	eapcr
Vg^O X	X	–	Jx	–	–	CCCC	St Augustine	e
Vg^O Y	Y	–	Ny	–	–	lind.	Lindisfarne	e
Vg^S Z	Z	Z	Jz	harl	–	–	Harleianus	e
VL 65	Z	–	–	–	65	–	–	pcr
Vg^O Δ	Δ	–	Nd, Ne, Nf	–	–	dunelm.	Dunelmensis	e
Vg^O Θ	Θ	–	Om	–	Θ^M	theod.	Theodulfianus	eapcr
Vg^O Π	Π	–	–	–	–	–	Parisinus	r
Vg^O Σ	Σ	–	–	–	–	–	Triveriensis	r
VL 91	–	Λ	Sl	–	91, Λ^L	leg^2	Legiomensis	eapcrl
Vg^S Φ^B	B	Φ^B	Te	–	–	–	–	apc
Vg^S Φ^E	–	Φ^E	–	–	Φ^E	–	–	p†
Vg^S Φ^G	K	Φ^G	–	–	Φ^G	Grandv.	Karolinus, Grandivallensis	eapcr
Vg^S Φ^T	–	Φ^T	Tt	–	Φ^T	–	–	eapcr
Vg^S Φ^V	V	Φ^V	Cv	vallic	Φ^V	vall.	Vallicellianus	eapcr

included in the 'Name' column. In addition to the 'Scope' references used in the Old Latin table above, l refers to the Epistle to the Laodiceans, only present in the Stuttgart Vulgate.

As the manuscripts are presented in Chapter 10 in alphabetical order of siglum in the Stuttgart Vulgate, the table below is ordered by the Oxford Vulgate, with Greek letters appearing at the end of the sequence. As with the table above, a few rows have been duplicated for ease of reference.

Additional Manuscripts Cited in Vetus Latina Editions

Some of the Vetus Latina editions include information from manuscripts not present in the *Register*, or not identified by their normal numerical siglum, when the editor cites them as witnesses but does not consider their evidence to be Old Latin. Vulgate manuscripts are sometimes identified by the same siglum as in the Oxford or Stuttgart Vulgates; these are not included in the table below (see instead Appendix 1). Most other sigla consist of a Greek letter to indicate the textual group and a superscript letter to identify the individual manuscript. Some manuscripts are included without a siglum. It should be noted that not every manuscript is cited for each Epistle and the same manuscript may be identified by multiple sigla.

Siglum	Manuscript	Other siglum	Scope
E	El Escorial, Real Biblioteca, M.III.3		r
H	Munich, Bayerische Staatsbibliothek, Clm 9544		p
I	St Gall, Stiftsbibliothek, 908	Vg^{Sp} s	p
J	Orléans, BM, 19; Paris, BnF, lat. 2389	Vg^{Sp} k	p
J	Ravenna, Archivio arcivescovile, s. n.	Vg^{S} r	cr
K	Kassel, Landesbibliothek, theol. oct. 5		r
M	Monte Cassino, Archivio della Badia, 521 AA		c
N	Rome, Biblioteca Nazionale Vittorio Emanuele, Sess. 96		r
P	Paris, BnF, latin 11505	Z^{P}	c
Q	Paris, BnF, latin 93		pcr
R	Karlsruhe, Badische Landesbibliothek, Aug. 222		r
V	Würzburg, Universitätsbibliothek, M.p.th.f. 69		p
W	Würzburg, Universitätsbibliothek, M.p.th.f. 12		p
X	Madrid, Biblioteca de la Universidad Complutense, 31	VL 109	pcr
Y	Wolfenbüttel, Herzog-August Bibliothek, Weissenburg 99		pc
s	St Gall, Stiftsbibliothek, 907	Vg^{Sc} S	r
Γ^{A}	Milan, Biblioteca Ambrosiana, E. 53 inf.	Vg^{S} B	pr
Γ^{B}	Milan, Biblioteca Ambrosiana, E. 26 inf.	VL 135	pr
Γ^{C}	Milan, Biblioteca Ambrosiana, B. 48 sup.	Vg^{S} Q	p
Γ^{M}	Milan, Biblioteca Ambrosiana, E. 51 inf.		r
Δ^{B}	Burgos, Seminario de San Jerónimo, s.n.		pcr
Δ^{L}	León, Archivio Catedralicio, 6		pcr
Δ^{M}	Madrid, Real Academia de la Historia, Aemil. 20		pcr
Z^{C}	Paris, BnF, latin 11533		pr

(*continued*)

Continued

Siglum	Manuscript	Other siglum	Scope
Z^E	Düsseldorf, Universitätsbibliothek, Ms. B 3		pr
Z^H	London, BL, Harley 1772	VL 65	pr
Z^L	Düsseldorf, Universitätsbibliothek, Ms. A 14		p
Z^M	Metz, BM, 7		pr
Z^P	Paris, BnF, latin 11505		pr
Z^R	Munich, Bayerische Staatsbibliothek, Clm 14179		p
Z^W	Warsaw, Bibliotheka Narodowa, akc. 12400		r[1]
Z^Z	Munich, Bayerische Staatsbibliothek, Clm 14345		p
Θ^A	Le Puy, Cathédrale, s.n.		pcr
Θ^M	Paris, BnF, lat. 9380	$Vg^O \Theta$	pcr
Θ^S	Stuttgart, Württembergische Landesbibliothek, HB. II,16		pc
Λ^H	Madrid, Real Academia de la Historia, 2–3 (text, not gloss)	cf. VL 95	cr
Λ^L	León, Biblioteca de la Real Colegiata de San Isidoro, 2 (text, not gloss)	cf. VL 91	pcr
N^C	Colmar, BM, 15	$Vg^O N$	p
N^M	Gotha, Forschungsbibliothek, Membr. I, 20		p
N^W	Berlin, Staatsbibliothek, theol.lat. fol. 366		p
Ξ^P	Paris, BnF, nouv. acq. lat. 1132	$Vg^O \Pi$	r
Ξ^V	Valenciennes, BM, 99		r
Π^F	Monte Cassino, Archivio della Badia, 521 AA		r
Π^L	Monte Cassino, Archivio della Badia, 552 AA		p
Π^W	Vienna, Österreichische Nationalbibliothek, lat. 903		p
Σ^A	Montpellier, Bibliothèque de la Ville, 6		pc
Σ^C	Madrid, Biblioteca de la Universidad Complutense, 31		pcr
Σ^O	Madrid, Museo Arqueológico, 485		pcr
Σ^T	Madrid, Biblioteca Nacional, Vitr. 13-1 (Tol. 2-1)	$Vg^O T$	pcr
Σ^W	Warsaw, Bibliotheka Narodowa, akc. 12400		p[2]
Υ^C	Cambrai, BM, 386		r
Υ^T	Trier, Stadtbibliothek, MS 31	$Vg^O \Sigma$	r
Φ^M	Monza, Biblioteca Capitolare, g-1/1		pr
Φ^Z	Zürich, Zentralbibliothek, Car. C. 1		pcr
Ψ^L	Vatican City, BAV, Palat. lat. 3-5		p
Ω^C	Paris, BnF, lat. 254	VL 6	pcr
Ω^D	Dijon, BM, 12–15	Vg^O div	pcr
Ω^O	Oxford, Bodleian Library, MS Laud. lat. 43	$Vg^{Or} O$	cr
Ω^W	London, BL, Royal I.B.12	$Vg^O W$	pr
θ^B	Bern, Burgerbibliothek, A.9		pr
θ^V	Vercelli, Archivio Capitolare, XI		pr
θ^W	Vercelli, Archivio Capitolare, VII		pr
κ^K	Copenhagen, Univ. Bibliotek Arnamagnaeske Legat, AM. 795 4to	Vg^O haf	r
κ^P	Paris, BnF, lat. 6, 1–4	VL 62	pr
κ^V	Vatican, BAV, Vatic. lat. 5729		pr
λ^A	Ivrea, Biblioteca Capitolare, LXXIX		p
λ^D	*Codex Demidovianus*	VL 59	pr

[1] In the Pauline Epistles, this has the siglum Σ^W.
[2] In Revelation, this has the siglum Z^W.

λ^M	Douai, BM, 14		r
λ^P	Paris, Bibliothèque de l'Assemblée Nationale, 1		pr
μ^A	Milan, Biblioteca Ambrosiana, A. 24 bis inf.		pr
μ^B	Bergamo, Curia vescovile, s.n.[3]		pr
ρ^A	Milan, Biblioteca Ambrosiana, C. 228 inf.		pr
ρ^D	Verona, Biblioteca Capitolare, LXXXVIII		r
ρ^P	Paris, BnF, latin 9451		pr
ρ^S	St Gall, Stiftsbibliothek, 365		pr
ρ^V	Verona, Biblioteca Capitolare, LXXXII		p^4r
ρ^W	Würzburg, Universitätsbibliothek, M.p.th.f. 62		pr
σ^G	St Gall, Stiftsbibliothek, 64		p
σ^H	St Gall, Stiftsbibliothek, 83		pr
σ^R	Fulda, Hochschul- und Landesbibliothek, Aa. 11	Vg^{Se} s	pr
σ^U	London, BL, MS Add. 11852	Vg^{Oa} U	pr
σ^W	Stuttgart, Württembergische Landesbibliothek, HB. II,54		pr
σ^X	St Gall, Stiftsbibliothek, 72		p
σ^Z	Zürich, Zentralbibliothek, Car. C. 57		p
τ^{56}	Paris, BnF, nouv. acq. lat. 2171	VL 56	pcr
τ^{68}	Toledo, Catedral, Biblioteca del Cabildo, 35–8	VL 68	pc
τ^{69}	León, Archivo Catedralicio, 2	VL 69	pr
τ^{70}	Madrid, Real Academia de la Historia, Aemil. 22	VL 70	pcr
τ^{71}	Paris, BnF, lat. 2269	VL 71	pc
τ^{72}	Toledo, Catedral, Biblioteca del Cabildo, 35–4	VL 72	pr
τ^{73}	London, BL, MS Add. 30846	VL 73	pr
-	Aarau, Staatsarchiv, Stift Zurzach, Mappe 3949 Fasc. Nr. 41		p
-	Autun, BM, 27 Palimpseste		r
-	Basle, Universitätsbibliothek, B.II.5		p
-	Hanover, Kestner-Museum, 3926		p
-	Mainz, Domschatz, 972		p
-	Milan, Biblioteca Ambrosiana, A. 28 inf.		p
-	Monte Cassino, Archivio della Badia, 271 K Palimpsest		pr
-	Monte Cassino, Archivio della Badia, Compact. XIII. 1		p
-	Munich, Bayerische Staatsbibliothek, Clm 4577		p
-	Munich, Bayerische Staatsbibliothek, Clm 6230	Vg^O M	c
-	Munich, Bayerische Staatsbibliothek, Clm 9545		p
-	St Gall, Stiftsbibliothek, 11		p
-	Vatican, BAV, Vatic. lat. 5755		p
-	Verona, Biblioteca Capitolare, LXXXII		p^5
-	Verona, Biblioteca Capitolare, LXXXVIII	ρ^D	p^6
-	Vienna, Österreichische Nationalbibliothek, lat. 732		p
-	Vienna, Österreichische Nationalbibliothek, lat. 1190[7]		p
-	Vienna, Österreichische Nationalbibliothek, lat. Ser. nov. 2065		p
-	Vienna, Österreichische Nationalbibliothek, lat. Ser. nov. 3750		p
-	Würzburg, Universitätsbibliothek, M.p.th.q. 32		pr

[3] The Pauline editions give the library as Bergamo, S. Alessandro in Colonna, 242.

[4] In earlier Epistles, this manuscript has no siglum.

[5] In later Epistles, this has the siglum ρ^V.

[6] In Revelation, this has the siglum ρ^D.

[7] According to Fröhlich 1995–8, this manuscript is a copy of Paris, BnF, latin 45 and 93 (Q in the table above).

Additional Gospel Manuscripts

According to Fischer 2010, there are sixty-nine gospel manuscripts with an agreement of less than 90 per cent with the editorial text of the Stuttgart Vulgate (see page 125 above). Fifty of these are included in the Catalogue in Chapter 10. The remaining nineteen are listed below in alphabetical order of library. Details are given of online images, the exact percentage agreements, and references in CLA.

Augsburg, Universitätsbibliothek, Fürst. Oettingen-Wallerstein'sche Bibl., 1.2.4°.2.
   Maihingen Gospels, sometimes *Harburg Gospels*. Fischer: Gr 87.7 per cent (ranging from 76.2 per cent in Mark[24] to 93.6 per cent in Matthew[12]). (CLA VIII 1216).

Autun, Bibliothèque municipale, 3.
   Gundohinus Gospels. Fischer: Gg 89.5 per cent.
   Images: <http://bvmm.irht.cnrs.fr/> (41 images). (CLA VI 716).

Bern, Burgerbibliothek, 671.
   Fischer: Hb 85.7 per cent.

Cambridge, University Library, Ii.VI.32.
   Book of Deer. Fischer: Hc 88.9 per cent.
   Images: <http://cudl.lib.cam.ac.uk/view/MS-II-00006-00032>.

Cambridge, University Library, Kk.I.24; London, British Library, Sloane 1044, fol. 2; London, British Library, Cotton Tiberius B.V, fol. 26.
   Fischer: Eh 86.6 per cent. (ranging from 74.1 per cent in Luke[32] to 94.4 per cent in Luke[33]).
   Images: i) <http://cudl.lib.cam.ac.uk/view/MS-KK-00001-00024/>; ii) <http://www.bl.uk/catalogues/illuminatedmanuscripts/ILLUMIN.ASP?Size=mid&IllID=15071>. (CLA II 138).

Dublin, Royal Irish Academy, D.II.3, foll. 1–11.
   Stowe St John. Fischer: Ht 88.5 per cent.
   Images: <http://www.isos.dias.ie/libraries/RIA/RIA_MS_D_ii_3/tables/1.html>. (CLA II 267).

Dublin, Trinity College, MS 59.
   Book of Dimma. Fischer: Hi 86.4 per cent. In Metzger 1977, this manuscript is identified as VL 43. (CLA II 275).

Erlangen, Universitätsbibliothek 10 (H 62).
   Fischer: Cf 89.3 per cent (ranging from 80 per cent in Matthew[11] to 95.7 per cent in Luke[32]).

Images: <http://bvbm1.bib-bvb.de/webclient/DeliveryManager?custom_att_2=simple_viewer&pid=5167279> (Vol. 1); <http://bvbm1.bib-bvb.de/webclient/DeliveryManager?custom_att_2=simple_viewer&pid=5098862> (Vol. 2).

Fulda, Hochschul- und Landesbibliothek, Bonifatianus 3.
Cadmug Gospels. Fischer: Hf 82.7 per cent (ranging from 76.6 per cent in Matthew[14] to 89.6 per cent in Mark[22]).
Images: <http://fuldig.hs-fulda.de/viewer/image/PPN325292043/1/>. (CLA VIII 1198).

Hereford, Cathedral Library, P.I.2.
Hereford Gospels. Fischer: Hh 87 per cent. (CLA II 157).

London, British Library, MS Add. 30845.
Missale Silense. Fischer: Wn 83.9 per cent.

London, British Library, MS Add. 40618.
Fischer: Ha 86.7 per cent (ranging from 77.7 per cent in John[44] to 92 per cent in Luke[31]).
Images: <www.bl.uk/manuscripts/Viewer.aspx?ref=add_ms_40618>. (CLA II 179).

Maaseik, Sint-Catharinakerk, s.n.
Maaseyck Gospels, Codex Eyckensis. Fischer: Gm 89.8 per cent (ranging from 84 per cent in Mark[23] to 96.3 per cent in Matthew[12]).
Images: Coppens et al. 1994 (facsimile), (CLA X 1558–9).

Oxford, Bodleian Library, Laud. lat. 102.
Fischer: Fg 89.6 per cent.
Images: <http://bodley30.bodley.ox.ac.uk:8180/luna/servlet/view/all/what/MS.+Laud+Lat.+102> (37 images).

Oxford, Bodleian Library, Rawlinson G.167.
Fischer: Ho 85.9 per cent. (CLA II 256).

Paris, Bibliothèque nationale de France, latin 13246.
Missale Bobiense, Bobbio Missal. Fischer: Gb 86.3 per cent. Cited in Vetus Latina as M-Bo.
Images: Legg 1917 (facsimile). (CLA V 654).

Paris, Bibliothèque nationale de France, lat. 14407.
Fischer: Pk 89.9 per cent (ranging from 78.9 per cent in Mark[24] to 94.4 per cent in Matthew[11]).
Images: <http://gallica.bnf.fr/ark:/12148/btv1b90807747>.

Vatican City, Biblioteca Apostolica Vaticana, Barberini lat. 570.
Barberini Gospels, Wigbald Gospels. Fischer: Ev 86.4 per cent (ranging from 75.6 per cent in Mark[24] to 92.8 per cent in Matthew[13]).
Images: <http://digi.vatlib.it/view/MSS_Barb.lat.570>. (CLA I 63).

Würzburg, Universitätsbibliothek, M.p.th.f. 61.
Fischer: Hw 84.5 per cent (ranging from 76.7 per cent in Matthew[12] to 92.4 per cent in Matthew[11]).
Images: <http://vb.uni-wuerzburg.de/ub/mpthf61/index.html>. (CLA IX 1415).

Bibliography

Abbreviations used in the Bibliography

CMCS	Cambrian (formerly Cambridge) Medieval Celtic Studies
CNRS	Centre national de la recherche scientifique
HTR	*Harvard Theological Review*
IEA	Institut des études augustiniennes
JTS	*Journal of Theological Studies*
NovT	*Novum Testamentum*
ns	new series
NTS	*New Testament Studies*
os	old series
PRIA	*Proceedings of the Royal Irish Academy*
REA	*Revue des études augustiniennes (et patristiques)*
RevBén	*Revue bénédictine*
RevBib	*Revue biblique*
RHT	*Revue d'histoire des textes*
RTAM	*Recherches de théologie ancienne et médiévale*
RTL	*Revue théologique de Louvain*
SISMEL	Società Internazionale per lo studio del Medioevo Latino
UP	University Press
VigC	*Vigiliae Christianae*
VL	Vetus Latina
ZNW	*Zeitschrift für die neutestamentliche Wissenschaft*
ZWT	*Zeitschrift für wissenschaftliche Theologie*

Aalders, G.J.M. (1932). *Tertullianus' Citaten uit de Evangelien en de oudlatijnsche Bijbelvertalingen*. Amsterdam: H.J. Paris.

Aalders, G.J.M. (1937). 'Tertullian's Quotations from St. Luke.' *Mnemosyne* 5: 241–82.

Abel, F. (1971). *L'Adjectif démonstratif dans la langue de la Bible latine*. Tübingen.

Abbott, T.K. (1884). *Evangeliorum versio antehieronymiana ex codice Usseriano (Dublinensi) adiecta collatione codicis Usseriani alterius*. Dublin: UP.

Ackroyd, P. and Evans, C.F., ed. (1970). *The Cambridge History of the Bible. I. From the Beginnings to Jerome*. Cambridge: UP.

Adams, James N. (2007). *The Regional Diversification of Latin 200BC–AD 600*. Cambridge: UP.

Adams, James N. (2013). *Social Variation and the Latin Language*. Cambridge: UP.

Adkin, Neil (2000). 'Biblia Pagana: Classical Echoes in the Vulgate.' *Augustinianum* 40: 77–87.

Aland, Kurt (1969). 'Bemerkungen zum Schluss des Markusevangeliums.' In *Neotestamentica et Semitica*, ed. E. Earle Ellis and Max Wilcox. Edinburgh: T&T Clark, 157–80.

Aland, Kurt, ed. (1972). *Die alten Übersetzungen des Neuen Testaments, die Kirchenväterzitate und Lektionare*. Berlin & New York: De Gruyter.

Albl, Martin C. (1999). *'And Scripture Cannot Be Broken.' The Form and Function of the Early Christian Testimonia Collections*. Leiden: Brill.

Alexander, J.J.G. (1978). *A Survey of Manuscripts Illustrated in the British Isles. Insular Manuscripts 6th to the 9th Century*. London: Harvey Miller.

Alexander, J.J.G. and Fox, Peter (1990). *The Book of Kells: Ms. 58 Trinity College Library, Dublin*. Facsimile edition. 2 vols. Lucerne: Faksimile Verlag.

Allgeier, A. (1948). 'Haec vetus et vulgata editio. Neue wort- und begriffsgeschichtliche Beiträge zur Bibel aus dem Tridentum.' *Biblica* 29: 353–90.

Alton, E.H., Meyer, P., and Simms, G.O. (1950). *Evangeliorum Quattuor Codex Cenannensis*. Facsimile edition. Bern: Urs Graf.

Amphoux, Christian-Bernard (1993). 'Les premières versions latines de Luc 5 et leur contribution à l'histoire du texte.' In Gryson 1993: 193–211.

Amphoux, Christian-Bernard (2013). 'Les lieux de rédaction des lettres de Paul d'après la tradition manuscrite.' *BABELAO* 2: 87–104.

Andorf, J. (1964). 'Der Codex Teplensis enthaltend «Di schrift dez newen gezeugz».' Unpublished dissertation. Freiburg.

Andrée, Alexander (2008). 'The Glossa ordinaria on the Gospel of John: A Preliminary Survey of the Manuscripts with a Presentation of the Text and its Sources.' *RevBén* 118: 109–34 & 289–333.

Andrée, Alexander (2011). 'Anselm of Laon Unveiled. The *Glosae super Iohannem* and the origins of the *Glossa ordinaria* on the Bible.' *Medieval Studies* 73: 217–60.

Andrist, Patrick (2007). 'Les *testimonia* de l'*Ad Quirinum* de Cyprien et leur influence sur la polémique antijudaïque postérieure.' In *Cristinesimi nell'Antichità*, ed. A. D'Anna and C. Zamagni. Hildesheim: Ohms, 175–98.

Armstrong, Jonathan J. (2008). 'Victorinus of Pettau as the Author of the Canon Muratori.' *VigC* 62: 1–34.

Auerbach, Erich (1965). *Literary Language and its Public in Late Latin Antiquity and the Middle Ages*. (Translated by Ralph Manheim from *Literatursprache und Publikum in der lateinischen Spätantike und im Mittelalter*, Bern: Franke 1958). London: Routledge & Kegan Paul.

Auwers, Jean-Marie (1996). 'Le texte latin des évangiles dans le codex de Bèze.' In Parker and Amphoux 1996: 183–216.

Auwers, Jean-Marie (2011). 'Chromace d'Aquilée et le texte biblique.' In *Chromatius of Aquileia and his Age*, ed. Pier Franco Beatrice and Alessio Persic. Turnhout: Brepols, 343–59.

Ayres, Larry M. (1994). 'The Italian Giant Bibles: aspects of their Touronian ancestry and early history.' In Gameson 1994: 125–54.

Ayuso Marazuela, Teófilo (1953). *La Vetus Latina Hispana, vol. 1: Prolegómenos: Introduccion General, Estudio y Análisis de las Fuentas*. Madrid: Instituto Francisco Suárez.

Ayuso Marazuela, Teófilo (1955–6). 'La Biblia visigótica de la Cava dei Tirreni.' *Estudios bíblicos* 14: 49–65, 137–90, 355–414; 15: 5–62.

Ayuso Marazuela, Teófilo (1960–1). 'La Biblia Visigótica de San Isidoro de León.' *Estudios bíblicos* 19: 5–24, 167–200, 271–309; 20: 5–43, 243–59, 359–406.

Ayuso Marazuela, Teófilo (1965). *La Biblia Visigótica de San Isidoro de León. Contribución al Estudio de la Vulgata en España.* Madrid: Instituto Francisco Suárez.

Backhouse, Janet (1994). *The Lindisfarne Gospels.* 2nd edn. London: Phaidon.

Bains, D. (1936). *A Supplement to Notae Latinae (Abbreviations in Latin MSS of 850–1050 AD).* Cambridge. Reprinted with Lindsay 1915 in 1963.

Bakker, Adophine H.A. (1933). *A Study of Codex Evang. Bobbiensis (k).* Amsterdam: Noord-Hollandsche Vitgeversmaatschappij.

Bardy, Gustave (1920). 'Le texte de l'épître aux Romains dans le commentaire d'Origène-Rufin.' *RevBib* 17: 229–41.

Bardy, Gustave (1948). *La question des langues dans l'église ancienne.* Paris: Beauchesne.

Bartoli Langeli, Attilio, et al., ed. (2001). *Il Vangelo dei principi. La riscoperta di un testo mitico tra Aquileia, Praga e Venezie.* Udine: Paolo Gaspari.

Baumstark, A. (1930). 'Die Evangelienzitate Novatians und das Diatessaron.' *Oriens Christianus* (third series) 5: 1–14.

Becker, Ulrich (1963). *Jesus und die Ehebrecherin. Untersuchungen zur Text- und Überlieferungsgeschichte von Joh. 7,53–8,11.* Berlin: Töpelmann.

Belsheim, J. (1878). *Codex Aureus siue quattuor euangelia ante Hieronymum latine translata.* Christiania: P.T. Malling.

Belsheim, J. (1879). *Die Apostelgeschichte und die Offenbarung Johannis in einer alten lateinischen Übersetzung aus dem «Gigas librorum» auf der königlichen Bibliothek zu Stockholm.* Christiania: P.T. Malling.

Belsheim, J. (1881). *Das Evangelium des Matthäus nach dem lateinischen Codex ff^1 Corbeiensis.* Christiania: P.T. Malling.

Belsheim, J. (1883). *Der Brief des Jakobus in der lateinischen Übersetzung aus der Zeit vor Hieronymus.* Christiania: P.T. Malling.

Belsheim, J. (1885). *Epistulae Paulinae ante Hieronymum latine translatae ex Codice Sangermanensi graeco-latino, olim Parisiensi, nunc Petropolitano.* Christiania: Cammermeyer.

Belsheim, J. (1887). *Codex f^2 Corbeiensis siue quattuor euangelia ante Hieronymum latine translata.* Christiania: Aschehoug.

Belsheim, J. (1892). *Evangelium secundum Matthaeum ante Hieronymum translatum e codice olim Claromontano nunc Vaticano.* Christiania: Dybwad.

Belsheim, J. (1893). *Acta apostolorum ante Hieronymum latine translata ex codice latino-graeco Laudiano Oxoniensi.* Christiania: Dybwad.

Belsheim, J. (1904). *Codex Veronensis Quattuor Euangelia ante Hieronymum Latine translata.* Prague: Grégr.

Benoît, André and Prigent, Pierre, ed. (1971). *La Bible et les Pères: Colloque de Strasbourg 1969.* Paris: Presses Universitaires de France.

Berger, Samuel (1889). *Le palimpseste de Fleury. Fragments du Nouveau Testament en latin.* Paris: Hachette.

Berger, Samuel (1893). *Histoire de la Vulgate pendant les premiers siècles du moyen âge*. Paris. Reprint (1976). Hildesheim: Olms; New York: Burt Franklin.

Berger, Samuel (1895). 'Un ancien texte latin des Actes des apôtres retrouvé dans un manuscrit provenant de Perpignan.' *Notices et extraits des manuscrits de la Bibliothèque Nationale et autres bibliothèques* 35.1: 188–208.

Berger, Samuel (1902). *Les préfaces jointes aux livres de la Bible dans les manuscrits de la Vulgate*. Paris: Imprimerie Nationale.

Bergren, T.A. (1991). *A Latin-Greek Index of the Vulgate New Testament Based on Alfred Schmoller's Handkonkordanz zum Griechischen Neuen Testament with an Index of Latin Equivalences Characteristic of 'African' and 'European' Old Latin Versions of the New Testament*. Atlanta: Scholars Press.

Berschin, Walter (2007). 'Die griechisch-lateinische Paulus-Handschrift der Reichenau "Codex Paulinus Augiensis".' *Zeitschrift für die Geschichte des Oberrheins* 155: 1–17.

Berti, G. (1954). 'Il più antico lezionario della Chiesa.' *Ephemerides liturgicae* 68: 147–54.

Best, Ernest and Wilson, R. McL., ed. (1979). *Text and Interpretation: Studies in the New Testament presented to Matthew Black*. Cambridge: UP.

Bévenot, Maurice (1957). 'An «Old Latin» Quotation (II. Tim. 3.2), and its Adventures in the Mss. of St. Cyprian's *De Unitate Ecclesiae* Chap. 16.' *Studia Patristica* 1. Berlin: Akademie Verlag, 249–52.

Bévenot, Maurice (1961). *The Tradition of Manuscripts. A Study in the Transmission of St Cyprian's Treatises*. Oxford: Clarendon.

Bianchini, Giuseppe Maria [Josephus Blanchinus] (1740). *Vindiciae Canonicarum Scripturarum. Vulgatae Latinae editionis I*. Rome: Hieronymus Mainardus.

Bianchini, Giuseppe Maria [Josephus Blanchinus] (1749). *Evangeliarium Quadruplex Latinae versionis antiquae seu veteris Italicae*. Rome: Antonius de Rubeis. Reprinted in PL 12 (1845).

Bibbia Amiatina (2003). *Bibbia Amiatina: Ms. Laurenziano Amiatino 1 Biblioteca Medicea Laurenziana di Firenze*. Florence: La Meta.

Biblia Augustiniana. ed. A.-M. La Bonnardière (1960–75). Paris: IEA.

Biblia Patristica. Index des Citations et Allusions Bibliques dans la Littérature Patristique, ed. J. Allenbach et al. (1975–2000). Paris: CNRS.

Bick, J. (1908). *Wiener Palimpseste, I. Teil: Cod. Palat. Vindobonensis 16, olim Bobbiensis*. Vienna: Akademie der Wissenschaften.

Bieler, L. (1947). 'Der Bibeltext des heiligen Patrick.' *Biblica* 28: 31–58, 236–63.

Bieler, L. (1964). 'The New Testament in the Celtic Church.' In *Studia Evangelica* 3, ed. F.L. Cross, Berlin: Akademie Verlag, 318–70.

Bieler, L. (1974). 'La transmission des Pères latins en Irlande et en Angleterre à l'époque préscolastique.' *Sacris erudiri* 22: 75–84.

Birch, Walter DeG. (1873). *The Latin Psalter in the University Library of Utrecht formerly Cotton MS Claudius C. VII*. Facsimile edition. London: Spencer, Sawyer, Bird.

Birdsall, J.N. (1970). 'The New Testament Text.' In Ackroyd and Evans 1970: 308–77.

Birdsall, J.N. (1986). 'The Geographical and Cultural Origin of the Codex Bezae Cantabrigiensis.' In *Studien zum Text und zur Ethik des Neuen Testaments*, ed. W. Schrage. Berlin & New York: De Gruyter, 102–14.

Bischoff, Bernard (1941). 'Zur Rekonstruktion des Sangallensis (Σ) und der Vorlage seiner Marginalien.' *Biblica* 22:147–58. Reprinted in Bischoff 1966:101–11.

Bischoff, Bernard (1946). 'Neue Materialien zum Bestand und zur Geschichte der altlateinischen Bibelübersetzungen.' In *Miscellanea Giovanni Mercati* Vol. 1, Vatican City, 407–36.

Bischoff, Bernard (1954). 'Wendepunkte in der Geschichte der lateinischen Exegese im Frühmittelalter.' *Sacris erudiri* 6: 189–281.

Bischoff, Bernard (1966). *Mittelalterliche Studien Band I*. Stuttgart: Hiersemann.

Bischoff, Bernard (1967). *Mittelalterliche Studien Band II*. Stuttgart: Hiersemann.

Bischoff, Bernard (1981). *Mittelalterliche Studien Band III*. Stuttgart: Hiersemann.

Bischoff, Bernard (1984). *Anecdota Novissima*. Stuttgart: Hiersemann.

Bischoff, Bernard (1990). *Latin Palaeography. Antiquity and the Middle Ages*. Translated by Dáibhí Ó Cróinín and David Ganz from *Paläographie des römischen Altertums und des abendländischen Mittelalters* (Berlin: Schmidt, 1979). Cambridge: UP.

Bischoff, Bernard (1994). *Manuscripts and Libraries in the Age of Charlemagne*. Translation by M. Gorman of selected papers. Cambridge: UP.

Bischoff, Bernard (1998). *Katalog der festländischen Handschriften des 9. Jahrhunderts I. Aachen-Lambach*. Wiesbaden: Harrassowitz.

Bischoff, Bernard (2004). *Katalog der festländischen Handschriften des 9. Jahrhunderts II. Laon-Paderborn*. Wiesbaden: Harrassowitz.

Bischoff, Bernard and Brown, V. (1985). 'Addenda to Codices Latini Antiquiores.' *Mediaeval Studies* 47: 317–64.

Bischoff, Bernard and Hoffman, J. (1952). *Libri Sancti Kyliani: Die Würzburger Schreibschule und die Dombibliothek im VIII. und IX. Jahrhundert*. Würzburg: Ferdinand Schöningh.

Bischoff, Bernard and Lapidge, M. (1994). *Biblical Commentaries from the Canterbury School of Theodore and Hadrian*. Cambridge: UP.

Bishop, Nancy (2004). 'The Barberini Gospels.' Unpublished PhD dissertation, University of Iowa.

Blass, F. (1896). 'Neue Texteszeugen für die Apostelgeschichte.' *Theologische Studien und Kritiken* 69: 436–71.

Bleskina, Olga N. (2012). 'Eighth-century Insular Gospels (NLR, Lat. F.v.I.8): Codicological and palaeographical aspects.' In *Western European Manuscripts and Early Printed Books in Russia*, ed. Leena Kahlas-Tarkka and Matti Kilpiö. Helsinki: Research Unit for Variation, Contacts and Change in English. http://www.helsinki.fi/varieng/series/volumes/09/bleskina/.

Blomkvist, Vemund (2012). *Euthalian Traditions. Text, Translation and Commentary*. Berlin & Boston: De Gruyter.

Bogaert, Pierre-Maurice (1982). 'Les particularités editoriales des Bibles comme exégèse implicite ou proposée. Les sommaires ou capitula donatistes.' In *Lectures bibliques. Colloque du 11 nov. 1980*. Brussels: Institutum Judaicum, 7–21.

Bogaert, Pierre-Maurice (1984). 'Épisode de la controverse sur le «Magnificat».' *RevBén* 94: 38–49. Posthumous publication of a 1906 article by De Bruyne.

Bogaert, Pierre-Maurice (1988). 'La Bible latine des origines au moyen âge. Aperçu historique, état des questions.' *RTL* 19:137–59, 276–314.

Bogaert, Pierre-Maurice (1998). 'La Bible d'Augustin. État des questions et application aux sermons Dolbeau.' In *Augustin Prédicateur (395–411)*, ed. Goulven Madec. Paris: IEA, 33–47.

Bogaert, Pierre-Maurice (1999). 'Ordres anciens des évangiles et tétraévangile en un seul codex.' *RTL* 30: 297–314.

Bogaert, Pierre-Maurice (2001). 'Les Quatre Vivants, l'Évangile et les évangiles.' *RTL* 32: 457–78.

Bogaert, Pierre-Maurice (2003). 'Aux origines de la fixation du Canon: Scriptoria, listes et titres. Le Vaticanus et la Stichométrie de Mommsen.' In *The Biblical Canons*, ed. J.-M. Auwers and H.J. de Jonge. Leuven, Peeters, 153–76.

Bogaert, Pierre-Maurice (2006). 'Les bibles d'Augustin.' *RTL* 37: 513–31.

Bogaert, Pierre-Maurice (2012). 'The Latin Bible, c. 600 to c. 900.' In Marsden and Matter 2012: 69–92.

Bogaert, Pierre-Maurice (2013). 'The Latin Bible.' In Carleton Paget and Schaper 2013: 505–26.

Bogaert, Pierre-Maurice (2014a). 'Les bibles monumentales au XIe siècle.' In *L'exégèse monastique au Moyen Âge*, ed. G. Dahan and A. Noblesse-Rocher, Paris: IEA, 27–55.

Bogaert, Pierre-Maurice (2014b). 'Le texte de *l'Apocalypse* chez les Pères latins.' In *Les visions de l'Apocalypse*, ed. François Vinel. Turnhout: Brepols, 13–34.

Boismard, Marie-Émile (1950). 'Critique textuelle et citations patristiques.' *RevBib* 57: 388–408.

Boismard, Marie-Émile (1987). 'Critique textuelle et problèmes d'histoire des origines chrétiennes.' In Gryson and Bogaert 1987: 123–36.

Boismard, Marie-Émile (1993). 'Le codex Palatinus (e) des Évangiles.' In Gryson 1993: 228–41.

Boismard, Marie-Émile and Lamouille, A. (1984). *Le texte occidental des Actes des apôtres. Reconstitution et réhabilitation*. Paris: Recherche sur les Civilisations.

Bolgiani, Franco (1962). *Vittore di Capua e il 'Diatessaron'*. Turin: Accademia delle scienze.

Bolz, Bogdan (1971). *Najdawniejszy kalendarz gnieźnieński według kodeksu MS 1*. Poznań: Państwowe Wydawnictwo Naukowe.

Bonnardière: see La Bonnardière.

Bonnassieux, F.-J. (1906). *Les Évangiles synoptiques de saint Hilaire de Poitiers: Étude et texte*. Lyon.

Borse, Udo (1966). 'Des Kolosserbrieftext des Pelagius.' Doctoral Dissertation. Bonn: Rheinische Friedrich-Wilhelms-Universität.

Botte, B. (1949). 'Itala.' In *Dictionnaire de la Bible, supplément IV*. Paris, cols. 777–82.

Bouton-Touboulic, Anne-Isabelle (2006). 'Autorité et Tradition. La traduction latine de la Bible selon Saint Jérôme et Saint Augustin.' *Augustinianum* 45.1: 185–229.

Bover, J.M. (1927). 'Un fragmento de la Vetus Latina (Act. 1,15–26) en un Epistolario del Siglo XIII.' *Estudios Eclesiásticos* 6: 331–2.

Boyle, Leonard E. (1984). *Medieval Latin Palaeography: A Bibliographical Introduction*. Toronto: UP.

Boynton, Susan and Diane J. Reilly, ed. (2011). *The Practice of the Bible in the Middle Ages: Production, Reception, and Performance in Western Christianity*. Columbia: UP.

Braun, René (1985). 'L'influence de la Bible sur la langue latine.' In Fontaine and Pietri 1985: 129–42.

Braun, René (1992). *Approches de Tertullien*. Paris; IEA.

Braun, René, Fredouille, J.-C., Chapot, F., et al. (1999). *Chronica Tertullianea et Cyprianea 1975–1994*. Turnhout: Brepols.

Brearley, D. (1987). 'The *Expositio Iohannis* in Angers BM 275. A commentary on the Gospel of St John showing Irish influence.' *Recherches augustiniennes* 22: 151–221.

Breay, Claire and Meehan, Bernard, ed. (2015). *The St Cuthbert Gospel*. London: British Library.

Bredehorn, K. (1999). 'Aus fuldischen Handschriften: Codex Waldeccensis. Fragmente einer griechisch-lateinischen Bibelhandschrift.' *Archiv für mittelrheinische Kirchengeschichte* 51: 455–514.

Breen, Aidan (1996). 'The Biblical text and sources of the Würzburg Pauline glosses (Romans 1-6).' In *Irland und Europa im früheren Mittelalter*, ed. Próinséas Ní Chatháin and Michael Richter, Stuttgart: Klett-Cotta, 9–16.

Brown, Michelle P. (2002). *Das Buch von Lindisfarne: The Lindisfarne Gospels*. Facsimile edition. Two vols. Lucerne: Faksimile-Verlag.

Brown, Michelle P. (2003). *The Lindisfarne Gospels. Society, Spirituality and the Scribe*. London: British Library.

Brown, Michelle P. (2006). *In The Beginning: Bibles Before the Year 1000*. Washington, DC: Smithsonian Books.

Brown, Michelle P. (2007). 'The Barberini Gospels. Context and Intertextual relationships.' In *Text, Image, Interpretation*, ed. A.J. Minnis and J. Roberts. Turnhout: Brepols, 89–116.

Brown, Michelle P. (2011). *The Lindisfarne Gospels and the Early Medieval World*. London: British Library.

Brown, Peter (1980). *The Book of Kells*. London: Thames and Hudson.

Brown, Peter (2003). *The Rise of Western Christendom: Triumph and Diversity, AD 200–1000*. 2nd edn. Oxford: Blackwell.

Brown, T.J. (1969). *The Stonyhurst Gospel of Saint John*. Facsimile edition. Oxford: UP (Roxburghe Club).

Brown, T.J. and Verey, C.D. (1972). 'Northumbria and The Book of Kells.' *Anglo-Saxon England* 1: 219–46.

Bruce, F.F. (1979). 'The Gospel Text of Marius Victorinus.' In Best and Wilson 1979: 69–78.

Bruce-Mitford, R. (1969). 'The Art of the Codex Amiatinus.' *Journal of the Archaeological Assocation* (third series) 32: 1–25.

Bruce-Mitford, R. (1989). 'The Durham-Echternach Calligrapher'. In *St Cuthbert, His Cult and His Community to AD1200*, ed. G. Bonner, D. Rollason, and C. Stancliffe. Woodbridge, 175–88.

Bruckner, Albert (1972). *Die Bibel von Moutier-Grandval. Der Codex und die Schrift*. Bern: Schweizer Landesbibliothek.

Bruyne: see De Bruyne.

Buchanan, E.S. (1907). *The Four Gospels from the Codex Corbeiensis . . . together with . . . the Fleury Palimpsest*. Oxford: Clarendon.

Buchanan, E.S. (1911a). *The Four Gospels from the Codex Veronensis b*. Oxford: Clarendon.

Buchanan, E.S. (1911b). 'An Old-Latin Text of the Catholic Epistles.' *JTS* os 12: 497–534.

Buchanan, E.S. (1912). *The Epistles and Apocalypse from the Codex Harleianus.* London: Heath Cranton & Ouseley.

Buchanan, E.S. (1914a). *The Epistles of St Paul from the Codex Laudianus.* London: Heath Cranton & Ouseley.

Buchanan, E.S. (1914b). *The Four Gospels from the Irish Codex Harleianus.* London: Heath Cranton & Ouseley.

Buchanan, E.S. (1916). *The Catholic Epistles and Apocalypse from the Codex Laudianus.* London: Heath Cranton & Ouseley.

Bulletin de la Bible latine. (1964–), ed. P.-M. Bogaert. In *RevBén.* Denée: Abbaye de Maredsous.

Bullough, D.A. (2004). *Alcuin. Achievement and Reputation.* Leiden: Brill.

Buonaiuti, E. (1916). 'Le citazioni bibliche in Ottato di Milevi.' *Rivista di Scienza delle Religioni* 1: 145–6.

Burkitt, F.C. (1896). *The Old Latin and the Itala.* Cambridge: UP.

Burkitt, F.C. (1900). 'The Vulgate Gospels and the Codex Brixianus.' *JTS* os 1: 129–34.

Burkitt, F.C. (1908). '"Chief Priests" in the Latin Gospels.' *JTS* os 9: 290–7.

Burkitt, F.C. (1910a). 'Saint Augustine's Bible and the Itala.' *JTS* os 11: 258–68, 447–58.

Burkitt, F.C. (1910b). 'A Gothic-Latin fragment from Antinoë.' *JTS* os 11: 611–13.

Burkitt, F.C. (1920). 'Itala Problems'. In *Miscellanea Amelli.* Monte Cassino & Rome: Typographia Pontificia, 25–41.

Burton, Philip H. (1996). 'Fragmentum Vindobonense 563: Another Latin-Gothic Bilingual?' *JTS* ns 47: 141–56.

Burton, Philip H. (2000). *The Old Latin Gospels. A Study of their Texts and Language.* Oxford: UP.

Burton, Philip H. (2002). 'Assessing Latin-Gothic Interaction.' In *Bilingualism in Ancient Society*, ed. J.N. Adams, M. Janse, et al., Oxford: UP, 393–418.

Burton, Philip H. (2007). *Language in the* Confessions *of Augustine.* Oxford: UP.

Burton, Philip H. (2008). 'On Revisiting the Christian Latin Sondersprache Hypothesis'. In Houghton and Parker 2008: 149–71.

Burton, Philip H. (2011). 'Christian Latin.' In Clackson 2011: 485–501.

Burton, Philip H. (2012). 'The Latin Version of the New Testament.' In Ehrman and Holmes 2012: 167–200.

Burton, Philip H., Houghton, H.A.G., MacLachlan, R.F., and Parker, D.C. (2011–). *Evangelium secundum Iohannem.* VL 19. Freiburg: Herder.

Bussières, Marie-Pierre (2011). 'Ambrosiaster's Method of Interpretation in the Questions on the Old and New Testament.' In Lössl and Watt 2011: 49–66.

Butzmann, H. (1964). *Die Weissenburger Handschriften.* Frankfurt am Main: Klostermann.

Cahill, Michael (2002). 'The Würzburg Matthew: status quaestionis.' *Peritia* 16: 1–25.

Caillet, J.-P. and Laffitte, M.-P., ed. (2009). *Les manuscrits carolingiens.* Brepols: Turnhout.

Cain, Andrew (2009). *The Letters of Jerome: Asceticism, Biblical Exegesis and the Construction of Christian Authority in Late Antiquity.* Oxford: UP.

Cain, Andrew (2011). 'Jerome's Pauline Commentaries between East and West: Tradition and Innovation in the Commentary on Galatians.' In Lössl and Watt 2011: 91–110.

Capelle, Bernard [Paul] (1910). 'Les homélies «De lectionibus evangeliorum» de Maximin l'arien.' *RevBén* 40: 49–86.

Capelle, Paul (1913). *Le texte du psautier latin en Afrique.* Rome: Pustet.

Capelli, A. (2011). *Dizionario di Abbreviature Latine ed Italiane.* 7th edn. Milan: Hoepli.

Caragliano, Tindaro (1946). 'Restitutio critica textus latini evangelii secundum Iohannem ex scriptis S. Ambrosii.' *Biblica* 27: 30–64, 210–40.

Cardoliani, A. (1950). 'Le texte de la Bible en Irlande du Ve au IXe siècle.' *RevBib* 57: 3–39.

Carleton Paget, James and Schaper, Joachim (2013). *The New Cambridge History of the Bible. I. From the Beginnings to 600.* Cambridge: UP.

Carmassi, P. (2008). 'Das Lektionar Cod. Guelf. 76 Weiss. Beispiele liturgischer Verwendung der heiligen Schrift im frühmittelalterlichen Gallien'. In P. Carmassi, ed., *Präsenz und Verwendung der Heiligen Schrift im christlichen Frühmittelalter.* Wiesbaden: Harrassowitz, 251–98.

Cavallera, Ferdinand (1920). 'Saint Jérôme et la Vulgate des Actes, des Épîtres et de l'Apocalypse.' *Bulletin de littérature ecclésiastique* VI 11: 269–92.

Ceresa-Gastaldo, Aldo (1975). *Il latino delle antiche versioni bibliche.* Rome: Studium.

Ceriani, A.M. (1866). *Monumenta sacra et profana e codicibus praesertim Bibliotecae Ambrosianae* 1.2. Milan: Bibliotheca Ambrosiana.

Chadwick, H. (1959). 'Rufinus and the Tura-Papyrus.' *JTS* ns 10: 10–42.

Chapman, H.J. (1908). *Notes on the Early History of the Vulgate Gospels.* Oxford: Clarendon.

Chapman, H.J. (1924). 'Did the Translator of St. Irenaeus use a Latin New Testament?' *RevBén* 36: 34–57.

Chapman, H.J. (1927). 'The Codex Amiatinus and Cassiodorus.' *RevBén* 39: 12–32.

Chapman, H.J. (1933). 'St Jerome and the Vulgate New Testament.' *JTS* 24: 33–51, 113–25, 283–99.

Charlet, Jean-Louis (1983). 'Prudence et la Bible.' *Recherches augustiniennes* 18: 3–149.

Charlier, Célestin (1945). 'Les manuscrits personnels de Florus de Lyon et son activité littéraire.' In *Mélanges Emmanuel Podechard*, Lyon: Faculté de théologie, 71–84. Reprinted in *RevBén* 119.2 (2009): 252–67.

Chase, F.H. (1895). *The Syro-Latin Text of the Gospels.* London: Macmillan.

Chazelle, Celia and Van Name Edwards, Burton, ed. (2003). *The Study of the Bible in the Carolingian Era.* Turnhout: Brepols.

Cherubini, Paolo, ed. (2005). *Forme e modelli della tradizione manoscritta della Bibbia.* Vatican City: Scuola Vaticana.

Cherubini, Paolo (2012). 'Le glosse latine antiche alla Bibbia di Cava.' In *Sit liber gratus quem servulus est operatus*, ed. P. Cherubini and G. Nicolaj. Vatican City: Scuola Vaticana, 133–49.

Chevalier-Royet, Caroline (2006). 'Les révisions bibliques carolingiennes.' *Temas Medievales* 14: 7–30.

Chevalier-Royet, Caroline (2007). 'Les révisions bibliques de Théodulf d'Orléans et la question de leur utilisation par l'exégèse carolingienne.' In *Études d'exégèse caro-lingienne*, ed. S. Shimahara. Turnhout: Brepols, 237–56.

Cimosa, Mario (2008). *Guida allo studio della Bibblia Latina, dalla Vetus Latina, alla Vulgata, alla Nova Vulgata* (with Carlo Buzzetti). Rome: Augustinianum.

Cipolla, C. (1913). *Il codice evangelico k della Biblioteca Universitaria Nazionale di Torino*. Turin: Molfese.

CLA. See Lowe (1934–71).

Clackson, J.P.T., ed. (2011). *A Companion to the Latin Language*. Chichester: Wiley-Blackwell.

CLLA. See Gamber (1968, 1988).

Coleman, A.M. (1927). *The Biblical Text of Lucifer of Cagliari (Acts)*. Welwyn: Lawrence.

Coleman, A.M. (1946). *The Biblical Text of Lucifer of Cagliari (Timothy I and II, and Titus)*. Oxford: A.T. Broome & Son.

Coleman, A.M. (1947). *The Biblical Text of Lucifer of Cagliari (Romans, I and II Corinthians, Galatians, Ephesians, Philippians, Colossians, I and II Thessalonians, and the Epistle to the Hebrews)*. Oxford: A.T. Broome & Son.

Coleman, Robert G.G. (1987). 'Vulgar Latin and the diversity of Christian Latin.' In *Latin Vulgaire—Latin Tardif 1*, ed. J. Herman, Tübingen: Max Niemeyer, 37–52.

Colker, M. (1991). *Trinity College Library Dublin. Descriptive Catalogue of the Medieval and Renaissance Latin Manuscripts 1*. Aldershot: Scolar Press.

Collins, A. (2007). *Teacher in Faith and Virtue. Lanfranc of Bec's Commentary on St Paul*. Leiden: Brill.

Colunga, Alberto and Turrado, Lorenzo, ed. (1946). *Biblia Sacra Iuxta Vulgatam Clementinam*. Madrid: Editorial Católica.

Contessa, Andreina (2003). 'Le Bibbie dell'Abata Oliba di Ripoll.' *Estudios Biblicos* 61: 27–64.

Contessa, Andreina (2008). 'Nouvelles observations sur la Bible de Roda.' *Cahiers de civilisation médiévale* 51: 329–41.

Contreni, John J. (1983). 'Carolingian Biblical Studies.' In *Carolingian Essays*, ed. U.-R. Blumenthal, Washington: Catholic University of America, 71–98.

Contreni, John J. (1992). *Carolingian Learning, Masters and Manuscripts*. Aldershot: Ashgate.

Contreni, John J. (1996). 'Carolingian Biblical Culture.' In *Johannes Scottus Eriugena. The Bible and Hermeneutics*, ed. G. van Riel, C. Steel, and J. McEvoy. Leuven: UP, 1–23.

Contreni, John J. (2012). 'The patristic legacy to c. 1000.' In Marsden and Matter 2012: 505–35.

Contreni, John J. and Ó Néill, P.P., ed. (1997). *Glossae divinae historiae. The Biblical Glosses of John Scottus Eriugena*. Florence: SISMEL.

Cooper, Stephen (2005). *Marius Victorinus' Commentary on Galatians*. Oxford: UP.

Cooper, Stephen (2011). 'Philosophical Exegesis in Marius Victorinus' Commentaries on Paul.' In Lössl and Watt 2011: 67–89.

Cooper, Stephen and Hunter, David G. (2010). 'Ambrosiaster *redactor sui*: The Commentaries on the Pauline Epistles (excluding Romans).' *REA* 56: 69–91.

Coppens, C., Derolez, Albert, Heymans, H., et al. (1994). *Codex Eyckensis. An Insular Gospel book from the Abbey of Aldeneik*. Facsimile edition. Maaseik: Town Council.

Cordolliani, A. (1950). 'Le texte de la Bible en Irlande du Ve au IXe siècle.' *RevBib* 57: 5–39.

Corsano, K. (1987). 'The First Quire of the Codex Amiatinus and the Institutiones of Cassiodorus,' *Scriptorium* 41: 3–34.

Corssen, P. (1887–9). *Epistularum Paulinarum codices graeci et latine scriptos Augiensem Boernerianum Claromontanum.* Two vols. Kiel.

Corssen, P. (1892). *Der cyprianische Text der Acta apostolorum.* Berlin.

Corssen, P. (1899). 'Bericht über die lateinischen Bibelübersetzungen.' In *Jahresberichte über die Fortschritte der klassischen Altertumswissenschaft* 101, ed. Conrad Bursian. Leipzig: Reisland, 1–83.

Courtenay, William J. (2012). 'The Bible in medieval universities.' In Marsden and Matter 2012: 555–78.

Cozza, J. (1867). *Sacrorum Bibliorum uetustissima fragmenta graeca et latina ex palimpsestis codicibus Bibliothecae Cryptoferratensis eruta, Pars 2.* Rome: Spithoever.

Cremascoli, G. and Leonardi, Claudio, ed. (1996). *La Bibbia nel Medioevo.* Bologna: Dehoniane.

Dahan, Gilbert (1997). 'La critique textuelle dans les correctoires de la Bible du XIIIe siècle.' In *Langages et philosophie,* ed. A. de Libera, A. Elamrani-Jamal, and A. Galonnier. Paris: Vrin, 365–92.

Dahan, Gilbert (1999). *L'exégèse chrétienne de la Bible en occident médiéval, XIIIe-XIVe siècle.* Paris: Cerf.

Dahan, Gilbert (2004). 'Sorbonne II. Un correctoire biblique de la seconde moitié du XIIIe siècle'. In *La Bibbia del XIII secolo,* ed. G. Cremascoli and F. Santi. Florence: SISMEL, 113–53.

Dahan, Gilbert (2010). 'Les commentaires bibliques d'Étienne Langton: exégèse et herméneutique.' In *Étienne Langton prédicateur, bibliste, théologie,* ed. L.-J. Bataillon et al. Turnhout: Brepols, 201–39.

Dahl, Nils Alstrup (1978). 'The Origin of the Earliest Prologues to the Pauline Letters.' *Semeia* 12: 233–77.

Dahl, Nils Alstrup (1979). '0230 (=PSI 1306) and the Fourth-Century Greek-Latin Edition of the Letters of Paul.' In Best and Wilson 1979: 79–98.

Dahlhaus-Berg, A. (1975). *Nova antiquitas et antiqua novitas. Typologische Exegese und isidorianisches Geschichtsbild bei Theodulf von Orleans.* Cologne: Böhlau.

Daniélou, Jean (1970). 'La littérature latine avant Tertullien.' *Revue des études latines* 48: 357–75.

Davies, Luned Mair (1996). 'The Biblical text of the Collectio Canonum Hibernensis.' In *Irland und Europa im früheren Mittelalter,* ed. Próinséas Ní Chatháin and Michael Richter. Stuttgart: Klett-Cotta, 17–41.

De Bruyn, Theodore S. (1992). 'Constantius the *Tractator*: Author of an Anonymous Commentary on the Pauline Epistles?' *JTS* ns 43: 38–54.

De Bruyn, Theodore S. (1993). *Pelagius' Commentary on St Paul's Epistle to the Romans.* Oxford: Clarendon.

De Bruyne, Donatien (1906). 'Épisode de la controverse sur le «Magnificat».' See Bogaert 1984.

De Bruyne, Donatien (1907). 'Prologues bibliques d'origine marcionite.' *RevBén* 24: 1–16.

De Bruyne, Donatien (1908). 'L'évangéliaire du VIIIe siècle conservé à Maaseyck.' *Bulletin de la Société d'Art et d'Histoire du Diocèse de Liège* 17: 385–92.

De Bruyne, Donatien (1910). 'Quelques documents nouveaux pour l'histoire du texte africain des Évangiles.' *RevBén* 27: 273–324, 433–46.

De Bruyne, Donatien (1911). 'Notes sur le manuscrit 6224 de Munich (Ms q des évangiles).' *RevBén* 28:75–80.

De Bruyne, Donatien (1912). 'Une poésie inconnue d'Aileran le Sage.' *RevBén* 29: 339–40.

De Bruyne, Donatien (1913). 'L'Itala de saint Augustin'. *RevBén* 30: 294–314.

De Bruyne, Donatien (1914). *Sommaires, divisions et rubriques de la Bible latine.* Namur: Godenne. [Published anonymously.] See also De Bruyne 2014.

De Bruyne, Donatien (1915). 'Étude sur les origines de notre texte latin de Saint Paul.' *RevBib* ns 12: 358–92.

De Bruyne, Donatien (1920a). *Préfaces de la Bible latine.* Namur: Godenne. [Published anonymously.] See also De Bruyne 2015.

De Bruyne, Donatien (1920b). 'Saint Jérôme et la Vulgate des Actes, des Épîtres et de l'Apocalypse.' *Bulletin de littérature ecclésiastique* 21: 269–92.

De Bruyne, Donatien (1921). *Les fragments de Freising (Épîtres de S. Paul et Épîtres catholiques).* Rome: Biblioteca Vaticana.

De Bruyne, Donatien (1923). 'Deux feuillets d'un texte préhiéronymien des Évangiles.' *RevBén* 35: 62–80.

De Bruyne, Donatien (1927a). 'Encore l'Itala de saint Augustin.' *Revue d'histoire ecclésiastique* 23: 779–85.

De Bruyne, Donatien (1927b). 'Sommaires antipélagiens inédits des lettres de saint Paul.' *RevBén* 39: 45–55.

De Bruyne, Donatien (1927c). 'Cassiodore et l'Amiatinus.' *RevBén* 39: 261–6.

De Bruyne, Donatien (1931a). 'Saint Augustin Reviseur de la Bible.' In *Miscellanea Agostiniana* (vol. 2), ed. A. Casamassa. Rome: Tipographia Polyglotta Vaticana, 521–606.

De Bruyne, Donatien (1931b). 'Étude sur le Liber de divinis scripturis.' *RevBén* 43: 124–41.

De Bruyne, Donatien (1933). 'Étude sur le Liber de divinis scripturis III. Un abrégé du VIIe siècle.' *RevBén* 45: 119–41.

De Bruyne, Donatien (2014). *Summaries, Divisions and Rubrics of the Latin Bible.* With introductions by Pierre-Maurice Bogaert and Thomas O'Loughlin. Turnhout: Brepols. [Reprint of De Bruyne 1914.]

De Bruyne, Donatien (2015). *Prefaces to the Latin Bible.* With introductions by Pierre-Maurice Bogaert and Thomas O'Loughlin. Turnhout: Brepols. [Reprint of De Bruyne 1920a.]

Declercq, Georges, ed. (2007). *Early Medieval Palimpsests.* Turnhout: Brepols.

de Hamel, Christopher F.R. (1984). *Glossed Books of the Bible and the Origins of the Paris Booktrade.* Woodbridge: Brewer.

de Hamel, Christopher F.R. (2001). *The Book. A History of the Bible.* London: Phaidon.

Dekkers, Eligius and Gaar, Aemilius (1995). *Clavis Patrum Latinorum. Editio tertia aucta et emendata.* Steenbrugge: Brepols.

Delcor, M. (1974). 'Le scriptorium de Ripoll et son rayonnement culturel. État de la question.' *Les cahiers de Saint-Michel de Cuxa* 5: 45–64.

Deproost, Paul-Augustin and Haelewyck, Jean-Claude (1993). 'Le texte biblique des Actes et l'authenticité des sommaires en prose dans l'*Historia apostolica* d'Arator.' In Gryson 1993: 583–604.

d'Esneval, A. (1978). 'La division de la Vulgate latine en chapitres dans l'édition parisienne du XIIIe siècle.' *Revue des sciences philosophiques et théologiques* 62: 559–68.

Despineux, M. (1988). 'Une version latine palimpseste du Ve siècle de l'Évangile de Nicodème (Vienne, ÖNB Ms 563).' *Scriptorium* 42: 176–83.

Devich, G. (1893). *L'Evangeliario Spalatense dell'Archivio Capitolare di Spalato.* Split: Zannoni.

Díaz y Díaz, M.C. (1988). 'Las glosas de un manuscrito litúrgico de Silos (Londres Brit. Libr. add. 30851).' In *Scire litteras. Forschungen zum mittelalterlichen Geistesleben*, ed. S. Krämer and M. Bernhard. Munich: Bayerische Akademie, 111–26.

Diehl, E. (1921). 'Zur Textgeschichte des lateinischen Paulus. I: Die direkte Überlieferung.' *ZNW* 20: 97–132.

Dobrovský, Josef (1778). *Fragmentum Pragense Evangelii S. Marci vulgo autographi.* Prague. Reprinted Prague: Nakladatelství Československé akademie věd 1953.

Dodd, Steven (1999). *Codex Biblicus Legionensis. Twenty Studies.* Translation of González 1999. León: Lancia.

Doignon, Jean (1975). 'Citations singulières et leçons rares du texte latin de l'Évangile de Matthieu dans l'«In Matthaeum» d'Hilaire de Poitiers.' *Bulletin de littérature ecclésiastique.* Toulouse: Institut Catholique, 187–96.

Doignon, Jean (1977). 'Une addition éphémère au texte de l'Oraison dominicale chez plusieurs Pères latins.' *Bulletin de littérature ecclésiastique.* Toulouse: Institut Catholique, 161–80.

Doignon, Jean (1978). 'Les variations des citations de l'Épître aux Romains dans l'œuvre d'Hilaire de Poitiers.' *RevBén* 88: 189–204.

Doignon, Jean (1979a). 'Le libellé singulier de II Corinthiens 3. 18 chez Hilaire de Poitiers. Essai d'explication.' *NTS* 26: 118–26.

Doignon, Jean (1979b). 'Les implications théologiques d'une variante du texte latin de 1 Corinthiens 15,25 chez Hilaire de Poitiers.' *Augustinianum* 19: 245–58.

Doignon, Jean (1980). 'Versets additionnels du Nouveau Testament perçus ou reçus par Hilaire de Poitiers.' *Vetera Christianorum* 17: 29–47.

Doignon, Jean (1989). 'Comment Hilaire de Poitiers a-t-il lu et compris le verset de Paul, Philippiens 3, 21?' *VigC* 43: 127–37.

Doignon, Jean (1991). 'Hilaire de Poitiers témoin latin le plus ancien d'un texte rare du logion *Matthieu* 10,38.' *RevBén* 101: 28–31.

Doignon, Jean (1993). 'Origine et essor d'une variante de 1 Th 5, 21 dans les citations de Jérôme, Augustin et Rufin.' In Gryson 1993: 306–15.

Doignon, Jean (1994). 'La chair du Christ comme dépouille triomphale. Une lecture de Col. 2,15 par Hilaire de Poitiers.' *Revue des sciences religieuses* 68: 447–52.

Dold, Alban (1923). *Konstanzer altlateinische Propheten- und Evangelienbruchstücke mit Glossen.* Beuron: Kunstverlag, 194–224.

Dold, Alban (1933). 'Funde und Fragmente.' *Zentralblatt für Bibliothekswesen* 50: 709–17.

Dold, Alban (1936). *Das älteste Liturgiebuch der lateinischen Kirche. Ein altgallikanisches Lektionar des 5./6. Jhs aus dem Wolfenbütteler Palimpsest-Codex Weissenburgensis 76.* Beuron: Kunstverlag.

Dold, Alban (1941). 'Neue Teile der ältesten Vulgata-Evangelienhandschrift aus dem 5. Jahrhundert.' *Biblica* 22: 105–46.

Dold, Alban (1944). *Die im Codex Vat. Reg. lat. 9 vorgeheftete Liste paulinischer Lesungen für die Meßfeier*. Beuron: Kunstverlag.

Dold, Alban (1950). 'Die Provenienz der altlateinischen Römerbrieftexte in den gothisch-lateinischen Fragmenten des Codex Carolinus von Wolfenbüttel.' In *Aus der Welt des Buches*, ed. Georg Leyh. Leipzig: Harrassowitz, 13–29.

Dold, Alban (1952). *Das Sakramentar im Schabcodex M 12 sup. der Biblioteca Ambrosiana*. Beuron: Kunstverlag.

Donaldson, Amy M. (2009). 'Explicit References to New Testament Variant Readings Among Greek and Latin Church Fathers'. PhD thesis. University of Notre Dame, Indiana.

Donaldson, Amy M. (2013). 'Explicit References to New Testament Textual Variants by the Church Fathers: Their Value and Limitations'. In Mellerin and Houghton 2013: 87–98.

Dorfbauer, Lukas J. (2013a). 'Der Evangelienkommentar des Bischofs Fortunatian von Aquileia (Mitte 4. Jh.).' *Wiener Studien* 126: 177–98.

Dorfbauer, Lukas J. (2013b). 'Fortunatian von Aquileia, Origenes und die Datierung des Physiologus.' *REA* 59: 219–45.

Dorfbauer, Lukas J. (2014a). 'Neues zu den Expositiunculae in Evangelium Iohannis evangelistae Matthaei et Lucae (CPL 240) und ihrem vermeintlichen Autor 'Arnobius Iunior'.' *RevBén* 124.1: 65–102.

Dorfbauer, Lukas J. (2014b). 'Neue Zeugnisse für die Überlieferung und Rezeption des Evangelienkommentars des Bischofs Fortunatian von Aquileia.' In *Edition und Erforschung lateinischer patristicher Texte*, ed. V. Zimmerl-Panagl, L.J. Dorfbauer, and C. Weidmann, Berlin: De Gruyter, 17–40.

Dorfbauer, Lukas J. (2015). 'Fortunatian von Aquileia und der Matthäus-Kommentar des «Frigulus».' *Mittellateinisches Jahrbuch* 50.1: 59–90.

Doyle, Peter J. (1967). 'A Study of the Text of St. Matthew's Gospel in the Book of Mulling and of the Palaeography of the Whole Manuscript.' PhD Dissertation, National University of Ireland.

Doyle, Peter J. (1972). 'The Text of Luke's Gospel in the Book of Mulling.' *PRIA* 73C6: 177–200.

Duft, Johannes (1990). 'Die griechischen Handschriften der Stiftsbibliothek St. Gallen'. In *Die Abtei St. Gallen Band I*, ed. P. Ochsenbein and E. Ziegler, Sigmaringen: Thorbecke.

Duft, Johannes et al. (1971). *Die Bibel von Moutier-Grandval, British Museum Add. MS. 10546*. Facsimile edition. Bern: Verein Schweizerischer Lithographiebesitzer.

Dulaey, Martine (1991). 'Jérôme "editeur" du *Commentaire sur l'Apocalypse* de Victorina de Poetovio.' *REA* 37: 199–236.

Dulaey, Martine (1993). *Victorin de Poetovio, premier exégète latin*. Paris: IEA.

Dunphy, Walter (2009). 'Rufinus the Syrian: Myth and Reality.' *Augustiniana* 59.1: 79–157.

Dunphy, Walter (2012). 'Ps-Rufinus (the "Syrian") and the Vulgate. Evidence wanting!' *Augustinianum* 52: 219–56.

Dunphy, Walter (2013). 'Glosses on Glosses: On the Budapest Anonymous and Pseudo-Rufinus. A Study on Anonymous Writings in Pelagian Circles (Part 1).' *Augustinian Studies* 44.2: 227–47.

Dunphy, Walter (2014). 'Glosses on Glosses: On the Budapest Anonymous and Pseudo-Rufinus. A Study on Anonymous Writings in Pelagian Circles (Part 2).' *Augustinian Studies* 45.1: 49–68.

Dunphy, Walter (2015). 'Glosses on Glosses: On the Budapest Anonymous and Pseudo-Rufinus. A Study on Anonymous Writings in Pelagian Circles (Part 3).' *Augustinian Studies* 46.1 (2015) 43–70.

Dyer, Joseph (2012). 'The Bible in the Medieval Liturgy c. 600–1300.' In Marsden and Matter 2012: 659–79.

ECM (2013). *Novum Testamentum Graecum. Editio Critica Maior. ed. Institut für Neutestamentliche Textforschung. IV. Die Katholischen Briefe/Catholic Letters.* 2nd edn. Stuttgart: Deutsche Bibelgesellschaft.

Ehrman, Bart D. and Holmes, M.W., ed. (1995). *The Text of the New Testament in Contemporary Research: Essays on the Status Quaestionis.* Grand Rapids: Eerdmans.

Ehrman, Bart D. and Holmes, M.W., ed. (2012). *The Text of the New Testament in Contemporary Research: Essays on the Status Quaestionis.* 2nd edn. Leiden: Brill.

Eklund, Sten (1970). *The Periphrastic, Completive and Finite Use of the Present Participle in Latin.* Uppsala: UP.

Elliott, J.K. (1984). 'Old Latin Manuscripts in Printed Editions of the Greek New Testament.' *NovT* 26: 225–48. Reprinted in J.K. Elliott, *A Survey of Manuscripts Used in Editions of the Greek New Testament.* Leiden, Brill: 1987, 259–80.

Elliott, J.K. (1992). 'The Translations of the New Testament into Latin: The Old Latin and the Vulgate.' In *Aufstieg und Niedergang der Römischen Welt* II.26.1 (Religion), ed. Wolfgang Haase and Hildegard Temporini. Berlin & New York: De Gruyter, 198–245.

Enciso, J. (1954). 'La serie «Ubi» en los Sumarios de los códices bíblicos españoles.' *Estudios Bíblicos* 13: 91–5.

Esposito, Mario (1990). *Irish Books and Learning in Medieval Europe.* Aldershot: Ashgate.

Étaix, Raymond (1986). 'Note sur la tradition manuscrite des Homélies sur l'Évangile de saint Grégoire le Grand.' In Fontaine et al. 1986: 551–9.

Eymann, Hugo (1996). *Epistula ad Romanos: Einleitung.* VL 21. Freiburg: Herder.

Fahey, Michael Andrew (1971). *Cyprian and the Bible: A Study in Third-Century Exegesis.* Tübingen; J.C.B. Mohr.

Falluomini, Carla (1999). *Der sogenannte Codex Carolinus von Wolfenbüttel (Codex Guelferbytanus 64 Weissenburgensis).* Wiesbaden: Harrassowitz.

Falluomini, Carla (2007). *Digitale Edition der Handschrift Cod. Guelf. 64 Weiss.* Editiones Electronicae Guelferbytanae. Online transcription at <http://diglib.hab.de/edoc/ed000006/index.php?transcript=palimpsest_Ulfilas_Falluomini>. Wolfenbüttel: Herzog-August Bibliothek.

Falluomini, Carla (2010). 'Il codice gotico-latino di Gießen e la Chiesa vandalica.' In *Lingua et ingenium. Studi su Fulgenzio di Ruspe e il suo contesto*, ed. A. Piras. Ortacesus: Sandhi, 309–40.

Falluomini, Carla (2012). 'The Gothic Version of the New Testament.' In Ehrman and Holmes 2012: 329–50.

Falluomini, Carla (2015). *The Gothic Version of the Gospels and Pauline Epistles.* Berlin & New York: De Gruyter.

Farr, Carol A. (1997). *The Book of Kells: Its Function and Audience.* London: British Library & Toronto: UP.

Farr, Carol A. (2011). 'Irish Pocket Gospels in Anglo-Saxon England.' In *Anglo-Saxon Traces,* ed. Jane Roberts and Leslie Webster. Tempe: Center for Medieval and Renaissance Studies, 87–100.

Feder, Alfred L. (1916). *Hilarii Pictavensis Opera IV: Tractatus mysteriorum.* Vienna: Tempsky.

Féliers, Jeanne-Huberte (1966). 'L'utilisation de la Bible dans l'œuvre d'Evodius.' *REA* 12: 41–64.

Felle, Antonio Enrico (2006). *Biblia epigraphica: la sacra scrittura nella documentazione epigrafica dell'«Orbis christianus antiquus».* Bari: Edipuglia.

Férotin, M. (1901). 'Deux manuscrits wisigothiques de la bibliothèque de Ferdinand 1er, roi de Castille et de Léon.' *Bibliothèque de l'École des chartes* 62: 374–87.

Férotin, M. (1912). *Le Liber Mozarabicus Sacramentorum et les manuscrits mozarabes.* Paris. Reprinted in *Bibliotheca Ephemerides liturgicae* 1995.

Ferrari, Michele Camillo (1999). 'Der älteste Touronische Pandekt Paris, Bibliothèque nationale de France Lat. 8847 und seine Fragmente.' *Scriptorium* 53.1: 108–13. Reprinted in *Analecta Epternacensia* ed. L. Deitz and R. Nolden (Luxembourg: Stadtbibliothek, 2000), 17–26.

Ferreres, Lambert (2004). 'La Bible de Pacien.' In *Pacien de Barcelone et l'Hispanie au IVe siècle,* ed. D. Bertrand, J. Busquets, and M. Mayer Olivé. Paris: Cerf, 163–71.

Figuet, Jean (1992). 'La Bible de Bernard: données et ouvertures.' In *Bernard de Clairvaux. Histoire, mentalités, spiritualité.* Paris: Cerf, 237–69.

Fischer, Bonifatius (1952). 'Die Lesungen der römischen Ostervigil unter Gregor dem Grossen.' In Fischer and Fiala 1952: 144–59. Reprinted in Fischer 1986:18–50.

Fischer, Bonifatius (1955). 'Der Vulgata-Text des Neuen Testamentes.' *ZNW* 46: 178–96. Reprinted in Fischer 1986:51–73.

Fischer, Bonifatius (1957). *Die Alkuin-Bibel.* Freiburg: Herder.

Fischer, Bonifatius (1961). 'Algunas observaciones sobre el "Codex Gothicus" de la R.C. de S. Isidoro en León y sobre la tradición española de la Vulgata.' *Archivos Leonenses* 15.29–30: 5–47.

Fischer, Bonifatius (1962). 'Codex Amiatinus und Cassiodorus.' *Biblische Zeitschrift* 6: 57–79. Reprinted in Fischer 1985:9–34.

Fischer, Bonifatius (1963a). 'Ein neuer Zeuge zum westlichen Text der Apostelgeschichte.' In *Biblical and Patristic Studies* ed. J.N. Birdsall and R.W. Thomson. Freiburg: Herder. 33–63. Reprinted in Fischer 1986:74–105.

Fischer, Bonifatius (1963b). 'Bibelausgaben des frühen Mittelalters'. In Franceschini et al. 1963: 519–600. Reprinted in Fischer 1985:35–100.

Fischer, Bonifatius (1964). 'Zur Liturgie der lateinischen Handschriften vom Sinai.' *RevBén* 74: 284–97. Reprinted in Fischer 1986:141–55.

Fischer, Bonifatius (1965). 'Bibeltext und Bibelreform unter Karl dem Großen.' In *Karl der Große. Lebenswerk und Nachleben. II. Das geistige Leben,* ed. B. Bischoff, Düsseldorf: Schwann, 156–216. Reprinted in Fischer 1985:101–202.

Fischer, Bonifatius (1971). 'Die Alkuin-Bibeln' in Duft et al. 1971:49–98. Reprinted in Fischer 1985:203–403.

Fischer, Bonifatius (1972). 'Das Neue Testament in lateinischer Sprache. Der gegenwärtige Stand seiner Erforschung und seine Bedeutung für die griechische Textgeschichte.' In Aland 1972: 1–92. Reprinted in Fischer 1986:156–274.

Fischer, Bonifatius (1975). 'Zur Überlieferung altlateinischer Bibeltexte im Mittelalter.' *Nederlands Archief voor Kerkgeschiedenis* 56: 19–33. Reprinted in Fischer 1985:404–21.

Fischer, Bonifatius (1977). *Novae Concordantiae Bibliorum Sacrorum iuxta vulgatam versionem critice editam.* 5 vols. Stuttgart: Frommann–Holzboog.

Fischer, Bonifatius (1980). 'Ein altlateinisches Evangelien-Fragment.' In *Text—Wort—Glaube.* ed. M. Brecht, Berlin: De Gruyter, 1980, 84–111. Reprinted in Fischer 1986:275–307.

Fischer, Bonifatius (1985). *Lateinische Bibelhandschriften im frühen Mittelalter.* Freiburg: Herder.

Fischer, Bonifatius (1986). *Beiträge zur Geschichte der lateinischen Bibeltexte.* Freiburg: Herder.

Fischer, Bonifatius (1987). 'Zur Überlieferung des lateinischen Textes der Evangelien.' In Gryson and Bogaert 1987: 51–104.

Fischer, Bonifatius (1988–91). *Die lateinischen Evangelien bis zum 10. Jahrhundert. I. Varianten zu Matthäus* (1988); *II. Varianten zu Markus* (1989); *III. Varianten zu Lukas* (1990); *IV. Varianten zu Johannes* (1991). Freiburg: Herder.

Fischer, Bonifatius (2010). 'Die lateinischen Evangelien bis zum 10. Jahrhundert. Zwei Untersuchungen zum Text.' *ZNW* 101: 119–44.

Fischer, Bonifatius and Fiala, V., ed. (1952). *Colligere Fragmenta. Festschrift A. Dold.* Beuron; Kunstverlag.

Fischer, Hans (1928). *Die lateinischen Pergamenthandschriften der Universitätsbibliothek Erlangen.* Erlangen: Universitätsbibliothek.

Folliet, G. (1997). '«(Deus) omnia cooperatur in bonum» Rom 8,28. Les citations du verset chez Augustin.' *Sacris Erudiri* 37: 33–55.

Fontaine, Jacques and Pietri, Charles, ed. (1985). *Le monde latin antique et la Bible.* Paris: Beauchesne.

Fontaine, Jacques et al., ed. (1986). *Grégoire le Grand: Actes du colloque international du CNRS, Chantilly 1982.* Paris: CNRS.

Forsyth, Katherine, ed. (2008). *Studies on the Book of Deer.* Dublin: Four Courts.

Franceschini, Ezio, et al. (1963). *La Bibbia nell'alto medioevo.* Spoleto: Centro Italiano di Studi sull'Alto Medioevo.

Frede, Hermann Josef (1958). *Untersuchungen zur Geschichte der lateinischen Übersetzung des Epheserbriefes.* Unpublished dissertation, Bonn.

Frede, Hermann Josef (1961). *Pelagius, der irische Paulustext, Sedulius Scottus.* Freiburg: Herder.

Frede, Hermann Josef (1962–4). *Epistula ad Ephesios.* VL 24/1. Freiburg: Herder.

Frede, Hermann Josef (1964). *Altlateinische Paulus-Handschriften.* Freiburg: Herder.

Frede, Hermann Josef (1965). 'Der Paulustext des Pelagius.' *Sacris Erudiri* 16: 165–83.

Frede, Hermann Josef (1966–71). *Epistulae ad Philippenses, Colossenses.* VL 24/2. Freiburg: Herder.

Frede, Hermann Josef (1971). 'Bibelzitate bei Kirchenvätern. Beobachtungen bei der Herausgabe der «Vetus Latina».' In Benoît and Prigent 1971: 79–96.

Frede, Hermann Josef (1972). 'Die Zitate des Neuen Testaments bei den lateinischen Kirchenväter.' In Aland 1972: 455–78.

Frede, Hermann Josef (1973). 'Ein Paulustext aus Burgund.' *Biblica* 54: 516–36.

Frede, Hermann Josef (1974). *Ein neuer Paulustext und Kommentar.* Freiburg: Herder.

Frede, Hermann Josef (1975–82). *Epistulae ad Thessalonicenses, Timotheum.* VL 25/1. Freiburg: Herder.

Frede, Hermann Josef (1976a). 'Probleme des ambrosianischen Bibeltextes.' In *Ambrosius Episcopus* ed. Giuseppe Lazzati. Milan: UP, 365–92.

Frede, Hermann Josef (1976b). 'Beobachtungen zur Überlieferung der Paulus-Ausgabe des Peregrinus.' In *New Testament Language and Text*, ed. J.K. Elliott. Leiden: Brill. 198–208.

Frede, Hermann Josef (1981). 'Neutestamentliche Zitate in Zeno von Verona.' In *New Testament Textual Criticism: Its Significance for Exegesis*, ed. E.J. Epp and G.D. Fee. Oxford: Clarendon, 297–304.

Frede, Hermann Josef (1983–91). *Epistulae ad Titum, Philemonem, Hebraeos.* VL 25/2. Freiburg: Herder.

Frede, Hermann Josef (1986). 'Der Text des Hebräerbriefs bei Liudprand von Cremona.' *RevBén* 96: 94–9.

Frede, Hermann Josef (1987). 'Lateinische Texte und Texttypen im Hebräerbrief.' In Gryson and Bogaert 1987: 137–53.

Frede, Hermann Josef and Stanjek, Herbert (1996–7). *Sedulii Scotti Collectaneum in Apostolum.* Freiburg: Herder.

Fredouille, Jean-Claude (1985). 'Les lettrés chrétiens face à la Bible.' In Fontaine and Pietri 1985: 25–42.

Fredouille, Jean-Claude (1996). '«Latin chrétien» ou «latin tardif»?' *Recherches augustinennes* 29: 5–23.

Frere, Walter Howard (1934). *The Roman Gospel Lectionary.* Oxford: UP.

Frere, Walter Howard (1935). *The Roman Epistle Lectionary.* Oxford: UP.

Friedl, Antonín (1929). *Kodex Gigas.* Prague: Emporium.

Friedrichsen, George W.S. (1926). *The Gothic Version of the Gospels: A Study of its Style and Textual History.* Oxford: UP; London: Humphrey Milford.

Frisius, Mark A. (2011). *Tertullian's Use of the Pastoral Epistles, Hebrews, James, 1 and 2 Peter and Jude.* Peter Lang: New York.

Fröhlich, Uwe (1995–8). *Epistula ad Corinthios: Einleitung.* 3 fasc. VL 22. Freiburg: Herder.

Galdi, Giovanbattista (2011). 'Latin Inside and Outside of Rome.' In Clackson 2011: 565–81.

Gamber, Klaus (1959). 'Das Lektionar und Sakramentar des Musäus von Massilia (†461).' *RevBén* 69: 198–215.

Gamber, Klaus (1962). 'Die älteste abendländische Evangelien-Perikopenliste.' *Münchener Theologische Zeitschrift* 13: 181–201.

Gamber, Klaus (1968). *Codices liturgici latini antiquiores.* 2nd edn. Freiburg: UP.

Gamber, Klaus (1988). *Codices liturgici latini antiquiores. Supplementum, Ergänzungs- und Registerband*, ed. Bonifacio Baroffio et al. Freiburg: UP.

Gamble, Harry Y. (1977). *The Textual History of the Letter to the Romans.* Grand Rapids: Eerdmans.

Gamble, Harry Y. (1995). *Books and Readers in the Early Church. A History of Early Christian Texts.* New Haven & London: Yale UP.

Gameson, Richard, ed. (1994). *The Early Medieval Bible: Its Production, Decoration and Use.* Cambridge: UP.

Gameson, Richard (2001-2). *The Codex Aureus: An Eighth-Century Gospel Book, Stockholm, Kungliga Bibliotek[et], A. 135.* Facsimile edition. Copenhagen: Rosenkilde and Bagger.

Gameson, Richard (2002b). 'The Insular Gospel Book at Hereford Cathedral.' *Scriptorium* 56: 48–79.

Gameson, Richard (2010). *Manuscript Treasures of Durham Cathedral.* London: Third Millennium.

Gameson, Richard, ed. (2012). *The Cambridge History of the Book in Britain. Vol. 1: c.400–1100.* Cambridge: UP.

Gameson, Richard (2013). *From Holy Island to Durham: The Contexts and Meanings of the Lindisfarne Gospels.* London: Third Millennium.

Gamper, Rudolf and Lenz, P., Nievergelt, A., Erhart, P., Schulz-Flügel, E. (2012). *Die Vetus Latina-Fragmente aus dem Kloster St. Gallen. Faksimile, Edition, Kommentar.* Zürich: Urs Graf.

Ganshof, François L. (1974). 'Charlemagne et la révision du texte latin de la Bible.' *Bulletin de l'Institut Historique Belge de Rome* 44: 271–81.

Ganz, David (1990). *Corbie in the Carolingian Renaissance.* Sigmaringen: Thorbecke.

Ganz, David (1994). 'Mass Production of Early Medieval Manuscripts: The Carolingian Bibles from Tours.' In Gameson 1994: 53–62.

Ganz, David (2001). 'The annotations in Oxford, Bodleian Library, Auct. D. II. 14.' In *Belief and Culture in the Middle Ages*, ed. Richard Gameson and Henrietta Leyser. Oxford: UP, 35–44.

Ganz, David (2012). 'Carolingian Bibles.' In Marsden and Matter 2012: 325–37.

García de la Fuente, Olegario (1994). *Latín bíblico y latín cristiano.* Madrid: Editorial CEES.

Gasquet, Aidan T. (1914). *Codex Vercellensis.* Rome: Pustet.

Gaudemet, Jean (1985). 'La Bible dans les conciles.' In Fontaine and Pietri 1985: 289–310.

Geerard, Maurice, ed. (1992). *Clauis apocryphorum Noui Testamenti.* Turnhout: Brepols.

Ghiglione, Natale (1984). *L'evangelario purpureo di Sarezzano (sec. V/VI).* Vicenza: Neri Pozza.

Ghiglione, Natale (1990). *Asterischi: circa le 'Nuove ricerche sul Codice biblico latino purpureo di Sarezzano' pubblicate da Sergio M. Pagano.* Milan: EIMA.

Gibson, Margaret T. (1989). 'The Twelfth-Century Glossed Bible.' *Studia Patristica* 23. Leuven: Peeters, 232–44.

Gibson, Margaret T. (1992). 'The Place of the Glossa ordinaria in Medieval Exegesis.' In *Ad litteram. Authoritative Texts and their Medieval Readers*, ed. M.D. Jordan and K. Emery, Jr. Notre Dame: UP, 5–27.

Gibson, Margaret T. (1993). *The Bible in the Latin West.* Notre Dame: UP.

Gilson, J.P. (1905). *The Mozarabic Psalter (MS. British Museum, Add. 30,851).* London: Henry Bradshaw Society.

Glaser, Elvira and Claudine Moulin-Fankhänel (1999). 'Die althochdeutsche Überlieferung Echternacher Handschriften.' In *Die Abtei Echternach 698–1998*, ed. M.C. Ferrari et al., Luxembourg: Cludem, 103–22.

Glauche, Günter (2000). *Katalog der lateinischen Handschriften der Bayerischen Staatsbibliothek München: Die Pergamenthandschriften aus dem Domkapitel Freising: Bd. 1. Clm 6201–6316.* Wiesbaden: Harrassowitz.

Glaue, P. and Helm, K. (1910). 'Das gotisch-lateinische Bibelfragment der Großherzoglichen Universitätsbibliothek Gießen.' *ZNW* 11: 1–38.

Glunz, Hans Hermann (1930). *Britannien und Bibeltext. Der Vulgatatext der Evangelien in seinem Verhältnis zur irisch-angelsächsischen Kultur des Frühmittelalters.* Leipzig: Tauchnitz.

Glunz, Hans Hermann (1933). *History of the Vulgate in England from Alcuin to Roger Bacon.* Cambridge: UP.

Gochee, William J. (1970). 'The Gospel Text of the Latin Liturgy: AD 400–800.' PhD dissertation, University of Chicago.

Gochee, William J. (1973). 'The Latin Liturgical Text: A Product of Old Latin and Vulgate Textual Interaction.' *Catholic Biblical Quarterly* 35: 206–11.

Godu, G. (1936). *Codex Sarzanensis.* Monte Cassino: Typis Archicoenobii Montis Casini.

González, A. Viñayo, ed. (1997). *Codex Biblicus Legionensis. Biblia Visigótico-Mozárabe de San Isidoro de León.* Facsimile edition. León: Lancia.

González, A. Viñayo (1999). *Codex Biblicus Legionensis: Veinte Estudios.* León: Lancia.

Gorman, Michael M. (1997). 'The Commentary on Genesis of Claudius of Turin and Biblical Studies under Louis the Pious.' *Speculum* 72.2: 279–329.

Gorman, Michael M. (2000). 'The Myth of Hiberno-Latin Exegesis.' *RevBén* 110: 42–85.

Gorman, Michael M. (2002a). *Biblical Commentaries from the Early Middle Ages.* Florence: SISMEL.

Gorman, Michael M. (2002b). 'Source Marks and Chapter Divisions in Bede's Commentary on Luke.' *RevBén* 112: 46–75.

Gorman, Michael M. (2003a). 'The Codex Amiatinus: A Guide to the Legends and Bibliography.' *Studi Medievali* serie terza 44: 863–910.

Gorman, Michael M. (2003b). 'The Earliest Latin Commentary on the Gospels.' *Augustinianum* 42: 253–312.

Gorman, Michael M. (2009). 'Rewriting Augustine: Alcuin's Commentary on the Gospel of John.' *RevBén* 119.1: 36–85.

Gorman, Michael M. (2011). 'Patristic and pseudo-patristic citations in the *Collectio Hibernensis*.' *RevBén* 121: 18–93.

Grasso, Natale (1951). 'Il testo biblico segnito da Prudenzio in «Hamartigenia» prae. 11–13.' *Misc. di Studi di Lett. crist. ant.* [Catania] 3: 124–35.

Grasso, Natale (1972). 'Prudenzio e la Bibbia.' *Orpheus: Rivista di Umanità classica e cristiana* 19: 79–170.

Gray, L.H. (1952). 'Biblical citations in Latin Lives of Welsh and Breton Saints Differing from the Vulgate.' *Traditio* 8: 389–97.

Green, Roger P.H. (2006). *Latin Epics of the New Testament: Juvencus, Sedulius, Arator.* Oxford: UP.

Green, Roger P.H. (2007). 'Birth and Transfiguration: Some Gospel Episodes in Juvencus and Sedulius.' In *Texts and Culture in Late Antiquity*, ed. J.H.D. Scourfield. Swansea: Classical Press of Wales, 135–73.

Green, William M. (1959). 'A Fourth Century Manuscript of Saint Augustine?' *RevBén* 69: 191–7.

Gribomont, Jean (1961). 'Les éditions critiques de la Vulgate.' *Studi medievali* 3.2: 363–77.

Gribomont, Jean (1985a). 'Les plus anciennes traductions latines.' In Fontaine and Pietri 1985: 43–65.

Gribomont, Jean (1985b). 'Cassiodore et la transmission de l'héritage biblique antique.' In Fontaine et Pietri 1985: 143–52.

Gribomont, Jean (1986). 'Le texte biblique de Grégoire.' In Fontaine et al. 1986: 467–75.

Gribomont, Jean (1987). 'Aux origines de la Vulgate.' In Stramare 1987: 11–20.

Gros, M.S. (2002). 'Les fragments de l'Épistolier latin du Sinaï. Étude liturgique.' *Ecclesia Orans* 19: 391–404.

Grosjean, Paul (1955). 'Sur quelques exégètes irlandais du VIIe siècle.' *Sacris Eruditi* 7: 67–98.

Gryglewicz, Felix (1964). 'The St Adelbert Codex of the Gospels.' *NTS* 11: 256–78.

Gryson, Roger (1978). 'Les citations scripturaires des œuvres attribuées à l'évêque arien Maximinus.' *RevBén* 88: 45–80. Reprinted in Gryson 2008: 351–86.

Gryson, Roger (1982). *Le recueil arien de Vérone*. Steenbrugge-Den Haag; Kluwer.

Gryson, Roger (1988). 'La vieille-latine, témoin privilégié du text du Nouveau Testament. L'exemple de Matthieu 13, 13–15.' *RTL* 19: 413–32. Reprinted in Gryson 2008: 497–516.

Gryson, Roger (1990). 'La version gothique des évangiles. Essai de réévaluation.' *RTL* 21: 3–31. Reprinted in Gryson 2008: 517–45.

Gryson, Roger, ed. (1993). *Philologia Sacra. 1. Altes und Neues Testament. 2. Apokryphen, Kirchenväter, Verschiedenes*. Freiburg: Herder.

Gryson, Roger (1997). 'Les commentaires patristiques latins sur l'Apocalypse.' *RTL* 28: 305–37, 484–502. Reprinted in Gryson 2008: 827–79.

Gryson, Roger (1999). *Altlateinische Handschriften/Manuscrits Vieux Latins. Première partie: Mss 1–275*. VL 1/2A. Freiburg: Herder.

Gryson, Roger (2000–3). *Apocalypsis Johannis*. VL 26/2. Freiburg: Herder.

Gryson, Roger (2004). *Altlateinische Handschriften/Manuscrits Vieux Latins. Deuxième partie: Mss 300–485*. VL 1/2A. Freiburg: Herder.

Gryson, Roger (2007). *Répertoire général des auteurs ecclésiastiques latins de l'antiquité et du haut moyen âge*. VL 1/1 (5th edn). Freiburg: Herder.

Gryson, Roger (2008). *Scientiam Salutis. Quarante années de recherches sur l'antiquité chrétienne*. Leuven: Peeters.

Gryson, Roger and Bogaert, P.-M., ed. (1987). *Recherches sur l'histoire de la Bible latine*. Louvain-la-Neuve: Faculté de Théologie.

Guignard, Christophe (2015). 'The Original Language of the Muratorian Fragment.' *JTS* ns 66.2.

Gurtner, Daniel M., Hernández, Juan, and Foster, Paul, ed. (2015). *Studies on the Text of the New Testament and Early Christianity*. Leiden: Brill.

Gwynn, J. (1913). *Liber Ardmachanus, The Book of Armagh*. Dublin: Hodges Figgis & co.

Haddan, A.W. and Stubbs, W. (1869). *Councils and Ecclesiastical Documents relating to Great Britain and Ireland*. Vol. 1. Oxford: Clarendon.

Haelewyck, Jean-Claude (1988). 'Le texte occidental des Actes des Apôtres. À propos de la reconstitution de M.-E. Boismard et A. Lamouille.' *RTL* 19: 342–53.

Haelewyck, Jean-Claude (1996). 'Les premières versions latines de la Bible.' In *Les premières traditions de la Bible*, ed. C.-B. Amphoux and J. Margain, Lausanne: Zebre, 121–36.

Haelewyck, Jean-Claude (1999). 'La version latine de Marc.' *Mélanges de science religieuse* 56.3: 27–52.

Haelewyck, Jean-Claude (2003). 'La Vetus Latina de l'Evangile de Marc. Les rapports entre les témoins manuscrits et les citations patristiques.' In *The New Testament Text in Early Christianity*, ed. C.-B. Amphoux and J.K. Elliott. Lausanne: Zebre, 151–93.

Haelewyck, Jean-Claude (2005). 'Marc 1, 1–11. La tradition latine (vetus latina et vulgate).' In *Évangile de Marc. Les types de texte dans les langues anciennes*, ed. J.-C. Haelewyck and S. Arbache. Lille: Universitaire Catholique, 17–26.

Haelewyck, Jean-Claude (2013–). *Evangelium secundum Marcum*. VL 17. Freiburg: Herder.

Haelewyck, Jean-Claude (2013a). 'Un nouveau témoin vieux latin de Marc. Le ms. Durham, Cathedral Library A.II.10 + C.III.13 + C.III.20.' *RevBén* 123.1: 5–12.

Haendler, Gert (1968). 'Die ältesten lateinischen Bibelzitate in Tertullians Frühschriften aus dem Jahre 197.' In *Theologie in Geschichte und Kunst*, ed. S. Herrmann and O. Söhngen. Witten: Luther-Verlag, 50–60.

Haendler, Gert (1989). 'Zur Arbeit an altlateinischen Bibelübersetzungen.' *Theologische Literaturzeitung* 114: 1–12.

Hagen, H. (1884). 'Ein Italafragment aus einem Berner Palimpsest des VI Jahrhunderts.' *ZWT* 27: 470–84.

Hahneman, Geoffrey M. (1992). *The Muratorian Fragment and the Development of the Canon*. Oxford: Clarendon.

Hälvä-Nyberg, Ulla (1988). *Die Kontraktionen auf dem lateinischen Inschriften Roms und Afrikas bis zum 8. Jh. n. Chr.* Helsinki: Suomarlainen Tiedeakatemia.

Hammond, Caroline P. (1978). 'A Product of a Fifth-Century Scriptorium Preserving Conventions used by Rufinus of Aquileia.' *JTS* ns 29.2: 366–91.

Hammond Bammel, Caroline P. (1979). 'Products of Fifth-Century Scriptoria Preserving Conventions used by Rufinus of Aquileia: Nomina Sacra.' *JTS* ns 30.2: 430–62.

Hammond Bammel, Caroline P. (1984). 'Products of Fifth-Century Scriptoria Preserving Conventions used by Rufinus of Aquileia: Script.' *JTS* ns 35.2: 347–93.

Hammond Bammel, Caroline P. (1985). *Der Römerbrieftext des Rufin und seine Origenes-Übersetzung*. Freiburg: Herder.

Hammond Bammel, Caroline P. (1990). *Der Römerbriefkommentar des Origenes. Kritische Ausgabe der Übersetzung Rufins. Buch 1–3*. Freiburg: Herder.

Hammond Bammel, Caroline P. (1996). *Origeniana et Rufiniana*. Freiburg: Herder.

Hammond Bammel, Caroline P. (1997). *Der Römerbriefkommentar des Origenes. Kritische Ausgabe der Übersetzung Rufins. Buch 4–6*. Freiburg: Herder.

Hammond Bammel, Caroline P. (1998). *Der Römerbriefkommentar des Origenes. Kritische Ausgabe der Übersetzung Rufins. Buch 7–10*. Freiburg: Herder.

Hanson, R.P.C. (1970). 'Biblical Exegesis in the Early Church.' In Ackroyd and Evans 1970: 412–54.

Harbert, B. (1989). 'Romans 5,12: Old Latin and Vulgate in the Pelagian Controversy.' *Studia Patristica* 22, ed. E.A. Livingstone. Leuven: Peeters, 261–4.

Harmon, Steven R. (2003). 'A Note on the Critical Use of Instrumenta for the Retrieval of Patristic Biblical Exegesis.' *Journal of Early Christian Studies* 11.1: 95–107.

Harnack: see von Harnack.

Harris, J. Rendel (1888). 'The "Sortes Sanctorum" in the St. Germain Codex (g1).' *American Journal of Philology* 9: 58–63.

Harris, J. Rendel (1891). *The Codex Sangallensis (Δ). A Study in the Text of the Old Latin Gospels*. Cambridge: UP.

Harris, W.V. (1989). 'Ancient Literacy.' Cambridge & London: Harvard UP.

Harrison, Rebecca R. (1986). *Jerome's Revision of the Gospels*. PhD thesis. University of Michigan.

Hawk, Brandon W. (2012). 'A Fragment of Colossians with Hiberno-Latin Glosses in St. Gall Stiftsbibliothek, Cod. Sang. 1395.' *Sacris Eruditi* 51: 233–56.

Heer, J.M. (1908). *Die Versio Latina des Barnabasbriefes und ihr Verhältnis zur altlateinischen Bibel*. Freiburg: Herder.

Heer, J.M. (1910). *Evangelium Gatianum*. Freiburg: Herder.

Heine, Ronald E. (2002). *The Commentaries of Origen and Jerome on St Paul's Epistle to the Ephesians*. Oxford: UP.

Heine, Ronald E. (2004). 'The Third Century: A Literary Guide.' In Young, Ayres, and Louth 2004: 117–60.

Heinsdorff, Cornel (2003). *Christus, Nikodemus und die Samaritanerin bei Juvencus. Mit einem Anhang zur lateinischen Evangelienvorlage*. Berlin & New York: De Gruyter.

Helderman, Jan (1992). 'Die Engel bei der Auferstehung und das lebendige Kreuz. Mk 16,3 in *k* einem Vergleich unterzogen.' In *The Four Gospels*, ed. F. van Segbroeck et al. Leuven: Peeters, 2321–42.

Hemphill, Samuel (1911). 'The Gospels of Mac Regol of Birr: A Study in Celtic Illumination.' *PRIA* 29C: 1–10.

Hen, Yitzhak (2003). 'A Merovingian Commentary on the Four Gospels (Pseudo-Theophilus, CPL 1001).' *REA* 49: 167–87.

Hen, Yitzhak and Meens, Rob, ed. (2004). *The Bobbio Missal. Liturgy and Religious Culture in Merovingian Gaul*. Cambridge: UP.

Henderson, George (1987). *From Durrow to Kells: The Insular Gospel Books 650–800*. London: Thames & Hudson.

Henne, Philippe (1993). 'La datation du *Canon* de Muratori.' *RevBib* 100: 54–75.

Henning, Hans (1913). *Der Wulfila der Bibliotheca Augusta zu Wolfenbüttel (Codex Carolinus)*. Hamburg: Behrens.

Henss, W. (1973). *Leitbilder der Bibelübersetzung im 5. Jahrhundert. Die Praefatio in Evangeliencodex Brixianus (f) und das Problem der gotisch-lateinischen Bilinguen*. Heidelberg: Akademie der Wissenschaften.

Herbert, Lynley Anne (2012). '"Lux Vita": The Majesty and Humanity of Christ in the Gospels of Sainte-Croix of Poitiers.' PhD thesis, University of Delaware.

Higgins, A.J.B. (1951). 'The Latin Text of Luke in Marcion and Tertullian.' *VigC* 5: 1–42.

Hilhorst, A. (1994). 'Le texte sur la résurrection de Jésus dans le ms. k de la *Vetus Latina* (Mc. 16,3).' *RevBén* 104: 257–9.

Hill, C.E. and Kruger, M.J., ed. (2012). *The Early Text of the New Testament.* Oxford: UP.

Hoffmann, Hartmut (2009). *Die Würzburger Paulinenkommentare der Ottonenzeit.* Hannover: Hahnsche.

Hofmann, J.B. and Szantyr, A. (1963, 1965). *Lateinische Syntax und Stilistik.* 2 vols. Munich: Beck.

Holder, Alfred (1914). *Die Handschriften der Badischen Landesbibliothek in Karlsruhe; 6: Die Reichenauer Handschriften.* Leipzig & Berlin: Teubner. Reprinted Wiesbaden: Harrassowitz, 1971.

Hoogterp, P.W. (1930). *Étude sur le latin du Codex Bobiensis (k) des Évangiles.* Wageningen.

Höpfl, H. (1913). *Beiträge zur Geschichte der Sixto-Klementinischen Vulgata nach gedruckten und ungedruckten Quellen.* Freiburg: Herder.

Hopkins-James, Lemuel J. (1934). *The Celtic Gospels. Their Story and their Text.* Oxford: Clarendon.

Horsley, G.H.R. and Waterhouse, E.R. (1984). 'The Greek nomen sacrum XP- in some Latin and Old English Manuscripts.' *Scriptorium* 38: 211–30.

Hoskier, H.C. (1919). *The Text of Codex Usserianus 2.* London: Quaritch.

Houghton, H.A.G. (2008a). 'Augustine's Adoption of the Vulgate Gospels.' *NTS* 54.3: 450–64.

Houghton, H.A.G. (2008b). *Augustine's Text of John. Patristic Citations and Latin Gospel Manuscripts.* Oxford: UP.

Houghton, H.A.G. (2009). 'A Newly Identified Old Latin Gospel Manuscript: Würzburg Universitätsbibliothek M.p.th.f.67.' *JTS* ns 60.1: 1–21.

Houghton, H.A.G. (2010a). 'The St Petersburg Insular Gospels: Another Old Latin Witness.' *JTS* ns 61.1: 110–27.

Houghton, H.A.G. (2010b). '"Flattening' in Latin Biblical Citations.' In *Studia Patristica* 45, ed. J. Baun, A. Cameron, M. Edwards, and M. Vinzent. Leuven: Peeters, 271–6.

Houghton, H.A.G. (2011). 'Chapter Divisions, Capitula Lists, and the Old Latin Versions of John.' *RevBén* 121.2: 316–56.

Houghton, H.A.G. (2012). 'The Use of the Latin Fathers for New Testament Textual Criticism.' In Ehrman and Holmes 2012: 375–405.

Houghton, H.A.G. (2013). 'Patristic Evidence in the New Edition of the Vetus Latina Iohannes.' In Vinzent, Mellerin, and Houghton 2013: 69–85.

Houghton, H.A.G. (2014a). 'The Electronic Scriptorium: Markup for New Testament Manuscripts.' In *Digital Humanities in Biblical, Early Jewish and Early Christian Studies*, ed. Claire Clivaz, Andrew Gregory, and David Hamidović, Leiden: Brill, 31–60.

Houghton, H.A.G., ed. (2014b). *Early Readers, Scholars and Editors of the New Testament.* Piscataway: Gorgias.

Houghton, H.A.G. (2014c). 'A Flock of Synonyms? John 21:15–17 in Greek and Latin Tradition.' In *Texts and Traditions. Essays in Honour of J. Keith Elliott*, ed. Peter Doble and Jeffrey Kloha. Leiden: Brill, 220–38.

Houghton, H.A.G. (2014d). 'The Biblical Text of Jerome's *Commentary on Galatians*.' *JTS* ns 65.1: 1–24.

Houghton, H.A.G. (2015a). 'The Text of John in Fortunatianus of Aquileia's Commentary on the Gospels.' *Studia Patristica. Papers from the Fifth British Patristics Conference*, ed. Markus Vinzent.

Houghton, H.A.G. (2015b). 'A Longer Text of Paul: Romans to Galatians in Codex Wernigerodensis (VL 58).' In Gurtner, Hernández, and Foster 2015: 331–46.

Houghton, H.A.G. (2016). 'The Gospel according to Mark in Two Latin Mixed-Text Manuscripts.' *RevBén* 126.1 (2016).

Houghton, H.A.G. and Parker, D.C., ed. (2008). *Textual Variation: Theological and Social Tendencies*. Piscataway: Gorgias.

Howlett, David (1996). 'Seven Studies in Seventh-Century Texts.' *Peritia* 10: 1–70.

Hulley, K.K. (1944). 'Principles of Textual Criticism Known to Jerome.' *Harvard Studies in Classical Philology* 55: 87–109.

Insular Gospels (2001). *The Insular Gospels of the 8th Century in the Collection of the National Library of Russia, Saint Petersburg*. (Electronic version of Manuscript Lat. F.v.I.8). CD-ROM. St Petersburg: Spaero/NLR.

Itala: see Jülicher, Matzkow, and Aland.

Janini, J. (1976). 'Officia Silensia. Liber Misticus, I. A Sancta Maria usque ad Ascensionem (cod. Londres, British Museum, Add. 30844). Edición y notas.' *Hispania Sacra* 29: 325–81.

Janini, J. (1977). 'Officia Silensia. Liber Misticus, II. A Paschate usque ad Pentecosten (cod. Londres, British Museum, Add. 30846). Edición y notas.' *Hispania Sacra* 30: 331–418.

Janini, J. (1980). *Liber misticus de Cuaresma y Pascua (Cod. Toledo, Bibl. Capit. 35.5)*. Toledo: Fuentes.

Janini, J., Gonzálvez, R., and Mundó, A.M. (1977). *Catálogo de los manuscritos litúrgicos de la catedral de Toledo*. Toledo: Instituto provincial.

Jimenez Zamudio, Rafael (2009). 'Técnicas de traducción en las antiguas versiones latinas de la Biblia.' *Estudios latinos* 29.1: 75–115.

Jones, Leslie Webber (1935). 'The Text of the Bible and the Script and Art of Tours.' *HTR* 28: 135–79.

Jones, Leslie Webber (1947). 'The Scriptorium at Corbie.' *Speculum* 22: 191–204, 375–94.

de Jonge, Henk Jan (1980). 'Erasmus and the comma Johanneum.' *Ephemerides Theologicae Lovanienses* 56: 381–9.

Jongkind, Dirk (2015). 'On the Marcionite Prologues to the Letters of Paul.' In Gurtner, Hernández, and Foster 2015: 391–409.

Jülicher, Adolf (1914). 'Kritische Analyse der lateinischen Übersetzung der Apostelgeschichte.' *ZNW* 15: 163–88.

Jülicher, Adolf, Matzkow, W., and Aland, K. (1963–76) *Itala. Das Neue Testament in altlateinische Überlieferung. I. Matthäus-Evangelium*. 2nd edn. (1972); *II. Marcus-Evangelium*. 2nd edn. (1970); *I. Lucas-Evangelium*. 2nd edn. (1976); *IV. Johannes-Evangelium* (1963). Berlin: De Gruyter.

Jullien, M.-H. (2004). 'Alcuin et l'Italie.' In *Alcuin, de York à Tours*, ed. P. Depreux and
    B. Judic. Rennes: UP, 394–406.

Kaczynski, Bernice M. (1988). *Greek in the Carolingian Age. The St. Gall Manuscripts.*
    Cambridge: Medieval Academy of America.

Kaestli, Jean-Daniel (1996). 'Le Protévangile de Jacques en latin. État de la question et
    perspectives nouvelles.' *RHT* 26: 41–102.

Kamesar, Adam (2013). 'Jerome.' In Carleton Paget and Schaper 2013: 653–75.

Kannengiesser, Charles (2004). *Handbook of Patristic Exegesis.* 2 vols. Leiden: Brill.

Kashouh, Hikmat (2011). *The Arabic Versions of the Gospels.* Berlin: De Gruyter.

Kelly, Joseph F. (1988). 'A Catalogue of Early Medieval Hiberno-Latin Biblical
    Commentaries.' *Traditio* 44: 537–71.

Kelly, Joseph F. (1989). 'A Catalogue of Early Medieval Hiberno-Latin Biblical
    Commentaries.' *Traditio* 45: 393–434.

Kendrick, T.D., et al. (1956–60). *Euangeliarum quattuor Codex Lindisfarnensis.*
    Facsimile edition. Two vols. Olten & Lausanne: Urs Graf.

Kessler, Herbert L. (1977). *The Illustrated Bibles from Tours.* Princeton: UP.

Klauser, T. (1972). *Das Römische Capitulare Evangeliorum.* 2nd edn. Münster:
    Aschendorff.

Klein, Peter K. (1972). 'Date et scriptorium de la Bible de Roda. État des recherches.'
    Les cahiers de Saint-Michel de Cuxa 3: 91–102.

Klein, Peter K. (2001). *Die Trierer Apokalypse. Codex 31 der Stadtbibliothek Trier.*
    Graz: ADEVA.

Klein, Peter K. and Laufner, Richard (1975). *Trierer Apokalypse: vollständige
    Faksimile-Ausg. im Originalformat des Codex 31 der Stadtbibliothek Trier.* Facsimile
    edition. Graz: Akademische Druck.

Klijn, A.F.J. (1969). *A Survey of the Researches into the Western Text of the Gospels and
    Acts. Part Two: 1949–1969.* Brill: Leiden.

Kloha, J.J. (2006). 'A Textual Commentary on Paul's First Epistle to the Corinthians.'
    PhD dissertation, University of Leeds.

Kloha, J.J. (2013). 'The New Testament Text of Nicetas of Remesiana, with reference to
    Luke 1:46.' In Vinzent, Mellerin, and Houghton 2013: 115–29.

Knust, Jennifer Wright (2006). 'Early Christian Re-Writing and the History of the
    Pericope Adulterae.' *Journal of Early Christian Studies* 14.4: 485–536.

Knust, Jennifer Wright and Wasserman, Tommy (2014). 'The Biblical Odes and the
    Text of the Christian Bible.' *Journal of Biblical Literature* 133.2: 341–65.

Kockelkorn, R. (2000). *Evangeliorum quattuor codex Petropolitanus (Lat. F.v.I.8).*
    Luxembourg: Bibliothèque nationale.

Kraft, Benedikt (1924). *Die Evangelientexte des Hl. Irenaeus.* Freiburg: Herder.

Kraft, R.A. (1977). 'A Note on Paleography and its Perils: The Date of the Old Latin Ms
    'ff' (=66) of the Epistle of James.' In *Studia Codicologica*, ed. K. Treu, Berlin:
    Akademie-Verlag, 273–7.

Krans, Jan (2013). 'Who Coined the Name "Ambrosiaster"?' In *Paul, John, and
    Apocalyptic Eschatology*, ed. Jan Krans, Bert Jan Lietaert Peerbolte, Peter-Ben Smit
    and Arie Zwiep. Leiden: Brill, 274–81.

La Bonnardière, Anne-Marie (1957). 'L'épître aux Hébreux dans l'œuvre de saint
    Augustin.' (*Biblia Augustiniana* NT fasc. 17). *REA* 3: 137–62.

La Bonnardière, Anne-Marie (1975). 'La Bible «liturgique» de saint Augustin.' *Théologie Historique* 35: 147–60.

La Bonnardière, Anne-Marie, ed. (1986). *Saint Augustin et la Bible*. Paris: Beauchesne.

Lagrange, M.-J. (1916). 'La Vulgate latine de l'Épître aux Romains et le texte grec.' *RevBib* 13: 225–35.

Lagrange, M.-J. (1917). 'La Vulgate latine de l'Épître aux Galates et le texte grec.' *RevBib* 14: 424–50.

Lagrange, M.-J. (1918). 'La révision de la Vulgate par S. Jérôme.' *RevBib* 15: 254–7.

Lai, Andrea (2011). *Il codice Laudiano greco 35. L'identità missionaria di un libro nell'Europa altomedievale*. Cargeghe: Documenta.

Laistner, M.L.W. (1937). 'The Latin Versions of Acts Known to the Venerable Bede.' *HTR* 30: 37–50.

Lambot, C. (1931). *North Italian Services of the Eleventh Century. Recueil d'ordines du XIe siècle provenant de la Haute-Italie*. London: Henry Bradshaw Society.

Lampe, G.W.H., ed. (1969). *The Cambridge History of the Bible. II. The West from the Fathers to the Reformation*. Cambridge: UP.

Lancel, Serge (2002). *Saint Augustine*. London: SCM.

Lawlor, H.J. (1897). *Chapters on the Book of Mulling*. Edinburgh: Douglas.

Legg, J.W. (1917). *The Bobbio Missal. A Gallican Mass Book. Vol. 1 Facsimile*. London: Henry Bradshaw Society.

Lehmann, P. (1908). 'Neue Bruchstücke aus «Weingartener» Itala-Handschriften.' In *Sitzungsberichte der Bayerischen Akademie der Wissenschaften*. Munich, 43–9.

Lehmann, P. (1933). 'Funde und Fragmente.' *Zentralblatt für Bibliothekswesen* 50: 50–76.

Lehmann, P. (1939). 'Mitteilungen aus Handschriften, VI.' In *Sitzungsberichte der Bayerische Akademie der Wissenschaften*. Munich, 11–14.

Lemoine, Louis (2004). 'Autour du scriptorium de Landévennec.' In *Corona Monastica. Moines bretons de Landévennec*, ed. L. Lemoine and B. Merdrignac. Rennes: UP, 155–64.

Leonardi, Claudio and Orlandi, Giovanni, ed. (2005). *Biblical Studies in the Early Middle Ages*. Florence: SISMEL.

Liere: see van Liere.

Light, Laura (1984). 'Versions et révisions du texte biblique.' In Riché and Lobrichon 1984: 55–93.

Light, Laura (1994). 'French Bibles c. 1200–30. A New Look at the Origins of the Paris Bible.' In Gameson 1994: 155–76.

Light, Laura (2001). 'Roger Bacon and the Origin of the Paris Bible.' *RevBén* 111: 483–507.

Light, Laura (2011). 'The Bible and the Individual: The thirteenth-century Paris Bible.' In Boynton and Reilly 2011: 228–46.

Light, Laura (2012). 'The thirteenth century and the Paris Bible.' In Marsden and Matter 2012: 380–91.

Linde, Cornelia (2012). *How to Correct the Sacra Scriptura? Textual Criticism of the Latin Bible between the Twelfth and Fifteenth Century*. Oxford: Society for the Study of Medieval Languages and Literature.

Lindsay, W.M. (1910). *Early Irish Minuscule Script*. Oxford: Parker.

Lindsay, W.M. (1915). *Notae latinae. An account of abbreviations in Latin MSS of the early minuscule period (c.700–850)*. Cambridge. Reprinted with Baines 1936 in 1963.

Lobrichon, Guy (2003). *La Bible au Moyen Âge*. Paris: Picard.

Lobrichon, Guy (2004). 'Le texte des bibles alcuiniennes.' *Annales de Bretagne et des Pays de l'Ouest* 111.3: 209–19.

Lobrichon, Guy (2012). 'The early schools, c. 900–1100.' In Marsden and Matter 2012: 536–54.

Lo Bue, F. (1955). 'Old Latin Readings of the Apocalypse in the "Wordsworth-White" Edition of the Vulgate.' *VigC* 9: 21–4.

Lo Cicero, Carla (2002). 'Rufino traduttore di Basilio: emulazione e citazione bibliche.' In *Tra IV e V secolo. Studia sulla cultura latina tardoantica*, ed. Isabella Gualandri. Milan: Cisalpino, 97–117.

Loewe, R. (1969). 'The Medieval History of the Latin Vulgate.' In Lampe 1969: 102–54.

Löfstedt, Bengt (1989–1991). *Sedulius Scottus: Kommentar zum Evangelium nach Matthäus*. Two vols. Freiburg: Herder.

Löfstedt, E. (1959). *Late Latin*. Oslo: Instituttet for Sammenlignende Kulturforskning.

Lössl, J. and Watt, J.W., ed. (2011). *Interpreting the Bible and Aristotle in Late Antiquity: The Alexandrian Commentary Tradition between Rome and Baghdad*. Farnham & Burlington: Ashgate.

Loi, Vincenza (1974). 'Vetus Latina, «testo occidentale» dei Vangele, Diatessaron nelle testimonianze di Novatiano.' *Augustinianum* 14: 201–21.

Lomiento, G. (1966). 'La Bibbia nella compositio di S. Colombano.' *Vetera Christianorum* 3: 25–43.

Lowden, John (2012). 'Illustration in biblical manuscripts.' In Marsden and Matter 2012: 446–82.

Lowe, Elias Avery (1920). *The Bobbio Missal. A Gallican Mass Book. Vol. 2 Text*. London: Henry Bradshaw Society.

Lowe, Elias Avery (1923). 'On the Date of Codex Toletanus.' *RevBén* 35: 267–71.

Lowe, Elias Avery (1925). 'Some Facts about our Oldest Latin Manuscripts.' *Classical Quarterly* 19: 197–208.

Lowe, Elias Avery (1928). 'More Facts about our Oldest Latin Manuscripts.' *Classical Quarterly* 22: 43–62.

Lowe, Elias Avery (1934–71). *Codices Latini Antiquiores. A palaeographical guide to Latin manuscripts prior to the ninth century*. 11 vols and supplement. Oxford: Clarendon.

Lowe, Elias Avery (1937). 'The Codex Cavensis. New Light on its Later History'. In *Quantulacumque. Studies Presented to K. Lake*, ed. R.P. Casey, S. Lake, and A.K. Lake, London, 325–31. Reprinted in Lowe 1972: 1.335–41.

Lowe, Elias Avery (1952). 'The Uncial Gospel Leaves Attached to the Utrecht Psalter.' *The Art Bulletin* 34: 237–8. Reprinted in Lowe 1972: 2.385–8.

Lowe, Elias Avery (1964a). 'Two New Latin Liturgical Fragments on Mount Sinai.' *RevBén* 74: 284–97. Reprinted in Fischer 1986:106–40.

Lowe, Elias Avery (1964b). 'Codices rescripti. A List of the Oldest Latin Palimpsests with Stray Observations on their Origin.' *Studi et Testi* 135: 67–113.

Lowe, Elias Avery (1965). 'Two Other Unknown Latin Liturgical Fragments on Mount Sinai.' *Scriptorium* 19: 3–29.

Lowe, Elias Avery (1972). *Paleographical Papers 1907–1965*, ed. L. Bieler. Oxford: Clarendon.

Luce, A.A., Simms, G.O., Meyer, P., and Bieler, L. (1960). *Evangeliorum Quattuor Codex Durmachensis*. Facsimile edition. Olten: Urs Graf.

Lundström, Sven (1985). *Die Überlieferung der lateinischen Irenaeusübersetzung*. Uppsala: Almqvist & Wiksell.

Lunn-Rockliffe, Sophie (2007). *Ambrosiaster's Political Theology*. Oxford: UP.

Lunn-Rockliffe, Sophie (2011). 'Prologue Topics and Translation Problems in Latin Commentaries on Paul.' In Lössl and Watt 2011: 33–48.

MacLachlan, R.F. (2014). 'A Reintroduction to the Budapest Anonymous Commentary on the Pauline Letters.' In Houghton 2014b: 93–106.

Magrini, Sabina (2007). 'Production and Use of Latin Bible manuscripts in Italy during the thirteenth and fourteenth centuries.' *Manuscripta* 51.2: 209–57.

Maître, Claire (2004). *Catalogue des manuscrits d'Autun*. Turnhout: Brepols.

Maltby, Robert (2006). 'Gerunds, gerundives and their Greek Equivalents in Latin Bible Translations.' In *Latin vulgaire—latin tardif* 7, ed. Carmen Arias Abellán. Seville: UP, 425–42.

Manselli, Raoul (1963). 'Gregorio Magno e la Bibbia'. In Franceschini et al. 1963: 67–102.

Marazuela: see Ayuso Marazuela.

Marone, Paola (2005). 'Note sul testo biblico di Ottato.' *Studi e materiali di storia delle religioni* 71: 309–36.

Marone, Paola (2008). 'Optatus and the African Old Latin.' *TC—A Journal of Biblical Textual Criticism* 13 (='Ottato e la revisione del testo biblico dell'Afra.' *Rivista Biblica* 55 (2007) 335–44).

Marsden, Richard (1998). '*Manus Bedae*: Bede's contribution to Ceolfrith's Bibles.' *Anglo-Saxon England* 27: 65–85.

Marsden, Richard (1999). 'The Gospels of St Augustine.' In *St Augustine and the conversion of England*, ed. Richard Gameson. Stroud: Sutton, 285–312.

Marsden, Richard (2012). 'The Bible in English.' In Marsden and Matter 2012: 217–38.

Marsden, Richard and Matter, E. Ann, ed. (2012). *The New Cambridge History of the Bible. II. From 600 to 1450*. Cambridge: UP.

Martimort, A.G. (1992). *Les lectures liturgiques et leurs livres*. Turnhout: Brepols.

Martin, E.J. (1923). 'The Biblical Text of Firmicus Maternus.' *JTS* os 24: 318–25.

Martin, H.J. and Vezin, J., ed. (1990). *Mise en page et mise en texte du livre manuscrit*. Paris: Cercle de la Librairie-Promodis.

Marzola, M. (1953, 1958). 'Ricostruzione teologico-critica degli Atti degli Apostoli, Epistole paoline della cattività, I e II ai Tessalonicense e Apocalisse nel testo latino usato da Sant'Ambrogio.' Text: *Scrinium Theologicum* 1: 95–123 [1953]; Commentary: *Analecta Ferrarensia*. Ferrara: Archiepiscopal Seminary, 143–272 [1958].

Marzola, M. (1965, 1971). *Bibbia Ambrosiana neotestamentaria (ricostruzione teologico-critica)*. 2 vols. Turin: Società Editrice Internazionale.

Mattei, Paul (1995). 'Recherches sur la Bible à Rome vers le milieu du IIIe siècle: Novatien et la Vetus Latina.' *RevBén* 105: 255–79.

Matthaei, C.F. (1782–8). *Novum Testamentum*. 12 vols. Riga.

Matzkow, Walter (1933). *De uocabulis quibusdam Italae et Vulgatae christianis quaestiones lexicographicae*. Berlin: UP.

Maxwell, Kathleen (2014). *Between Constantinople and Rome. An Illuminated Byzantine Gospel Book (Paris gr. 54) and the Union of Churches*. Aldershot: Ashgate.

Mayr-Harting, H. (1991). *Ottonian Book Illumination*. 2 vols. London: Harvey Miller.

Mazzini, Innocenzo (1973). 'Due esempi di traduzione biblia pregeronimiana: *moechatio* ed *hauritorium*.' *Vetera Christianorum* 10: 319–25.

McGurk, Patrick (1955). 'The Canon Tables in the Book of Lindisfarne and in the Codex Fuldensis of Victor of Capua.' *JTS* ns 6.2: 193–4. Reprinted in McGurk 1998.

McGurk, Patrick (1956). 'The Irish Pocket Gospel Book.' *Sacris Erudiri* 8.2: 249–69. Reprinted in McGurk 1998.

McGurk, Patrick (1961a). *Latin Gospel Books from AD400 to AD800*. Paris: Érasme. Introduction reprinted in McGurk 1998.

McGurk, Patrick (1961b). 'Citation Marks in early Latin Manuscripts.' *Scriptorium* 15: 3–13. Reprinted in McGurk 1998.

McGurk, Patrick (1963). 'The Ghent Livinus Gospels and the Scriptorium of St Amand.' *Sacris Erudiri* 14: 164–205. Reprinted in McGurk 1998.

McGurk, Patrick (1987). 'The Gospel Book in Celtic Lands before AD850: Contents and Arrangement.' In *Ireland and Christendom: The Bible and the Missions*, ed. P. Ní Chatháin and M. Richter. Stuttgart: Klett-Cotta. Reprinted in McGurk 1998.

McGurk, Patrick (1993). 'The Disposition of Numbers in Latin Eusebian Canon Tables.' In Gryson 1993: 246–51. Reprinted in McGurk 1998.

McGurk, Patrick (1994a). 'The Oldest Manuscripts of the Latin Bible.' In Gameson 1994: 1–23. Cambridge: UP. Reprinted in McGurk 1998.

McGurk, Patrick (1994b). 'An Edition of the Abbreviated and Selective Set of Hebrew Names Found in the Book of Kells.' In O'Mahony 1994: 102–32. Reprinted in McGurk 1998.

McGurk, Patrick (1995). 'Theodore's Bible: The Gospels.' In *Archbishop Theodore: Commemorative Studies on his Life and Influence*, ed. M. Lapidge, Cambridge: UP, 255–9. Reprinted in McGurk 1998.

McGurk, Patrick (1996). 'Des recueils d'interprétations de noms Hébreux.' *Scriptorium* 50.1: 121. Reprinted in McGurk 1998.

McGurk, Patrick (1998). *Gospel Books and Early Latin Manuscripts*. Aldershot: Ashgate.

McKee, Helen (2000a). *Juvencus: Codex Cantabrigiensis Ff.4.42*. Facsimile edition. Aberystwyth: CMCS.

McKee, Helen (2000b). *The Cambridge Juvencus Manuscript, Glossed in Latin, Old Welsh, and Old Irish: Text and Commentary*. Aberystwyth: CMCS.

McKee, Helen (2000c). 'Scribes and Glosses from Dark Age Wales: The Cambridge Juvencus Manuscript.' *CMCS* 39: 1–22.

McKitterick, Rosamond (1989). *The Carolingians and the Written Word*. Cambridge: UP.

McKitterick, Rosamond, ed. (1994a). *Carolingian Culture: Emulation and Innovation*. Cambridge: UP.

McKitterick, Rosamond (1994b). 'Carolingian Bible Production. The Tours Anomaly.' In Gameson 1994: 63–77.

McKitterick, Rosamond, ed. (2008). *Charlemagne: The Formation of a European Identity*. Cambridge: UP.

McNally, Robert E. (1959). *The Bible in the Early Middle Ages*. Westminster: Newman.

McNamara, Martin (1987). 'The Echternach Gospels and MacDurnan Gospels: some common readings and their significance.' *Peritia* 6–7: 217–22.

McNamara, Martin (1990). *Studies on the Text of Early Irish Latin Gospels (A.D. 600–1200).* Steenbrugge-Dordrecht: Kluwer.

McNamara, Martin (1992). 'Non-Vulgate Readings of Codex AMB. I.61 SUP.' *Sacris erudiri* 33: 183–257. See also Gryson 1993:1.177–92.

McNamara, Martin (1994). 'Sources and Affiliations of the Catechesis Celtica.' *Sacris erudiri* 34: 185–237.

McNamara, Martin (2001). 'Bible Text and Illumination in St Gall Stiftsbibliothek 51, with Special Reference to Longinus in the Crucifixion Scene.' In *Pattern and Purpose in Insular Art,* ed. M. Redknap, N. Edwards, et al. Oxford: Oxbow, 191–202.

McNamara, Martin (2002). 'The Biblical text of Sankt Gallen 51 with particular reference to the Fourth Gospel.' In *Ogma. Essays in Celtic Studies,* ed. M. Richter and J.-M. Picard. Dublin: Four Oaks, 262–7.

McNamara, Martin (2004). 'The Latin Gospels, with Special Reference to Irish Tradition.' In *The Earliest Gospels,* ed. Charles Horton. London & New York: T&T Clark, 88–107.

Meehan, Bernard (1995). *The Book of Kells. An Illustrated Introduction.* 2nd edn. London: Thames & Hudson.

Meehan, Bernard (1996). *The Book of Durrow.* Dublin: Town House.

Meehan, Bernard (2012). *The Book of Kells.* London: Thames & Hudson.

Meershoek, Gerard Q.A. (1966). *Le latin biblique d'après saint Jérôme. Aspects linguistiques de la rencontre entre la Bible et le monde classique.* Nijmegen: Dekker & Van De Vegt.

Mees, M. (1966). 'Matthäus 5:1–26 in der altlateinischen Bibelübersetzungen.' *Vetera Christianorum* 3: 85–100.

Mercati, Giovanni (1925). 'Un paio di appunti sopra il codice purpureo veronese dei vangeli.' *RevBib* 34: 396–400.

Mercati, Giovanni (1953a). 'Papiri della Società Italiana 1306. Epistola Di Paolo.' *Pubblicazioni della Società Italiana per la ricerca dei Papiri* 13: 87–97.

Mercati, Giovanni (1953b). 'Sul frammento di San Giovanni ora ad Aberdeen.' *Pubblicazioni della Società Italiana per la ricerca dei Papiri* 13: 97–102.

Messerer, Wilhelm (1961). 'Zum Juvenianus-Codex der Biblioteca Vallicelliana.' In *Miscellanea Bibliotheca Hertzianae,* ed. Franz Graf Wolff Metternich and Ludwig Schudt. Munich: Schroll, 58–68.

Metz, Peter, ed. (1957). *The Golden Gospels of Echternach. Codex aureus Epternacensis.* New York: Praeger.

Metzger, Bruce M. (1972). 'Patristic Evidence and the Textual Criticism of the Church Fathers.' *NTS* 18.4: 379–400. Reprinted in Metzger 1980.

Metzger, Bruce M. (1977). *The Early Versions of the New Testament. Their Origins, Transmission and Limitations.* Oxford; Clarendon.

Metzger, Bruce M. (1979). 'St Jerome's Explicit References to Variant Readings in Manuscripts of the New Testament.' In Best and Wilson 1979: 179–90. Reprinted in Metzger 1980.

Metzger, Bruce M. (1980). *New Testament Studies: Philological, Versional and Patristic.* Leiden: Brill.

Metzger, Bruce M. (1987). *The Canon of the New Testament.* Oxford: UP.

Metzger, Bruce M. (1994). *A Textual Commentary on the Greek New Testament.* 2nd edn. Stuttgart: Deutsche Bibelgesellschaft.

Meyer, G. (1965). 'Ein neuer Zeuge des ρ-Typus der Vetus Latina im zweiten Korintherbrief 7,3–10,18.' *RevBén* 75: 40–53.

Meyer, G. and Burckhardt, M. (1960). *Die mittelalterlichen Handschriften der Universitätsbibliothek Basel. Beschreibendes Verzeichnis, Abteilung B: Theologische Pergamenthandschriften. Bd. 1.* Basel: UP.

Meyvaert, P. (1995). 'Bede's *Capitula Lectionum* for the Old and New Testaments.' *RevBén* 105: 348–80.

Meyvaert, P. (1996). 'Bede, Cassiodorus and the Codex Amiatinus.' *Speculum* 71: 827–84.

Millares Carlo, Agustín (1925). 'De paleografía visigótica: a propósito del Codex Toletanus.' *Revista de Filología Española*: 252–72.

Millares Carlo, Agustín (1931). *Contribución al 'Corpus' de códices visigóticos.* Publicaciones de la facultad de filosofía y letras 1. Madrid: UP, 94–130.

Millares Carlo, Agustín (1963). *Manuscritos visigóticos. Notas bibliográficas.* Madrid & Barcelona.

Milne, C.H. (1926). *A Reconstruction of the Old-Latin Text or Texts of the Gospels Used by Saint Augustine.* Cambridge: UP.

Minard, P. (1945). 'Témoins inédits de la vieille version latine des Évangiles. Les canons à initia des évangéliaires de Sainte-Croix de Poitiers et de la Trinité de Vendôme.' *RevBén* 56: 58–92.

Minard, P. (1947). 'Le Capitulare Evangeliorum de l'Évangéliaire oncial de Sainte-Croix de Poitiers.' *Ephemerides liturgicae* 61: 211–28.

Miquélez, Remedios and Martínez, Pilar (1935). 'El códice complutense o la primera Biblia visigótica de Alcalá.' *Anales de la Universidad de Madrid,* Letras 4: 204–19.

Mizzi, J. (1954). 'The Latin Text of Matt. V–VII in St. Augustine's «De Sermone Domini in monte».' *Augustiniana* 4: 234–78.

Mizzi, J. (1962). 'The Latin Text of the Gospel Quotations in St. Augustine's «De Diversis Quaestionibus LXXXIII Liber Unus».' *Augustiniana* 12: 245–90.

Mizzi, J. (1963). 'The Vulgate text of the Supplemental Pages of Codex Bezae Cantabrigiensis.' *Sacris Erudiri* 14: 149–63.

Mizzi, J. (1965). 'A Comparative Study of Some Portions of Cod. Palatinus and Cod. Bobiensis.' *RevBén* 75: 7–39.

Mizzi, J. (1968). 'The African Element in the Latin Text of Mt. XXIV of Cod. Cantabrigiensis.' *RevBén* 78: 33–66.

Mizzi, J. (1978). 'The Old-Latin Element in Jn. I,29 – III,26 of Cod. Sangallensis 60.' *Sacris Erudiri* 23: 33–62.

Mohrmann, Christine (1932). *Die altchristliche Sondersprache in den Sermones des hl. Augustin.* Nijmegen: Dekker & van de Vegt.

Mohrmann, Christine (1949). 'Les origines de la latinité chrétienne à Rome.' *VigC* 3: 67–106, 163–83.

Mohrmann, Christine (1958–77). *Études sur le latin des chrétiens.* 4 vols (2nd edn of vol. 1 1961). Rome: Storia e Letteratura.

Mommsen, Theodor (1886). 'Zur lateinischen Stichometrie.' *Hermes* 21: 142–56.

Monat, Pierre (1982a). 'Étude sur le texte des citations bibliques dans les Institutions divines: la place de Lactance parmi les témoins des «Vieilles Latines».' *REA* 28: 19–32.

Monat, Pierre (1982b). *Lactance et la Bible. Une propédeutique latine à la lecture de la Bible dans l'Occident constantinien.* 2 vols. Paris: IEA.

Monat, Pierre (1985). 'Les testimonia bibliques de Cyprien à Lactance.' In Fontaine and Pietri 1985: 499–507.

Monceaux, Paul (1923). *Histoire littéraire de l'Afrique chrétienne depuis les origines jusqu'à l'invasion arabe. VII. Saint Augustin et le Donatisme.* Anastatic reprint of 1963. Brussels: Culture et Civilisation.

Morey, C.R. (1931). 'The Gospel-Book of Landevennec: The Illumination of the Landevennec Gospels.' *Art Studies: Medieval Renaissance and Modern* 8: 258–62.

Morgan, Nigel (2012). 'Latin and vernacular Apocalypses.' In Marsden and Matter 2012: 404–26.

Morin, Germain (1893). *Liber Comicus sive Lectionarius Missae quo Toletana Ecclesia ante annos mille et ducentos utebatur.* Maredsous: Abbaye de Maredsous.

Morin, Germain (1908). 'Un lectionnaire mérovingien avec fragments du texte occidental des Actes.' *RevBén* 25: 161–6.

Morin, Germain (1909). 'Un texte préhiéronymien du cantique de l'apocalypse XV, 304: L'hymne Magna et mirabilia.' *RevBén* 26: 464–7.

Morin, Germain (1910). 'Le plus ancien comes ou lectionnaire de l'Église romaine.' *RevBén* 27: 41–74.

Morin, Germain (1911). 'L'évangéliaire de Wurtzbourg.' *RevBén* 28: 296–330.

Morin, Germain (1913). 'Le lectionnaire mérovingien de Schlettstadt et son texte occidental des Actes.' In *Études, textes, découvertes. Contributions à la littérature et à l'histoire des douze premiers siècles.* Maredsous & Paris: Abbaye de Maredsous.

Morin, Germain (1934). 'Sur la date et la provenance de l'ordo scrutiniorum du Cod. Ambros. T 27 sup.' *RevBén* 46: 216–33.

Morin, Germain (1937). 'Le plus ancien monument qui existe de la liturgie gallicane: le lectionnaire palimpseste de Wolfenbüttel.' *Ephemerides liturgicae* 51: 3–12.

Muncey, R.W. (1959). *The New Testament Text of St. Ambrose.* Cambridge: UP.

Mundó, A.M. (1954). 'Frammenti palinsesti del «Liber Commicus» visigotico.' *Analecta gregoriana* 70: 101–6.

Mundó, A.M. (1956). 'El Commicus palimpsest Paris lat. 2269. Amb notes sobre litúrgia i manuscrits visigòtics a Septimània i Catalunya.' In *Liturgica I: Cardinal I. A. Schuster in memoriam.* Montserrat: Abbey of Montserrat, 151–275.

Mundó, A.M. (1965). 'La datación de los códices litúrgicos visigóticos toledanos.' *Hispania Sacra* 18: 16.

Munier, Charles (1972). 'La tradition manuscrite de l'Abrégé d'Hippone et le canon des Écritures des églises africaines.' *Sacris Erudiri* 21: 43–55.

Munier, Charles (1974). *Concilia Africae. A.345–A.525.* Turnhout: Brepols.

Mütherich, Florentine (1976). 'Manoscritti romani e miniatura carolingia.' In *Roma e l'età carolingia.* Rome: Multigrafica, 79–86.

Mynors, R.A.B. and Powell, R. (1956). 'The Stonyhurst Gospel.' In *The Relics of St Cuthbert*, ed. C.F. Battiscombe, Oxford: UP, 356–74.

NA28 (2012). *Nestle-Aland Novum Testamentum Graece*, ed. Institut für neutestamentliche Textforschung. 28th edn. Stuttgart: Deutsche Bibelgesellschaft.

Nardin, Giuseppe et al., ed. (1993). *Commentario storico paleografico artistico critico della Bibbia di San Paolo fuori le Mura.* Rome: Libreria dello Stato.

Nauroy, Gérard and Vannier, Marie-Anne, ed. (2008). *Saint Augustin et la Bible*. Bern: Peter Lang.

Nees, Lawrence (1983). 'The Colophon Drawing in the Book of Mulling.' *CMCS* 5: 67–91.

Nees, Lawrence (1987). *The Gundohinus Gospels*. Cambridge: Medieval Academy of America.

Nees, Lawrence (1999). 'Problems of Form and Function in Early Medieval Illustrated Bibles from Northwest Europe.' In Williams 1999: 121–78.

Nellessen, Ernst (1965). *Untersuchungen zur altlateinischen Überlieferung des Ersten Thessalonicherbriefes*. Bonn: Hanstein.

Nellessen, Ernst (1968). 'Der lateinische Paulustext im Codex Baliolensis des Pelagius-kommentars.' *ZNW* 59: 210–30.

Nellessen, Ernst (1970). 'Lateinische Summarien zum Hebräerbrief.' *Biblische Zeitschrift* ns 14: 240–51.

Nestle-Aland: see NA28.

Netzer, Nancy (1994). *Cultural Interplay in the Eighth Century: The Trier Gospels and the Making of a Scriptorium at Echternach*. Cambridge: UP.

Nordenfalk, Carl (1938). *Die spätantiken Kanontafeln*. 2 vols. Göteborg: Isacsons.

Nordenfalk, Carl (1947). *Before the Book of Durrow*. Copenhagen: Munksgaard.

Norelli, Enrico (1990). 'La tradizione ecclesiastica negli antichi prologhi latini alle epistole paoline.' In *La tradizione: forme e modi*. Rome: Augustinianum, 301–24.

North, J. Lionel (1995). 'The Use of the Latin Fathers for New Testament Textual Criticism.' In Ehrman and Holmes 1995: 208–23.

Norris, Oliver (2014). 'The Sources for the Temptations Episode in the *Paschale Carmen* of Sedulius.' In Houghton 2014b: 67–92.

Ó Cróinín, Daíbhí (1989). 'Is the Augsburg Gospel Codex a Northumbrian Manuscript?' In *St Cuthbert, his Cult and his Community to AD 1200*, ed. Gerald Bonner, David Rollason, and Clare Stancliffe. Woodbridge: Boydell, 189–201.

Ó Cróinín, Daíbhí (2000). 'Bischoff's Wendepunkte Fifty Years On.' *RevBén* 110: 204–37.

O'Donnell, James J. (1979). *Cassiodorus*. Berkeley: California UP.

O'Loughlin, Thomas (1993). 'Julian of Toledo's Antikeimenon and the Development of Latin Exegesis.' *Proceedings of the Irish Biblical Association* 16: 80–98.

O'Loughlin, Thomas (1994). 'The Latin version of the Scriptures in Iona in the late seventh century: the evidence from Adomnán's De locis sanctis.' *Peritia* 8: 18–26.

O'Loughlin, Thomas (1996). 'Tyconius' Use of the Canonical Gospels.' *RevBén* 116: 229–33.

O'Loughlin, Thomas, ed. (1999a). *The Scriptures and Early Medieval Ireland*. Steenbrugge: Brepols.

O'Loughlin, Thomas (1999b). 'Tradition and Exegesis in the Eighth Century. The Use of Patristic Sources in Early Medieval Scriptural Commentaries.' In O'Loughlin 1999a: 217–39.

O'Loughlin, Thomas (2007). 'Division systems for the Gospels: The Case of the Stowe St John.' *Scriptorium* 61: 150–64.

O'Loughlin, Thomas (2009). 'The Biblical text of the Book of Deer (C.U.L. Ii. 6.32): Evidence for the remains of a division system from its manuscript ancestry.' *Scriptorium* 63: 30–57.

O'Loughlin, Thomas (2010). 'Harmonizing the Truth: Eusebius and the Problem of the Four Gospels.' *Traditio* 65: 1–29.

O'Loughlin, Thomas (2012). *Gildas and the Scriptures*. Turnhout: Brepols.

O'Loughlin, Thomas (2014). 'The Structure of the Collections that Make up the Scriptures: The Influence of Augustine on Cassiodorus.' *RevBén* 124.1: 48–64.

O'Mahony, Felicity, ed. (1994). *Book of Kells. Proceedings of a Conference at Trinity College Dublin*. Dublin: College Library.

O'Malley, T.P. (1967). *Tertullian and the Bible. Language, Imagery, Exegesis*. Nijmegen: Dekker & Van De Vegt.

Orban, A.P. (1995). 'Juvencus als Bibelexeget und als Zeuge der «afrikanischen» Vetus Latina Tradition. Untersuchungen der Bergpredigt (Mt. 5,1–48) in der Vetus Latina und in der Versifikation des Juvencus (I. 452–572).' *VigC* 49: 334–52.

Osburn, Carroll D. (2005). 'Methodology in Identifying Patristic Citations in NT Textual Criticism.' *NovT* 47.4: 313–43.

O'Sullivan, William (1994). 'The Lindisfarne Scriptorium: For and Against.' *Peritia* 8: 80–94.

Oxford Vulgate: see Wordsworth, White, et al.

Pagani, Sergio M. (1976). 'Il Matteo latino in Tertulliano e Cipriano.' Dissertation, Catholic University of Milan.

Pagani, Sergio M. (1978). 'Le versioni latine africane del Nuovo Testamento: Considerazioni su Mt. 10,32-33 in Tertulliano e Cipriano.' *Bibbia e Oriente* 20: 255–70.

Pagano, Sergio M. (1987). 'Nuove ricerche sul codice biblico latino purpureo di Sarezzano.' *Benedictina* 34: 25–165.

Palazzo, Éric (2006). 'Tradition antique et «modernité» dans les évangiles de Sainte-Croix de Poitiers.' In *Artem quaevis alit terra*. Warsaw: UP, 67–80.

Pallás, José Maria Romeo (1991). 'La Biblia Cyprianea. Una muestra de su reconstrucción.' In *Actes del IXè simposi de la secció catalana de la SEEC*, ed. L. Ferreres. Barcelona: UP, 2.787–8.

Palmer, D.W. (1976). 'The Origin, Form and Purpose of Mark XVI.4 in Codex Bobbiensis.' *JTS* ns 27: 113–22.

Palmer, L.R. (1954). *The Latin Language*. London: Faber & Faber.

Parker, D.C. (1985). 'The Translation of OYN in the Old Latin Gospels.' *NTS* 31: 252–76. Reprinted in Parker 2009.

Parker, D.C. (1990). 'A Copy of the Codex Mediolanensis.' *JTS* ns 41: 537–41. Reprinted in Parker 2009.

Parker, D.C. (1991). 'Unequally Yoked: The Present State of the Codex Bobbiensis.' *JTS* ns 42: 581–8. Reprinted in Parker 2009.

Parker, D.C. (1992). *Codex Bezae. An Early Christian Manuscript and its Text*. Cambridge: UP.

Parker, D.C. (2008). *An Introduction to the New Testament Manuscripts and their Texts*. Cambridge: UP.

Parker, D.C. (2009). *Manuscripts, Texts, Theology*. Berlin & New York: De Gruyter.

Parker, D.C. (2012). *Textual Scholarship and the Making of the New Testament*. Oxford: UP.

Parker, D.C. and Amphoux, C.-B., ed. (1996). *Codex Bezae. Studies from the Lunel Colloquium*. Leiden: Brill.

Parkes, Malcolm B. (1992). *Pause and Effect. A History of Punctuation in the West.* Aldershot: Ashgate.

Peebles, B.M. (1967). 'Bible. Latin Versions.' In *New Catholic Encyclopaedia II.* New York, 426–57.

Pérez de Urbel, J. and González y Ruiz-Zorrilla, A. (1950, 1955). *Liber Commicus.* 2 vols. Madrid.

Perriccioli Saggese, Alessandra (2014). 'Le bibbia visigotica di Cava de' Tirreni, la sua copia ottocentesca e la riscoperta della miniatura.' In *Riforma della chiesa, esperienze monastiche e poteri locali,* ed. M. Galante et al., Florence: SISMEL, 329–38.

Petersen, William L. (1994). *Tatian's Diatessaron. Its Creation, Dissemination, Significance and History in Scholarship.* Leiden: Brill.

Petitmengin, Pierre (1968). 'Le Codex Veronensis de saint Cyprien. Philologie et histoire de la philologie.' *Revue des études latines* 46: 330–78.

Petitmengin, Pierre (1985). 'Les plus anciens manuscrits de la Bible latine.' In Fontaine and Pietri 1985: 89–127.

Petitmengin, Pierre (1990a). 'Le «Codex Amiatinus».' In Martin and Vezin 1990: 73–7.

Petitmengin, Pierre (1990b). 'La Bible de Rorigon.' In Martin and Vezin 1990: 78–83.

Petitmengin, Pierre (1993). 'Bible latine et Europe savante.' In *Patristique et antiquité tardive en Allemagne et France de 1870 à 1930,* ed. Jacques Fontaine et al. Paris: IEA, 73–92.

Petitmengin, Pierre (1997). '*Capitula* païens et chrétiens.' In *Titres et articulations du texte dans les œuvres antiques,* ed. Jean-Claude Fredouille. Paris: IEA, 491–509.

Petzer, Jacobus H. (1988). 'A Quantitative Analysis of the Relationship among Latin Manuscripts in Acts 6.' In *Koninkryk: Gees en Woord,* ed. J.C. Coetzee. Pretoria: NGKB, 98–112.

Petzer, Jacobus H. (1991a). 'Tertullian's Text of Acts.' *The Second Century* 8: 201–15.

Petzer, Jacobus H. (1991b). 'St Augustine's Text of Acts.' *Neotestamentica* 25: 33–50.

Petzer, Jacobus H. (1993a). 'Texts and Text Types in the Latin Version of Acts.' In Gryson 1993: 259–84.

Petzer, Jacobus H. (1993b). 'The Textual Relationships of the Vulgate in Acts.' *NTS* 39: 227–45.

Petzer, Jacobus H. (1993c). 'Variation in citations from the Old Testament in the Latin version of Acts.' *Journal of Northwest Semitic Languages* 19: 143–57.

Petzer, Jacobus H. (1995). 'The Latin Version of the New Testament.' In Ehrman and Holmes 1995: 113–30.

Philippart, G. (1972). 'Fragments palimpsests latins du Vindobonensis 563 (Ve siècle?). Évangile selon S. Matthieu, Évangile de l'enfance selon Thomas, Évangile de Nicodème.' *Analecta Bollandia* 90: 404–6.

Picard, Jean-Michel (2003). 'L'exégèse irlandaise des Épitres de saint Paul: les gloses latines et gaéliques de Würzburg.' *Recherches augustiniennes* 33: 155–67.

Piras, Antonio (2001). 'Bibbia e sermo biblicus negli scritti luciferiani.' In *La figura e l'opera di Lucifero di Cagliari,* ed. Sonia Laconi. Rome: Augustinianum, 131–44.

Plater, W.E. and White, H.J. (1926). *A Grammar of the Vulgate, being An Introduction to the Study of the Latinity of the Vulgate Bible.* Oxford: Clarendon.

Plinval, Georges de (1943). *Pélage. Ses écrits, sa vie et sa réforme.* Lausanne: Payot.

Plooij, D. (1936). *The Latin Text of the Epistles of St. Paul.* Leiden: Bezan Club.

Poleg, Eyal and Light, Laura, ed. (2013). *Form and Function in the Late Medieval Bible.* Leiden: Brill.

Popovic, Vladislav (1989). 'Les Évangiles de Split.' *Bulletin de la société nationale des antiquaires de France* 1987: 266–89.

Popovic, Vladislav (1990). 'Sur l'origine de l'évangéliaire latin de la British Library, Harley 1775.' *Comptes-rendus des séances de l'Académie des inscriptions et belles-lettres* 134.3: 709–35.

Popovic, Vladislav (1992). 'Du nouveau sur les Évangiles de Split.' *Bulletin de la société nationale des antiquaires de France* 1990: 275–93.

Portarena, D. (1946). *Doctrina scripturistica S. Filastrii Brixiensis episcopi et textus biblicus ab eo adhibitus.* Rome: Tipografia Pio X.

Porter, A.W.S. (1935). 'Cantica Mozarabica Officii.' *Ephemerides Liturgicae* 49: 126–45.

Powell, R. (1956). 'The Book of Kells, the Book of Durrow. Comments on the Vellum, the Make-up and other Aspects.' *Scriptorium* 10: 3–21.

Pulliam, Heather (2006). *Word and Image in the Book of Kells.* Dublin: Four Courts.

Quentin, H. (1922). *Mémoire sur l'établissement du texte de la Vulgate. Première partie: Octateuque.* Rome & Paris: Desclée & Gabalda.

Quentin, H. (1927). 'La prétendue Itala de saint Augustin.' *RevBib* 36: 216–25.

Quispel, Gilles (1943). *De bronnen van Tertullianus' Adversus Marcionem.* Leiden: Burgersdijk & Niermans.

Quispel, Gilles (1972). 'Mani et la tradition évangélique des Judéo-chrétiens.' *Recherches de science religieuse* 60: 143–50.

Radiciotti, P. (1998). 'Manoscritti digrafici grecolatini e latinogreci nell'Alto Medioevo.' *Römische historische Mitteilungen* 40: 49–118.

Rand, Edward K. (1929). *A Survey of the Manuscripts of Tours.* Cambridge: Medieval Academy of America.

Rand, Edward K. (1931). 'A Preliminary Study of Alcuin's Bible.' *HTR* 24: 323–96.

Rand, Edward K. (1934). *The Earliest Book of Tours with Supplementary Descriptions of Other Manuscripts of Tours.* Cambridge: Medieval Academy of America.

Ranke, Ernst (1847). *Das kirchliche Pericopensystem.* Berlin: Reimer.

Ranke, Ernst (1868). *Codex Fuldensis. Novum Testamentum latine interprete Hieronymo ex manuscripto Victoris Capuani.* Marburg: Elwert.

Rathofer, Johannes (1973). 'Die Einwirkung des Fuldischen Evangelientextes auf den althochdeutschen 'Tatian'. Abkehr von der Methode der Diatessaronforschung.' In *Literatur und Sprache im europäischen Mittelalter*, ed. A. Önnerfors et al., Darmstadt: Wissenschaftliche Buchgesellschaft, 256–308.

Ray, R. (1982). 'What Do We Know about Bede's Commentaries?' *RTAM* 49: 5–20.

Register: see Gryson 1999, 2004.

Regul, Jürgen (1969). *Die antimarcionitischen Evangelienprologe.* Freiburg: Herder.

Reichardt, Alexander (1909). *Der Codex Boernerianus der Briefe des Apostels Paulus mit einem Vorwort von Dr. Alexander Reichardt.* Leipzig: Karl W. Hiersemann.

Renna, T. (1990). 'The Triers Apocalypse and its Patristic Origins.' *Patristic and Byzantine Review* 9: 49–57.

Repertorium: see Gryson 2007.

Rettig, H.C.M. (1836). *Antiquissimus Quatuor Evangeliorum Canonicorum Codex Sangallensis Graeco-Latinus Interlinearis Nunquam Adhuc Collatus.* Zurich: Frideric Schulthess.

Reventlow, Henning L.G. Graf. (2009). *History of Biblical Interpretation 2. From Late Antiquity to the End of the Middle Ages*. Translated by James O. Duke from *Epochen der Bibelauslesung. 2. Von der Spätantike bis zum Ausgang des Mittelalters*. (Munich: Beck, 1994). Atlanta: SBL.

Revilla Rico, Mariano (1917). *La Políglota de Alcalá: estudio histórico-crítico*. Madrid: Imprenta Helénica.

Reynolds, L.D. and Wilson, N.G. (2013). *Scribes and Scholars. A Guide to the Transmission of Greek and Latin Literature*. 4th edn. (Refs. are to the 3rd edn of 1991.) Oxford: UP.

Ricci, Luigi G.G. (2000). *La Bibbia Amiatina. The Codex Amiatinus. Riproduzzione integrale su CD-ROM del manoscritto*. Florence: SISMEL.

Riché, Pierre (1976). *Education and Culture in the Barbarian West*. Translated by John Contreni from *Éducation et culture dans l'Occident barbare. VIe–VIIIe siècles* (Paris: Seuil, 1963). Columbia: UP.

Riché, Pierre and Lobrichon, Guy, ed. (1984). *Le Moyen Âge et la Bible*. Paris: Beauchesne.

Rivera Recio, J.F. (1948). 'El 'Liber Comicus' de Toledo. Ms. 35,8 de la Biblioteca Capitular.' *Estudios Bíblicos* 7: 335–59.

Robinson, Henry Wheeler, ed. (1954). *The Bible in its Ancient and English Versions*. 2nd edn. Oxford: Clarendon.

Rohr, W. Günther (2000). 'Die Griffelglossen im Echternacher Evangeliar Willibrords.' In *Analecta Epternacensia*, ed. L. Deitz and R. Nolden. Luxembourg: Stadtbibliothek, 9–16.

Rolando, G.M. (1945–6). 'Ricostruzione teologico-critica del testo latino del Vangelo di S. Luca usato da S. Ambrogio.' *Biblica* 26: 238–76, 321–35; 27: 3–17.

Rönsch, Hermann (1871). *Das Neue Testament Tertullians. Aus den Schriften des Letzteren möglichst vollständig reconstruirt*. Leipzig; Fuess.

Rönsch, Hermann (1875). *Itala und Vulgata*. 2nd edn. Marburg: Elwert.

Rönsch, Hermann (1882–3). 'Die Doppelübersetzungen im lateinischen Texte des cod. Boernerianus der Paulinischen Briefe.' *ZWT* 25: 488–517; 26: 73–98, 309–44.

Ropes, J.H. (1926). 'The Text of Acts.' In *The Beginnings of Christianity 1/3*, ed. F.J.F. Jackson and K. Lake. London: Macmillan.

Ropes, J.H. and W.H.P. Hatch (1928). 'The Vulgate, Peshitto, Sahidic and Bohairic Versions of Acts and the Greek MSS.' *HTR* 21: 69–95.

Roth, Dieter T. (2008). 'Matthean Texts and Tertullian's Accusations.' *JTS* ns 59: 580–97.

Roth, Dieter T. (2009). 'Did Tertullian possess a Greek copy or a Latin translation of Marcion's Gospel?' *VigC* 63: 429–67.

Roth, Dieter T. (2012). 'Marcion and the Early Text of the New Testament.' In Hill and Kruger 2012: 302–12.

Roth, Dieter T. (2015). *The Text of Marcion's Gospel*. Leiden: Brill.

Rouse, Richard H. (2000). *Manuscripts and Their Makers. Commercial Book Producers in Medieval Paris, 1200–1500*. Turnhout: Harvey Miller & Brepols.

Rouse, Richard H. and McNelis, Charles (2000). 'North African literary activity: A Cyprian fragment, the stichometric lists and a Donatist compendium.' *RHT* 30: 189–233.

Rouse, Richard H. and Rouse, M.A. (1974). 'The Verbal Concordance to the Scriptures.' *Archivum Fratrum Praedicatorum* 44: 5–30.

Ruggiero, F., ed. (1991). *Atti dei martiri scilitani. Introduzione, testo, traduzione, testimonianze e commento*. Rome: Accademia Nazionale dei Lincei.

Ruzzier, Chiara (2008). 'La produzione di manoscritti neotestamentari in Italia nel XIII secolo: analisi codicologica.' *Segno e Testo* 6: 249–94.

Ruzzier, Chiara (2013). 'The miniaturisation of Bible manuscripts in the thirteenth century.' In Poleg and Light 2013: 105–25.

Ruzzier, Chiara (2014). 'Quelques observations sur la fabrication des bibles au XIIIe siècle et le système de la *Pecia*.' *RevBén* 124.1: 151–89.

Sabatier, Pierre (1743). *Bibliorum Sacrorum Latinae Versiones Antiquae seu Vetus Italica. Tomus Primus; Tomus Secundus; Tomus Tertius.* [Vol. 1: Preface, Genesis–Job; Vol. 2: Psalms–2 Maccabees; Vol. 3: New Testament.] Reims: Florentain. Reprinted Turnhout: Brepols, 1976.

Saenger, P. (2008). 'The Anglo-Hebraic Origins of the Modern Chapter Division of the Latin Bible.' In *La fractura historiográfica. Edad Media y Renacimiento desde el tercer milenio*, ed. J. San José Lera, Salamanca: Seminario de Estudios Medievales y Renacentistas, 177–202.

Salmon, Pierre (1941). 'Le lectionnaire de Luxeuil. Ses origines et l'Église de Langres.' *RevBén* 53: 89–107.

Salmon, Pierre (1944, 1953). *Le lectionnaire de Luxeuil (Paris, ms. lat. 9427). 1: Édition et étude comparative; 2: Étude paléographique et liturgique.* 2 vols. Vatican City.

Salmon, Pierre (1963). 'Le texte biblique des lectionnaires mérovingiens'. In Franceschini et al. 1963: 491–517.

Sanday, W. (1885). 'Some Further Remarks on the Corbey St. James (ff).' *Studia Biblica* 1: 233–63.

Sanday, W. (1891). *The Books of the Bible and the Writings of Cyprian in the Phillipps Collection at Cheltenham.* Oxford; Clarendon, 217–323. Reprinted as a separate volume, Piscataway: Gorgias, 2006.

Sanday, W., Turner, C.H., et al., ed. (1923). *Nouum Testamentum Sancti Irenaei Episcopi Lugdunensis.* Oxford: Clarendon.

Sanders, G. and Van Uytfanghe, M. (1989). *Bibliographie signalétique du Latin des Chrétiens.* Turnhout: Brepols.

Sanders, H.A. (1922). 'Buchanans Publikationen altlateinischer Texte. Eine Warnung.' *ZNW* 21: 291–9.

Sanders, H.A. and Ogden, J. (1937). 'The Text of Acts in Ms. 146 of the University of Michigan.' *Proceedings of the American Philosophical Society* 77.1: 1–97.

Saxer, Victor (1985a). 'Bible et liturgie.' In Fontaine and Pietri 1985: 157–88.

Saxer, Victor (1985b). 'La Bible chez les Pères latins du IIIe siècle.' In Fontaine and Pietri 1985: 339–69.

Scalon, Cesare and Pani, Laura (1998). *I codici della Biblioteca Capitolare di Cividale del Friuli.* Florence: SISMEL.

Schaab, Rupert (1999). 'Bibeltext und Schriftstudien in St. Gallen.' In *Das Kloster St. Gallen im Mittelalter*, ed. Peter Ochsenbein. Stuttgart: Theiss, 119–36, 248–53.

Schäfer, K.T. (1929). *Untersuchungen zur Geschichte der lateinischen Übersetzung des Hebräerbriefs.* Freiburg: Herder.

Schäfer, K.T. (1935). 'Der griechisch-lateinische Text des Galaterbriefes in der Handschriftengruppe DEFG.' In *Scientia Sacra. Theologische Festgabe für K.J. Kardinal Schulte*, ed. Carl Feckes. Cologne & Düsseldorf: Bachem & Schwann, 41–70.

Schäfer, K.T. (1939). *Die Überlieferung des altlateinischen Galaterbriefes I.* In Personal- und Vorlesungsverzeichnis der Staatl. Akademie zu Braunsberg. Braunsberg.

Schäfer, K.T. (1951). 'Die Zitate in der lateinischen Irenäusübersetzung und ihr Wert für die Textgeschichte des Neuen Testaments.' In *Vom Wort des Lebens*, ed. N. Adler. Münster: Aschendorff, 50–9.

Schäfer, K.T. (1957). *Die altlateinische Bibel.* Bonn: Hanstein.

Schäfer, K.T. (1962). 'Pelagius und die Vulgata.' *NTS* 9: 361–6.

Schäfer, K.T. (1963). 'Der Paulustext des Pelagius.' In *Studiorum Paulinorum Congressus Internationalis Catholicus 1961.* Rome: Pontifical Biblical Institute, 2.453–60.

Schäfer, K.T. (1970a). 'Marius Victorinus und die marcionitischen Prologe zu den Paulusbriefen.' *RevBén* 80: 7–16.

Schäfer, K.T. (1970b). 'Marcion und die ältesten Prologe zu den Paulusbriefen.' In *Kyriakon. Festschrift Johannes Quasten*, ed. P. Granfield and J.A. Jungmann. Münster: Aschendorff, 1.130–50.

Schenker, Adrian (2013). 'Der Platz der altlateinischen Randlesarten des Kodex von León und der Valvanera-Bibel in der biblischen Textgeschichte (1–4Kgt).' In *Der Antiochenische Text der LXX*, ed. Siegfried Kreuzer and Marcus Sigismund. Göttingen: Vandenhoek & Ruprecht, 199–210.

Scherbenske, Eric (2010). 'The Vulgate *Primum quaeritur*, Codex Fuldensis, and the hermeneutical role of early Christian introductory materials.' *Studia Patristica* 54: 139–44.

Schildenberger, Johannes (1952). 'Die Itala des hl. Augustinus'. In Fischer and Fiala 1952: 84–102.

Schirner, Rebekka (2014). 'Donkeys or Shoulders? Augustine as a Textual Critic of the Old and New Testament.' In Houghton 2014b: 45–66.

Schirner, Rebekka (2015). *Inspice diligenter codices: Philologische Studien zu Augustins Umgang mit Bibelhandschriften und Übersetzungen.* Berlin: De Gruyter.

Schlossnikel, Reinhard F. (1991). *Der Brief an die Hebräer und das Corpus Paulinum. Eine linguistische, Bruchstelle' im Codex Claromontanus . . . und ihre Bedeutung im Rahmen von Text- und Kanongeschichte.* Freiburg: Herder.

Schmid, Anne (1992). 'Il codice di Gioveniano: Roma, Bibl.Vall. B 25 II.' Doctoral thesis: Università degli studi di Roma La Sapienza. Rome: Pittini.

Schmid, Ulrich B. (1995). *Marcion und sein Apostolos.* Berlin & New York: De Gruyter.

Schmid, Ulrich B. (2003a). 'How Can We Access Second Century Gospel Texts? The Cases of Marcion and Tatian.' In *The New Testament Text in Early Christianity*, ed. C.-B. Amphoux and J.K. Elliott. Lausanne: Zebre, 151–93.

Schmid, Ulrich B. (2003b). 'In Search of Tatian's Diatessaron in the West.' *VigC* 57.2: 176–99.

Schmid, Ulrich B. (2005). *Unum ex Quattuor. Eine Geschichte der lateinischen Tatian-überlieferung.* Freiburg: Herder.

Schmid, Ulrich B. (2012). 'The Diatessaron of Tatian.' In Ehrman and Holmes 2012: 115–42.

Schmid, Ulrich B. (2013). 'Marcion and the Textual History of *Romans*: Editorial Activity and Early Editions of the New Testament'. In Vinzent, Mellerin, and Houghton 2013: 99–113.

Schneider, H. (1938). *Die altlateinischen biblischen Cantica.* Beuron: Kunstverlag.

Schrijnen, J. (1932). *Charakteristik des altchristlichen Latein.* Nijmegen: Dekker & van de Vegt.

Schroeder, Jean (1983). 'Älteste Echternacher Bibelfragmente.' In *Mélanges offerts à Joseph Goedert,* ed. G. Trausch and É. Van der Vekene. Luxembourg: Bibliothèque nationale, 228–39.

Schultze, Viktor (1904). *Codex Waldeccensis (D^{W Paul}). Unbekannte Fragmente einer griechisch-lateinischen Bibelhandschrift.* Munich: C.H. Beck.

Schulz-Flügel, Eva (2000). 'Probleme der altlateinischen Bibelübersetzungen und ihrer Darstellung in einer wissenschaftlichen Edition.' *Editio* 14: 1–10.

Schumacher, Rudolf (1929). *Die beiden letzten Kapitel des Römerbriefes.* Münster: Aschendorff.

Schwank, B. (1961). 'Zur Neuausgabe von «Contra Varimadum» nach dem Codex Paris B.N. Lat. 12217 in Corpus Christianorum Series Latina XC.' *Sacris Erudiri* 12: 112–96.

Scrivener, Frederick H.A. (1859). *An Exact Transcript of the Codex Augiensis, a Graeco-Latin Manuscript of St Paul's Epistles deposited in the Library of Trinity College Cambridge . . . with a critical introduction.* Cambridge: UP.

Scrivener, Frederick H.A. (1864). *Bezae Codex Cantabrigiensis.* Cambridge: Deighton Bell. Reprinted Pittsburgh: Academic Press, 1978.

Scrivener, Frederick H.A. (1887). *Codex S. Ceaddae Latinus Evangelia SSS. Matthaei, Marci, Lucae ad cap. III, 9 complectens.* Cambridge: C.J. Clay.

Sharpe, John L. and Van Kampen, K., ed. (1998). *The Bible as Book. The Manuscript Tradition.* London: British Library.

Shepard, Dorothy (2012a). 'The Latin gospelbook, c.600–1200.' In Marsden and Matter 2012: 338–62.

Shepard, Dorothy (2012b). 'Romanesque display Bibles.' In Marsden and Matter 2012: 392–403.

Sillib, R. (1906). 'Ein Bruchstück der Augustinischen Bibel.' *ZNW* 7: 82–6.

Simonet, Jean-Louis (2010). 'Une lecture vieille latine des Actes des Apôtres dans un recueil liturgique de Graz.' *RevBén* 120: 12–30.

Simonetti, Manlio (1994). *Biblical Interpretation in the Early Church. An Historical Introduction to Patristic Exegesis.* Translated by John A. Hughes from *Profilo Storico dell' Esesgesi Patristica* (1981). Edinburgh: T&T Clark.

Sittl, Karl (1882). *Die lokalen Verschiedenheiten der lateinischen Sprache mit besonderer Berücksichtigung des afrikanischen Lateins.* Erlangen: Deichert.

Sloan, Michael C. (2012). *The Harmonious Organ of Sedulius Scottus: Introduction to his Collectaneum in Apostolum and Translation of its Prologue and Commentaries on Galatians and Ephesians.* Berlin & Boston: De Gruyter.

Smalley, Beryl (1935–6). 'Gilbertus Universalis, Bishop of London (1128–1134), and the Problem of the "Glossa ordinaria".' *RTAM* 7: 235–62; 8: 24–60.

Smalley, Beryl (1937). 'La Glossa ordinaria. Quelques prédécesseurs d'Anselme de Laon.' *RTAM* 9: 365–400.

Smalley, Beryl (1963). 'L'exégèse biblique dans la littérature latine.' In Franceschini et al. 1963: 631–56.

Smalley, Beryl (1978). 'Some Gospel Commentaries of the Early Twelfth Century.' *RTAM* 45: 147–80.

Smalley, Beryl (1983). *The Study of the Bible in the Middle Ages*. 3rd edn. Oxford: Blackwell.

Smith, Lesley (2001). *Masters of the Sacred Page. Manuscripts of Theology in the Latin West to 1274*. Notre Dame: UP.

Smith, Lesley (2009). *The Glossa Ordinaria. The Making of a Medieval Bible Commentary*. Leiden: Brill.

Smith, Lesley (2012). 'The Glossed Bible.' In Marsden and Matter 2012: 363–79.

Smith, L.F. (1924). 'A Note on the Codex Toletanus.' *RevBén* 36: 347.

Soden: see von Soden.

Souter, Alexander (1905). *A Study of Ambrosiaster*. Cambridge: UP.

Souter, Alexander (1911). 'The Type or Types of Gospel Text used by St Jerome and the Basis of His Revision, With Special Reference to St Luke's Gospel and Codex Vercellensis (a).' *JTS* os 12: 583–92.

Souter, Alexander (1922–31). *Pelagius' Expositions of Thirteen Epistles of St Paul*. 3 vols. Cambridge: UP.

Souter, Alexander (1922b). 'A Lost Leaf of Codex Palatinus (e) of the Old-Latin Gospels Recovered.' *JTS* os 23: 284–6.

Souter, Alexander (1924). 'A Fragment of an Unpublished Latin Text of the Epistle to the Hebrews with a Brief Exposition.' In *Miscellanea Francesco Ehrle I*. Studi e Testi 37. Rome, 39–46.

Souter, Alexander (1927). *The Earliest Latin Commentaries on the Epistles of St Paul*. Oxford: Clarendon.

Souter, Alexander (1932). 'Traces of an Unknown System of Capitula for St Matthew's Gospel.' *JTS* os 33: 188–9.

Souter, Alexander (1934). 'The Anonymous Latin Translation of Origen on St Matthew and Old Latin MS q of the Gospels.' *JTS* os 35: 63–6.

Souter, Alexander (1937). 'Portions of an Old-Latin Text of St. Matthew's Gospel.' In *Quantulacumque. Studies presented to K. Lake*, ed. R.P. Casey, S. Lake, and A.K. Lake. London, 349–54.

Souter, Alexander (1941). 'Notes on Incidental Gospel Quotations in Jerome's Commentary on St Matthew's Gospel.' *JTS* os 42: 12–18.

Spagnolo, Antonio and Marchi, Silvia (1996). *I manoscritti della Biblioteca capitolare di Verona: catalogo descrittivo*. Verona: Mazziana.

Sparks, H.F.D. (1954a). 'The Latin Bible.' In Robinson 1954: 100–10.

Sparks, H.F.D. (1954b). 'A Celtic Text of the Latin Apocalypse Preserved in Two Durham Manuscripts of Bede's Commentary on the Apocalypse.' *JTS* ns 5: 227–31.

Sparks, H.F.D. (1970). 'Jerome as Biblical Scholar.' In Ackroyd and Evans 1970: 510–41.

Spicq, Ceslas (1944). *Esquisse d'une histoire de l'exégèse latine au Moyen Âge*. Paris: Vrin.

Stansbury, Mark (1999). 'Early-Medieval Biblical Commentaries, Their Writers and Readers.' *Frühmittelalterliche Studien* 33: 49–82.

Stegmüller, Friedrich (1981). *Repertorium Biblicum Medii Aevi. Tomus I. Initia Biblica, Apocrypha, Prologi*. 2nd edn. Madrid: CSIC.

Steinová, Evina (2011). 'Biblical Material in the Latin Apocryphal Acts of the Apostles.' Unpublished Masters dissertation, University of Utrecht.

Stelzer, Wilbert. (2013). 'A New Reconstruction of Pelagius' Text of 2 Corinthians.' Unpublished doctoral dissertation, Concordia Seminary, St Louis.

Stern, L.C. (1910). *Epistolae B. Pauli glosatae glosa interlineali. Irisch-lateinischer Codex der Würzburger Universitätsbibliothek.* Halle: Niemeyer.

Stone, Robert C. (1946). *The Language of the Latin Text of Codex Bezae.* Urbana: Illinois UP.

Stramare, Tarcisio, ed. (1987). *La Bibbia 'Vulgata' dalle origini ai nostri giorni.* Rome: Abbazia San Girolamo, Libreria Vaticana.

Streitberg, W. (1910). *Die gotische Bibel I.* Heidelberg: Winter.

Stummer, F. (1928). *Einführung in die lateinische Bibel.* Paderborn: Schöningh.

Stuttgart Vulgate: see Weber, Gryson et al.

Sundberg, Albert C., Jr. (1973). 'Canon Muratori: A Fourth Century List.' *HTR* 66: 1–41.

Süss, W. (1932a). *Studien zur lateinischen Bibel I. Augustins Locutiones und das Problem der lateinischen Bibelsprache.* Tartu: UP, 86ff.

Süss, W. (1932b). 'Das Problem der lateinischen Bibelsprache.' *Historische Vierteljahrschrift* 27: 1–39.

Sutcliffe, E.F. (1948). 'The Name "Vulgate".' *Biblica* 29: 345–52.

Sutcliffe, E.F. (1969). 'Jerome.' In Lampe 1969: 80–101.

Szerwiniack, Olivier (1994). 'Des recueils d'interprétations de noms hébreux chez les Irlandais et le wisigoth Theodulf.' *Scriptorium* 48: 187–258.

Tamoto, Kenichi (2013). *The Macregol Gospels or The Rushworth Gospels. Edition of the Latin text with the Old English interlinear gloss transcribed from Oxford Bodleian Library, MS Auctarium D. 2. 19.* Amsterdam & Philadelphia: John Benjamins.

Tenney, M.C. (1947). 'The Quotations from Luke in Tertullian as Related to the Texts of the Second and Third Centuries.' *Harvard Studies in Classical Philology* 56–7: 257–60.

TeSelle, Eugene (1970). *Augustine the Theologian.* Herder and Herder. Reprinted Eugene: Wipf & Stock, 2002.

Tewes, Babette (2011). *Die Handschriften der Schule von Luxeuil. Kunst und Ikonographie eines frühmittelalterlichen Skriptoriums.* Wiesbaden: Harrassowitz.

Thiele, Walter (1955). 'Augustinus zum lateinischen Text des Jakobusbriefes.' *ZNW* 46: 255–8.

Thiele, Walter (1956–69). *Epistulae Catholicae.* VL 26/1. Freiburg: Herder.

Thiele, Walter (1958). *Wortschatzuntersuchungen zu den lateinischen Texten der Johannesbriefe.* Freiburg: Herder.

Thiele, Walter (1959). 'Beobachtungen zum Comma Iohanneum (1 Joh. 5, 7f.).' *ZNW* 50: 61–73.

Thiele, Walter (1965). *Die lateinischen Texte des 1. Petrusbriefes.* Freiburg: Herder.

Thiele, Walter (1968). 'Probleme des augustinischen Bibeltextes.' *Deutsches Pfarrerblatt* 68: 406–8.

Thiele, Walter (1969). 'Zum lateinischen Paulustext. Textkritik und Überlieferungsgeschichte.' *ZNW* 60: 264–73.

Thiele, Walter (1972). 'Probleme der Versio Latina in den katholischen Briefen.' In Aland 1972: 93–119.

Thiele, Walter (1981). 'Beobachtungen zu den eusebianischen Sektionen und Kanones der Evangelien.' *ZNW* 72: 100–11.

Thomson, Rodney M. (2001). *The Bury Bible*. Facsimile edition. Woodbridge: Boydell.

Thurn, Hans (1984). *Die Pergamenthandschriften der ehemaligen Dombibliothek.* Wiesbaden: Harrassowitz.

Tilley, Maureen A. (1997). *The Bible in Christian North Africa: The Donatist World.* Minneapolis: Fortress.

Tinnefeld, F.H. (1963). *Untersuchungen zur altlateinischen Überlieferung des I. Timotheusbriefes. Der lateinische Paulustext in den Handschriften DEFG und in den Kommentaren des Ambrosiaster und des Pelagius.* Wiesbaden: Harrassowitz.

Tischendorf, Constantin (1847). *Evangelium Palatinum ineditum.* Leipzig: Brockhaus.

Tischendorf, Constantin (1850). *Novum Testamentum Latine, interprete Hieronymo, ex celeberrimo codice Amiatino.* Leipzig: Avernarius & Mendelssohn; reissued 1854.

Tischendorf, Constantin (1852). *Codex Claromontanus sive Epistulae Pauli omnes graece et latine ex codice Parisiensi . . . .* Leipzig: Brockhaus.

Tischendorf, Constantin (1861). *Anecdota Sacra et Profana.* Leipzig: Fries.

Tischendorf, Constantin (1869–72). *Novum Testamentum Graece ad antiquissimos testes . . . . (Editio octava maior.)* Leipzig: Giesecke & Devrient.

Tischendorf, Constantin (1870). *Codex Laudianus.* Leipzig: Hinrichs.

Tite, Philip L. (2012). *The Apocryphal Epistle to the Laodiceans.* Leiden: Brill.

Tkacz, Catherine Brown (1996). 'Labor Tam Utilis: The Creation of the Vulgate.' *VigC* 50: 42–72.

Tornau, Christian and Cecconi, Paolo (2014). *The Shepherd of Hermas in Latin. Critical Edition of the Oldest Translation Vulgata.* Berlin: De Gruyter.

Traube, Ludwig (1907). *Nomina Sacra. Versuch einer Geschichte der christlichen Kürzung.* Munich: Beck.

Turner, C.H. (1904a). 'A Re-collation of Codex k of the Old Latin Gospels (Turin G VII 15).' *JTS* os 5: 88–100.

Turner, C.H. (1904b). 'An Exegetical Fragment of the Third Century.' *JTS* os 5: 227–41.

Turner, C.H. (1927). 'Did Codex Vercellensis (a) Contain the Last Twelve Verses of St Mark?' *JTS* os 29: 16–18.

Turner, C.H., ed. (1931). *The Oldest Manuscript of the Vulgate Gospels.* Oxford: Clarendon.

Turner, C.H. and Burkitt, F.C. (1904). 'A Recollation of Codex *k* of the Old Latin Gospels.' *JTS* os 5: 88–107.

Turner, E.G. (1939). *Catalogue of Greek and Latin Papyri and Ostraca in the Possession of the University of Aberdeen.* Aberdeen: UP.

UBS5 (2014). *The Greek New Testament. Edited for the United Bible Societies.* 5th edn. Stuttgart: Deutsche Bibelgesellschaft.

Vaccari, A. (1961). 'Les traces de la Vetus Latina dans le Speculum de Saint Augustin.' *Studia Patristica* 4.2: 228–33.

Valgiglio, Ernesto (1985). *Le antiche versioni latine del Nuovo Testamento.* Naples: D'Auria.

van den Hout, M. (1951). 'Gothic Palimpsests of Bobbio.' *Scriptorium* 6: 91–3.

van der Horst, K., Engelbrecht, J.H.A., and Rathofer, J. (1982). *Utrecht-Psalter. Vollständige Faksimile Ausgabe im Originalformat der Handschrift 32, aus dem Besitz der Bibliotheek der Rijksuniversiteit te Utrecht.* Graz: Akademische Druck.

van Liere, Frans (2012). 'The Latin Bible, c. 900 to the Council of Trent.' In Marsden and Matter 2012: 93–109.

van Liere, Frans (2014). *An Introduction to the Medieval Bible*. Cambridge: UP.

Vercellone, C. (1860–4). *Variae Lectiones Vulgatae Latinae Bibliorum*. 2 vols. Rome: Spithöver.

Verey, Christopher D. (1969–70). 'A Collation of the Gospel Texts contained in Durham Cathedral MSS. A.II.10, A.II.16 and A.II.17 … .' Dissertation, University of Durham.

Verey, Christopher D. (1973). 'Some Observations on the texts of Durham Cathedral MSS. A.II.10 and A.II.17.' *Studia Evangelica* 6: 575–9.

Verey, Christopher D. (1998). 'A Northumbrian text family.' In Sharpe and Van Kampen 1998: 105–22.

Verey, Christopher D., Brown, J., and Coatsworth, E. (1980). *The Durham Gospels together with Fragments of a Gospel Book in Uncial*. Facsimile edition. Copenhagen: Rosenkilde & Bagger.

Verheyden, J. (2003). 'The Canon Muratori: A Matter of Dispute.' In *The Biblical Canons*, ed. J.-M. Auwers and H. J. De Jonge. Leuven: Peeters, 487–556.

Verheyden, J. (2013). 'The New Testament Canon.' In Carleton Paget and Schaper 2013: 389–411.

Vernet, André (1989). *La Bible au Moyen Age. Bibliographie*. Paris: CNRS.

Vessey, Mark (2005). *Latin Christian Writers in Late Antiquity and their Texts*. Aldershot: Ashgate.

Vetus Latina. Die Reste der altlateinischen Bibel. Nach Petrus Sabatier neu gesammelt und herausgegeben von der Erzabtei Beuron (1949–). Freiburg: Herder.

Vetus Latina Arbeitsbericht. Vetus Latina. Gemeinnützige Stiftung zur Förderung der Herausgabe einer vollständigen Sammlung aller erhaltenen Reste der altlateinischen Bibelübersetzungen aus Handschriften und Zitaten bei alten Schriftstellern. Bericht der Stiftung und Forschungsbericht des Instituts (1967–). Beuron: Vetus Latina-Institut.

Vezin, Jean (1987). 'Les divisions du texte dans les Évangiles jusqu'à l'apparition de l'imprimerie.' In *Grafia e interpunzione del latino nel medioevo*, ed. Alfonso Maierù. Rome: Ateneo, 53–68.

Vezin, Jean (1993). 'A propos des manuscrits latins de Sinaï.' *Bulletin de la Société nationale des antiquaires de France*, 347–9.

Vineis, E. (1974). *Studio sulla lingua dell'Itala*. Pisa: Pacini.

Vinzent, M., Mellerin L., and Houghton, H.A.G., ed. (2013). *Biblical Quotations in Patristic Texts*. Studia Patristica 54. Leuven: Peeters.

Vives, J. (1957). 'Inscripciones Hispánicas y los «Capitula Biblica».' In *Estudios dedicados a Menendez Pidal* 7.1. Madrid: CSIC, 477–81.

Vogels, H.J. (1913). *Codex Rehdigeranus*. Rome: Pustet.

Vogels, H.J. (1918). 'Zur 'afrikanischen' Evangelienübersetzung.' *Biblische Zeitschrift* 12: 250–68.

Vogels, H.J. (1919). 'Eine Neuausgabe des Codex Vercellensis.' *Biblische Zeitschrift* 15: 301–18.

Vogels, H.J. (1920). *Untersuchungen zur Geschichte der lateinischen Apokalypse-Übersetzungen*. Düsseldorf: Schwann.

Vogels, H.J. (1922a). 'Die Lukaszitate bei Lucifer von Calaris.' *Theologische Quartalschrift* 103: 23–37.

Vogels, H.J. (1922b). 'Die Johanneszitate bei Lucifer von Calaris.' *Theologische Quartalschrift* 103: 183–200.

Vogels, H.J. (1924). 'Der Evangelientext des hl. Irenaeus.' *RevBén* 36: 21–33.

Vogels, H.J. (1925). 'Der Bibeltext der Schrift "De physicis".' *RevBén* 37: 224–38.

Vogels, H.J. (1926a). *Evangelium Palatinum. Studien zur ältesten Geschichte der lateinischen Evangelienübersetzung.* Münster: Aschendorff.

Vogels, H.J. (1926b). 'Die Vorlage des Vulgatatextes der Evangelien.' *RevBén* 38: 123–38.

Vogels, H.J. (1928a). *Vulgatastudien. Die Evangelien der Vulgata untersucht auf ihre lateinische und griechische Vorlage.* Münster: Aschendorff.

Vogels, H.J. (1928b). 'Übersetzungsfarbe als Hilfsmittel zur Erforschung der neutestamentlichen Textgeschichte.' *RevBén* 40: 123–9.

Vogels, H.J. (1933). 'Der Codex Claromontanus der Paulinischen Briefe.' In *Amicitiae Corolla*, ed. G.H. Wood. London: UP, 274–99.

Vogels, H.J. (1952). 'Codex VII der Cathedralbibliothek von Verona (b2).' In Fischer and Fiala 1952: 1–12.

Vogels, H.J. (1953). *Evangelium Colbertinum.* Bonn: Hanstein.

Vogels, H.J. (1955a). *Untersuchungen zum Text paulinischer Briefe bei Rufin und Ambrosiaster.* Bonn: Hanstein.

Vogels, H.J. (1955b). 'Der Bibeltext in drei pseudoambrosianischen Predigten.' *ZNW* 46: 60–8.

Vogels, H.J. (1956). 'Ambrosiaster und Hieronymus.' *RevBén* 66: 14–19.

Vogels, H.J. (1957). *Das Corpus Paulinum des Ambrosiaster.* Bonn: Hanstein.

Vogels, H.J. (1959). 'Die Überlieferung des Ambrosiasterkommentars zu den Paulinischen Briefen.' *Nachrichten der Akademie der Wissenschaften in Göttingen* 7: 107–42.

Vogt, K. (1965). 'Untersuchungen zur Geschichte der lateinischen Apokalypse.' Unpublished dissertation, Freiburg.

von Dobschütz, E. (1894). *Studien zur Textkritik der Vulgata.* Leipzig: Hinrichs.

von Dobschütz, E. (1912). *Das Decretum Gelasianum de libris recipiendis.* Leipzig: Hinrichs.

von Harnack, A. (1931). 'Studien zur Vulgata des Hebräerbriefs.' In *Studien zur Geschichte des Neuen Testaments und der alten Kirche I.* Berlin & Leipzig: De Gruyter, 191–234.

von Soden, Hans (1909). *Das lateinische Neue Testament in Afrika zur Zeit Cyprians nach Bibelhandschriften und Väterzeugnissen.* Leipzig: Hinrichs.

von Soden, Hans (1927). 'Der lateinische Paulustext bei Marcion und Tertullian.' In *Festgabe für Adolf Jülicher zum 70. Geburtstag.* Tübingen: Mohr, 225–81.

Vööbus, Arthur (1954). *Early Versions of the New Testament.* Stockholm: Estonian Theological Society.

Wachtel, Klaus and Witte, Klaus (1994). *Das Neue Testament auf Papyrus. II. Die Paulinischen Briefe.* Berlin & New York: De Gruyter.

Walther, Otto K. (1980). 'Codex Laudianus G.35. A Re-examination of the Manuscript.' Unpublished doctoral dissertation, University of St Andrews.

Wasserman, Tommy (2011). 'The "Son of God" was in the Beginning (Mark 1:1).' *JTS* ns 62.1: 20–50.

Weber, R., Gryson, R., et al., ed. (2007). *Biblia Sacra iuxta Vulgatam versionem*. 5th edn. Stuttgart: Deutsche Bibelgesellschaft.

Weitzmann, K. (1977). *Late Antique and Early Christian Book Illumination*. New York: Braziller.

West, Martin L. (1973). *Textual Criticism and Editorial Technique Applicable to Greek and Latin Texts*. Stuttgart: Teubner.

Westcott, Brooke Foss and Hort, F.J.A. (1882). *The New Testament in the Original Greek. Introduction—Appendix*. Cambridge & London: Macmillan.

White, Henry Julian (1888). *The Four Gospels from the Munich Ms. (q)...with a fragment from St John in the Hof-Bibliothek at Vienna (Cod. lat. 502)*. Oxford: Clarendon.

White, Henry Julian (1897). *Portions of the Acts of the Apostles, of the Epistle of St. James and of the First Epistle of St. Peter from the Bobbio Palimpsest*. Oxford: Clarendon.

White, Henry Julian (1902). 'Vulgate.' In *Dictionary of the Bible*, ed. Hastings. Vol. 4, 872–90.

Williams, John, ed. (1999). *Imaging the Early Medieval Bible*. Pennsylvania: UP.

Williams, Megan Hale (2006). *The Monk and the Book. Jerome and the Making of Christian Scholarship*. Chicago: UP.

Williams, P.J. (2004). *Early Syriac Translation Technique and the Textual Criticism of the Greek Gospels*. Piscataway: Gorgias.

Williams, P.J. (2012). 'Where Two or Three are Gathered Together: Evaluating Agreements between Two or More Early Versions'. In Hill and Kruger 2012: 239–60.

Willis, Geoffrey G. (1959). 'Some Interesting Readings of the Book of Mulling.' In *Studia Evangelica*, ed. F.L. Cross. Berlin: Akademie-Verlag, 811–13.

Willis, Geoffrey G. (1962a). *St. Augustine's Lectionary*. London: SPCK.

Willis, Geoffrey G. (1962b). 'St. Augustine's Text of the Epistle to the Hebrews.' *Studia Patristica* 6. Berlin: Akademie-Verlag, 543–7.

Willis, Geoffrey G. (1966a). 'Patristic Biblical Citations. The importance of a good critical text, illustrated from St. Augustine.' *Studia Patristica* 7.1, ed. F.L. Cross. Berlin: Akademie-Verlag, 576–9.

Willis, Geoffrey G. (1966b). 'Textual Divisions in the Book of Mulling.' *JTS* ns 17: 89–95.

Wilmart, A. (1913). 'Le *Comes* de Murbach.' *RevBén* 30: 25–69.

Wilmart, A. (1922). 'Un ancien texte latin de l'évangile selon saint Jean.' *RevBib* 31: 182–202.

Wilmart, A. (1937). *Codices Reginenses Latini. Band 1*. Vatican City: Biblioteca Apostolica.

Wilmart, A., Lowe, E.A., and Wilson, H.A. (1924). *The Bobbio Missal. A Gallican Mass Book. Vol. 3 Notes and Studies*. London: Henry Bradshaw Society.

Winstedt, E.O. (1907). 'Some Greek and Latin Papyri in Aberdeen Museum.' *Classical Quarterly* 1: 257–67.

Wlosok, A. (1961). 'Zur Bedeutung der nichtcyprianische Bibelzitate bei Laktanz.' *Studia Patristica* 4, ed. F.L. Cross. Berlin: Akademie-Verlag, 234–50.

Wolgarten, E. (1968). 'Die lateinischen Texte des Titusbriefs.' Unpublished Diplomarbeit, Bonn.

Wordsworth, John (1883). *The Gospels according to St Matthew from the St Germain MS. (g1) now numbered Lat. 11553 in the National Library at Paris.* Oxford: Clarendon.

Wordsworth, John (1885). 'The Corbey St. James (ff) and its Relation to Other Latin Versions and to the Original Language of the Epistle.' *Studia Biblica* 1: 113–50.

Wordsworth, John, Sanday, W., and White, H.J. (1886). *Portions of the Gospels according to St Mark and St Matthew from the Bobbio ms. (k) . . . together with other fragments of the Gospels from six mss. in the libraries of St. Gall, Coire, Milan and Berne.* Oxford: Clarendon.

Wordsworth, John, White, H.J., et al., ed. (1889–1951). *Nouum Testamentum Domini nostri Iesu Christe latine secundum editionem sancti Hieronymi.* 3 vols. Oxford: Clarendon.

Wormald, Francis (1954). *The Miniatures in the Gospel of St Augustine.* Cambridge: UP.

Wouters, A. (1988). *The Chester-Beatty Codex Ac. 1499. A Graeco-Latin Lexicon on the Pauline Epistles and a Greek Grammar.* Leuven: Peeters.

Wright, D.H. (1961). 'Some Notes on English Uncial.' *Traditio* 17: 441–56.

Yawn, Lila (2004). 'The Illustrated Giant Bible of Perugia (Biblioteca Augusta, Ms. L. 59). A Manuscript and Its Creators in Eleventh-Century Central Italy.' Unpublished PhD dissertation, University of North Carolina.

Young, Frances M. (1997). *Biblical Exegesis and the Formation of Christian Culture.* Cambridge: UP.

Young, Frances M., Ayres, Lewis, and Louth, Andrew, ed. (2004). *The Cambridge History of Early Christian Literature.* Cambridge: UP.

Zamudio: see Jimenez Zamudio.

Zangemeister, K. (1877). *Bericht über die im Auftrage der Kirchenväter-Commission unternommene Durchforschung der Bibliotheken Englands.* Vienna: Akademie der Wissenschaften.

Zelzer, Michaela (1970). 'Zur Sprache des Ambrosiaster.' *Wiener Studien* 4: 196–213.

Ziegler, L. (1876a). *Italafragmente der paulinischen Briefe.* Marburg: Elwert.

Ziegler, L. (1876b). 'Bruchstücke einer vorhieronymianischen Übersetzung der Petrusbriefe.' *Sitzungsbericht der Bayerische Akademie der Wissenschaften phil.-hist. Klasse* 5: 607–90.

Ziegler, L. (1879). *Die lateinischen Übersetzungen vor Hieronymus.* Munich: Riedel.

Zimmer, Friedrich (1887). *Der Galaterbrief im altlateinischen Text als Grundlage für einen textkritischen Apparat der Vetus Latina.* Königsberg: Hartung.

Zimmermann, H. (1960). *Untersuchungen zur Geschichte der altlateinischen Überlieferung des zweiten Korintherbriefes.* Bonn: Hanstein.

Index of Manuscripts

Named manuscripts are cross-referenced in the Index of Subjects. Bold references are to images or entries in the Catalogue of Manuscripts.

Index of Biblical Passages

Apocryphal books are given by title in the Index of Ancient Authors and Writings apart from the Epistle to the Laodiceans and 3 Corinthians which are included below after Revelation.

Index of Ancient Authors and Writings

This list is restricted to authors and works of the first millennium. Other writers will be found in the Index of Subjects. Items in bold indicate a direct quotation. Pseudonymous writings are listed after the author to which they are attributed. Certain anonymous writings are given by their title or incipit.

Index of Subjects

Names of manuscripts are cross-referenced to the holding institution in the Index of Manuscripts; this should be consulted directly for manuscripts named after their current location (e.g. the Bamberg Bible). Authors and works from the first millennium are listed in the Index of Ancient Authors and Writings.